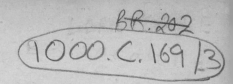

B.R. 516B (Restricted)

GEOGRAPHICAL HANDBOOK SERIES

FOR OFFICIAL USE ONLY

GREECE

VOLUME III

REGIONAL GEOGRAPHY

August 1945

NAVAL INTELLIGENCE DIVISION

LIST OF MAPS AND DIAGRAMS

SUMMARY OF CONTENTS OF HANDBOOK ON GREECE

CONTENTS

comprehensive and convenient form about countries which they may be called upon to visit, not only in war but in peace-time ; secondly, to maintain the high standard of education in the Navy and, by supplying officers with material for lectures to naval personnel ashore and afloat, to ensure for all ranks that visits to a new country shall be both interesting and profitable.

Their contents are, however, by no means confined to matters of purely naval interest.   For many purposes (e.g. history, administration, resources, communications, etc.) countries must necessarily be treated as a whole, and no attempt is made to limit their treatment exclusively to coastal zones.   It is hoped therefore that the Army, the Royal Air Force, and other Government Departments (many of whom have given great assistance in the production of the series) will find these Handbooks even more valuable than their predecessors proved to be both during and after the last war.

J. H. GODFREY

Director of Naval Intelligence

1942

The foregoing preface has appeared from the beginning of this series of Geographical Handbooks.   It describes so effectively their origin and purpose that I have decided to retain it in its original form.

This volume has been prepared for the Naval Intelligence Division at the Cambridge sub-centre (General Editor, Dr H. C. Darby). The account of the mainland (Chapters II–VII) has been written by Professor A. G. Ogilvie.   The remainder of the volume has been written mainly by Dr H. C. Darby, Miss J. B. Mitchell and Dr N. J. G. Pounds, with contributions from Mr G. R. Crone, Dr Elwyn Davies, Mr F. J. Monkhouse and Mrs Gwen Raverat.   The maps and diagrams have been drawn mainly by Miss K. S. A. Froggatt, Miss F. Hands, Miss M. Hart and Mrs Marion Plant.   The volume has been edited by Dr Elwyn Davies and Mr J. R. James.

E. G. N. RUSHBROOKE

Director of Naval Intelligence

August, 1945

PREFACE

IN 1915 a Geographical Section was formed in the Naval Intelligence Division of the Admiralty to write Geographical Handbooks on various parts of the world. The purpose of these handbooks was to supply, by scientific research and skilled arrangement, material for the discussion of naval, military and political problems, as distinct from the examination of the problems themselves. Many distinguished collaborators assisted in their production, and by the end of 1918 upwards of fifty volumes had been produced in Handbook and Manual form, as well as numerous short-term geographical reports. The demand for these books increased rapidly with each new issue, and they acquired a high reputation for accuracy and impartiality. They are now to be found in Service Establishments and Embassies throughout the world, and in the early years after the last war were much used by the League of Nations.

The old Handbooks have been extensively used in the present war, and experience has disclosed both their value and their limitations. On the one hand they have proved, beyond all question, how greatly the work of the fighting services and of Government Departments is facilitated if countries of strategic or political importance are covered by handbooks which deal, in a convenient and easily digested form, with their geography, ethnology, administration, and resources. On the other hand, it has become apparent that something more is needed to meet present-day requirements. The old series does not cover many of the countries closely affected by the present war (e.g. Germany, France, Poland, Spain, Portugal, to name only a few) ; its books are somewhat uneven in quality, and they are inadequately equipped with maps, diagrams, and photographic illustrations.

The present series of Handbooks, while owing its inspiration largely to the former series, is in no sense an attempt to revise or re-edit that series. It is an entirely new set of books, produced in the Naval Intelligence Division by trained geographers drawn largely from the Universities, and working at sub-centres established at Oxford and Cambridge. The books follow, in general, a uniform scheme, though minor modifications will be found in particular cases ; and they are illustrated by numerous maps and photographs.

The purpose of the books is primarily naval. They are designed first to provide, for the use of Commanding Officers, information in a

LIST OF PLATES

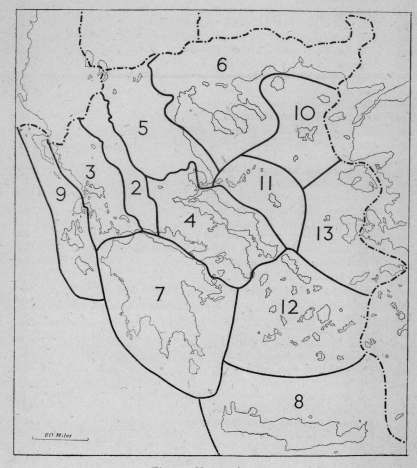

Fig. 1. Key to chapters

The map shows the boundaries of the regions described in the several chapters, the numbers of which are given.

2. The Dividing Mountains
3. Western Greece
4. Central Greece
5. Eastern Greece
6. North-eastern Greece
7. The Pelopónnisos

8. Crete (Kríti)
9. The Ionian Islands
10. The Thracian Islands
11. The Northern Sporádhes
12. The Kikládhes (Cyclades)
13. The Eastern Aegean Islands

Chapter I

INTRODUCTION

In the first two volumes of this Handbook, Greece as a whole has been surveyed in terms of general topics, e.g., climate, agriculture, railways. In this third volume, on the other hand, an attempt is made to describe the country in terms of its regional geography. A fundamental distinction is at once apparent between the mainland and the islands, covering respectively some 41,000 and 9,000 sq. miles. The total population of Greece in 1938 was estimated at rather more than seven millions, and some three-quarters of this total lived on the mainland. The size and importance of the mainland meant that it received inevitably the greater emphasis in the first two volumes. In this volume, the regional treatment of the islands has been expanded to include other aspects (e.g., coasts, history) so as to give a picture of each island. The result is that the amount of space given to the islands is proportionately greater than that given to the mainland, and, in particular, opportunity has been taken to describe Crete at comparatively great length.

Fig. 1 shows the regions dealt with in each chapter. For convenience, certain islands have been included with the accounts of the adjacent mainland (see p. 166). The major regions and their subdivisions bear little relation to the administrative divisions of the country which are given in Fig. 2.

The Mainland

The description of the mainland is based upon the regional division made in volume I (pp. 17–30). A chapter is devoted to each of the six main regions, the general features of which are summarized below. These regions have been further subdivided, and the sub-regions have been described in one of two ways. For some sub-regions an account is given under the headings of (*a*) physical characteristics and (*b*) land utilization ; other sub-regions have been further divided into smaller areas as seemed necessary.

The Dividing Mountains. The central mountain belt, extending southwards from Albania to the Gulf of Kórinthos, forms the backbone of northern Greece. It includes tracts of rounded summits and even gently rolling plateaux some 6,000 ft. high, but elsewhere rugged escarpments and deep ravines dominate the landscape. It forms the largest area of sparse population in Greece, and the only large settlements are those guarding the passes across the mountains.

Fig. 2.   The administrative divisions of Greece

Based on the 1 : 1,000,000 G.S.G.S. Series 2758 : Europe, and the population census of 1928.
Greece is divided into ten *dhiamerísmata* or geographical regions as shown in the inset map, and into thirty-nine *nomoí* or departments. The *nomós* of Thresprotía was formed out of parts of Ioánnina and Préveza after 1936.

There is little cultivation, but the upland pastures are grazed during the summer months by sheep and goats from the lowlands to the east.

Western Greece. The western slopes of the Dividing Mountains are, for the most part, peculiarly inhospitable, less because of their elevation, which is rarely above 6,000 ft., than because of their greatly varied relief. Outcrops of resistant limestone form parallel mountain chains, narrow, serrated, and with imposing precipices ; between them, belts of sandstones, shales and slates form deep valleys, on the slopes of which the bulk of the population is settled. In the south, near the Gulfs of Amvrakía and Pátrai, the country is lower and the rivers reach the sea across marshy flats. The density of population is low and agriculture is backward except in the small plains, especially that of Árta where drainage in recent years has transformed the countryside (Fig. 3).

Central Greece. This region is an oblong of mountains and plains lying east of the southern Píndhos and bounded by the Gulf of Kórinthos and the Aegean Sea. The highland regions consist of a series of mountain blocks, built of limestone, which have been largely deforested. In this region also, therefore, the population is concentrated largely on the alluvial plains. It is a land of sharp contrasts in relief, vegetation and density of population and these general features are continued eastward into Évvoia. In all, the region contains nearly a quarter of the Greek people, of whom about one-half live in Athens and Piraiévs.

Eastern Greece. The main feature of this region is the existence of four parallel zones that trend south-south-east from the northern frontier to the broken mountainous edge of Central Greece. Two of the zones are mainly lowland and the other two are mainly high mountain blocks that rise to over 6,000 ft. ; here is Ólimbos (9,570 ft.) the highest mountain in Greece. In the south the barrier between the eastern and western mountain zones is low and the two plains of Thessalía may be regarded as a single subdivision. The region shows great diversity in the distribution of population ranging from uninhabited summits to the intensively cultivated ' riviera ' coast south of Mount Pílion. The large settlements are commercial centres along the routeways. This is a region which has been strongly affected by the exchange of populations after 1923.

North-eastern Greece. Central and eastern Makedhonía, with Dhitikí Thráki, form a remarkable physical region where broad and once swampy plains are separated from one another by high crystalline plateaux. At the beginning of the twentieth century it was one of the most poverty-stricken parts of Europe but few regions have been

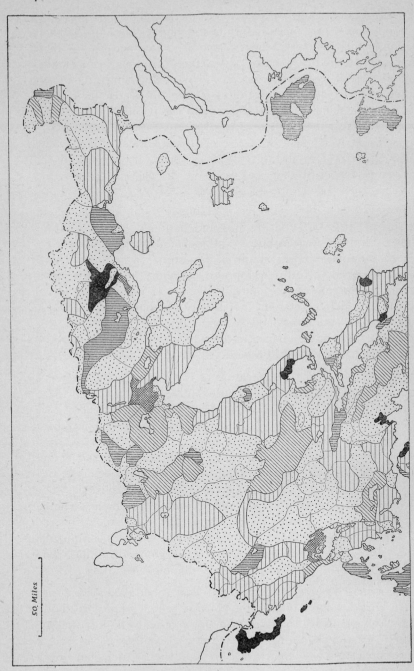

50. Miles

Fig. 3.   The distribution of population in northern Greece, 1928

Based on a map accompanying a paper by A. G. Ogilvie on 'Population Density in Greece' in *The Geographical Journal*, vol. 101, Nos. 5 and 6 (London, 1943).

The map and Fig. 4 are based on the census of Greece taken in 1928. The figures are calculated on the basis of natural districts or

no
ar
th
co
he
in

G.
th
bu
wi
m
isl
an
ha
co
ce

isl
fir
sep
Ae
an
Lí
se
th
an
Ae
litt
of

gr
Sk
Yí
of
Th
fer
Th
ro
the

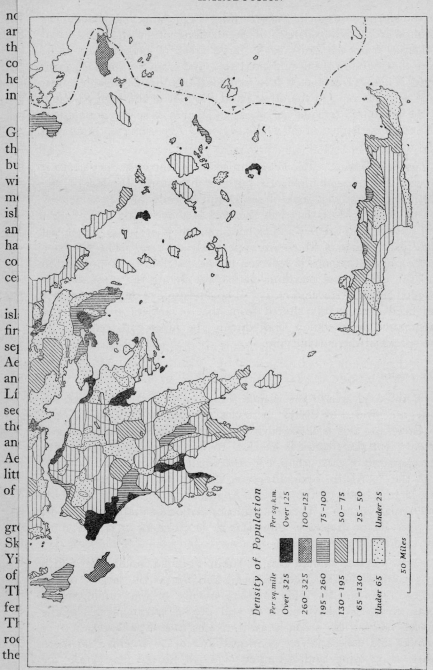

Density of Population

Per sq. mile	Per sq. km.
Over 325	Over 125
260–325	100–125
195–260	75–100
130–195	50–75
65–130	25–50
Under 65	Under 25

50 Miles

Fig. 4. The distribution of population in southern Greece, 1928

For source and comment, see Fig. 3.

The Kikládhes.   This group comprises some twenty major islands ranging in size from Ándros and Náxos to the much smaller Dhílos and Folégandros ; there are, besides, uninhabited islets and rocks. The barren rock-bound, flat-topped appearance of many of the islands indicates fairly clearly their origin.   They represent fragments of an ancient upland which, by a series of fractures and subsidences, has been all but submerged.   On the southern rim of the old hard rocks of the former upland is a line of volcanic activity curving south-eastwards from the Méthana peninsula in the Saronic Gulf, through the island of Mílos, to the still active vent of the Kaïméni islands in the crater of Thíra.   The main commercial centre of the group is the port of Síros (Ermoúpolis) and the island on which it stands has a density of 800 people per sq. mile.   Thíra comes next, with a density of 342 per sq. mile.   Most of the other islands have less than 100 people per sq. mile, and the smallest are uninhabited.

The Eastern Aegean Islands.   The three large islands of Lésvos, Khíos and Sámos lie near the coast of Asia Minor and are detached portions of the peninsulas of that country.   All three are mountainous but the lower hill country and plains are intensively cultivated and support a dense population.   Their position in the eastern Mediterranean has made them, throughout history, the intermediary between eastern and western trade and civilization.   In addition to the three islands there are the mountainous island of Ikaría, the small island of Psará off the north-west coast of Khíos, and the almost uninhabited group of Foúrnoi islets between Ikaría and Sámos.

Area and Population of the Chief Islands of Greece

	Area in sq. miles	Population	Density per sq. mile
Crete	3,174·5	386,427	121·7
Ionian Islands			
Kérkira	227·0	101,375	445·5
Levkás	112·7	26,691	235·7
Kefallinía	276·8	57,578	207·2
Itháki	39·8	7,183	181·3
Zákinthos	154·8	40,469	261·6
Erikoúsa	1·5	543	352·2
Othonoí	3·5	808	233·1
Paxoí	7·7	2,901	375·5
Samothráki	1·5	391	253·8
Meganísi	9·3	1,640	176·1
Kálamos	9·3	1,352	145·0
Kastós	2·7	301	111·4
Thracian Islands			
Thásos	153·7	11,573	75·1
Samothráki	69·5	3,866	54·4
Límnos	184·2	23,611	126·9
Áyios Evstrátios	17·4	786	44·0
Kikládhes			
Ándros	148·3	17,593	119·1
Tínos	75·3	11,260	150·2
Síros	33·2	27,663	834·0
Míkonos	29·0	4,188	145·0
Rinía	6·2	159	25·9
Dhílos	2·3	158	67·3
Kéa	39·8	3,713	93·2
Kíthnos	33·2	2,680	80·3
Sérifos	29·0	3,210	111·4
Náxos	170·7	19,981	116·5
Páros	75·3	9,369	124·3
Andíparos	14·7	612	41·4
Mílos	62·2	4,941	80·3
Sífnos	34·4	3,348	98·4
Kímolos	14·7	1,959	134·7
Folégandros	12·7	1,015	80·3
Síkinos	15·1	649	44·0
Thíra	29·0	9,884	341·9
Íos	39·8	1,797	44·0
Iráklia	7·3	286	38·8
Skhoinoúsa	3·9	260	67·3
Koufó	5·0	261	51·8
Dhenoúsa	5·8	235	41·4
Amorgós	47·5	3,164	67·3
Thirasía	3·9	657	170·9
Anáfi	14·7	565	38·8

	Area in sq. miles	Population	Density per sq. mile
Northern Sporádhes			
Skíathos	17·4	3,213	183·9
Skópelos	37·1	6,124	165·8
Iliodhrómia	23·9	1,005	41·4
Skíros	78·0	3,179	41·4
Eastern Aegean Islands			
Lésvos	623·2	137,160	220·1
Khíos	331·3	72,452	217·6
Sámos	189·6	58,558	308·2
Ikaría	99·2	10,783	108·8
Foúrnoi	11·2	973	85·5
Psará	15·8	788	49·2
Oinoúsai	5·4	2,440	450·7
Islands described with the Mainland			
Évvoia	1,382·2	140,851	101·0
Kíthira	101·2	8,770	85·5
Andikithira	8·1	322	38·8
Élafónisos	8·1	287	36·3
Ídhra	19·3	3,693	191·7
Póros	8·1	6,449	795·1
Spétsai	8·1	3,637	448·1
Salamís	35·9	15,100	419·6
Aiyina	31·7	8,832	279·7
Angístrion	5·4	664	121·7
Ammouliani	2·3	513	220·1
Other small islands	17·0	681	38·8
Uninhabited islands	159·8	—	—
Total	8,618·0	1,283,576	150·0

Source : *Annuaire Statistique de la Grèce*, 1931, pp. 24–5 (Athénes, 1931).

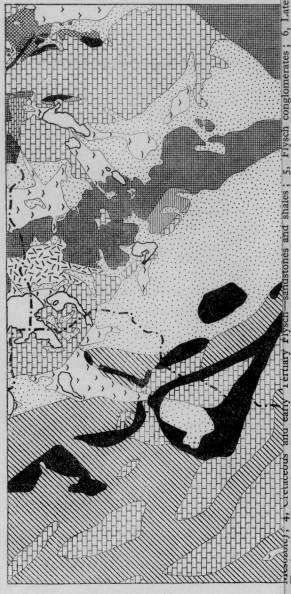

Mesozoic; 4, Cretaceous and early Tertiary Flysch—sandstones and shales; 5, Flysch conglomerates; 6, Later Tertiary gravels, sands, marls, clays, calc-sand and sinter; all unfolded; 7, Later Tertiary conglomerates; 8, Alluvium (in places Quaternary).

Chapter II

THE DIVIDING MOUNTAINS

The Northern and Central Mountains : The Highlands of Aitolía : Bibliographical Note

North of the Gulf of Pátrai is a mountain region unmatched in Greece for its continuity, its average height and its impenetrability. It extends for over 160 miles in a north-north-westerly direction to the high Albanian frontier and has a greatest breadth of some 50 miles. There are many summits exceeding 6,000 ft. and very few low passes, but the accessibility of these mountains and the degree to which they are habitable are less matters of altitude than of ruggedness.

The character of the whole region is dominated by its geological structure and the direction and character of its valleys (Fig. 5). In the north, the rocks are mainly of the impermeable type—sandstones and shales, serpentine and gabbro ; in the centre and south, i.e. in the Píndhos mountains and in Aitolía, belts of sandstone or shale alternate with very pure limestones. The high summits of the mountains are everywhere composed of limestone. The rocks have been compressed into a series of folds having approximately the same trend as the mountains. The pressure was from the east, so that the upfolds, or anticlines, tend to ' lean over ' to the west, and the limestone ridges usually present their most abrupt escarpments to the west. So great was the pressure that in some places masses of rocks have been thrust bodily over younger strata. As a result of the folding there are many fractures, marking lines of weakness in the rocks. Most of them are longitudinal, but others are transverse to the trend of the folds. North of the 39° parallel, a line which marks the axis of the Gulf of Amvrakía on the west and the Óthris mountains on the east, the general trend of the folds is ' Dinaric ' or north-north-west to south-south-east. To the south of this line, however, the trend changes and the folds run almost due south to the Gulf of Kórinthos.

Most of the rivers that drain this mountainous region adopted their present courses before the last great upheaval. This is apparent from the course of the river Mégdhova which rises east of the Píndhos ranges at only 2,600 ft. (Fig. 6). It then cuts obliquely across the highest mountain zone in a series of deep canyons, before joining the Akhelóös. The Akhelóös itself, while rising in the mountains, disregards their trend and flows in a long zig-zag course to the Gulf of Pátrai. In Aitolía, the rivers are not merely oblique to the main folds, but run directly across them. This factor, combined with the north to south trend of the structure in this area, the variations in rock types, and the consequent differences in settlement and land utilization, account for the two-fold division of the Dividing Mountains into :

    A1 The Northern and Central Mountains.
    A2 The Highlands of Aitolía.

THE NORTHERN AND CENTRAL MOUNTAINS (REGION A1)

Physical Characteristics

The northern and central mountains of Greece have no comprehensive name, although often referred to as the Píndhos. Near the Albanian frontier they are dominated by the Grámmos mountains (Fig. 6). Southwards, the broadening backbone comprises two distinct parts—the western and bolder mountains, including the plateau of Gamíla and the peak of Smólikas, and the eastern highlands, the most typical Vlach country in the Balkans. This Vlach highland extends to the Pass of Métsovon, beyond which the ranges of the Píndhos mountains run south-south-east for 68 miles to the pass near Karpenísion. Each of these sub-regions has local physical characteristics.

The Grámmos Mountains. Many of the summits on the frontier are over 6,500 ft. in height, in one area rising abruptly from the Albanian lowlands of Kolonje in a great fault scarp (Fig. 20). This striking feature is the result of a north-north-east to south-south-west fracture that has sharply truncated the folded sandstones and serpentines of the Grámmos mountains. The folds themselves run from north-west to south-east, a trend similar to that of the central Píndhos. The mountains are drained transversely by the river Sarandáporos, a southward flowing tributary of the river Aóös (Vijosë) and also by the headwaters of the river Aliákmon, flowing eastwards through deep longitudinal glens.

The Gamíla Plateaux and Smólikas. The basin of the Sarandáporos is dominated in the south by broad tabular masses of pure limestone that form plateaux nearly 8,000 ft. in height. The larger ones, with the regional name Gamíla, are penetrated by the rivers

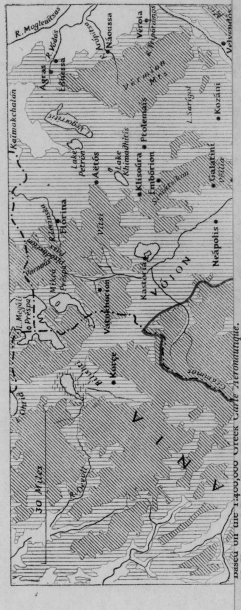

Based on the 1:400,000 Greek Carte Aéronautique.
K, Karvasará Bay ; TL, Tsoukalió Lagoon ; V, Váltos Bay
The contours are at 400 and 1,000 metres.

Aóös and Víkos which have cut formidable canyons some 4,000 ft. in depth (Plate 1). The high plateau surfaces, however, although of the bare, karstic type, have few well marked features. On the other hand, the smaller tableland in the east culminates in Smólikas, a peak 8,652 ft. above sea level, with rugged corries that betray its former glaciers (see vol. I, plate 14).

The Vlach Highlands. The rest of these northern mountains are of very different aspect. Here the erosion of a widespread exposure of sandstone and massive green serpentine has produced many dome-like mountains with no clear trends. Their summits generally are between 5,600 and 6,900 ft. in height. The valleys, which are drained westwards to the Aóös and eastwards to the Venétikos, lack any pronounced pattern and are usually narrow. The whole area is one of mature relief (see vol. I, Fig. 15 and Plate 5).

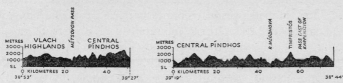

Fig. 7. Longitudinal profiles of parts of the Dividing Mountains
Based on the 1 : 250,000 G.S.G.S. Series 4088 : The Balkans. The profiles follow the watershed with few exceptions. The vertical exaggeration is just over three times.

The Píndhos Mountains. The high central zone of the Píndhos mountains, composed mainly of limestone, is illustrated in Fig. 7 and Plate 2. It extends for a distance of 68 miles from the Métsovon Pass in the north to the pass east of Karpenísion in the south. These two passes are not the lowest points through the mountains but they are reached by accessible valleys. The significance of the Métsovon Pass as one of the key points in the Balkan Peninsula has been shown in many wars, and never more clearly than in 1941 when the Italians' initial thrust was met and repelled from its approaches. Around the pass the slopes of the high Píndhos are drained by the headwaters of five divergent rivers—the Aliákmon, the Piniós, the Akehlóös, the Ákrakhthos and the Aóös (Vijosë). Tributaries of these rivers have cut profound canyons through the central zone, dividing it into various sub-ranges. In the south, for example, the canyon of the river Mégdhova separates a serrated limestone ridge from the rest of the chain, and this ridge ends in the peak of Mount Timfristós, 7,595 ft. high, an isolated bastion of the southern Píndhos. The relief of this central region has been further diversified by the existence within it of narrow and winding outcrops of sandstone and chert. These less resistant rocks have weathered for the most part into a series of deep and somewhat inaccessible glens.

On each side of the central limestone zone, often ending in an abrupt escarpment, there is a belt of lower land corresponding to outcrops of sandstones and shales (Plate 3). These rocks are preserved in roughly parallel downfolds, or synclines. Numerous springs occur at the foot of the limestone scarps, and their abundant waters, together with the rainfall and melted snow, account for the intricate network of valleys of all sizes. The western zone, flanked by the river Árakhthos, broadens southwards but its continuity is interrupted by two short ranges of limestone—the Tzoumérka and the Gávrovon mountains. The eastern zone, at its northern end, abuts on the Piniós valley, a narrow trough between limestone walls. Then, like its western counterpart, it broadens out southwards to link with the Óthris mountains. Its surface has been dissected by rivers flowing to the plain of Thessalía and by tributaries of the river Mégdhova, thus forming a maze of hills and valleys. Although the highest summits are some 2,000 ft. lower than the central chain, the plateau forms one of the main watersheds of Greece.

Land Utilization

There are no records of the climate of the high Píndhos, Ioánnina being the nearest meteorological station. Nevertheless, it is clear from travellers' accounts that the temperatures are considerably lower than those at corresponding heights in central and southern Greece. This is also the wettest part of Greece with an average annual precipitation exceeding 80 ins. in places. The snowfall is particularly heavy, and in some years snow covers the lower slopes until mid-April, while the summits are normally not free before mid-June. Frequent and violent thunderstorms are also experienced throughout most of the year. The vegetation indicates greater extremes of temperature on the eastern than on the western slopes, but on both there are well marked altitudinal zones. The tree-line varies from about 5,200 to 6,000 ft. and is perhaps kept low by goats and sheep. Near these levels, and especially on limestone, juniper bush is found ; together with box and holly, it forms an

Plate 1.   The limestone gorge of the river Aóös

Plate 2. Mount Peristéri at the northern end of the central Píndhos mountains

Plate 3. A broad longitudinal valley in the central Píndhos mountains
The valley is cut in weak shale and sandstone and is largely cultivated. In the
foreground, grain is being threshed by trampling.

[Facing page 15

undergrowth in the upper forests of silver fir. These trees have suffered more by ruthless felling than other types, especially on the western slopes where there was much lumbering during the nineteenth century, the logs being floated down the Árakhthos. Silver firs are found as low as 2,300 ft. On siliceous soils the fir is scattered among the upper forests of beech and Corsican pine, the former descending to 650 ft. and the latter to 3,000 ft. Large forests of beech, fir and Corsican pine still clothe the less accessible northern parts, and in spite of ruthless destruction during the nineteenth century the Píndhos mountains are probably the best wooded ranges in the country and one of the chief sources of timber in Greece. The lower forests, generally below 4,000 ft., are dominated by both deciduous and evergreen oaks, but certain areas have fine chestnut woods. In others, the hornbeam is common and notably in the inner valleys it occurs as dense bushwoods, while planes and poplars line the streams.

The contrast in climatic conditions east and west of the Píndhos is emphasized by the vegetation at lower altitudes. The evergreen maquis formation, and olive cultivation, are both absent from the slopes of Thessalía, whereas in the west, luxuriant bushwood including elements of true maquis prevails throughout the broad area of impermeable rocks. It occurs either alone or with oakwoods and, below the 1,600 ft. level, with olive groves. The bushwood extends up to about 2,600 ft. with heaths predominating in the higher parts. No better example of the correspondence of vegetation with altitude could be found than on the sides of the Mégdhova gorge, where the different zones are compressed into short stretches of very steep slope.

In the northern and central mountains many of the higher villages are purely pastoral and are vacated in the winter. This is especially true of those of the Vlachs who have only in very recent times, and then only partially, taken to cultivation. The relative size of villages is mainly determined by the type of land, together with the important consideration of water supply. Thus, on the porous limestones, springs or perennial streams are far apart and villages tend to be large ; on the other rocks, where water is nowhere far to seek, the settlements vary greatly in size and closeness. The contact lines between the two rock types form the most obviously attractive sites, where other conditions are favourable. Maize is the chief crop and is almost the only bread grain. Its presence indicates an abundance of water, summer showers, and warmth during the season of ripening. Other crops and fruit trees are confined almost entirely to the immediate vicinity of the villages.

The mountains form a vital feature in the economy of the lower lands that flank them ; for not only are the waters gathered on their slopes a great asset to the plains, especially those of Thessalía with their low rainfall, but, rising as they do above the tree lines, they possess large areas of meadows that are the summer pastures of immense flocks of sheep and goats. It is chiefly because of this that the high valleys contain many villages above 5,000 feet in altitude and that the largest body of pastoral people in the Balkan Peninsula, the Kutzo-Vlachs or Aromani, have their homes in this region (see vol. I, pp. 358–62).

The rich pastures also account for the influx of population in summer to all the high ranges and more particularly to the well-watered ranges north of the Pass of Métsovon. In this northern area the traditional pastoral life of the Balkan highlanders has been most fully preserved. Originally this type of life may have involved complete nomadism, whereas the Vlachs are now semi-nomadic with their real homes in the mountain villages which they occupy in summer only. The winter quarters of this group are in the low-lands of Thessalía, in towns such as Kalabáka and Tríkkala where they are engaged in trades or in transport. Many of them, however, live in tents or mere huts of branches, while their flocks of sheep and goats winter on the lowland pastures. The pastoral economy is directed toward the maximum production of milk, meat, wool, hair and skins, and the winter migration is necessary for the preservation of the stock as well as being a supplementary means of livelihood for the people. Hence the annual movements of the Vlachs are a direct adaptation to the climates of northern Greece. The lambs and kids born on the plains in December or January cannot be moved until weaned, though most of the young males are sold when one month old. The Vlach Highlands are reached on the summer migration, chiefly by way of the Piniós valley, or from the east by that of the upper Aliákmon. Not all the Vlach villages are in the highland ; some important places are at the lower limit of the Vlach district and are chiefly winter villages ; Grevená, 1,800 ft. in height and 5 miles from the Aliákmon, is typical. Such places offer inter-mediate pastures in early summer, and large numbers of the migrant Vlachs arrange to be there during the great festival of St. Akhíllios. This is held at the end of May (New Calendar) and marks the beginning of the full summer season. Before the end of July large quantities of cheese have been made and sent by mule to the Ioánnina market. It is produced from the milk of ewes, each of which yields some 280 pints annually, and from the less rich milk of goats. The wool and hair-clip from the flocks has also been marketed during this period. By the Feast of the Assumption, on 28 August, work has slowed down, the year's weddings are celebrated, village dances are held on the green, and betrothals are made for the next year. During October, snowfalls usually warn the Vlach shepherds to be ready for the downward migration which takes place about St. Demetrius's Day (8 November).

It is obvious that the summer population will be much greater than that recorded in the census of 1928, taken on 15-16 May, and it is probable that the difference would be greater in the northern part of the mountains. The following figures, however, show that the region contains a relatively large population that is more or less settled. In the Grámmos mountains there are some 15,000 people, or 34 per sq. mile, mostly living in large villages in the basin of the Sarandáporos, the chief being Pirsóyianni (population 910). In the Vlach Highlands the villages are also large and wide apart. Samarína, situated at the foot of Mount Smólikas at an altitude of 4,760 ft. and with a population of 603, is a good example (Plate 4). The total population is 17,000 and the density is 34 to the sq. mile. The upper valleys of the Piniós and the Metsovítikos, along the important Métsovon route, are much more populous, with some 17,000 people living in a narrow strip across the mountains. Here, the average density is 96 per sq. mile. The two largest villages flank the pass on either side, Métsovon on the west, with a population of 2,156 (see vol. I, plate 13), and Malakási on the east with a population of 832.

The population of the high central zone of the Píndhos mountains, southwards to the Mégdhova gorge, amounts to 16,000 and the average density is only 21 per sq. mile, reflecting the poor quality of the limestone pastures. It is surprising to find that towards the southern end of the chain there is a greater settled population just where the profound canyons of the Mégdhova and the Akhelóös are converging, with many large ravines leading to them. Numerous villages are perched on shelves and at the heads of remote glens ; the density of population rises to 50 per sq. mile along an arc following these two deep valleys, and there are some 27,000 inhabitants. This is the heart of Ágrafa, the largest of the traditional districts of the Píndhos. The name, which is officially retained by a village of Aitolía, embraces not merely the southern half of the Píndhos divide, but also the lower mountains of sandstone on both sides. The district also extends eastwards to include the intricate and forested region towards the Óthris mountains. The sandstone mountains have been partially cleared for agriculture and support 75 people to the sq. mile, but the eastern extension, covering 180 sq. miles, has a density of only 44 inhabitants per sq. mile. As a whole, Ágrafa is one of the most difficult areas to penetrate in Greece, and it remained substantially free of Turkish rule. It has, moreover, constantly played its part in providing men for numerous campaigns, and latterly has been the chief source of recruits for the *Evzone* regiments.

Among the mountains, district names which have no relation to modern administration are still current. These names are also used when referring to their inhabitants who have settled elsewhere in Greece. Some of the names may originally have been those of tribes, and the territory owned was probably delimited to include both agricultural and pastoral land for summer and for winter use. For example, the district known as Aspropótamos, from the name of the headstream of the Akhelóös, includes not only the canyons of this river but also the more open valley and lower country of the Klinovítikos, a north-flowing tributary of the Piniós.

THE HIGHLANDS OF AITOLÍA (REGION A2)

Physical Characteristics

The highlands of Aitolía form one of the most secluded regions in Greece. The central mountains are a series of parallel ranges of limestone whose rugged relief has suggested the name, ' the Alps of Aitolía '. Rivers, rising well to the east, traverse the high massif either directly or obliquely, and have cut for themselves a system of deep valleys. The trend of the river courses is therefore older than the mountains, but the shape of the valleys is youthful. They are, for the most part, deep canyons and none provides an easy route. Thus, although the limestone mountains of central Aitolía do not form the main watershed, they are a major barrier to communication.

Both the northern and southern edges of this region are lines of dislocation and depression. The northern one produced the Gulf of Amvrakía in the west and the Fokís depression, drained by the Sperkhiós, in the east. This line of crustal weakness also marks the south-eastern foot of Mount Timfristós and accounts for the pass near Karpenísion, the gateway from Fokís to Aitolía. But although

Plate 4. Samarína from the south-west
Behind the village is the shoulder of Mount Smólikas, composed of limestone.

Plate 5. The lower gorge of the river Mórnos viewed upstream
The whole floor is occupied by the river when in flood.

Plate 6. The gorge of the river Karpenisiotikos above its confluence with the
Kríkelopotamos

the altitude of this pass is comparatively low (4,070 ft.) the approach to it from the west is difficult, much more so than the route to the Métsovon Pass. At their southern end, the Dividing Mountains are terminated abruptly by the entrance to the Gulf of Kórinthos. The coast is clearly of faulted origin, but the truncation is oblique to the folds of the rocks, which are here bending round to the south-east. It is this oblique faulting that is responsible for the rough and inhospitable character of the coastal mountains.

The central limestone belt is a continuation of the limestone mountains of the Píndhos, but in Aitolía the trend of the folds changes to north-south. South of Karpenísion this high central massif forms a rough square some 15 miles across ; it then narrows south-eastwards to the river Mórnos, beyond which are other and lower limestone mountains along the coast. These rugged and almost inaccessible highlands culminate in the Khelidhón mountains, 7,218 ft. high. The one possible route, as yet not followed by a motor road, leads southwards from Karpenísion. It is a deep, longitudinal furrow, corresponding to an exposure of sandstone (Plate 6). Although the nature of the relief prevents roads from following river banks for long stretches, the valleys do form the obvious routes and also the small districts in which villages are grouped. On the other hand, the rivers in their canyons are subject to severe floods in winter and spring, and can only be regarded as obstructions to communications. Hence the importance of the few bridges, which are often masterpieces of medieval, or even Byzantine, engineering and architecture.

To the west of the longitudinal furrow, the limestone mountains are narrower and somewhat lower than the rest of the ' Alps ' ; the exception is the massive block of Panaitolikón, 6,313 ft. high, which overlooks Lake Trikhonís and is a prominent feature from the sea. Everywhere, these mountains command lower country to the west, more appropriately described under Akarnanía (see p. 29). The traditional boundary between Aitolía and Akarnanía is the Akhelóös, or Aspropótamos, the largest river flowing from the mountains of Aitolía (Plate 9).

To the east of the central limestone belt is a district of sandstones and shales, with here and there an isolated mass of limestone. It extends southwards from eastern Ágrafa (see p. 18) to occupy a broad area in Aitolía, and, as in Ágrafa, it is entirely mountainous. Its general altitude is below that of the central belt, but its highest ridge forms the main watershed of Aitolía. This runs south-eastwards from the pass near Karpenísion to the isolated and rugged Mount Vardhoúsia, 7,995 ft. high. Vardhoúsia is an example of an outlying mass of limestone. The watershed also rises to the summit of Mount Oxiá, 6,322 ft. high, which is named from the distinctive beech-forests on its slopes, probably the most southerly forest of beech anywhere in Europe. The surface of the watershed, although high, is mature and rounded, and marks one of the easiest lines of communication in eastern Aitolía. Elsewhere, the country is difficult to penetrate because the watershed offers no pass from east to west for a distance of 30 miles and the rivers flowing from it to the west-south-west are separated from one another by steep ridges. The approach from the coast is also difficult because of the limestone ridge, through which the river Mórnos breaks in a narrow gorge (Plate 5). The valley of the Mórnos is more accessible from the south-east than from Návpaktos near its mouth, and it is only in the gorge through the coastal limestones that the modern road has to leave the river banks.

The summit of Oxiá has a commanding view over most of eastern and southern Aitolía. Almost equidistant from it are the peak of Timfristós to the north with the Píndhos mountains behind, the magnificent double ridge of Vardhoúsia to the east, and the peak of Kaliakoúdha to the west ; the nearest and highest summit of the serrated limestone mountains. To the south, beyond the gulf, are the more distant peaks of the Pelopónnisos. Within this frame is a wide view of an intricate system of lower ridges, separated by the chasms of many rivers and still largely forested. The regional name for this labyrinth is Kravári, more strictly applied to the district between the Mórnos and the Évinos (Plate 7).

Land Utilization

On the slopes of Kravári, where cleared of forest, are occasional white villages, and many more isolated houses (*kalívia*)—the summer shielings on the pastures. The people, like those of Ágrafa, are reputed to be mistrustful of strangers : ' They will pay the stranger to be rid of him ' is the saying. The meagre resources of the country have forced many to emigrate, but some return with a little wealth and a knowledge of foreign languages.

Forestry is one of the chief occupations of the people, and some of the forests of these southern mountains have remained more intact than in many parts of the Píndhos. In the higher forests, up to 4,500 ft., fir is dominant, especially upon northern slopes ; the

Plate 7. The valley of the river Kókkinos

The view is from the south and shows the western ridge of Mount Vardhoúsia. Apart from the high limestone ridge, the scene is typical of the mountains formed of shale and sandstone, and the river-bed is choked with detritus. The valley is deforested.

Plate 8. The town of Karpenísion

The view is from the west and shows the summit of Mount Timfristós in the distance.

Plate 2. The gorge of the river Alphelóös upstream from the bridge at Tatárna

lower forests are of chestnut and oak, the former used for food, while the latter, in the more westerly areas, includes the Valona oak and so provides valuable tanning material.

Depredations have been serious even in the remote glens of Kravári, where logs are dragged down long distances to be floated on the rivers when in flood. On many slopes stripped in this way, the only woods are those kept above the settlements to preserve the villages from landslides or inundation. On the sandstones and, more especially, the shales, this is a serious danger and much good soil is lost in this way. All pasture and farm land must once have been under trees and, since there is little meadowland when compared with the northern mountains, the inhabitants have little pasture to spare for migrant shepherds.

The people of these southern highlands number some 60,000 and the average density of population is about 70 per sq. mile. The northern area, with the Karpenísion district, has this density, while the more rugged central part and the coastal slopes are less populous; and the Mórnos valley is the most densely peopled with 114 per sq. mile. This valley is favoured climatically, since most of the villages have vineyards, and maize is grown at the unusual height of 4,600 ft. The villages are almost always built high above the dangerous rivers, usually on shelves that represent the old smooth surface before these mountains were so deeply dissected.

Within the mountains there is only one place that looks at all like a town. This is Karpenísion, with a population of 2,576, the capital of the eparchy of Evritanía (Plate 8). Its superior nodality over all other settlements is shown by the importance of its annual fair, held on the first three days of August. At this time the population of the town is probably doubled. Its market serves a very wide region of pastoral interest, and, in addition, a vigorous and regular trade in skins and leather is maintained. Karpenísion is reached by three important routes : first, from the east, over the main watershed and along a small cultivated plain near the town ; secondly, from Agrínion in the south over the pass near the large village of Proussós, with a small but famous monastery ; and thirdly, by a fairly direct but difficult route from Amfilokhía on the Gulf of Amvrakía. The directness of the last route is due to the existence of three single-arch bridges, of Turkish or earlier construction, all nearly in the same latitude. These span respectively the Akhelóös by the Tatárna bridge, the Agrafiótis by the Manoli bridge, and the Mégdhova at Viviani.

BIBLIOGRAPHICAL NOTE

1. The most complete general bibliography is contained in the volume of the *Enzyklopädie der Erdkunde* entitled ' Länderkunde von Südeuropa ' by O. Maull (Leipzig and Wien, 1929). Select bibliographies follow the chapters by J. Sion in *Péninsules Méditerranéennes* (Paris, 1934) which is vol. VII, Part 2 of the *Geographie Universelle*, edited by P. Vidal de la Blache and L. Gallois.

2. The following works stand out among the earlier modern accounts of travel in Greece, since the authors, while primarily concerned with the identification and survey of classical sites, included careful topographical descriptions in their texts :
E. Curtius, *Peloponnesos*, 2 vols. (Gotha, 1851–2) ;
W. M. Leake, *Travels in the Morea*, 3 vols. (London, 1830) ;
             Travels in Northern Greece, 4 vols. (London, 1835) ;
L. Pouqueville, *Voyage en Morée*, 3 vols. (Paris, 1805) ;
F. Stählin, *Das hellenische Thessalien* (Stuttgart, 1924) ;
W. J. Woodhouse, *Aetolia* (Oxford, 1897) ;
and, for territories acquired by Greece since 1832,
H. F. Tozer, *Researches in the Highlands of Turkey*, 2 vols. (London, 1869).

3. The following contain the results of scientific exploration :
Expédition scientifique de Morée, 1831-8, 8 vols. (Paris) ; six works by A. Philippson, viz. : *Der Peloponnes* (Berlin, 1892) ; *Thessalien und Epirus* (Berlin, 1897) ; *Beitrage zur Morphologie Griechenlands* (Stuttgart, 1930) ; ' Der Isthmos von Korinth ', *Zeitschrift der Gesellschaft für Erdkunde*, vol. 25, pp. 1–98 (Berlin, 1890) ; ' Bericht über eine Reise durch Nord- und Mittel Griechenland ', *ibid.*, pp. 331–406 ; ' Der Kopaïs-see in Griechenland und seine Umgebung ', *idem*, vol. 29, pp. 1–108 (Berlin, 1894).

4. Comparable studies for other regions are :
J. Ancel, *La Macédoine, son évolution contemporaine* (Paris, 1930) ;
J. Cvijič, ' Grundlinien der Geographie und Geologie von Makedonien und Altserbien ', *Petermanns Mitteilungen, Ergänzungsheft* 162 (Gotha, 1908) ;
A. G. Ogilvie, ' A Contribution to the Geography of Macedonia ', *The Geographical Journal*, vol. 55, pp. 1–34 (London, 1920) and ' Physiography and Settlements in Southern Macadonia ', *The Geographical Review*, vol. 11, pp. 172–197 (New York, 1921) ;
J. H. Schultze, ' Neugriechenland ', *Petermanns Mitteilungen, Ergänzungsheft* 233 (Gotha, 137) ;
J. H. Schultze, ' Greek Colonisation in Thrace and Macedonia ', *Scottish Geographical Magazine*, vol. 53, pp. 81–89 (Edinburgh, 1937).

5. The geological maps (Figs. 5, 14, 23 and 29) have been compiled mainly from the following sources :
A. Bittner, M. Neumayr and F. Teller, ' Geologische Übersichtskarte des festländischen Griechenland und der Insel Euboea (1876), 1 : 400,000 ', *Denkschriften der Kaiserlichen Akademie der Wissenschaften : Mathematische-Naturwissenschaftliche Klasse*, vol. 40, Part 2 (Vienna, 1880) ;
S. Bončev, *Geologische Karte der Ostlichen und Zentralen Balkanhalbinsel*, 1 : 800,000 (Sofiya, 1936) ;
J. Bourcart, ' Carte géologique des Confins Albanais, 1 : 200,000 ', *Revue de Géographie*, vol. 10, Part 1 (Paris, 1922) ;
L. Burgerstein, M. Neumayr and F. Teller, ' Geologische Übersichtskarte der nordwestlichen Küstenländer des Aegaeischen Meeres, 1 : 500,000 ', *Denkschriften der Kaiserlichen Akademie der Wissenschaften : Mathematische-Naturwissenschaftliche Klasse*, vol. 40, Part 2 (Vienna, 1880) ;
K. Osswald, *Geologische Übersichtskarte von Griechisch-Makedonien*, 1 : 300,000', Sheets I and II, published by the Geological Survey of Greece ;
A. Philippson, 'Geologische Karte von Epirus und West-Thessalien, 1 : 300,000', and ' Geologische Karte von Südost-Thessalien, 1 : 300,000 ', in *Thessalien und der Epirus* (Berlin, 1897) ;
' Geologische Karte des Peloponnes, 1 : 300,000 ' (4 sheets), with *Der Peloponnes* (Berlin, 1892).
Carte Géologique Internationale de l'Europe, 1 : 1,500,000, Sheets 39 (D VI) and 40 (E VI).

Chapter III

WESTERN GREECE

The Uplands of Ípiros and Váltos : Lower Ípiros : The Peninsula of Akarnanía :
The Interior Valley of Akarnanía : The Lake Basin of Aitolía : The Coastal
Plains of Aitolía : The Coastal Mountains of Akarnanía

Western Greece extends from the Albanian frontier to the Gulf of
Pátrai, and from the slopes of the Dividing Mountains to the shores
of the Ionian Sea. It forms the administrative region of Ípiros in
the north, containing the *nomoí* of Ioánnina, Thesprotía, Árta and
Préveza, and of western Stereá Ellás in the south, corresponding
mainly with the *nomós* of Aitolía and Akarnanía (Fig. 2). Throughout, there is a broad similarity of relief and geological structure—
limestone ridges are separated by intervening valleys or lowlands
where shales and sandstones occur—and the trend of the coastline
has everywhere been determined by faulting.

The remoteness of Ípiros from the rest of Greece, and its backwardness, features which have characterized the whole history of
this region, are explained by its position and by the relief of the
land. To the west it extends along the shores of the Ionian Sea
from the Straits of Kérkira to the Gulf of Amvrakía. To the
north it borders Albania, to the north-east Makedhonía, to the
south-east, Thessalía, and to the south it adjoins the *nomós* of Aitolía
and Akarnanía. The country is mountainous throughout, possessing
but one considerable plain of low altitude. This lowland faces the
Gulf of Amvrakía, and seems to offer an easy entrance into Ípiros,
but the shore is made almost unapproachable by the silt of two
rivers, the Loúros and the Árakhthos. The western coast, on the
other hand, is not inaccessible, but its trend is parallel to the
mountain ranges, which are real barriers to communication. The
greatest of these ranges, the Píndhos mountains forms the eastern
boundary of Ípiros.

The backwardness of Ípiros is, in part, due to its long subjection
to Turkish rule. From 1881 until 1912 the Graeco-Turkish
frontier followed the river Árakhthos, and western Ípiros was
therefore under the Turks for three decades longer than Thessalía
and the Píndhos. The Albanian frontier is determined by no
natural feature and was the subject of much dispute before the
final demarcation of November 1921 (see vol. I, Fig. 104). It runs

across the grain of the country and cuts into two approximately equal parts a natural region that extends from the Gulf of Amvrakía to the plains of central Albania. Most of the physical features of Ípiros, therefore, have their counterpart in southern Albania, and the population living on either side of the frontier is very mixed.

The dominant orographical features of Ípiros result from the structure of the country. Firstly, the whole region is underlain by rocks arranged in folds that run approximately parallel to the coast. Secondly, these rocks consist of thick permeable limestones and of impermeable sandstones and shales. In general, the limestones make up the high mountains, while the sandstones and shales correspond to a series of intervening broad vales or deep narrow valleys. Where the vales are wide they have been dissected by numerous streams and are rarely level for any considerable distance. Fig. 5 shows that to the west of the limestone bastions of the Dividing Mountains there are three continuous zones of shale, alternating with three of limestone. In addition to the large plain of Árta there are several smaller strips of alluvial land, sensibly flat and at various heights above sea level. These are often scarcely distinguishable from the larger *polja*, or flat-floored depressions due to the solution of limestone. The scale of the orographical features diminishes in general from east to west, but the ruggedness of the scenery prevails right to the coast, and, in spite of the proximity of the Ionian islands, there are few parts of the Greek coastal lands where seafaring has been so little developed.

The great depth of the valleys is probably the result of rapid uplift of the whole area, ages after the rocks were pressed into folds in the Oligocene or Miocene periods. In the absence of detailed geological surveys, however, the extent to which this elevation was accompanied by fractures remains uncertain. It seems that before the uplift this was already a region of parallel, but lower, mountain chains ; and the floors of the valleys which separated the ridges still exist as shelves, high above the present river beds. These now form the sites of many of the villages which consequently are difficult to reach. The instability of the earth's crust in this region, and the likelihood that there are many deep dislocations, is shown by the frequency of earthquakes. In 1936, for example, the total number of earthquake shocks in Greece was 165—probably a normal condition. Of these, 33 (or 20%) were recorded in Ípiros (including Levkás with 9). That the coastal belt is the least stable area seems to be indicated by the number of shocks at Préveza (3) and Árta (8), but the tremors also affected the interior as far as Ioánnina and Karpenísion.

Although the grain of the relief runs from north-west to south-east the general altitudes are higher along two lines transverse to this direction. The first of these higher zones lies near the Albanian frontier, and the second extends from the coast, opposite the southern end of Kérkira, to the northern end of the Píndhos mountains. Thus the land below 1,000 ft. includes the lower valley of the Thíamis and most of south-western Ípiros. The climate and vegetation in these parts, therefore, are markedly Mediterranean in character.

Ípiros contains 5% of the Greek population (363,041 in 1938), 7% of the total area of the country (3,686 sq. miles), but only 4·5% of the cultivated land. The population density is low (only 98 per sq. mile) and there are no really large urban agglomerations in the whole area. Agriculture differs little throughout the area. There is a small production of wine and grapes in the *nomoí* of Ioánnina and Préveza, and even a small raisin industry in the town of Préveza. Maize predominates everywhere and there is also a certain amount of wheat, but cereals are not generally grown to any large extent. There are only 61,000 agricultural holdings, 92% of which are less than 12 acres in size. Formerly there was a considerable number of large estates, but these were expropriated by the government and distributed as small holdings to the peasants. Farm equipment is relatively simple and there are few iron ploughs. The use of fertilizers is negligible ; the system of crop rotation is poor, and maize is often grown on the same land year after year. Sometimes the land is irrigated, but more often not, and in a region of plentiful rainfall, rivers and lakes, much more could be done to conserve the water. In general, therefore, agriculture is more backward than in other parts of Greece, and partly because of the infertility of the soil the yields per acre are lower than in the rest of the country. On the other hand, the livestock industry is important.

Western Stereá Ellás, lying to the south of the Gulf of Amvrakía, comprises the whole of Akarnanía as well as the lowland of Aitolía, and unlike Ípiros it has a considerable area of agricultural land and has always been relatively populous. Climatically it resembles Iliá and the neighbouring Ionian islands and it shares in their modern concentration upon the growing of currants. Moreover, it suffers like them from the effects of recent earthquakes.

On the basis of its relief, which has largely been determined by fractures, Western Greece can be divided into seven well marked regions (Fig. 6). The first two are the largest and lie mainly in Ípiros, the remaining five are in western Stereá Ellás. They are :

B1. The Uplands of Ípiros and Váltos.
B2. Lower Ípiros.
B3. The Peninsula of Akarnanía.
B4. The Interior Valley of Akarnanía.
B5. The Lake Basin of Aitolía.
B6. The Coastal Plains of Aitolía.
B7. The Coastal Mountains of Akarnanía.

THE UPLANDS OF ÍPIROS AND VÁLTOS (REGION B1)

This region lies mainly in the north and east of Ípiros and includes almost all the land above 1,000 ft. It corresponds with the *nomós* of Ioánnina, includes eastern Árta, and extends along the western edge of the Dividing Mountains into the district of Váltos in Akarnanía. It is divisible into five physical units :

The Basin of Ioánnina
The Northern Districts
The Eastern Fringe
The Upper Valley of the Loúros
The Western Mountains and Furrow

The Basin of Ioánnina

The most easterly of the limestone belts of Higher Ípiros broadens to enclose the basin of Ioánnina. This is one of the few parts of Ípiros where the scenery is not rugged (see vol. I, Plate 5). In spite of the high altitude of its floor (1,550 ft.) the basin forms part of an old worn surface which, since its elevation, has not been attacked by serious erosion. It is a *polje* plain, once entirely filled by a lake and hence covered with fine silt, but with some ridges of conglomerate. It is 14 miles long and 1 mile wide at the narrowest part, and at its broad eastern end contains the triangular lake of Ioánnina, 24 sq. miles in area and not more than 35 ft. deep. Several rocky hills rise from the plain, one still an island, while another forms the peninsular site of the fortress of Ioánnina built in its present form by Ali Pasha (see vol. II, pp. 383–5). From this promontory the town has spread landwards. Its relatively large size, with a population of 20,540, is the clearest indication of the degree to which it dominates north-western Greece. It is the natural focal point of the region, but its growth has also depended upon the fertility of the basin.

The surrounding country is extremely bare and the lake is insalubrious. The basin is dominated on the north-east by the faulted and straight ridge of limestone, the Mitsikéli mountains, which rise to 5,935 ft. The range ends abruptly opposite Métsovon and gives easy access to the valley of the river Metsovítikos, and so to the main pass across the Píndhos. Near the southern shore of the lake an isolated crag rises to 2,480 ft., the site of the ancient town of Tekmon, and at its foot is one of the *katavóthra* that act as outlets for the lake. To the south-west, the broad and bare plateau of Tomarokhória rises to rounded summits some 3,500 ft. high ; it is uninhabited except for summer shepherds and a few people who live in the fertile hollows covered with red earth. The plateau is separated from the high limestone massif of Tómaros to the south-west by a steep sided valley, drained in part by the headwaters of the river Loúros. Dodona, the site of the sanctuary of Zeus and the most ancient oracle in Greece, lies in the valley (Plate 10). Its importance was in all probability greatly enhanced by the imposing relief of the surrounding mountains and the high frequency of thunderstorms.

An easy route from the basin of Ioánnina leads southwards over an arm of the former lake bed and enters the valley of the Loúros. A second route strikes northwards past the secondary lake of Mirádhia to the *polje* of Dholianá, the source of the Thíamis, and so to Albania. Originally the Lake of Ioánnina was drained northwards by a tributary of the Thíamis, and, at a later stage, by *katavóthrai*, west of Lake Mirádhia. Today, the drainage is by a tunnel that has been driven through the northern end of the Tomarokhória plateau, thus connecting with the valley of the Thíamis.

The basin of Ioánnina has a rather extreme climate, with mean temperatures over 75° F. for July, August and September and below 44° F. for December, January and February, while in exceptional years the lake has been frozen over for as long as 3 months. The average annual rainfall is 47 ins. and there is no real drought— the warmth of summer and the plentiful water supply ensure heavy crops of maize. Some wheat, grapes and wine are also produced. These plants have largely replaced deciduous oak forests and the only prominent woods that remain are made up of evergreen oaks,

such as ilex and Kermes.   The average density of population in the
district is 220 per sq. mile.

The Northern Districts

From Mount Tómaros, abrupt ridges, often with symmetrical
bare slopes and sharp tops, extend north-north-west to the Albanian
frontier.   This almost entirely mountainous area contains, however,
an important depression that lies across the northern end of the
basin of Ioánnina.   It is some 13 miles long, 1,300 to 2,300 ft. in
height, and is formed of two *polja*.   The one in the north-east is
drained by the Aóös, and is separated by rolling country from that
of the Thíamis in the south-west.   The natural focus of this district
is the plain of Dholianá, extremely marshy but very fertilé where
drained, and forming an oasis of foliage and fruit.   The Thíamis
enters the plain from a cavern and leaves it southwards in a gorge.
West of Dholianá the plain narrows to the low Pass of Delvinákion
(1,870 ft.) through which runs the main road to Sarandë.   The
average density of population is 120 per sq. mile.

The Eastern Fringe

The Dividing Mountains are separated from the other ranges of
Ípiros by a belt of country which, owing to its geological nature,
presents similar physical features throughout.   This is the eastern
zone of impermeable sandstones and shales.   Beginning as a narrow
strip of hill and wooded land east of the Mitsikéli mountains it
extends for 90 miles, varying greatly in width, to the rift valley of
Aitolía.   The northern end of the Píndhos mountains marks a
transverse fracture, along which the river Metsovítikos has cut its
valley in these easily eroded rocks.   Farther south the Árakhthos
has carved its deep gorge, and between it and the nearly isolated
bastion of the Tzoumérka mountains the shaly slopes have been torn
into thousands of ravines and larger valleys.   There are, however,
high ledges bearing numerous villages where the ground is well
watered from the limestone above.   Some of the settlements are
large, like Prámanda, with over 2,000 inhabitants, and are surrounded by orchards and terraced fields, with occasionally woods of
oak nearby.
South of the limestone mountains of Tzoumérka the exposure of
impermeable rocks broadens to 13 miles to reach the Akhelóös.

Plate 10.   The valley of Dodona

The view shows the small fields after harvest, and nut trees on the lower parts of steep fans below the limestone slopes.

Plate 11.   The village of Delvinákion (Pogónion)

The village is at the head of a tributary of the Drínos river and near the Albanian frontier.   The church, in the foreground, stands at the entrance to a gap in the limestone mountains.

[Facing page 28

Plate 12. The gorge of the river Loúros

The river is low ; the road from Árta to Ioánnina is hidden by the plane trees on the left.

The altitudes decline, but the relief remains extremely rough. This area forms the old district of Radhovízi, still in Ípiros. The belt then continues with little change of scenery, but with a breadth of only 8 miles, into the district of Váltos in Akarnanía. Still farther south the much dissected upland retains its height of 2,500 ft., only near its eastern and western edges ; in the middle it has been much lowered by the tributaries of the Akhelóös. This river here flows in wide meanders on a narrow flood plain, a band of shingle fringed with plane trees. The river owes its other name ' Aspro ' either to the whiteness of the stones or to its milky waters. Just below its confluence with the Mégdhova, where there are hot springs of some repute, the Akhelóös turns across the grain of the rocks into a long canyon nearly 1,000 ft. deep. Throughout this large tract there is an average density of 49 people per sq. mile, but in the broad southern part and in Váltos it is only about 38. Here, many of the settlements are mere hamlets or even isolated houses, occupying clearings in oak-forest. The collecting of tanning material from the Valona oak provides a source of livelihood, but most of the people are shepherds and the limestone uplands of Gávrovon (5,845 ft.), an outlier of the central Píndhos mountains, offer convenient summer pasture.

The Upper Valley of the Loúros

West of the Árakhthos the next belt begins with the high precipices of the Xerovoúni mountains overlooking the river. They are composed of limestones of three different types and form a high block of country, some 10 miles across, in which the river Loúros has cut a deep canyon (Plate 12). The Xerovoúni drop from the main crest (5,282 ft.) to a tableland with occasional cultivated hollows. This in turn gives way northwards to the well-peopled district of Katsanokhoria, the threshold of the basin of Ioánnina. From this northern area the road comes easily down to the river Loúros which it follows southwards in the canyon to the Plain of Árta. The region benefits from the outcrop of impermeable strata of red chert which cause many springs, and which, in places, widen the valley of the Loúros, thus making it suitable for settlement. Most of the villages, however, are on the high tableland and their fields are on the red earth of the hollows. The population of the whole area is about 22,000 giving an average density of 96 per sq. mile.

The Western Mountains and Furrow

This belt, stretching from the Albanian frontier to the plain of Árta, has a twofold character. On the west is the most imposing and longest of all the limestone mountains, though not the highest : on the east is the much lower land of sandstone and shales narrowing southwards to deep and wooded valleys. The summits of the western mountains are mostly between 4,000 and 5,000 ft. above sea level and stand above precipices facing westwards. The difficulty of penetrating this country is lessened slightly by three gaps, but their gorge-like nature makes road building almost impossible. The most northerly gap is the transverse gorge of the Thíamis, inaccessible and avoided by the road which climbs over the high ground to the south. The most southerly is the gorge of the Akhéron, which is equally forbidding. The steep eastern slopes of these limestone mountains are well wooded, with oaks and firs on the higher parts.

The furrow to the east is a continuation of the similar country in Albania, drained by the river Drino. The frontier crosses it at an acute angle and would shut off the Greek district of Pogonianí but for the access to it by the Pass of Delvinákion (Plate 11). The impermeable sandstones and shales have been carved up into a hilly land by the many affluents of the Drino and by the several longitudinal tributaries of the Thíamis. Patches of oak-wood are frequent, and in the north beech is common. The numerous villages, with the maize-fields and fruit and nut-trees, usually stand on terraces or higher shelves, the majority lining the foot of the mountains where they benefit from spring water. In the south, the western mountains and the limestone belt of the central Píndhos converge, and the broad hilly land that intervenes is replaced by the narrow and forested valley of the Xiropótamos, an alcove of the Plain of Árta (Fig. 8). The average density of population for the whole region is 62 per sq. mile.

LOWER ÍPIROS (REGION B2)

Fundamentally this region is built of limestone, and the degree of its habitability depends upon the extent to which these rocks are covered either by alluvium or by the residual red earth of the *doline*. The chief exception to this is on the outcrops of sandstone and shales. The hills throughout have been largely denuded of woods ; scattered ilex and maquis, or humbler scrub, form the

prevailing vegetation while bare cliffs and crags are common features.
The cultivation of every hollow containing soil shows the advantage
of the low altitude. Olive groves and vineyards are common, but
the vine is not grown in the district around the mouth of the Thíamis.
The hills north of the Thíamis are more varied in scenery, because
here the sandstones and shales are more in evidence. They are
drained chiefly by the river Kalpatiótiko which, with a tributary,
cuts two transverse gorges through the most westerly high ridge.
The villages are evenly spread among these hills and along the great
bend of the Thíamis. On the basis of physical features the region
may be subdivided into four :

The Lower Thíamis Valley
Thesprotía
The Coastal Hills of Préveza
The Plain of Árta

The Lower Thíamis Valley

The Thíamis crosses the most westerly ridge of Higher Ípiros
in a deep incised meander, passes between low hills of Tertiary
rocks, and then emerges upon its delta. The river now has a single
mouth which is extending rapidly in the sheltered waters of Váltos
Bay, and in so doing, the delta has embraced two islands of limestone.
Part of the delta is swamp but most of it is cultivated for maize and
wheat. The low hills behind, and the edges of the plain, have many
olive groves and other fruit trees, especially round the largest place,
Filiátes. This corner of the Greek mainland has a population
density of 127 per sq. mile.

Thesprotía

The nomós of Thesprotía, established in 1936, corresponds to this
area and to the ancient district of the same name. It is drained
chiefly by the Kokkitós, whose valley is separated from the Ionian
Sea by a series of coastal hills.

The Kokkitós Valley. The heart of Thesprotía is the lowland
lying immediately west of the high mountains. It begins close to
the southward bend of the Thíamis as a low saddle and a small *polje*,
and then continues to the sea as an almost flat plain, $2\frac{1}{2}$ miles wide
and 21 miles long. It consists of two distinct sections. The upper
part lies sunk between parallel north-south scarps, probably marking

faults. The alluvial floor is well drained by the Kokkitós which is
pressed close to the western edge, and slopes gently southwards
from 500 to 150 ft. The western wall rises some 800 ft. from the
plain and is cut by deep ravines ; on the east, the much higher
mountains have no deep valleys and present continuous precipices
of pale limestone. The lower slopes are less steep because they are
formed of sandstones—a point of geological interest, since they
are much younger than the Mesozoic limestones which have been
thrust over them. The junction between the different strata is
marked by springs. The lower part of the plain begins opposite
the huge chasm cut in the mountains by the Akhéron, a V-shaped
gash some 3,600 ft. deep ; it then extends southwards for six miles
and finally turns westwards for the last six. The plain broadens
irregularly on both sides and most of the floor is very low. This
section is evidently an old arm of the sea which the Akhéron has
gradually filled up with its alluvium. The highest parts are along
the banks of the river in the middle of the plain, and, until recently,
there were swamps on either side. The process of silting was aided
by the obstruction of two ridges of rock, one forming the coast
and the other, less continuous, farther inland. Between the two
ridges the swamps of Ammoudhiá still remain, just behind the
cliffed coast. The ancient name of Fanári Bay (at the mouth
of the Kokkitós) ' Glykys Limen ' (or sweet harbour) was due to the
freshness of its water, proof of the great volume of the river. Drainage of the inland swamps has now been largely effected by elaborate
works, including the installation of pumps on both banks of the
river close to the shore.

The plain of the Kokkitós and Akhéron has an average population
density of 194 per sq. mile, but it must be remembered that many of
the inhabitants are partly dependent on the surrounding mountain
slopes. Most of the villages are on the eastern side and stand well
above the plain. By far the largest is Paramithiá with a population
of 2,390 ; it has a Turkish fortress commanding the entrance to the
plain. The upper vale has always been devoted mainly to cereal
crops and tree fruits ; in the lower swampy part, rice alone was
regularly cultivated, but with proper cultivation various irrigated
crops may now be produced (Plate 13).

The inhabitants of this valley are mainly Chamurian Moslems
who belong to the Cham branch of the south Albanian Tosks (see
vol. I, pp. 363–5). In the mid-eighteenth century these people
(the Souliotes) were a semi-autonomous community, regarded by

Plate 13. The swamps of the lower Akhéron, before drainage

Plate 14. Coastal hills and islands north of Párga
The ridge behind the village of Moúrtos (right) is some 1,600 ft. high. The coastline indicates submergence and the caves in the foreground are due to solution of pure limestone.

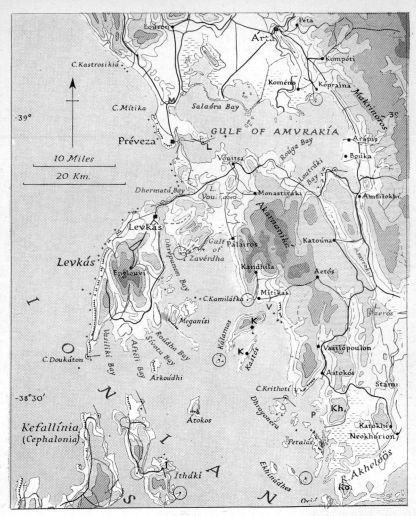

Fig. 8.   The Gulf of Amvrakía and the peninsula of Akarnanía
Kh, Khounovoúna Hills ;   *Ko*, Mt. Koutsouláris ;   *L*, Cape Laskára ;
M, Mázoma Lagoon ;   *P*, Platiyáli Bay ;   *V*, Voúrkos Bay

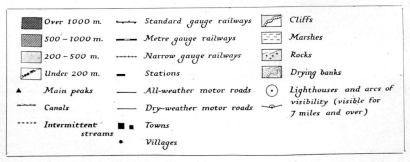

Over 1000 m.	**Standard gauge railways**	**Cliffs**
500 – 1000 m.	**Metre gauge railways**	**Marshes**
200 – 500 m.	**Narrow gauge railways**	**Rocks**
Under 200 m.	**Stations**	**Drying banks**
Main peaks	**All-weather motor roads**	**Lighthouses and arcs of visibility (visible for 7 miles and over)**
Canals	**Dry-weather motor roads**	
Intermittent streams	**Towns**	
	Villages	

Fig. 9.   Key to Figs. 8, 16, 25, 31, 34 and 35

[*Facing page* 33

the Turks as a counterpoise to the Venetian control of Párga and Préveza. But from 1791 they had to resist Turkish attempts at suppression, and, in spite of their heroism, they lost their independence in 1821.

The Coastal Hills. The hills between the valley of the Kokkitós and the sea occupy a rough parallelogram whose sides have been delimited by fractures. The district is built of folded limestones, the trend of which corresponds to the ridges, as shown, for example, by the headlands flanking Platariá Bay (Plate 14). One peak, east of this bay, reaches 3,163 ft. but the general summit levels usually lie between 2,000 and 2,500 ft. The rivers are short and intermittent, the greater part of the drainage being underground. Although the coastal slopes in many parts bear forests of Valona oak up to 1,200 ft. most of the hills are covered with maquis, which provides winter pastures for large flocks of sheep and goats. Agriculture and settlements are mainly restricted to the coast and the hollows of the interior. On the coast the settlements depend upon the small plains at the heads of the bay and on the gentle slopes of the riviera coast near Párga. In these places there is all the variety of Mediterranean cultivation, including, since water is plentiful, the growing of citrus fruits. The largest villages are Párga and Pérdhika (see vol. I, Plate 27), each with over 1,400 inhabitants, but Igoumenítsa, with a population of 1,340, is the capital of the new *nomós* of Thesprotía and the terminus of the road to Ioánnina.

Among the several enclosed *polja*, that called the plain of Margarítion from the name of its largest village is the most important. In many ways it resembles the plain of the Kokkitós but is much smaller. The long flat floor, only 33 ft. above sea level, is continued at either end by smaller basins, separated from the main depression by rocky barriers. The one in the south is marshy and lies only a mile from the coast. The plain is irrigated with well water, and the fruit and grain crops support six villages. The average density for the whole district is 106 people per sq. mile.

The Coastal Hills of Préveza

South of the Akhéron the ends of the limestone ranges have been truncated by a straight, faulted coastline with a scarp rising from the sea to 1,800 ft. Similarly, from north of Cape Kastrosikiá, other fractures run inland and have brought the mountains to an abrupt end. The high ground continues inland to the valley of the Loúros and is drained southwards through a series of parallel valleys. Much of this country is largely covered by scattered woods of oak, mixed with maquis. Along the valleys there is often much cultivation supporting large villages, while settlements are sprinkled widely over the higher parts.

The mountains are prolonged southwards by the hills that end in the peninsula of Préveza. These are remnants of a sheet of porous Pliocene strata, up to 500 ft. in height, around which large expanses of lower raised beaches have been preserved to form the peninsula. The higher hills are covered with maquis or poorer vegetation, but they are partly under cultivation, with olives on the east. The flatter ground is everywhere under crops, and several square miles north of Préveza form a continuous olive grove. These conditions extend to the peninsula east of Préveza (Plate 15).

Control of this peninsula and of the straits has always called for a settlement of importance and the site of Préveza has been occupied by a town since the time of Pyrrhus, about 290 B.C. (see vol. II, pp. 279-81). The isthmus, 5 miles to the north, was selected by the Roman emperor Augustus as the site of his new city, Nicopolis, built and named to commemorate the victory of Actium in 31 B.C.

The Plain of Árta

The depression occupied by the Gulf of Amvrakía and the plain of Árta is due to subsidence along transverse fractures. It has been shut off from the open sea by the raising of Pliocene strata which have later been subjected to wave action. The enclosed depression is a rough parallelogram, with sides some 20 and 13 miles long, and the original gulf must have had this general shape interrupted only by two narrow limestone islands that prolong the mountain chains of Préveza south-eastwards. The reduction of the gulf is due to the

Fig. 10. The western corne

Based on photographs.
The view is taken from the crag of Ayía Kateríni in the south, the limits of the vie follow the mountain foot. The valley near the centre, between limestone ridges,

deposition of silt in its shallow waters by the rivers Árakhthos and Loúros during floods. The Árakhthos has been the more active and has carried the greater load, consisting of heavy gravel from the impermeable rocks. The fan of its deposits, shown by the contours on Fig. 11, has been built up higher than that of the Loúros which, coming from limestone, is much more regular in its flow and carries little silt. As a result, the Loúros has been forced to hug the north-western corner of the depression. The Árakhthos traverses the last spur of limestone in a gap of its own making, now occupied by the town of Árta and in earlier days by Amvrakía, and then turns to the south-east in which direction it is extending its bed. Most of this eastern part of the plain is high enough to be dry, well peopled and cultivated, but hitherto damage has repeatedly been caused by the river shifting its bed.

The Loúros, on the other hand, with much water but little silt, is impeded on reaching the plain, and the congestion becomes worse as it passes westwards owing to the abundant flow of water from tributaries and many springs from the ends of the limestone ridges (Fig. 10). Consequently along its course there are marshes which are partly below sea-level. The waves of the gulf have raised a series of spits in front of the plain, attached to the two deltas and supported by two islets. Behind the spits are broad lagoons, abounding in fish and large prawns, and the home of vast numbers of aquatic birds, notably pelicans. Salt is obtained by evaporation in the Tsoukalió Lagoon.

The task of putting in harness the two contrasted rivers of the plain has been undertaken in recent years by British engineers, and the prospective results of their work comprised not merely the drainage and protection of nearly all the land requiring these benefits, but also provision for the perennial irrigation of most of it by water from the Loúros. Protection is effected by embankments along

f Árta before drainage

imately WNW and ENE. The river Loúros enters from the gap (right) to Xiropótamos. The distant lowland (left) is drained by several small rivers.

the Árakhthos, on its right bank where it follows the hill-foot, and on both banks below this ; the left bank of the Loúros has also been raised except for the last 5½ miles to its mouth, where the swamps still remain. Drainage of the upper marshes involves pumping at a station situated at the head of the last reach of the Loúros. Irrigation has been effected partly by the regulation of the Loúros from its entrance to the plain, and partly by the diversion of some of its waters from the point where the river turns westwards near Áyios Spirídhon. A main canal, 30 ft. above sea level and with four branch canals, has also been built around the Árakhthos fan, and canals also drain the Strongilí marshes. The future agricultural benefits of the plain are indicated by the fact that the acreage of irrigated land has much increased at the expense of poor grazing and marsh.

Before the drainage operations the cultivated land coincided mostly with the older fan of the Árakhthos, south-west of Árta, and only in lesser measure along the banks of the present river, which are farther east. There was also some cultivation along the Loúros. This area was given, in almost equal proportions, to field-crops, orchards, and vineyards. The latter produced table-grapes as well as wine, while the orchards include a large number of orange trees. Indeed, oranges are more important to Árta than to the rest of the mainland of Greece.

The population density of this rich plain is 263 per sq. mile. Most of the villages are on the plain itself and no doubt will now be much healthier from the partial drainage of the swamps. Around the margin, the entrance to each valley in the mountains is marked by a settlement ; while Flámboura, near the mouth of the Loúros, with a population of 1,530, is a strategic place guarding the entrance from the coast. Árta itself controls the routes to Akarnanía, Central Greece and Thessalía. It is a compact little town of 1,468 inhabitants and possesses a citadel and a fine Byzantine or Turkish bridge.

The Peninsula of Akarnanía (Region B3)

Physical Characteristics

The eparchy of Vónitsa and Xíromeros possesses distinct individuality, and the keynote of the scenery is expressed in the name Xíromeros or drylands. Much of the country is hilly and the high ground is composed of permeable pale yellow limestones which are

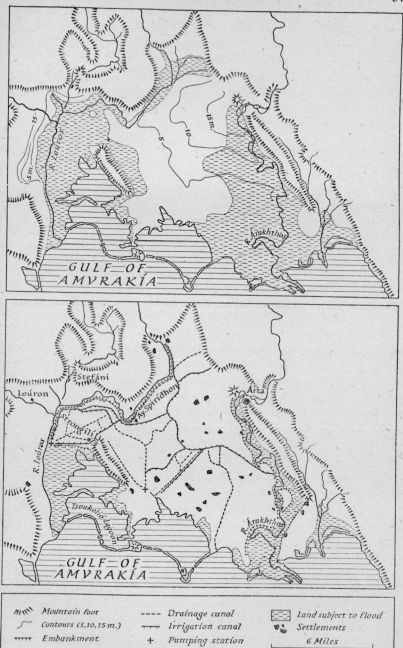

Fig. 11.   Drainage of the plain of Árta

Based on engineering plans and the 1 : 100,000 G.S.G.S. Series 4087, Sheet C1854.
The upper map shows the condition of the plain before drainage but with the
settlements omitted ; contours have been inserted to show the slope of the ground
in some localities only.   The viewpoint of Fig. 8 is a rocky hill south-west of
Strongilí.

gently folded like those of southern Ípiros. The well-watered parts of the peninsula are either the many small karstic basins, or the several larger and separate plains around the margin. Some of these peripheral lowlands are composed of low terraces of Pliocene marls or sands, while others are of deltaic alluvium. The region was once continuous with Ípiros before transverse fractures led to the formation of the Gulf of Amvrakía. Stretches of the west coast are also due to faulting, while the eastern boundary is a great furrow that is linked to the rift-valley of southern Aitolía (see p. 40). The general grain of the country in this broken peninsula is from north to south, corresponding to the rock folds, and the most prominent orographical features are the bare rocky sides of the flat-topped ridges and plateaux (Fig. 10). The average summit level of these uplands is between 3,600 and 5,000 ft., and the highest point is in the massive Boúmistos ridge, 5,161 ft. above sea level. Most of the rivers have only intermittent flow, and all the hills and plateaux are pockmarked by enclosed and often rocky depressions, varying in size from mere sink-holes to wide karstic basins.

The indented coast is evidence of submergence, fortunately offset by subsequent elevation in the north where there are some stretches of Pliocene sediments forming valuable cultivable land. The islands of Kálamos and Kastós are fragments of the same limestone that composes so much of the mainland, while the hilly peninsula in the north-west, attaining a height of 1,653 ft., was also an island before its recent emergence. It is now linked by a raised beach which forms the largest plain in Akarnanía, and which extends between the bays of Vónitsa and Pálairos. This lowland encloses the shallow reed-girt lake of Voulkariá, and is comparable in origin and physical characteristics with the neck of land that has linked the peninsula of Áktion to the mainland. Again, in the south, the archipelago of the Ekhinádhes Islands (including the Dhragonéra group, see p. 345) consists of small outlying fragments of limestone, while other remnants, now some distance inland, rise from the delta of the Akhelóös on both sides of the river.

Land Utilization

The peninsula as a whole was originally covered with oak-forest, mainly of Valona and ilex, and only a century ago these woods were still a source of timber for ship-building. In the western half they have now been replaced by maquis or, in places, by scrub of

Kermes oak. On flatter ground the wild pear is widely distributed, cypresses adorn the villages, and the plane, sometimes with the ash, characterizes the damper hollows. The eastern half of the peninsula, though everywhere the lower, is hilly, and is still mainly wooded in the north and in the south, but the larger central section is a fairly smooth plateau, 650 to 1,300 ft. in height with considerable areas of good, red, residual soil. It is largely under maize and other grains, vines and tobacco, and is one of the more populous parts of the peninsula. In the mountainous west the small villages are situated so as to overlook the little plains which are generally karstic depressions. Vátou, with 233 inhabitants and some 300 ft. above its flat *polje*, is a typical example of such settlements. The plain, only a square mile in area, is 2,510 ft. above sea-level and is surrounded by cliffs from 500 to 2,000 ft. in height (Fig. 12).

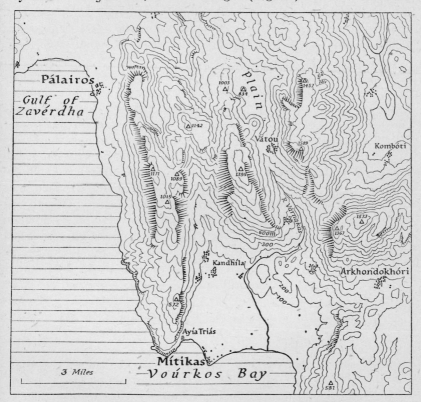

Fig. 12. The coastal plain of Mítikas and the *polje* of Vátou
Based on the 1 : 100,000 *Epitelikós Khártis tis Elládhos*, Sheet θ IV.

Two openings, leading to Voúrkos Bay and Astakós Bay respectively, break the continuity of the western coastal wall. The former resembles a box with the seaward side missing, the other three being precipices ; this plain of the ancient Alyzia now supports some 4,000 people, living in villages on the inner slopes and in the small port of Mítikas. One of the villages, Arkhondokhóri, occupies a high gap in the mountains, and this way inland is still guarded by two medieval towers on hill tops. The second opening, towards Astakós, in some ways resembles a Norwegian fiord, with half of the funnel occupied by deep water (Plate 16). The curving valley floor rises gently inland and, like the bay, is bounded on the west by precipitous slopes rising to over 3,000 ft. Half of the population of some 4,000 are in the port of Astakós, which is now favoured by two good roads, to north and east. In the valley, which is healthy and benefits from concentrated land and sea breezes, vineyards and fields of maize and wheat are flanked by dense maquis, with a profusion of almond trees, gone wild, near the coast.

The landscapes of the north-west are more varied. The unusual features are the lowland recently covered by the sea, and the complete absence of dwellings on it, doubtless from risk of malaria. Except for the port of Vónitsa at the northern end of the isthmus (population 2,416) and that of Pálairos (2,223) at the southern end, there are only four villages and none of these is on the flats. Between Lake Voulkariá and Loutráki Bay the scene varies greatly over short distances. Oak-woods cover the lower hills, some of which are composed of sandstones and marls, while between the hills and on the coastal plains fields of grain are mingled with many fine and varied deciduous trees. The higher ground, containing masses of gypsum, is covered with maquis. The average density of population for the whole region is 67 per sq. mile, but it is much lower than this on the western promontory.

The Interior Valley of Akarnanía (Region B4)

Physical Characteristics

Separating the peninsula of Akarnanía from the ridges of Váltos (see p. 29) is a long north-south furrow, the origin of which is due to a combination of dislocation and solution. Moreover, it is likely that the ancestor of the river Árakhthos followed it, prior to the formation of the Gulf of Amvrakía (Fig. 8).

Plate 15. The countryside around Ayía Thomas, east of Préveza

This aerial view is from the east and shows olive orchards and fields, bare after harvest, on the low terrace facing Préveza. Behind are the uncultivated slopes of the higher terrace.

Plate 16. The head of the Bay of Astakós

The view is to the south-east ; Astakós is partly visible in the foreground. The hills along the far side of the gulf are of limestone, about 1,000 ft. high ; owing to submergence, the lower parts of the valleys form inlets of the gulf. The much steeper slope in the foreground rises to hills which are some 2,000 ft. in height.

[Facing page 40

Plate 17. Amfilokhía at the head of Karvasará Bay

The view looks south-west. The road from Árta (left) passes south, through the ravine, towards Agrínion. The slope behind is of almost pure limestone.

Plate 18. The town of Aitolikón, from the south

The town is on an island in a lagoon and is connected to the mainland on either side by two causeways ; the ends of the two causeways are just out of view.

[Facing page 41

At the south-eastern corner of this gulf the limestone plateaux come forward to the sea and are cut by three deep valleys. That on the west, the narrow gorge of the perennial river Nísas, converges with the second in the inlet of Loutráki ; this central valley is wider, except at the northern end, and is a straight line of *doline* and *polja*, one containing a swamp. The third valley starts as Karvasará Bay, with the little port of Amfilokhía at its head (Plate 17). Its steep sides are like those of Astokós Bay, but instead of a valley plain leading gently inland, an abrupt step marks the entrance to a long valley of interior drainage occupied by Lake Amvrakía (see vol. I, Plate 31, which shows the eastern arm). The bottom of the lake bed is below sea-level and the lake surface varies in extent and level. On the west it is hemmed in by the sinuous edge of the plateaux and on the east by a straight ridge of fine-grained yellowish limestone, including beds of lithographic-stone. This ridge, which is thickly covered with oak-woods, rises to 2,600 ft. and extends southwards for 12 miles, ending abruptly near the river Akhelóös. The occurrence of sulphur at both ends of the corridor is obviously associated with fracturing. Thus in 1847, and again in 1865, a submarine solfatara was active in Karvasará Bay, killing fish and covering them with sulphur. Then in 1881 a violent eruption of sulphuretted hydrogen took place in the Lagoon of Aitolikón, accompanied by great disturbance of the water. Moreover, emanation of sulphur may have caused the formation of the gypsum in the hills to the west of the valley.

Land Utilization

Although the floor of the valley is quite uneven it forms an easy route for a good road, which winds among cornfields, vineyards and orchards. The situation of Amfilokhía at the entrance to this corridor gives it control of two of the three routes into Akarnanía ; one leads west from Karpenísion and the other follows the shores of the gulf from Árta. The two roads converge on the considerable plain of Xirókambos with its scattered woods and cultivated land. High on the ridge behind Amfilokhía, and joined to it by walls, are the ruins of an ancient city. This was Limnaea whose site emphasizes the strategic character of the seaport. The modern town contains 3,516 of the 14,000 inhabitants of the corridor and its western slope.

The Lake Basin of Aitolía (Region B5)

Physical Characteristics

The lake basin of Aitolía, the natural extension of the interior valley, forms the core of the whole region and has always been the chief seat of population. It is a rift-valley cutting across the trend of the various rock formations, and in many respects the physical features resemble those of Makedhonía inland from Thessaloníki. The truncated ends of the sandstone ridges face the plain from the north, while on the south stand remnants of the same strata, forming the Arákinthos range, only the narrow western edge being of limestone. At one time the rift was filled by a single lake, the overflow from which was probably directed upon the present Lagoon of Aitolikón, thereby cutting the deep defile (Klisoúra), 2 miles long and with nearly vertical walls, across the Arákinthos mountains. The much wider outlet of today, followed by the river Akhelóös, is mainly a product of subsequent dislocations.

The Arákinthos mountains present a steep and straight fault-scarp to the valley and a less regular slope to the south, and although not exceeding 2,466 ft. in height and 9 miles in width they form a real barrier because of their deep valleys. To the north-east, the pyramid of Panaitolikón (6,312 ft.) dominates the region, and the limestone zone to which it belongs flanks Lake Trikhonís on the east, thus sealing off the rift valley by a country of hills somewhat lower than the Arákinthos. The ridges, from 1,000 to 3,000 ft. in height, form a dissected plateau that extends eastwards to the valley of the Évinos. Lake Trikhonís now stands 59 ft. above sea-level, but its bottom is 131 ft. below. The outlet westwards through swamps and Lake Lisimákhia (29 ft. in depth) has hardly any slope and is intermittent, so that the level of the lake may be reduced in summer through evaporation by as much as 16 ft. The western part of the hollow has, in fact, gradually been filled up by deposits from the Akhelóös, which now hugs the higher ground to the west of its fan and which provides water for irrigation. Finally, west of the river, is the variable Lake Ozerós lying under the limestone escarpment of Akarnanía and separated from the Akhelóös by a narrow, undulating barrier covered with oak-woods. Through this ridge the lake receives some water from a distributary of the Akhelóös. The whole system, therefore, represents a very immature drainage and one which calls for artificial aids in the interests of agriculture and of health. Whether the Akhelóös could be

deepened permanently at the key-point in the defile by which it
leaves the basin is uncertain, and in any case the plain will be liable
to changes of level or of slope due to earthquakes, such as the one
which destroyed Agrínion (then named Vrakhokhori) in 1887.

Land Utilization

The greater part of the rift-valley is still occupied by lakes or
swamps, but the terraces and alluvial land within its walls provide
for intensive agriculture practised by a large population. The plain
falls into several divisions. First, there is the small triangle at the
outlet of the valley leading from the Gulf of Amvrakía. This lies
to the west of the Akhelóös and is immune from its floods ; it was
the land of the ancient Stratos, built on the site of the present village
and crowning the terminal spur above the river. Next is the plain
of Agrínion, composed partly of the fan of the Akhelóös—its western
half subject to inundation and uncultivated—and partly of the
steeper fan of the Ermítsa which separates the two lakes. This
district is extended by lake terraces for 5 miles along the northern
shore of Lake Trikhonís. On the southern side of the valley such
land is restricted to a narrow strip of fans all the way from the
Akhelóös to within 2 miles of the head of the lake. Finally, at the
south-eastern end, is a small separate plain, hemmed in by hill
and lake.

The mean density of population on these separate plains, about
160 per sq. mile, corresponds to fairly intensive cultivation. The
chief agricultural features are the large production of good tobacco,
and, in recent times, the extension of currant growing. But the
attractiveness of the scenery is greatly increased by the varied
broad-leafed trees and orchards of fruit and olive trees, together
with fields of maize and other grains.

All but a few of the villages occupy hill-foot sites and make use
of hill pastures as well. Agrínion, which in its present position
probably dates from the Middle Ages, is a pleasant garden town
that has doubled its population in the last fifty years to 14,562.
It is reached from Mesolónghion by two routes : the road and
railway by way of the Akhelóös gap and, more directly, by the road
that comes through the Klisoúra defile and then crosses the reed-beds
and thickets between the lakes on a many-arched viaduct or causeway, built by the Turks some 250 years ago. One of the points of
interest in the region is the abundance and great variety of birds,

especially those of marsh and woodland. The lakes are said to teem with fish of several kinds, yet, oddly enough, there is little fishing, and even on Lake Trikhonís there are few boats.

The dissected plateau east of Lake Trikhonís is more densely peopled than the plain, for, in spite of the height of its ridges and the loss of its forests, the valley sides retain sufficient good soil for heavy crops of maize, vines and tobacco. The district, including the plain at the head of the lake, has a density of 190 per sq. mile. Thérmon, with 2,357 inhabitants, on the site of the ancient capital of the Aetolian League (see vol. I, pp. 147–8), predominates among the numerous villages. The Arákinthos mountains are largely smothered in dense bush and remnants of oak-forest, and except for the huts of shepherds and charcoal-burners they are devoid of settlements.

THE COASTAL PLAINS OF AITOLÍA (REGION B6)

Physical Characteristics

The twin deltas of Akhelóös and Évinos, separated from one another by the Aitolikón Lagoon, make up the very immature coastal plain of the Gulf of Pátrai. It was the Parakheloïtis of ancient times, a district where feuds arose over boundaries that altered with natural changes of the river ; it is an amphibious tract of mud-floored lagoon under 3 ft. in depth. Mud banks merge into salt-marsh and then fresh-water marsh covered with broad reed-beds that are burned each summer to promote growth. All this is outlined by a flimsy and incomplete screen of sandspits with dunes.

Land Utilization

The vegetation is gradually winning land from lagoon and gulf, a process that might be accelerated artificially. So far, however, the chief human effort has been the construction of salt-pans west and south of Mesolónghion and the building of the road and branch railway to the landing stage on a sandspit 3 miles from the town. The highest ground is everywhere the most valuable ; the best of it, along the inner margin of the flats, is given to currant vines, the chief wealth of the district, and the industry of this fertile strip is served by a railway. Mesolónghion (population 10,000) is now the only town (see vol. II, pp. 302–3) and is built on a grid-plan with a fringe of summer bathing huts along the lagoon front ; but in ancient times control of this region was contested by two cities.

These were, Oinidai (vine-lands) in the west on a hill beyond the Akhelóös, and Kalydon in the east on a spur overlooking the Évinos. The former had walls 4 miles long enclosing its own harbour ; the latter had a separate port, Krionéri, at the extreme end of the plain. Need for safe refuge in the Middle Ages called Aitolikón into being, and today this remarkable place, with its 400 houses, completely covers an islet in the throat of its lagoon (Plate 18). It has survived partly because of its people's reputation as seamen and fishermen, and partly because it possesses fine olive groves across the water. For a long time it was reached only by stone bridges ; today it is a junction on the Krionéri metre gauge railway.

The lagoons have always been the scene of active fisheries in which labyrinth-traps play a large part ; and fish roes, as well as fish, form a special export of Mesolónghion. The traditional boat for this industry and for local transport is the dugout canoe which is punted with tridents.

THE COASTAL MOUNTAINS OF AKARNANÍA (REGION B7)

Physical Characteristics

The lake region of Aitolía has been described as a hinterland without a coast, and the mountainous belt to the east as a coast without a hinterland. This goes far to explain the eastward pressure of the ancient Aitolians into territory of the Locrians, and their desire to develop the port of Návpaktos. The twin mountains, Varásovon (3,002 ft.) and Klókova (3,408 ft.) rise abruptly from the sea, east of the Évinos delta, and the little plain between them is a gateway only to rough country, crossed transversely by the canyon of the Évinos (Plate 19). The two mountains are composed of limestone, used in the building of Pátrai harbour, and are isolated by faulting from the surrounding mountains. East of Klókova the foreland of Andírrion provides scenery that is familiar all along the northern coast of the Pelopónnisos, but not elsewhere on the northern side of the gulf. It consists of a detached portion of yellow sands and gravels forming deeply gullied hills with a maquis covering and little cultivation. The hills rise from a narrow fringe of plain near the shore and merge into the higher sandstone country of the interior.

Land Utilization

The ancient town of Návpaktos occupies a striking situation on the terminal spur of a long ridge that rises inland to Mount Rígani

(4,839 ft.).   It resembles many ancient Greek cities in its site and plan, with the walls spreading from the lofty acropolis to the shore and enclosing the harbour.   Although destroyed by an earthquake in A.D. 557 much still remains visible, since the Venetians rebuilt the outer walls.   The existing town, with 4,208 inhabitants, was doomed to relative insignificance by the poverty of its connexions with the interior.   It was formerly linked to the small port of Krionéri by a most difficult road that notched the pale precipices of Klókova and Varásovon ; today, the new road still contours Klókova at a giddy height, but circumvents Varásovon by passing northwards to the Évinos (see vol. II, Plate 96).   The two flanking plains of Návpaktos are intensively cultivated, with irrigation partly derived from copious springs.

For Bibliographical Note, see p. 22.

For sources, see p. 22.

Chapter IV

CENTRAL GREECE

The Barrier Mountains : The Megára and Elevsís Plains and Salamís : The Peninsula of Attikí and Aíyina : The Kifissós and Asopós Basins : The Oíti and Kallídhromon Mountains and Lokrís : The Valley of the Sperkhiós : Óthris and its Marginal Lands : Évvoia

The oblong of mountains, plains and islands lying east of the highlands of Aitolía and the southern Píndhos forms Central Greece. It was, and is, the heartland of the Hellenes. The northern part corresponds mainly to the *nomós* of Fthíotis and Fokís, but includes also the southern fringe of Thessalía. The narrower seaward area consists of the more peninsular *nomós* of Attikí and Voiotía, together with the island of Évvoia. In the south-west the region extends to the Isthmus of Kórinthos and so includes a small part of Korinthía. In all, the region contains nearly a quarter of the Greek people, of whom about one half live in Athens and Piraiévs.

Fig. 14. A highland profile of Central Greece
Based on the 1 : 250,000 G.S.G.S. Series 4088 : The Balkans. The vertical exaggeration is just over three times. The profile has not been drawn in a continuous straight line ; changes in direction are indicated where points of latitude are marked.

Central Greece is largely shut off from the Gulf of Kórinthos by high mountains (Fig. 14), and most of its plains, whether coastal or inland, face the Aegean Sea. Furthermore, the fragmentation of the rocks has divided it into a number of compartments, in which the modern population is largely concentrated. The intervening mountains, although essential to the life of the country, have been largely deforested and stripped of their soil. It is, therefore, a land of abrupt contrasts in relief, vegetation and density of population.

While the coastline and the boundaries of mountain and basin correspond mainly with recent fractures, the less obvious physical features depend upon the nature and structure of the rocks. For the most part the northern and western region is composed of limestones of Mesozoic age and their folds generally trend from west to east, i.e., somewhat obliquely to the direction of the major physical features. In Attikí and southern Évvoia, however, other rocks are exposed and lie closely folded in various directions, usually transverse to these two peninsulas. This broad structural division of Central Greece into two major regions was adopted in Vol. I, Chap. I of this Handbook. In this more detailed account, however, Central Greece is divided into eight regions (Fig. 15). These are :

C1. The Barrier Mountains.
C2. The Megára and Elevsís Plains and Salamís.
C3. The Peninsula of Attikí and Aíyina.
C4. The Kifissós and Asopós Basins.
C5. The Oíti and Kallídhromon Mountains and Lokrís.
C6. The Valley of the Sperkhiós.
C7. Óthris and its Marginal Lands.
C8. Évvoia.

THE BARRIER MOUNTAINS (REGION C1)

The Barrier Mountains are conveniently described under the following sub-regions :

The Upper Mórnos Basin
Gióna and Parnassós
Mount Elikón
The Eastern Mountains

The Upper Mórnos Basin

From Cape Psaromíta a line running approximately northwards for 37 miles to the Sperkhiós valley divides the two main regions of Stereá Ellás. It is a physical boundary, and, as the western limit of the full Hellenic civilization in classical times, it was of great cultural significance. For 18 miles in the north, the boundary follows the prominent ridge which culminates in Vardhoúsia (7,995 ft.—see vol. I, Plate 4). To the east is the even higher wall of Gióna (8,242 ft.), separated by the deep, straight cleft of the upper Mórnos. The head streams of the Mórnos enter the furrow from a broad pass (3,900 ft.) leading eastward to the valley of Kifissós. This high crossways has often been contested by armies in the past, and in the future, roads will doubtless make use of it to give access to the surrounding mountains of Oíti, Gióna and Vardhoúsia. The country offers both to mountaineer and to tourist the nearest approach

SKÍROS

ÉVVOIA

miropótamos

C.Kafirévs

Stíra

Marmári

Óchi

Káristos

KÉA

in Greece to the scenery of the Alps, with fantastic ridges of limestone rising from the gentler slopes of sandstone and dark forests. Farther south, the Mórnos turns west and has cut a deep valley through the limestone mountains. In classical times the gap was controlled by a fortress town on its northern brink ; the modern counterpart is Lidhoríkion, 2 miles to the south-east, connected by motor-road to the small port of Pánormon. The road follows the valley of the Velítsa, a north-flowing tributary of the Mórnos, above which a dozen villages are picturesquely situated. The density of population is 62 per sq. mile and is much the same as on the lower mountains of the seaboard.

Gióna and Parnassós

The Barrier Mountains consist of a series of separate faulted blocks, composed almost entirely of limestone. They stand *en echelon* from west to east, each block being successively farther south. The two highest massifs, Gióna and Parnassós, are also the broadest and dominate Central Greece in every way. The most impressive features are the forbidding cliffs and buttresses of their flanks. Each mountain has a small culminating part, over 6,500 ft. in height, that has been sculptured by ice—in Gióna a true comb-ridge, in Parnassós (8,061 ft.) a group of peaks above the eastern wall (see vol. I, Plate 17). Apart from these Alpine features both mountain groups consist of plateaux, characterized by open valleys which are often over 1,500 ft. deep and which were eroded when the mountains stood much lower (Plate 20). The limestones, long subjected to solution, have a very rough surface, with abrupt sink-holes and broader *doline* floored with red earth. In the southern part of Gióna four *doline*, comparable only with those of Crete, are sunk from 1,300 to 1,900 ft. beneath the surrounding ridges. On the plateau of Parnassós, north of Dhelfoí, there is a large *polje* on which grain is cultivated at an altitude of 3,600 ft. Both mountains bear remnants of fir- and pine-woods in the remoter parts, and they also provide pasture for large flocks in summer.

Between the two limestone massifs the erosion of a belt of folded red shales has produced a deep valley, a gateway to Central Greece ; it is followed by a road, made by the Allies in 1916–18, linking the port of Itéa with Brállos across the Ámbliani Pass (2,820 ft.) near its northern end. South of this pass the road runs above an open basin with many vineyards, from which a dark ravine, 2,600 ft.

deep, leads westwards to Mount Gióna, and an even deeper canyon leads southwards to the coast (see vol. I, Plate 40). Above the valley a high shelf surrounds the end of Mount Gióna and continues seawards to form the bush-covered waste flanking the Gulf of Kríssa. On the east a similar plateau, triangular in shape, lies between the Gulfs of Kríssa and Andíkira, facing the former in a straight fault-scarp, 2,600 ft. high, in contrast to the indented shore opposite. From its surface, Mount Soumaliés rises to 4,186 ft., a block of limestone that has been severed by fracture from Parnassós. Between the two mountains the deep glen of the river Xiropótamos (Pleístos) provides a route to the lower basin of the river Kifissós, via Dhelfoí and Arákhova.

On the western shelf there are several large villages, including Ámfissa (Sálona) with 5,294 inhabitants. They overlook a forest of cultivated olive trees upon the flat floor of the broadening canyon, and the great production of the finest olives accounts for the comparatively dense population (Plate 21). Itéa, at the head of the Gulf of Kríssa, is the port for Dhelfoí and offers good anchorage to coasting vessels. Galaxídhion, on the western side of the gulf, is uncommon in having few contacts with the soil. Its 3,000 inhabitants are mostly sailors and ship-builders and owners. The eastern plateau has its own oasis, that of Dhesfína (population 3,029) in a large *polje* with good red soil.

The valley of the Xiropótamos was the holiest ground of ancient Greece, and even now is one of the most impressive localities. Delphi, standing on a terrace 820 ft. above the chasm and far below the sun-scorched precipice of Parnassós, has a magnificent site befitting the priceless treasures of architecture, sculpture and precious metals that gradually accumulated as gifts from all the states of Greece (see vol. I, pp. 431–3 and Plate 104). East of Delphi the terrace rises, carrying the road to the head of the valley (2,900 ft.) and to Arákhova, a very distinctive village with 3,572 inhabitants. It lies immediately beneath the summit of Parnassós with vineyards below it, and is renowned in Central Greece for its wine, and the wonderful view it commands. Carpets of special colour and design are woven by the women from the wool of large flocks which roam all over Parnassós during the summer (see vol. II, Plate 1).

Mount Elikón

For the next twenty-five miles the country between the Gulf of Kórinthos and the plain of Kopaís is dominated by Mount Elikón.

Plate 19. Mount Klókova and Mount Varásovon, from Pátrai
Mount Klókova is on the right ; behind are the Arákinthos mountains.

Plate 20.   Mount Parnassós

The view is northward from the brink of the scarp above Delphi. White limestone, folded nearly vertically, can be seen in the centre and on the right.   The plateau surface provides summer pasture

Plate 21. The valley of the Xiropótamos and the bay of Itéa
The view is from below Delphi and has the southern spurs of Mount Gióna in the
background. Olive groves cover the valley floor.

Plate 22. Mégara, from the south

The western edge is marked by the transverse saddle of Dhístomon north of the small port of Andíkira, where there has been some mining of bauxite. The mountains are built of limestones, some grey and some cream-coloured, which are thinly veiled by bush and remnants of fir-woods. The lower ranges in the north, and the wider valleys elsewhere, correspond to the outcrops of red shale and sandstone. These impermeable rocks determine the location of springs and, therefore, the sites of the few villages. The coast, however, is formed of the fractured edges of limestone. The mountains culminate in the graceful cone of Paliovoúna (5,735 ft.) which is one of the many parallel chains. East of this central peak the general altitude falls to below 3,000 ft., allowing for a route by winding valleys from Levádhia to Domvraína, and then rises again to form a narrower plateau, pitted with sink-holes, overlooking the plain of Thívai. The lower coastal mountains are separated from the main blocks by the valley of the river Askrís and the *polje* of Domvraína to which it flows. The depression is drained underground to the remarkable Gulf of Domvraína, with its screen of islets and two rocky peninsulas. On the eastern peninsula, the imposing precipices of Korombíli rise to 2,976 ft. and, like the straight scarp forming the western coast of Livadhóstratas Bay, provide further evidence of the fractured margins of the Gulf of Kórinthos.

The district serves mainly as pastoral land and is very thinly peopled ; but in the south the depression of the river Askrís and Domvraína, largely covered with olive and vineyards, supports some 5,000 inhabitants.

The Eastern Mountains

From Livadhóstratas Bay the next series of mountains extends eastward for 18 miles as the Kithairón and Pástra mountains ; only 3 miles to the south the Patéras mountains are linked in turn with the higher and broader Párnis, with a total length of 37 miles ; finally, from Cape Melangávi on the Gulf of Kórinthos, the Yeránia mountains reach from sea to sea, the last barrier to the Isthmus. Thus, within a breadth of from 12 to 18 miles, there are three parallel ranges with two intervening depressions. The most northerly has always been difficult to negotiate, but a pass between the Kithairón and Pástra mountains serves the main road from Elevsís to Thívai. The longitudinal furrows, marking the main fractures, are rocky and do not offer continuous routes ; moreover the whole region is covered either with maquis or with forests of Aleppo pine, except for the higher ranges of Kithairón which are under fir woods. Hence the populous centres of Attikí and Voiotía are separated from one another by wild and sparsely peopled country, the abode chiefly of shepherds, charcoal burners, and collectors of resin, as well as of deer, pigs, foxes and probably still of wolves. The most northerly furrow, however, widens in the two oval basins of Oinóï and Skoúrta where there is a population of some 6,000 peasants, cultivating grain, olives and vines.

The Patéras mountains (3,710 ft.) are broader and smoother than Kithairón ; a branch of them turns south-eastwards to the coast separating the plains of Elevsís and Mégara, while to the east only a low ridge connects them with Mount Párnis. This is a very uniform plateau, composed of shales, chert and serpentine, and presenting a bold and straight front to the plains of Attikí, and deeply cut by valleys opening upon them. Mount Yeránia (4,465 ft.) is a very striking example of an upraised fault-block with smooth top and steep sides. Its structure is complex and includes shales in the western peninsula which give soil for the growing of crops and for olive and almond trees. The southern fault-scarp is most pronounced where it forms the great cliff along the coast almost 2,000 ft. high and continued under water. It was known to the ancient Greeks as the Skironian defile and later as the Kakí Skála (bad step). On this the modern road and railway have been built and maintained, not without difficulty (see vol. II, Plate 98). In the west the fracture is marked by the warm springs (91° F.) and spa of Loutráki.

The Mégara and Elevsís Plains and Salamís (Region C2)

South of the limestone escarpment of the eastern mountains, and lying between the Isthmus of Kórinthos on the west and the peninsula of Attikí on the east, is a small but fertile region, contrasting strongly with the barrenness of the surrounding country (Fig. 16). It is divided by the terminal spurs of the Patéras mountains and by the sea into :

The Plain of Mégara
The Plain of Elevsís
Salamís

Plate 23. Lake Marathón
The view shows the artificial lake, behind its dam, and the plateau north of it.
The end of Mount Párnis appears on the left ; on the right is the ravine from which
the river Oinóis was diverted.

Plate 24.   The first defile of the river Kifissós
The narrow strip of alluvium along the river is cultivated.   The limestone of the
hillside is fissured by solution.

[Facing page 52

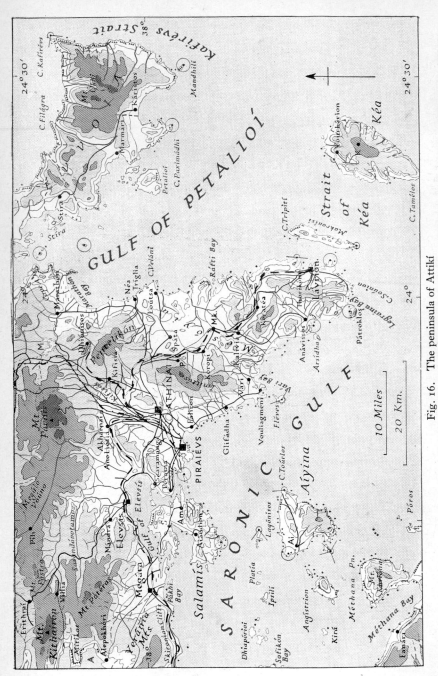

Fig. 16. The peninsula of Attikí

Based mainly on the 1 : 250,000 G.S.G.S. Series 4088 : The Balkans, and the 1 : 100,000 *Epitelikós Khártis tis Elládhos*.
A. Gulf of Alkionídhes ; *Aí.* Aíyina ; *Am.* Ambeláki ; *Cape A.M.* Cape Ayía Marína ; *M.* Marathón Lake ; *Mk.* Markópoulon ;

[*Facing page*

The Plain of Mégara

The lowlands of Mégara are wedge-shaped in plan, narrowing towards the east, and are composed of sandy marls and friable limestones, much broken by faults. In the west the ground is high, and the deeply gullied hills, clothed with pines, slope steeply to the sea. East of this divide, however, the slope is gentle and the pines give place to vineyards and then to olive groves with which the plain of Mégara is almost completely covered. Various cereal crops are also grown and the flat area near the town, watered from numerous wells, is notably fertile. It was known in ancient times as the White Plain, presumably from the pale loamy alluvium which covers it. Mégara is situated a mile inland and is closely built upon two isolated hills (Plate 22). The town conceals most of the remains of the ancient Mégara, its chief monument now being the aqueduct that brought water over the saddle between the two hills. The people are largely farmers and apart from the town (with a population of 11,110) there are no settlements on the plain.

The Plain of Elevsís

The abrupt end of the Patéras mountains leaves little space for the road and railway along the shore to the Plain of Elevsís. This plain and its gulf are enclosed by the Páteras mountains on the west, by the Párnis mountains on the north, and by the Aigáleos hills on the east. The latter form the end of the folded limestone that extends from the Yeránia mountains through the northern ridge of Salamís. The oval shaped gulf has been formed by submergence, making Salamís an island ; the rivers which debouch from Mount Párnis on to the plain must formerly have been much more vigorous streams, since they have covered it with rather steep and stony fans. In these reddish conglomerates many artesian wells have been bored in order to increase the productivity of the plain.

The situation of Elevsís is closely comparable with that of Mégara : it stands at the south-western corner of a plain, but, unlike Mégara, Elevsís has a great deal to show of its ancient glory as the seat of the Mystery (see vol. I, pp. 433–4). Nevertheless, the outward attraction of these remains is somewhat lessened by modern industries. These are the making of cement from the neighbouring limestone, and of soap from the olives of this and adjoining districts. The population numbers 6,416, to which the agricultural village of Asprópirgos adds another 3,391.

From Elevsís the railway must go north-eastwards to pass between Párnis and Aigáleos, but the road, following the ancient Sacred Way, leads south-eastwards over a gap in the hills. Near the gap, which commands a fine view of Athens, are the monastery and magnificent church of Dháfni set amid pinewoods.

Salamís

The island of Salamís consists of a series of east-west ridges linked by strips of raised alluvium. The hills are covered by woods of pine, especially in the southern peninsula, and the lowlands are largely under vineyards. The name Kouloúri, applied to the island and to its capital at the head of the Gulf of Salamís, means a baker's crescent, and the island gets this shape apparently from subsidence of the central section. The principal settlements are, the capital (Salamis) on the west coast, and Ambeláki and the naval arsenal both on the east coast (see vol. I, p. 61, and vol. II, p. 233).

THE PENINSULA OF ATTIKÍ AND AÍYINA (REGION C3)

The peninsula of Attikí forms an isosceles triangle, with the Aigáleos hills and the greater mass of Pentelikón at the base and Cape Soúnion at the apex. To this must be added the country of plateau and hills in the north-east with its bulge to Cape Ayía Marína (Fig. 16). The region has a total area of some 550 sq. miles, yet only a part of this heartland of classical Greece offers favourable economic opportunity. Hence the great interest which the Athenians had in overseas policies and adventures.

The outstanding fact about the relief of Attikí is that the chief plains open upon the Saronic Gulf ; the east coast offers few spots attractive for settlement except for the small plain of Marathón and the mining district of Lávrion. Although the geological structure of Attikí is complicated, owing to the fact that the rocks have been folded at two distinct epochs, the major relief features are mainly the result of prolonged erosion and only exceptionally of recent fractures. The bolder hills are composed of marble which is resistant to weathering ; the lower hills are of less resistant rocks, such as slates or crystalline schists or the still softer Tertiary sediments ; and the plains are mostly formed of gently sloping aprons of detritus from the hills. In general, the trends of these ridges are nearly the same as the directions of the rock-folds. There are only two important rivers : the Kifisós, flowing from Párnis south-westwards between Pentelikón and the Aigáleos hills, and the Oinóis which, like the stroke of a T, crosses south-eastwards to the Bay of Marathón, but has been beheaded in the interests of the water supply of Athens. The incised valley of the Oinóis has been dammed at a place 4 miles above the village of Marathón, thus forming the large reservoir of Athens, known as the Lake of Marathón (Plate 23 and vol. I, Plate 89).

The comparatively great extremes of temperature in Attikí virtually exclude the orange from the orchards and also emphasize the intensity of the summer drought. An interesting feature of the climate is the remarkable clarity of the atmosphere, especially near dawn and dusk, although in summer, mirage due to heat and haze due to dust are commonly experienced.

The peninsular triangle is sub-divided by the straight ridge of Imittós which starts opposite Athens and extends southward to the Saronic Gulf. Much of its marble structure is but thinly veiled by vegetation, and there are many bold crags on the flanks and in the passes between its several summits of which the northern-most is the highest (3,365 ft.). The eastern slope is the barer and steeper, for it is one of the exceptional fault-scarps of Attikí ; on the western side the lower slopes are clad in pinewood and orchards. Attikí and Aíyina, therefore, is divisible into four major districts :

The Western Lowlands and Athens
The Eastern Peninsula
North-eastern Attikí
Aíyina

The Western Lowlands and Athens

The only really flat part of the western lowlands is the alluvial belt of the Kifisós, ending in Fáliron Bay. From this plain the ground rises westwards to the Aigáleos mountains, and near the sea it is occupied by Piraiévs and its suburbs. The harbour is enclosed by a former island of Miocene strata converted to a peninsula by marine accumulation, and now mostly covered by the rapidly extending city. East of the Kifisós several blocks of limestone rest upon the crumpled slates of the lowland and form a row of isolated hills, parallel with the river. They are Tourkovoúnia (1,112 ft.) in the north, then Likavitós (909 ft.) and the Akropolis (512 ft.). Under this last hill, modern Athens has grown from a mere village in 1821 to a city some 11 sq. miles in area. In so doing it has enveloped Mount Likavitós, and its new satellite towns or villages together make an almost continuous urban area round the Tourkovoúnia. Farther north, and still separate, is the large refugee settlement of Néa Ionía (population 16,460) containing the bulk of the carpet makers from the Izmir district of Turkey. South-west of the Akropolis is the largest of the new towns, Kallithéa, which by 1928 had a population of 29,446 and which by 1943 is estimated to have grown to some 80,000. This in turn almost touches Néon Fáliron and so links with Piraiévs (see vol. II, pp. 375–82). There have also been considerable increases in the towns west of the Kifisós, and the greater part of the western lowland, for 12 miles inland from Piraiévs, has become at least a semi-urban district, mostly of a very drab character. This drabness is, of course, offset by the hills within the built-up area, by the surrounding mountains, and by the olive-groves of the Kifisós valley.

South of Athens the western lowland, with its smooth coast, narrows to the three capes that mark the end of the ridge of Imittós ; agricultural land gives place southward to pine woods and seaside resorts, including Vouliagméni with its hot sulphurous baths. This hilly promontory is a barrier to communications, and the main route to eastern Attikí lies to the north.

The lowland continues northwards between Imittós and Pentelikón and is covered with sloping sheets of detritus, varying in composition from red conglomerates to fine yellow loams. In the north the land is mostly smooth, as at the Tatóï aerodrome, but is trenched by the Kifisós and the ravines of its tributaries flowing from Mount Párnis. Here there is much cereal cultivation but also poor pasture with scattered pine trees. This upper plain offers an easy passage for both road and railway from Attikí to northern Greece. At the western foot of Pentelikón the twin towns of Kifisiá and Amaroúsion (population 15,140), like Khalándri to the south (7,084) may be regarded as outer satellites of Athens.

The Eastern Peninsula

South of Pentelikón is a flat and fertile district that forms an eastern arm of the Kifisós lowland. While mainly given to cereals it has many vineyards and vegetable gardens watered from numerous wells. To the south-east it narrows to a pine-clad gap before opening on to the most valuable of the Attikí plains, the Mesóyia (' Midland '), so-called because it is hemmed in by hills. It is enclosed by the worn stumps of ancient crystalline rocks, mainly marble, which merge into the almost mountainous district around Lávrion in the south, and only in the west is the boundary sharply defined by the scarp of Imittós. Elsewhere the easily eroded sediments of which the plain is formed lap round the edges of these hills. Since the formation of the Gulf of Petalioí, deep valleys have been cut back through the eastern hills, but as yet none has trenched the surface of this plain. Its flat surface, 390 ft. high, is uniformly covered by thick red loam which may be watered from many wells ; and it is, therefore, the most fertile district in Attikí. The Mesóyia is prolonged southward as a winding vale in the centre of the narrowing peninsula so that the medial hollow of smooth agricultural land is some 17 miles long in all. It is everywhere under cultivation. Although wheat and barley occupy part of the land, vineyards are the great feature and they have extended enormously with the growth of Athens which provides a local market for wine. Hence the original villages, usually of Albanian farmers as in other parts of Attikí, have become agricultural towns; they lie on or near the railway and road to Lávrion.

The hills to the south and east, in spite of the complexity of their structure, are generally flat-topped and reveal parts of at least two ancient surfaces of erosion broken by deep, winding and usually narrow valleys. Several mountains do, however, stand much higher than the others, notably Mount Paníon (2,087 ft.). The indented coast is evidence of submergence (see vol. I, Plate 49), but horizontal remnants of raised terraces at 112 ft. and 200 ft. indicate that emergence has also taken place. The Temple of Soúnion stands on the 200 ft. terrace. The hills of the eastern peninsula are generally covered either by pine-woods or maquis and consequently there are very few settlements among them ; this also applies to the coast, which is difficult to reach in most parts and which is thinly populated except for the mining district of Lávrion.

The mineral wealth of the hills opposite Makronísi have made the Lávrion district famous since very early times, but its prosperity has not been continuous. The mines, old and new, occupy an area of some 20 sq. miles and they are perhaps the best known silver-lead workings in the world. Part of the modern operations consists in re-smelting the ancient refuse, but in addition to lead and silver, important amounts of zinc, manganese and some copper are now produced (see vol. II, pp. 117–18). About 8,000 people are more or less dependent on the industry, including a polyglot element in the population of Lávrion (6,135). As a source of marble for classical Athens, Lávrion was third in importance, after Pentelikón and Imittós. The fine distinctions of grain and of colour in the marble are due to the degrees of purity and massiveness of the strata. Thus, while the pure white marble of the island of Páros was preferred for statues in Athens, the stone of Pentelikón, finer in grain but with a faint suggestion of golden yellow, was used for most of the buildings on the Acropolis and elsewhere. The Temple of Athene at Soúnion is built of Lávrion marble, white in colour with fine yellow and grey streaks ; while again, the parallel grey-blue stripes in the marble of Imittós seem to have attracted the Romans more than the Greeks. Another industry of the peninsula is the evaporation of salt from salt-pans at the head of Ayíos Nikólaos Bay ; it supports some 400 people at Anávissos.

North-eastern Attikí

The gable-like ridge of Pentelikón (3,680 ft.) forms a massive barrier extending eastward almost to the sea, but there is room for a coastal road to Marathón Bay. The lower slopes are composed of deeply gullied red conglomerate, largely covered with pine-forests. North of Pentelikón lies a stretch of country over 100 sq. miles in area, of monotonous configuration (Plate 23). It is a rolling plateau, 1,300 to 1,800 ft. high, cutting across folded crystalline rocks and dissected by rivers draining to Lake Marathón and by short ravines leading to the coast. Pine-woods still cover much of its surface. The district is very thinly peopled and the coastal slopes from Cape Ayía Marína to Cape Kálamos is almost uninhabited.

The curved southern edge of the plateau embraces the smallest of the plains of Attikí, that of Marathón (see vol. I, Plate 85). The long rocky finger of the cape—the ancient Kynosura—has provided a protecting screen for the deposit of silt by the river Oinóis which now has its flow regulated by the reservoir in the plateau ; but the eastern half of the plain remains a malarial swamp. The population of some 2,000 people is concentrated in Marathón, three miles up the valley. With river water and wells the alluvial fan is intensively cultivated, producing a variety of tree-fruits and vines.

Aíyina

This island doubtless owes its triangular shape to submarine fractures, since the coasts do not correspond to features of geological

structure. The southern part consists of trachyte like that of
Méthana, and this contains the summit (1,752 ft.), one of the
finest viewpoints in Greece. The broad northern part is built of
late Tertiary rocks, largely marls and soft limestones. Yet, in
spite of the weakness of these, much of the land stands above 800 ft.
with the hills pitted by sink-holes, and only the north-western
corner of the island is lowland. None of the rivers of Aíyina is
permanent and water must be conserved. Maquis and patches of
pine-forest cover the rough hills, but the lowland is under intensive
cultivation.

In classical Greece, Aíyina had great importance as the home of a
trading community, and this character has persisted throughout its
history. It was the last stronghold of the Venetians against the
Turks, and for a short time it was the capital of Modern Greece,
when the town had twice its present population (5,035 of the total
of 8,832 for the island). The ancient glory of Aíyina is evident from
its temples, including that of Zeus on the highest summit, Óros
(see vol. I, p. 416). The recent decline of the rural population is
shown by the terraces now covered by maquis, and by the olive- and
almond-trees that have run wild. The plain is still farmed by the
people of Aíyina by a remarkable method. Hampered by a bed of
calc-sinter under the thin soil, they have for ages been digging out
the marl underneath and spreading it above, using the caverns as
stores and tanks. Thus they produce corn, wine, many tree-fruits
and even some cotton. Moreover they are still sailors, and they
take part in the sponge-fisheries ; they also maintain their ancient
manufacture of earthenware. Aíyina is the capital of an eparchy
in the *nomós* of Attikí and Voiótia. The eparchy also includes smaller
islands to the west, but of these the hilly Angístrion is alone inhabited
(population 664).

THE KIFISSÓS AND ASOPÓS BASINS (REGION C4)

From the gap south of Mount Oíti a great corridor extends east-
south-east for some 80 miles to the shores of the Gulf of Évvoia.
For the greater part of its length it is drained by the river Kifissós,
and, in the south-east, by the shorter Asopós. In general, this
composite depression runs parallel to the trend of the rock-folds,
and forms a series of faulted basins, narrow in the west, broad in
the east, separated by rocky sills through which rivers have cut
defiles. On the south, the corridor is bounded by the escarpments

of the Barrier Mountains (see p. 48) and on the north by the coastal ranges of Lókris (see p. 65). The numerous basins, supporting an average density of 153 people per sq. mile, are :

The Amfíklia Basin
The Elátia Basin
The Dhávlia Basin
The Kopaïs
The Upper Asopós Basin
The Plains of Thívai and Tanágra, and the Coastal Hills

The Amfíklia Basin

Between the Kallídhromon mountains (see p. 64) on the north and the imposing masses of Gióna and Parnassós on the south lies the first of the basins of the depression, 5 miles across at its broadest part. The alluvial floor rises very gently from 950 ft. and then more steeply on the northern side to 1,600 ft. and, except for the ravines of the Kifissós and its tributaries, the surface is entirely smooth. This basin, the ancient Doris, has always been populous owing to its fertility and supports an average density of 184 people per sq. mile. The villages, with their vineyards and orchards, hug the mountain foot and stand at least 300 ft. above the river. The rest of the basin is almost all under grain, with meadows and trees along the rivers. Bróllos and Graviá, at the western end of the basin, mark the northern and southern exits respectively, both of them lying on the motor road that leads south to Itéa. Amfíklia (Dhadhíon) is a picturesque little town which, with its neighbouring monastery, stands on a steep fan backed by a deep ravine of Parnassós. It has 3,801 inhabitants, or almost one-third of the total population of the basin. At this point the mountains approach one another and the Kifissós crosses its first limestone threshold in the short defiles that formerly divided Doris from Fokis (Plate 24). The railway from Amfíklia to Thívai crosses the barrier in a cutting.

The Elátia Basin

The next basin is somewhat larger than that of Amfíklia, but is of similar shape. The tributaries from Parnassós form an immense and steep fan of coarse and infertile debris fit only for poor pasture. At the mountain foot there are two large villages, Tithoréa (Velítsa) and Ayía Marína. From the latter, the face of Parnassós turns south, but a narrow ridge continues eastward severed from Par-

nassós by the wooded gorge of some former river ; the gorge gives
a side entrance to the small basin of Dhávlia, 3 miles to the south
(see below). Similarly, at the north-eastern corner, the Kalli-
dhromon mountains proper come to an end in a gap leading to
Atalándi. The control of this gap gave importance to the ancient
city of Elátia (Dhrakhmáni), still the largest place in the basin, with a
population of 1,719. It dominates the northern half of the plain
which is everywhere under grain and large vineyards. Since the
Kifissós and its tributaries are somewhat incised in the floor of the
basin, irrigation is restricted to small areas, especially in the eastern
alcoves, and the basin as a whole supports only 103 people per sq.
mile.

The Dhávlia Basin

From the Elátia depression the Kifissós cuts through a narrow
limestone plateau that forms the northern edge of the Dhávlia
basin. This broad and fertile valley of ancient Daulis, rectangular
in shape and about 14 sq. miles in area, is the gateway of Voiótia
and has been guarded in the past by several cities. The ruins of
Daulis, near the modern Dhávlia, look down the valley from the
slopes of Parnassós ; on the south is Chaeroneia (see vol. I, p. 427)
while on the long crag to the north are the ruins of Orchomenus, a
natural fortress and one of the centres of Mycenean civilization
(see vol. I, p. 441). The soils of the plain are rich and well watered,
and agriculture continues all the year, with cotton, rice and millet
as the chief summer crops.

The Kopaïs

The Kopaïs is one of the largest *polja* in Greece and covers an
area of 135 sq. miles. The enclosed hollow was due in the first
instance to crustal disturbance, and subsequently to erosion and
solution of limestone. The natural outlet for the water is underground through a barrier of limestone separating the basin from
the sea. The barrier is a series of bare karstic ridges and, south
of the highest (Mount Ptóön), a deep furrow containing the isolated
lakes Ilikí and Paralímni, now connected and drained superficially
to the sea (Fig. 17). The bottom of the lake which originally
formed in the Kopaïs gradually became raised by sedimentation to
the level of the chief sink-holes ; the water was then so shallow
that evaporation in summer almost dried it up. This seasonal
alternation of lake and swamps was the condition prior to 1886, when

the land was artificially drained. It is evident, however, that the Kopaïs had been drained as long ago as the second millenium B.C., when the plain was settled by the Minyae. It was these people who founded Orchomenus to the west and who probably built the fortress of Gla in the north-east corner of the plain (see vol. I, p. 434). Their rulers may have derived their knowledge of canalization from Egypt or Mesopotamia, and it was their engineers who improved the natural outlets of the basin near Gla.

The modern drainage system gathers nearly all the water by marginal canals, taking it to a new eastern outfall—a tunnel 732 yards long leading to Lake Ilikí (Plate 25). The surface of this lake was raised to enable it to overflow to Paralímni, and this in turn was raised from 115 to 180 ft. above sea level. The outfall to the sea drops partly in a tunnel, giving a potential source of water power. This successful drainage of some 61,000 acres of white marl, with its rich cover of dark humus, formed a most valuable addition to the farm land of Greece. The country is well suited to grain, including maize, and grass on which horses and cattle as well as turkeys are reared. The principal aim of irrigation, however, is cotton growing ; but it must be noted that the drainage system did not introduce any new supply of water, which, in summer, is derived almost entirely from the Melás. This river, which alone has a vigorous flow throughout the year (c. 5 cu. metres per second) rises in springs in the north-western alcove of the plain. It follows the northern rim of the basin, marked by a wave cut cliff, to a similar alcove in the north-east where it disappears in sink-holes. Much of the water from these emerged, as some still does, in the springs south of Lárimna (Fig. 17). The Kifissós, which becomes much reduced in summer, is used for irrigation only in its lowest part.

Only the straight roads and canals relieve the monotony of crops and flat earth ; the tillers of the drained plain have remained in the old settlements on the western and southern margins, and these marginal settlements have grown as a result of the drainage. Those villages on the south depend for their economy upon mountain and plain, and the whole district has been influenced by the hill town of Levádhia, capital of Voiótia from late classical times and the successor of Orchomenus and Thebes. The modern town has 12,585 inhabitants, and depends upon the spinning and weaving of cotton, using local water power. Its position on both sides of a ravine leading to the south-western corner of the plain has helped to make it the hub of the rich agricultural district of Voiótia (Plate 26).

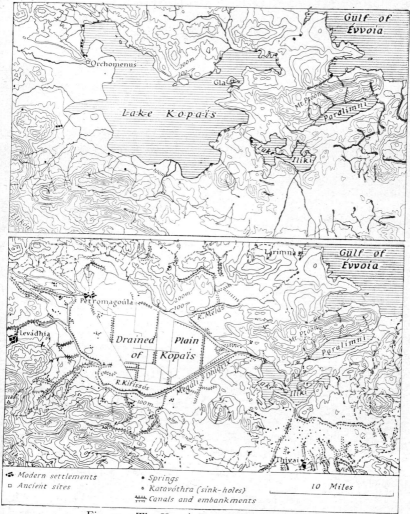

Fig. 17. The Kopaïs Basin in 1894 and 1933

Based on a map by A. Philippson in *Zeitschrift der Gesellschaft für Erdkunde*, Band 29 (Berlin, 1894) and the 1 : 100,000 G.S.G.S. Series 4087, Sheet C3648. The upper map shows ancient settlements only.

Plate 25. Lake Ilikí
The view is from the north and shows the western part of the lake with Mount
Kithairón behind.

Plate 26. The town of Levádhia
The view shows the upper part of the town ; the mountain slopes are partly
terraced for cultivation.

The Upper Asopós Basin

South of Levádhia the Elikón mountains come to an end and give place to a plateau drained by the head streams of the Asopós. The district is isolated from the Gulf of Kórinthos by the Kithairón mountains (see p. 51). The plateau is some 22 by 7 miles in extent and its undulating surface varies between 1,000 and 1,300 ft., with the river Asopós flowing indolently eastward in a shallow valley. It is a surface of erosion, developed on easily eroded Pliocene sands, marls and conglomerates and is covered with a red or brown soil. The northern edge is a youthful and ravined fault scarp overlooking the Kopaïs and Aonian plain some 700 ft. below ; and it is partly covered by the vineyards and orchards of neighbouring villages. The villages of this monotonous and partly wooded plateau are mostly along its northern and southern edges, and not along the valley of the Asopós, which is not followed by a route. Most of the area now serves as pasture where, in ancient times, were the fields of famous cities such as Plataea, Thespia, and Leuctris. On a spur of the northern escarpment stands Thívai, on the site of ancient Thebes ; the acropolis of Cadmus and other buildings have been destroyed, partly by repeated earthquakes (see vol. I, pp. 443–4). Although Thívai, with 7,289 inhabitants, has doubled in size in forty years, its small manufactures do not compare with the notable silk industry which formerly flourished here (Plate 27).

The Plains of Thívai and Tanágra and the Coastal Hills

The eastern end of the great composite depression is flanked by the rough ridge of Ktipás ending in a fine peak, 3,350 ft. high, which stands like a gate post of the Evripós. But west of this lies the Aonian plain of Thívai between the Theban escarpment and Lake Ilikí, with a smaller arm almost continuous with the Kopaïs. Although partly swampy and malarial, this plain produces valuable crops in winter and summer, while the slopes above are clothed with fig and olive orchards. Mount Ktipás is mainly composed of limestone, but this rock rests upon serpentine from which magnesite is quarried.

From the plain the railway and road to Athens pass eastwards over a low saddle, to the south of which the limestone ridges of Sorós and Terméssos rise from a plateau. The river Asopós penetrates these oak-forested hills in a winding gorge to reach the plain of Tanágra, and, after crossing the plain, plunges northward into another ravine to the sea at Khalkoútsi. Tanágra, at the western edge of the plain, is now a village but was once the capital of Voiótia and was famous for its clay statuettes. Its plain, sur-rounded by pine woods, is floored with easily eroded sediments and its red soil is under grain, vines and olives. From its brink, 500 ft. high, the land falls away to the Gulf of Évvoia ; the slope is covered with dense maquis and pines and below it are three small and rich coastal areas that match the similar garden land across the strait. These are the coastal plains of Oropós and Avlís, and, north of the Evripós, the peninsula of Khália.

THE OÍTI AND KALLÍDHROMON MOUNTAINS AND LOKRÍS (REGION C5)

The northern frame of the faulted basins drained by the Kifissós is a series of mountains, less elevated than those on the south, but, nevertheless, a formidable barrier to the next depression—that of the river Sperkhiós and the northern Gulf of Évvoia. The region is conveniently subdivided into :

The Oíti Mountains
The Kallídhromon Mountains
The Mountains and Hills of Lokrís

The Oíti Mountains

The triangular block of Mount Oíti is composed mainly of lime-stone and is an outlier of the Dividing Mountains. The northern face of this great massif overlooks the Sperkhiós valley as a scarcely gullied fault-scarp (Plate 28). Above the scarp there is a maze of dry valleys with fir- and pine-woods, and finally, a plateau 6,200 ft. high with crags rising to 7,060 ft. The eastern face is cut by deep gorges, and that of the Kifissós (see p. 60) is followed for a short distance by the railway from the Sperkhiós to the Pournaráki Pass (1,770 ft.). The southern slopes of Oíti, composed of less resistant rocks, are much more gentle than the northern and eastern faces, and are drained by the numerous head-waters of the Mórnos (see p. 48).

The Kallídhromon Mountains

East of the railway tunnel near Brállos, the land rises to a mountainous range where the crests in several places exceed 4,000 ft. in height. The most dominant is that of Kallídhromon (4,501 ft.)

Plate 27.   Thívai and the Aonian plain
The gap in the centre of the distant hills leads to Lake Paralímni.

Plate 28.   Mount Oíti and the Sperkhiós valley
The view is from west of Lamía (cf. Plate 29).   It shows the northern escarpment
of the mountain where the valley is narrowest.

[Facing page 64

Plate 29.   The pass of Thermopylae
The view is from the east and shows Mount Oíti in the background.   The white calc-sinter is encroaching upon the marshes.

Plate 30.   Mount Óthris
In this part of the mountain the oak forests have been greatly thinned.

[Facing page 65

which has given its name to the range. The folded and broken structure of limestones, slates and red chert has caused great variety in relief, and in addition, the range is bounded by fault scarps both north and south. That on the north is marked by the light-grey cliffs, some 2,600 ft. high, which overhang the Thermopylae and which were called the Trachinian rocks (Plate 29). The fracture at the foot accounts for the two hot sulphurous springs, with a temperature of 111° F. (43·8° C.), which have been used as baths at many periods and give the name to the narrow defile between cliffs and sea (see vol. I, p. 444). The higher northern slopes are wooded with fir and some oak ; the southern slopes, of reddish, weathered limestone, bear only scrub and phrygana.

The Mountains and Hills of Lokrís

The Kallídhromon mountains in their eastern part are separated from Mount Knimís (3,071 ft.) and lesser ranges along the coast by a lower zone which extends over 25 miles from the Maliaic Gulf to the plain of Atalándi. Although this district is made of non-resistant Pliocene marl and conglomerate it rises to nearly 2,500 ft. and has been reduced by erosion of the Xiriás and other rivers to a labyrinth of ravines. Only at the two ends near Thermopylae and Cape Arkítsa is it little dissected and cultivated to any extent ; elsewhere, oak-woods and maquis cover the hills. The rivers break through the higher coastal ranges in gorges to form the narrow coastal plain of Mális. On the east, the zone ends at the triangular coastal plain of Atalándi, and on the south-east it abuts upon the hills of limestone which extend from the coast to the threshold of the Elátia basin. Near the junction of the two types of country a road leads directly from Elátia to Atalándi following narrow hollows, probably due to fracture.

The limestone country to the east, though quite different from that of the Pliocene rocks, is almost as much a waste, and, since goats greatly outnumber men, vegetation is largely reduced to bush of Kermes oak, with some woods of ilex. Only on the coastal slopes do maquis and Aleppo pines appear. Inland, cream-coloured cliffs stand above shaly, scrub-covered slopes where occasional hollows of red earth are cultivated for grain, olives and pears. Dark serpentine occurs along the southern margin of the plain of Atalándi and appears again near the east coast. Associated with it are mines of iron and nickel on the ridge of Ptóön near Lárimna. Above all this country rises a single prominent mountain, Khlomón (3,543 ft.), of hard dolomitic limestone and offering a wide panorama. The separation of this land from Évvoia is still intermittently in progress, as is shown by the frequency of earthquakes. Thus two shocks in April 1894 resulted in a straight fracture, 37 miles long, from Cape Gátza nearly to Cape Knimís, when part of the land on the coastal side of the fissure was displaced.

The density of population of the entire area of mountains and hills is only 33 per sq. mile, but in winter there are additional shepherds from the southern Píndhos. The coastal plain of Atalándi, with the strip beyond Cape Arkítsa, is all under cultivation and there is a concentration on tobacco, grain, olives and vines. The town of Atalándi, at the inner corner of the plain, has a population of 3,578.

The Valley of the Sperkhiós (Region C6)

Physical Characteristics

The river Sperkhiós is the relatively recent tenant of its valley, which was prepared for it by subsidence of the earth's crust. Great fractures extend from the mountainous backbone of Greece to the Aegean Sea, forming the sides of the valley and also bounding the Maliaic Gulf and the straits north of Évvoia. Hot springs mark the faults, at Ipáti, Thermopílai, Platístomon and Aidhipsós. They are either alkaline or sulphurous and all deposit cones of white sinter.

The upper basin lies on the broad belt of sandstones and shales that spreads from the mountains of Ágrafa to the foot of Mount Vardhoúsia, and it is seamed by deep valleys, especially those of the upper Sperkhiós and the Vistrítsa which joins it near the head of the plain. All these rivers are laden with gravel, sand and silt when in flood, and the main river is apt to change its bed and to leave ponds behind. Hence the villages stand back from the marshy banks, if only to avoid the dangers of malaria ; nevertheless, it is the detritus and plentiful water which makes the valley so fertile. East of the upper basin, the valley is enclosed on the north by the Óthris mountains, rising gradually eastwards from 2,700 to 3,600 ft. ; and on the south by the scarp of Mount Oíti, almost unbroken for 18 miles, and prolonged by that of Kallídhromon to the sea. The floor is nearly flat and varies from $2\frac{1}{2}$ to $4\frac{1}{2}$ miles in width.

In 480 B.C. the mouth of the Sperkhiós lay at Kómma, now 7 miles inland, south of which was the separate delta of the Asopós (of

Fthiótis). Thus the cliff of the Trachinian rocks, some 2,500 ft. high, overlooked the Gulf just where the hot springs emerge from its foot. Consequently this Pass of Thermopylae was then only a narrow strip of shore. Later, the delta thrust eastwards and the active mouth of the Sperkhiós is now 5 miles to the north-east of Thermopílai.

Land Utilization

The mountains have a marked effect upon climate : in winter they promote a downward flow of cold air, followed sometimes by severe frost, and in summer the heat is oppressive, the more so from the absence of a well-developed sea breeze. Moreover, the hot and desiccating *livas* wind, equivalent of the alpine *föhn*, is also a common feature of this plain. Thus, winter cold excludes the more delicate fruits, while summer heat ripens such crops as cotton, rice and maize for which the river and the springs from the southern limestones provide ample water. These crops prevail on the lower plain, where the fields pass gradually to meadows and then to marsh which serve as pasture for flocks in winter. The main part of the floor, however, is given to wheat ; fruit trees with vineyards are widespread and notably so on the marginal fans and over the lower plain. There is also some mining of chromite from the serpentine of the northern slopes, and salt is evaporated at the delta. The economic opportunities of the valley have resulted in the high average density of 228 people per sq. mile. The mountainous upper basin, somewhat larger in area, has less than half this density of population. The railway, which crosses the valley obliquely, has brought considerable benefit to the district, and especially to Lamía, the capital of the *nomós*, through which a branch-line leads to the port of Stilís. Lamía, with some 15,000 inhabitants, although now possessing few vestiges of its ancient form, has always dominated transit both from north to south and from east to west. It occupies a hollow in a spur of Mount Óthris, and is flanked by two crags the higher of which bears the fort ; from these the town spreads fan-wise to the plain.

Ipáti, at the west end of Mount Oíti, is a remarkable village, obviously built to withstand siege. Its ancient acropolis, still marked by part of a Byzantine castle, stands beside a great ravine in the mountain, and the village overlooks the cultivated fan 3 miles in radius ; the spa stands by the river 1,600 ft. below.

Óthris and its Marginal Lands (Region C7)

Between the plains of Thessalía in the north and the valley of the Sperkhiós and the narrow seas in the south is a varied land of mountain, plateau and plain. In plan it is a rough triangle nearly 800 sq. miles in area, most of which in ancient times was known as Achaea of Fthiótis and formed part of Thessaly. From 1832 to 1881 the frontier of Greece and Turkey lay across the region, and detrimental effects of this national division are still to be found locally. Today the northern part constitutes the districts of Fársala and Almirós in Thessalía, and the remainder belongs to the *nomós* of Fokís and Fthiótis.

The mountain groups are the greater Óthris and the lesser Kassidhiáris and Narthákion hills. They are of only moderate height and their surface is rugged in few places ; yet they have always directed movement along a few important routes around and between them, and have thus given special significance to the three controlling towns, Fársala, Vólos and Lamía, widely spaced on the northern, eastern and southern margins respectively. The major obstacle to travel is the Óthris mountains in the south-east, their southern slopes rising steeply from the Maliaic Gulf. Several summits exceed 5,000 ft. in height, but they are rounded in form, and the Óthris has formed a barrier chiefly on account of the density of the forest of oak which still covers the greater part of the mountains. The larger part of the region is lower and more accessible ; it consists of a broad plateau, from 1,000 to 2,000 ft. high, from which the Kassidhiáris and Narthákion mountains in the north-west, and several other hills, rise to 3,600 ft. The region as a whole is narrowest in the west, where it extends to meet the mountains of Ágrafa, as a threshold between the plain of Thessalía and the Sperkhiós, and is therefore used by the principal road and railway. In the north-east a lower and still narrower extension of the plateau abuts on the Mavrovoúni hills which separate the two chief plains of Thessalía ; on the east the highland falls to the plain of Almirós and the Gulf of Pagasaí, while on the south it forms the deeply indented coast of the Straits of Oreoí.

The region differs considerably in aspect and tradition from all parts of Greece lying farther south. The reasons for this are mainly physical, but are also due to the longer hold of Turkish influence, seen in the prevalence of large estates and the consequent depression of the peasants until quite recent times (see vol. II, p. 52). The differences, however, are not prominent on the maritime fringes, which became Greek territory in 1832 ; moreover, the rock structure and relief, the climate and vegetation, all resemble those features in the south. For convenience of description the region can be divided into :

The Óthris Mountains
The Northern Margin
The Eastern and Southern Margins
The Western Margin.

The Óthris Mountains

The chief contrasts in the scenery of the Óthris depend upon the rocks which lie in broad folds in an east-west direction. In general, the relief is subdued in character (Plate 30), but the thick limestones are barer and are cut by deeper valleys than in the intervening area from which these rocks have been removed. Here the underlying slates, shales and sandstones, together with intrusive eruptive rocks, notably serpentine and gabbro, have been closely folded. A striking element in the scenery throughout this large central area is the red colour of the exposed strata. Ores of copper and chrome, which are associated with outcrops of igneous rocks, have led to mining operations in the south-west.

Most of the rivers which radiate from the high Óthris are short, but those flowing north-westward join the Khiliadhiótikos, which, as the Enipévs, is the longest tributary of the Piniós. The Khiliadhiótikos runs for some 12 miles to the north-east and so divides the Óthris from the northern ranges. Since it flows in a gorge, deepening northward, the river valley does not form a route, but the lower plateau surface which it crosses offers fairly easy passage from the flat-floored basin containing Lake Xiniá in the west to the plain of Almirós in the east. The presence of the ruined remains of Achaean fortress towns along both flanks of this interior routeway seems to indicate that its control was an important matter in ancient times. Today, however, the belt is almost unpopulated ; like the higher slopes it is mainly forested and has no importance as a route.

The prevalence of deciduous oak-woods on the Óthris indicates that the climate here, unlike that of the nearby coast, is marked by no real drought in summer ; indeed snow may lie, and even fall, as late as March. In limestone districts the more stately deciduous trees are replaced by juniper, ilex and Kermes oak, and these same evergreens form an undergrowth to the deciduous forests. They are also found in the deforested areas of the west and north-east. In the very few villages a tough cloth is made, the material of the heavy cloaks of rural Greece ; but the mountains are chiefly the haunt of deer and wild pigs, and support only a few shepherds and charcoal burners.

The Northern Margin

The north-western bastion of this region consists of a miniature replica of Óthris, but here the outcrops of limestone cover most of the district and form the prominent relief features. This is especially so in the south-west, where the well-wooded Kassidhiáris and Narthákion hills, rising to over 3,300 ft., overlook the upper plain of Thessalía. An abundant flow of water from the limestone has rendered part of the plain swampy. The town of Fársala stands at the foot of the straight northern edge of these hills, and, although a market town, it has lost much of its former prominence as a nodal point. The ancient city, enclosed by walls reaching to its acropolis, covered twice the area of the modern town of some 4,000 inhabitants (Plate 31).

The long and narrowing area of the plain on which Fársala lies is drained by the Enipévs and is followed eastwards by the railway to Vólos. On the north the plain is hemmed in by the Mavrovoúni plateau, and on the south-east by a hilly and well wooded barrier consisting mainly of gneiss but capped by limestone summits rising to over 2,000 ft. The water system of the plain is now regulated by a dam built in the gorge where the river Enipévs leaves the southern hills (Fig. 19). To the east of the gorge a low pass, dominated by the village of Erétria, gives access to the plain of Almirós.

The Eastern and Southern Margins

The coastal plain of Almirós was known to the ancients as the Krokic plain of Fthiotis and was then controlled by the two cities, Thebes of Fthiótis and Halos, situated on its northern and southern margins respectively. This lowland has gradually extended sea-wards and now ends in an almost straight beach 8 miles in length. The development of coastal shipping and of railways has lessened both the importance of the plain and the value of the coastal road from Lamía to Vólos through Almirós. The town of Almirós (7,680 inhabitants), now somewhat isolated, occupies a central position in the lowland, on the line that divides the plain into two sections. The larger part, lying to the west, slopes gently seawards from the hillfoot (1,000 ft.) and consists of a sheet of gravel laid down by a former river. This permeable surface, cut by deep ravines, is largely covered by scrub of Kermes oak and herbs, fit only for pasture. To the east lies the nearly flat coastal plain, where irrigation has led to the intensive cultivation of the fine, deep soil. It inherits from Turkish times a reputation for excellent tobacco and there are many fruit orchards as well. The importance of commercial crops is indicated by the density of population for the coastal plain, which is 194 per sq. mile. Apart from Almirós, which possesses over half the total population of the plain, there are two large refugee settlements, one near Almirós and another, Néa Ankhíalos, at the north end of the beach, replacing the classical town of Pirasos. From this new town a road leads along the steep slope of the mountain to Vólos. There is no modern equivalent of Halos in the south and the traces of this large ancient port now lie a mile inland, as a result of silting.

South of the plain of Almirós, the fringe of the Óthris region is a rough land with a deeply indented coast ; mica-schists form the lower ground, notably around Pteleón Bay, while the higher hills are built of marble as in the peninsula of Tragovoúni and the pyramid of Khlomón (2,930 ft.) with its precipices commanding the shore of Vólos strait. This district is partly separated from Óthris by the broad and cultivated valley leading to Soúrpi. From this valley, the road crosses the watershed to Pteleón, the ancient site on a bluff by the sea, the present village, 2 miles inland, in an amphitheatre of fruit trees. The seaward slopes here, and throughout the southern side of the Óthris, have all the advantages of the Mediterranean climate, but the cultivable land is restricted to several small terraced plains, each with orchards and tilled fields. Among these is the one which faces the bay of Gardhíki (Plate 32) ; it serves Pelasyía built on a high terrace, with its acropolis standing, just above the limit of the olive trees, at 1,740 ft. To the west of this plain the faulted edge of the Óthris yields much water from springs and from several gorges in the limestone, and the coastal terrace to Stilís is under irrigation. The produce includes maize, wheat, tobacco, cotton and fine olives ; oranges are also grown but they sometimes suffer from frost. Stilís, with a population of 2,735, is the largest place and the terminus of the standard gauge Lamía-Stilís line. It is supplemented as a port by Ayía Marína, from which a road climbs steeply to the copper mines near Limogárdhi.

The Western Margin

The narrow western end of the Óthris region is of great strategic importance as the main gateway to southern Greece from the north. Much of it is nearly flat, and only the southern slopes are truly mountainous. To cross this district from the south, the railway from Lamía winds and tunnels north-westward to a height of 1,900 ft. It then makes use of a central depression, 1,500 ft. above sea level ; its floor is nearly flat and almost half of it is occupied by the residual lake Xinía, 10 sq. miles in area and only 16 ft. deep. Such water as escapes from this lake, through a swamp, flows in a deepening valley through the foothills of Ágrafa north-westward to the plain of Thessalía. East of the lake, recent artificial drainage has improved conditions of health, and provided excellent land, for the hill-foot villages. Although Lake Xinía is rich in fish, which flourish in its greenish waters, complete drainage seems desirable.

Occurrences of chromite are associated with the serpentine rock in this western plateau. The ore is extracted at Metallíon, 2 miles east of Lake Xinía, and is carried by light railway to Makrirrákhi station on the main line ; it is also found at several places on the southern edge of this district, overlooking the Sperkhiós valley.

North of Lake Xinía the land is composed mainly of limestone, from which water emerges both north and south. It is penetrated by the effluent from the lake, thus offering passage for the railway in an oblique descent to the plain below Dhomokós. This ancient town, on the brink of the escarpment, controls the northern end of the almost straight road from Lamía, but the smallness of its population (1,793) scarcely indicates its early importance. The immense view from the acropolis (1,970 ft.), across the western plain of Thessalía, has always impressed the Greeks from the south, accustomed only to small plains—hence the name Thaumakoi (' the place of wonder ').

ÉVVOIA (REGION C8)

Évvoia owes its island origin to the great rifts that produced the Gulfs of Petalioí and Évvoia on the west, and the Straits of Oreoí and Tríkeri on the north. The subsidence that led to the formation of these long arms of the Aegean Sea was followed by unequal uplift of the whole block, which gave the island a tilt to the south-west. On the east coast the occurrence of raised beaches up to 410 ft. above sea level indicates rapid and recent upheaval ; on the other

Plate 31. Fársala and the upper plain of Thessalía

The view shows the lower part of the town and the road leading to the railway.

Plate 32. The plain of Gardhíki and the end of the Óthris mountains

On the left, above the sloping plain, is Pelasyía and behind it is the site of Larissa Kremaste.

Plate 33.   The town of Aidhipsós in northern Évvoia

Plate 34.   The plain of Oreoí

The view, from the west, shows the landing place and the pine-clad hills of northern Évvoia behind the plain.   This old alluvial fan, of some 4 miles radius, is cut by the river Kállas which is seen behind Istaía among the orchards near the apex of the fan.

hand, the islets of the west coast are evidence of depression. In the southern part of the island both shores possess features characteristic of submergence, but with the longer inlets on the west.

The major relief features consist of a number of mountain ranges and lower hills, and, except in the north, their trends correspond to two general directions—north-west to south-east or longitudinal, and north-east to south-west or transverse. The longitudinal ranges are the result of folding during the Alpine earth-storm ; the transverse correspond to more ancient crumpling. The rocks that make up the island are chiefly Mesozoic limestones, but igneous rocks occur at several places, and in the south there are also crystalline schists and marble. The basins between the ranges are floored with various sediments of Tertiary and Quaternary age, including some of the most productive seams of lignite in Greece.

The climate of Évvoia resembles that of eastern central Greece, with strongly marked contrasts in temperature and precipitation between summer and winter. Snow lies on the high peaks until June, and partly as a result of the considerable range of altitudes from sea-level to the summit of Mount Dhírfis (5,738 ft.) the island clearly exhibits various zones of vegetation. These are : (1) the lower pine forests, extending up to 1,200 ft. or 1,300 ft. ; (2) chestnut forests up to 2,100 or 2,300 ft. ; and (3) fir-forests up to 4,500 ft. The woods are not, of course, limited to the trees mentioned, nor is the island mainly under woodland. Much of the lower land is now cultivated, or is covered with maquis which occupies at least one-third of the island.

The total population is 140,850 and this, in an area of 1,382 sq. miles, gives a mean density of 101 per sq. mile. But the population is most unevenly distributed, living generally in large and widely separated villages, with comparatively few settlements on the coast. Although the people of Évvoia depend mainly on agriculture and stock-keeping, farming generally is not intensive. This is well seen by comparing this island with Crete, which is just over twice its area ; in 1937 the total value of agricultural and pastoral produce, however, was only 27% of that in Crete. Nearly two-thirds of the cropped area are under cereals which contribute less than one-third of the value. The olive is the richest product ; vineyards cover 14% of the area and yield 14% of the income, mainly as wine. Among the flocks, goats exceed sheep in numbers, and the dairy yield is comparatively high. The chief tree fruit is the almond, followed by citrus fruits and figs.

For convenience in further description, Évvoia may be divided
into three parts by transverse lines drawn from the west coast at
Límni and Alivéri Bay respectively. These are :

Northern Évvoia
Central Évvoia
Southern Évvoia

Northern Évvoia.

Northern Évvoia consists of three separate groups of mountains,
the peninsula of Likhás, the Teléthrion mountains, and the Xirón
massif. They increase eastwards in area and height, and in their
structure resemble the mainland to the north. The peninsula of
Likhás, rising to 2,428 ft., is composed mainly of pine-covered
limestones, but is partly fringed by marls with the olive-groves of
two large villages. Yiáltra is one of them and is noted as a summer
resort. East of the Gulf of Aidhipsós, ancient crystalline schists
form the Teléthrion mountains (3,205 ft.) largely forested with pines
and chestnuts. Hot alkaline springs emerge close to the eastern
shore of the gulf from a fan of calc-sinter, and their high curative
powers made Aidhipsós famous throughout ancient Greece (Plate
33). The high temperature (169° F.) and the quality of the water
are evidence of the fractures which define the coast and the steep
scarps of Teléthrion. The district culminates in the large massif
of Mount Xirón (3,251 ft.), north of Límni, a boss of dark gabbro
enveloped by limestone ; associated with the igneous rock is the
magnesite mined by the Anglo-Greek Magnesite Company, near
Límni (see vol. II, pp. 115-16). These mountains merge into the
surrounding tangled hills of Pliocene sediments which reach to
2,000 ft. in places, and which fall steeply to the coast. They are
mostly under pine-woods or maquis, but in the valleys there are
damp meadows and tall bracken, and part of the surface is cultivated.

The river Kállas, or Xiriás, has built up a fan on the north coast
of the island, somewhat raised and dissected except at its malarial,
seaward edge. Nevertheless, it has many wells and is all cultivated.
Istiaía, with a population of 3,320, stands at its apex, and the small
port of Oreoí, with 946 inhabitants, on its western edge (Plate 34).
The average density of population for the whole of northern Évvoia
is 83 per sq. mile, but the density rises to three times this figure on
the lowland.

Central Évvoia

Central Évvoia is by far the largest part of the island, and possesses the highest mountains and the greatest plains. Near the Aegean coast the longitudinal ranges extend for over 30 miles to Cape Kími and include the three mountain masses of Pixariá (4,396 ft.), Dhírfis (5,738 ft.) and Skotiní (4,650 ft.). Rising from the shores of the Gulf of Évvoia between Limní and Politiká, some 18 miles apart, is the longitudinal range that contains Mount Kandhílion (4,019 ft.). Its great fault-scarp is one of the most imposing precipices in Greece, and it is the haunt of goats and the home of a few monks. In the south of central Évvoia the widening of the island is due to the presence of transverse ranges, marked on the west and east by Ólimbos (3,733 ft.) and Oktoniá (2,188 ft.) respectively. These mountains separate the several big lowlands of Évvoia—the basin of the river Kirévs in the north ; the double basin of Psakhná and Yídhes in the centre ; and the south-eastern lowlands that extend right across the island from Kími to Alivéri Bay. In addition, smaller plains line the coast from Alivérion to Khalkís.

The north-flowing river Kirévs has cut for itself a hilly basin, mostly covered with pines and maquis, but with some cultivation and a few large villages. Cereals and vines are grown, with other fruits here and there, and especially on the irrigated coastal plain near Mandoúdhion (population 2,000). Magnesite is quarried from the hills of serpentine which make up most of the basin. The terraced plain of Psakhná, open to the gulf, is scarcely separated from the larger plain of Yídhes which rises gently eastwards to the foothills of Dhírfis, Skotiní, Moúles and Ólimbos. Both plains are floored by deposits of gravel, except in the lowest parts, and are dissected by ravines. Here, tracts of Kermes oak and other bush are separated by cultivated land, mainly devoted to cereals. Below Psakhná, with 2,963 inhabitants, on the pine-clad edge of a terrace, the plain is alluvial and is partly under vines and other fruit trees. The average density of population for both plains is 106 per sq. mile.

The western extension of Ólimbos is penetrated by the river Lílas, which traverses the plain of Yídhes in a defile and has the largest river basin in Évvoia. It reaches the gulf just south of the narrows, and its delta has provided Khalkís with most valuable fruit land and with a water supply. The surrounding low hills are composed of limestone and serpentine, from which magnesite is obtained. The town of Khalkís, on the eastern shores of Evripós Strait (Plate 35), is the capital of the island and owes its importance to its position. The Venetian walls have fallen into ruin, but it remains a picturesque and prosperous town with 16,967 inhabitants and a vigorous trade in agricultural and dairy produce (see vol. II, pp. 272–5). A further 9,000 people are supported by the little orchard-covered plain behind it. The complex currents of the Evripós (= swift current) seem to be due to a combination of tide and seiche.

From the southern slopes of Ólimbos steep-sided ravines lead down to fans, covered with olive groves, and then to a coastal plain. The narrow plain of Néa Psará (Erétria) in the west is succeeded by the triangular plain of Amárinthos, composed partly of river fans, and hemmed in on the east by the grey limestone precipices of Mount Servoúni. From Arálimas cove a straight fracture runs almost due north to Metókhi Bay on the Aegean coast, and on either side of it the mountains differ markedly. To the east is the rectangular and tabular Mavrovoúni, a karst plateau of pure limestone, with many *doline* ; west of it are rugged ridges and ravines produced by the alternation of limestones and shales. Above the general level of these eastern ridges rise the abrupt peak of Mount Skotiní, the graceful, isolated cone of Dhírfis, and beyond it the parallel ridges that continue to the Pixariá mountains. The entire seaward slope is riven by huge gorges, and the higher parts are still covered with forests of fir. The inhabitants of the sparse pastoral villages give an average population density of 40 per sq. mile.

The mountainous frame of the lowlands of Kími, the richest district in Évvoia, consists of the fractured edge of limestone blocks on the north, west and south-east, with lower hills of sandstone and slate in the south-west. Within this frame the andesitic rocks of a volcano rise in bare cones to a height of 1,358 ft. Elsewhere, the basin is composed of an assortment of Tertiary rocks, including much marly limestone and sands. These, rising steeply from the curved beach, are trenched by the rivers Maníkia and Avlomárion which water and drain the small plain south of the volcanic hills. Kími, with a population of 3,358, stands at the north-east corner of the basin with its famous vineyards on the slopes above. To the west, iron ore has been worked from the ridges of serpentine and sandstone ; and an important lignite mine lies 3 miles to the west among the highest slopes of Tertiary strata.

The verdant lowland is one of the most favoured spots in Greece.

The trees—plane, poplar, willow, walnut, cypress and olive—grow to an unusual size ; the production of grapes is enormous, and that of olives and many other fruits is also remarkable. The district has always been noted for its richness, and the number of Frankish and Venetian castles is unmatched throughout Évvoia. The mean density of population is 420 per sq. mile, and it is the most populous part of the island.

Southern Évvoia

The axis of this narrow southern part runs almost due south and then swings to the south-east, but the ancient crystalline rocks of which it is composed lie in folds that are respectively oblique and transverse to these directions. It is a hilly land, sloping steeply to the coast, with many summits approaching 2,000 ft. in height and all over-topped by Mount Ókhi, 4,563 ft. above sea level. This peak, and the ridge extending towards Cape Kafirévs, are formed by specially hard schist, but most of the higher ridges are of marble and its pale colour relieves an otherwise monotonous landscape. The surface is almost uniformly covered by maquis, except for a few luxuriant stream banks on which plane trees flourish.

The north-south trend in the northern part is emphasized by a medial depression which continues the basin of Kími southwards and is followed by the easy road to Alivérion (and Khalkís). The valley lies mainly in slates and sandstones but it extends into the marble of the south on the line of three *doline* and the fiord-like Gulf of Almiropótamos. Here is a large artesian spring and on the coast farther north are salt springs above sea level, indicating an active underground water system along a line of weakness. The northern hollow (3 by 1½ miles) is filled, half by cultivated alluvium and half by the variable Lake Dhístos. Overlooking this are the ruins of the ancient city and the late Venetian castle and citadel of Dystos.

Cultivated land, in general, is restricted to scattered pockets of residual red earth on the marble and to small patches of alluvium on the schists. There is, however, one larger area of alluvium in a valley west of Mount Ókhi. Two of the several coastal plains have some importance : the smaller, that of Stíra, sheltered by Stíra islet, and the much bigger plain of Káristos in the south. Both have Tertiary beds as well as alluvium and, with plenty of springs, they are prosperous oases ; at both, too, there are ancient and modern quarries of greenish-coloured marble, much prized by the Romans. The best stone, however, is found at Marmári between these places. Káristos, with a population of 1,866, is a summer resort, less than 100 years old, lying at the foot of Mount Ókhi (Plate 36). The average density of population for the whole of southern Évvoia is 85 per sq. mile.

For Bibliographical Note, see p. 22.

Plate 35.   The Strait of Evrípos
The view is from Khalkís and towards the mainland.

Plate 36.   Mount Ókhi and Káristos, from the south

Plate 37. The entrance to the Aliákmon valley from the Siniátsikon mountains west of Siátista

The lower ridge is typical of the Anaselítsa country, of which it is a bay in the mountains.

Plate 38. The northern corner of the lower plain of Thessalía and the mountains north of Tírnavos

The river Máti emerges from permanent springs in the limestone. The river is now used to irrigate the northern part of the plain.

Chapter V

EASTERN GREECE

The Western Corridor : The Plains of Thessalía : The Western Mountain Belt :
The Eastern Corridor : The Eastern Mountain Belt

The region of Eastern Greece forms an oblong belt of country,
approximately 110 miles long and 45 miles broad, lying east of the
Dividing Mountains. The greater part is drained to the Aegean
Sea by two of the few long rivers that are wholly in Greece—the
Aliákmon and the Piniós ; both are transverse to the trend of
structure and relief, which suggests that they flowed in this direction
before the uplift of the mountains. Several areas near the frontier,
however, and one in the lower plain of Thessalía are drained into
lakes that have only subterranean outlets.

The country is divided between upper, or western, Makedhonía
in the north, and the greater part of Thessalía in the south, and the
boundary separating the two provinces roughly follows the watershed between the Piniós and Aliákmon basins. The Piniós basin,
excluding the part tributary to the Xiriás (Sarandáporos), west of
Mount Ólimbos, became Greek territory in 1881 ; but the whole of
the Aliákmon basin, now included in Makedhonía, was only acquired
in 1913. This historical and administrative division of the country
into two transverse belts does not, however, imply that the watershed between the two rivers is a serious physical obstacle.

The major features of relief comprise four zones, comparable in
size, and broadly parallel throughout their entire length. Their
general trend, like that of the east coast, is south-south-east and they
run from the frontier to the broken, mountainous edge of Central
Greece. Two of the zones are mainly lowland, and the other two
are mainly high mountain blocks, the edges of the zones for the most
part marking profound geological faults ; similar fractures farther
east, followed by subsidence, produced the Aegean Sea in its present
form. In the south, the barrier between the western and eastern
lowland zones becomes so slight that the two plains of Thessalía
may be viewed as a single geographical region. There are, therefore,
five major physical regions in Eastern Greece (Fig. 18) :

D1. The Western Corridor.
D2. The Plains of Thessalía.

D3. The Western Mountain Belt.
D4. The Eastern Corridor.
D5. The Eastern Mountain Belt.

The Western Corridor (Region D1)

Physical Characteristics

The western zone is one of almost continuous lowland, starting in Albania in the ill-drained plain of Bilishti which gathers the waters of the upper Devoll. At the frontier the ground rises from the swampy plain to a ridge that overlooks the long corridor known as Anaselítsa or Vóïon (an eparchy of Kozáni). This district varies in height from 1,600 to 3,000 ft. and is drained and dissected by the Aliákmon and its tributaries. Southwards, beyond an ill-marked watershed, it merges into the Khasiá, drained by the Piniós and its affluents, and finally the corridor falls steeply to the plain of upper Thessalía. Khasiá and Anaselítsa together form a strip of similar country, over 60 miles long and with an average breadth of 18 miles.

Owing to the difficulty of movement among the mountains of Ípiros on the west and Makedhonía and northern Thessalía on the east, the corridor between them has always been used as an easy approach to Central Greece from the north, and in 1941 the German army made one of its main attacks by this route. It forms, indeed, the longest easy route in the whole of Greece.

Unlike the other zones of Eastern Greece, this lowland belt has been little affected by earth-fractures with transverse trends, although such faults from south-west to north-east are, in fact, followed by several right bank tributaries of the Aliákmon. The geographical unity of this region is due to its peculiar relief. Though exceedingly hilly in character it was once a smooth plain composed of thick and almost flat-bedded sediments of Miocene and Pliocene age, sandstones and sands, marls, shales and conglomerates (Plate 37). On this, an intricate river system, tributary to the Aliákmon and Piniós, has developed and cut into the plain to depths up to some 1,600 ft. leaving remnants of the old surface along watersheds and as hilltops. Hence there are remarkable recurrences of similar forms throughout some 1,150 sq. miles of country. Flat land is generally uncommon and is chiefly confined to divides and to valley floors, but Anaselítsa is less deeply cut into than Khasiá and it contains several tracts that are merely undulating or even flat, notably on the western margin around Grevená, on the eastern

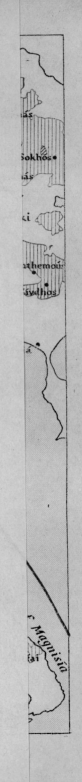

margin, and also near Lake Kastoría. Because of the weakness of many of the rocks, erosion is rapid with steep slopes and frequent landslides. Yet the total rainfall is low, probably under 27 ins., for the region is flanked by high mountains.

Land Utilization

The rainfall is sufficient for the growth of deciduous oak and beech forests, with juniper and Kermes oak as the chief evergreens. This type of vegetation still covers large areas of Khasiá and lesser ones in Anaselítsa. Wheat and maize are the main crops of the lowlands, with rye and barley in the higher parts, and tobacco and other crops wherever the soil is retentive of moisture : vines increasingly clothe the steeper slopes near the villages. But with the exception of a few favoured districts this corridor region has remained backward and, for its altitude, thinly populated. Its relative accessibility to warlike operations in the past partly accounted for this, but it was also subjected to the full incidence of Turkish rule and most of the villages were *tchiftliki* in which the Greek labourers led a miserable life. Moreover, from 1881 to 1913 the international frontier crossed the region from east to west, and retarded development.

The results of the exchanges of population in 1922 in this region were considerable, but very much less than those farther east ; the evacuation of the Moslem population, which constituted about one-fifth of the total, was barely balanced by the immigration of some 14,000 refugees. These were settled in about 30 new villages, and a score of old ones in which they joined the previous inhabitants. The largest places in the region from north to south are Kastoría, Neápolis, Siátista and Grevená. Kastoría is a town with a remarkable site and surprising links. Closely built of white houses on the neck of a high limestone peninsula jutting eastward into the oval lake, it contains the ruins of sixty-nine Byzantine churches, evidence of its former importance as a great commercial centre. In the fur trade, which is its speciality, the people of Kastoría still have close relations with furriers in Leipzig, Paris, London and New York, where they are known for their skill in matching and fine sewing of small clippings. The greenish, muddy waters of the lake, only 26 ft. deep, provide for a considerable fishery. The banks, apart from the peninsula, are marshy and the neighbouring villages suffer badly from malaria. This is especially true of the

settlements to the south-east since mosquitoes are carried there by the
prevailing north-west wind. Neápolis lies near the right bank of
the Aliákmon and possesses two notable forts of former importance
and a large new co-operative tobacco factory. Siátista stands on a
high terrace (2,790 ft.) at the eastern mountain edge, near the gap
which leads to Kozáni. It consists of twin villages with 4,600
inhabitants, and the neighbouring vineyards are famous for the
white wine they produce. Hellenism here found a stronghold in
Turkish times, and Siátista was long an important market with
foreign connexions. Grevená stands out among the villages of the
western edge of the corridor as a centre of routes and an important
Vlach settlement, with a population of 3,747. A great influx to the
town takes place annually when the flocks are on the way from the
plains of Thessalía to the northern Píndhos. The Vlach caravans
arrive in time to take part in the fair of St. Akhíllios, from 29 May
to 5 June, an opportunity for family reunions.

The north-western part of this region is very much more populous
than the south-eastern ; the division runs through Siátista and
Grevená, and the respective densities are 98 and 34 per sq. mile.
The reasons for the great excess in the higher area are not clear, but
contributory causes may be a better water supply and closer connexions with the summer pastures in the mountains : moreover,
the political changes may still have had some influence at the census
of 1928.

The Plains of Thessalía (Region D2)

Physical Characteristics

The upper and lower plains of Thessalía belong to separate zones
but the hills that divide them form such an insignificant barrier
that the whole region must obviously be considered together. The
two plains occupy areas in which progressive crustal subsidence
continued over a long period, so that the bedrock rests at unknown,
but doubtless considerable, depths. It is covered by masses of
easily eroded sediments laid down by deposit from surrounding
rivers, first in lakes and later on intermittently flooded land. The
plains are each roughly sickle-shaped, convex to the south-west,
and the upper plain is somewhat the larger. They are bounded
on the west by a uniform, curved wall, the first range of the Dividing
Mountains, which is composed of thick beds of limestone and chert
broken by the deep defiles of many rivers—notably the Portaïkós

and the Pámisos. On the north, a number of spurs of the Khasía mountains extend southwards, composed of sandstone in the west and crystalline schists and limestones in the east, and between them lie bays of the plain (Plate 39). The largest of these is the Kalabáka Bay, followed by the Piniós, narrowing north-westward into the Píndhos. On the south are the plateaux of the Óthris, and in the east, the foothills of Mount Óssa.

Since the upper plain receives the more powerful rivers, falling steeply from well-watered mountains, its surface features are composed of a number of convergent fans, with slopes of gravel near their heads and finer materials farther out, becoming clay between the fans. The Piniós brings to the lower plain all the drainage of the upper plain, but it carries only fine silt, and the Xiriás (Titarísios), from the north, is the only river capable of building a large fan. It should be noted that large tracts alternate naturally between inundation, when rivers have been in spate, and sun-baked or dusty aridity after the summer drought.

Land Utilization

Thessalía, the largest region of plains in Greece, has been regarded as a granary from classical times, and the generally backward character of the farming that has prevailed until the most recent decades may well cause surprise. To this, two main causes have contributed : first, the general inability of the population to control the waters, and secondly, the Turkish land system which lasted so long. Moreover, it must be remembered that this lowland, the forecourt of approach to Greece, was always looked upon as a rich prize in itself, and in consequence was the scene of almost unremitting warfare for centuries before the Turkish conquest in 1393. Whether ruled nominally from Byzantium, Albania or Serbia, or partitioned among Greek, Vlach or Frankish principalities, the feudal landlords frequently failed to live at peace with their neighbours. With such a history, the population of Thessalía is of very mixed origin, but in language and culture it has always been Greek. The Turkish agrarian system, by which the owners of large estates (*tchifliki*) had complete control of their serfs and their lives, receiving perhaps one-third of their produce and ejecting them at will, was sufficient in itself to prevent any real social or agricultural improvement ; and these conditions persisted until 1881. Even the removal of the Turks brought very meagre improvements at first, for the wealthy Greeks who acquired the estates were with few exceptions little better in their treatment of the land and its people than their Turkish masters had been. Nevertheless, by 1900, agricultural yields were beginning to increase and some additions to the cereals (wheat, barley, and maize) to which land had so long been devoted were making their appearance, notably sugar beet ; attention was also given to the road system, and railway construction had already taken place. Expropriation laws from 1916 onwards enabled the government to break up many large estates in Thessalía, and thus to induce social changes, so that by 1922, when the refugees began to reach Greece, little land was available for them. Consequently under 35,000 were absorbed altogether, of whom a proportion lived in urban settlements such as Vólos, Lárisa and Fársala. Altogether, thirty-three agricultural settlements were established in the *nomós* of Lárisa, twelve being in the eparchy of Elassón, and only six in the *nomós* of Tríkkala.

The total population of the upper, and larger, plain is about 161,000, and that of the lower is about 67,000 ; the density on the former is 163 per sq. mile as compared with 122 on the latter. This difference reflects not only the greater fertility of the better-watered plain, but also a somewhat less oppressive rule here under the Turks as well as a much greater Vlach element in the population, with interests other than agriculture. Throughout these plains, the settlements are large and, generally, sprawling villages which grew around the old *tchifliki ;* they are so situated as to be comparatively safe from flooding (Fig. 19). The towns of the upper plain are Tríkkala, Kalabáka, Kardhítsa, Fársala and Dhomokós ; the last two, in view of their connexions with the south, have already been described (see pp. 70, 72). Those of the lower plain are Lárisa and Tírnavos. With the exception of Lárisa all the ancient towns stood upon, or at the foot of, the hills.

Strategic control of the main western approach from the Dividing Mountains in ancient times rested on the twin Homeric fortresses of Trikka and Ithome, crowning forward bluffs of the foothills and flanking the gorge of the Piniós. Ithome on the south, still marked by a ruined Byzantine castle, is now represented only by the large village of Fanárion ; but Tríkkala, the successor of Trikka, remains the chief town of the upper plain, with about 19,000 inhabitants of Greeks and Vlachs, the latter being in majority in winter. It is the principal market for the pastoral produce of the Píndhos region and the farm crops of the plain. The town is laid out on both banks of the Lithaíos, the ancient Lethe, which hugs the foot of the acropolis, its banks fringed with plane-trees ; many churches are clustered on the slopes above the houses. The ancient importance of the town as a famous sanctuary of Asclepius is recalled only by the presence of the two healing springs, and now by the name of a principal street (Asklepiós Street). The significant features now are the evidences of ecclesiastical prominence in this archiepiscopal seat and the vivid activity of the bazaar. Facing the town, ten miles across the plain, are the ' Gates of Tríkkala ', the defiles of the rivers Portaïkós and Pámisos which are followed by routes from Tríkkala to the mountains of Ágrafa.

Kalabáka stands at the apex of the bay of the Piniós where there is still room for cultivation and large groves of mulberry trees between the mountains and the river bank ; the stony flood-bed of the river here, at the head of the fan, is 1,000 yds. wide. The site is unique from the grandeur of the bare precipice of conglomerate behind the town ; crowning the pinnacles are the remarkable monasteries of Metéora (see vol. I, p. 437 and Plate 90). The ancient town, Aeginium, occupying this strategic place was famous for the many attacks it had to resist. Again, from A.D. 1309, when the town was called Stagus, it has contained a Metropolitan church of importance. But Kalabáka, although it is the terminus of the railway, is a small place of 2,695 inhabitants in cramped surroundings and necessarily overshadowed by Tríkkala, only 13 miles away.

Unlike the other towns, Kardhítsa is situated 5 miles from the foothills, and the remains of the ancient citadel of Metropolis, corresponding to it, stand high among the wooded ridges. Kardhítsa is a Turkish foundation but, with independence, it was largely replanned on the Greek pattern ; it has only recently been rendered immune from occasional inundation. It is the chief agricultural market for the southern part of the plain and the mountains of Ágrafa ; and benefitting from the coming of the railway, it has doubled its population (13,883) in the last fifty years.

These three towns, as well as Fársala and Dhomokós, are clearly differentiated from the villages by their compactness and plan. Kardhítsa, for example, with its parallel streets, covers about the same area as Palamás, 10 miles to the north-east, a loose agglomeration with winding lanes ; but it has over three times its population.

The sites of Tírnavos and Lárisa may be compared respectively with those of Tríkkala and Kardhítsa. The former dominates the northern alcove and the fan of the Xiriás. The town is backed by the steep, bare ridge of the northern mountains (Plate 38) and stands near the defile of this river. It is a medieval town with several interesting churches and a bridge that has always been important. In addition to its agricultural resources it has small cotton and silk industries ; the population numbers 7,158.

The elbow of the meandering Piniós has probably been the site of a town from prehistoric times, and the name Lárisa is a very ancient word meaning fortress. But, for defence, the place had to rely upon artificial works except on the river front. The natural dangers have included not only floods and malaria but also earthquakes—the latest in 1944. Rebuilt by the Turks with the name Yenisher (= new town) the town, although nearly flat, possessed a certain oriental picturesqueness ; but since the departure of the Turks its appearance has become almost squalid, except for a rather pretentious square and a few of the older houses and minarets. Lárisa is the provincial capital, and the second town in Thessalía with a population of 23,889 (see vol. II, pp. 386–7).

No picture of life of these plains as it has been for many centuries would be complete without the pastoral element ; for in winter the population has always been greatly augmented by herdsmen with their flocks of sheep and goats, while the towns of the upper plain, notably Tríkkala, house a largely increased population of Vlachs. The shepherds are to be seen in winter living either in tents or, more often, in small reed huts. They have in the past consisted partly of semi-nomadic Vlachs, named by the Greeks *Arvanitovlachi*, and partly of complete nomads. These latter, whether Albanian Vlachs, termed Farseriotes, or Greek-speaking *Sarakatzanaei*, have preserved a clan system of unusually marked patriarchal character.

The present agricultural output of the two plains may be partially discerned from the 1937 statistics of the *nomoí* of Tríkkala and Lárisa, which correspond largely to the western and eastern plains. It is significant that Tríkkala had 69% of its cultivated area under cereals, with 39% in wheat, 17% in maize, 6% in oats and 5% in barley. Lárisa had 70% under cereals, with 52% in wheat and 9% each in oats and barley, the maize being insignificant, indicating the drier summer conditions of the east. Heavier rainfall accounts for Tríkkala having four times the area in forage crops and twice the number of cattle shown for Lárisa, as well as twice the cotton, and three times the area under sesame. Vines in Tríkkala are grown in patches along the western margin, and in Lárisa on the plain itself, including a large tract of the Xirías fan east of Tírnavos.

Plate 39.   Kalabáka from the south-west

Behind the town is Mount Koukoúla, one of the three neighbouring massifs of conglomerate on which the Meteora monasteries stand. The monastery of Ayía Stéfanos (extreme right) is reached by a bridge over a chasm. The railway terminus is in the foreground.

[Facing page 86

Plate 40. The river Enipévs near its confluence with the Piniós
From the banks, built up by the river in flood, the ground slopes away on both
sides. The background is formed by the Antikhasia mountains to the north.

Plate 41. The confluence of the river Piniós with the Xirías above the entrance
to the defile of Mousalar
The Piniós is seen flowing from left to right. The view is westward to the
mountains behind Tírnavos.

Such, however, is the predominance of cereals and so much land is fallow at one time that the general aspect is that of a steppe, with scattered deciduous bushes and the white asphodel often prominent. The water courses, however, are frequently lined with tall plane and poplar trees. Future developments will doubtless be dictated by the economic needs of Greece, but changes like those affected by reclamation in the northern plain of Italy might be expected, with areas given to rice, hemp and sugar beet, more systematic growing of deciduous fruit trees and perhaps greater attention to cotton, while the soya bean might be added to sesame as an oil-yielding crop. With the area subject to flood reduced, and less reliance placed upon fallowing, limitation of winter pastures must necessarily follow, and this will eventually lead to some alteration in the migratory habits of the shepherds.

The ridge which separates the two plains, while still a considerable feature in the north where it is penetrated by the Piniós and the main Tríkkala–Lárisa road, dwindles south-eastwards to a mere sill in which the railway follows a wide gap with hardly a cutting. Nearing Lake Voïvïís the sill again becomes a ridge, exceeding 2,000 ft. in altitude, but lack of soil, rather than height, is the cause of its cover of dark bushy woodland and its name, Mavrovoúni. To the south, the furrow of the Enipévs provides the Fársala–Vólos railway with an almost level route (Plate 40), except for a short climb where the ridge impinges on the northern flank of the Óthris mountains.

Drainage and Irrigation

The full development of the plains of Thessalía can become possible only when the flood waters are under control, and the Greek government, with the help of British engineers, has already taken the necessary steps to make this effective. Fig. 19 shows the natural hydrography and the new system of control. The task was a complex one and has been partially completed. In the western plain there are gentle slopes from all directions towards the north-east corner where the exit of the Piniós is a steep-sided valley nearly 2,000 ft. deep and half a mile wide. Many of the rivers have variable channels, and owing to the abrupt decline in slope where they emerge from the mountains the floods are a real danger to the towns and villages on the fans, notably Tríkkala, where the Litháios is one of the rivers to be provided with a diverted course : the town was devastated by flood in 1907. Similarly, the Pámisos has been given a new channel of 5 miles, with direct flow to the Piniós. The plan, then, is first to divert rivers, secondly to enclose channels by protective embankments, and thirdly, to drain marshes by many low-level ditches. In addition, the smaller hill-streams have to be collected by seven high-level drains along the hill-foot ; and all this involves the building of a number of siphons where channels intersect. By early 1939, some 13,000 acres had thus been protected from flood.

On the eastern plain the task is complicated by the following features : first, there is no regular outlet from Lake Voïviís at the lowest level of the plain, under 160 ft. ; secondly, the Piniós below its defile has deserted its older direct entrance to this plain and turned into the hills, flowing north, and then east, in a gorge over 900 ft. deep. Thence it follows a meandering course, with many swampy cut-offs, round the fan of the Xiriás. Again, north of Lárisa, there is an area of uncertain drainage due to past changes in the direction of flow. When the plain was some 100 ft. higher, the Piniós seems to have flowed directly north-east to the vale of Témbi in the valley that carries the railway and road ; later, it must have turned to Lake Voïviís, but finally it has returned to the north. It now follows a defile nearly 4 miles long and 500 ft. deep, and then crosses a small plain before reaching its last great gorge of Témbi. Most of these peculiar changes are doubtless connected with the instability of the earth's crust, of which the frequent earthquakes are evidence.

The level of Lake Voïviís will now decline further, since with the diversion of streams formerly tributary to the lake, evaporation will become more effective. Further hydrographic changes have been effected to safeguard the towns of Lárisa and Tírnavos from flooding. Protective embankments have been built enclosing the meander strip of the Piniós, and the river has also been diverted from Lárisa. Similarly, the Xiriás has been provided with embankments in order to protect Tírnavos which stands on the left bank of the river immediately below its entry upon the plain (Plate 41).

During the summer drought the only water available over most of both plains has been that derived from numerous wells of the lever pattern, a characteristic element of the scene ; but in the future a large system of irrigation is contemplated by hydraulic control. In the eastern plain 50,000 acres had been protected in

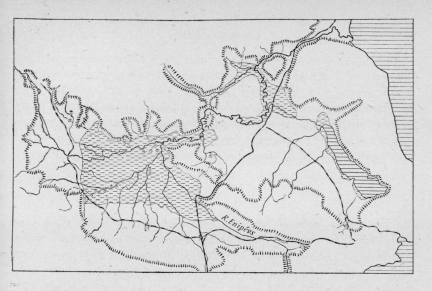

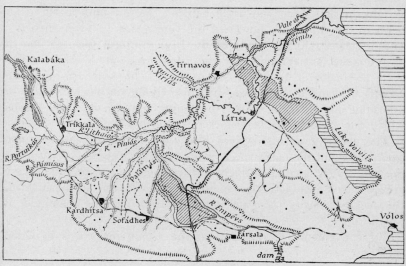

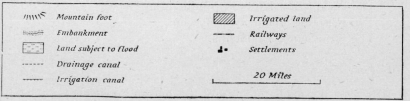

Fig. 19. Drainage of the plains of Thessalía

Based on engineering plans and the 1 : 250,000 G.S.G.S. Series 4088, The Balkans Sheet S3060.
The upper map shows the plain before drainage ; settlements have been omitted.
Note that the stippled areas on the upper map show land formerly subject to flood, while the areas shaded diagonally on the lower map show land under regulated irrigation.

1939 and 20,000 acres of this represented additional cereal land. To regulate irrigation in the upper plain a dam has been constructed on the Enipévs in the Óthris mountains (see p. 70). Thus, with full control of the water the agricultural future of the plains is likely to be secured. The soils are mostly deep and loamy, rich in humus, and although the percentage frequency of frost between November and April is 17, the physical conditions favour heavy crops of grain.

THE WESTERN MOUNTAIN BELT (REGION D3)

This region consists for the most part of up-thrust masses of crystalline and metamorphic rocks, beginning as the high Babá mountains (8,530 ft.) west of Bitolj (Monastir). In Greece this zone is affected by south-west to north-east fractures which have resulted in several low passes and the division of the belt into several districts, each with local names. As far south as the great bend of the Aliákmon, however, the summits are above 5,900 ft. ; but thereafter, to the defile of the upper Piniós, they decline in altitude, and farther south still, the zone forms only low hills separating the plains of Thessalía (see p. 87). The northern mountain groups are flanked on the west by lower mountain blocks, mainly of limestone and severely broken by faults, and also by Lake Préspa which now covers a sunken block of the crust.

The entire mountain system has a population of about 50,000 and, in view of the narrowness of the strip and the rugged nature of the country, it is comparatively well peopled, suggesting that many villagers have also activities on the plains. In the northern third, the average density is 72 per sq. mile, and over the remainder it falls to 47.

For convenience of description, the region may be subdivided into four areas :—

The Lake Préspa District
The Pisodhérion-Klisoúra Mountains
The Klisoúra-Aliákmon Mountains
The Kamvoúnia Mountains.

The Lake Préspa District

The most debatable territory of the Balkan Peninsula is probably that surrounding Lake Préspa, for it has long been contested by Albanians, Slavs and Greeks. One of the main bodies of the

Plate 42.   Vlásti

The view, from the south-west, shows an enclosed plain at 3,800 ft. and, behind the village, the pass leading to Embórion.

Plate 43.   Flórina from the south-west

The view extends just beyond the frontier on the plain, but the high mountains and the gap of the Crna river are not visible.

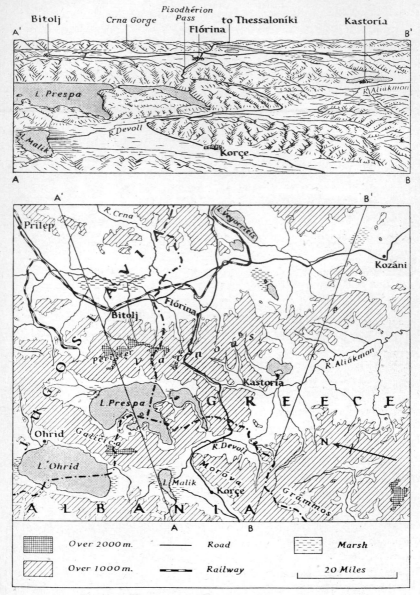

Fig. 20.   The frontier district of western Makedhonía
This map is based on the 1 : 400,000 Greek *Carte Aéronautique*.
The lines AA' and BB' show the lateral limits of the view above.

Vlachs was also established in the mountains to the west, in the two important towns of Muskopole and Shipiska ; the former was a university town of some 50,000 inhabitants when it was sacked by the Albanians in 1769. The restless history of the district is partly the result of the convergence of routes upon the shores of Lakes Ohrid and Préspa (Fig. 20), and the convergence is due to the same crustal dislocations which so strongly affected the surrounding mountains. The deeply sunk fault-block containing Lake Ohrid lies entirely in Jugoslavia and Albania, but the southern shore of Lake Préspa is in Greece, the frontier being demarcated so as to leave Korçe (Koritza), the real route centre, in Albania. This large lake, 2,776 ft. above the sea and about 100 ft. deep, has a peculiar outline and is now without a visible outlet. The main part of the basin is a sunken wedge-shaped block overlooked on the east by the straight fault-scarp of the Varnoús mountains which are built of granite, and on the west by a great slab of white limestone which narrows towards Kastoría and which is broken transversely into three, the two arms of Préspa corresponding to the fractured depressions. One of these is now occupied by Lake Mikrí Préspa, cut off from the main lake by a sandspit half a mile wide. Each has once been an outlet, but water now reaches both Lake Ohrid and the Devoll plain, presumably by underground channels. Since the ends of both inlets are in Albania this is an awkward frontier.

The Pisodhérion-Klisoúra Mountains

Parallel to Mikrí Préspa a deep, and now dry, valley through the limestone plateau carries the one road leading across the Varnoús range. At Vatokhórion the road meets the longitudinal Livadho-pótamos and follows it on its climb to the Pisodhérion Pass (4,856 ft.) whence the Lerínska valley carries it down to Flórina. The Varnoús forms a real barrier and this is the only low pass for 25 miles from the frontier. The actual summits are rounded, since they are remnants of the old mature surface, but the faulted sides of this granitic and gneissic range are cut into the wildest scenery. Yet the mountains are inhabited, each deep valley having at least one village. From the peak named Vítsi (6,981 ft.), 12 miles south-east of Pisodhérion, where the gneiss has a broad capping of flat-bedded limestone, the crest declines to the Klisoúra (= Pass) at 3,770 ft., above which is perched the large Vlach village of this name, a place of former commercial importance and once a Byzantine frontier fort. The pass dominates the routes converging upon Kastoria to the west, and today a metalled road runs to Édhessa and north-eastern Greece.

The Klisoúra-Aliákmon Mountains

South of Klisoúra the mountains again rise to similar heights on the Muríki and Siniátsikon ranges, divided by a pass, above the village of Vlásti (Plate 42), which leads to Embórion (see p. 95). South of the Siniátsikon range lies a lower plateau, 3,000 ft. in height, with the villages of Eratíra and Galatiní on its western edge. From this rises a fairly uniform series of mountains ; it begins with the table-mountain of Véllia and extends for 22 miles to the defile of the Aliákmon. These mountains, however, are broken by two gaps that seem once to have carried transverse rivers north and south of the massif of Voúrinos. The first is under 2,300 ft. in height, and the site of Siátista at its western entrance (see p. 82), the modern road from Grevená to Kozáni, and the proposed railway between those towns, marks its importance as a route. The second gap is of similar altitude, but so far has no first-class road.

The origin of the defiles of this long mountain zone has not been completely studied, but it is clear that the gap of the Aliákmon is an elbow of capture. When the Aegean basin foundered, the great river began cutting backwards with renewed energy due to steepened slope and so captured the drainage of the lowland zone to west. The process has continued progressively northwards, the rivers formerly flowing by the Devoll valley to the Adriatic being successfully diverted. The next stage will be the tapping of Lake Préspa by the Aliákmon. In the great bend the transverse section is no longer a canyon, but the northward reach, just below the elbow, is gorge-like and inaccessible. This constriction causes the river to flood its banks in the gap itself, and the modern road from Grevená via Karperón to Sérvia keeps high on the right bank.

The Kamvoúnia Mountains

From Karperón a main road strikes south-east to Elassón and Tírnavos, directly across the next and last section of the mountain zone. Here, in the Kamvoúnia mountains, the crystalline rocks are mica-schists dipping to the north-east, and the region is a massive, rolling and well wooded plateau—an ancient mature surface, nearly 15 miles square, with summits from 3,600 to 4,900 ft. Three valleys cross the district and are widely open from west to east. At the head of the middle one is the large village of Dheskáti, with a fertile plain and long famous as a centre of brigandage. The name Kamvoúnia is also given to the range which strikes off north-eastward (see p. 96). Southwards the plateau becomes lower, more dissected and less wooded, and is penetrated by the defiles of the Piniós and Xiriás rivers.

THE EASTERN CORRIDOR (REGION D4)

The third longitudinal zone starts as the plain of Pelagonia in Jugoslavia, drained somewhat ineffectively by the river Crna. Southwards, beyond a lower watershed in the district of Eordhaía, a series of basin plains with only slight differences of level carries the zone across the Aliákmon. The drainage is partly northwards to the deep mountain lake of Vegorrítis, or Óstrovon, and partly southwards to the Aliákmon ; but it is most immature and the basins contain shallow residual lakes such as Petrón and Khimadhítis, or the swamps of the one-time lake Sarigól. Beyond the Aliákmon the lowland nature of the zone is interrupted by transverse mountains caused by dislocations along lines from south-west to north-east. These uplands are a north-eastern extension of the Kamvoúnia range, rising to 4,900 ft., and then a lower range hemming in the upper basin of the Xiriás. For a more detailed description it is convenient to subdivide the region into four areas :

The Plain of Pelagonia
The Plain of Eordhaía
The Middle Aliákmon Basin
The Sarandáporos (Xiriás) Basin.

The Plain of Pelagonia

The ancient Pelagonia, once the bed of a large lake, is now drained by the upper Crna river. About nine-tenths of it lie in Jugoslavia, the frontier crossing it just south of the bend of the river where it forms an elbow of capture before entering the mountains to the north-east. The Greek section of the plain is relatively well drained by a fan of rivers gathered up by the Eléska and carried northwards to the Crna, and their valleys are slightly etched in an apron of easily eroded lake-sediments that slopes gently from 2,600 ft. to 1,650 ft. Throughout its length the plain is overlooked by great rectilinear fault-scarps, those of the Varnoús in the west and of the Kaïmakchalán mountains in the east, the latter rising much less steeply. The Greek part of the plain has an area of some 135 sq. miles, and is important both for its fertility and for the access it offers by rail and road to Bitolj, the Roman *Via Egnatia*, and by the Pisodhérion road to Albania.

This plain was completely under Turkish sway and its Slav and Greek inhabitants were in a depressed condition before 1923. But, since the replacement of about one-third of the population by Anatolian refugees, the countryside has been transformed ; mud hovels have given place to brick and tile cottages, and the plain, which was largely a steppe, is now completely cultivated, yielding varied crops in farms of from one to three acres. Wheat takes about one-third of the land and vines one-fifth. Next in importance come maize, barley, rye and tobacco, but in suitable places there are irrigated meadows for forage, and an increasing number of fruit trees are grown, especially apples, walnuts and pears.

The fourteen villages evacuated by the Turks were on the western border of the plain, or along the *Via Egnatia* ; renamed, they are now the homes of Anatolian Greeks. There are also several new villages, one being ' New Caucasus ', indicating far-travelled immigrants. Few of the Macedo-Slavs took advantage of the Conventions for exchanges of population with Bulgaria, and they constitute more than one-third of the population of the *nomós* of Flórina, forming the largest minority in Greece (see vol. I, p. 354). The only town is Flórina, situated picturesquely on the floor and slope of a valley, amid its orchards, just within the hills ; it controls access to the Pisodhérion Pass, and is now reached by a short branch line from the main railway (Plate 43). During the exchanges of population it lost some 5,000 Turks and is now an almost purely Greek and Vlach town of nearly 11,000 inhabitants. Its only factory makes woollen knit-goods. Lignite is exploited at the southern edge of the lacustrine deposits, where the railway leaves the plain near Vévi. The population of the Greek part of the plain, with Flórina, has an average density of 197 per sq. mile.

The Plain of Eordhaía

A low, but rocky, plateau forms a threshold between the plain of Pelagonia and the plain of Eordhaía. This feature is the result of dislocation extending from Kastoría north-eastwards to the northern end of Lake Vegorrítis, and along it the gneiss of the west and the limestones of the eastern mountains both project to meet at Aëtós. The rise from the north is gentle but on the south-east there is a straight escarpment, some 1,000 ft. high, overlooking the plain of Eordhaía. Subsidiary faults have caused local subsidence and have led to the formation of the lakes Khimadhítis (now partly a marsh), Petrón and Vegorrítis : the latter just touches the plain and is described on p. 103. The plain extends south-eastwards for 26 miles, varying in breadth from 6 to 12 miles, and about 300 ft. in altitude. It is the floor of a former lake, now dry except for occasional stretches and the swamp of Sarigól in the south. It is floored by gravel, sand, loam, and mud, and for a long time the greater part of it was a pale-coloured steppe. Today, it contains about forty villages situated on or near its margins, and in the middle of the northern part is the small town of Ptolemaïs, formerly Kaialar, with 6,600 inhabitants. This plain was the home of the most westerly compact body of Turks introduced after the conquest, and in 1912 Moslems numbered three-quarters of the population. The steppe, therefore, is now very largely cultivated by immigrant peasants. Of a total population of 44,000, some 39,000 are Greeks, two-thirds being refugees largely from northern Anatolia, the remainder being Slavs and Vlachs. The Slavs living about Lake Petrón are interesting in that they speak a dialect akin to Slovene rather than Serb or Bulgar. By far the greatest area is under wheat, with maize and a little barley and rye. Much attention, however, is given to tobacco, especially near Ptolemaïs, and the Greeks from Pontus are skilful growers.

The villages near the lakes and the swamp of Sarigól suffer badly from malaria. Elsewhere on the plain, surface water is only seen intermittently, and the villages are supplied from wells ; at Ptolemaïs, near the bottom of a large undrained hollow, the new well had to be 843 ft. deep to get a supply sufficient for the town. The average density of population for the plain is 142 per sq. mile, and the people live for the most part in nucleated settlements around the margins. Embórion (Plate 44) on the west is typical, with 1,078 inhabitants.

The Middle Aliákmon Basin

South of Eordhaía a belt of rocky hills, stretching from west-south-west to east-north-east rises in summits some 1,000 ft. high, but among these are small, well-cultivated plains supporting a dozen hamlets. Then the plain reappears, dominated by Kozáni at its northern edge. From this town, at a height of 2,300 ft., the plain slopes gently southwards for 9 miles to the Aliákmon river,

1,200 ft. lower : it is somewhat dissected by parallel streams flowing permanently, and there are two transverse belts of open woodland between which the land is well tilled by the people of Kozáni and of a score of villages. Kozáni is a town of 12,700 inhabitants, sheltered by hills from the north, and its location is determined primarily by routes. At this point the western highway from the Klisoúra defile divides, one road continuing north-eastwards over the Vérmion mountains to Véroia and another following the edge of the plain south-eastwards, to Sérvia and so on to Lárisa. It has long been a centre of Hellenism, with its school founded in 1668, and is now a town of administrative importance ; in commerce, it is noted especially for saffron which until the present century was widely cultivated here. This trade was largely in Turkish hands and the emigration brought about considerable changes in the basin since two-fifths of the population were Moslems ; now it is entirely Greek, and the Anatolians have brought to it a carpet industry. Today the plain is best known for its vines and tobacco, each of which occupies 4% of the cultivated land of the *nomós*. The vineyards around the town are very large and the quality of the grapes, like those of Siátista across the mountains, is surpassed only by those of central and southern Greece. On this northern part of the plain the population density (135 per sq. mile) is very similar to that of the Eordhaía district. The part of this basin south of the Aliákmon, slopes more steeply to the river from the foot of the Kamvoúnia and Piéria mountains. It extends parallel to the river for 15 miles from Rímnion to Velvendós, noted for its large vineyards and irrigated orchards, beyond which the Aliákmon enters its gorge. The intensity of cultivation is reflected in the large population of this small lowland, over 9,000, with a density of 205 per sq. mile. Sérvia, the centre, with 3,250 inhabitants, is an attractive place backed by rugged slopes, and surrounded by fine plane trees and fields of maize and tobacco ; but it has suffered many times from wars, for it commands the southward passage from Makedhonía to Thessalía.

The Sarandáporos (Xiriás) Basin

The highway that strikes south from Sérvia makes a steep ascent to a saddle (2,950 ft.) in the Kamvoúnia, known as the Sarandapórou Sténa. Thence it follows the Sarandáporos, here called the Titarísios, to reach the broad rolling basin which gathers all the western drainage of Mount Ólimbos and bears the regional name

Tripoliana. It is not clear why this basin, with its many rivers and the centre of the ancient district of Perraibia, contains only six fairly large villages on its edges and elsewhere quite small settlements. The total population is under 11,000 and the density is only 54 per sq. mile.

Tripoliana is hemmed in on the south by a low rocky spur which is penetrated in gorges by the Sarandáporos in the west and the Elassonítikos in the east. Between them two important roads meet—the Sérvia–Elassón road and the modern road following a very old route from Thessaloníki. The little town of Elassón, with a population of 3,015, stands at the exit of the Elassonítikos from its gorge through the barrier and possesses great strategic importance as the key to the plain of Lárisa ; for in addition to the routes mentioned above, a third road reaches the town from Grevená and at least two others lead southwards. Its military value was amply demonstrated in the campaigns of 1897, 1912 and 1941. The ancient Elasson, mentioned by Homer, has disappeared and the present town is chiefly noted for its annual fair, its monastery and its Byzantine bridge ; its inhabitants include a colony of Vlachs.

The last barrier before the wide plains is the ridge which joins the Khasiá mountains to the Ólimbos range, and it is surmounted by two roads : one following the river Titarísios through its defile to Tírnavos, the other crossing the Meloúna Pass and reaching the plain 6 miles north of Tírnavos. The whole of this district of hills and valleys has a population of under 14,000, or 44 per sq. mile.

THE EASTERN MOUNTAIN BELT (REGION D5)

The last of the great longitudinal zones of Eastern Greece embraces high mountain blocks separated only by occasional defiles. The general altitudes of the summits are among the greatest in Greece, including with many others the well-known Pílion, Óssa and Ólimbos. Profound dislocations bound both sides of the long, narrow block, accounting for the general smoothness of the Aegean shores and the inner edge of the mountains. The original folding of the more or less crystalline rocks that compose the region is transverse to these long fault-lines, thus accounting for the parallelism and great depth of the numerous short valleys. The scenery on both escarpments is wild and the paths tortuous, yet most of the summits, as parts of an old erosion surface, are monotonous in their gentle slopes.

It is convenient to subdivide this region into its various mountain groups. From south to north these are :

The Peninsula of Magnisía and the Vólos Plateau
Mavrovoúni, Ossa and the Vale of Témbi
Mount Ólimbos
The Mountains of Piéria
The Vérmion Mountains
Lake Vegorrítis and the Vódas Basin

The Peninsula of Magnisía and the Vólos Plateau

Throughout the southern part of Magnisía the high ridge of the peninsula falls steeply to the Gulf of Pagasaí ; nevertheless, villages are more numerous on this western-facing side than on the deeply incised and longer slopes towards the Aegean. Farther north, the southern slopes of Mount Pílion, together with the plain of Vólos, constitute one of the most favoured areas of Greece, benefiting from the mildness of winter, in contrast to the inland plains, and from the proximity to a good port.

The small plain facing Vólos on the north and west is composed of convergent fans of alluvium, varying in steepness, soil and water supply. Behind it, the transverse plateau which separates the eastern plain of Thessalía from the Gulf of Pagasaí belongs structurally to Mount Pílion and consists mainly of marble and mica-schist. The folds of these rocks lie across the barrier and so therefore do the ridges and valleys. Since the summits are between 1,300 and 2,000 ft. in height the Piláftepe Pass that leads across the plateau is of great importance. The gap was probably once a river valley, determined by a fracture, and it permits the road and railway from the plain at Velestínon to pass directly eastwards to the gulf, without climbing more than 300 ft.

With the gap as easy access to an immense hinterland, the well-protected gulf and plain have formed a focus of trade from earliest times and it is not surprising that Jason, regarded by the ancients as the father of navigation, should be associated with this place as king of Iolcus, or that the Argos was built of indestructible timber from Mount Pílion. Vólos stands upon the site of Iolcus, and on the promontory which faces it stood Pagasae as well as the later Demetrias, nearly as large as the modern town opposite. Vólos itself is now a compact town of 42,000 inhabitants, built on the grid plan on the fans of two torrents which enclose it, as they also defined the site of Iolcus ; Áno-Vólos, an older place, stands on the crags behind. The commercial importance of Vólos is obvious ; and so too is the dependence of its industries upon the produce of Thessalía, chiefly grain, wool, hides, tobacco and fruit. The population includes many landowners of the plains, successors of the Turkish beys. From the port, a 600 mm. (1 ft. 11⅝ in.) gauge line, sometimes called the ' steam railway ', runs eastwards to Miléai, the most easterly of a number of summer resorts on this ' riviera coast '. From the outskirts of Vólos the hillsides, up to some 1,600 ft., are almost completely covered by olive trees, interspersed with the denser foliage of the orange and quince, and the red roofs of numerous houses and the small landing places on the shore. Among and above these woods are the villages, partly surrounded by vine-yards and served by long aqueducts for watering the orchards. Beyond the settlements the tall maquis of arbutus, heath and purple cistus extends to cover most of the mountain from sea to sea, but the higher parts of Mount Pílion bear forests of oak and chestnut and, above some 1,000 ft., also beech. Thus the district is dependent upon its fruits and especially its output of fine olives for preserving. The riviera coast and the small plain of Vólos, excluding the port, have the remarkably high density of 422 people per sq. mile.

Mavrovoúni, Óssa and the Vale of Témbi

North of Mount Pílion the rounded or flat summits culminating in Mavrovoúni are covered by dense oak-forest ; and on the steep seaward slope the villages, often perched high above the straight, cliffed coast, are almost hidden by luxuriant vegetation. Then opposite the gap south of Mount Óssa the sea-cliffs give way to a coastal plain with a long beach, olive orchards and fields but no settlements. An inland plain forming a wide gap between Mavrovoúni and Óssa, some 500 ft. above sea level, is also cultivated and has large vineyards and mulberry orchards : the villages possess-ing these lands stand in a cluster on the southern slopes of Óssa and are the homes of nearly 8,000 people. The chief place is Ayiá at the terminus of a motor road from Lárisa.

North of the gap and Cape Dhermatás, where the coastline swings north-westwards, the country becomes much more mountainous, and the contrast of climate and vegetation on the east and west more pronounced. The luxuriance of oak, chestnut and beech forests on the eastern slopes of Óssa suggests a remarkably regular distribution of rainfall throughout the year. The character of the scenery on

Óssa is largely due to the presence of resistant magnesian and
crystalline limestones which rest in folds upon the gneiss and mica-
schist. The mountain rises, opposite Cape Dhermatás, to a pyramidal
peak, 6,391 ft. high ; and immediately below its western precipices
the small town of Spiliá stands on a low divide, floored with red
earth, between the Gavronéri and Megálo streams. These flow
respectively north-east to Stómion and south-west to Sikoúrion.
Thus the peak is severed from the rest of the massif—a broad
shouldered, steep-sided plateau. On the slope towards the Vale of
Témbi is Ambelákia, a village reputed throughout Europe during the
eighteenth and nineteenth centuries for its industry and trade.
The commodity was red, handspun cotton yarn and the chief markets
were Austria-Hungary and Germany, where the villages had their
own representatives in many cities. The cotton and the Turkey-red
dye were both Greek products. Ambelákia faces the western
entrance to the Vale of Témbi where the slopes of Mount Óssa are
accessible ; farther east they are seamed by huge rocky ravines and
almost vertical walls 1,000 ft. high hem in the Piniós, while on the
north of the vale there are similar cliffs of bluish-white limestone.
Thus for a stretch of 3 miles there is barely room for the road on
the right, and the railway on the left, bank. The narrowness of this
defile (Plate 46) withholds from the inner plain the mild features of
Mediterranean climate and the associated plants ; and in the gorge
the true maquis is seen to reach its limit, mingled with ancient
hawthorn and fine plane trees on the river banks. Témbi is a classic
example of an ' antecedent ' river gorge, the river having succeeded
in maintaining its outlet by erosion during the progressive vertical
uplift of the mountain masses. Below the gorge the river cuts deeply
into its old delta, formed when the land stood some 260 ft. lower, and,
deserting a former direct outfall, it turns south-east over the white
limestone south of Cape Platamón. Here begins the beach and
coastal plain that extends along the Gulf of Thérmai.

Mount Ólimbos (Olympus)

The grandeur of Mount Ólimbos is most impressive from the east
or from the north, for on both these sides immense precipices of
pale rock rise above a zone of dark coniferous forest to the highest
summit in Greece (9,570 ft.). For most of the year these heights
are capped with snow (see vol. I, Plate 3). To the west, the mountain presents an almost flat-topped profile above a long uniform
slope. In general form, the massif is a dome, abruptly shorn on its

Plate 44.   The western corner of the plain of Ptolemaïs with the village of
Embórion
The view is northward.   The ridge in the background conceals Lake Roudnik.

Plate 45.   Portariá, north-east of Vólos
The view shows the upper part of this summer resort, with the slope of Mount
Pílion.

Plate 46. The river Piniós in the vale of Témbi
The road and railway are concealed by the plane trees on the left.

Plate 47. The Vlach village of Kokkinoplós
The village is at 3,820 ft. near the watershed west of Mount Olímbos.

eastern flank by a great fault. Like Óssa, Ólimbos is composed of limestone, partly dolomitic, partly semi-crystalline, which rests upon gneiss and green schists. All these rocks lie in east-north-east to west-south-west folds that determine the bastions and ravines of the eastern flank ; they are traversed by faults of two ages, and the more recent ones give the mountain its outline. The eastern edge is a great fault-scarp, and the outer fractures make steps in the apron of conglomerates that lie below. Ólimbos arose, up-thrust bodily, as the Aegean Basin foundered, and is the youngest of the high mountains, its summit plateau an old worn surface warped by the compression. Subsequent erosion, aided by earthquakes, has notched the scarp into great ravines ; that of the river Mavrólongos is cut in the floor of a glacial corrie 3 miles across, and others also bear traces of glaciation.

To the south Káto (lower) Ólimbos is made of the same rocks, limestone to east, schists to west, but the old surface here has been raised only to 4,900 ft. : it contains a flat basin at 2,950 ft. occupied by the fields of three villages, while a smaller karstic hollow, now good agricultural land, was filled by a lake at least until 1904. Mediterranean climatic influences that are suppressed in the plain owing to temperature inversion seem to penetrate at these inter-mediate heights, for the monastery of Ayía Triás at 3,300 ft. on the south-western slope of Ólimbos has large olive groves surrounded by plants of the maquis.

The south-eastern slopes of Káto Ólimbos are well peopled ; of the seven villages, four are approximately at the 1,650 ft. level and repeat the features of many on Óssa and Pílion. Rapsáni is reached by a winding motor road from the outlet of Témbi. East of Ólimbos itself three villages, including the large Litókhoron on the Mavrólongos, stand at the top of the fan-like alluvial apron amid vineyards and orchards, and each has its *skála* on the beach.

The Mountains of Piéria

From Ólimbos the mountains continue north-westwards, forming an undulating divide with transverse valleys leading down to the lowland of Piéria ; one of these, that of the Elikón, is followed by a motor road from Elassón over a pass at some 4,130 ft. Two other passes are marked by the large Vlach villages of Kokkinoplós (Plate 47) and Livádhion overlooking the basin of Tripoliana to the south ; and from them Vlach colonists have gone to Sérvia, Elassón and Kateríni.

Beyond the Elikón the plateau curves to the north-east, enclosing the head-streams of this, the chief river of Piéria flowing directly eastwards in a deep and remote valley, its southern slope completely forested with beech and oak. The plateau, however, is above the level of woods and offers wide summer pastures. It rises as the mountains of Piéria to about 7,200 ft. and then declines gradually, to a wooded surface, for some 19 miles, finally to be truncated by the steep fault-scarp facing north over the Kambanía. The sparse villages, with less than 3,000 inhabitants, including a Vlach group, were originally settled by colonists from Albania and have in turn supplied many townsmen to Véroia. Parallel to this highland runs the Aliákmon in a canyon 15 miles in length, its lowest defile. In origin it is like the gorge of Témbi, but it is a far more serious barrier and is followed only by the roughest mule track. Patches of terrace, marking stages in the cutting of the gorge, hang above the river at 1,300 ft. and other levels, but they are hard to reach. On the left bank the slope rises rapidly in steps to the plateau surface which continues that of the mountains of Piéria : this is the beginning of the Vérmion mountains and on ledges just below its edge the winding highway from Kozáni to Véroia climbs to 4,430 ft.

The Vérmion Mountains

The Vérmion is among the greatest mountain wastes of Greece. It extends for some 30 miles to the next defile, that of the river Vódas, and is nowhere less than 12 miles broad ; its summits are from 5,500 to 6,650 ft. in the south, but they decline somewhat in the north. Like so many of the neighbouring mountain blocks the Vérmion has a rolling upper surface with steep and deeply trenched sides. It is built of Cretaceous limestones, sandstones and shales, closely folded by thrusts from the north-east, but its shape is determined by the marginal fractures from north to south. Limestone predominates and many of the higher slopes are bare of vegetation, or merely thinly-veiled karst with dry valleys ; but the rock junctions are marked by vigorous springs. Moreover, the climate, especially east of the watershed, is mild for the height : snow vanishes early, and the pastures are rich. While many slopes are clad in dense bush, both evergreen and summer-green, which attracts hosts of charcoal burners, the valleys have luxuriant forests, especially in the east with an upward transition from chestnut to oak, beech and fir—the haunt of herds of deer and wild pig. The total population of the small and sparse settlements is only 5,000. In spite of many natural advantages the higher Vérmion is a shepherds' paradise and little more. The misrule of Ali, Pasha of Janina, seems to have caused the evacuation of several large Vlach villages, once occupied all the year but now in ruins.

Lake Vegorrítis and the Vódas Basin

The same rocks that compose the Vérmion extend both north and north-west nearly to the frontier, and in the latter direction the structure, already complex from over-thrusting, is riven by transverse faults. One of these, truncating the rocks in a long scarp edge, marks the western shore of Lake Vegorrítis (Plate 48). The lake is over 23 sq. miles in area, and has no visible outlet. While the features of the high Vérmion are repeated in the ridge (6,549 ft.) which overlooks the lake from the north, the plateaux flanking it, although bleak, are much lower (2,300–2,900 ft.) ; their good soils are cultivated, especially for vines, and support a considerable population. Much has been written about Vegorrítis because of the fluctuations of its level, but there are accurate records only from a minimum of 1,726 ft. in 1900 to a maximum of 1,775 ft. in 1923. This variation has practical importance since the north shore is flat and the railway had to be moved as a result of submergence.

The eastern arm of the lake lies in the entrance to the gap between the Vérmion and the slopes leading to the high Nice. This was the last defile of the *Via Egnatia* and since it is now used by modern road and railway it is of great importance. The entire defile is a transverse river valley, like those of the Piniós and Aliákmon, and it was once the outlet of the great lake that covered Eordhaía ; but the water of Vegorrítis seeps away in unknown fissures, and the choking of these doubtless accounts for the rising level of the lake at intervals. For 5 miles the defile is dry ; then it joins a broader valley leading from a large oval hollow in the mountains with a flat swampy floor, a karst basin probably fed from below by the waters of the lake and by those of the northern mountains. This is the source of the river Vódas. For the next 5 miles this river flows in a broad valley through orchards, vineyards and grass meadows lined with planes and poplars ; it is unique, for the floor has been gradually built-up of calc-sinter or travertine. The process can be seen at work where the Vódas comes over a high step in the valley, its foam leaving a white crust on stones and plants. Thus the falls at Ágras (formerly Vladovo) are steadily being pushed forward from the fault-scarp which first caused them. The vale continues to the limit of the Vérmion where the Vódas again tumbles for 330 ft. in many falls to the plain. The brink of this travertine cliff is the site of Édhessa, the earliest capital of Macedonia, and its Slavonic name Vodená (' waters ') is descriptive of its location (see pp. 115–7 and Plate 49). The waterfall marks the faults running from north to south at which the limestones give place eastward to older Carboniferous rocks and serpentine, and then beyond to volcanic tuff in the Moglenítsas valley. North of the Vódas defile the limestones continue in the slopes rising to the Nice, which carries the frontier and forms the background of the plain of Enotía (Almopía).

For Bibliographical Note, see p. 22.

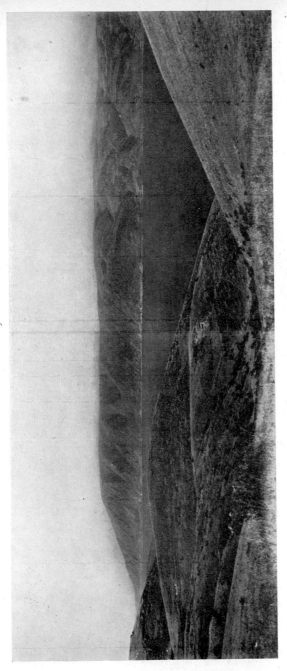

Plate 48. Lake Vegorritis from the north-east

The straight western side is formed by a young fault-scarp, cut by few ravines.

Plate 49. Édhessa from the east

The various branches of the river on the escarpment are hidden by the trees ; most of the town is on the flat above. In the fore-ground are the stalks of the previous year's maize crop.

Chapter VI

NORTH-EASTERN GREECE

The Lowlands of Piéria : Enotía (Almopía) : Western Kambanía : Eastern Kambanía ; Khalkidhikí and Thessaloníki : The Axiós-Strimón Divide : The Plain of the Strimón : The Trans-Strimón Mountains and Basins : The Mountains of Dráma : The Plain of Dráma and Kaválla : The Trans-Néstos Mountains of Makedhonía and Dhitikí Thráki : The Plain of Dhitikí Thráki : The Eastern Frontier Zone

Central and Eastern Makedhonía with Dhitikí Thráki form the fringe of the Balkan Peninsula for over half its breadth ; the Turkish frontier lies some 250 miles east of Édhessa and the average width of the Greek territory is about 44 miles. Thus many of the geographical characteristics of this northern Aegean coastland are found to extend beyond the frontier into Jugoslavia, Bulgaria and Turkey.

In climate and vegetation the belt is transitional between Mediterranean and Central European types, but it also merges into the steppe type in the east. As an Aegean region, however, where plains and lowlands are easily accessible, the cultural outlook has always been towards the Greek world, although until after 1919 a large part of the population was Turkish or Slav, and in Dhitikí Thráki Turks still remain. This accessibility does not imply any outstanding traffic between land and sea. There are, in fact, few coastal lands so well populated and with so long a shore that are so ill-provided with seaports. In general it may be said that the people live inland and have landsmen's interests. Thessaloníki and Kaválla provide the exceptions : Thessaloníki is the second city and port of Greece because of its situation where two major routes intersect, meeting the sea at the head of a navigable gulf. The same advantages have been effective throughout history, and geographical position no doubt contributed to the expansion of Macedonia from the nucleus of that kingdom at the north-western corner of the Aegean. Moreover, when the Roman Empire extended to the whole Peninsula, many cultural and economic consequences resulted from the fact that the main route between Rome and Byzantium traversed this territory. Similarly, convenience of communication with Constantinople, as well as richness of the plains, insured complete mastery of these lands by the Turkish empire.

The physical character of the North Aegean lowlands, more particularly their climate and soil and the distribution of their waters, have brought them fame and ill-fame at once. They produce the finest quality of tobacco and they are notorious for the prevalence and severity of malaria. Tobacco cultivation developed under the Turks, but reduction of malaria has had to wait for the efforts of a modern Greek government and sufficient years of peace to effect the necessary drainage. This feat of engineering, however, was mainly the result of that unique episode in modern European history, the systematic settlement of a new Greek population from Turkey and neighbouring countries, carried out chiefly by the Refugee Settlement Commission (see Fig. 21 and vol. I, Chapter XIII). There were about 562,000 newcomers to eastern and central Makedhonía and 108,000 to Dhitikí Thráki.

The orographical features of this region resemble those of Eastern Greece. It is a region of mountains and plains, sharply defined by the fractures which separated the various blocks in very recent geological times, i.e. long after the formation and folding of the rocks now seen in the mountains. The pattern of the relief, then, is prominently marked by the straight edges of the mountains ; and the height of these mountains depends upon the degree to which they were elevated after the separation of the blocks. Four of the five large rivers—the Aliákmon, Axiós, Strimón and Néstos— traverse the mountains in gorges either within the region or on its margin, maintaining directions they had before the upheaval. At that time, the low undulating plateaux that are now high ranges were separated by the waters of one or more great lakes, at first brackish and later fresh. These covered the present basins and their margins, and also, presumably, the area now occupied by the deep North Aegean Basin. Within the framework of mountain slopes, composed of hard rocks of various kinds, the lowland consists of two types. The lowest ground, which is nearly flat, often marshy and sometimes not drained to the sea, is composed of sand, silt or mud. It can generally be regarded as land that has become progressively drier and more accessible throughout historic times. Surrounding this is a zone of higher ground which may be termed hill-foot terrace land. It is built of thick beds of weak sediments, lying nearly horizontal, that may vary from heavy gravels near the mountain foot, through sands, to heavy clays ; in places they include thin layers of fresh-water limestone. These marginal strata were mostly deposited in Pliocene or later times.

The ' terrace lands ' slope away from the hill foot and are more or less dissected by rivers, the majority being torrents of intermittent

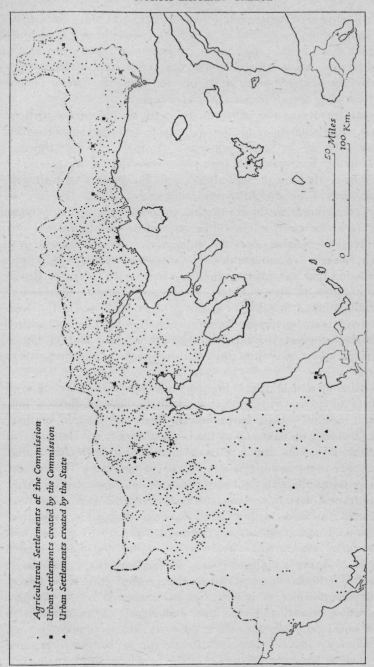

Fig. 21. The settlement of refugees in northern Greece up to 1926

Based on a folder map in *Greek Refugee Settlement* (League of Nations, Geneva, 1926).

- .   *Agricultural Settlements of the Commission*
- ■   *Urban Settlements created by the Commission*
- ◄   *Urban Settlements created by the State*

50 Miles
100 Km.

flow. The water-courses often have precipitous sides, and crossing them is not easy ; moreover, many such areas are so much cut up in this way that land fit for cultivation is patchy and able to support only small villages. The greater rivers have entirely removed considerable areas of higher sediments by lateral erosion and the zone is therefore not always continuous.

Two elements in the environment account for the severity of malaria : the climate, and the abundance of stagnant or slowly moving water in the spring and early summer. Of the climate it may be noted that mean temperatures exceeding 68° F. prevail on the plains from June to September, and this amount of heat suits the life-cycle of the *Anopheles* mosquitoes admirably ; the epidemic season corresponds to these months, although infection may begin earlier from insects that have hibernated (see vol. I, pp. 271-80). The effects of malaria upon the indigenous population are serious enough, but twice in a recent decade *Anopheles* was able to feed upon a population that was not immune from the parasite. In the British Army of 1916-18 the numbers of cases of malaria admitted to hospital amounted to 24%, 35% and 37% of the Force in the years 1916, 1917 and 1918 respectively. Again, it has been estimated that of the refugees who settled in Makedhonía and Dhitikí Thráki after 1922, about one-tenth died of this disease in the first two or three years.

Makedhonía and Dhitikí Thráki are perhaps most widely known for their tobacco. Although the quantity they produce is only 2 or 3% of the world's output of the leaf, the tobacco of these regions includes the material of the highest quality of ' Turkish ' or ' Oriental ' cigarettes, and it is consequently of great relative value. This quality is the result of experiments carried on by Turkish and Greek peasants for well over two centuries, during which a plant coming from American regions with heavy summer rainfall has been acclimatized in lands with marked summer drought. Thus have been evolved new types of small growth (from 20 to 30 ins.) and thin aromatic leaves, in contrast to the taller and thicker-leafed plants of countries with heavy rains in the hot season. This is a triumph of cultivation upon which the greatest care is bestowed, and the maintenance of quality has been assured by government precautions, necessitated by the exchanges of population in Makedhonía and in view of the great extension of tobacco growing undertaken by the refugees. It should be noted, however, that many of these had been producers of the best tobacco in Anatolia.

Although the meteorological records of this region are few and mostly short, the successful growth of fine Turkish tobacco is clear evidence that the summers are both hot and dry, i.e. that during the four important months, June to September, the mean temperature exceeds 68° F. and that the relative humidity is about 45%, with little cloud. During these months rain falls only as occasional thunder showers ; more frequent rains would spoil tobacco of this type. The merchants cling to the long-familiar Turkish names such as *Basma*, denoting a particular shape of leaf ; and the full title of a tobacco includes not merely a place-name, as with a wine, but also one of the terms *jebel*, *yaka* or *ova*, meaning respectively mountain, foothill and plain. This important distinction, indicating the geographical location of the fields, is also a mark of quality. The mountain, or *jebel*, tobacco may be grown from 1,000 to 3,000 ft. in hollows sheltered from north winds, and it yields delicate and mild leaves without aroma. The *yaka* fields are broadly on hill-foot land, frequently alluvial fans, and give the very best aromatic leaves. The *ova* location is on the sloping edge of a low plain well above flood level ; the heavier and moister soil there yields thicker and larger leaves which generally bring a lower price.

The tobacco soils are well drained and rich in potash, phosphorus, and iron which so often gives the soil its reddish character ; moreover, lime is plentiful, derived often from the stones which for other reasons are also essential ingredients. Sheep and goats supply the manure, which is skilfully applied. The seed is sown with wood-ash in prepared beds in early March (later in the hills) and the seedlings are transplanted to the ploughed fields from mid-May to mid-June. The picking goes on from mid-July to mid-September, and the leaves are then threaded as festoons for drying and marketing. A fuller account of the value of tobacco crops in the agricultural economy of Greece is given in vol. II, pp. 62–3.

Makedhonía contains 23% of the Greek population, 26% of the total area of Greece and 30% of the cultivated land. Dhitikí Thráki, on the other hand, has only 5% of the population, 6·5% of the total area and 8% of the cultivated land. In each case the population density is rather below the average for the country, and the combination of low density and comparatively high proportion of agricultural land makes the region more than self-sufficient in grain. Land holdings, however, are very small—of the total of 258,000, about 86% are under 12½ acres and a further 10 or 11% are under 25 acres.

In the following account north-eastern Greece is divided for the purpose of description into thirteen regions. These are shown on Fig. 22 and are listed below :

E1. The Lowlands of Piéria.
E2. Enotía (Almopía).
E3. Western Kambanía.
E4. Eastern Kambanía.
E5. Khalkidhikí and Thessaloníki.
E6. The Axiós–Strimón Divide.
E7. The Plain of the Strimón.
E8. The Trans-Strimón Mountains and Basins.
E9. The Mountains of Dráma.
E10. The Plain of Dráma, and Kaválla.
E11. The Trans-Néstos Mountains of Makedhonía and Dhitikí Thráki.
E12. The Plain of Dhitikí Thráki.
E13. The Eastern Frontier Zone.

THE LOWLANDS OF PIÉRIA (REGION E1)

Physical Characteristics

Framed by Mount Ólimbos and the mountains of Piéria is an equilateral triangle of lowland based on the shores of the Gulf of Thérmai. It is bisected by the river Mavronéri which gathers most of the drainage. The inland half is terrace land, extending from 300 ft. above sea level to its upper edge at from 1,000 to 1,600 ft., and is deeply cut by hundreds of streams of all sizes. Seawards from this the ground slopes gently to a virtually flat plain, ending in a strip of fresh and salt marshes and many small lagoons. These are ponded back by a long series of sand bars built by storm waves, the spits constantly growing northward with great accretion at the north-east corner. At this point the terrace near the end of the mountains of Piéria reaches the coast, and the storm waves, with considerable fetch from the inner gulf, have formed a large hook at Cape Atherídha enclosing the Toúzla lagoon, now used for evaporating salt.

Land Utilization

All the shore is virtually uninhabited, except for the huts at landing places : among them, Vromeróskala serves the capital, Kateríni, 4 miles inland and is frequented by coastal steamers. Nor is there

Based on
The conto

any continuous coastal road fit for motor traffic, but the railway follows the shore turning inland to reach Kateríni. This small town, with 10,138 inhabitants, has a central position and a semi-rural aspect, and it is, in fact, an important agricultural market, especially for tobacco. It is also a market for grain, butter, cheese, honey, meat and vegetables, and has three flourmills, an electric power station and an ice factory. Piéria is the chief producer of tobacco in Makedhonía, apart from the eastern districts, with some 17,000 acres cultivated and an annual yield of 4,400 tons of leaf. The tobacco soils occur chiefly on the lower alluvial fans behind the sandy coastal plain which is mostly either woodland or pasture subject to floods.

The villages of the lowland are located chiefly upon these fans or else far up the valleys of the piedmont terraces ; several new or expanded villages with refugee populations lie in the north-east corner of the plain. This was the one place where evacuation of Moslems had taken place. Near one of these settlements, Moskhopótamos (1,550 inhabitants), 12 miles west of Kateríni, a lignite mine is reached by a light railway. The average density of population for the lowlands of Piéria is 145 per sq. mile.

Enotía (Almopía) (Region E2)

Physical Characteristics

The Hellenized form of the former Vlach village, Nunte, is now the name of this remarkable district called Meglen by the Slavs and Karajova by the Turks. It is a triangular plain, lying between Édhessa and the northern frontier, about 80 sq. miles in area and 650 ft. in height (see vol. I, Plate 20). In origin it is a sunken slab divided from the surrounding up-thrust blocks by fractures. Thus hemmed in by high mountains, the district was virtually unknown until this century and its people were, in fact, unfriendly to strangers.

Just as Mount Ólimbos dominates Piéria, so the character of Enotía is determined principally by the Nice mountains which rise abruptly from the plain on the north-west to form the frontier with Jugoslavia. To the west are the Kaïmakchalán mountains, rising to 8,281 ft. on the frontier. These were the scene of prolonged and bitter fighting from 1916 to 1918, and here the Serbian attack first overcame enemy resistance which crumbled rapidly and led to the Balkan Armistice. Kaïmakchalán is north of Lake Vegorrítis and is partly hidden by the peak of Piperítsa, rearing a massive head above luxuriant beech and fir forests. The western end of the Nice range is formed of gneiss, but the structure of this intensively folded and overthrust massif, which extends north-eastwards for 30 miles, is most varied throughout (Fig. 23). Acid lava and tuff cover the other rocks at higher levels and form about half of the summits ; and the tuffs also compose the hilly barrier, shutting in the basin on the south-east. This is trenched by the Moglenítsas river draining it by a gorge, and also by a broader valley used by the highway and light railway that now link the basin with the outer plains. Thus the entrance to Enotía is by a defile and the visitor receives a sudden and vivid impression of a rich plain backed by a mountain wall which, in Greece, can probably be matched in grandeur only by the view of Ólimbos from the sea. The mountains to the west and east rise more gradually and are much lower : those on the west are composed of limestone and are a continuation of the Vérmion ; the Páïkon mountains on the east are also largely made of limestone which changes to marble as they pass towards the Axiós valley.

Land Utilization

Enotía is one of the richest and most intensively cultivated plains of Greece, owing to its fertility, its seclusion, its soil and abundant water, and also to its highly favourable local climate. Presumably a prevalence of descending air makes for unusually high temperature and sunshine during most of the year, though winter cold excludes Mediterranean plants. Calm weather in summer leads to thunderstorms which add to the rainfall. The mountain torrents emerge on to the plain over large alluvial fans, providing power for water mills and sufficient water to irrigate about half the area ; but the streams are hard to constrain when in spate and often spread their gravel and sand unduly. Nevertheless, the forty-two villages produced in 1928, 200 tons of raw silk, 400 of tobacco, and 500 of red pepper (pimento) as well as wheat (with a high yield for Greece), maize, sesame, cotton, beans, grapes and a variety of vegetables. Land is commonly cropped twice in the year and in places three times, while fruit orchards and mulberry trees for feeding the silk worms surround the villages. Such is the work of a population of over 25,000, consisting almost entirely of newcomers from Anatolia and Thrace, for the old inhabitants were chiefly Moslem. Except for a small number of Turks, the majority of the emigrants were Pomaks, i.e. Bulgarian-speaking Moslems (see vol. I, p. 355) and they included the land-owning beys who lived in Suboskon, now

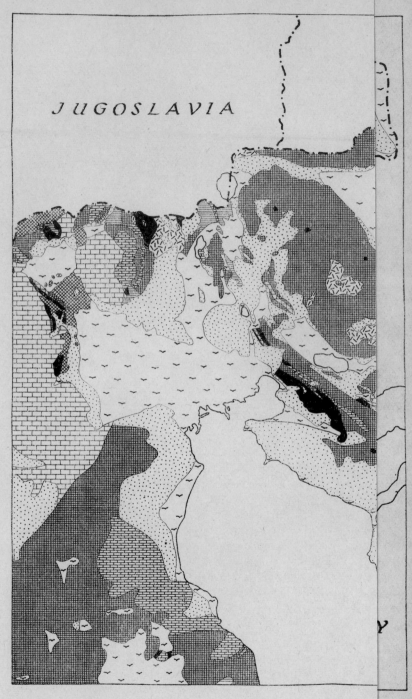

JUGOSLAVIA

For sources, see p. 22.
A, Acid lava (trachyte) ; B
1, Sandstones, shales and c
calc-sand and sinter ; all u

Ardhéa, the administrative and geographical centre of the plain. The incomers simply renamed and reoccupied the villages, and the old agriculture was carried on as before with few changes. Ardhéa is the terminus of a branch line of the railway from Skídhra through Flórina, and has 2,781 inhabitants. The mean density of population on the plain is 210 per sq. mile.

On the mountains to the west there are a number of small semi-pastoral villages and a considerable cover of beechwoods ; similarly, the Páïkon mountains are mainly forested with beech, but are cleared for pasture in the north where there are several Vlach villages. From this plain the direct distance to the river Axiós at the frontier is only 19 miles and the way is easy, crossing a low narrow plateau some 2,000 ft. high, north of the Páïkon massif. This supports several villages (including Nótia) which were formerly occupied by Moslem Vlachs who practised agriculture and who differed from their compatriots in dialect and in calling themselves Vlachs and not Aromani. These people, too, have been replaced by Greeks. Livádhia, on high ground to the south of the plain, is a closely-built Vlach village ; the people held themselves aloof from their former neighbours and still live their traditional life. In spite of the altitude of 3,900 ft. the 200 families remain here all the year, but the shepherds and their flocks of some 100,000 sheep and goats winter by the lower Axiós and, as with other Vlachs, the Feasts of St. Demetrius and St. George are the dates respectively for the downward and upward migrations.

WESTERN KAMBANÍA (REGION E3)

Physical Characteristics

This part of the Kambanía lies west of the lowest course of the river Axiós or Vardar, and is a plain some 31 miles by 25 miles in extent bounded on three sides by mountains (Fig. 24). The dominant feature was once the large lake of Yiannitsá, now drained ; and any change of slope, however gentle, is of great importance. Within the mountain frame, the area of real plain is reduced by two projections of piedmont terrace land. First, that already described in Piéria extends northwards, hilly and wooded, to Neókastron ; and secondly, the southern and eastern slopes of the Páïkon mountains overlook a triangular apron of similar character ending at Néa Khalkidhón where the Édhessa and Véroia roads meet. On this more restricted plain the rivers Aliákmon and Axiós have both laid

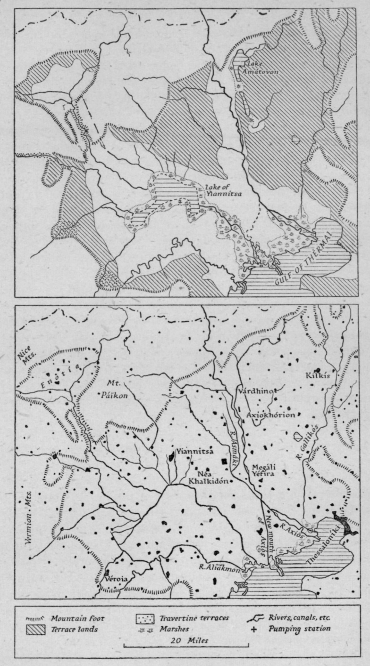

Fig. 24.   Drainage of the Kambanía

Based on engineering plans and the 1 : 250,000 G.S.G.S. Series 4088 : The Balkans, Sheet S3072.

The upper map shows the plain before drainage and the lower map shows it after drainage.   The terrace land is indicated on the upper map only : all settlements are shown on the lower map.

down their loads in the past, the former building an elongated fan and delta north-eastwards and the latter southwards. Convergence of these deposits impounded the other waters of the western plain to form a great but shallow lake which was gradually converted into peat-forming fens, with, however, sufficient open water to support fisheries and countless waterfowl. Within historical time, both the Axiós and Aliákmon have changed their courses widely, each with progress to the right, a feature observable on all the rivers draining western Kambanía. The Aliákmon turned from its old course at Kapsokhóra, on the railway, to the south-east, shifting its banks and building its fingered delta rapidly, always farther south. From Megáli Yéfira, at the bridge of the Athens railway, it has now been given a new and more direct outfall.

The plain on the west of the lake bed is composed of the fan built by the Moglenítsas, similar in size and height to that of the Aliákmon, and of numerous smaller fans. At three places on this western margin there are remarkable terraces of travertine or calc-sinter which form the sites of the three towns Véroia, Náousa and Édhessa. This form of lime carbonate appears to come from the milky-green water of the lime-laden rivers Tripótamos, Arápitsa and Vódas where they tumble in cascades over escarpments, the lime being deposited on plants and stones from the splashing water as it evaporates ; but there is reason for believing that it may be the deposit from hot springs in the standing water of the great lake of Pliocene times.

The recent task of engineers in the western Kambanía was to drain Yiannitsá Lake, reclaiming its bed for agriculture and reducing the incidence of malaria. Owing to the low altitude of the impounded waters this involved pumping, for which a station was constructed at the deltaic barrier, 6 miles south-west of Néa Khalkidhón. The left bank of the Aliákmon from its defile to its new mouth was protected by an embankment against flooding. From a point east-north-east of Véroia, part of the river's water is led north-westwards for 9 miles in a new canal to flow through an embanked course in the drained area, meeting convergent channels from the north and then being carried south-east to the sea near the artificial mouths of the Aliákmon and the Axiós (see p. 119).

Land Utilization

In 1912, Moslems amounted to 48% of the total population in the north-western area of the plain and its margins, 39% in the north-eastern and 20% in the southern parts. The remainder were almost entirely Greek in language and sentiment, though many were of Slavonic descent. Thus there was a large exchange of population, the immigrants coming from Asia except in the north-east where they are from Eastern Thrace and Bulgaria. A score of new villages of cottages, laid out on the grid plan, are easily distinguished and a minority of the old places remain without refugee population. To help in the settlement, malaria clinics were established, and many deep wells were bored, those on the old Aliákmon fan being artesian. So in western Kambanía the old agriculture proceeds to a great extent in new hands, and with new advantages which will be enhanced when some 115 sq. miles of drained fenland are in full production. The population density in 1928 was 173 per sq. mile.

Although the plain is not shut off from the sea the winter is not free from frost, and there is no olive cultivation except on surrounding terraces ; yet there is an abundance of varied fruit trees about the villages and a large production of figs and mulberries. Huge quantities of mulberry leaves are gathered for the silk industry of the western margin. Perhaps three-quarters of the land, however, is given to cereals, wheat being the chief crop ; in summer, sesame is prominent together with cotton and tobacco.

The two ancient towns of Véroia and Édhessa occupy corners of the Kambanía, controlling routes and standing on well-watered sinter-terraces above the plain. The sinter, or travertine, favours plant growth and each place is like a stairway of verdure and fruit gardens. Édhessa is withdrawn somewhat from the plain, for its approach is a 3-mile stretch of broad valley within the hills. Véroia, the old Macedonian city of Berea, lies west of the Aliákmon gorge, and it was to this town that St. Paul and Silas withdrew from Thessalonica. It is built mostly on the second of its sinter-terraces, and its many church cupolas and minarets stand above orchards of fig, almond and olive trees ; behind it a terrace, 130 ft. higher, is covered with orchards and vines, cotton and sesame, and it was here that the fabulous gardens of the Phrygian King Midas were supposed to have been situated. The town has grown rapidly in the last decade and in 1938 had about 17,000 people, including Greeks, Vlachs and a colony of Spanish Jews. Water-power, derived from the falls, is used by an electric station and two silk-spinning mills. It may be noted in passing that the power of the lower Aliákmon, estimated at 123,000 kW., is still to be harnessed.

Édhessa seen from the east is a striking sight, owing to the contrast which the bareness of the flanking slopes offers to the verdure of the scarp which it caps (Plate 49). The ancient town seems to have been built on the slope with the fortress on top, where the narrow streets of sinter-built houses now stand. The modern fringes, however, are more open and include refugee quarters and factories—two for carpets, one for silk and the older mills for grinding pimento, together with the power station for which the falls provide from 6,000 to 16,000 kW. The population in 1928 was 13,115 of whom 7,000 are refugees.

Náousa, lying between Véroia and Édhessa, is built on the highest of four travertine terraces, at about 1,000 ft. above sea level—a healthy site with many branches of the Arápitsa stream tumbling through and around it to falls capable of yielding 22,000 kW of electricity. Some of this is used for two large cotton mills, and at least two woollen mills, as well as for the making of silk fabrics and for rope-works. It is a closely built town of Turkish type, but only a minority of the townsfolk were Moslem. These have been more than replaced by refugees and the population now exceeds 10,000 ; there is a considerable Vlach colony of whom many go up to the Vérmion in summer. Here again, there is intensive cultivation of the watered terraces ; the vines are famous and of commercial importance (the red wine resembles Chianti) while the silk industry accounts for large mulberry orchards and a big export of cocoons.

Philip of Macedon founded Pélla as his capital, in a situation that gave easy access to the eastern Kambanía ; it lies close to the swamp of recent times. Little remains of the city, but the neighbouring village now bears the name. In some ways, however, the former Turkish town of Yiannitsá (Yenidje Vardar) is its counterpart, 7 miles to the west ; but in spite of its population of 12,000 it remains a huge sprawling village with some outgrowth of refugee type. The old Greek villages in the piedmont valleys of the north are great producers of mulberry leaves and of silk cocoons ; their chief centre is Gouménissa, east of the Páïkon mountains. Thus the western Kambanía consists of a well peopled fringe surrounding a drained lake basin, still without settlements, that continues to hinder direct communications—a condition that will doubtless be improved in the near future. The plain is encircled by a metalled road, and on the south and west by the railway which comes near, but not into, Véroia and Náousa ; to reach Édhessa it takes a sinuous

course, with tunnels, up the hillsides to the north of the valley.
The Aliákmon is now the chief obstacle to routes, and it is crossed
by only one road and one railway bridge.

EASTERN KAMBANÍA (REGION E4)

Physical Characteristics

The plain continues without interruption east and north from
western Kambanía to embrace the lower basins and deltas of the
Axiós and Gallikós (Fig. 22). This last river flows along the
foot of rocky plateaux to its delta which nearly reaches the outskirts of Thessaloníki. In the north the Kambanía is hemmed in
by the barrier plateau that extends north-eastward toward the
Kroúsia plateau, and in it there are two gaps—the Tsingánska
Klisoúra or ' Gipsy Defile ' cut by the Axiós and followed by the
northern railway, and the wider Kalindría Gap, the occasional
outlet of Lake Doïráni from the north, carrying the eastern railway
southward towards Thessaloníki, as well as a main road.

In the south, the low plain repeats the characteristics of the
Yiannitsá district, and similarly, the terrace lands north of the
Axiós and Gallikós delta are like those to the west. Moreover, the
southern edge of the terraces is a continuation of the same line that
runs from Yiannitsá to Néa Khalkidhón, interrupted only by the
2½-mile gap cut by the Axiós. This terraced margin of the real plain
was followed by the *Via Egnatia* to Thessalonica, and is now used
by the railway. The rest of the Kambanía is made up of somewhat
complex association of low plateaux, terraces and hitherto ill-drained
bottom lands. The lowland between the Axiós and Gallikós
corresponds geologically to one of the most intensively folded strips
of Greece, with manifold overthrusting from the east. The many
low hills are formed by parallel outcrops of varied rocks—chiefly
phyllites, marble and sandstones of Palaeozoic ages—but their
denuded surface is largely masked by the lake beds of late Tertiary
age. The rolling plateau is bevelled at two distinct heights, below
920 ft. and below 590 ft. respectively, and the deeper hollow is
partly occupied by lower terraces of Pleistocene age which rise from
the silt and fen bottoms now drained for the first time.

Improvements in the physical conditions of this region are the
result of several hydrographic changes (Fig. 24). First, some
17 sq. miles of lake and fen have been drained by means of a north-
south canal, inclined from each end to a central cut north of Várdhino

and then led south for 8 miles to join the Axiós below Axiokhórion. Thus, the one-time lake Amátovon has been drained. Secondly, neighbouring lands have been protected from flooding by the embankment of the Axiós. Thirdly, the many tributaries from Mount Páïkon and the western terraces have been gathered into the artificial river, Asmáki, and led to the Axiós at the point of its diversion to a new mouth. Fourthly, from this point, below the bridge on the Flórina railway, the Axiós has been led south to the sea and away from its old south-eastward course which had long been bringing too much silt to the port of Thessaloníki. Thus the mouths of the Aliákmon and the Axiós are now only 3 miles apart, with the Yiannitsá outlet between them, all being south of the narrows opposite Karaburnú.

Land Utilization

The outstanding features of the climate are the low annual rainfall of under 20 in., the extremes of temperature throughout the year, and the not infrequent fierce northerly winds. Together these factors partly account for the marked absence of trees on the open plains, while the lower marginal hills, except in sheltered valleys, have only pseudo-maquis or phrygana types of vegetation. Nor is there a good water supply ; the Axiós is a large river with a channel apt to change at every spring flood, and the Gallikós, which drains impermeable plateaux to the east, scarcely flows in summer. As a result the villages are chiefly dependent on wells and springs, and many wells have been bored by the Settlement Commission : thus, for reasons of shelter and water, most of the villages occupy hollows in the plateau and terraces.

Before 1920 the Kambanía was in many ways a dreary land with numerous sordid villages, and the greater part of the country was uncultivated owing to the length of the fallow period. But the changes effected by the settlement have been great, and the promise of high productivity from the loamy soils which cover much of the district has already been substantiated. The plain is naturally best adapted to cereals (especially wheat) which cover two-fifths of the cultivated area ; leguminous plants also do well, while the chief summer crop is sesame. The settlers, however, notably specialists from Thrace and Bulgaria, have made a commercial success of tobacco and vine cultivation respectively.

The population north of the *Via Egnatia* and east of the Axiós in 1912 was Turkish with a Slav minority, and so has been completely replaced, largely by Thracian Greeks. West of the Axiós about one-third were Greeks and one-fifth Slavs, who have remained, so in this area, too, refugees are in majority. There are very few new villages but many have been entirely replanned and others extended : some of those in the south are now very large. Nearly every settlement has received a new name and has to some extent changed its aspect. Kilkís is the only real town, with 8,000 inhabitants. It stands on a small plateau near the Gallikós, and was largely rebuilt after its destruction in the war of 1912 ; as a market it serves the northern plain and also the hill villages to the east. The total populations and average densities are 32,000 in the north with a density of 88 ; and 61,000 with a density of 280 per sq. mile in the south where the largest of the new settlements are to be found.

KHALKIDHIKÍ AND THESSALONÍKI (REGION E5)

Physical Characteristics

The curious shape of the Khalkidhikí Peninsula with its three long fingers is explained chiefly by fracturing of Plio-Pleistocene age and the covering of the more deeply sunken blocks by the Aegean Sea. These cataclysms are so recent, geologically, that the coasts are steep and offer few easy landward approaches. The coast and the relief show two dominant trends, north-west to south-east and west to east (Fig. 25). Fractures following the former direction define most of the coast as well as the edges of the series of plateaux that extend from the central finger, the Sithoniá or Lóngos Peninsula, to the river Gallikós. In the north, these plateaux continue the zone of intensely overthrust rocks of the eastern Kambanía. On the other hand, the plateaux ending respectively at Karaburnú on the west and Cape Elévthera on the east are bounded by fault-scarps that run from west to east, the former facing north, the latter south. Linking these two plateaux the main watershed runs from south-west to north-east in sympathy with earlier foldings.

The part of Khalkidhikí facing the Gulf of Thérmai, including the Kassándra Peninsula, differs from the remainder in many respects. In it the harder rocks are thickly covered by lake sedi-ments, and land-forms like those of the piedmont terraces prevail, with friable soils developed in most parts. The curving Kassándra Peninsula, once an island, is now linked to the mainland by wave-built sand spits enclosing a lagoon and forming an isthmus chosen as the site of the Athenian colony of Potidea. Today, Néa Moud-

Plate 50.   Mount Áthos from the north-west

The view is from the summit ridge of the peninsula west of Kariaí and shows the
forest of oak, chestnut and fir in winter.

Plate 51.   The lowest defile of the river Strimón

The view is from the slope below the site of Amfípolis.   It shows the bush-
covered eastern slope of the Kerdhíllion mountains, with scattered fields and
alluvial fans meeting the Strimón.

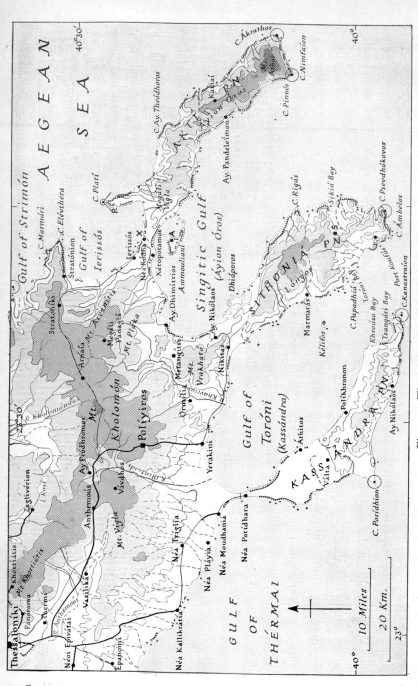

Fig. 25.   The peninsula of Khalkidhikí

Based mainly on the 1 : 250,000 G.S.G.S. Series 4088 : The Balkans, and the 1 : 100,000 *Epitelikós Khártis tis Elládhos.*
P. Platí harbour ; S. Sikiá ; X. Xérxes Canal.

[*Facing page* 121

haniá, which has replaced Políyiros as the centre of the *nomós*, stands on the northern edge of the isthmus. The varied but generally weak sediments form a plateau rising to 1,100 ft., and are cut by innumerable intermittent streams. The coast of this district is smooth and marked by cliffs, except for the low Cape Epanomí, a triangle of sand spit and lagoon and a hot-bed of malaria. Karaburnú, farther north, is a high headland bringing the gulf to its waist of 3 miles. The cape marks the end of the fault scarp that runs east to Vávdhos, overlooking, at first, a swampy coastal plain of silt, and then, beyond the village of Vasiliká, the hill-girt basin of Anthemoús (Galatísta). The greater part of Khalkidhikí and the two eastern peninsulas consist of metamorphic and igneous rocks. The backbone is the rounded ridge of Kholomón composed of granite ; it extends from the gap of Políyiros to that of Arnaía, beyond which it is prolonged by a similar massif to Cape Elévthera. South-east of Políyiros is Mount Vrakható, and through the surrounding hills the river Khavriás flows in a gorge to the Gulf of Toróni.

All three fingers of the peninsula were formerly islands and the isthmuses are formed of weak sediments ; that of Kassándra is a mere sandspit, that of Sithoniá is hilly and over 300 ft. high, and that of Aktí, locally known as ' The Xerxes ', is now some 45 ft. higher than the level in 482 B.C. when the Persian general, Xerxes, cut a canal across it. The peninsula of Sithoniá is rugged hill country exceeding 1,600 ft. in the middle : the steep-sided Aktí peninsula has a narrow crest which rises gradually and then abruptly on the white marble pyramid of Mount Áthos to 6,670 ft. (Plate 50). There are many evidences of the extreme youth of the coasts, and the frequent earthquakes show that movements along faults are still active, especially on the east. For example, on 28 September 1932, there was great destruction at Ierissós and at Stratoníki (see vol. I, Plate 1) where the first help to the stricken population was rendered by five destroyers of the British fleet ; many other villages and some of the Áthos monasteries were damaged, while about Ierissós new mineral springs appeared and changes of altitude occurred ; these shocks affected the eastern part of the Balkan Peninsula. Again in 1936, of the 165 seismic records for Greece, nine were from Ierissós.

Land Utilization

The natural vegetation of Khalkidhikí is ' Mediterranean ' over the lower western part and on all seaward slopes except for the higher parts of Aktí. Thus Kassándra and Sithoniá are still largely clad

in forest of Aleppo pine. Elsewhere, this woodland has given place to maquis, more or less luxuriant, or, in more arid areas, to phrygana. The interior mountains, originally under deciduous forest, have still considerable areas of oak and chestnut woods which, however, have been badly treated. Mount Áthos rises through the beech zone to that of the fir. The water courses are lined by plane trees and oleander, especially near the sea.

In ancient Greece, Athenian colonies were set up in Khalkidhikí especially on the coastal plain of the Gulf of Toróni ; agriculture was not the only attraction, for minerals were also extracted, and in the mining village of Stáyira, near Stratoníki, Socrates was born. In spite of these early settlements, the broken relief has always made the region difficult of access, and since it does not lie across any of the major routes, the peninsula has remained backward and isolated. Its principal fame has been as a refuge for the monastic settlements of the Eastern Church. Today, mining is again one of the chief occupations of the people. At Vávdhos and inland from Yerakiní, magnesite and chrome ore are associated with intrusions of gabbro ; iron pyrites occurs in the southern part of Kassándra and is found with manganese at Stratoníki, while north of Stratoníki a smaller mine was recently worked for gold, copper, silver and lead.

The open steppe-like slopes of western Khalkidhikí alone attracted the Turks, and this area was long occupied and poorly farmed by them under the *tchiflik* system. It was this land and part of the plain to the north that became available for Greek refugees from Anatolia and Thrace. The majority settled in some forty new or enlarged hamlets with new deep wells, and cultivated crops similar to those of the Kambanía, with the addition of cotton and olives ; but the population density is still only 93 per sq. mile. This figure is exceeded on the plain near Thessaloníki and on the slopes of Mount Khortiátis where the density is 98. Among the new villages here is Paraia where the English Quakers established a weaving mill using the cotton yarn of Naóussa and Édhessa. Elsewhere, Khalkidhikí has had few immigrants. The old villages and the outlying farms of the monasteries are widely spaced and the population of 25,000 on the mainland and 17,000 in the peninsulas is much less dense.

The twenty monasteries and twelve subordinate houses of the Holy Mountain, in their various magnificent settings of precipice and forest, never fail to arouse interest in the western stranger ; apart from the scenic harmony, the ancient convents themselves and the life of their monks constitute for the visitor a museum of medieval religion, art and custom that is unique. The monks, who before 1914 numbered about 7,000, were drawn largely from Greece, with others from Serbia, Bulgaria, Roumania and Russia, and the monasteries were maintained partly by supplies and money from these countries, and partly by the monks themselves who worked on farms. Moreover, the bishops and a numerous regular clergy received their training on the Holy Mountain. Before and throughout the Turkish period this monastic republic was independent ; and the Holy Synod, seated in Kariaí, continues to have full autonomy, except that its administration is supervised by a resident representative of the Greek Government. The wealth of the Communities is now reduced, and also the numbers of monks. Whatever the future may hold for Áthos as a religious power, the monasteries will remain outstanding monuments of Byzantine architecture, and their libraries, although depleted, still contain precious manuscripts of the early Christian church.

Most of the monasteries are visible from the sea ; those on the steeper western and southern side, indeed, appear almost as parts of the cliffs, notably Simónos Pétra, while Áyios Pávlos occupies a ledge in the great western ravine of Mount Áthos itself, overlooking a white waste of marble blocks shaken from the high crags by an earthquake. Those on the east side are less boldly situated, many of them overlooking small bays with beaches and space for intensively cultivated gardens and orchards. Mount Áthos is a three-sided pyramid of pale marble flecked with dark firs and crowned by a chapel ; it is thus one of the most widely visible peaks of the Aegean. A more detailed description of the administration of this autonomous province is given in vol. I, pp. 257 and 335–6.

The inevitability of a great town at the head of the Gulf of Thérmai, and at the extreme corner of the Kambanía has already been indicated ; but the exact site and shape of Thessaloníki have been determined by the ridge of Khortiátis and by the dislocation at its foot. The ridge is a narrow faulted block aligned with Sithoniá, extending from the middle of Khalkidhikí to the river Gallikós. Among its varied rocks is a hard band of crystalline limestone of which the peak of Khortiátis is composed. This graceful summit, dominating the gulf and city, is high enough (3,940 ft.) to carry woods of chestnuts and oaks, and to provide ice from ponds in winter to be stored and brought to town in summer. In Roman times its springs fed a massive aqueduct, which supplied the city.

The southern flanks of the long ridge are of green schist and intrusive gabbro covered with Kermes oak and the humbler phrygana vegetation. The most westerly spur of this slope is the site of Thessaloníki, refounded with this name in 315 B.C. It has been rebuilt many times since, suffering destruction from numerous sieges and assaults, from occasional earthquakes (fourteen of which were destructive between 1545 and 1902) and from terrible fires (e.g. in 1890, and again in August 1917).

The modern outgrowth of Thessaloníki has been naturally confined to the widening strips of plain on either side, in the residential suburb of Kalamariá reaching now some 3 miles to the south, and in the industrial quarter with the railway convergence upon the port on the west. Factories have increased greatly in numbers in recent years, and although many are small, they are most varied. The largest group is concerned with textiles, dealing in whole or in part with fibres of local origin—wool, cotton and silk ; there are thirty-eight hosiery or knitwear works, four weaving, and seven carpet, mills. Another large group makes food products, including twenty makers of Turkish Delight or *Loukoumi*. The bee-keepers of Khalkidhikí send wax to six factories ; and local hides go to twelve tanneries or leather works. Most of these establishments use imported materials in part, and there is a third, varied, group entirely dependent on imports and making goods for the northern Greek market.

By 1940 this second city of Greece and fifth of the Balkan lands was well on the way to rapid material progress, only to find its sobriquet ' the coveted city ' was fully justified. In this year the census recorded a population in the deme of 300,000 as against 236,524 in 1928. The composition of its population had undergone a transformation. Formerly the Sephardic Jews predominated in its affairs, and probably in numbers also ; in 1928, however, they formed only about one-fifth (*c.* 50,000) of the citizens, and there were no Turks or other Moslems. Thus, for the first time in four centuries, Thessaloníki was virtually a Greek city. A full account of the town, port facilities and trade is given in vol. II, pp. 241–51, and buildings of historical interest are described in vol. I, pp. 444–5.

THE AXIÓS-STRIMÓN DIVIDE (REGION E6)

The broad plain of the Axiós is separated from the plain of the Strimón by a belt of high hills best described as a dissected plateau. It is part of a zone of gneissic rocks that extends from eastern

Khalkidhikí far into Jugoslavia. At each of its ends this upland mass is flanked by a narrow corridor of low altitude, both marked by dislocations of the rocks. That in the south may be called the ' Lake Corridor ', and the northern one the ' Doïráni-Strimón Trench ' ; a third and similar trench is drained by the Strumitsa in Bulgaria. The region may be subdivided, therefore, into :

The Kroúsia-Kerdhillíon Mountains
The Lake Corridor
The Doïráni-Strimón Trench.

The Kroúsia-Kerdhillíon Mountains

East of the Kambanía of Thessaloníki there is a large expanse of hill country running from north-west to south-east for which there is no common name ; nevertheless, it has a continuity and general similarity throughout its length of 56 miles and its breadth of 18 miles. The summits, however, which range from 2,600 to 3,600 ft. in height, bear various local names between the Kroúsia mountains in the north and the Kerdhíllion mountains near the Gulf of Strimón. The hills rise in a steep escarpment from the plain of the Strimón and fall gently to the south-west, but the tilted plateau is far from smooth for it is deeply dissected by many valleys that are avoided by roads and paths. This hill country is a geological unit, a tilted fault-block consisting of gneiss penetrated in part by granite, serpentine and gabbro, and in places it bears the ores of antimony, copper, chromium and magnesium ; there are, however, no important mines.

Since most of the rocks are impermeable few of the streams have much water in summer, nor have the valley slopes much soil. In consequence, the many small villages tend to stand high, each in a hollow with a spring, and each with its fields widely scattered on the smoother patches of ground. The cultivated strips are separated by deciduous bush that has largely replaced the former woods of oak, chestnut and hornbeam, now restricted to the higher ridges. Exceptions are found in the north-west where the sediments and lower relief of the Gallikós basin give rise to more continuous agricultural land and to a denser population, and in the south where again the landscape is different. Here, near the large village of Sokhós, a minor fault-scarp faces south and overlooks a shelf some 1,650 ft. in height with fields extending to its edge. Eastwards the shelf becomes a narrow basin with no superficial drainage and containing the residual Lakes Mávrovon and Lántza, the underground outlet of which is presumably in one of the marble belts that occur here. Both of these districts are now traversed by motor roads leading to the Strimón plain, but the main route through the hills from Thessaloníki to Sérrai is in the centre, crossing the watershed in the saddle of Lakhanás at 1,970 ft. The density of population in these hills varies from 33 to 41 per sq. mile, being greatest in the north.

The Lake Corridor

The ' Lake Corridor ' is separated from the Kambanía by a gently sloping threshold, but it is shut off from the Gulf of Strimón by a narrow, high barrier, where gneissic rocks have not disappeared from sight, and through which imperfect drainage is effected by a short canyon 1,000 ft. deep. The corridor, apart from this canyon, is 2½ to 6 miles wide, and 40 miles long, with one marked bend in its almost parallel sides. It is a former lake basin, perhaps an extension of that of the Kambanía, and its two residual lakes, Korónia or Langadhá and Vólvi or Besikíon, occupy about half of its almost flat floor. Near the western end of the former is a hot sulphurous spring, indicating a central fracture in addition to those which delimit the corridor.

The sides of the corridor are the scarped edges of the Kerdhillíon hills on the north and those of the Khortiátis ridge and the hills of Khalkidhikí on the south. Both rise in terraces and so present a striped appearance of alternating bush, or, in the east, forest, and tilled land ; but south of Lake Vólvi the hills give place to a terraced plain with more continuous cultivated and many large villages. Although these lakes provide small quantities of fish for Thessaloníki, their presence is harmful on account of malaria, but complete drainage would be a difficult operation in view of the eastern barrier and of a rise of over 325 ft. to the western watershed ; finally, the depth of the eastern lake is over 65 ft. The lake shores, then, have few settlements, and the population is found either on the flanking terraces of the corridor or on the floor of its higher western end where the land is intensively farmed from a dozen villages and the small town of Langadhás with 5,700 inhabitants. The road from Thessaloníki to Sérrai starts by following the line of the Roman road continuing the *Via Egnatia* and crosses the Khortiátis ridge in a low pass at 950 ft., but on reaching the corridor it is met first by the road from Sokhós through Langadhás and secondly by the old road

Plate 52. Southern side of the Lake Corridor (western end)

The view shows the lower end of the Khortiátis ridge, with meagre phrygana, and wheat fields and fruit trees on the plain.

Plate 53. Southern side of the Lake Corridor (between the lakes)

which follows the southern edge of the lakes. Furthermore, a light railway built by the British Army, starting near this cross-roads and running to the sea at Stavrós, has been maintained. The population numbers 37,000, of whom 27,000 are in the part west of Lake Vólvi with a density there of 163 per sq. mile (Plates 52 and 53.)

The Doïráni-Strimón Trench

Lake Doïráni is drained intermittently to the Axiós through the defile used by the railway from Thessaloníki to İstanbul, and today it is only the shallow (30 ft.) vestige of a greater and much deeper lake that once reached towards the Strimón. The threshold of hard rock through which the Axiós has cut its gorge farther west rises to an isolated peak, the Dub, which commands the oval lake on the south-west and became historic as a stronghold of Austro-Bulgar resistance to many costly British assaults during 1917 and 1918. These battles caused the destruction of the picturesque fishing village of Doïráni which has not been rebuilt. From the Dub the Greek frontier traverses the lake and mounts to the crest of the Belashitsa mountains which it follows to their end. This great ridge is literally a slice of gneissic rock 30 by 5 miles in extent that has been thrust rapidly upwards between fractures, and probably as late as the Glacial period, to a height of over 6,500 ft. During this event the wet climate helped torrents to carve deep ravines in the sides and to build cones, clogging the trench to the south and creating a valley watershed over which the railway now climbs at about 820 ft. (Plate 54). The northern slopes are densely forested almost to the summits, but on the Greek side a belt of summer pasture stands above the woods of oak, beech and fir. At the scarp-foot a score of large villages are aligned at or near the heads of the fans which provide easily irrigated fields and orchards ; but there is also much woodland of oak and chestnut which increases with the eastward descent to the plain of the Strimón. This foot-hill belt from lake Doïráni to the Strimón has an average density of 223 people per sq. mile.

THE PLAIN OF THE STRIMÓN (REGION E7)

Physical Characteristics

The Strimón enters upon its lowland course through the faulted Rúpel defile at the eastern end of the Belashitsa mountains (Fig. 26, and vol. I, Plate 12) ; it maintained this entrance during the uplift of the mountains. The importance of this gateway to Greece explains the demarcation of the frontier of 1919 beyond the northern entrance to the defile ; from a tactical standpoint this was fully justified by the successful defence of the Rúpel against the German attack of 20 May 1941, since the vital invasion was effected not at this point but west of the Belashitsa. The defile is 5 miles long and it is followed only by a road, since, for reasons of security, connexion between the Greek and Bulgarian railway systems is lacking.

In shape the plain is almost a parellelogram, and the short barrier in the south corresponds geologically with the Belashitsa in the north. Both are formed of the same gneissic rock and both are penetrated by the Strimón in defiles. This southern barrier, although low, has impeded the drainage of the plain and explains its incomplete utilization and its malarious reputation in the past. The two longer sides differ considerably from one another. To the west the escarpment is continuous, although scored by countless ravines in the gneiss and similar rocks, and is covered by deciduous forest or the bush which has replaced it. The eastern frame is a line of separate mountain blocks and the gaps between them are floored with terrace deposits that also form a continuous foothill slope facing the plain (Fig. 27). The terraces are composed of weak sediments deeply gullied by intermittent torrents (see vol. I, Plate 21). West of the Strimón this feature is prominent only in the south.

Where the Strimón emerges from the Rúpel defile it has built out a great fan that now reaches across the plain to the scarp of the Kroúsia mountains. Thus the drainage from the western tributaries was impeded to form malarial swamps. By the construction of a dam these have now been replaced by the artificial Lake Kerkíni, which is a reservoir filled by the flood water, and by the streams of the surrounding mountains, which even the recent engineering works have been unable to drain. From this corner the river keeps near the southern side of the plain, and until the recent drainage operations the lowest part of the basin was occupied by the shallow Lake Akhinós which was constricted in the middle by two convergent tributary fans of alluvium. Thus the plain proper has been built up by the overflowing Strimón and its tributaries, chiefly those from the east, and while it is flat in appearance its gentle slopes are important.

From the northern entrance at a height of 165 ft. the surface declines along the axis of the plain by 130 ft. in the first 25 miles ;

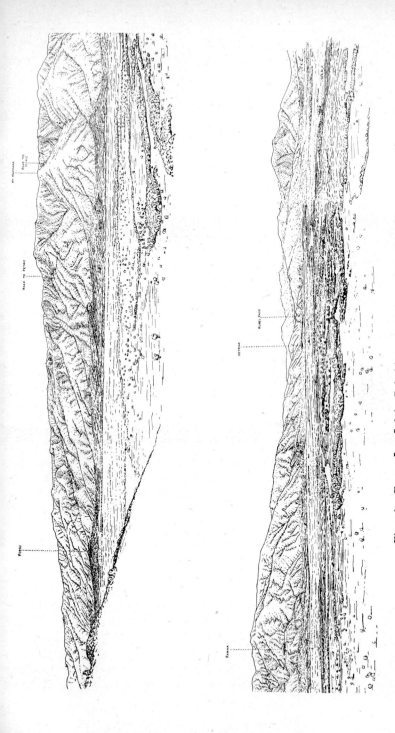

Fig. 26. Eastern part of the Belashitsa mountains and the Rupel Pass.

The drawing was made from a spur of the Kroúsia mountains in July 1916. The marshes in the foreground are now replaced by Lake Kerkíni. The Tsingélion mountains are seen on the right. The upper and lower halves of the panorama are continuous (west to east).

Plate 54.   The Belashitsa mountains near their western end

The view is from the south and shows two large alluvial fans under cultivation except where that on the left is still being

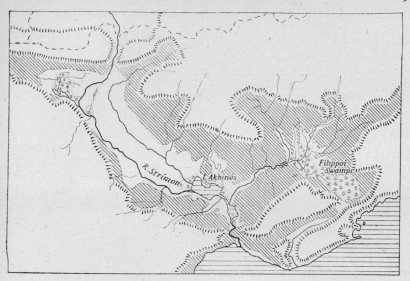

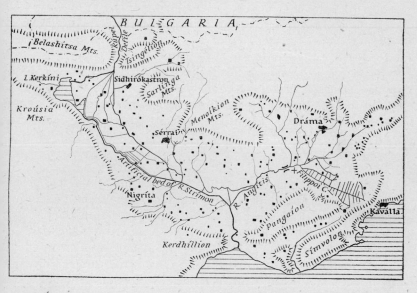

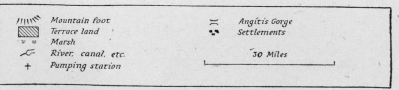

Fig. 27.   Drainage of the plains of the lower Strimón

Based on engineering plans and the 1:250,000 G.S.G.S. Series 4088, Sheet 4272.
The upper map shows the plain before drainage; it indicates the terrace-land but
settlements have been omitted.   The lower map shows the regulating Lake
Kerkíni and all the settlements, but not the terrace-land.

thereafter, over the similar distance to the exit defile, the slope is much less upon the now drained floor of Lake Akhinós, and its former margins. To drain this lower area, thereby providing 46 sq. miles of new agricultural land and improving the bordering tracts, the principal task was to deepen the channel in the defile leading to the sea (Plate 51). This has now been done, and the river in the drained area is confined to an embanked course, while the requisite protection from flooding by the tributaries has also been constructed. Among these, the Angítis is the most important since it is the effluent of the large basin of Dráma beyond the mountains ; moreover, the recent drainage of the swamps in that plain is necessarily associated with the works on the Strimón. As a result of all these operations some change may be expected at the river mouth. Unlike the Axiós and Néstos, the Strimón has only a small delta, for the plain and lake acted as traps for the detritus ; but silting at the mouth will now develop and demand constant attention if a harbour is to be maintained.

The second main engineering accomplishment is the provision of water for the irrigation in summer of at least 1,700 sq. miles, and so for a very large increase in agricultural output. This is effected by regularizing the natural flooding of the north-west corner. The impounded water of Lake Kerkíni rises in spring to the maximum level of 115 ft., at which height this reservoir contains 311 million cubic metres. The water is then gradually passed out by sluices to the irrigation canals.

Land Utilization

In the past the population of the lower Strimón basin has always preferred the surrounding terraces and fans to the plain, the density ratio being approximately three to one, and this despite the periodic renewal of the soil of the plain. The defects of the plain were, of course, the risk to crops from spring floods and to man from the malaria that followed. Furthermore, during the summer drought the surface water became saline and deleterious to men, animals and crops. From the surface incrustation in some parts, saltpetre was formerly collected. Hence the villages depended upon wells, for the water was always plentiful underground, and the repopulation of the plain by refugees was made possible by the boring of some fifty new wells on the plain itself, about half of which were artesian.

From classical times the basin has been one of the most populous areas of Macedonia. It was noted not only for its crops but also for the timber of the hills ; Alexander the Great, for instance, had sea-going vessels built on Lake Akhinós. The basin yielded great revenues to the Turks ; but economic decline and depopulation were induced by the *tchiflik* system, the insecurity of overland trade in the latter part of the nineteenth century, the Balkan wars, and finally the war of 1916–18. In 1912 the region was occupied by a mixed people, some 40% Turkish, mainly living in the south, and the remainder chiefly Greeks and Bulgars, dominant in the north. Thus in 1922 the greater part of the region was left empty, and the plain therefore became one of the principal areas of refugee settlement in Greece. By 1926 the Bulgar minority had been reduced to 15% in the north and to 6% in the south. The Greek immigrants came in slight majority from Asia, the rest from Thrace and Bulgaria, thus bringing some variety of agricultural knowledge and habit ; and the wars, in any case, had broken the traditional system of husbandry. When first entered by British forces in 1916, the plain was still bright in places with fields of opium poppy and cotton, for the latter crop had previously brought fame to the district from the quality of its fibre. But these soon disappeared, together with greater areas of other crops, and the proportion of derelict land became larger than ever ; thus in 1920 only about one-tenth of the plain and the terrace land was under cultivation. The refugees when they came made the plain look still more like the steppe to which many of them had been accustomed, for they cut down most of the tall, deep-rooted shade trees that had surrounded the villages.

The older population remained chiefly on the terraces and foothills, in villages now enlarged to house immigrants as well, and this zone was more quickly and more fully cultivated than the flat land where most of the refugee settlements had to be built, usually on grid plans. Here a large proportion of the land had to wait for drainage and irrigation, and its full accomplishment is still awaited. Already, as an indication of the agricultural benefits of drainage, a five-fold increase in the yield of hay, produced experimentally, may be quoted. Just before the improvements the greater part of the cultivated land was devoted to cereals, over one-third being under wheat and about one-tenth each under barley and maize ; the latter crop will doubtless increase with irrigation.

The terrace lands east of the Strimón are among the best tobacco-growing grounds in Greece, and although the total production is much less than in the basin of Dráma, cultivation of the leaf is still the speciality of some of the villages where tobacco has always been grown ; thus around Pappás and Áyion Pnévma (Mónoikon), on terraces east of Sérrai and between 790 and 1,180 ft. 50 and 80% of the land respectively was devoted to tobacco. Cotton cultivation also has made a good start on lower ground, and by 1937 occupied 6% of the arable land of the *nomós* of Sérrai ; moreover, the refugees have been encouraged to cultivate fruits, including the olive and the vine. The total population of the lowland, including the eastern gap followed by the river Angítis, is 145,000, and the average density is 215 per sq. mile.

The basin possesses three towns, Nigríta, Sidhirókastron and Sérrai, all situated on terraces. Nigríta, located immediately above the swamps of Akhinós, with a large area under vines, mulberry and tobacco surrounding it, has always been a Greek town, and has grown as the market of a considerable district ; but it was burned by the Bulgar army in 1913 and then rebuilt. It suffered somewhat from isolation, and only in recent years have metalled roads linked it directly with Sérrai and with the highway from Sérrai to Thessaloníki. Increased by refugees, the population now numbers some 9,000. The village of Thermá, south-east of Nigríta, with hot mineral springs which mark the boundary fault of the basin, may well be a future watering place for the cooler months.

The other two towns are on the railway ; indeed they have always been on a main route, for the old road from Thessaloníki to Belgrade followed the Strimón and not the Axiós, passing through Sérrai and Sidhirókastron. This latter town, the ' Iron Castle ', was a stronghold both of medieval Bulgaria and of the Turks, controlling the Rúpel defile, 4 miles to the north-west. The fortress crowns the cliff of the ravine from which the river Krushovítis emerges on to the plain, and the town occupies the hollow before the gorge (Plate 55). Its population first became predominantly Greek about 1920, and the number, doubled by influx of refugees, rose in 1928 to nearly 10,000. The position of Sidhirókastron makes it a local market, administrative centre and a garrison town, and its importance would be increased by railway connexion with Bulgaria.

Sérrai, the Seris of ancient times and a place of importance in the Byzantine, Serbian and Ottoman Empires, is built at the hill foot below an acropolis ; the flanking ravines have no permanent streams, but the town stands on alluvial fans sloping rather steeply to the south. The buildings represent replacements, very varied in age, since Sérrai has suffered in many wars, and for two years was frequently under British shell fire. In marked contrast are the new quarters of the refugees in the south-west which nearly double the area of the town. The Serbian Emperor Stephen Dushan made this his advanced capital about 1350 as a challenge to the Turks, under whom the town later came to have great commercial importance ; this probably culminated in the early nineteenth century when the annual fairs drew caravans from most of Bulgaria and Serbia. The population then was probably about 25,000 ; in 1920 it was 14,486 and in 1928 it was 29,640. This figure includes a large number who are farmers in the vicinity, for manufactures are unimportant. Sérrai is still the chief commercial centre of its basin and capital of a *nomós* (see vol. II, pp. 387–8).

It is perhaps remarkable that there has been no town near the mouth of the Strimón since the fall of Amphipolis, the ancient Athenian colony. The site of this ruin is attractive, on a high terrace surrounded, as the name indicates, on three sides by the last meander of the river ; and with full benefit from the sea breeze in summer a healthy town may again rise here. A Greek naval or military harbour named Amfípolis has been constructed at the eastern edge of the delta and was connected in 1940 with the main railway. The port is linked by road with Sérrai, with Kaválla and with Thessaloníki by the coastal plain and the lake corridor.

The Trans-Strimón Mountains and Basins (Region E8)

There is no general name for the mountains that rise to the north-east of the plain and gulf of Strimón, for these do not constitute a single range and they differ completely from the uniform scarped plateau to the west. Five separate mountains are set in line but vary greatly in aspect ; and they may be likened to molars embedded in gums represented by the terraces at their foot, but with one lost from the series, leaving the wide Angítis gap that leads to the basin of Dráma. The island of Thásos (see p. 367) may be regarded as the sixth of this series of mountains. Their mutual contrasts are partly due to the rocks ; thus, starting in the north, numbers one, three, four and Thásos are composed mainly of marble ; numbers two and five are of granite and gneiss. The longer axes of all but Thásos lie transversely (i.e. WSW–ENE) as determined by the fractures that separate them, and all but the coastal range rise above 5,900 ft. (Fig. 22). Their names, from north to south, are :

The Tsingélion and Alí Butús Mountains
The Sarlínga and Alí Babá Mountains
The Menoíkion Mountains
The Pangaíon Range
The Símvolon Range

The Tsingélion and Alí Butús Mountains

The northern frontier which descends from the Belashitsa mountains for strategic reasons to include both ends of the Rúpel defile in Greece thereby encloses a part of the Bulgarian basin of Melnik, and again reaches the high summits 11 miles east of the Strimón. Thus Mount Tsingélion (or Chengel), the prolongation of the Belashitsa, is all in Greece. The gneiss that forms both slopes of the Rúpel defile gives place eastwards, as the crest rises, to marble which is nearly bare of soil and vegetation. Tsingélion therefore appears from the plain as a delicately sculptured mountain, brilliantly luminous when not under cloud ; and this applies also to its higher eastward extension, Alí Butús, with its steep crags and spurs facing west at the head of the basin drained by the Krushovitís to the Strimón (Fig. 26). Access to this basin from the plain is through deeply cut terraces behind Sidhirókastron ; much of its soil is coarse permeable rubble, and its villages are few and poor. Five hot mineral springs which are spaced out on a fault that crosses the Tsingélion north-eastwards from Thermopiyí may have a future as watering places.

The Sarlínga and Alí Babá Mountains

The elliptical mass of Sarlínga-Alí Babá is a squat dome of granite, its sides deeply cleft by valleys. The contrast with the neighbouring marble mountains is emphasized by the luxuriant growth of forests, especially on the north where oak gives way to beech with both fir and pine. The lower slopes, composed of lake sediments, are even more sharply incised by gullies, but they pass into the terrace land of the plain. The road from Sérrai to Káto Nevrokópion climbs steadily northwards, keeping to the west of the deep ' Green Valley ', so called from the numerous orchards and the exceptionally high olive gardens of Elaión at 1,300 ft. It avoids the great ravine that delimits the Menoíkion mountains, succeeds in crossing the watershed below 3,440 ft. and so descends to the enclosed basin of Nevrokópion.

The Menoíkion Mountains

Menoíkion, or the Boz of Sérrai (see vol. I, Plate 22), is a block of marble, and forms part of the massive framework of this rock which encloses the Basin of Dráma on three of its sides. The Turkish name Boz is also applied to the still higher peak north of Dráma. Boz means ' riddled with holes ', and the marble is, in fact, pitted by sink-holes of all shapes and sizes, rendering it difficult to traverse. The Menoíkion slab is tilted gently to the south-west, but is very steep on the other sides, especially the west. With thin vegetation and no surface water the mountain does not offer even a summer home for shepherds, but the springs near its foot benefit the villages of the terraced apron below. The total settled population of these northern mountains is under 6,000.

Between the Menoíkion and Pangaíon masses the broad Angítis (Angísta) Gap forms not merely an important route (the railway from Sérrai to Dráma passes along it) but also a large expanse of farmland, for it is the continuation of the marginal terraces of the Strimón. The chief exception is at the narrower eastern end where the soft sediments give place to a low marble threshold in which the river Angítis flows for 2½ miles in a straight canyon (see vol. I, Plate 7). The entrance to this gorge is the critical point for the drainage of the basin of the Dráma. There is a large population, partly of refugees, with many well distributed villages, since the district has advantages of climate and soil, helped by a little irrigation, that made it famous in the past for cotton, tobacco and vines. The vineyards were devastated by phylloxera during the wars of 1912–18 and only a few have been replanted, but cotton production remains considerable.

The Pangaíon Range

The Pangaíon, when seen from the sea, is without special grandeur, but from west or east its summit fully justifies the Turkish name Pilav, i.e. ' heap of rice '. The white marble is but thinly veiled, owing to long continued charcoal-burning and summer herding by the Vlachs. In places, however, the vegetation still pleases the eye ; fern and juniper grow near the top, beech woods in the hollows, and near the foot, chestnut and heath. At the two ends of the mountain the lower slopes are of the underlying gneiss, and this is the rock which in ancient times brought fame to the Pangaíon as a source of gold ; the metal was probably recovered mainly from the stream-beds and not worked *in situ.*

The vale of Marmarás, separating the Pangaíon from the coastal ridge of Símvolon, is one of those features of Greece so strange to the northern visitor accustomed to valleys made by their rivers

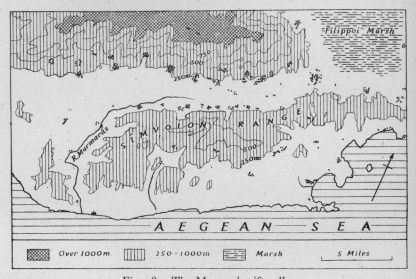

Fig. 28. The Marmarás rift valley

Based on the 1 : 100,000 G.S.G.S. Series 4087, Sheets C4272 and C4872. The map includes all settlements. The lowest contour just fails to show that the valley is blocked at both ends and that the lower Marmarás flows in a rocky gorge. The Fílippoi Marsh is shown as it was before drainage.

(Fig. 28). It is a rift valley bounded by parallel faults, floored by rich alluvium and drained, not as would appear natural, through one of its ends, but by the narrow defile of the river Marmarás southwards through the Símvolon block. Strange, too, in Makedhonia, before the big irrigation scheme, was land that remained green throughout the summer. But here the streams sufficed for continuous cultivation, with meadows and tall maize surrounded by tobacco fields on the fans. Hence the villages containing, after the immigration, over 9,000 inhabitants, are closely aligned on both edges of the narrow trough ; in 1928 it was an over-populated area, but the intention was to move some of the newcomers to the swamps of Fílippoi, when drained.

The Símvolon Range

The Símvolon is a range of hills composed of granite in the east where narrowest, and gneiss with a little marble in the west where twice as broad, and although deeply cut by valleys with intermittent streams, it possesses a rather even crest. The climate is Mediterranean, and summer drought determines both the vegetation of maquis and the sparseness of population. Near the Strimón, the low coast is backed by inhabited and cultivated terrace land ; but at Cape Dhévtero it turns to the east-north-east and becomes the straight faulted edge of the rocky Símvolon, with only narrow beaches. This stretch ends abruptly at Cape Vrasídhas where the Gulf of Kaválla begins. Here, subsidence has brought the sea into the lower valleys, and the shore is deeply indented, while one granite hill-top has been left in the gulf to form Xeronísi. The natural harbour of Elevtherón Bay has now been developed for military purposes and is connected with the road system. It is backed by a considerable alluvial plain on which stand several villages and where careful cultivation is dependent upon water from wells. The narrow eastern end of the Símvolon range is cut by the Pass of Kaválla, 690 ft. above the sea and just over a mile northwest of the port.

THE MOUNTAINS OF DRÁMA (REGION E9)

The mountain frame that encloses the Basin of Dráma consists of a series of crystalline blocks. Those in the west have already been described in Region E8 ; the remaining masses are :

The Falakrón Mountains and the Northern Plateau
The Boz of Dráma
The Chal Dag

The Falakrón Mountains and the Northern Plateau

The Falakrón continue the line of the Menoíkion, though at a lower altitude, to the Boz of Dráma, thereby hemming in the basin of Nevrokópion, and forming the southern edge of the rolling plateau that continues far into Bulgaria. This barrier ridge is heavily wooded and uninhabited ; but it is crossed by roads from Sérrai and Dráma. The metalled road from Dráma to Nevrokópion makes use of a pass, 2,600 ft. high, where the village of Granítis marks an outcrop of this rock ; while a branch road, crossing a more easterly saddle near Vólax at 3,300 ft. makes straight for the crossing of the

Néstos at Potamoí. These communications were demanded to counter the undoubted failure of colonization on the northern plateau where, as in the Greek territory north of the Rúpel defile, the failure of the settlement was largely due to the proximity of the frontier which made both districts open to military invasion. The vulnerability to attack was clearly demonstrated in 1941. The northern plateau with its varied rocks and soils is well watered and largely forested, but the former Bulgarian and Turkish peasants had cultivated more of it than did smaller numbers of colonists. The basin-plain of Nevrokópion is a flat-floored hollow immediately behind the ridge of Falakrón, a structural depression that may owe its origin partly to solution of limestone, for it is drained underground to the Dráma plain. Here, in contrast to the highlands, cultivation is intense, and most of its 21 sq. miles of flat surface came under the plough after the exchange of population, producing good crops of cereals, beans and potatoes, with vines on the slopes. The villages, with a total population of 9,000 inhabitants, are characteristically situated on fans in the angles of the surrounding hill-foot.

The Boz of Dráma

The Boz of Dráma rises to a summit of 7,493 ft. and is visible for a great distance from land and sea. The southern side has only a sparse vegetation and is cut by several precipitous ravines ; on the north, however, the mountains present regular and thickly wooded slopes to the river Néstos. A motor road now circumvents Mount Boz, striking north from Dráma to Papádhes, a mile beyond a new bridge across the Néstos. By this way, the previous inaccessibility of the trans-Néstos highland has been partly overcome. Between this road and the railway corridor (see below) to the south-east, the mountains are under 3,250 ft. in height, with well-wooded sides and many permanent streams. This district is composed partly of mica schists and is better peopled than the neighbouring mountains, most of the villages lying in the valleys. The Platania gap, which separates the Boz from the Chal Dag or Karsí mountains, continues the trend of the Angítis gorge to the plain of the river Néstos. It rises to a summit altitude of only 985 ft. and is of great importance as a railway route.

The Chal Dag

The Chal Dag is a plateau with its summit ridges climbing gradually from about 3,250 ft. in the south to 3,900 ft. in the north.

These broad ridges are pitted with small cultivated depressions, floored with red soil, while in the north-east at Lekáni there is a large *polje*, or flat-floored depression, some 4 sq. miles in area and 2,300 above sea level. Here, water lies in temporary lakes and nourishes an oasis with green meadows. The former beech and oak forests have mostly been reduced by animals and woodmen to dense bush, but they still remain on the eastern slopes. Deep valleys dissect the plateau, giving access to the many villages, that stand between 1,600 and 2,600 ft., and utilize spring water emerging at the outcrop of the underlying schists. The settlements are marked by lines of tobacco fields with red-soil and before the exchange they were peopled entirely by Turks. The colonization by Greeks was not a success ; thus in fifteen villages the 10,779 Turks of 1913 had been replaced in 1928 by only 3,670 Greeks and consequently much land has reverted to nature.

THE PLAIN OF DRÁMA, AND KAVÁLLA (REGION E10)

Physical Characteristics

This structural basin has received the waters and the detritus of the surrounding mountains, first in a lake that filled the basin, and later upon its drying floor : hence the wide-spread alluvial fans of the hill-foot, especially in the north, and the vast marshes of the southern area. The surrounding mountains have risen progressively and there is evidence that even now the plain continues to sink relatively to these. The greater movements were no doubt marked by earthquakes, and the account of St. Paul's experience at Philippi (Fílippoi) is probably the most widely read record of any seismic disturbance ; this site is on the eastern boundary fault at the foot of the Chal Dag.

Land Utilization

Apart from the vicinity of Fílippoi the favoured part of the plain has always been the northern half, and it includes the finest and most productive tobacco land in Europe. The settlements here and the farming system still bear the imprint of Turkish times and, as in the plain of Strimón, the upper edges contain the old free villages and the best tobacco land, while the lower and flatter ground was formerly the domain of the *tchiflik*. The whole of this northern plain was peopled by Turks and Bulgars, and many of the latter remained under the terms of the voluntary exchange with Bulgaria (see vol. I, pp. 369–78). Thus the aspect of the marginal villages has changed but little, new red-roofed houses of the refugees simply being added to the older, stone-built and flat-roofed dwellings about the central market place. The *tchiflik* villages of the lower land, however, have been replaced by new settlements built on a grid plan. At the hill-foot the stony soil is under grain or is left for pasture ; next follows a zone of red loam in which tobacco is the main crop and, even if it does not take first place in area, it dominates the work of field and village ; finally, the flatter land, liable in the past to partial inundation, is devoted to cereals and to pasture. A similar arrangement of village and cultivation marks the edges of the southern plain as well, including, on its eastern side, the terrace land that narrows toward the Plataniá gap. In 1937 almost one-third of the cultivated area in the *nomós* was given over to tobacco (another third being under wheat), and the proportion on the best land is, of course, much higher. The yield was 98,000 quintals and the value 712 million drachmas. Climate, soil and imparted skill combine in this remarkable production. A considerable crop of olives seems to indicate a milder winter climate than in the *nomós* of Sérrai where very few are grown.

The elimination of the swamps of the southern plain as one of the chief malarial districts in Greece was the main project of recent engineering operations, but in addition 16 sq. miles have been protected from periodic inundation and a further 46 sq. miles have now improved drainage (Plate 56). These projects depend upon the manipulation of the bottle neck, i.e. the entrance to the Angítis canyon (Plate 57), and also upon the works on the lower Strimón. The great gain in agricultural land was intended to benefit the settlers who had made little of their occupation of surrounding districts, especially those of the high country to the north and east. It is clear that the drained marshes of Filíppoi, like the Akhinós land, will eventually provide that rarity in Greece, permanently damp soil, while elsewhere the risk of saline incrustation will be eliminated. In 1928 the average density of population on this plain, including Dráma, was 337 per sq. mile.

It seems natural that eastern Makedhonía should possess two related towns, one inland and dependent on the wealth of the basin, the other acting as the seaport. This has always been the case, but Drabescus, the Byzantine ancestor of Dráma, was not the inland capital, since Philippi had flourished under that name from 358 B.C., and as a Thasian town, Krenides, for at least 500 years before that.

Plate 55. Sidhirókastron and the river Krushovítis

The view shows the river, with many small branches at low water in summer, entering the Strimón plain. The river separates the town from its irrigated gardens. The Kroúsia mountains are concealed by the dust-haze prevalent in summer.

Plate 56. The plain of Dráma

The view shows drainage works in the marshes of Fílippoi.

Plate 57.   The plain of Dráma from the entrance of the Angítis canyon
Behind the limestone ridge, in the foreground, is flat alluvial land backed by a low
terrace ; the mountains beyond are concealed by haze.   At this place the pumping
station for the drainage of the southern plain has since been erected.

Plate 58.   The old town and Turkish castle at Kaválla

Only at its final disappearance about 1750 did Dráma take its place. Neapolis which later became Kaválla, the port of Krenides and Philippi, occupied a very significant position in the Roman Empire as the most easterly good port on the Greek mainland, with a short passage to Asia Minor. Thus it resembled the present Brindisi in relation to the Suez Canal. It was, presumably, owing to its proximity to Asia Minor that St. Paul landed here and made the first European conversions at Philippi, while the reputed origin of the name Kaválla, curious in a seaport, was the practice of crusading knights to leave their horses here on embarkation. These towns were also related, from Roman times, to the course of the great road from Thessaloníki which passed along the eastern edge of the plain and which was controlled by Philippi at a defile between mountain and swamp ; then, like the modern road, it crossed the terminal spurs of the Símvolon to Neapolis, before following the inner edge of the Thracian plains. The economic position is now different, for Dráma is on the railway while Kaválla is not ; and the merchants of the inland town tend to exploit this advantage at the expense of the port. Of Philippi there remain only scattered ruins, but enough to indicate its former splendour founded upon the rich gold field of antiquity. The nearby village of Ráhcha, however, has been re-named Krinídhes after the colony of Thasian miners. Many have searched for the sources of the gold with little success ; the lodes presumably were in the mica-schist underlying the marble of Chal Dag.

The site of Dráma, like that of the prosperous villages along the northern edge of the plain, commands a group of alluvial fans where a powerful spring emerges from the limestone. With increasing importance the town has expanded from a closely built centre in the Turkish style to suburbs on the grid plan. Its population of over 29,000 is more than double that of 1913. Dráma, while a military and administrative centre, is above all a tobacco market.

Kaválla, like many ancient Mediterranean ports, occupies a promontory site. Its acropolis is a Turkish fortress, built on older foundations, and it crowns the granite hill that is joined to the mainland by flat ground (Plate 58). Around it clusters the old oriental town, while on the low ground and the lower mainland slopes is the commercial town adjoining the harbour. Here are the market, the cigarette factories and, rearing gaunt windowless walls from the harbour, the tobacco warehouses. In 1913 Kaválla had 23,000 inhabitants, of whom 5,000 lived by tobacco. In 1928 the population had grown to nearly 50,000 by the influx of refugees, and the newly built quarters range along the hillsides both east and west. The economic position of the town as mistress of the tobacco trade, exporting from a quarter to a third of the Greek product, may well be considered precarious in view of the fluctuations in price of the leaf. In recent years these prices have been determined by the great importing firms, chiefly in Germany and the United States. The port facilities of Kaválla are described in vol. II, pp. 266-9.

THE TRANS-NÉSTOS MOUNTAINS OF MAKEDHONÍA AND DHITIKÍ THRÁKI (REGION E11)

The Trans-Néstos mountains of Makedhonía form a physical unit with the mountains of Dhitikí Thráki, extending in unbroken line along the Bulgarian frontier to the valley of the Évros (Maritsa). The Néstos, though only in its lower course the boundary between Makedhonía and Dhitikí Thráki is a serious barrier to communications, since it flows in impassable canyons except in the small basin of Paranéstion. At this point the railway that has followed the Korpillón defile crosses the river. The boundary between the two provinces, leaving the Néstos where it enters the plain, runs almost due north to join the Bulgarian frontier at its southern salient on Mount Koúla. West of this line the inhabitants were either Turks or Bulgars, the majority of the latter being Moslems and named Pomaks (see vol. I, pp. 355-6). Thus the result of the Convention of Lausanne was the complete evacuation of this western district in contrast with the mountains east of the line where the similar population remained, as they were entitled to do. The resulting differences in agricultural methods and densities of population makes it necessary to subdivide the region into :

The Trans-Néstos Mountains of Makedhonía
The Mountains of Dhitikí Thráki

The Trans-Néstos Mountains of Makedhonía

The Greek frontier reaches its most northerly point (41° 33′) in the mountains about 12 miles beyond its crossing of the river Néstos, and from there it follows the watershed of the Rodhópi mountains to a point north of Alexandroúpolis, some 90 miles distant in a straight line. This watershed divides the tributaries of the upper Évros (Maritsa) from the rivers flowing directly to the Aegean, but the physical features on the two slopes are similar, for they are those of the greatest single massif of ancient crystalline rocks in the Balkan Peninsula, the larger part being in Bulgaria.

A view northwards from the Boz of Dráma shows a wilderness of dome-like summits and intricate valleys largely swathed in beech woods, and satisfies the observer at once that it has few of the features typical of Makedhonía. Instead of the alternation of scarped mountain and enclosed basin, there is the monotony of subdued relief with wide accordance of summit levels and many small rolling plateaux. These remnants of worn surfaces rise northwards to heights exceeding 5,900 ft. on the frontier ; the whole district, however, is deeply etched by a maze of valleys. The nomenclature of these features seems to be uncertain owing to the almost complete change of population ; and it is in this demographic aspect that the difference from the mountains of Dhitikí Thráki chiefly lies. The Moslems, long settled in these mountain woodlands, had become completely adapted to their environment, cultivating small areas around the villages in suitable crops, making use of various nut trees and growing other fruits ; but principally they depended upon their flocks for saleable goods. The Settlement Commission wished to establish some 10,000 families of Greek refugees in place of the evacuated population ; but whatever the number actually introduced only a minority remained after a few years. Their failure to adapt themselves to a new environment seems to have been due partly to the fact that there were no old inhabitants to pass on local knowledge. Moreover, many of the small villages had fallen into ruin and the fields had become overgrown before their arrival. In the higher northern area the nearness of the frontier probably engendered a feeling of insecurity, and above all the inaccessibility of the villages was disliked by the newcomers. Thus the settlement did not succeed and the total population of this large district shows a great decline from that of the previous period. In the meantime the vacant land benefitted one element, the Vlachs, who were able to feed their flocks with little restriction. Over this broad mountainous area of some 700 sq. miles there is an average population of only 13 per sq. mile, although in the more accessible basin of Paranéstion the density rises to 65 per sq. mile.

The Mountains of Dhitikí Thráki

Although the Rodhópi is so strongly contrasted with much of Makedhonía, detailed survey has shown that there is one physical feature common to both—the directions imparted to the rivers by structural causes. Thus the main rivers, instead of running at right angles to the watershed, flow south-south-east, while many tributaries run from east to west, from east-north-east to west-south-west, or in the reverse directions, just as they do in Makedhonía. The three principal rivers reaching the plain of Dhitikí Thráki are the Néstos, coming as the Mesta from Bulgaria, the Eskejé emerging from the mountains at Xánthi, and the Kurú emerging at Políanthos. The general south-eastward course of the main streams has probably been imparted to them by warping of the plateau surface, but to complicate this it seems that while the whole of the Rodhópi block rose in height the parts near the fractures that delimit the southern edge were thrust upwards more rapidly. Two results of this are, first, that the plains are overlooked by abrupt fault-scarps which are continuous for 50 miles from the Gulf of Kaválla, and secondly, that the rivers reach the plain through narrow gorges, those of the lower Néstos and lower Kurú being respectively over 10 and 6 miles long. The railway was driven through the former only at the expense of several tunnels (see Plate 59 and vol. I, Plate 10).

In the mountains that contain the drainage basin of the Eskejé and the Kurú, a rough triangle of some 3,000 sq. miles, the interior consists partly of decomposed granite which shows up in yellow patches where the vegetation is broken. It has been more fully eroded by the many streams than the southern heights, and while still generally wooded with beech, juniper and oak, the trees are usually pollarded, and there are many clearings. The Moslem peasants live here as their ancestors have done for centuries. Cultivation is carefully carried out, often upon walled terraces, with tobacco accompanying the varied fruit trees and subsistence crops of rye and maize ; stock include many cattle with the more numerous sheep and goats. Scattered farms are common and the villages, although lacking in plan, generally cluster around the simple mosques. The market and geometric centre is Ekhínos, with 1,900 inhabitants, on the Kurú about half way from Xánthi to the frontier, and on one of the three roads that cross the Rodhópi. The road has little traffic and follows the Kurú to its source before descending to Raikovo in Bulgaria.

Immediately east of the Kurú the frontier approaches to within 6 miles of the southern plain and for the next 18 miles the natural features offer little military protection to Greece. At first, the Kartál mountains rise to 4,862 ft., east of which a road leads directly north from Komotiní to the Balkan Turesi Pass at some 2,300 ft.

Plate 59.   The lower gorge of the river Néstos

The view shows the river emerging from the gorge cut in crystalline limestone.   The bridge is that of the coastal road : the railway enters the first tunnel in the background.

[Facing page 144

Plate 60.　The town of Xánthi

The view is from the west and shows the lower part of the old town.　The river
Eskejé is crossed by the railway on the farther bridge.　The refugee quarters are
off the view on the right.

Plate 61.　The upper part of Xánthi, from the south-east

All this narrow mountain zone, with short streams on crystalline rocks, suffers from drought ; the forest has been decimated and the bush-covered slopes support only a small population. Farther east, however, the highland spreads out and forms a large plateau, dissected by intricate valley systems which divide it into roughly equal areas, and which drain it to north, south, east and west. The central part, culminating at 3,402 ft. is named Boukatí Dag, but there are many other local names. To the south-west the plateau is linked by lower hills to the coastal ridge of Chóban Dag which extends westwards from near Alexandroúpolis (Dedéagach) to Mount Ísmaros. This last ridge rises steeply from the shore to 2,224 ft. and maintains an altitude of over 1,600 ft. for 9 miles to the north-west (see p. 152).

The whole of the highland thus delimited belongs structurally to the Rodhópi massif, and is composed mainly of igneous and metamorphic rocks. But in several parts Tertiary volcanics cover considerable areas, especially trachyte and andesite similar to those found in Samothráki, Límnos and Imroz. Indeed the structure of Samothráki (see p. 376) has been closely compared with that of the neighbouring mainland, and the sea between them, now mostly from 20 to 40 fathoms deep, covers the foundered surface that recently joined the two.

The central part of the plateau is largely covered with deciduous forest of beech, oak and chestnut, or open woodland in which the only houses are the shepherds' huts, either of the Vlachs or the villagers themselves ; large flocks spend the summer in the more open parts of the woodland. The real settlements, with greater clearings, are near the edges of the plateau. In aspect and economy they resemble those described in the mountains farther west, since the population is predominantly Turkish and long settled. Few villages number more than 400 inhabitants and only two have over 1,000, of which one is the only Greek refugee village in the district. Throughout the whole plateau there are few roads of any kind, though bridle paths are numerous ; the plateau is, therefore, remote from progressive influences and its conservative people would doubtless prefer to keep it so.

THE PLAIN OF DHITIKÍ THRÁKI (REGION E12)

From the Gulf of Kaválla the plain extends eastwards for 56 miles, but it is almost severed by the lagoon or lake of Vistonís and Pórto

Lágo Bay into two nearly equal parts. Each possesses one considerable town, Xánthi to the west and Komotiní (Gumuljína) to the east, which are situated symmetrically in relation to the lagoon and the hill foot. As in so many cases, this lowland may be described literally as a ' sunkenland,' but to what depth the block, once continuous with the Rodhópi, has subsided is not known. A well-bore reaching 722 ft. below sea level east of the lagoon revealed only weak deposits, the lowest being sea-sand. The north-north-west axis of the lagoon probably marks a zone of subsidence somewhat greater than has occurred on its flanks. Thus the outline of the plain is substantially the result of crustal movement, though the work of waves has smoothed the outline of the shore. The Néstos alone among the rivers has built out to sea, but it is not responsible for the whole of the projection towards Thásos ; other rivers reach the coast only intermittently, while the Eskejé brings no water to the lagoon and the Kurú is merely a trickle, except during flood. While all the streams from the mountains have added their quota of deposits to the plain, their water sinks from the surface ; thus underground water is widespread and on the lower land is easily tapped in wells, many of which are artesian in character. The deposits building the plain have been warped and certain harder beds remain as zones of somewhat hilly ground, while elsewhere broad hollows tend to be waterlogged. For more detailed description, it is convenient to divide the lowland into :

> The Western Plain
> The Vistonís Lagoon
> The Eastern Plain

The Western Plain

The eastern shore of the Gulf of Kaválla, to Keramotí Bay, projects at right angles from the hill foot ; sandbars screen lagoons and make it smooth, but its trend is probably due to fracture, for it is aligned with part of the Thásos coast and is parallel to a large fault in the island. The straight shore is succeeded by the curve of Keramotí Bay, with flanking sandspits that give some protection to the anchorage. Beyond this and the strait between Keramotí and Thasopoúla island the real delta of the Néstos begins ; in antiquity the river mouth was some 9 miles farther east, close to Cape Baloústra. All this coast, like the delta itself, is intensely malarial. The villages, therefore, are well inland, except for Keramotí, and, at the western end, the new village of Néa Karváli was founded, despite official warnings, by Anatolian refugees who later suffered severe mortality. The inland villages, though healthier, also have a bad reputation for malaria, and the largest, Khrisoúpolis (Sarí Sabán), was the place to which the last Sultan was wont to banish political prisoners. Yet the new population in most villages was larger than the number of the previous Moslem inhabitants. In spite of the exchange, the aspect of the places has altered little, and the use of the land not at all, for the Turks had developed their agriculture here, as across the Néstos in Dhitikí Thráki, with the chief aim of producing the finest tobacco, and Greek refugees, mostly with knowledge of its culture, have continued the practice. Thus there is the same sequence of villages and farm types from hill foot to plain as on the eastern plain. The lowest fields and the swamps form the winter pasture of the Vlach shepherds, while the thickets and reed beds are the haunts of myriads of birds. The population west of the Néstos numbers 13,000 and the density is 135 per sq. mile.

Along the 7 miles of foothills, between the Néstos and Xánthi, there are nine villages of great interest to connoisseurs of oriental tobacco, since between them they produce from 500 to 700 tons of the very finest quality of leaf, the ' Xanthí-yaka ' of commerce. The mountain slopes are of limestone and the fine red soil with stony detritus, as well as the slope and exposure, give the best conditions for the crop. Presumably the growers, all Turkish except in one new village, have special skill, for physical factors are very similar both farther west and east. Just below, and on less steep and stony fields, ' Xanthí-kuchük-yaka ' is grown, of very good quality, but not so valuable as the ' Xanthí-yaka ' ; throughout the upper edge of the plain, tobacco is almost a mono-culture but it takes up less of the lower and moister land. With the tobacco fields, the striking features of the landscape are, first, the old irregular Turkish villages with gardens, fruit trees and mosques, in marked contrast with the bare and severely utilitarian Greek refugee settlements, built on the grid plan ; secondly, the considerable stretches of arid grassland on the higher parts of the plain, fit only for pasture ; and thirdly, perhaps, the number of storks—on their nests on the housetops or hopefully following behind the plough. These birds have always had protection from the Turks as killers of snakes and other vermin.

The settlement of some 11,000 refugees on farms in this part of the plain was not easy. At the hill foot, land was expensive and mostly cultivated ; farther from the hills the higher ground lacked sufficient water. It was found possible, however, to settle many in the areas alternately damp in winter and dry in summer by extending the old villages, most of which are on land of this kind. The lowest land was *tchiflik* domain, very damp and malarial, but good for cattle and buffaloes and for some crops. Here then, the new villages are found, built upon such hillocks as rise above flood level, and usually on the sites of the *tchifliki*. Thus the population on the whole is more evenly spread on the plain than it was in Turkish times. It numbers, east of the Néstos, 36,000, with a density of 148 per sq. mile.

The low bluff of Cape Baloústra was occupied in very early times by a large rectangular town of unknown origin but certainly destroyed by the Thracians and rebuilt as the Ionian colony of Abdera ; this possessed great commercial importance, but later under Macedon it declined, chiefly for political reasons ; a contributory cause may well have been malaria, of which there is literary evidence. Under Byzantium the small town of Polystylon occupied the same site, but now little of either town remains visible. The name Ávdhira, however, has been given to the nearest village, 3 miles inland on high ground. The local Turkish capital was Yenije, situated half-way from Xánthi to Vistonís and long the centre of the tobacco trade, although in a malarial locality. It is now simply a large village named Yenisaía, and with its 1,800 inhabitants has yielded place to the healthier Xánthi.

The Byzantine town of Xanthea grew up beneath a fortress on a crag, built to defend the exit from the Eskejé defile that was repeatedly used by invaders from Bulgaria. In Turkish times it was a mere village and was mainly a healthy summer resort for the people of Yenije. However, the place was clearly marked for dominance in the district ; possessing spring water, a well-drained site on the river fan, and finally, standing on the obvious bridge point for the railway. So gradually, the business and the cigarette factories of Yenije were moved there (Plates 60 and 61). Xánthi now has some 36,000 inhabitants of whom one-third are Moslem. The old oriental centre clusters round the market places and adjoins the quarter built about 1900, more in the European style, mainly for Moslem refugees from Bulgaria. Beyond these quarters lie the monotonous gridded streets of the latest Greek immigrants, more than doubling the extent of the town, which gained over 17,000 people by the settlement.

The Vistonís Lagoon

The Vistonís Lagoon must be regarded as an awkward interloper in the life of the plain since it is inaccessible from the sea, it interrupts land traffic except by two narrow passages, and its shores form a hot-bed of malaria. For all this, however, the valuable fisheries provide an important compensation. The combination of features bringing this about are unique. The fish are caught in the narrow and islet-studded gap between the sandspits that is bridged by the main Xánthi-Komotiní road. In these shallow passages fixed traps of woven reeds are erected from October to February. When the fresh-water affluents of the lagoon dry up in spring, sea water enters and with it huge quantities of young fish of several species. In the rich feeding ground of shallow warm water, growth is rapid, and the only toll of the fish is that taken by the numerous herons and pelicans of the marshes. Then, in November, the passage of the first deep depression produces the weather sequence that leads to the capture of the fish. Strong south winds drive in sea water, raising the level of the lagoon and also bringing heavy rain to the mountains ; turgid floods follow, together with cold northerly wind, and these combine to drive the fish to the strait, and their death. With the sea fish there come also large carp which have lurked in the fresher water of the marshes during the summer. Finally, Vistonís is an important source of eels for the German market from December to March when the home supply ceases there. The eels are caught either as they swim seawards at night or attempt to return at dawn. Their further fate is the result of Teutonic organization ; stored alive until ordered, they travel by rail in special tank wagons to Germany. During the winter eels are also taken by shepherds from Bulgaria, using spears and salting the catch. The profits of all these fisheries are shared between the Áthos monastery of Vatopédhi and the government, and the average seasonal catch amounts to some 12,500 cwt. of fish.

The Eastern Plain

The eastern plain differs from the western chiefly in the absence of large rivers and in the high coastal hills which dominate part of it ; this eastern area, which is shaped like a horseshoe, has a separate drainage system, sending one permanent river—the Filiourí—directly to the sea. The upper margin is for the most part quite different, since the straight fault-scarp that forms the abrupt mountain edge in the west comes to an end north of Komotiní ; in its place, around the horseshoe, is a zone of terrace land composed of conglomerates and weaker Tertiary sediments which merges more gradually into the higher slopes of crystalline rocks. The western half of this plain, however, mirrors the features of the Xánthi plain in general, except for the coast where several small islands have been tied to the mainland and to each other by wave-built bars that enclose lagoons ; those nearest to Pórto Lágo are used for the evaporation of salt. The sea bottom also shelves more steeply than farther west.

Prior to the Balkan Wars, the aspect of the plain was thoroughly oriental, in many respects recalling Anatolia. Much of it consisted of large estates, and while the *tchifliki* themselves and the Turkish villages were, and still are, picturesque in their tree-girt irregularity, much land was uncultivated save at considerable intervals. The semi-waste land, now greatly reduced, led to the erroneous impression that a steppe climate prevailed, and this was enhanced by the use of the camel as a beast of burden. Camels, though still used, will doubtless soon disappear, but during the war of 1916–18 about 250,000 of them are said to have been employed in army transport in western Thrace.

As in the plain of Xánthi, the land formerly little used was the highest, i.e. where water was lacking, so that the Settlement Commission, as a prelude to establishing some 17,000 immigrants, had to undertake the boring of many deep wells, again partly artesian, which gave much purer water than the shallow wells elsewhere. Then the settlers in the lower land had to be placed in old villages or in new ones in the malarial parts ; and hence arose the same sharp contrast already noted on the other plain, that of the bare new refugee ' diceboards ' with the old homesteads that seem to fit into the landscape ; it is the English ' bungaloid growth ' of the 1920's in acute form. More fundamental, however, is the change in the land itself : fallow land has virtually disappeared, for intensive farming is essential where the new inhabitants have to live from small holdings, and, over most of the plain, mosaics of cultivated strips penetrate the land of the Turks which shows little sign of agricultural change. The exception is the north-west corner, from the hill foot to the Pórto Lágo–Komotiní road, where refugees found practically no place, and this again includes the best tobacco land. In general the effect of these changes upon crop production has been, first, to increase the growing of wheat, a winter crop, as compared with those grown in summer in the fields subject to flooding, i.e. maize, barley, rye, and sesame, and secondly, to extend viticulture and to reintroduce cotton, both under government supervision. The agriculture of the terrace-land round the eastern bay of the plain shows minor variations from that of the smoother area. Much of this ground possesses very good black soil, which, however, is underlain by an unusual hard-pan that inhibits the growth of fruit trees. The population of the eastern plain, some 35,000, is nearly equal to that of the plain of Xánthi, but the density is much lower, 116 as compared with 148 per sq. mile.

Komotiní, like Xánthi, must have been founded in connexion with the fortress which guarded a route over the Rodhópi ; but the ruins of the acropolis are here 5 miles from the town, which is well away from the hill foot. In this case the Byzantine concern was partly the pass of Balkan Turesi ; but doubtless the town, then as now, was the market for the plain, and the old walls are still seen adjoining the business quarter. The Turks gave the place a typical oriental character, naming it Gumuljína, extending it on both banks of the intermittent river Bokloutzá, and converting churches into mosques. During the nineteenth century and especially with the coming of the railway, the town was greatly extended on the European pattern, both east and west, to house increased Greek and other elements, while the business centre was also altered. Finally, three separate refugee suburbs were added on the grid plan to house the 10,000 new arrivals who brought the population up to over 31,000, of whom half were Greek. This extension has rendered the water supply somewhat inadequate. Komotiní is the capital of Dhitikí Thráki and of the Rodhópi *nomós* (see vol. II, pp. 385–6). The proximity of the frontier made it a garrison town, and but for the arrival of the refugees this relation to the frontier would have retarded its growth ; under Turkish rule the trading region of Gumuljína extended far over the Rodhópi. Today it remains the local market for crops and stock, and there are woollen and leather manufacturers in the town ; the railway encourages the use of Alexandroúpolis as its sea port.

The railway and main road leading south-eastwards from Komotiní diverge and meet again before entering the defile through the coastal range of Chóban Dag to Alexandroúpolis, but from the corner of the plain a new road also leads directly over the summit to Makri. The Chóban, though a somewhat broken range of hills, is yet a climatic divide, as is evident from the vegetation. The northern and gentler slope has only the humble cover of phrygana type and Kermes oak, while the steep seaward face is clad in luxuriant maquis, and the villages of this outlying riviera are surrounded by fruit trees of many kinds, and especially olives. Among the existing place-names, Marónia, Mesimvría and Mákri are those of classical towns famous for their wines ; and the people of this southern slope have always been Greek. The vineyards which, like those of most of northern Greece, suffered from phylloxera during the wars, were recently being reconstituted. It would seem likely that this coast in the future will be a winter resort for people from colder Balkan lands, as Yalta in the Crimea is for the Russians ; the fine view of Samothráki is an added attraction, and even in summer the strong sea breeze mitigates the heat. The neighbouring town of Alexandroúpolis, however, would not belong to the group since it lies on the margin of another malarial region, the Évros marshes.

The Eastern Frontier Zone (Region E13)

Physical Characteristics

By the attainment of the Évros or Maritsa frontier in 1922, Greek territory came to include a portion of the greatest lowland in the Balkan Peninsula and, within it, the important bifurcation of routes at the elbow of the river. But the strategic point, the ancient fortress town of Edirne or Adrianople, was withheld from Greece and remains Turkish. Thus a tongue of Greece extends northwards over the end of the Rodhópi, and so includes a tract of the country most typical of Eastern Thrace and Bulgarian Rumelia. This comprises low, rolling, and largely treeless hills composed of soft sediments of Tertiary and later age, and many valleys often with a strip of flat floor, apt to be marshy for half the year ; the hills may be likened in general to the chalk downs of England. The simple pattern of the valleys is evidence of the geological youth of the drainage system ; and the Évros valley itself, below Edirne, dates only from the foundering of the land blocks that produced the North Aegean Basin. The presence of a hot spring with a spa at Loutrós, midway between Alexandroúpolis and Férrai, doubtless indicates the fracture that prepared this southerly course for the river.

It is owing to the structural origin of the gap between the Rodhópi and the hills bordering the Gulf of Saros that the Évros has not succeeded in building a salient delta. As it is, the river sand and mud have built up the narrowing depression, while the straight 15-mile line, from Alexandroúpolis to the sea cliff 7 miles south of Enez, approximates to the one-fathom line.

The Évros receives its last main tributary at a point about 20 miles directly north-east of its mouth, the distance by river being much longer ; this is the Ergene, draining Eastern Thrace. Some 5 miles below the confluence the river is crossed by the last road bridge leading from Péplos to İpsala, and forthwith begins to distribute its waters, meandering freely on an ever widening deltaic plain which at high flood disappears almost entirely under water. Above the Ergene confluence the Évros swings from side to side on a flood plain from 1 to 2 miles wide. Farther upstream there are many swampy tracts between one or other edge of the flood plain and the river bank which, as is usual in such rivers, has been raised by flood deposits. Moreover, in a reach of 17 miles there are, during floods, three parallel rivers instead of a single channel ; this stretch lies north of the bridge of the İstanbul railway, east of Dhidhimótikhon, up to the frontier near Edirne. Thus the Évros is a real barrier to communications, for it is the high water state which affects the emplacement of roads and bridges ; yet in most summers there are periods when the river may be forded at several points. It also forms a suitable frontier, though in detail there may be doubt about the boundary, since the main channel, especially in the lower reaches, changes its course. Two major right bank tributaries of the Évros are the Kizíl and the larger Árdhas. The Kizíl, from the point where it ceases to be the Greek boundary with Bulgaria, turns from its northward mountain course and flows east-south-east to Dhidhimótikhon on the Évros, for the last 9 miles on a flood plain of its own making. The Árdhas, on the other hand, has no plain normally subject to inundation ; this river, on leaving the mountains and crossing the frontier, spreads out upon a very broad sandy bed which is slightly sunk in the floor of its flat valley, a cultivated plain with a greatest width of 5 miles.

Land Utilization

The wooded mountain and plateau land that terminates the Rodhópi and separates the plain of Komotiní from the Évros has already been described (see p. 145). As a whole it has only a small population, but in the north-eastern valleys leading to the Évros this was not always the case. Here, depopulation was a result of the Second Balkan War, when the Bulgars in 1913 destroyed numerous villages. Twenty years later there had been no considerable reconstruction and the highlands west of Souflíon remained for the most part as the summer haunt of shepherds and charcoal burners.

By far the most distinctive country in the *nomós* of Évros is the large expanse of hill slopes, partly wooded but mostly open downland, which lies between the forested mountains and the flood plain of the Évros. Although it corresponds in some ways to the terrace lands of the basins of Makedhonía it is much more extensive than any of these, much less torn by gullies and less liable to ruin by torrents. This district has been noted for a hundred years at least for the continuity and excellence of its agriculture. It is particularly adapted by both climate and soil to cereal cultivation, but great attention is also paid to other crops including fruit trees in many varieties which are planted in open order among the fields. The mulberry predominates in the district between Souflíon and Dhidhimótikhon, since this is a great source of silk and the most productive in Greece ; moreover, the area has long been occupied by Greeks. The success of this old industry is evidence not only of the care devoted to it but also of the abundance of damp soil in the valleys and of the warmth of the air in April and May, bringing on the leaves to feed the growing caterpillars. The yield of leaves for the *nomós* in 1937 was 21,300 tons and the weight of cocoons over 400 tons. Wheat fields, however, dominate the landscape, occupying two-fifths of the agricultural land, followed by maize and barley ; tobacco, on the other hand, is unimportant. The *nomoí* of Évros and the Rodhópi have about the same number of cattle, grey beasts like those common on the Russian steppe, but in Évros their condition is notably better, doubtless on account of the pastures of the flood plain.

This region was the first to receive the flood of refugees who crossed the land frontier and, while many had later to be directed farther west, large numbers remained to swell the population of some fifty villages or towns. The single new town (as opposed to villages) in all northern Greece is Néa Orestiás, founded with over 3,000 inhabitants on the railway midway between Edirne and Dhidhimótikhon, a challenge to the importance of the latter and an offset to the old Orestiás or Karagach at the bridgehead of the former. These towns, as well as Souflíon and Férrai, stand well above the flood level of the Évros, on or above the terrace that carries the railway and the road. They are occupied mainly by farmers but have urban functions, and Souflíon has two silk-spinning mills. The town, as the centre of the silk trade, has long been Greek, and in 1911 had over 10,000 inhabitants ; it suffered however from the placing of the frontier at its door and declined seriously, so that in 1928 it had less than 8,000 people. Dhidhimótikhon clusters round the ruins of a Byzantine fortress that crowns a rock above the river Kízil, and was the residence of successive emperors and Sultans. But its glory has departed, and the life of the town, with nearly 9,000 inhabitants (mainly Greek), does not seem to be greatly affected by the advantage it possesses in relation to routes. Here, the main road up the Évros sends a branch along the Kízil valley to join the Bulgarian roads of the Arda (Árdhas) basin, while 6 miles to the east a road-bridge crosses the Évros ; it is also near to the junction town of Píthion on the İstanbul railway.

Férrai, the smallest of the towns, is built on a hillside overlooking the flood plain of the lower Évros. Under the Turks it possessed some administrative importance and for a time it had a commercial advantage over Dedéagach (Alexandroúpolis). While the railway from Edirne reached Dedéagach, the line afterwards built from Thessaloníki did not at first do so, since, in order to avoid the coast for military reasons, it penetrated the Irén defile with but two short tunnels and then turned into the hills, and with steep gradients reached the Évros at Férrai. In the war of 1916–18 the Bulgars seem to have expelled the Greek population of Férrai and by 1928, even after the refugee settlement, the population was still under 3,000. Alexandroúpolis is built on the grid plan at the western edge of the deltaic fan of an intermittent stream. It owes its growth to the railway which first reached it from Edirne in 1872. Its population of over 14,000 was mainly Greek in 1928. It is a seaport without a natural harbour, and the roadstead is exposed to all but northerly winds (see vol. II, pp. 269–72). The commercial function of the port, apart from a slight but regular coastal traffic, is the export of grain in August and September to other Greek ports. In the future, with an artificial harbour, with happier international relations, and with a large extension of its hinterland, Alexandroúpolis probably will play a much greater part in the trade of the Aegean.

The hilly section of the northern salient of this region has a population of 36,000, the majority occupying the valleys of the Árdhas and Kízil. The inhabitants of the Évros valley and the coastal strip, excluding Alexandroúpolis, number 47,000. The rather uniform density over most of this belt is 83 per sq. mile, but in the area nearest to Edirne it exceeds 200.

For Bibliographical Note, see p. 22.

Chapter VII

THE PELOPÓNNISOS

The Isthmus and the Threshold : The Mountains and Plains of Eastern Akhaía and Korinthía : The Peninsula of Argolís and the Adjacent Islands : The Plain of Argolís : Eastern Arkadhía : Western Arkadhía : South-eastern Pelopónnisos and Kíthira : The Lowlands of Lakonía : The Saddle of Lakonía : The Basin of Megalópolis : The Barrier of Cynúria : The Hills of Ilía and Western Akhaía : The Plains of Ilía and Western Akhaía : The Nédha Mountains : The Corridor of the River Arkadhéïka : The Kontovoúnia and the Peninsula of Messinía : The Basins of Messinía : The Taïyetos Mountains and the Máni Peninsula

The Pelopónnisos is one of the largest peninsulas of the Mediterranean with an area of 8,356 sq. miles and a population, in 1938, of 1,185,046. Its relief, structure and drainage are complex and varied. It is mainly a highland region ; more than half of the area is above 1,500 ft. in height and much of the lower land is rugged. The separation of the Pelopónnisos from the mainland, and its upheaval to present altitudes, are geologically recent events. Consequently, there are strong resemblances in structure and relief between the mountains of the Pelopónnisos and those of central Greece east and west of the Isthmus. The peninsula is unique in Greece in having an almost continuous coastal plain in the north-west but, although this extends for some 200 miles, much of it is very narrow. On the other hand, the three basin plains of Messinía, Lakonía and Argolís, each open to a gulf, are compact, isolated units. All but two of the rivers are short, and these exceptions, the Alfiós and Evrótas, drain a great structural depression in opposite directions. This furrow determines the three-fold division that was adopted for the brief physical description of the Pelopónnisos in Chapter I, vol. I of this Handbook.

The greatest of these divisions, the northern and eastern highlands, includes the bulk of the mountains and a specially large area that is without superficial drainage. Its form is due to the great fractures which surround it, and especially to those radiating from the north-west. The highest part is in the north, where the mountains run from east to west transverse to the folds of the rocks. In the south, on the other hand, the trends of the mountains and of the structure nearly coincide, running from north-north-west to south-south-east. At the end of the Pliocene period, i.e. perhaps a million years ago, much of the Pelopónnisos was still covered by a shallow sea or by lakes, and the rest was a land of subdued mountains or hills. The marginal sea or lakes covered thick deposits of soft rocks that had long been accumulating in the depressions. One of these depressions was the ancestor of the northern gulfs of Pátrai, Kórinthos and Aíyina, and lay a little farther north than its successors. Then the final breaking of the crust began, with uneven upheaval and subsidence of the various blocks ; the bottoms of the new gulfs sank, as the bordering land was thrust up. The northern mountains had their height increased by at least 5,750 ft. and the others by lesser amounts. The new land around the margins consisted mainly of the clays, marls, sands and conglomerates that had formed under the surrounding sea or lakes. Inland, much of the older rock was of limestone (Fig. 29). Before the period of uplift it had been saturated with water and was drained normally by rivers ; but following upon the upheaval, the water table sank to deeper levels, and these areas came to be drained only by subterranean channels. Such land became karst (see vol. I, Fig. 12).

Among the fractures that affected the interior of this region some run approximately from west to east and others from north to south. One of the former is of special importance because it led to the break in the mountains west of the Gulf of Argolís. Today, it provides the main route across the Pelopónnisos and is followed by the railway to Trípolis. Many of the more important fractures demarcate the various regions that have been adopted in this chapter for purposes of description.

The central corridor of the Pelopónnisos was described in vol. I of this Handbook as a single physical feature because it is followed by the two longest rivers, the Alfiós and the Evrótas, and because it is an almost continuous strip of lowland through the mountains. The term ' furrow ' would perhaps be more suitable than corridor, since the latter implies easy human movement throughout the whole length and this does not exist. Thus there is neither a railway nor a continuous metalled road from end to end. The river Alfiós has succeeded in penetrating the central barrier by way of a gorge, too steep and narrow to be followed by road or railway.

The corridor is, in the geological sense, a young feature, marking the dislocation of the folded rocks that make up the highlands. Most of the long hollow, therefore, does not coincide with these folds : in the north it cuts transversely across them, and in the south it meets them at very acute angles. But although its existence, geologically, has been short, four major periods in its history can be

Fig. 29.   The geology of the Pelopónnisos

For sources, see p. 22.

A, Acid lava (trachyte) ; B, Serpentine, diabase, porphyrite, gabbro ; C, Gneiss, mica-schist and other metamorphic schists ; D, Marble. 1, Sandstones, shales and conglomerates (mostly folded Mesozoic) ; 2, Red chert (flint) ; 3, Limestones (mostly folded Mesozoic) ; 4, Cretaceous and early Tertiary Flysch—sandstones and shales ; 5, Flysch conglomerates ; 6, Later Tertiary gravels, sands, marls, clays, recognized. Each has left its mark on the landscape, and it is through them that the corridor has acquired its present uneven floor, consisting of separate basins divided by thresholds or barriers.

(1) The oldest and greatest fractures produced the straight and high mountain side of Taïyetos, facing east, and also the bold edge of the mountains of Arkadhía, looking west to the basin of Megalópolis.

(2) Following the formation of the corridor by dislocation it was for a long time the bed of a lake, or perhaps two lakes. Next, it gradually became filled up, first with sand and then, as the mountain blocks began to be elevated, by coarse gravels brought down by the torrents. These streams built fans along the margins of the depression. As a result of this stage the lower slopes of the corridor in many parts consist of brightly coloured cliffs and gullies cut in the conglomerates (cf. pp. 185–9).

(3) When the lake finally dried up, rivers proceeded to cut away the lake deposits, and in due course began to work upon underlying rock. It is probable that the ancestor of the Evrótas at one time drained the greater part of the depression, and that part which it has since lost, the Alfiós has subsequently gained (see vol. I, Fig. 17). The saddle of Lakonía and the high terraces on the margins of the basins of Lakonía and Megalópolis were cut by rivers during this phase.

(4) Lastly, the most recent upheaval of the Pelopónnisos was accompanied by many violent fractures. They led to the relative subsidence of the plains of Ilía in the north-west, the basin of Megalópolis in the centre and the basin of Spárti in the south.

The relief of south-western Pelopónnisos, as in the rest of the peninsula, is due mainly to recent earth-movements involving large fractures. The area is still subject to severe earthquakes which have their origin in displacements along the eastern wall of the Ionian deep. This great submarine escarpment runs parallel and close to the south-west coast of the Pelopónnisos (see vol. I, Fig. 6). The trend of the rocks, all intensively folded, is approximately north to south. In general, limestones are less in evidence than elsewhere in Greece. This fact, combined with the relatively high rainfall, humidity and temperatures, make it the most favoured hill-country for cultivation in the Pelopónnisos. Moreover, although forests are restricted in area, the maquis often exceeds 12 ft. in height.

The landscape of the Pelopónnisos has been considerably altered from that of ancient times by the progressive deforestation of the

coniferous and oak forests, and, during the nineteenth century, by
the propagation of the currant vine on the western lowlands. The
very irregular distribution of population has always characterized
the peninsula. The cities of Corinth, Argos, Sparta and Messene,
each with its watered plain, were centres of isolated and populous
areas throughout the early history of Greece. These lowlands are
still well peopled and today, in addition, the north-western plain is
also a region of dense population. The highlands and part of the
lowlands are used chiefly for pasture, and in these pastoral areas the
population is sparse—from 50 to 70 per sq. mile. In the agricultural
lowlands, on the other hand, the density ranges from some 150 to
over 500 per sq. mile, the latter figure being reached where water is
specially abundant and cultivation most intensive.

In ancient Greece, the principal external connexions of the
Pelopónnisos cities were with the Aegean and the lands of the
eastern Mediterranean. But with Roman, and later Frankish and
Venetian, influences, the north-western lowlands came to be linked
more directly with the western world. In the nineteenth century,
the people of north-western Pelopónnisos began to exploit the
climatic advantages of their region by establishing the monopoly of
the currant in international trade.

For convenience of detailed description the Pelopónnisos is
divided into eighteen regions, of which the first seven are in the
north-eastern peninsula, six are in the central corridor and the north-
west, and the remaining five are in south-western Pelopónnisos
(Fig. 30). They are :

F1.   The Isthmus and the Threshold.
F2.   The Mountains and Plains of Eastern Akhaía and
      Korinthía.
F3.   The Peninsula of Argolís and the Adjacent Islands.
F4.   The Plain of Argolís.
F5.   Eastern Arkadhía.
F6.   Western Arkadhía.
F7.   South-eastern Pelopónnisos and Kíthira.
F8.   The Lowlands of Lakonía.
F9.   The Saddle of Lakonía.
F10. The Basin of Megalópolis.
F11. The Barrier of Cynuria.
F12. The Hills of Ilía and Western Akhaía.
F13. The Plains of Ilía and Western Akhaía.

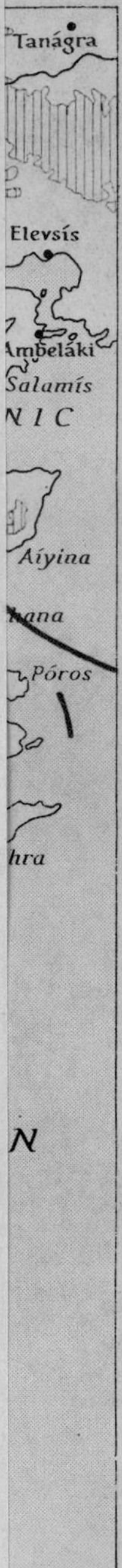

Tanágra

Elevsís

Ambeláki

Salamís

N I C

Aíyina

ana

Póros

hra

N

F14. The Nédha Mountains.
F15. The Corridor of the River Arkadhéïka.
F16. The Kontovoúnia and the Peninsula of Messinía.
F17. The Basins of Messinía.
F18. The Taÿetos Mountains and the Máni Peninsula.

THE ISTHMUS AND THE THRESHOLD (REGION F1)

Physical Characteristics

The great earth-movements that so profoundly affected the landscape of Greece were responsible for the formation of the Gulf of Kórinthos and the Saronic Gulf (Aíyina). In the region between the two gulfs, however, these movements were less pronounced, and just as the Yeránia mountains were left standing on the north, so the abrupt crag of Akrokórinthos (1,880 ft.) and the ridge of Ónia (1,970 ft.) were left on the south. They are joined by the Isthmus of Kórinthos which is composed of Pliocene marls and other weak strata. From the northern and southern shores of the gulfs, and from those of the Isthmus itself, the land rises inland in a series of easy steps, gullied by many wet-weather streams. The terraces are separated from one another by low, parallel fault-scarps. Transverse faults, well seen on the walls of the canal (see vol. II, Plate 84) have also affected the relief of the Isthmus.

Two valleys lead northwards to the Gulf of Kórinthos, crossing the threshold of the Pelopónnisos—the Lévkon to the east and the Longopótamos to the west. The Lévkon is the more accessible and its valley forms an easy route for the road and railway from Kórinthos. At Khiliomódhion the route turns westwards across the upper basin of the Longopótamos with its alluvial plain of Áyios Vasílios and then enters the lowest pass leading to the Plain of Argolís, with an altitude no higher than 750 ft. From here it strikes southwards along the deep valley of the Dervéni river.

Near the Isthmus the lower of the faulted terraces are covered with fertile alluvium, but the largest expanse of alluvium forms the coastal plain, known as the Vokha, which begins immediately west of Kórinthos. It is also the most fertile region since it receives silt-laden water not only from periodic streams but also from the Asopós. This river, augmented by canal water from Lake Stimfalía, is perennial and feeds the irrigation system on the plain.

Land Utilization

The higher parts of the Isthmus and its vicinity, formerly covered with pine woods, are now under sparse brushwood and thin phrygana that serve as winter pasture. The greater area, however, is devoted to wheat and barley, but the thin soils and scanty rainfall prevent heavy crops ; where the soils are better and deeper as, for example, near the upper edge of each terrace and along the stream banks, there are vineyards. The Isthmus, therefore, apart from Kórinthos and the Vokha, has only a moderately dense population. The pale silt of the Vokha is entirely cultivated with currants and tree fruits of many kinds, and there are over 16,000 inhabitants on this favoured plain. The largest village is Sikionía, with some 3,000 inhabitants, and once the rival of Corinth. The density of population on the Vokha is 417 per sq. mile, while that of the adjoining Isthmus, including the population of Kórinthos, is 267.

Kórinthos, until destroyed by earthquake in 1858, stood on the site of the ancient city on the high terrace below the acropolis— Akrokórinthos (see vol. I, p. 430). The new town by the sea, with a population of 9,944, has a grid-plan of broad tree-lined streets. The importance of Kórinthos rests, as always, upon transit trade, but in modern times this is slight. The ancient city grew upon the dues it levied on passage across the Isthmus, and it remained great as long as sailors avoided the journey around the Pelopónnisos ; hence its decline during the Middle Ages. The Isthmus has always been an obvious place to defend and a wall across it, parallel to the canal, has existed at least since 400 B.C. Its importance as a meeting place was marked by the Isthmian Games, held south of the wall.

The higher threshold to the south is thinly peopled except in the basin of Áyios Vasílios, the ancient Kleonae, where the red earth of the alluvial plain is productive both of cereals and of vines.

THE MOUNTAINS AND PLAINS OF EASTERN AKHAÏA AND KORINTHÍA (REGION F2)

Physical Characteristics

The three groups of mountains which dominate the northern Pelopónnisos, Erímanthos (7,283 ft.), Aroánia (7,726 ft.) and Killíni (7,792 ft.) stand in a west-east line 31 miles long. The peak of Killíni is only 13 miles from the coast ; the seaward descent from Aroánia is almost as steep, but from Erímanthos the projection of Mount Panakhaïkón extends northwards culminating at 6,322 ft., some 9 miles from Cape Dhrépanon. All three mountains are composed mainly of limestone, and their rugged peaks bear the traces

Plate 62. Akrokórinthos from the east

The limestone crag, bearing the acropolis, rises from weak Pliocene rocks cut by gullies. In the foreground are olive orchards.

[Facing page 162

Plate 63.   The isthmus of Kórinthos (Corinth) and the canal from the west

The regular fields of the coastal plain behind the strip of blown sand contrast with the less continuous cultivation and pine trees of the terrace-land elsewhere.

of former glaciation. In the western group the rock is light grey and fissured ; in the other two, this light grey limestone overlies a dark and massive type.

The three giants rise from a mountainous surface with maturely rounded summits, many of which are above 5,000 ft. This mature highland is broadest in the west where it includes Panakhaïkón. In the east the mountains come to an abrupt end along an almost straight escarpment that extends from Dhimínion on the Gulf of Kórinthos to Míloi on the Gulf of Argolís. This line is a marked geological boundary (Fig. 29). Relief, river systems, and water supply are all affected by the structure and character of the rocks. As well as the permeable limestones there are beds of reddish chert, greenish sandstones, shales and mica-schist. The whole system has been intensively folded and in Erímanthos many bands of chert and shales have a north-north-east trend giving abundant springs at their junction with the limestone.

It is the appearance of the less resistant rocks of the northern slope, however, which render these mountains unique in Greece. These consist of thick beds of conglomerate resting upon pale marls, sands and clays. They have been uplifted to great, but varying, heights. From the area of Mount Panakhaïkón they have been largely worn away and remain as patches up to about 40 sq. miles in area ; but from the river Vouraïkós eastwards they occupy almost the entire slope below 5,600 ft. The whole series has been broken by innumerable faults, in general running parallel to the coast. These have divided the rocks into slabs, arranged like a stair, some of the steps tilted forwards and others backwards. All this dislocation doubtless happened during earthquakes, of which the more recent are recorded. Thus in 373 B.C. Helikon, situated east of the Selinoús river, disappeared into the sea, and Bura on a coastal plateau was rent by a chasm. Torrential erosion has torn a labyrinth of canyons in the conglomerate, and ramifying ravines in the softer marl. The Kráthis, for example, emerging from a dark cleft in Mount Aroánia runs throughout in a canyon about 2,000 ft. deep. Rivers are recognized as agents of erosion in their names, for example Dhiakoptón means ' cut through ' and Fónissa means ' biter.' Yet some of the slabs remain intact, like the small plateau of Vrostína (3,966 ft.) near Cape Akráta.

The steep, parallel rivers flow directly to the sea, having cut their valleys deeper as the land rose. In flood, they build out fans on and beyond the narrow coastal plain, but all except the Vouraïkós dry up when the snow has melted. This river, the canyon of which is followed by a rack-railway to Kalávrita, has a wide and marshy valley in its upper course, and its source marks the lowest pass (c. 3,500 ft.) between the Erímanthos and Aroánia mountains (Plate 67).

Although most of the rivers flow directly to the Gulf of Kórinthos, the Pliocene conglomerates lying north and north-east of Killíni have been tilted ' backwards ' (i.e. southwards), causing curious drainage effects. Thus, from sources well to the north of Killíni, two rivers flow towards the interior, one on each side of the mountain. They enter depressions that are due partly to fracture and partly to solution of limestone. Each of the hollows is occupied periodically by a large lake which is drained underground. On the west the deep depression of Feniós has been nearly dry in recent years, but during various times in the past it has been filled by a lake some 25 sq. miles in area (Plate 64). The drainage of this basin is almost certainly westward to the Ládhon (see p. 175). The depression to the south-east of Mount Killíni contains Lake Stimfalía, and it is probable that the water from this lake partly nourishes the springs on the Plain of Argolís. Farther east is the parallel furrow of Phlius, drained by the river Asopós directly to the gulf (Plate 65).

Land Utilization

The three high mountains form the only considerable tract in southern Greece with a real mountain climate. They are under snow except during August and September. Precipitation is frequent and well distributed, and Mount Erímanthos is probably the wettest part of the Pelopónnisos. The summits therefore have swards with alpine plants and provide summer pasture for flocks. Below 6,500 ft. there are remnants of a once continuous forest of fir and Black pine ; lower down, these are mixed with deciduous and Kermes oak, while the natural vegetation of the lowest slopes and the coastal plain was Aleppo pine and maquis, with plane trees and oleanders along the river banks. The prevailing dark tints of these trees contrast with the brilliant red of the conglomerate and the blinding white of the marl in the ravines.

The great range of altitude has always offered variety of exploitation, but the rugged relief and the trend of the valleys inevitably limited movement. Except along the coast there is no continuous road or track across the ' grain ' of the country. On the other hand the towns and villages on the coast have always maintained the closest relations with their immediate hinterlands, by difficult

Plate 64.   The Feniós depression

The view shows the narrow northern part of the depression from the west.   The former lake bed, cultivated but without settlements, has a raised beach above the farther rim.   The foreground, and the saddle opposite leading to Lake Stimfalía, are composed of granite.   The slopes of Mount Zíria, on the left, and the other mountains are of limestone

Plate 65.   The canyon of the river Asopós

The view is south-west of Sikionía on the Gulf of Kórinthos, and shows eroded marls and sands, with some cultivation in the valley floor.

[Facing page 164

Plate 66. The monastery of Megaspílaion in the gorge of the river Vouraïkós The cliffs are of conglomerate. The buildings date from the 17th century and replace the medieval monastery. Above the cliff is a building which was used as a fort during the War of Independence.

though well-beaten paths. These tracks avoid the valleys and have no steady gradients. This is a land of seasonal change of habitation, where families may move as a whole or in smaller groups according to the work of the season. The narrow coastal strip is the only really flat land and it is not continuous : it exceeds 1 mile in width only in the part east of Aíyion. It is almost entirely given over to currant vines and to the drying floors of beaten earth. On marl, the currant fields also extend up the slopes to 1,000 ft., and in the higher vineyards the grapes are used for wine. Various tree-fruits are grown around the villages, where fine olive groves often mingle with the vineyards. The hill villages grow their own wheat and some maize, and may export pears, nuts and almonds. Caves, natural and hewn, are common features in the canyons ; many have been the homes of hermits, and the monastery of Megaspílaion in the Vouraïkós valley is justly famous (Plate 66). It is reached by railway from Dhiakoftó.

The total population of the region facing the gulf was some 71,000 at the time of the 1928 census, but a quarter of these were on the coastal strip, giving a mean density there of 288 per sq. mile. Elsewhere, except on the high summits, the figure is between 130 and 140, but in the basin of the river Kráthis the density falls to 49 per sq. mile.

Aíyion, with a population of 11,011, is the only real town and the only harbour on the coast. It stands on a marl cliff where excavated caves serve as reservoirs and stores. Kalávrita in the Vouraïkós valley is only a village of 1,790 inhabitants, but it is the capital of the highland eparchy. With its railway to the coastal plain it is becoming a popular summer resort amid the fir-forests. The village replaces the ancient Kynaetha, and nearby are the ruins of a Frankish castle commanding the gorge. A recent development is the working of lignite in the high exposure of marl that flanks the river valley.

Conditions of scenery and life are somewhat different in the district lying south and east of Aroánia and Killíni. The population of this region was about 37,500 in 1928 with an average density of 59 per sq. mile. Since almost the whole tract is of limestone, the deeply cut valleys—apart from the three basins of Feniós, Stimfalía and the upper Asopós—are usually dry, with widely separated springs. The villages are therefore far apart, most of them being placed high on the slopes of the valleys and basins. There is sufficient rainfall and soil to give a cover of fir-forest, but most of the trees have recently been felled. A virgin wood on Mount

Killíni, with moss and lichen on the trunks, bears witness to the moist conditions on the mountain. This south-eastern district depends largely upon its flocks, but on the valley floors and on outcrops of shale or schist, grain and some vines are grown. The three basins of Feniós, Stimfalía and the upper Asopós, however, have flat and moist floors covered with fertile loam, and all are cultivated (Fig. 32). The villages in these basins contain some 15,000 people, almost half the total, and about equally divided among the three. The largest plain is that of Feniós, at present nearly covered with wheat or maize crops ; but in 1888 it was occupied by a lake which oscillated periodically according to the state of two sink-holes. The villages, therefore, are on the slopes of the basin, amid their vines and fruit trees. The second plain is today half covered by Lake Stimfalía and again the villages are high, if only from fear of malaria. The basin of Phlius (the upper Asopós) is surrounded by escarpments of conglomerate. The chief village, Neméa, is famous for its wine : other villages to the north stand evenly spaced, where water emerges from the escarpment that forms the rim of the region. These three basins are all associated in legend with the activities of Hercules, who is said to have canalized the river of Feniós to a sink-hole. By order of the Emperor Hadrian, a tunnel was driven from Lake Stimfalía to an aqueduct leading to Corinth, and this still feeds the river Asopós, to the benefit of the coastal plain.

THE PENINSULA OF ARGOLÍS AND THE ADJACENT ISLANDS (REGION F3)

Though an obvious physical unit this region has never possessed a single name. The landward boundary of the peninsula on the north is formed by the sharp edges of a plateau, and both the road and railway from Kórinthos to Árgos lead westwards to avoid this obstruction. The straight northern edge of the escarpment extends westwards from Cape Spirí for about 23 miles. The region is extremely hilly and most of the plains are minute and lie on or near the coast. But the broader northern plateau differs from the more varied and more strictly peninsular section to the south. The dividing line follows the route from Návplion to Epídhavros, the only easy way across the peninsula (Fig. 31). The following account is divided into :

The Northern Plateau
The Southern Peninsula and the Adjacent Islands

Plate 67. Kalávrita from the north-west

Mount Aroanía is seen through the valley, which marks the southern limit of the Pliocene conglomerate.

[Facing page 166

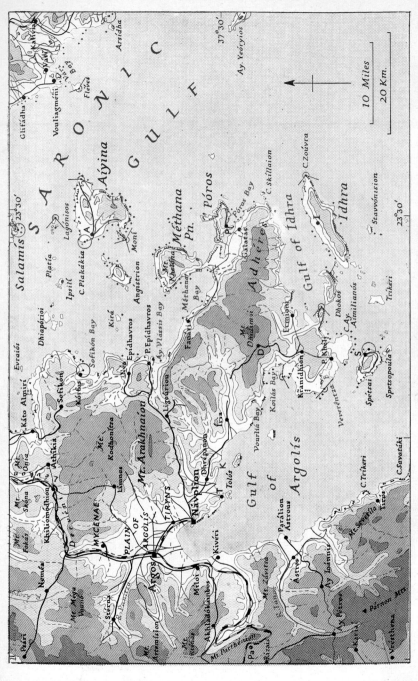

Fig. 31. The peninsula and plain of Argolis

Based mainly on the 1 : 250,000 G.S.G.S. Series 4088 : The Balkans, and the 1 : 100,000 *Epitelikós Khártis tis Elládhos.*

The Northern Plateau

The general level of the plateau in the central area is over 3,300 ft., rising to the Arakhnaíon mountains (3,629 ft.) along the southern rim. Elsewhere the plateau falls gently to some 1,700 ft. near the edges and then abruptly to the sea or to lowland. It consists of cream-coloured and semi-crystalline limestones lying in gentle folds from west to east. Although there are numerous deep valleys, the tracts between them clearly belong to a once continuous surface of erosion. Yet in detail there are all the rugged marks of typical karstic country, and the paths are extremely rough. The seaward parts still retain some of their forests of Aleppo pine, or they are covered with maquis ; but as a whole this is one of the barest and most forbidding tracts of Greece, and one where thin phrygana and Kermes oak rarely veil the rock surface.

So negative are the qualities of this plateau that it has no well recognized name. Although flanked by much used routes it is seldom visited by strangers. The vegetation affords meagre pasture for flocks, including many from Arkadhía which winter here. The population, numbering some 7,000, is divided among a few large villages, lying in upland hollows or in the upper valleys of small streams. In these basins there is often a red residual earth favouring the cultivation of grain and vines. The only village reached by a road from Kórinthos is Sofikón (population 1,786) where resin from the pines of the promontory is collected.

The Southern Peninsula and the Adjacent Islands

The remainder of the peninsula has all the characteristics of a faulted and tilted block. It rises on both sides from a deep sea and is tilted towards the south-west. Rivers have dissected the surface deeply and have emphasized the complexity of the structure. The rocks consist chiefly of massive black limestone which is closely folded and forms ranges of rugged hills, trending with the peninsula. Separating these ranges from the broad plateau to the north is a curving strip of lower land, marking an outcrop of shale and sandstone, and extending from the plain of Argolís to the coast at Néa Epídhavros. In the south-eastern corner of the peninsula, the Adhéres hills are also formed of shales and sandstones. Springs are limited in occurrence to the junction of the limestone with such rocks. The most celebrated is at the Sanctuary of Epidaurus, where the water, containing Epsom and Glauber's salts, may well have determined the site.

Most of the islands around the peninsula are composed of the same rocks, in varying proportions, but with limestone dominant. This applies to Póros, Ídhra, Dhokós, and Tríkeri, to the three small islands within the Gulf of Argolís, and to the hills south-east of Návplion—a former island now attached by the spread of alluvium. On the other hand, trachytic lava of recent age forms the tip of Póros island, and all of the peninsula of Méthana, except for the western and southern corners. The volcanic dome of Méthana is mainly composed of a coarse-grained rock, but in the north-west there is a cone, with its crater about 250 ft. deep, from which a stream of glassy lava extends to the sea. This is the result of the last eruption, in the third century B.C. Just east of this is a hot sulphurous spring (97° F. or 36° C.), and another occurs at Vromolímni in the south. The island of Spétsai and part of the neighbouring mainland are built of Pliocene conglomerate.

The climate is mild and dry and the limestone makes the surface largely waterless. As a result the vegetation is chiefly sparse phrygana, yielding to maquis on the impermeable rocks, with wild pear prevalent in the stony valleys. On Spétsai, Póros and the south-western headlands there are pinewoods, and Méthana has pines among its maquis. Ídhra and Dhokós, on the other hand, are bare. The mildness of the winter largely accounts for the influx of flocks from Arkadhía.

Agriculture is limited to a few interior lowlands and to several coastal plains. Among the former is the furrow across the peninsula. Centrally placed in it is the plain of Ligoúrion, drained southwards through defiles, and devoted to olive production. To the east is the tiny and almost enclosed plain named Ierón, with its famous sanctuary of Asclepius, the god of healing (see vol. I, p. 434). From it a gorge, with the Sacred Way, leads to the valley plain of Palaiá Epídhavros, well watered and growing citrus fruits. Within the hills, about 3 miles east of Koilás Bay, is the deep and circular depression of Dhídimoi, with its flat red floor under vines, grain, tobacco and olives. The majority of the people live near the coast. In contrast with the stony plain of the river Íria on the west, which is fit only for pasture, that of ancient Troizen, in the lee of Méthana and Póros, is covered with fine silt. Its well watered soils are under vines, citrus fruits and cereals. Screened from sea breezes, it is a hothouse in summer and somewhat malarious, but its lemon trees are most productive. Méthana, despite the steepness of its slopes, is partly terraced to grow vines and olives, watered from cisterns. In the south, hollows among the hills of conglomerate about Kranídhion have famous vineyards and olive groves, and the district is as famous for its honey as the narrow coastal plain east of Ermioní is for its olive oil.

The life of the south coast is dominated by the three towns Kranídhion, Pórto-Khéli and Ermioní on the mainland, and Spétsai, Ídhra and Póros on the islands. All are dependent on the sea and between them they largely control the sponge fisheries. Most of their inhabitants are descended from Albanian refugees of the fifteenth and sixteenth centuries (see vol. I, p. 362), and they are seamen and merchants by long tradition. From their ports, well sheltered and strategically placed, they developed their carrying trade from the Black Sea to the Atlantic, and in 1821 Ídhra alone had 4,000 inhabitants. Together with the people of Spétsai, they bore most of the initial cost of the War of Independence. With the establishment of security and the arrival of the steamship, much of their trade passed to Síros, which in turn had to yield to Piraiévs. The population of the islands has therefore declined steadily—to about 24,000 in 1889 and to 18,325 in 1928. This latter figure includes the Naval Training Centre at Póros.

THE PLAIN OF ARGOLÍS (REGION F4)

Physical Characteristics

The alluvial plain at the head of the Gulf of Argolís is roughly triangular (Fig. 31). It is bounded by fractures on both sides, but the steep escarpments have been worn back by the erosion of many streams. The mountains that enclose the plain consist mainly of limestone, and forward bastions of this rock are : (1) the acropolis of Árgos in the west, (2) that which has Mikínai at its foot, in the north-east, (3) the isolated massif near Návplion in the south-east. Tírins, too, stands upon a small and isolated limestone block. On the east of the plain, however, there are low hills of shales, and the northern rim is composed of Pliocene conglomerate. The plain is built chiefly of the alluvial fans of intermittent torrents. When these dry up there remains a steady flow of ground water, now tapped by some 2,000 wells. There is but one perennial river, emerging to the surface south-west of Árgos, and flowing only 3 miles to the sea. Alluvium has filled up the former strait between the hills of Návplion and the mountains and thus extended the plain to the coast at Tolós.

Land Utilization

Argolís merits its Homeric description ' thirsty '. The average rainfall is only about 20 in., of which three-quarters fall in the winter half year. Moreover, the variability is great. Vegetation is therefore meagre, and water must be used with care. Of the notable towns of ancient Greece, four stood at or near the eastern margin of the plain—Mycenae, Midea, Tiryns and the port of Asine, the latter sheltered by a promontory and the island of Tolós (Romví). The sea may also have reached Tiryns during Mycenean times. Árgos, in a central position, alone seems to have had a continuous history ; its original site was just north of the present town and below the strong acropolis. Nauplia (Návplion) was the port of ancient Argos and, although later deserted, it has been a fortified seaport at least since Byzantine times (see vol. II, pp. 303–4). Under Turkish rule it was the port of Tripolitsa (Trípolis), capital of Morea (Plate 68).

In spite of the disadvantages of malaria in the coastal swamp and of occasional drought, this plain has always been noted for its prosperous agriculture, and even under the Turks its exports were varied and considerable. The district suffered during the War of Independence, but a century of progress saw an increase in population from 17,791 in 1828 to 38,278 in 1928. In this census year the mean density of 399 per sq. mile was surpassed only on the plain of Messinía. The bulk of the inhabitants live in some thirty compact villages on the eastern side of the plain ; the western part, where it is not too dry, is cultivated by the people of Árgos, now a purely rural town of some 13,000 inhabitants. The refugee settlement of Néa Kíos was founded on the coast after partial drainage of the marshes. The upper, and drier, plain is used chiefly for the growing of wheat and barley. Elsewhere, there are large and well-tended vineyards and olive groves, but the favourite crop on the eastern side is tobacco, the rich but stony soil and the abundant wells ensuring a good crop. Finally, the demand for vegetables and melons in Athens is partly met from the watered gardens of the south.

EASTERN ARKADHÍA (REGION F5)

Physical Characteristics

This well defined region is one of the largest enclosed depressions in the Balkan Peninsula and it differs considerably, both in climate

Plate 68. Návplion, with the corner of the plain of Árgos

The Palamídi fort crowns the ridge on the left. In the foreground are vegetable and fruit gardens · in the background are the bare mountains west of the Gulf of Argolis.

[Facing page 170

Plate 70. The village of Langadhiá

The village, with over 3,000 inhabitants, rises for 650 ft. from a tributary of the river Ládhon ; the valley is deeply cut in shale. The plateau behind has a cap of limestone. Many of the households depend upon earnings made elsewhere in Greece.

[Facing page 171

Plate 69. The walls of Mantinea

The view is west-south-west towards the Maínalon mountains which are here completely deforested.

and history, from the other basins of the Pelopónnisos. The two parallel ranges that enclose it, 11 miles apart, are the Maínalon mountains (6,496 ft.) on the west, and the Artemísion mountains (5,761 ft.) on the east. The distance between the lower northern and southern rims is about 28 miles, but the line of the depression is continued northwards by the Stimfalía and Feniós basins (see p. 166). The average height of the floor of the basin is 2,070 ft. above sea level.

The surrounding mountains are of folded limestone, except in a part of the southern rim. The once continuous massif was broken by parallel faults and the intervening block sank. Rivers, working normally upon the lowered mass, produced an undulating surface. Then, with general upheaval and a sinking of the water-table, superficial drainage ceased and chemical solution prevailed. The basin is now in an advanced stage of karstic development, all but small fragments of the original floor—a sheet of rock about 1,000 ft. thick—having been dissolved. A fine-grained red-brown earth today remains, covering most of the floor. Across this surface, streams flow sluggishly towards the sink-holes which at times get clogged. As a result the plains have often suffered inundation and parts are undrained at present.

The basin contains several separate solution-hollows, more or less separated by rock barriers (Fig. 32). The larger group, in the south, forms the plains of the ancient Tegea and Mantinea, and merge into a single flat surface. The northern group forms the basin of Orchomenus.

The slopes of the mountains are scored by many ravines which carry torrents. The Artemísion mountains, of pale fissured rock, are distinguished from the Maínalon range, of black, massive limestone, by the great screes which line the slopes. On all sides there are many *doline* (enclosed hollows) of all sizes and at all heights, some making alcoves in the plain.

The water on most of the plains comes either from direct precipitation or from underground sources. Lake Táka overflows to a sink-hole at its southern rim, and the river Dholianá (Sarandapótamos) flows to a sink-hole in the east. The southern end of this plain marks the easiest way across the Pelopónnisos, because the passes to the east and west are comparatively low, less than 2,700 ft. They are the result of transverse faults.

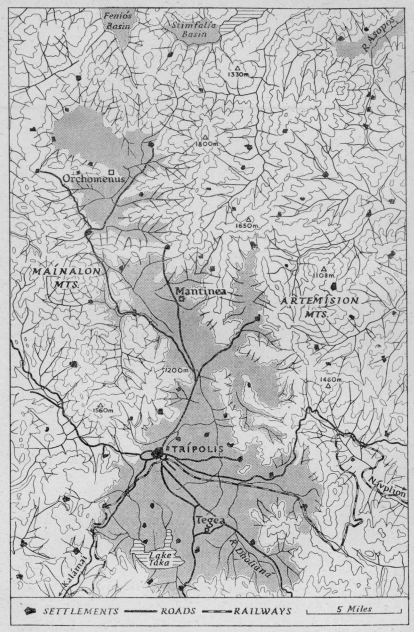

Fig. 32.   Solution hollows in the mountains of Eastern Arkadhía
Based on the 1 : 100,000 *Epitelikós Khártis tis Elládhos*, Sheets K.7 and Λ 7.
The floors of the solution hollows are shown by the stipple.   All the mountain
streams shown are intermittent.

Land Utilization

This region differs considerably in climate from areas open to sea influences. In winter, cold stagnant air often accumulates, thus explaining the abnormally low mean temperature for January at Trípolis (41° F. or 5·1 C.). The July mean is 75·6 F. or 24·2 C., giving a rather extreme range. In summer, there are frequent thunderstorms, especially in June, and the associated hailstones are sometimes big enough to kill sheep. The Maínalon mountains form a sharp divide between the wetter and the drier parts of the Pelopónnisos. The forest of fir which formerly clothed this range is still in evidence on the eastern slope ; but the Artemísion range and other ranges on the east are treeless, and are covered only by pseudo-maquis and phrygana. On the plains, once under oak woods, there is now little natural vegetation except for poplars, willows and reeds along the streams.

The inhabitants of these lands can be sure of their crops, provided that they prevent the sink-holes from becoming choked. The danger is surfeit, not scarcity, of water. Owing to the prevalence of malaria most of the villages are built on foothills or isolated crags. The houses are of stone, of two or even three storeys, with large balconies. Round the villages are deciduous (non-evergreen) fruit trees, especially the walnut—the olive being excluded by cold. Cultivation of the plains is directed chiefly to the production of wheat and maize, together with vines, tobacco, melons and vegetables. The wine made in this region is unusually light for Greece. Although the silk industry no longer flourishes here, mulberry trees are grown for their fruit and foliage, especially in the southern part ; the foliage is used as cattle fodder. On the damper parts hemp was formerly grown, not for the fibre but for the drug (*hashish*), which was a valuable source of revenue ; it was all exported. In view of its accessibility, the southern part of the basin has always been commanded by an important town. In ancient times this was Tegea, situated on the low hills separating Lake Táka from the larger plain. It had disappeared by the thirteenth century A.D. and was replaced a hundred years later by Trípolis.

The northern end of the larger plain was ruled from ancient Mantinea, whose walls stand close to the eastern edge of the plain (Plate 69). Its existence must have depended on the clearance of neighbouring sink-holes. The third of the ancient cities was Orchomenus, still farther north ; from its acropolis between two enclosed plains it was able to control the surrounding region, as well as the routes to Corinth on either side of Mount Killíni and that to western Arkadhía between Aroánia and Maínalon.

Trípolis was founded about the fourteenth century to replace these towns. Under the Turks, as Tarabolussa or Tripolitza, it became the seat of the Pasha of Morea, thus as the capital justifying its central position. Taken by the Greeks in 1821 and destroyed by the Turks in 1828, it was later rebuilt, and supplied with water from Valtétsi, 6 miles away. In spite of the towering slopes behind it, Trípolis is not an impressive town ; but it is important as a market and for its administrative functions as the capital of Arkadhía. Its traditional manufacture of farm implements, dependent on imported materials, has continued to the present day.

Including Trípolis, with its 14,897 inhabitants, the total population of these basins numbers about 40,000, of whom nearly 6,000 live in the northern basin of Orchomenus. The average density on the larger plain is 155 per sq. mile.

WESTERN ARKADHÍA (REGION F6)

Physical Characteristics

The most remote and inaccessible part of the Pelopónnisos is the mountainous region lying west of the Maínalon range and south of a line through Erímanthos and Aroánia. The northern area, though historically belonging to Arkadhía, is now part of Akhaïa. In general, the valleys are so deep that travel is difficult, and, in consequence, the region has always been isolated and backward. Most of it is drained by the river Ládhon, tributary of the Alfiós.

When viewed from any of the high peaks the general aspect is that of a maze of mountains and valleys. But survey and closer study reveal two facts : first, that if the deep valleys were to be filled in, the relief would be far from striking since the summits are rounded ; secondly, that the network of valleys forms a rectangular grid of lines approximately north-south and east-west (Fig. 33). The region represents an old worn surface truncating the outcrops of intensively folded and overthrust rocks. These trend roughly from north to south and are chiefly limestones. The general summit level, which gives uniformity to the landscape, lies between 3,600 and 4,000 ft. To the west of the Maínalon mountains, however, is the Frankovoúno range, in places exceeding 5,000 ft. Between these twin ranges of limestone is a deep and secluded furrow, drained southwards by the river Elissón and northwards by the lower course of the Maloítas.

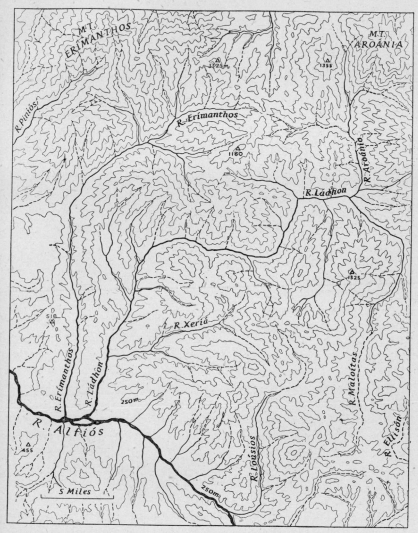

Fig. 33. The drainage pattern of Western Arkadhía

Based on the 1 : 100,000 *Epitelikós Khártis tis Elládhos*, Sheet K.6.

The rectilinear pattern of the drainage has been determined mainly by great faults running from north to south, and from east to west. The source of the river Ládhon lies just off the map, a few miles east of its confluence with the river Maloítas. It begins in the great *kefalaria* of tepid water that emerges from the limestone and is presumably the outflow of the Feniós Basin. The contour interval is 250 metres. In general the summits of the hills are smooth and rounded and represent the remnants of an old, worn surface.

Land Utilization

In contrast to the regions east of the Maínalon mountains there is here an abundance of permanent rivers fed by numerous springs. The amount of rain and snow everywhere exceeds 30 in. per annum, especially on the higher mountains. Summer thunderstorms and late autumn rains followed by snow are features of this mountain climate. On all gentle slopes there is a good soil cover and the natural vegetation is comparatively luxuriant. Originally there must have been continuous forests of fir on the higher slopes and deciduous oak on the lower. Conifers still largely clothe the two high ranges in the east—on the Maínalon up to 5,570 ft. Remnants of oak forest are much more widespread, but generally they occur as mere groves. Replacing the forest, Kermes oak is found, sometimes as open woodland, but more generally as bush. Most of the plateaux have in summer a carpet of herbaceous plants along with the woody growth.

Western Arkadhía is predominantly dependent upon its flocks, the chief product for export being cheese. Nevertheless nearly all the numerous villages are continuously occupied, although shepherds spend the winter elsewhere. The greater number go to Argolís, since so much of the lower pastures of Ilía have been replaced by the currant vine. But the inhabitants manage to grow most of their own food, for while the cultivable land is not extensive it is well distributed. It consists mainly of terrace land built of detritus, and is found wherever the valleys are not actually canyons. Thus it is prominent along the two east-west depressions in the north and in the north-south valleys of the Maloítas and the Aroánia (Fig. 33). In smaller valleys, steeper detrital remnants are terraced for cultivation. In such places, wheat, barley, maize, beans and vegetables are grown, with vines, walnuts and deciduous tree-fruits.

This highland in the past must have been seriously overpopulated, for under Turkish rule it was a refuge and immigration from other parts of the Pelopónnisos was doubtless continuous. Hence, with the coming of national freedom, there was a return to more profitable lands. The outward movement was accelerated by the development of currant production in the lowlands of Ilía. Arcadians travel far as skilled artisans but, like many mountaineers, they tend to return to their birthplace, and the appearance of the villages and the comparatively high standard of comfort indicate the presence of income not earned locally. The settlements are commonly perched high on valley slopes, near springs, and are therefore found along

[*Facing page* 176

Plate 71. The village of Dhímitra (Dívritsa)

The village has about 1,000 inhabitants and faces south in the middle valley of the river Ládhon. The terraced fields mark a patch of detritus clinging to the slope.

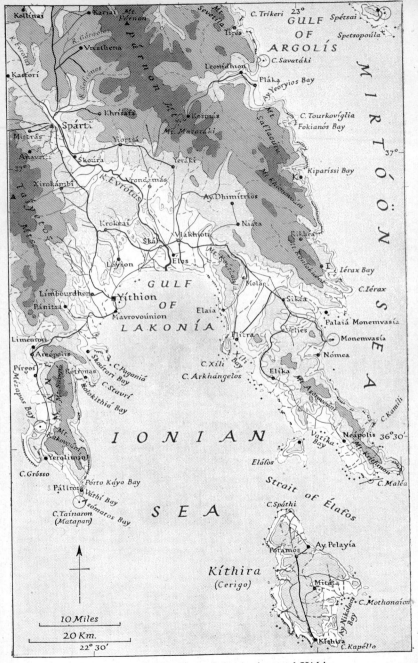

Fig. 34.   South-eastern Pelopónnisos and Kíthira

Based mainly on the 1:250,000 G.S.G.S. Series 4088 : The Balkans, and the
1:100,000 *Épitelikós Khártis tis Elládhos*.

K. Kiparíssi.   For key, see Fig. 9.

the junctions of limestones with impermeable rocks. These spring lines are associated with the narrow belts of chert, north of the river Ládhon, and the larger areas of greenish sandstones and shales to the south. Very few villages are on the river banks from fear of flood or malaria. Magoúliana (4,290 ft.) in the Frankovoúno mountains is said to be the highest village in the Pelopónnisos. Its climate and woods and the fine view of the Maínalon across the basin of Vitína have favoured its development as a summer resort, and Arkadhía may well develop a tourist industry.

The relief has not encouraged the growth of any central town ; indeed the largest places, Langádhia (3,049 inhabitants) (Plate 70), Trópaia (2,234), Dhimitsána (2,010) and Ipsoús or Stemnítsa (1,346), are not real towns. They are all near the southern edge of the mountains and overlook the central corridor of the Pelopónnisos. The higher northern area, however, is more densely populated, with 114 per sq. mile. It is less deeply dissected ; the summer pastures are richer and emigration has probably been less. In the eastern belt of the region, which has the highest mountains, the density is about half as great.

SOUTH-EASTERN PELOPÓNNISOS AND KÍTHIRA (REGION F7)

South-eastern Pelopónnisos is a wedge-shaped highland, some 1,300 sq. miles in area. It extends from the southern rim of the basin of Trípolis to Cape Maléa, 75 miles to the south. The region is dominated by Mount Párnon, 6,350 ft. above sea level. The general outline of the area has been determined by two nearly parallel fractures separating it from the sea and the valley of the Evrótas. Before being thrust upwards between these dislocations its surface had been worn smooth, and such ruggedness as it now exhibits is the result of later erosion. The character of the coast-line, however, shows that there has been subsequent depression, especially in the peninsula (Fig. 34).

The folds of the rocks, except in the peninsula, trend south-south-east, continuing those of eastern Arkadhía. The axis of the Maínalon range is continued in the Párnon mountains, and the folds of the Artemísion mountains are prolonged to meet the coast obliquely. The whole area, apart from the margins and the peninsula, is remarkably uniform in its relief. It is a worn-down and extremely monotonous surface, dissected by youthful valleys, with the Párnon ridge rising gently from it. Both sides of the ridge still have forests of fir and Austrian pine. Elsewhere, oak-woods, once prevalent, have been largely replaced by Kermes oak, phrygana and maquis.

It is convenient to describe the region under six subdivisions, each of which possesses local physical characteristics. The subdivisions are :

The Northern Basins
Skiritis and the Western Slopes
The Párnon mountains
Kinouría
The Peninsula
Kíthira

The Northern Basins

The basin of Arkadhía is bounded on the south by an intricate series of hills and valleys where the rocks are broken by great transverse faults. These same faults explain the existence of two small basins at the southern foot of the Maínalon and Artemísion mountains respectively—the basins of Frankovrisis and Akhladhókambos. The plain of Frankovrisis is named from the ' spring of the Franks ' which emerges at its edge and is the source of the river Alfiós (see p. 186). The smaller plain of Akhladhókambos in the east is skirted by the railway that runs from Míloi on the Gulf of Argolís westwards to Trípolis. The large village of Akhladhókambos stands on the main road on the northern edge of the plain, high above the fields of grain and the olive trees. Arid limestone slopes flank the plain on both sides, but water flows vigorously from the foot of the mountains directly to the sea at Míloi.

Skiritis and the Western Slopes

The rivers from the Párnon mountains tend to flow westwards to the valley of the Evrótas, but farther north they are directed towards the plain of Trípolis. The watershed between these west and north flowing rivers is ill-defined and the area was long debated between Sparta and Tegea. Its ancient name was Skiritis ; today it forms part of southern Arkadhía and has no general name. Throughout the western slopes of south-eastern Pelopónnisos, and in Skiritis, the chief distinctions of scenery and life depend upon the water-supply. North of the latitude of Spárti, mica-schists are dominant and nearly all the villages are sited on this rock or on shales and sandstones in the hollows of Skiritis. The landscape tends to appear reddish from the weathered schist, but there are remnants of oak-wood, and cultivated areas are considerable. The villages are large, with fruit orchards set close by. On the other hand, the hard lime-stones that form the steeper slopes and the plateau are but thinly veiled by Kermes oak and phrygana. Southwards, the desolation is increased because the outcrops of schist are much smaller, and on these again the bigger villages are found. From the higher settle-ments people go to the plain of Spárti, either for the winter or to help with various harvests ; others are itinerant artisans, away for most of the year. The whole belt contains about 20,000 people and the mean density is 50 per sq. mile, but is higher in the north than in the south.

The Párnon Mountains

This residual ridge, rising from a plateau, is impressive because of its isolation rather than on account of its height. Only on the east does it present bold precipices. Yet for 15 miles the summits are above 5,000 ft., the highest being 6,350 ft. The northern part is composed of blue-grey marble of coarse texture, with some mica-schist ; the southern part consists of the same dark limestone that flanks the ridge on both sides. Above the fir woods, which in places rise to 5,900 ft., alpine grasses provide valuable fodder, and the whole mountain is lined by sheep tracks.

Kinouría

The coast from the high bluff south of Míloi to Cape Iérax is as bold as any in Greece. It is the steep edge of a typical karstic plateau that has been broken by a fault. The disappearance of the eastern part by foundering has caused the underground water of the remainder to flow steeply to the sea, and this has made the surface more waterless than ever. In many cases caverns have become unroofed to form canyons. The greater part of this coastal plateau still remains, however, as the smoothed surface of erosion truncating the folded rocks. It slopes gently, from the foot of Párnon at 2,600 ft., to 1,970 ft., but is warped upwards nearer the sea which it overlooks in places from nearly 4,000 ft. (Plate 72). In the south, where the Párnon ridge is much lower, the canyons are directed westward from the coastal summits and end in deep *doline* on the lowlands bordering the Gulf of Lakonía.

The inaccessibility of Kinouría has led to the preservation in the northern part of Tzakonian speech, a dialect derived from ancient Doric (see vol. I, p. 322). Intercourse between the coastal settlements is by the sea, and some of the people on the plateau are more in touch with the plain of Lakonía than with the coast. Agriculture in Kinouría is almost limited to the deep valley mouths near the sea, where alluvium, water and warmth favour Mediterranean cultivation. Fields of grain are sometimes found on the plateau, the best in the *doline*, the worst, with miserable return, among the stones. On the high land, however, flocks are the mainstay, together with the gathering and peddling of plants for drugs and dyes. Conditions are a little better in the north where there is the considerable deltaic plain of Ástros. The rich loam soils of the plain, watered by the river Tános and by abundant springs, grow cereals and olives. But the land is malarial and the modern village of Ástros is less important than Áyios Ioánnis, 8 miles up the valley. Together they have some 1,600 inhabitants. A former islet, joined to the plain by alluvium and crowned by a ruined fort, shelters the anchorage of Parálion Ástrous. This northern district around Ástros supports over 15,000 people and has an average density of 106 per sq. mile.

The remainder of Kinouría is three times larger and has almost the same population. Leonídhion, at the mouth of a very narrow gorge and with a tiny olive-girt plain, is the largest settlement with 2,906 inhabitants. It is the capital of the eparchy of Kinouría and largely depends for its wealth on the success of its merchants abroad. The fir-covered plateau rim above Kiparíssi is 4,200 ft. above sea level and the precipice overlooking the village is 3,500 ft. high. There is no canyon here and only a minute plain with olive and locust trees. The bay is sheltered and is used for the export of locust beans. Behind Iérax, farther south, the same products are raised in a deep valley. Both the valley and the bay are completely sheltered from the open sea and represent a partly submerged *dolina*. The rugged hills behind this southern promontory are a haunt of wolves.

The Peninsula

The peninsula has a much more varied landscape than the remainder of the region, not only because its milder winter leads to a more luxuriant growth of maquis, but also because it includes several plains. These are underlain by weak Pliocene sediments whereas the upland surface is composed of mica-schist and massive black or grey limestone. The highland descends abruptly to the sea on the east coast ; and on the west, groups of flat-topped hills fall steeply to the Gulf of Lakonía. Their continuity, however, is broken by the plains of Moláoi in the north and Vátika in the south. On this coast, marine abrasion platforms at 330 ft. and 130 ft. indicate a former submergence followed by halting emergence, and the ruins of buildings several feet under water point to a sinking of the land in historical times.

The population numbers 21,000 and the mean density is about 70 per sq. mile, but the terminal part, Vatíka, is more densely peopled because, like the similar point of Argolís, it forms the home of sailors.

The scenery of the east coast is like that of Kinouría on a smaller scale. A gap in the hills opposite the large bay of Palaiá Monemvasía carries the main road from Moláoi to Monemvasía. The plain at the head of the bay, covered with wheat, vines, olives and locust trees is flanked on the north by a bluff bearing the acropolis of Epídhavros Limíra. On the south, Monemvasía stands on a high rock projecting a mile to sea and joined to the mainland by a low isthmus. This stronghold, originally a refuge of the Epidaurians from the Slavs, was later fully built by the Franks whose structures remain as monuments to its importance. Profiting by the decline of Corinth, it flourished under the Venetians as the centre of Levantine trade, but it fell from glory under the Turks. Memory of its commerce is retained in the names of its wine—Malvoisie or Malmsey—corruptions of Monemvasía. The present village, with barely 600 inhabitants, is far from filling the medieval walls.

On the western side of the peninsula, the plain of Moláoi comes to the sea along the shores of Xíli Bay. It broadens inland towards the lower end of the Párnon ridges. The origin of this triangular hollow is partly due to the solution of the surrounding limestone, which underlies the non-resistant sediments. These consist of white marls and permeable calc-sandstone known locally as *pori*. Hence the ancient name, Levka (white), of the plain. The southern part is dissected and hilly and is under orchards of fig, olive and locust trees, vineyards and wheat. The flat northern part is covered with sticky loam and is watered from alluvial fans and is imperfectly drained to sink-holes ; here, wheat and maize are grown. The villages stand around the edge of the plain, the chief being Moláoi, capital of the eparchy, with over 3,000 inhabitants.

South of the limestone crag of Cape Xíli (1,050 ft.), the coast and all the inland hills are patchily cultivated for grain, vines and olives. Near the island of Eláfos, limestone reaches the coast, and at its contact with schist yields iron-ore that has been worked intermittently since ancient times. Elafónisos or 'Stag Island' is a triangular slab of dark limestone, 715 ft. high, with its western cape cut by cliffs and its slopes notched by raised beaches. It was once part of the mainland, and sunken ruins in the straits are witness of subsidence in historical times. The islanders are mainly shepherds. The plain of Vatíka to the south is formed by flat-bedded *pori* rocks, greenish-grey in colour, but covered with reddish sand. It is similar in height and origin to the plain of Moláoi. The soil is not naturally very fertile but, watered from numerous wells, it is fully cultivated with grains and vines, olives and other fruit trees. On the slope near Neápolis, and indeed wherever an irrigating spring exists, onions are grown successfully. Vegetable gardens and fruit trees, including the orange, surround the many villages of the hilly peninsula of Cape Maléa. Neápolis is the chief settlement, with 1,750 inhabitants. It stands on the site of the ancient Boiai, but the modern village is less than 100 years old. It represents a deliberate concentration of the majority of the seamen of Vatíka near a safe anchorage for coasting vessels. At this place the cable to Kíthira leaves the mainland. Sponge fishing is practised in shallow waters around the cape.

Kíthira

Kíthira is related in structure to the Párnon Peninsula, from which it is separated by a strait 10 miles wide and everywhere less than 165 fathoms deep. The island is 18½ miles long and 11 miles wide ; the greater part is over 1,000 ft. above sea-level, the highest point rising to 1,658 ft. close to the west coast. Kíthira is known to have been occupied by the Phoenicians for the prosecution of the 'purple fishery', and presumably it has had a settled population ever since. The ancient capital was situated on a crag overlooking Áyios Nikólaos Bay, and here, in a church, are the Doric pillars of the famous temple of Aphrodite of Kíthira.

In general, the surface of the island is that of a smooth and high plateau. The seaward slopes are steep, and at the foot they are undercut in most places by the sea. The main physical feature is a broad ridge of dark limestone running from north-west to southeast. On its flanks there are precipices ; within it are grottoes, and where the limestones meet the sea the coast is indented. The western slope is seamed by straight ravines, but without corresponding inlets. The eastern promontory of the island marks the end of another broad ridge, parallel to the first and attaining 1,475 ft. Between the two ridges the lower country has been eroded from rocks of Pliocene age, chiefly marls and sandstones. It descends in terraces to Áyios Nikólaos Bay in the south-east.

The island has a typical Mediterranean climate, with very little rain between April and September and with an average of only thirty-seven rain-days in the other six months. Whatever its original vegetation, Kíthira is now without natural woods, and the bush varies in character between maquis and phrygana. The bare appearance of the island from the sea is somewhat misleading ; the interior plateau has large numbers of orchards, many of them irrigated from springs or wells, and yielding exports of fine oil, figs and oranges. Grapes and melons are also sent abroad. Wheat and barley are grown for home use ; cheese, made from the milk of sheep and goats, and honey, for which the island is famous, are exported. The fisheries also are productive, and the catching of quails during migration is an important source of revenue to the islanders.

The distribution of population is unlike that in most of the Pelopónnisos. The settlements comprise over 100 villages or hamlets, the majority with less than 100 inhabitants. All but a few lie in a north-south strip along the plateau and are linked by winding roads made or improved during the British occupation (1815–64). Roads also lead down to landing places at Ayía Pelayía and Dhiamófti on the east coast, and to Milopótamos on the west coast. The capital of the island is Kíthira, dominated by a Venetian fortress and with a population of 907. Below the town is the small harbour of Kapsáli.

In the past century there has been a considerable change in the population of the island. At the end of the British occupation it numbered some 13,000, but in the following period much emigration took place, and in 1900 the population was only 6,000. By 1928, however, it had risen to 8,770, giving an average density of 85 per sq. mile.

The narrow, rocky island of Andikíthira, or Cerigotto, lies 17 miles to the south-east of Kíthira and has an area of 8 sq. miles. It rises to a height of 1,230 ft. on its south-western side, and has a sterile aspect except for the cultivated inner valleys. The coast consists of steep, inaccessible cliffs and the only port is Potamós (see vol. I, Plate 47), 1¼ miles south-east of Cape Kefáli, the northern extreme of the island. According to the census of 1928, Andikíthira had a population of 322, living in 12 villages or hamlets. Of these, only Potamós and Galanianá have over 50 inhabitants.

The Lowlands of Lakonía (Region F8)

These lowlands consist of three distinct parts :
The Low Plateaux
The Coastal Plain of Élos
The Plain of Spárti

The Low Plateaux

From the southern part of the Taÿetos chain the plateau of Vardhoúnokhoria extends eastwards for 5 miles and bounds the plain of Spárti on the south. It is composed of folded limestones and mica-schists, with intrusive igneous rocks ; but because it is part of the former smooth floor of the corridor, Pliocene marls partly cover these hard rocks. The altitude of the plateau is nowhere more than 1,600 ft. The river Evrótas runs first in a shallow canyon along its eastern edge and then cuts a winding course through it. To the east of this hilly plateau is a lower tableland of different aspect. It is composed of beds of Pliocene conglomerate, of marl and of *pori* sandstone. The surface, once smooth and tilted southwards, is now cut by numerous parallel ravines.

The plateau of Vardhoúnokhoria is a varied district with sharp alternation of bush-covered hills and fertile hollows. There are patches of Valona oakwood, a source of revenue from tanning material ; many mulberry orchards recall that the silk industry of Morea was most persistent in Lakonía ; and wheat, olives and vines are plentiful. The southern part is the borderland of Máni (see p. 201), and tower-like houses are common. Yíthion (formerly Marathousi) is the seaport for the whole Evrótas valley and is approached by a main road that crosses the plateau along the foot of the mountains. As the chief port of Lakonía, Yíthion has a long history. Its ancient neighbour inland was Krothai, near which the Romans worked the green porphyry rock as a much prized ornamental stone. The modern town, built on a sloping site, is the capital of an eparchy and has a population of 6,700 (see vol. II, p. 305). The eastern tableland is largely barren, but the lower hills, of *pori* and marl, are partly under cereals. The villages in this district are situated at the foot of the Párnon slopes.

The Coastal Plain of Élos

The name of this coastal plain, Élos (swamp), has passed into history in the appellation of the slaves of ancient Sparta (Helots). The fine silt and the ground-water combine to produce immense reeds and there are still some scattered oaks. This natural vegetation has been largely replaced by intensive agriculture. Water for irrigation is obtained from the Evrótas and also from the *kefalaria* at the limestone edge, and productive orchards, including orange and lemon trees, are the result. With recent improvements in the management of this water, excellent cotton is grown and new villages have arisen, among them Élos. The population of the little plain is about 5,500 and the density 142 per sq. mile.

The Plain of Spárti

The ancient name ' hollow Lakedaemon ' is an apt description of the plain of Spárti. The edges of the plain are sharply defined. These are : (1) the short transverse scarp of the Vardhoúnokhoria in the south, (2) the fault-scarp of the Taïyetos mountains on the west, and (3) the parallel fault-scarp of the Párnon mountains on the east. The latter, while much the lower, rises from 600 to 1,000 ft. above the plain. It is composed of yellowish sandy marl but is generally capped with bright red conglomerate. Since it has been torn by deep ravines it presents, in the strong sunlight, a striking background to the greenness of the vale, and especially to the trees lining the Evrótas. Near the river are several hillocks, each crowned with a pink-washed chapel. Some of them were the sites of ancient settlements.

In the northern part of the plain, the alluvial fans of the torrents from Taïyetos slope gently and the abundant water from the mountains can be used almost everywhere. This water and the great heat bring prosperity to the gardener. In the southern part, the tributaries are somewhat incised, leaving an undulating surface. To the traveller this plain appears mainly as a high orchard in which olive trees are interspersed with quince, mulberry and orange. But beneath and among these fruit trees, vast quantities of vegetables are raised, and on many fields maize succeeds wheat or barley in the same year. Vineyards may also be seen against the lush background of poplar, willow, reeds or oleander that line the streams, or against the cypresses near the farms. The richness of this plain is surpassed only by that of Messinía, where there is a more maritime climate.

Spárti, refounded on the outskirts of the ancient city near the
Evrótas, is a small town with a population of 5,800. Its straight
streets are lined with acacias and eucalyptus. It is mainly an
agricultural market and the administrative centre for the *nomós* of
Lakonía. The ruined and medieval Mistra, which now gives its
name to a large fruit-growing village below, remains a monument
of Byzantine architecture. It was built in the thirteenth century
under the shadow of a fortress on the slope of Taïyetos, 1,200 ft.
above the level of the plain (Plate 73).

THE SADDLE OF LAKONÍA (REGION F9)

Physical Characteristics

The plateau of Skiritis (see p. 178) sinks westwards to a lower
plateau, here called the saddle of Lakonía. It separates the plain
of Spárti from the basin of Megalópolis, and, as an upland block,
it forms the floor of the central corridor for a distance of 18 miles.
Near the northern end of the plateau, the alluvial plain of Frankovrisi
forms the only stretch of really flat land. It is drained by the
Alfiós which cuts a gorge, followed by the railway, to the basin of
the Megalópolis. In the southern end of the plateau, the upper
Evrótas and its tributaries have formed a maze of ravines that make
the area difficult to cross (Fig. 35).

Land Utilization

The significance of the saddle of Lakonía is due to its function
as a crossways, but, as yet, modern routes do not make full use of
it. The only existing motor-road out of Lakonía runs due north
from Spárti, over the plateau of Skiritis, to Trípolis. A very poor
road does, however, connect Spárti with Kastorí, Longaníkos and
Megalópolis, and a future railway is likely to take the same course.
From east to west the plateau already carries the road and the
railway from Trípolis to Messíni.

The most favoured districts are in the north and south ; first,
the plain of Frankovrisi, where the prosperity of the villages is
dependent upon the excellent vineyards, wheat fields and orchards
of olives and mulberries ; secondly, at the foot of the northern
Taïyetos is an equally prosperous upland, almost continuous with
the plain of Spárti.

Plate 72. The high coast of Kinouría at Pláka, the small port of Leonídhion

Plate 73. Mistra and the plain of Spárti
In the foreground are the medieval ruins and, below them, is part of the modern village. On the right are the slopes of Mount Taíyetos and in the distance, to the south-east, is the plateau of Vardhoúnokhoria.

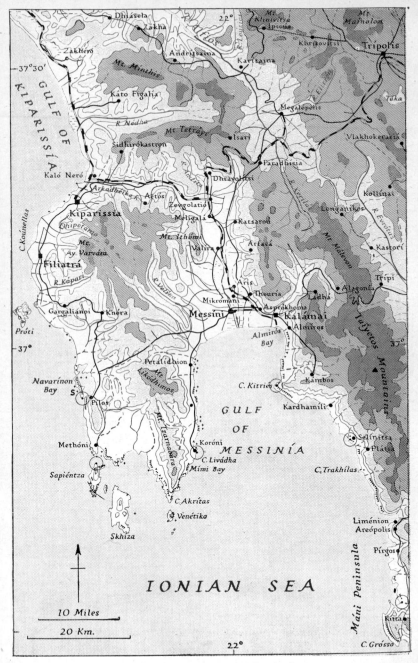

Fig. 35. South-western Pelopónnisos

Based mainly on the 1:250,000 G.S.G.S. Series 4088 : The Balkans, and the
1 : 100,000 *Epitelikós Khártis tis Elládhos.*

S. Sfaktiría island.   For key, see Fig. 9.

The Basin of Megalópolis (Region F10)

Physical Characteristics

The term ' basin ' may be applied literally to this district for it is an almost symmetrical hollow with a generally flat bottom 1,350 ft. above sea level (Fig. 35). It measures 11 by 5 miles and is surrounded by steep-sided and faulted mountains rising at least 2,500 ft. above it. In the rim there are three lips of lower height ; the saddle of Lakonía in the south-east ; the saddle of Messinía in the south-west, and the saddle of Cynuria in the north-west. These stand 650 ft., 850 ft. and 650 ft. respectively above the general level of the plain. The basin is drained by the Alfiós which has cut a gorge in the saddle of Cynuria.

The basin is the gathering ground for a large number of streams and rivers from the surrounding hills. Chief among them are the Alfiós, entering the basin through a limestone gorge ; the Koudhou-farina, from a ravine in the saddle of Lakonía, and the Xerílas from the northern Taïyetos mountains. In general, the tributaries from the west are short ; those from the east are longer, especially the Vrendheádhes and the Elissón, which carry much silt.

The floor of the basin is entirely covered by Pliocene marl, containing some lignite, but over it a continuous layer of yellow sandy loam has been laid. On the fragments of high terraces around the basin there still remain red, stony deposits, common to much of the corridor.

Land Utilization

The natural vegetation has long disappeared from the plain, but on the slopes are considerable remnants of oak-forests, together with maquis and Kermes bush. Since the rivers are incised and the deposits permeable, springs are few and the soil suffers from dryness. Thus, although a sufficient water supply is available from wells, fields cannot easily be irrigated. Almost the whole plain, therefore, is under cereals with a fair proportion in vineyards, including currants. Among the fruit trees the olive, fig and mulberry predominate. Similar products are seen on the lower slopes of the mountains, but here the fruits are walnut, apple, pear and cherry. Vineyards are important on the valley sides in the north, including those of the river Loúsios as far as Dhimitsána.

This basin is a focus of routes, and strategic control naturally determined the position of certain places, especially in the Middle

Ages. Entrance was then controlled by the fortresses of Karítaina (p. 189) in the north and Leondárion in the south. The Frankish castle of Leondárion stands on the extreme northern bluff of the Taïyetos mountains. Like Mistra, the fortress was built to keep the Slavs of Taïyetos in check (see vol. I, p. 175) and the town became the leading place in the district ; the Turks for a time made it the capital of Morea. Megalópolis, or ' Great City ', from which the basin takes its name, was planned by Epaminondas the Theban in 371 B.C. as a capital of a united Arkadhía. It was built in four years on both banks of the Elissón and was peopled by compulsory immigration ; its walls, 5 miles long, included a theatre for 20,000 spectators. Geographically, the location of a capital on this site was good, but the scale of building was unwarranted. Within a century the city was deserted, and, although twice rebuilt, it disappeared during the Slav invasion of the eighth century. Although again planned as a small town in the modern kingdom of Greece, its population (2,373) has taken forty years to double itself.

The basin received many Turkish immigrants in the past and this still affects the appearance of some of the villages. The total population of the plain and nearby slopes is 17,660, and the density —119 per sq. mile—is distinctly low for a fully cultivated area.

The Barrier of Cynuria (Region F11)

Physical Characteristics

The barrier of Cynuria is a comparatively low ridge, some 10 miles wide, guarding the northern entrance to the basin of Megalópolis. It is composed mainly of limestone with belts of chert, trending from south-south-west to north-north-east. The Alfiós has cut a gorge across the barrier, impracticable for road or railway (Plate 74). Within the gorge it receives one large tributary, the Loúsios, a short distance below its entrance at Karítaina.

Land Utilization

In spite of its importance as a barrier the district has no modern name. Its classical name was Cynuria, from the name of the tribe who lived here during the fourth century B.C. The extent to which it obstructs movement may be seen from the course of the existing road. This leaves Karítaina and, crossing to the south bank of the Alfiós by a medieval bridge, climbs to a summit 4,650 ft. high before descending with many bends to Andrítsaina and so to the

Plate 74. The gorge of the river Alfiós below Karítaina, looking upstream

Plate 75. The river Alfiós and the crag of Karítaina
The river flows sluggishly westward to its gorge by the crag (centre). The road
to Andrítsaina climbs over the shoulder of the Diafortis mountains on the left.

Plate 76. Mézapos Bay on the west coast of the Máni peninsula
The slopes, of marble, carry little vegetation, which is less meagre on the shelf
near a village (left), and in the valley.

[Facing page 189

more open valley below. This, or older roads to the west and north, have always been controlled from the rock at the entrance to the gorge. This was the site of Brenthe, which came to be called Karítaina on becoming a refuge for the mountaineers of Gortyn against the Slavs. The castle of Geoffrey de Bruyères is one of the finest feudal strongholds in Greece. The village, with a population of 925, clusters on the slope below the crag (Plate 75).

THE HILLS OF ILÍA AND WESTERN AKHAÏA (REGION F12)

Physical Characteristics

From the bastion of Mount Panakhaïkón a bold escarpment runs southwards to the summit of Erímanthos, and then, turning southwestwards, ends abruptly near Boukovína. At this point the mountain edge overlooks the valley of the Piniós. To the west of this escarpment is a broad expanse of hill-country, intricately cut by valleys. It is composed mainly of closely folded shales, sandstones and conglomerates, over which pale-coloured limestones have been thrust. Its surface reaches 2,300 ft. in the higher summits, but in one place the remarkable narrow ridge of Mount Skóllis rises to 3,333 ft. When seen endwise, from north or south, Skóllis appears as a sharp cone, but from the west it is a long arête of cream-coloured limestone. At the foot of these hills is a shelving apron of Pliocene sands and marls, in part so smooth and low that it merges into the coastal plain. Bordering Mount Panakhaïkón, however, these younger strata have been raised nearly 2,000 ft. and, capped by conglomerates, they form the rugged hills near Pátrai.

South of the river Piniós the hills are built entirely of sands, marls and conglomerates, and not one of the many rivers has uncovered the underlying strata. The conglomerates form immense beds, in places 1,900 ft. thick. They are found to the north of the Alfiós and are broken by step-faults running west-north-west to east-south-east. As a result, the country rises northwards in four main steps to a height of 2,600 ft. west of Mount Erímanthos. The southward courses of the rivers Erímanthos and Ládhon are carved deeply into these rocks. Those of the Ládhon Selíis, flowing to the Piniós, and many tributaries of the lower Alfiós, run either directly across the fault-steps or parallel to them. Innumerable parallel ravines open upon each river, cutting the country into a kind of tabular maze. South of the river Alfiós conglomerates do not occur and sands form the valley slopes up to nearly 2,000 ft.

Land Utilization

The higher rainfall on these hills, as compared with the interior, and the presence of many impermeable strata combine to make this a well-watered land. Consequently, it must once have all been under oak or Aleppo pine ; but the northern part is now almost bare and is largely covered with maquis. This is luxuriant, especially on the impermeable rocks, where it has not been consumed by charcoal burners ; asphodel meadow then takes its place. The southern part still contains two of the largest remnants of forest in the Pelopónnisos ; that on the highest of the table lands, known as Kapellis, is of deciduous oak, while the lower terraces and slopes are largely under Aleppo pine, with *Pinus pinea* also in the west, and ilex and wild pear. The maquis, too, is rich, especially in heaths.

The amount of cultivated land is small in view of the physical advantages of the region, and doubtless the greater attractions of the plain account largely for this. The main crops are wheat, with maize in the bottom land, vines for wine, and fruit trees marked by variety rather than numbers.

THE PLAINS OF ILÍA AND WESTERN AKHAÏA (REGION F13)

Physical Characteristics

This region is unique in forming the only large coastal plain of the Pelopónnisos. In the south its boundaries are sinuous, since the plain penetrates inland up the valleys of the Alfiós and Piniós. There the descent to the lowland is rather steep, but farther north, and especially between the rivers Vérga and Pírros the slope is very slight. Alluvium is dominant in the south, but this is replaced northwards by sandy marls.

The origin of the plain is simple. The Pliocene beds fall gently seaward and presumably extend to about the 50-fathoms line. On this shelving shore the waves have thrown up barrier beaches upon which sand dunes have formed. These have linked together four points—the former rocky islands or peninsulas of Mavrovoúni near Cape Pápas, Kounoupéli 5 miles to the south, Khlemoútsi (between Cape Killíni and Cape Tripití), and Katákolon. Hot sulphurous springs—indicating dislocation—are found at Kounoupéli and Khlemoútsi. The large lagoons formed behind each of the sand bars have been nearly filled up by the silt-laden rivers.

Such an amphibious fringe would scarcely be habitable were it not that the land has risen slightly. As a result, the lower courses of the rivers lie embedded in the plain to a depth of at least 15 ft. Thus, south of the peninsula of Khlemoútsi, all the rivers reach the sea and the land is well drained. On the plain facing the Gulf of Pátrai the rivers of the western half are incised in marl rock, while the narrow eastern part consists of the alluvial fans of the steep rivers draining Mount Panakhaïkón and therefore resembles the plain east of Cape Dhrépanon.

From the gorge of Cynuria (see p. 188) to the sea, the Alfiós flows in a rather open valley with a broad and variable stony bed. The coastal plain proper begins at the confluence of the Alfiós and the Klávdhios, at Olimbía, and forms the real end of the central corridor. Northwards it is cut off from the broader coastal lowlands by the peninsula of Katákolon, and southwards it is hemmed in close to the shore by the Lapíthas mountains.

Land Utilization

The plain of Ilía is seldom mentioned in the ancient history of Greece, although Olympia almost equalled Delphi as a sanctuary of the Hellenic world and the record of victors at the Olympic Games extends over twelve centuries. Most of the ruins for long lay deeply buried by the silt of the Klávdhios, overlooked by hills of marl clothed in tall maquis and pines. This part of Greece became important for its accessibility from western Europe. The peninsula of Khlemoútsi in the thirteenth century offered a reasonable harbour (Glaréntza or Killíni) and the site for the great Castel Tornèse, while Andreville on the plain (now Andravídha with 3,090 inhabitants), with its Frankish cathedral, was the Frankish capital of Morea.

Ilía and the adjoining lowland of Akhaïa have long been famous for their live stock. The rich maquis, the winter herbage, and in places the lush grass, have always supported large flocks of sheep and goats as well as horses and mules and many cattle—a small breed, for which the plain was noted in Homeric times. Moreover, the distance to high summer pasture is not great. But a mainly pastoral economy, coupled with imperfect drainage in some parts, did not favour close settlement in the lowland ; nor did the dangers of attack by sea and land. In liberated Greece, however, a new inducement to settlement arose in the cultivation of the currant vine. From about 1850 a steady movement of immigrants to these plains has taken place from other parts of the Pelopónnisos, and especially from the mountains. Many new villages have been built and old ones enlarged, while great tracts of maquis and some woodland have been cleared. Vines have also been planted along the valleys and up their lower slopes to about 1,000 ft. Prosperity was increased after 1890 when the railway from Pátrai was built.

The scene, then, is dominated by currant fields lined by cactus hedges, and each field has its bare drying floor set apart. Brightly coloured villages contrast with the dark cypresses and fruit trees. It is probable that other forms of agriculture have been somewhat neglected, but there is a considerable production of wheat, and maize is grown in damper soils. Olive trees are widespread, though not in profusion, and other fruits are grown locally. After the currant, however, the main interest is still the raising of animals. Hence the need for pasture has probably restricted other developments.

The most intensive cultivation is found south of the Piniós. Here the silt is well drained and of great depth, and each of the two areas separated by the peninsula of Katákolon has its own important towns. Thus, near the Piniós are Gastoúni, the live-stock market, Amaliás, the currant market, and Killíni, the seaport. Pírgos, a town of 19,336 inhabitants, is both the capital of the *nomós* of Ilía and the centre of the southern plain. The delta of the Alfiós is moister than that of the Piniós and is flanked by long lagoons behind sandspits, of which the southernmost is covered with pines. Malaria is prevalent and Pírgos stands raised on an outcrop of marl. Most other settlements lie just off the plain, where, with spring-water from the marl, the villagers cultivate orchards of citrus fruits. The plain of Ilía, including the peninsula of Khlemoútsi, and a strip 5 miles wide along the north bank of the Piniós, together have a population of over 87,000 and a density of 340 per sq. mile.

Extending northwards to the river Pírros, is a somewhat smaller district which has the much lower density of 129 per sq. mile. The eastern part, on the marl, and entirely in Akhaïa, is devoted to wheat with scattered vineyards. The largest place is Káto Akhaïa with a population of 2,153. In the western area the cultivable plain is narrow and includes woods of Valona oak. The headland of Mavrovoúni and the sands inside the dunes to the south of it are under a forest of pines—*Pinea* and Aleppo. Between the two woodlands is a series of lagoons and swamps. Throughout all this area the camps of shepherds are to be seen during the winter.

East of Káto Akhaïa, and along the southern shores of the Gulf of Pátrai, the lowland consists of two small alluvial plains that are much

more populous. They are dominated by Pátrai which stands between them. Here, the currant fields are again nearly continuous,
and tree-fruits are common. They support some 16,000 inhabitants,
excluding the population of Pátrai, and the density is 225 per sq.
mile. The site of Pátrai itself is a bluff of marl rock thrust forward
to the sea. It is crowned by a castle of Venetian and Turkish construction, with the closely built upper quarter on the slope and the
' European ' town near the shore. Of ancient origin, Pátrai owed its
greatness largely to the decline of Corinth, and for a time it played
the part in western trade that Monemvasía did in the eastern. Its
almost complete destruction in the War of Independence led to a
decline in population from 16,000 to 4,000. By 1860, however,
the number was restored, and since the construction of the railway,
giving it leadership in the currant trade of Pelopónnisos the population has doubled. With 61,278 inhabitants in 1928, Pátrai is the
fourth city of Greece (see vol. II, pp. 251–7).

THE NÉDHA MOUNTAINS (REGION F14)

Physical Characteristics

The dominant features of this district are the two parallel ranges of
mountains about 8 miles apart (Fig. 35). They extend eastwards
from near the coast for some 12 miles and are separated by the
valley of the river Nédha. Near the headwaters of this river the
mountains are joined by a horse-shoe ridge overlooking the basin
of Megalópolis. Most of the summits are about 4,000 ft. in height,
with a few in the east exceeding 4,500 ft. The passes are all relatively
high. Like the mountains of western Arkadhía the rocks consist of
pale, fissured limestone and belts of red chert. The northern chain,
Dhiafortes in the east and Mínthis in the west, is partly separated
from the Alfiós by a more broken and lower range ending abruptly
at the coast as the Lapíthas mountains.

The river Nédha and its tributaries acquired their present courses
when the mountain block was much lower and smoother. This old
surface is partly preserved at a height of 1,600 ft., and many villages
stand upon it. With later uplift, the Nédha has cut deeply ; its
lower course flows in a canyon, and its tributaries follow the bands
of chert. A series of deep, parallel valleys has been formed and
these make the landscape almost alpine in its ruggedness. The
northern, marly foothills are also deeply ravined.

The alluvial coastal plain broadens northwards from the mouth of the Nédha and encloses the lagoon of Kaïáfa behind a pine-clad spit. This lagoon is connected with the much larger lagoon of Agoulinítsa, and so with the mouth of the Alfiós. The sand-bar that hems in Kaïáfa lagoon carries the railway northwards to Pírgos.

Land Utilization

The natural vegetation of these mountains was oak forest of which a few patches, and many single trees, remain. Ilex is found everywhere, even near the summits.

The abundance of spring-water favours the growing of wheat, maize and vines near the villages, and especially on the outcrops of chert; but the real mainstay of the people is stock-keeping. While some remote villages in the upper basin of the Nédha have fallen into ruin, those nearer the coast share in the prosperity of the plain. The population of the whole basin is over 10,000 with the very high density, for mountainous land, of 180 per sq. mile. Cultivation is more common on the marls of the northern slope, a district dominated by the high, attractive and comfortable little town of Andrítsaina (population 1,802). It is from here that visitors usually cross the mountains to visit the Doric temple of Bassae. The columns crown a high, southern spur of the main ridge, and the building has been described as seeming to grow out of the rock (see vol. I, p. 426).

The coastal plain, although malarial, is nevertheless the most productive part. Orange groves, currant fields, and orchards of other fruits are watered from springs at the edge of the plain, and wheat and maize are grown in the fields. Fishing by trap is practised in the lagoon of Agoulinítsa, the fishermen living in pile-dwellings on its banks. Between the lagoons of Agoulinítsa and Kaïáfa stands the dark limestone rock of Samikón, capped by an ancient citadel some 500 ft. above the defile it was built to control. At the foot of this cliff the large cave facing the lagoon of Kaïáfa emits hot sulphurous water, used in the spa.

THE CORRIDOR OF THE RIVER ARKADHÉÏKA (REGION F15)

Physical Characteristics

South of the river Nédha the coastal plain narrows to 600 yds. and is hemmed close to the sea by steep slopes of pale-coloured limestone. Farther south, however, the limestones give way to a tableland of red conglomerate and marl through which the river Arkadhéïka cuts a narrow way to the sea. The present valley is merely a notch in a wide basin that rises gently to a flat watershed some 670 ft. above sea-level. To the east of the watershed the valley of the river Pírnax leads to the upper basin of Messinía. The gravels that formed the conglomerate were laid down, before the basin of Messinía existed, by a much longer river than the Arkadhéïka (see vol. I, Fig. 17).

Land Utilization

The soils of the conglomerate are very infertile and, apart from some cereals, the valley is devoted to pasture and the population is small. East of the watershed, however, limestone reappears, with fertile alluvial hollows and more numerous settlements. The importance of this depression lies in its use as a corridor for road and railway.

THE KONTOVOÚNIA AND PENINSULA OF MESSINÍA (REGION F16)

Physical Characteristics

This group of mountains is roughly triangular, with its straightest and steepest edge to the west. The escarpment is made less impressive, however, by the plateau known as the Kámbos that causes the westward bulge in the coastline about Filiatrá. This plateau is a wave-cut platform, descending abruptly from 1,000 ft. to a narrow coastal plain. The northern side of the mountains exhibits a broad expanse of red chert, deeply trenched by a tributary of the river Arkadhéïka. East of the gorge, the highland extends to the outlying Mount Ithómi. The main drainage is to the Gulf of Messinía in parallel valleys deeply cut in limestone or chert (Fig. 35).

The coastal plateau of the Kámbos is flanked on the south by a lower tableland of Pliocene rocks extending to Navarínon Bay (see vol. II, Plate 80). The plateau then reappears, and extends almost to Cape Akrítas, repeating the characteristics of the Kámbos. Again shales and massive limestone have been cut down to a smooth platform, and again there is the same seaward tilt and similar altitudes : it is also the counterpart of the high terrace on the peninsula of Máni. From its surface Mount Likódhimos rises gently in the east to a height of 3,140 ft. The plateau falls directly to the coast and, in consequence, the rivers lie in deep, narrow valleys. There is no coastal plain, except at Methóni and where the Xeriás enters Navarínon Bay. On the north of this bay a high ridge of cream-coloured limestone rises sharply from the sea. Its continuity has been broken, isolating Sfaktiría and Sapiéntza islands. Próti, farther north, is also composed of this rock, while Skhíza and its small neighbours are of sandstone. On the east coast of the peninsula the plateau descends to the sea in a series of steps, mainly composed of marl.

Land Utilization

Only scattered trees now remain to mark the forest of deciduous oaks that once covered much of this area, but here and there is a wood of ilex. Elsewhere, the impermeable rocks are covered with maquis, and the limestone with phrygana. The greater part of the Kontovoúnia is used for pasturing sheep and goats, and so also are Mount Likódhimos and many parts of the Kámbos. But throughout the peninsula, vineyards, olive-groves and grain have encroached on to the higher slopes, except those of limestone. The wine made from the lower vineyards is among the strongest and sweetest in Greece.

Most of the higher settlements are small and lie in the northern and eastern valleys of the Kontovoúnia, where springs flow freely. Everywhere cultivated land increases with the passage from the harder rocks to the sandy marls, common at lower altitudes. These, like the small alluvial plains, are always marked by the olive and vine, and, where springs emerge, by citrus fruits. The proportion of these varies locally. Thus currants are dominant on the western coastal plain from Kiparissía southwards, together with fine oranges and lemons. Currants, olives and wheat are the chief products on the wide plain inland from Navarínon ; currants and oranges mark the alluvial plain of Methóni. Perhaps the most luxuriant fruit-orchards to be found on the coast of the Pelopónnisos are those of the eastern slopes of the peninsula. Here, springs from the marls are abundant and forests of olive trees alternate with vineyards or groves of orange and lemon trees. Cactus hedges grow as high as the houses, and in the south date palms flourish, though the fruit does not ripen.

The produce is usually taken to market in caïques by the Maniate sailors of Petalídhion. This little port is close to the ancient Coron which served nearby Asine, so the name of the largest place on this coast, Koróni (population 2,094) is misleading. The people numbering about 13,000 on this strip of coast, live in a score of large villages. The density of rural population, 470 per sq. mile, is surpassed only on the Plain of Messinía.

The largest fruit-growing region lies between Kiparissía and Pílos. Among the many settlements six towns are outstanding. From north to south they are Kiparissía with 4,443 inhabitants, Filiatrá (9,293), Gargaliánoi (7,094), Khóra (3,582), while Methóni (1,991), with its own small plain, completes the series. All these places suffered severely from earthquake in 1886, but all have prospered greatly from the currant and fruit trade. Kiparissía and both Old and New Pílos (see vol. I, p. 442) have had special fame as the principal ports of Messinía in their time. Kiparissía, rising picturesquely to its acropolis, is now the railway terminus. Filiatrá, a well-planned and prosperous town, stands 200 ft. above the sea, while Gargaliánoi on the plateau (1,000 ft.) overlooks an immense expanse of sea and land. Both towns are served by motor roads. Khóra lies below crags of conglomerate from which it obtains a fine supply of water for irrigation. Pílos, which has taken the name of the ancient city across the bay instead of Navarínon (i.e. ton Avarinon = of the Avars or Slavs), is dominated by a Veneto-Turkish fortress.

The Basins of Messinía (Region F17)

Physical Characteristics

The northern extension of the Gulf of Messinía is a rectangular hollow, bounded on the west and north by the Kontovoúnia and on the east by the northern Taïyetos mountains. It is divided by a low ridge into two parts, of which the southern is the larger. These two mountain-girt plains form the heart of Messinía.

The wall of the Taïyetos, here named Kokkála, is a most impressive barrier. It is composed of black limestone and rises in a straight fault-scarp from the lowest part of the plain to an almost level top 3,600 ft. high. Much of the slope is scored by horizontal terraces, that seem to mark stages in the upheaval of the Taïyetos.

The walls of the Kontovoúnia are less impressive because their foot stands some 1,000 ft. higher. From their base a broad apron of sandy deposits slopes gently towards the gulf, to end in a cliff some distance from the shore. Much of the lower basin is thus a sloping tableland of yellow-sands, red-brown at the surface and deeply trenched by parallel valleys. A narrow strip of similar aspect lies near the eastern edge of the basin and between the two is the alluvial plain, swampy in its lower part. In the eastern alcove, near the gulf, the torrential river Nédhon emerges from its deep glen, tearing ravines in the conglomerate at its lower end, and building up its fan, the site of Kalámai. Winter rains and swollen streams inundate the land behind the dunes all along the shore of the gulf. This lower basin is distinguished from all others in the Pelopónnisos in having two great *kefalari* near its upper end. It is these which bring from the limestones of Taÿyetos the water that feeds the lower Pámisos. One of them, named Flóros, received annual sacrifices in ancient times.

Between the two basins is a low plateau, composed of folded shales, through which the river Pámisos flows in a gorge. The upper basin is hemmed in on the north by the Nédha mountains. The nearly flat floor, 200 ft. high, is composed entirely of alluvium, the very low fans of many streams. There are no terraced deposits around the margin, a fact which indicates that the basin is of very recent formation. The district obtains some of its water from limestones and so always has a supply, but winter floods inundate part of the floor. The valleys in the west lead to the corridor of the river Arkadhéïka and those in the east to the saddle of Messinía (see pp. 194, 187). The railways that make use of these gateways unite on the plain.

Land Utilization

This district has been well-named a sun-bitten paradise ; sun and water combine to produce ' hot-house ' conditions, as nowhere else in the Pelopónnisos. There are, however, considerable differences in production throughout the region, largely determined by regional variations in soils and water supply. On the upper plain, the light coloured silt is deep and frequently renewed ; currants and wheat are grown, and maize where moisture is retained in summer. In the east the somewhat stony and drier soils bear olive and fig trees over crops of barley and lupin. There are many villages both on the plain and hillside. The largest is Meligalá, on the railway, with a population of 2,270. The houses and the divisions between the fields are built mainly of stone.

On the sloping tableland of the lower basin, about 80 sq. miles in area, wheat, currants and olives cover the broad strips of red soil between the parallel ravines, and olive trees also grow upon the terraces. The villages are many and near the lower edge of the tableland, where they house the owners of the rich flood plain, they become large. The flood plain is without settlements, partly because of the malarial nature of the land and partly because of its value. The exception is Messíni (Nisíon) the largest and most southerly of the settlements, with a population of 6,723. It arose under the Franks who guarded it by the castle of Mikrománi, across the river. The town is reached by a branch railway from Kalámai. Cultivation is most intensive ; no space is wasted and no period of the year is unused. Currants are dominant, but various tree-fruits are of great value, especially figs and oranges. Cotton, too, is grown with good quality and yield.

The ancient and the modern capitals of Messinía occupy very different situations. The former was placed so as to control both the basins, standing high above the threshold between them. The acropolis stood on the summit of Mount Ithómi, a cap of pale limestone, while the city and its gardens lay on the southern slopes of cultivable soil. Kalámai, the modern capital, stands on the site of the ancient Pharae which achieved fame as a medieval, and then a Turkish, stronghold against the unruly Maniates (see vol. II, pp. 262–6). It lies beneath the ruined fortress on the banks of the river Nédhon, banks which for safety must be raised periodically, as this turbulent river builds up its stony bed. The town is surrounded by a forest of fruit trees, and has both rural and urban functions. In the forty years to 1928 the population of this commercial and administrative centre and seaport increased from 10,696 to 29,039—a growth which measures the prosperity of Messinía as a whole, and of the two basins in particular. The alluvial plains and their immediate fringes, without Kalámai and the western tableland, contain 45,000 inhabitants who are dependent upon the produce of this fertile soil. The mean density of population is almost 560 per sq. mile, the highest rural density in Greece.

THE TAÏYETOS MOUNTAINS AND THE MÁNI PENINSULA
(REGION F18)

Physical Characteristics

Nowhere around the Mediterranean are mountains as high as the Taïyetos so close to the sea. They lie only 8 miles inland and rise to 7,877 ft., the highest point in the Pelopónnisos. These figures imply gradients commonly associated with the Swiss Alps. From the basin of Megalópolis in the north to Cape Taínaron (Matapan) in the south, the range extends for a distance of 66 miles.

In structure, the Taïyetos is an upfold of the several rocks of the Pelopónnisos. Crystalline schists and marble are overlaid by slates and limestones of different types. With the last uplift, great fractures formed along both sides of the range, the western one marking the shores of the Gulf of Messinía, and the high eastern edge of the plains of Messinía (see p. 197). Transverse fractures split up the range into several sections and the central part was elevated more than the others.

Over much of the Máni peninsula and the southern and central Taïyetos mountains the cover of sedimentary rocks has been removed. But the most remarkable feature of erosion is the great coastal terrace that lies below the western escarpment. In the north, in the promontory of Cape Kitriés, it is over 5 miles wide and 1,300 ft. high at its inner edge. Southwards, it declines in height and narrows to a minimum breadth near Trakhílas Bay (see vol. I, Plate 45). Then it widens again and ends near Cape Grósso at an altitude of 320 ft. This very long terrace, originally cut level by the waves, has therefore been raised unequally. Ravines were subsequently cut deeply into it by rivers, and finally a certain amount of sinking has produced inlets at the mouths of the ravines, aided probably by solution of the marble. The seaward edge of the terrace is an escarpment which has been steepened in several headlands of sea cliffs (Plate 76).

The northern Taïyetos falls into three longitudinal divisions. The eastern ridge is narrow and straight, rising gently southwards to 5,285 ft. above the Langádha gorge (see below). It is composed of dark limestones, schists and shales. The western ridge does not exceed 4,250 ft. in height, but is comparatively broad, bulging westwards to look down on the southern plain of Messinía (see p. 197). It is formed entirely of massive limestones. Between the two ridges much lower country has been worn out of sandstones and fissured limestone by two river systems—that of the Nédhon flowing south-west in a great gorge to Kalámai, and that of the Xerilás draining northwards to the Alfiós. In spite of these local variations in relief, the northern Taïyetos, as a whole, has the appearance of a massive dissected plateau tilted towards the north.

The high central Taïyetos is some 23 miles long and flanks the sunken basin of Spárti. The highest peaks are of massive limestone, with, to the west, lower crests of marble and mica-schist. Vast ravines have torn the eastern flank, and between them are bold limestone bluffs. At the northern end of this section is the Langádha Pass (4,200 ft. high), which gives direct access from Spárti to Kalamaí. At this place one of the eastward flowing rivers has pushed its source back through the main ridge.

The southern Taïyetos mountains consist of two ridges, the eastern of limestone, the western of marble. In a distance of 18 miles they decline in altitude from 5,900 ft. to 3,000 ft., and then end in a furrow only 750 ft. high, which severs them from the peninsula of Máni. The pass is used by a road from Areópolis to Yíthion.

The Máni peninsula is a continuation of the Taïyetos mountains. The main summits are composed of marble and decline from 3,600 ft. in the north to 1,020 ft. only 2 miles from Cape Taínaron (see vol. I, Plate 46). Limestone ridges strike off to the east coast and from the bold headlands of Paganiá and Stavrí.

Land Utilization

Although the rainfall on the western side of the Taïyetos mountains is considerable, the vegetation is generally meagre because the marble and limestone retain little soil. Westerly gales have also had an adverse effect on forest growth. The only woodland consists of Black pine and fir down to 3,500 ft.; below this, patches of deciduous oak and hawthorn occur on both sides of the range and Valona oak and chestnut also grow on the east. Above the tree-line (about 6,250 ft.) there is little meadow, and brushwood is everywhere thin.

Few flocks are maintained and the people are therefore dependent upon agriculture, for which conditions are generally unfavourable. In the northern Taïyetos, settlements based upon subsistence agriculture are most numerous in the central hills, especially along the valley of the Xerilás. The total population, however, is small, and the villages are in touch with the basins of Megalópolis and Messinía rather than with Lakonía. Farther south, the most prosperous mountain villages are those on the high shelf of mica-schist west of Spárti. Outstanding examples of overpopulation are to be found on the lower western slopes of Taïyetos and on the coastal terrace, and in the peninsula of Máni. As one passes southwards, the amount of soil and water becomes progressively less. This is the land of the Maniates who from an early period have been virtually cut off from civilizing influences. They differ in their history, dialect and customs from all other Greeks and claim descent from the ancient Lakonians. In the Taïyetos mountains, too, the descendants of Slavonic invaders have remained distinct.

The villages of Máni are clusters of square towers built for defence and indicating the perennial unrest which, like the blood-feud, persisted until recent times ; clan warfare prevailed and insurrections were rarely subdued by the central power. With all this is linked the perpetual hunger in the villages. The pods of white lupin can alone be relied on as food for men and pigs ; wheat gives poor yields, and so do the recent introductions, the olive and vine : the chief fruit is the fig. While the Maniates are not fishermen they depend greatly on the quails which they net in large numbers during August and September to be preserved for winter consumption or exported from Geroliménas. Porto Kalio is named from this bird. Although emigration has caused some decline in population the density on the south-western slope of Máni remains at 132 per sq. mile.

For Bibliographical Note, see p. 22.

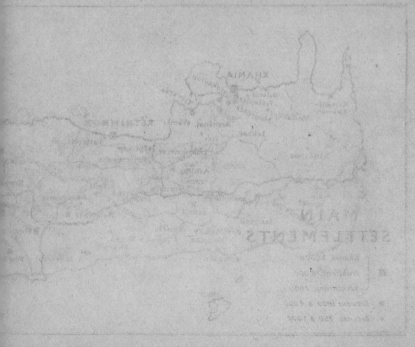

Chapter VIII

CRETE (KRÍTI)

Geology and Physical Features : Climate : Vegetation : Fauna : Regional Divisions : Coasts, Islets and Ports : The Cretan People : Historical Outline : Economic Geography : Communications : Bibliographical Note

The island of Crete lies between latitudes 34° 55′ and 35° 41′ N, and between longitudes 23° 30′ and 26° 19′ E. Its northernmost point (Cape Spátha) is some 60 miles from Cape Maléa on the Greek mainland. In general shape the island is a narrow oblong about 160 miles long, while its breadth varies from 36 to 7½ miles. Its area is about 3,200 sq. miles. It is thus the fifth largest island in the Mediterranean and by far the largest of the Greek archipelago.

The province (*dhiamerísmata*) of Crete is administered by a Governor-General, who ranks as a Minister in the Greek Cabinet. The province, according to the census of 1928, consists of four *nomoí* or departments, each under a nomarch or prefect. Within the *nomoí* there are 20 eparchies, 5 demes and 534 communes (Fig. 36). It should be remembered that the eparchy is no longer an administrative unit (see vol. 1, pp. 253–57).

Nomoí	Eparchies	Demes	Communes
Khaniá	5	1	143
Rethímni	4	1	128
Iráklion	7	1	179
Lasíthi	4	2	84

The eparchies are as follows :

Khaniá
 Kidhonía
 Kísamos
 Apokóronas
 Sélinon
 Sfakiá

Iráklion
 Témenos
 Pedhiás
 Kainoúrion
 Malevízion
 Monofátsion
 Piryiótissa
 Viánnos

Rethímni
 Rethímni
 Milopótamos
 Amári
 Áyios Vasílios

Lasíthi
 Lasíthi
 Merabéllo
 Sitía
 Ierápetra

GEOLOGY AND PHYSICAL FEATURES

Geological Structure

Crete owes its geological structure to the Tertiary earth-movements that affected southern Europe (see vol. I, p. 3). It is the remains of an arc of folds that stretched from the Pelopónnisos to south-west Asia Minor. The folds trend east-west except towards the western end of the island where the trend changes, first to the south-west and then to the south. The surface of this land-bridge was probably that of an uneven limestone tableland, but fractures, dislocations, upheavals and subsidences broke up the arc. Crete was isolated and itself suffered several major fractures, represented by the isthmuses that now separate the higher masses of Lévka Óri, Psilorítis, Lasíthi and Sitía. The various segments that thus came to compose Crete underwent upheaval and tilting towards the north and north-east. The result is that the interior mountains present abrupt slopes to an almost harbourless south coast which in turn plunges precipitously into the Mediterranean. From out to sea, the southern margin of the island appears as a serrated and furrowed glittering limestone wall. The northern slopes towards the Aegean are more gradual, and the submarine declivities here are also less steep. Thus the 100-fathom line along the north and east coasts lies on an average about $3\frac{1}{2}$ miles from the shore, while on the south and west coasts it is only about 1 mile away (Fig. 46). Moreover, local fractures and subsidences resulted in the faces of the mountains (particularly to the north) being broken into a series of plains and plateaux descending more or less like steps to the coast.

Faulting also was responsible for the origin of the curious upland basins of Crete—the plain of Omalós in the Lévka Óri, the plain of Nídha in the Psilorítis mountains, and the plain of Lasíthi amid the mountains of that name. Some of the great chasms, too, were formed by faulting (e.g. the gorge of Roumelí that reaches the south coast), and subsidences also explain some of the most striking coastal features (e.g. Soúdha Bay). Moreover, there is evidence of local coastal movements in late geological, and perhaps even in historical, times. It is clear at any rate that the instability of the earth's crust in this part of the world has continued up to the present day, for earthquakes have been frequent in Crete throughout historical times ; most are slight, but occasionally they have been severe, e.g. those of 29 May 1508 and 12 October 1856.

Rock Types

The main rock types in Crete are shown on Fig. 38. Broadly speaking, they are four in number—that is, apart from small areas of igneous rock near the eastern end of the Asidhéroto range and to the south of the Lasíthi mountains. These igneous areas include a variety of rocks such as serpentine, gabbro, syenite, together with some granite ; their age is largely Jurassic and Cretaceous but may extend into the Eocene period. The interrelation of the four main rock groups are greatly complicated by thrusting and dislocation, and much work yet remains to be done on the geology of Crete before the relationships of the various rock groups are clear.

1. *Metamorphic Rocks.* These form the basement of the island. They include phyllites, slates, mica-schists and quartzites, and are made up largely of highly folded and metamorphosed Triassic rocks, but they probably also include some older rocks. They generally appear only on the lower slopes of the limestone plateaux (as in Sitía) or where streams have eaten away the overlying limestones. In the western part of the island, however, in Kísamos and Sélinon, they cover an extensive portion of the surface. The slopes on these metamorphic rocks are more or less rounded and gentle. As the rocks are impervious, surface drainage is abundant during the wet seasons, and the ground is furrowed by many valleys separated by soft rounded ridges. The rocks decompose into clayey or sandy soils that are yellowish or reddish in colour.

2. *Jurassic, Cretaceous and Eocene Rocks.* Upon the crystalline rocks rests an immense mass of light-grey to jet-black coarse-grained limestones, often several thousand feet in thickness. They are generally unstratified and are of Jurassic, Cretaceous and Eocene age. Locally they include sandstones and conglomerates, and there is considerable variation in the limestone itself. It is this limestone that forms the main mountain blocks, e.g. that of Lévka Óri, and gives its character to the island. The sharp, hard outlines, greyish-white crests, immense precipices, gorges, ridges and step-like plateau formations of this rock are the main features, both in a distant view and in the closer detail of the island. The pervious and soluble nature of the limestone has given rise to well-marked features, and parts of Crete have much in common with, say, the karst areas of Jugoslavia. On the one hand, the limestone country is characterized not by normal surface river-systems but by underground drainage, caves and swallow-holes ; numerous caves form

one of the outstanding features of Crete. On the other hand, solution and erosion have formed shallow hollows (*polja*) on the rock surface, some large, some small ; they are well developed, for instance, on the level plateau of eastern Sitía. Decomposition results in the formation of a little reddish-yellow soil which is rapidly washed down into these hollows to form oases of fertile soil on an otherwise bare and arid surface.

3. *Marine Upper Tertiary Rocks.* These are predominantly conglomerates, but they also include limestones, marls, chalks and sandstones. They occupy nearly all the lower areas. Thus the isthmus of Ierápetra is almost entirely, and that of Rethímni is largely, composed of them. Their typical forms are broad, flat-domed and rather featureless ridges with smooth sides. Their surfaces are stony, but their sides and slopes often retain a good deal of soil.

4. *Quaternary and Continental Upper Tertiary Rocks.* The alluvial areas are not extensive but are very fertile. The plain of Mesará is the largest, and after that comes the plain of Khaniá. The upland plains and polja depressions are floored by alluvial soil ; so are the river valleys. Finally, there are narrow alluvial strips at places along the coast, and more particularly along the shores of the bays of Kísamos, Réthimnon and Iráklion. The soil is generally rich red or brown, turning blue with exposure to the air, and it is often pebbly or gravelly.

Outlying Islands

The composition of the small islands around the Cretan coast resembles in general that of Crete itself. They are nearly all of limestone formations and are rocky, the larger and higher ones (Gávdhos, Día, the Yianisádhes) having their crests mainly of the older and harder varieties, the smaller and lower islands (Koufonísi, Gaïdhouronísi, Graboúsa, the northern parts of Gávdhos, and others) being mostly of the more recent Tertiary formations—chalky limestones and clayey gravels.

Drainage System

Rivers. Crete has no large perennial rivers. By far the greater number of its watercourses carry only seasonal torrents. They are dry except for a short time in winter and spring or after thunderstorms, when they become liable to floods. Those streams with a constant flow vary greatly from season to season. In winter they are broad and swift and sometimes impassible, but in August they are reduced to trickling brooks winding through empty stony beds with oleanders or clumps of plane trees, or else they become merely a series of water-holes. The main sources of their supply are the winter snows which, when they melt, often find their way underground to appear at lower levels as strong springs. Many of the local features of the drainage of Crete are explained by the presence of large stretches of limestone. Here are all the features of karst regions—underground streams, caves and swallow-holes. Thus, in eastern Sitía, surface streams are almost entirely absent ; almost as soon as a stream appears on the surface it disappears again into a sink-hole, to reappear at a lower level, usually near the coast. Over the extreme western end of the island, in Sélinon and Kísamos, the river regime is exceptional owing to the impervious nature of the soil and the heavier rainfall. For the most part the streams in this area flow constantly from their sources to the sea.

The heads of the Cretan streams are mostly to be found in innumerable wild glens in the mountains. Their upper courses often converge in a fan-like fashion into broad and shallow basins. From here they reach the sea either through deep gorges in limestone areas or through the softer country of other rocks. Even in the latter areas, however, the beds are usually considerably below the level of the surrounding country, and the valleys are deep, steep-sided and narrow. Thus most streams, almost throughout their entire length, offer serious obstacles to lateral communication.

The main watershed lies on the whole nearer to the south coast, and the majority of the larger streams flow to the north coast. Except for the Mesará district, where the presence of a long subsidiary coastal range has created exceptional conditions (see p. 237), the south coast streams are short and steep. They flow in deep gorges often with a rapid current ; here, for example, are the great chasms of Roumelí and Askífos. The east and west coasts, even for their length, are poorly provided with streams owing to the proximity of coastal mountains.

Springs. Crete abounds in springs, the result of the frequent juxtaposition of limestone and impervious rocks. The wholly limestone areas of the Psilorítis mountains and the plateau of eastern Sitía form almost the only exceptions. The springs of Crete are remarkable. Around the bases of the great limestone masses they well out as from holes in the sides of mighty reservoirs, e.g. at Mesklá near the head waters of Plataniás on the northern slopes of

Lévka Óri.   There is, of course, great variation of spring flow from place to place and from season to season.

Of special interest are the three salt-springs or *almiroí*, all similar in site and character.   Each is situated near the south-west angle of a bay on the north coast.   That near the corner of Yeoryioúpolis Bay issues from several sources, and has the weakest flow ; its waters join the Vrisón near the mouth of the river.   The *almíra* of Merabéllo flows into the sea about a mile south of Áyios Nikólaos on the west coast of the gulf ; it has a fairly strong flow.   Finally, that of Malevízion lies at the foot of Mount Stroúmboulas near the corner of the Gulf of Iráklion, and it provides a strong-flowing deep stream to the sea.   Various conjectures have been put forward to explain their salinity—either that their waters pass through saline beds or that there is some connexion with the sea.

In addition to springs, there are many wells in Crete, up to a hundred feet in depth, and windmills are frequently employed to raise water for irrigation and other purposes.

Marshes.   These are not frequent or of any great extent.   The mouths of a few streams (e.g. that of Stómios in Sitía) are marshy, and the river Yéros (Mesará) and the Plataniás (Khaniá) expand to form swamps in places.   There is a salt marsh near the head of Soúdha Bay, and the upland plains and hollows are more or less marshy in spring before the melting snow has drained away.   But, in general, the steepness and rockiness of the soil, the presence of large areas of limestone, and the lack of large perennial streams, give little opportunity for the formation of large and permanent marshes.

Lakes.   Except for one or two large, water-filled, elevated basins in the south-western Sélinon district, Crete has only one moderately-sized stretch of water, Lake Kournás in the west of the Rethímni district.   It lies at about 60 ft. above sea-level, some 2 miles south of the shore of Yeoryioúpolis Bay, and is fed by strong springs near its south-western corner.   The lake is about one mile across, and is backed by the precipitous steeps of the spurs of Lévka Óri.   It is extremely deep and its water is fresh and clear.

CLIMATE

Crete has in general the warm wet winters and hot dry summers of the Mediterranean climate but its insularity, its long narrow shape, and its great mountain masses combine to make its climate in some respects anomalous for its position and very varied for its size. Insularity gives a more equable climate than the mainland enjoys, but its size makes the extremes of heat and cold greater than in the other Aegean islands. A linear position athwart the rain bearing winds, and the mountainous interior of the island, explain its relatively high total rainfall. North-westerly winds are prevalent at all seasons, but winds sweeping down in the lee of mountain masses are often strong and have great importance locally.

Pressure and winds

In winter, depressions move eastwards in the Mediterranean along well defined tracks and one of these lies to the north, and another to the south, of Crete. Depressions passing to the north bring the island within a current of southerly air drawn in from the African region, thus southerly and south-westerly winds are frequent from November to April (see table on p. 214). These southerly winds bring rain, especially to the south coast, and even in winter they are warm and dust-laden. Offshore they may rise to gale force ; southerly gales are a great danger to shipping and much reduce the usefulness of the small harbours on the south coast. Depressions passing to the south of Crete draw in air from the Aegean and the Balkans, and the winds are northerly and north-westerly. Like those from the south, these north-westerly winds bring rain ; crossing the Aegean Sea they become moisture-laden and much of the rain of northern Crete is orographical in type, dropped as the winds rise over the mountains. In spring the north-westerlies are frequently of gale force. These gales are often sudden in onset, though they may be heralded by low cloud gathering on the mountains. They are accompanied by a hazy sky and it may be two or three days before they blow themselves out. The wind rises over the mountains and sweeps down the lee slopes in fierce gusts, whipping up a ' white squall ' in the offshore waters of the south coast.

In summer the winds of the Aegean Sea (the Etesians) are almost entirely northerly in direction and are strong and constant in character. They blow along the isobars, which show a steep pressure gradient from the plains of Russia and the plateaux of the Balkans to Persia and north-west India. The winds of Crete at this season are gentle land and sea breezes superimposed on this northerly planetary system. Thus the on-shore sea breezes of the north coast are considerably strengthened, and are known as the *Vorrás*—

the local equivalent of the Etesians. They blow nearly every afternoon with great regularity, bringing coolness and moisture to the
coastal plain. They die away soon after sunset, and at night are
replaced by offshore winds felt some 10 miles out to sea. Southerly
winds may sometimes become established in late spring and summer
for two to five days at a time, and at this season they are so dry and
hot that they do much damage to crops, burning the young shoots
and shrivelling the fruit.

Local winds are of great variety and importance in the island.
The mountains act as a barrier to the gentle sea breezes but strong
winds from north or south sweep up the windward slope, and,
surmounting the crest, rush down the lee side often with great
violence. The south coast is particularly open to severe squally
winds of this character, making navigation difficult and dangerous.
The intermontane basins and river plains are sometimes swept in
spring by similar winds which, descending from high snow-clad
mountains, check the vegetation growth on account of the low
temperatures they bring.

Temperature

The temperature range in Crete is less than on the mainland :
Iráklion has a mean monthly maximum of 99° F. and a mean
monthly minimum of 38° F. as compared with 98·6° F. and 32° F.
at Athens. The summers in the island are as hot as on the mainland because the more southerly latitude masks the effect of insularity. July and August have the highest mean temperatures
(though absolute temperatures of over 100° F. are more often reached
in June, or even September, than in July) as shown in the table
below.

Average Monthly Temperatures, 1900–29 (in °F)

Station	Ht. in ft.	Jan.	Feb.	Mar.	Apr.	May	June	July	Aug.	Sept.	Oct.	Nov.	Dec.	Year
Khaniá	46	52	53	56	60	67	72	78	78	73	67	61	55	65
Iráklion	118	54	54	57	62	68	75	79	79	75	69	63	57	66
Anóyia	2,546	45	44	49	56	61	70	73	72	67	61	55	48	58

Source : E. G. Mariolopoulos and A. N. Livathinos, *Atlas Climatique de la Grèce* (Athènes, 1935).

In July the on-shore northerly breezes lower the temperature in
the afternoon but the mean temperature of June is kept low because
mornings and evenings are still cool. The rise in temperature in
spring is less rapid than on the mainland because of the prevalent
north wind and the presence of snow on the mountains. The
fall of temperature in the autumn is also more gradual since the

warm surrounding sea keeps up the temperature in the island in
September, and the equability of the climate as compared with
mainland Greece is, in fact, due to high temperatures in Crete
throughout the winter. Frost is very rare in the lowlands, though,
of course, it is common in the highlands.

Percentage Frequency of Days of Frost 1900–1929

Station	Jan.	Feb.	Mar.	April	Nov.	Dec.	(Nov.–April)
Khaniá	0·2	0·8	0·0	0·0	0·0	0·0	0·2
Iráklion	0·0	0·5	0·0	0·0	0·0	0·0	0·1
Anóyia	6·5	12·1	3·8	0·6	0·8	1·8	4·3

Source : E. G. Mariolopoulos and A. N. Livathinos, *Atlas Climatique de la
Grèce* (Athènes, 1935).

Precipitation

Rain. The amount of rainfall in Crete is only about half that of
the western coasts of mainland Greece, but in spite of its more
southerly latitude it is slightly more than that of Eastern Greece
(Árta 42.5 ins. ; Iráklion 20.1 ins. ; Athens 15.1 ins.). Almost
half the total amount falls in November and December, but January
is also wet ; the summer months, June, July and August are driest,
and in the east and south of the island July and August are rainless
in normal years (see table on p. 212). Much of the rainfall is
torrential, occurring in short sharp showers ; more rain falls in
Crete in its 70 rain days than in Eastern Greece in its 109 rain days.
In March, especially, heavy downpours may last for two or three
days ; such downpours are probably associated with the slow
passage of a depression when warm, moist southerly air meets with
cooler, but also damp, northerly air. Thunderstorms are frequent
and severe in autumn, when moisture-laden air rising over the
heated land surface creates conditions of great instability.

Snow. Falls of snow are occasionally experienced from November
to April but are most frequent in January and February. In the
lowlands it melts immediately, although after a heavy fall the
plateau of Sitía sometimes has a good cover for several days. In
the mountains the snow-line is usually found in winter between
1,600 ft. and 2,000 ft. but in a severe season it may descend to
1,300 ft. The high mountain plains of Omalós and Nídha are
often snow-covered most of the winter but are freed about April,
while snow lies on the highest peaks until May. There is no
permanent snow in Crete, though patches may occasionally survive
in sheltered places and crevices throughout much of the summer.

Average Monthly Rainfall, 1894–1929 (in inches)

Station	Ht. in ft.	Jan.	Feb.	Mar.	Apr.	May	June	July	Aug.	Sept.	Oct.	Nov.	Dec.	Year
Khaniá	46	5·0	3·9	2·6	1·1	0·6	0·1	0·0	0·1	1·3	1·5	4·8	6·6	27·6
Iráklion	118	3·3	2·8	1·8	1·1	0·9	0·0	0·0	0·3	0·7	1·5	3·9	3·6	19·9
Sitía	—	3·5	2·7	1·8	0·6	0·6	0·0	0·0	0·0	0·0	1·5	3·1	3·7	17·5
Anóyia	2,546	8·3	6·7	4·7	2·1	2·4	0·2	0·1	0·6	0·7	2·8	6·2	9·1	43·9
Ierápetra	10	2·1	1·1	0·7	0·3	0·2	0·2	0·0	0·0	0·2	0·6	1·2	1·5	8·1

Average number of rain days, 1894–1929

Station	Ht. in ft.	Jan.	Feb.	Mar.	Apr.	May	June	July	Aug.	Sept.	Oct.	Nov.	Dec.	Year
Khaniá	46	17·2	15·8	11·7	8·4	5·0	1·4	0·1	0·6	4·6	6·7	12·9	18·5	103·0
Iráklion	118	18·0	15·0	12·1	7·5	6·3	1·8	0·1	0·7	1·9	7·1	9·7	16·2	96·8
Sitía	—	6·8	5·8	3·9	1·8	2·4	0·3	0·03	0·1	0·2	3·1	5·1	8·4	·37·4
Anóyia	2,546	22·2	17·9	15·1	10·1	8·6	2·6	0·5	1·6	4·4	10·3	15·1	21·2	129·7
Ierápetra	10	12·5	9·0	6·1	3·9	1·7	0·4	0·0	0·0	0·9	3·7	5·5	11·5	55·5

Average Frequency of Thunderstorms (days per 1,000)

Station	Ht. in ft.	Jan.	Feb.	Mar.	Apr.	May	June	July	Aug.	Sept.	Oct.	Nov.	Dec.	Year
Khaniá	46	43·0	42·4	28·0	22·2	15·6	2·0	0·0	0·0	28·8	60·2	44·4	77·4	30·3
Melidhónion	341	88·8	57·5	40·3	20·8	44·4	12·5	0·0	4·0	16·7	104·8	83·3	88·8	47·9
Iráklion	118	33·3	37·0	34·5	15·3	19·4	4·4	0·0	0·0	4·4	47·3	33·3	38·7	21·9
Anóyia	2,546	58·1	50·9	32·3	37·8	38·7	15·6	2·2	2·2	31·1	88·2	66·7	73·1	41·4

Source : E. G. Mariolopoulos and A. N. Livathinos, *Atlas Climatique de la Grèce* (Athènes, 1935).

Percentage Frequency of Days on which Snow falls

Station	Ht. in ft.	Jan.	Feb.	Mar.	Apr.	Nov.	Dec.	Year
Khaniá	46	3·5	3·2	1·0	0·3	1·0	1·6	0·9%
Melidhónion	341	3·2	5·0	1·6	0·3	0·3	2·6	1·1
Iráklion	118	6·8	13·6	5·5	1·0	1·0	1·6	2·5
Sitía	—	1·6	1·0	0·3	0·0	0·0	0·3	0·3
Ierápetra	10	0·3	0·6	0·6	0·0	0·0	0·0	0·2

Source : E. G. Mariolopoulos and A. N. Livathinos, *Atlas Climatique de la Grèce* (Athènes, 1935).

Sunshine

Clear skies and bright sunshine are particularly characteristic of the Cretan climate. Although the relative humidity, averaging about 66%, is greater than in the eastern mainland, more hours of sunshine are recorded in Iráklion than in Athens owing to the effect of latitude. The skies are, on the average, only $\frac{4}{10}$ cloud covered (contrast $\frac{7}{10}$ in England) and the atmospheric conditions give great clearness and range to vision and sound, especially in the mountains. With a persistent south wind the air may become hazy and murky, but real fog and mist are almost unknown.

Regional Variations

Climatic variations in Crete are great for an island of its size. The mountain masses obviously have a climate that is much modified by altitude, as shown by the data for Anóyia, the only meteorological station above 1,000 ft. The average monthly temperatures in winter are lower than on the coast ; the differences are less in summer, in fact some of the narrow mountain valleys can then be very hot and stuffy whereas the heat of the coastal plains is tempered by sea breezes. The more severe winter is shown by the high frequencies of frost days in January and especially in February, but unfortunately no records exist of snow days. The greater rainfall is most marked ; and some rain falls in the summer months owing to the local instability showers, characteristic of mountain regions in this season. The relatively high frequency of thunderstorms recorded at Anóyia and Melidhónion (an inland station of the western peninsula) in June and September, and their occurrence in July and August, illustrate this point.

The coastal lowlands are not all alike ; the north coast is more exposed than the south coast, and Khaniá and Iráklion have lower winter temperatures and a greater rainfall than Ierápetra. The

Meteorological Table for Iráklion (Lat. 35° 20′ N., Long. 25° 09′ E. Height above M.S.L. 89 ft.)

Month	Pressure at M.S.L. Mean For Month mbs.	Air Temperature Average†† °F	Daily Max. (mean) °F	Daily Min. (mean) °F	Highest each month (mean) °F	Lowest each month (mean) °F	Highest recorded °F	Lowest recorded °F	Relative Humidity§ %	Cloud Amt. 0–10	Rain Average Fall in.	Rain No. of Days‡	Rain Max. fall in 24 hrs. in.	Wind N	N.E.	E.	S.E.	S.	S.W.	W.	N.W.	Calm
January	1018	54	60	48	69	41	76	34	71	6·2	3·7	14	2·7	8	3	1	2	17	22	6	23	18
February	1017	54	60	48	70	40	77	32	70	6·4	3·0	12	2·2	12	4	0	2	15	16	6	29	16
March	1016	57	64	50	77	43	86	35	67	5·3	1·6	7	1·3	10	6	1	1	14	11	5	25	27
April	1014	62	70	54	84	47	98	42	63	4·2	0·9	4	1·0	8	8	1	3	14	10	3	26	27
May	1014	68	76	60	88	53	100	48	64	3·5	0·7	3	1·6	11	8	1	2	7	7	4	28	32
June	1014	74	82	67	95	59	114	52	61	1·4	0·1	0·7	0·3	13	6	0	0	4	5	5	37	30
July	1012	78	85	72	94	65	106	62	60	0·7	0·0	0·1	0·5	9	2	0	0	1	2	7	59	20
August	1012	78	85	71	92	66	104	56	61	1·0	0·0	0·4	1·3	8	2	0	0	0	2	6	57	25
September	1016	75	82	68	88	61	102	56	64	2·0	0·7	2	3·0	10	4	0	1	2	4	5	47	27
October	1018	69	77	62	90	55	96	50	68	4·0	1·7	5	2·3	12	6	0	2	7	16	3	29	25
November	1017	63	71	56	81	48	87	42	70	5·8	2·7	8	2·6	11	6	0	3	16	17	4	22	21
December	1017	58	64	51	72	45	80	38	74	6·1	4·0	13	5·2	9	4	0	3	19	23	5	21	16
Means	1015	66	73	59	99*	38**			66	3·9				10	5	0	2	10	11	5	33	24
Totals											19·2	69										
Extreme of values							114	32					5·2									
Years of observations	1909–29	1909–29				1909–29	1909–29				1909–29			1920–29								

Source: *Mediterranean Pilot*, vol. IV, p. 421 (London, 1941).
Hours of observations: 0800, 1400, 2100 or 2000 local time.
†† ½ (Max. and Min.).
* Mean of highest each year.
** Mean of lowest each year.
† ½ (0800 + 2100 or 2000).
‡ Day with trace or more of rain.

south coast, sheltered from north winds, has very high summer temperatures, and the plain of Mesará, lying between the Psilorítis mountains to the north and the Kófinas mountains to the south, is unbearably hot in summer. The Kófinas mountains, however, shelter the plain from the scorching south wind and to them therefore the Mesará owes in part its fertility. The eastern promontory of Sitía is also distinctive. It is drier, and is more tempered by the sea and more exposed to gales, than the western part of the island. In spring and summer the plain of Sitía is almost as dry as the plains of the south coast, and the climate of this region has more affinities with the south than with the plains around Khaniá and Iráklion in the north-west.

VEGETATION

Flora

The flora of Crete is, relative to the area of the island, fairly rich and its affinities are clearly with the floras of the Pelopónnisos and Anatolia. There are only a few plants showing special connexion with North Africa, and almost all these have a limited range in Cyrenaica. This relationship reflects not only the existing climatic conditions but also the geological history of the island. Severance from Greece and a former Aegean continental mass was, however, sufficiently far distant in time to allow the development of some peculiar features in the flora. Approximately 1,450 species of seed-bearing plants are now known from Crete, and of these about 140 are endemic, that is are entirely limited to the island. The largest families are those of the daisies (*Compositæ*, with 180 species), peas (*Leguminosæ*, with 150 species), grasses (*Granineæ*, with 120 species), dead-nettles (*Labiatæ*, with 80 species), pinks (*Caryophyllaceæ*, with 70 species), umbellifers (*Umbelliferæ*, with 70 species), and crucifers (*Cruciferæ*, with 60 species). There are also considerable numbers of species of the lily and orchid families. These last two families, together with several others, are mainly responsible for the bulbous, tuberous, and rhizomatous plants, which form a feature of the herbaceous vegetation of Crete (as of other parts of the Mediterranean region) and which largely account for the carpets of brightly coloured flowers in the spring and early summer months. The most interesting areas floristically, and those where the majority of the endemics occur, are the four principal mountain groups : Lévka Óri, in the west, the richest area botanically ; Psilorítis with

Mount Ídhi, in the centre ; Lasíthi, in the east ; together with the Sitía mountains and peninsula still farther east. Nearly all the endemics are plants of rocky or stony habitats, and they occur especially in rocky ravines in the hill, montane, or high-mountain altitudinal zones.

General Character

While the flora of Crete may be considered rich, the natural vegetation at the present time is poor, in the sense that most of it has been either destroyed or highly modified by man in the course of the long history of human occupation of the island. The natural climax vegetation (that is the general type of plant community which shows maximum stability under given climatic conditions) is, for most of the surface of Crete, moderately tall forest or tall brushwood. Once this natural cover of forest and tall brushwood has been destroyed, the Mediterranean climatic conditions and the grazing activities of sheep and goats make regeneration difficult or impossible. Soil erosion quickly occurs on all slopes, and the forests are replaced by low brushwoods or open and impoverished communities growing on a rocky or stony substratum. The limited plains, with richer and deeper soil, have long been under cultivation. The general appearance of Crete is thus one of aridity except in the spring and early summer. The summer drought and heat, the predominance of pervious limestones, and the continued effects of interference with the natural plant cover in its attempts to re-establish itself, result in a rather monotonous brown or straw-coloured dried-up surface over much of the country throughout the summer months ; exceptions occur only in the ravines, in the mountain valleys, and where there is a permanently high water-table.

Forests

The forests of Crete were once very extensive but have now been almost completely destroyed. Much that is called ' forest ' in official statistics is only open woodland or brushwood from which most of the tall trees have disappeared. Even the brushwoods are depleted for fuel. Some of the oak forests have suffered from the ravages of the gipsy moth (*Porthetria dispar*). Forest fires have been responsible for much damage. It is, however, the grazing of large numbers of sheep and goats that is the main cause of the lack of forests today over so much of Crete. These animals effectively prevent regeneration by eating to the ground every seedling that may establish itself in any but the most inaccessible places. It follows that there is no development of saplings to replace trees destroyed by man or by fire, or to replace those dying more or less naturally from old age or disease. Consequently, forests in Crete are now limited to a few relics, mainly in the mountains.

The most interesting woods in Crete are those of the wild cypress (*Cupressus sempervirens* var. *horizontalis*). This species was at one time very widely spread both in the lowlands and the hills, especially on the south side of the western half of the island. Both historical evidence and the present occurrence of isolated specimens indicate that cypress forests formerly extended on both the north and south sides of the island almost to sea level. There still are, or were till recently, sparse cypress woods between 1,000 and 2,500 ft. on the south slopes of the Lévka Óri, and in places they extend upwards to about 5,000 ft. The trees here, for the most part, occur scattered, singly or in small groups. Some are fine specimens and their horizontally spreading branches give the impression of Lebanon cedars, very different in appearance from the tapering cypress which is so widely cultivated. Trees up to 100 ft. in height and 10 ft. in circumference have been recorded from this district. On exposed crests, the trees become gnarled and dwarfed, and elsewhere their natural beauty is marred by the lopping of branches. The undergrowth, which is sometimes quite dense but not tall, consists predominantly of small thorny or prickly and hairy shrubs with herbs of the Cretan phrygana (see pp. 219–20). It has been suggested that the cypress would be an excellent tree for re-afforestation of much of the Cretan hill and mountain country, if flocks and herds were rigidly controlled.

While the cypress is, or was, the characteristic tree of western Crete, pines (the Aleppo pine, *Pinus halepensis*, and the Black pine, *P. nigra*) are characteristic of, and, as forest elements, now almost limited to, central and eastern Crete. Two large pine forests are recorded in fairly recent literature, but both have now been very largely destroyed by fire and ruthless exploitation. One of these was in the eastern part of central Crete on the southern slope of the Lasíthi mountains almost as far as Kalámi ; the other lay in eastern Crete to the north of Mount Thriftí. As in Greece, the pines are frequently tapped for resin. The Aleppo pine has a light canopy, and the trees are frequently well spaced. Naturally, the undergrowth is thick and composed of mainly evergreen, hard-leaved shrubs and climbers. The Black pine has a closer canopy and, when the trees are allowed to grow thickly, the light is insufficient to allow the development of much undergrowth. The stone or umbrella pine (*Pinus pinea*) is seen in some places particularly near the coast or elsewhere in the lowlands, but it is not a native and was probably introduced by the Venetians.

The holm oak (*Quercus ilex*) is an evergreen oak growing on limestones and, in places, also on Tertiary non-calcareous beds. In western Crete there are the holm-oak woods in southern Apokóronas and here the gipsy moth has wrought terrible havoc. Although there are a good many holm-oak trees on both the western and eastern slopes of Psilorítis, there is no forest till one reaches the eastern slopes of the Lasíthi range, where what is probably the largest holm-oak forest in the island is found. The Kermes oak (*Quercus coccifera*), in its several varieties, dominates sometimes in communities intermediate between light forest and brushwood. Good examples are to be seen on the north side of the Lévka Óri. The trees stand well apart from one another, and there is some mixture of holm-oak, Cretan maple (*Acer creticum*), wild olives (*Olea europæa* var. *oleaster*), and a privet-like shrub (*Phillyrea media*).

All the above named trees are evergreen (the Cretan maple only imperfectly so). Deciduous forest, in which all or the majority of trees shed their leaves in the autumn, is rare in Crete. On the south side of the island are small light woods of hairy oak (*Quercus lanuginosa*), but these have been much damaged by cutting. In the hill and lower montane zones (500 to 800 m.) the sweet or Spanish chestnut (*Castanea sativa*) occurs locally.

Brushwood Communities

The Cretan brushwoods are for the most part composed of evergreen shrubs. Well developed maquis (forming the typical tall Mediterranean evergreen brushwoods dominated by species with leathery leaves) are now very rare in the island, though they occasionally occur near the coast, and brushwoods in some of the lower ravines might best be classified as a variety of maquis. Nevertheless, characteristic maquis plants are widely distributed in Crete, even if they are not grouped together as dense tall brushwood. Such species include : strawberry tree (*Arbutus Unedo*), locust, carob, or St. John's bread (*Ceratonia siliqua*), wild olive, Mediterranean heaths (*Erica arborea* and *E. verticillata*), myrtle (*Myrtus communis*), Mediterranean juniper (*Juniperus oxycedrus*), and others. Brushwood along some of the streams also appears to be partly related to the maquis though there is a mixture with woody and herbaceous plants that require a high water-table. Here, with planes (*Platanus orientalis*), reeds (*Arundo donax*), shrubs of the Chaste-tree (*Vitex agnus-castus*), and willows (*Salix* spp.), there is sometimes a shrub belt of junipers, myrtles, and Spanish broom (*Spartium junceum*), together with Jerusalem sage (*Phlomis fruticosa*) and the three-lobed sage (*Salvia triloba*). If the streams are followed inland to the mountains they nearly always lead to narrow rock gorges, where, on the rock shelves and in the clefts of the steep, shaded sides, there is often a rich vegetation of shrubby and herbaceous plants including many rarities with attractive flowers. The plants found here include a woody flax (*Linum arboreum*), the composites *Stæhelina fruticosa* and *S. arborescens*, the legume *Ebenus cretica*, a spiny mullein (*Verbascum spinosum*), a wild cabbage (*Brassica cretica*), and many other species.

Crete has been described as the land of scent and spines, with the comment that the abundance of spiny plants is such that people everywhere wear boots up to their knees, which they would certainly not otherwise do in a hot climate. This description applies especially to the Cretan phrygana—a more or less open community of low shrubs and sub-shrubs amongst which bulbous and other herbaceous plants grow at certain seasons. This low shrubby and sub-shrubby community has three marked characteristics : the predominance of hemispherical bushes, the great number of spiny or prickly plants, and the numerous odoriferous half-shrubs and herbs. Many of these last are members of the dead-nettle family, producing essential oils which evaporate into a still atmosphere on hot days. Five plants are, in varying proportions, nearly always dominant in the Cretan phrygana : the spiny burnet (*Poterium spinosum*), growing as a compact mass of branched thorns ; a spurge, *Euphorbia acanthothamnos*, poisonous, growing up to 2 ft. high, and provided with forked spines ; a gorse-like plant, with strong spines and deep yellow flowers, *Calycotome villosa ;* a spiny broom, *Genista acanthoclada*, very much branched ; and a shrubby kidney-vetch, *Anthyllis hermanniæ*, with sub-spinescent branches. Associated with these are the spiny mullein and a variety of hawthorn (*Cratægus monogyna* var. *hirsutior*) which sometimes grows into a small tree. Growing amongst the spiny bushes, and there finding protection from the grazing animals, are many herbaceous plants such as vetches (*Vicia* spp.), pinks (*Dianthus* spp.), milkworts (*Polygala* spp.), scented labiates, and many others. This Cretan phrygana is the most widespread plant community now found on the island. With local modifications it extends from near sea level far up into the mountains. Sometimes it is very dense, but on rocky ground it becomes more open. It rarely grows more than 2 to 3 ft. in height, and is usually much lower than this. On all the chief mountain groups, the Cretan barberry (*Berberis cretica*) is found as a low, spiny shrub, with black berries. It grows from about 3,000 ft. up to almost the top of the highest peaks. Amongst other shrubby or sub-shrubby species of Crete, the following may be noted : the Cretan rock-rose (*Cistus villosus* var. *creticus*) from which the aromatic gum ' ladanum ' was formerly collected either by whipping the plants with leather thongs or from the beards of he-goats which had grazed on the shrubs ; a sage (*Salvia pomifera*), called ' phascomilia ' by the Cretans, which bears large greenish galls, containing a sweet liquid, which when chewed are said to quench the thirst ; and the styrax (*Styrax officinalis*), known in Crete as ' astirakas ' or ' stiraki ', which has large white scented blossoms and which yields storax, a resin much used in ancient times as incense.

Herbaceous Communities

Natural herbaceous communities are rare in Crete as there are no extensive grasslands in the island. In places where even the low-growing phrygana shrubs have been cut or dug up for fuel, and everything palatable eaten by sheep and goats, a poor community of scattered herbs may be the only vegetation. Such a community is not infrequently dominated by asphodel (*Asphodelus microcarpus*). In some of the mountain basins there are fairly considerable grazing areas which, however, have not been botanically analysed in detail. There is a very considerable ruderal flora in Crete. Most of these plants are annual herbs growing along paths and in waste places near habitations. The weed flora of arable fields is also rich in species and individuals, owing to the primitive methods of cultivation and to the sowing of imperfectly cleaned seed.

FAUNA

Changes, probably of recent geological date, in the climate, vegetation, and physical features of Crete have perhaps been responsible for great changes in its fauna. The elephant, pigmy hippopotamus, antelope, and other animals, whose bones are found embedded in the limestone floors of some Cretan caves, have disappeared, though the deer seem to have lingered into historical times (cf. the legends of Dictynna and deer connected with the promontory of Rodhopoú). There are now only seventeen species of mammals in the island, nine of which are peculiar to Crete ; all except one (the spiny mouse) are European in character. The largest and most interesting is the *agrimi* or wild goat (*Capra aegagrus*), which haunts the remotenesses of the Asprovoúni and perhaps of Psilorítis also. It is not the same as the ibex of the Alps and Pyrenees ; it weighs about 90 lb. and has fine tapering horns about $2\frac{1}{2}$ ft. long, curving slightly backwards with pointed tips. The colour is brown with a dark stripe down the back. It is as active as a chamois, but in winter it is driven by the snows to lower levels and is then shot. It existed in ancient times on various islands of the archipelago—more recently on Andímilos, and on Yioúra in the Northern Sporádhes.

Of rodents the chief are : rabbits (plentiful on the island of Día) ; hares (a small light-coloured variety resembling those of Kefallinía and found all over the island) ; besides mice, rats, etc. There are several small kinds of carnivora : a small pale-hued badger, with a useful skin ; a small marten, plentiful and killed in winter for its fur ; a large variety of weasel, peculiar to Crete and fairly common ; and a wild-cat resembling that of Sardinia. Shrews and hedgehogs are found in the lowlands ; bats haunt the caves ; and there are scorpions and some small non-venomous snakes. Cretan snails are a Levantine delicacy. The insects of Crete are numerous and apt to be troublesome. Cicadas abound in the trees ; at certain times flying ants swarm in the air and may cause beasts and human beings intense discomfort ; flies, fleas and bugs are very numerous, but mosquitoes are not common except in the valleys. There are, in addition, the usual domesticated animals. The Cretan dog, a rough-coated medium-sized animal resembling a lurcher, is peculiar to the island : it is a good hunter, and less savage than Albanian and Turkish dogs. In the towns other dogs, mostly mongrels, are to be seen.

The mountains and the variety of scenery attract numerous birds, and except for regular game varieties these are not killed by the inhabitants. A good many of these birds are not native, but come from Europe either as winter guests or as migrants on their way to Africa. Such are the snipe, heron, woodcock, and numerous smaller birds. The raven (a small variety), grey crow, black-headed jay and chough, as well as a great many smaller birds, including songsters like the thrush and nightingale, are indigenous. A great many of these smaller birds frequent the upland plains and scrubby slopes. The owl haunts the lowlands, as do some of the falcons and hawks. These latter, however, are also found in the mountains ; but chief among birds of prey are the griffon-vulture and the lammergeyer (bearded vulture), which hover amongst the great heights. Dove, rock-pigeons, bitterns, and ducks are found, and in various parts quail and partridges (the latter e.g. on Akrotíri) are plentiful. In addition to these, some sea-birds are found around the coasts.

REGIONAL DIVISIONS

Physically the island includes three types of country—lowland, hill country and mountain. The lowland occupies less than 4% of the total area, and the greater part of that is included in the plain of Mesará. Along the north coast there are small strips of coastal plain, the chief of which lies around Khanía ; in addition, there are the upland basins (Omalós, Nídha, Lasíthi and a few others) set amid the mountains.

The hill country stretches across the three isthmuses of Rethímni, Iráklion and Ierápetra, and these separate the four main mountain masses from one another. For the most part, these three isthmuses consist of tangled country, intersected by valleys and ravines, with heights mounting in places to over 2,000 ft. Generally speaking, they correspond with the less resistant Tertiary formations (chalky limestones, marls and conglomerates) ; and their features are much softer than those of the towering heights of hard limestone which lie on either side of them.

From west to east the great mountain masses are : (1) the Lévka Óri, rising to 8,045 ft. ; with this may be included the western uplands of Sélinon and Kísamos ; (2) the Psilorítis mountains, rising to 8,058 ft., the highest point in the island ; (3) the mountains of Lasíthi, which reach 7,047 ft., and finally (4) the less impressive mountains of Sitía, whose highest point is only 4,839 ft. above sea level. It is these mountain groups, especially the first three, that give Crete its essential character. Their massive groupings, with serrated crests, steep slopes, and towering cliffs, make them conspicuous from great distances ; and at close range their great height (as compared with the breadth of the island) and their steepness give them a dominating and even overpowering appearance. In winter, they are clad for some months, even to low levels, with snow ; and, though most of this has gone by early spring, the main heights are snow-clad till June, and retain flecks of snow in crevices and hollows throughout the year. In summer, their crests of glittering whitish limestone are no less conspicuous, and are even harsher and more savage-looking ; the upper parts are scrub-covered or quite bare, the lower slopes are usually sparsely clad with trees.

For the purpose of more detailed description, Crete may be divided into the following regions and sub-regions (Fig. 39) :

A. The Western Hill-country :
    (1) The Kísamos Basin.
    (2) The Sélinon Basin.
    (3) The Western Coastlands.
    (4) The Northern Peninsulas.

B. The Lévka Óri :
    (1) The Western Massif.
    (2) The Central Mountains.
    (3) The Eastern Massif.

C. The Uplands and Plains of Khaniá :
    (1) Ridges and Plateaux.
    (2) The Coastal Plain.
    (3) The District of Apokorónas.
    (4) The Peninsula of Akrotíri.

D. The Isthmus of Rethímni :
    (1) Northern Drainage Area.
    (2) Southern Drainage Area.

E. The Milopótamos District

F. The Psilorítis Mountains

G. The Depression of Iráklion

H. The Mesará Depression

I. The Asteroúsia Mountains

J. The Lasíthi Area
    (1) The Central Highlands.
    (2) The Northern Hills and Plateaux.
    (3) The Southern Slopes.

K. The Isthmus of Ierápetra

L. The Sitía District :
    (1) Western Sitía.
    (2) The Central Furrow.
    (3) Eastern Sitía.

The population figures of the towns and villages are those of the census of 16 May 1928.

A. THE WESTERN HILL COUNTRY (Fig. 40)

This is an area of tangled ridges, mostly below 3,000 ft. but occasionally rising above. The southern half, which includes the highest areas, is composed of red, brown and purple schists, while in the north there are Tertiary marls, clays and sandstones. The ranges are therefore softer-featured than the limestone heights of the Lévka Óri to the east. Exceptions to these general features are found in the restricted limestone areas where the sharp rocky profiles most usual in Crete appear. These limestone areas include : (1) the two peninsulas of Kórikos and Rodhopoú ; (2) Mount Mána (2,897 ft.), south of Kastélli Kisámou, and the bold grey ridges that run north-west, south-east and north-east from it ; and (3) the coastal hills of the south which really form a westward extension of the Lévka Óri. Generally speaking, the whole area is bare, the predominant vegetation type consisting of high bush thicket and low scrub, except of course where cultivated types appear.

The watershed between the north and south flowing rivers is formed by a broad belt of high country averaging 2,200 ft. in height and extending from Mount Apopigádhi to the west coast. To the north lies the Kísamos basin, to the south that of Sélinon, both names being those of eparchies. A third, smaller, drainage area comprises the narrow belt along the west coast. Any regional division of such a confused region must be artificial, but these three areas divided by watersheds form a convenient basis for description. To them must be added a fourth division—the two great peninsulas of the north.

A.1. The Kísamos Basin

The ridges of the Kísamos basin are roughly parallel and run north to south. They descend from heights averaging 2,200 ft. near the watershed area to 800–500 ft. before they slope to the narrow plain along the shore of the Gulf of Kísamos. The coastal plain is composed of pebbly sands and gravels through which most of the streams disappear before reaching the sea. It is fertile and well cultivated, wider in the east than in the west. There is a fair number of villages, the largest settlement being Kastélli Kisámou itself, with a population of 1,280. From the plain, the arrangement of the background presents the appearance of an amphitheatre as the ridges nearer the coast rise in height to those behind, and as the eastern and western ranges continue northwards into the

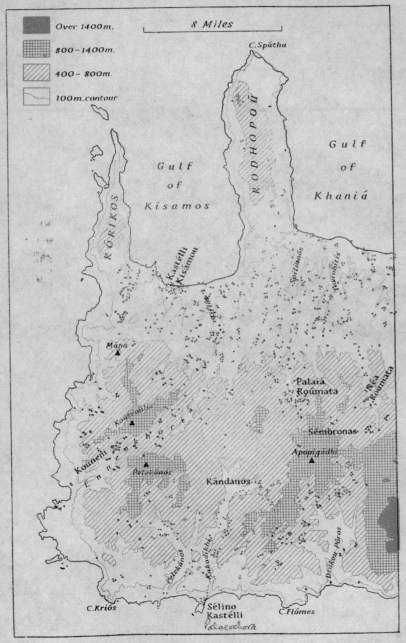

Fig. 40. Settlement in the western part of Khaniá nomós (Crete)
Based on the 1 : 50,000 Crete, M.D.R. 612 (1943).

The red dots show settlements ; owing to reduction from the
original maps they do not necessarily indicate individual houses.

peninsulas of Rodhopoú and Kórikos respectively. The ridges of the basin are composed mostly of Tertiary marls with occasional coverings of shales, gravels and schist boulders. Their surface is undulating, save where occasional outcrops of harder limestone give rise to some bold isolated heights. The valleys, though narrow, are fertile, and the light Tertiary slopes, sheltered and warm, favour cultivation. Settlement continues from the plain inland up the valleys, in particular up the Tiflós valley-system which drains the northern end of the Enneakhoriá furrow. The upper courses of these streams are deep and steep-sided ravines, containing oleander and other brushwood and plane trees. Eastward, the region continues into the ridge and valley district of Khaniá, and it is difficult to draw a boundary between the two areas.

A.2. The Sélinon Basin

This is a more confused region, but in general the ridges trend north-east to south-west. Its schistose hills are either cultivated or capable of cultivation to high levels. The region broadly consists of two shallow upland basins separated by a north-south ridge (rising to over 3,000 ft.) that runs southward from Mount Apopigádhi. The westerly basin is drained by the Kakodíkhi, the Pelekános and other streams that descend from the northern watershed or from the western mountains of Pelekános. Villages are numerous, the largest being Kándanos (977) situated in a fertile area floored by recent yellow clays and sands and drained by the Kakodíkhi river. The eastern basin is that of the Dhrákou Póros which likewise has cultivation and villages. The lower courses of these rivers cut through the coastal limestone belt in gorges to reach the sea across a very narrow plain. The intervening ridge between the lower valleys of the Kakodíkhi and the Dhrákou Póros spreads out into a series of spurs forming a fan-like plateau also separated from the sea by a narrow marginal plain.

A.3. The Western Coastlands

The westward face of the coastal chain presents a fairly even slope to the sea, and is furrowed by numerous torrent beds often containing cultivable soil. Southwards from Mount Mána (2,897 ft.), the chain continues at over 3,000 ft. until it culminates in Mount Koutroúlis (3,511 ft.), which overlooks the Enneakhoriá furrow. This great gap in the western range is one of the most important features of western Crete. Its general direction is

south-west to north-east, and it forms a groove connecting the
western coastlands with the Kísamos basin. It is hemmed in by
long parallel ranges running in that direction. The form of the
depression is not simple, for the watershed between the north-
east and south-west flowing rivers within it rises to 1,940 ft. The
valley floor is undulating, abounds in springs, and is well cultivated.
It contains numerous villages of which Koúneni is the largest with
445 inhabitants (Enneakhoriá = ' nine hamlets ').

South of the Enneakhoriá gap the ground rises abruptly to an
upland known as Pelekános (3,878 ft.). This mass and that of
Koutroúlis stand like two great towers overlooking the depression
between. To the south, the Pelekános mountain descends and
splits into numerous barren ridges and spurs, some running south-
west and terminating in bold bluffs (1,500 ft.) overlooking a narrow
coastal plain, others running south to form the western limits of
the Sélinon Basin.

A.4.   The Northern Peninsulas

The peninsulas of Kórikos (2,500 ft.) and Rodhopoú (2,600 ft.)
are, in the main, limestone masses. Their barren slopes and cliffs,
scarred by deep fissures and ravines, give them a wild and desolate
appearance. They are almost uninhabited, save in the south where
they join the mainland. Here there are villages and cultivation,
continuous with those of the Kísamos basin.

B.   THE LÉVKA ÓRI (Fig. 41)

The Áspra Voúna or, more classically, the Lévka Óri (White
Mountains), are sometimes also called the Sfakianakes Madháres
or ' Sphakiot Bleak Mountains '. These names suggest both the
grey limestone rock and its rugged character. The block forms the
largest and most massive of all the Cretan mountains. On the west
it rises abruptly from the valley of the Dhrákou Póros, above the
headwaters of which it is linked to the western hills of Sélinon by
the district around Apopigádhi. To the south the mass falls with
startling abruptness in great cliffs to the sea, and here is the wildest
and grandest part of the Cretan coast. To the north, the Lévka
Óri fall in trackless steeps of naked and rugged rock to the plateaux
above Khaniá. Finally, to the east, the lower flanks of the massif
thrust themselves out to meet the western spurs of the Psilorítis in
the peninsula of Rethímni.

Over 1400m.

800–1400m.

400–800m.

100m. contour

8 Miles

C. Dhrápunon

Yeoryioúpolis Bay

Lake Kournás

Episkopí

petrés

Mourskláis

Trípali

Aryiroú-polis

hés

Kallikrátis

ndlíon

Krionerítis

Skalotí

Rodhákinon

Plakiás Bay

lo

not necessarily indicate

The highest parts of the region are wild and deserted, with little or no surface cover, with some mountain pasture and much exposed bare rock. The lower areas have scattered trees and scrub. Very high bush thicket, consisting mainly of oleander, grows on the slopes between the gorges. The oleander (= *sfakos*) is so widespread here that it has given the name ' Sfakia ' to the whole district. In the gorges themselves, cypress, oak, plane, walnut and wild fig are usual, and most of these trees grow thick and tall. Agriculturally, the whole region of Lévka Óri is a poor country. The rearing of sheep and goats occupies the first place, the beasts moving upwards in spring, but the southern slopes are usually too steep even for pasturage. Cultivation is possible only on the upland plains and on the limited coastal flats.

Seen from the south, the massif clearly reveals three main groups —western, central and eastern. These are separated from one another by two great gorges—that of Roúmeli in the west and Áskifos in the east. These two valleys provide the only passages across the massif from north to south.

B.i.   *The Western Massif*

The western group of heights rises to sharp rugged peaks of 6,000–7,000 ft. which are deeply notched by great ravines and chasms towards the coast. The highest points are Volakiás (7,271 ft.) and Psiláfi (6,509 ft.). North of the main heights lies the upland plain of Omalós. This is one of the geographical curiosities of Crete. It is nearly circular in form, with a diameter of 2 miles or more, and it is enclosed by a ring of mountains rising to over 7,000 ft. on the south and to 5,000 ft. elsewhere. The plain is probably due to faulting and has been eroded into a rounded basin whose almost level floor, covered by alluvial soil, lies about 3,420 ft. above sea level. Around rise, to 1,500–3,500 ft. above the level of the plain, stony limestone hills with bare tops and steep, rocky sides, thinly covered with bushes. In winter the basin is filled with snow, often 6 ft. deep ; in spring, this melts and forms a marsh which appears to drain away, partly through a large hole (*katavóthra*) near the northern end, thus enabling some of the plain to be cultivated in the summer by temporary residents from the Lákkoi district. Until a few years ago the plain was largely under cereals, but now potatoes are the dominant crop. Around the edges of the plain, the rocky, scrubby slopes have good spring pasture, and there are several huts for seasonal occupation (Plate 78). The plain is approached by passes from the Dhrákou Póros valley (3,694 ft.), from the upper Roúmeli gorge (4,026 ft.), and from the upper Plataniás valley (3,566 ft.).

The western mass as a whole is severed from the main central area by the deep chasms of the Roúmeli in the south and the upper Plataniás in the north, the heads of these gorges being separated by only a narrow neck which links the two mountain groups. The Roúmeli gorge is the most remarkable in Crete. It may have once corresponded to a fault, but water and weathering have deepened the original cleft to an almost vertical-sided cut. The walls are composed of limestone with hard concrete-like conglomerate which forms ledges resistant to erosion. For the greater part of its course, down to its mouth, mountains of 3,000–6,000 ft. rise close on either hand, and the lower slopes fall in precipices of 1,500 ft. or so to the bed of the gorge. The bottom of the gorge is strewn with immense boulders, between and over which flows a rapid stream, swift and deep in winter, weaker in summer and autumn, when, however, it is liable to sudden and dangerous floods after rain and thunderstorms. The track itself is slippery and dangerous in many places, and has to cross the river repeatedly by stones or fords. At one point the track actually lies in the stream bed. Towards its mouth the ravine opens on to a small, cultivated, gravelly delta, and the stream rushes over a steep pebbly beach into a wild open bay between two bluffs. On the southern outer slopes near the gorge, scattered pines occur, but in the gorge itself there are only a few cypresses.

B.2. The Central Mountains

To the east of the Roúmeli gorge, the main Lévka Óri rise almost sheer to form a series of conical peaks of about 7,000–8,000 ft. The main heights are as follows : Pákhnes (8,045 ft.), Trokháres (7,877 ft.), Sorós Griás (7,647 ft.), Kástro (7,277 ft.), Zaranokefála (7,021 ft.), Melidaoú (6,998 ft.) and Mávri (6,789 ft.). They stand above a massive plateau of about 6,000 ft. and enclose several basins or depressions with blind valleys leading into them. These are rocky, barren, encroached upon by talus heaps, and lie deep in snow during winter. To the south, the western portion of the central massif falls direct into the sea, with precipitous cliffs upwards of 2,000 ft. Eastwards, there is a narrow plateau (about 2,000 ft.) between coast and massif ; here are the rough, stony plains of Arádhaina and Anópolis ; they carry some fertile soil, however, that is cultivated with vines, cereals and other crops to support a

Plate 77. The plain of Omalós

The view shows the sharp contrast between the flat cultivated plain and the bare limestone mountains which surround it.

Plate 78. The house of a Lakkiot on the edge of the Omalós basin

The house is dry-built of stone and serves as a temporary dwelling occupied in summer by migrant farmers from the Lakkoi district (see p. 227).

Plate 80. Vegetation on the limestone slopes near Áyios Ioánnis

The photograph was taken in the country east of the Roúmeli gorge, and shows the small rounded bushes which are typical of the limestone

Plate 79. The Roúmeli gorge

fair population. Serving this area is the little port of Khóra Sfakíon, with a population of 407. This lower plateau region is cut by the gorges of Arádhaina, Kávis and Sfakianó—all with perpendicular sides some hundreds of feet in depth. Along its eastern margin, the central mass diminishes in height but not in boldness or ruggedness. Deep gorges furrow the surface until the great Áskifos gorge is reached. Like the Roúmeli gorge, it is probably the result of faulting, and it provides the second routeway from north to south across the Lévka Óri. On either side, lofty barren limestone mountains fall in vertical or overhanging cliffs to form the sides of the ravine, and the passage narrows in places to 10 or even 6 ft. The bottom contains no stream and is rough and often slippery. Higher up the valley, at about 2,500 ft., the gorge opens suddenly on to the plain of Imbros above which a pass at 2,680 ft.—the highest point in the passage—leads to the plain of Áskifos, with the village of that name (789). This forms an amphitheatre of 3 to 4 miles circumference lying at about 2,200 ft. in the midst of a triangle of mountains about 6,000 ft. high. It is snowbound in winter, and is marshy towards the centre, but around its edges the rocky hills are inhabitable and the whole plain is cultivated with vines, cereals and other crops. To the north, ridges and valleys with intermittent streams descend to the district of Apokorónas. Like most of the southern lower hill-sides, the heights around the gorge of Áskifos are dotted with pines.

B.3. The Eastern Massif

Beyond the valley of Áskifos stretch the lower but still striking heights of the eastern Lévka Óri. The highest points are Angathés (4,957 ft.), Trípali (4,898 ft.) and Krionerítis (4,305 ft.). Among these heights are small cultivated upland plains (e.g. Asféndhon and Kallikrátis) which are approached by steep ascents and narrow passes. To the south is a stony inclined plain, about a mile wide, between the sea and the line of craggy steeps behind. Cultivation is possible and there are several tiny villages of a few hundred people each, e.g. Rodhákinon and Skalotí. In the middle of this coast is the rocky promontory of Frangokástello, crowned with Venetian ruins. Towards the east, spurs thrust out into the Rethímni isthmus to join with the outliers of the Psilorítis massif.

C. The Uplands and Plains of Khaniá (Fig. 41)

The great mass of Lévka Óri descends to the north coast in a series of ridges and plateaux that develop into foothills and spurs as the sea is approached. The whole region may be conveniently divided into four parts for the purposes of description : (1) ridges and plateaux, (2) the coastal plain, (3) the eastern area of Apokorónas, and (4) the peninsula of Akrotíri.

C.1. Ridges and Plateaux

The western portion of this region is a continuation of the Kísamos district to the west. Its background is formed by the heights around Apopigádhi, and from these proceed a number of narrow but rather flat-topped ridges which sink with soft undulating knolls towards the coastal plain. They are intersected by narrow ravines, often draining broader upland basins, and they discharge several streams into the Gulf of Khaniá. The main stream is that of the Tavroнítis whose headwaters drain a number of upland basins with tiny villages—Palaiá Roúmata, Néa Roúmata and Sémbronas. In winter it is a roaring torrent, but in summer it tends to become a series of waterholes. As the prevailing rock of the area is schist, there is a good deal of surface soil and water. Olives and grain do well in the open upper valleys, while the lower valley-slopes grow vines.

Eastwards is the basin of the Plataniás, the largest stream of western Crete. It rises in springs on the high slopes of the western Lévka Óri, to the north of the plain of Omalós, and is perhaps fed by underground drainage from that plain. A series of deep pre-cipitous ravines unites just above Mesklá (619) to form a broad valley enclosed by ridges that rise to 2,000 ft. The stream here is rapid and clear, and it continues as a brawling highland stream until, below Fournés (653), its course leads out into more open and level country near Alikianoú (707) ; this plain of Alikianoú is an extension of the coastal lowlands of Khaniá.

To the east of the Plataniás valley system is a broad plateau area which lies at the base of the steep slopes of the Lévka Óri to the south, and which falls abruptly to the plain of Khaniá to the north. The surface of this plateau area is by no means uniform. The greater part is composed of limestone, and these districts are highest, but the whole of the middle part, as well as the lower outside slopes, are of quartzite and talc schists, and towards the plain of Khaniá these are succeeded lower down by Tertiary rocks. Several smaller plateaux are distinguishable. At the highest levels (2,000–1,500 ft.) are plateaux like those of Madharó, Drakóna and Thérisson. Lower down (at about 1,150 ft.) are those of Panayía and Maláxa. Between

[Facing page 230

Plate 81. The village of Vrisos

The village lies in the valley of the Vrisón near where the road to Khóra Sfakíon cuts across the Lévka Óri massif, the higher parts of which can be seen in the distance.

Plate 82. Mount Vígles in the Akrotíri peninsula

Plate 83. The plain of Nídha

The plain, lying at about 5,000 ft., is too high for cultivation and stands in contrast with that of Omalós (*cf.* Plate 77).

these two main plateau groups the surface dips to the depression of Katokhóri (1,000–700 ft.) in the schist region. The limestone surface of these plateau regions is rather bare, and, though there are numerous springs, the whole area is dry in summer. There is, however, much good soil in the valleys and in pockets on the plateaux. Vines do well up to 1,400 ft. Olives and cereals (oats and barley) are also grown, as well as temperate-climate fruits (apples, pears, cherries). In the wilder parts, large flocks of sheep and goats are pastured. The schist slopes facing Khaniá, and the schist areas generally, are covered with heath and green scrub which even in summer retains a fresh and bright appearance, and the whole of this region forms a lower dark-green belt in striking contrast with the background of bare and whitish mountains.

C.2. The Coastal Plain

Below the plateau area lies the plain of Khaniá—a belt of softly rolling lowland extending westwards from Soúdha Bay. It is drained by the Kladhisós, a narrow stream with a pebbly bed. The gentle undulations of the plain are intensively cultivated, and almost every crop grown in Crete is represented here. The orange, the olive, the grape-vine and the carob are the most widespread ; but cotton, maize, tobacco and vegetable crops are also grown. The area is covered with fertile irrigated fields enclosed by low irrigation banks or equally low stone walls. This intensive cultivation leaves little room for non-cultivated types of surface-cover ; groups of cypresses and isolated date palms form the main trees. Villages are numerous throughout the whole area, and Khaniá itself, with a population of 26,604, is the capital of Crete.

Westwards, towards the mouth of the Plataniás, the plain of Khaniá passes into hilly ground, more rocky, but still with cultivation. The outstanding height of Monodhéndri is an outlier of the upland country to the south. The plain of Khaniá is separated from that of Alikianoú by a watershed of only 130 ft. The river Plataniás, in the latter plain, is shallow but has a rapid perennial flow which serves the irrigated fields of the valley. West of the Plataniás mouth, the coastal plain narrows very considerably, but there are extensions of lowland up the stream that cross it to the Gulf of Khaniá, e.g. up the valley of the Tavronítis and the Spilianós.

C.3. The District of Apokorónas

The north-eastern slopes of the Lévka Óri overlook the district of Apokorónas. The barren limestone edge, furrowed by gorges, gives place to foothills (800–900 ft.) of schists, gravelly clays and Tertiary conglomerates, abounding in springs, and more or less fertile. Lower still, these hills pass into the undulating plain of Apokorónas, composed of coarse Tertiary limestone and marls. The area is drained to the north by the Koíliaris, and to the south by the Vrisón ; the watershed between the two valley-systems is 500–600 ft. above sea-level. The area as a whole is a country of rolling hills and valleys, extremely fertile and well watered, producing amongst other things cereals, vines, olives and market-garden produce ; villages are fairly numerous. To the north-east rises a limestone upland that culminates in a height of 1,736 ft. and terminates in Cape Dhrápanon. Its surface is rough and barren with only occasional patches of cultivable soil in depressions. On the north-east, the fall of this upland to the sea is steep and in places precipitous.

C.4. The Peninsula of Akrotíri

This peninsula is joined to the mainland by a low isthmus only 2¼ miles wide. The greater part consists of Tertiary rocks—marls below, overlaid with coarse, whitish limestones and conglomerates. Its surface is for the most part barren and covered with heather, stunted scrub and scattered trees. Cultivable soil is largely restricted to the hollows (doline) where red clayey alluvium has collected ; cereals form the main crop, but there are also olives, and there is pasturage for cattle. Over a dozen villages are to be found in the area.

To the north-east, the surface rises into a range of hard grey limestone, bold and rocky, split by deep gorges and containing several caves. This range reaches a maximum height of 1,732 ft. near the east coast and falls precipitously into the sea (Plate 82).

D. THE ISTHMUS OF RETHÍMNI (Fig. 42)

Lying between the higher masses of the Lévka Óri and the Psilorítis mountains is the isthmus of Rethímni, a lower region of irregular hills and plateaux. The watershed between the drainage to the north and south respectively lies along a central bridge of hilly country. It does not correspond with the lines of the ranges, and leaves the greatest heights now on the south and now on the north, but it forms a convenient basis for describing the area. The greatest heights are in the southern area.

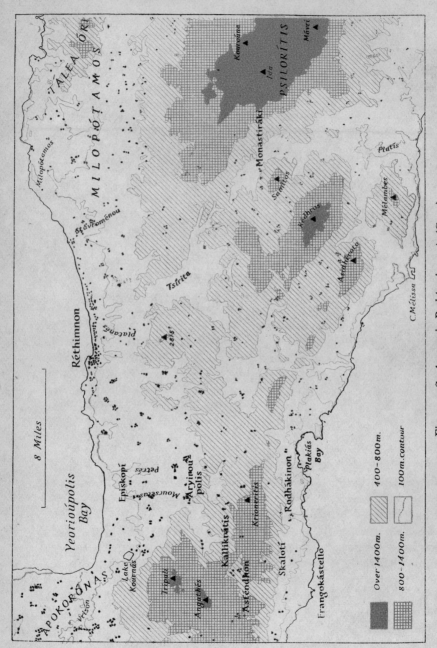

Fig. 42. Settlement in Rethímni nomós (Crete)

Based on the 1 : 50,000 Crete, M.D.R. 612 (1943).

Over 1400m.

800–1400m.

400–800m.

100m.contour

C.Mélissa

D.1.   Northern Drainage Area

The northern part of the isthmus drains down to a narrow coastal plain of sands, red gravels and Tertiary debris. But the general slope of the district is masked by numerous ridges, plateaux and valleys extending from the Lévka Óri on the west and from the spur of the Psilorítis on the east. The main rivers, from west to east, are the Moursélas, the Petrés, the Tsírita (known as Sfakoríako in its lower course, and joined near the coast by the Platanés), and finally the Stavroménou. The rocks include Tertiary marls, and limestones in the west, and both these and schists in the east ; there are also outliers of more massive limestones. Much of the surface is over 1,200 ft. and at one point it rises to 2,815 ft. In the north-west of the area is Lake Kournás, the largest lake in Crete. It lies about 2 miles inland and is enclosed on three sides by high hills with precipitous slopes in places. The surface of the lake is about 63 ft. above sea-level. It is now used as a storage reservoir for irrigation purposes.

The country is too broken to form an agricultural area of first-class importance, but still there is considerable cultivation. The coastal plain is very fertile and a wide variety of crops is grown, sometimes very intensively with the aid of irrigation. Behind this coastal strip, the larger valleys also contain much cultivable soil, and there is a fair amount of pasturage. The largest town in the whole area is Réthimnon itself, with a population of 8,632. There are also some fair sized villages, particularly in the west, e.g. Episkopí (945) and Aryiroúpolis (767).

D.2.   Southern Drainage Area

This is a more mountainous region. The relief is complicated, but it consists essentially of a series of ranges curving from the Lévka Óri towards the outliers of the Psilorítis massif in the east. The ranges are broken in places by narrow transverse valleys connecting long east-west intermontane valleys. Towards the east the ranges become higher and more discontinuous. The most important of these eastern heights are the Asidhéroto (3,727 ft.) and the Mélambes (3,107 ft.), both rising to rocky crests. To the north of these lies the more important and conspicuous highland of Kédhros (5,287 ft.) which is a blunt conical mass of limestone, bold and dry, but giving rise to seasonal springs. To the south, this falls steeply ; to the north and west, it is continued in the form of limestone and schist spurs into the irregular country of the northern slope. To the

east, it and the nearby Samítos highland (3,327 ft.) are separated
from the Psilorítis massif by the valley and gorge of the Platís which
provides a routeway between Réthimnon and the plain of Mesará.

The valleys of this southern drainage area as a whole are well-
watered and fertile. Thus the upper valley of the Platís, particularly
around Monastiráki, carries a fair amount of cultivated land (cereals,
vines and fruit trees) and supports fairly numerous villages ; the
same is true of the trough between the Kédhros and Asidhéroto
ranges. There is, however, but little settlement along the coast
which is steep-to and difficult ; an exception to this is the small
cluster of villages in the hinterland of Plakiás Bay.

E.   The Milopótamos District (Figs. 42, 43)

The district of Milopótamos is geographically an extension of the
isthmus of Rethímni and lies between the Psilorítis massif and the
sea. It consists of two distinct areas—lowland and upland. In
the south is the fertile Tertiary basin of the river Milopótamos and
its tributaries. The tributaries flow from the steep northern slopes
of the Psilorítis, and their valleys, though narrow, are fertile. Both
they and the main stream usually dry up in summer to a series of
waterholes. Considerable cultivation is carried on, and the basin
has always been an area of settlement, and prosperity. The usual
Cretan crops occupy most of the cultivated area—cereals, vines,
olives, together with oranges, walnuts and other fruit trees. The
valley is fairly thickly populated, and the largest settlement is
Anóyia with a population of 2,904 ; there are several villages, a
number each with about 500 inhabitants, and some smaller than this.

Towards the eastern end of the basin, the country rises and the
Tertiary limestones pass into harder forms while dark schists
occasionally appear. This higher eastern area is really a buttress of
the Psilorítis massif, and it extends to the coast to form the promontories at the western end of the Gulf of Iráklion. Here is the
divide between the Milopótamos district and the plain of Iráklion.
It is a region of rough, craggy hills with a number of rather small
barren plains, and it rises to 2,625 ft. in the striking limestone cone
of Stroúmboulas. Cultivation is restricted and villages are few.
This hilly country sweeps round to the west to form a coastal range
that separates the Milopótamos basin from the sea. The coastal
range consists of a series of tangled ridges with sharp rocky summits
of whitish limestone rising to a maximum height of 3,536 ft. in the

Tálea Óri. Towards the valley on the south, it presents a rapid descent with cliffs ; while to the sea on the north, it falls precipitously with only a few rugged inlets.

F. THE PSILORÍTIS MOUNTAINS (Fig. 43)

The mountain system of Psilorítis, known to the ancients as Ida, occupies a large part of central Crete, and constitutes a formidable barrier between the eastern and western halves of the island. Though rising in Mount Psilorítis (or Mount Ida) itself to 8,058 ft., the highest point of the island, the mass as a whole is not so large and impressive as that of the Lévka Óri. Its average elevation, too, is lower. The basis of the whole massif is a fairly uniform plateau, about 4,600 ft. high, composed of stratified limestone interspersed with schists. Upon this platform rise a number of high crests separated by deep valleys. Apart from Psilorítis, the outstanding heights are Mávri (6,499 ft.), Alikadám (6,299 ft.), Koudhoúni (6,102 ft.), Kouroúna (6,070 ft.) and Skínakas (5,744 ft.). Below these bare heights there is scrub and pasture land, while the lower slopes of the massif as a whole have villages with cultivation (olives, corn, figs).

The outer edges of the massif towards the south and west form gigantic steep slopes. On the west, across the valley of the Platís, they look towards the outlying Kédhros. On the south, however, between the main massif and the Mesará plain, there are some outliers which rise to 2,900 ft. in Sanídha mountain. This southern area is drained by various tributaries of the Yéros (Mesará), the chief of which is the Koutsoulídhis. Where the valleys open out, there are villages with pasturage and cultivation, e.g. Zarós (1,136). The eastern face of the Psilorítis is also fairly steep, but is broken by ravines ; and numerous low Tertiary spurs extend out into the isthmus of Iráklion (Plate 84). To the north and north-east, the fall is more gradual ; here, faults and dislocations have produced a series of ridges and terraces that fall to the valley of the Milopótamos and to the higher country in the east of the Milopótamos district.

In the very heart of the massif, at a height of about 5,000 ft., lies the plain of Nídha, a geographical curiosity resembling the plains of Omalós and Lasíthi. It is best approached from the north by a track leading through the village of Anóyia. It is oval in shape and is some 1½ miles long. In the south-west, it is covered with masses of rough stone and scrub. The remainder is filled to a good depth with reddish yellow alluvial soil ; this part is very flat but it is too high for cultivation, although in summer it is covered with luxuriant vegetation (Plate 83). In winter, it lies deep in snow which melts about the end of April, the water being drained off by *katavóthra*.

G. The Depression of Iráklion (Fig. 43)

Between the mountains of Psilorítis and Lasíthi, lies what is virtually a gigantic col—the plateaux and ridges backing the Iráklion district. They are highest in the watershed region, where they rise above 2,000 ft. in places, the highest points being those of Oxí Kefála (2,654 ft.) and Monodhéndri (2,635 ft.). Composed mainly of Tertiary deposits, and with only a few outstanding limestone caps and schist ridges, these hills present mostly blunted forms. Towards the south, the uplands of the watershed region break into a multitude of small plateaux and isolated hills falling in steep sandy and gravelly ridges to the plain of Mesará. On the north, the uplands slope more gradually as a series of flattened ridges composed of white Tertiary marls, sands and sandy gravels. Here and there, between the upland slopes and the coast, are small strips of alluvial land.

Numerous northward-flowing streams (e.g. the Yiófiros) have cut deep fertile valleys into the general surface. In the west, the rivers issue from the steep eastern slopes of the Psilorítis ; in the centre, from the lateral uplands of the watershed area ; and in the east from the Lasíthi mountains. The streams are for the most part intermittent with a good flow of water in winter.

The somewhat featureless appearance of the landscape north of the watershed area is relieved by only one striking projection. This is Mount Yúktas, an isolated peak, conspicuous from the sea, and situated about 7 miles south of Iráklion itself. It is a mass of limestone (2,746 ft.), bare, rugged and grey, rising from the soft rounded forms of marl and yellow limestone. Anciently reputed to be the birthplace of Zeus, it contains on its northern side a notable cave, and its summit has often proved useful as a fortress. Another feature of the area is the upland plain of Pedhiádha towards the east. This is roughly triangular in shape, about 4 miles across, and has an average elevation of 1,100 ft. Its rather uneven surface is composed of pebbly clay and quartz gravel, and it is surrounded on all sides by gentle hills except on the east where the Lasíthi Mountains rise abruptly.

The whole depression of Iráklion forms a uniform area of culti-

Plate 84.   The eastern face of the Psiloritis mountains

The view looks west over the village of Pirgou and shows the steep eastern edge of Psiloritis, broken by ravines.

Plate 85.   Mount Yúktas
In the foreground is the river Yiófiros.

Plate 86.   The village of Áno Arkhánai
This village is one of the largest on the isthmus of Rethímni ;   the photograph was
taken from Mount Yúktas.   in the e depression of Jaldia

vation, approximately 200 sq. miles in extent, and it may be significant that Cnossus, the seat of the early Minoan civilization, lay here, some 3½ miles from the sea. Today, the low broad ridges and hills, although somewhat dry, are generally cultivable almost to the summits. The valleys too are fertile, likewise the greater part of the plain of Pedhiádha. The main crops, apart from grain, include the vine, olives, and the usual fruits of the Mediterranean lands. The largest town in the region is the port of Iráklion with a population of 33,404, but apart from this there is no village of any size along the coastal plain ; the main villages are situated along the inland border of the low-lying land. The remainder of the region, however, is one of the most continuously settled parts of Crete. Áno Arkhánai and Thrapsanós are the largest villages with populations of 3,160 and 1,192 respectively, and there are other villages that approach them in size (Plate 86). Villages are also fairly numerous in the plain of Pedhiádha. The largest settlement is Kastéllion (930) which is built on a mound near the northern end of the plain ; most of the villages avoid the cultivated plain and are set around its margin.

H.   The Mesará Depression (Fig. 43)

The east-west plain of Mesará is about 30 miles long and about 5 to 6 miles wide. It forms a long trough between the uplands of the Iráklion district to the north and the mountains of Asteroúsia to the south, and it derives its rich alluvial soil from these mountains on either side. The result is one of the most fertile plains, not only in Crete but in the whole Aegean area. It is drained westward by the Yéros which flows into Mesará Bay, and eastwards by the Anapodháris which reaches the sea beneath the overlooking heights of the Lasíthi Mountains to the east. The divide between the two streams is 948 ft. in altitude, but the watershed is so slight as to be scarcely visible to the eye, and from it the plain slopes to east and west (Plate 87).

The Yéros, the largest river in Crete, is perennial and is fed by streamlets that flow down the steep slopes on either side ; those of the north lie in narrow glens. The upper and middle course of the river has a very gentle gradient and meanders across an alluvial plain through which it has cut a deep and steep-walled bed (20 to 30 ft.), pebbly and set with scrub. Four miles or so from its mouth, the hills on either side close in, and here the river cuts across a ridge in a steep and narrow gorge. It then enters the low flat coastal plain of Timbákion, through which it winds to the sea near the inner corner of Mesará Bay.

The eastern part of the depression is drained by the Anapodháris and its tributaries ; two of the largest drain the western slopes of the Lasíthi mountains—the Kolokíthis and the Barítis. In its middle course the Anapodháris is constricted by approaching hills, and its lower course turns sharply and cuts straight southwards in a gorge through the upland that connects the mountains of Lasíthi and those of Asteroúsia. Except in these parts, its basin is wide and gentle, and its bed broad and stony. In winter, it carries a great and swift volume of water, but in summer it is reduced to a brook winding through a pebbly bed.

The Mesará plain as a whole includes much first-class arable land, but its development has laboured under certain disadvantages. The exodus of the Moslem population in 1898 left it largely deserted, and the lack of adequate communications has been a further draw-back. At present, however, it is one of the most densely peopled districts in Crete ; cereals, vine, carobs, olives and the usual Mediter-ranean fruit trees are grown, and there is much cattle-grazing on the hill-sides. On the coastal plain of Timbákion there is intensive garden cultivation. Villages are frequent throughout the whole area. In the west, they are situated not in the valley of the Yéros itself, but along the northern and southern margins. On the north, the largest villages include Timbákion (1,855) ; and on the south Pómbia (1,214). In the east, the main settlements are along the Kolokíthis and the Barítis ; here, the villages are rather small, and include not more than a few hundred inhabitants each.

I. The Asteroúsia Mountains (Fig. 43)

The east-west mountain belt of Asteroúsia separates the plain of Mesará from the sea, and forms a westward extension of the lime-stone highlands of Lasíthi. In its eastern part, heights of over 3,000 ft. are found, but its main summit, Mount Kófinos, is towards the middle. The steep grey limestone crest of this mountain rises to 4,038 ft. and is visible far out to sea. The seaward face of the range is steep and furrowed by torrents, raging in winter but dry in summer ; the projecting headlands often end in high cliffs, and at one place only, near its eastern end, is it broken by a deep gorge of a stream flowing into Tsoútsouros Bay. The northern face is

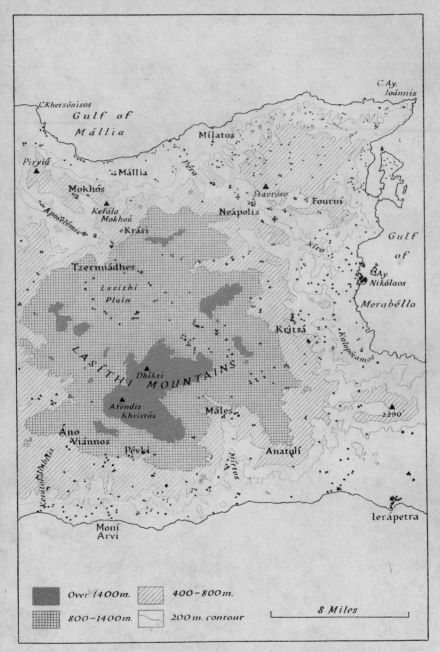

Fig. 44. Settlement in the western part of Lasíthi nomós (Crete)

Based on the 1 : 50,000 Crete, M.D.R. 612 (1943).

The red dots show settlements ; owing to reduction from the original maps they do not necessarily indicate individual houses.

more gentle, but even so it falls moderately sharply to the Mesará depression. Towards its western end, the mountain belt sinks to 700 to 800 ft. and becomes complex, the whole of the angle of Cape Líthinon being occupied by uneven spurs. The hills here are rounded and composed of chalk, while the higher ones are capped with grey limestone. Cape Líthinon itself is a bold projecting bluff and, within a short distance to the north of it, the bay of Mesará is faced by low cliffs and spurs of Tertiary rock.

The greater part of the mountain belt consists of limestone slopes with scattered trees, low scrub and mountain pastures. In the more favoured areas, grain and vines of good quality thrive, and there are a number of mountain villages, for the most part confined to the valleys along the northern slopes.

J. THE LASÍTHI AREA (Figs. 43, 44)

This region forms a rough square, stretching from the line of coast between the promontories of Khersónisos and Ayios Ioánnis across the island to the south coast, the length of each side being about 20 miles. It is almost entirely occupied by the Lasíthi mountains and their spurs. Despite its mountainous nature, there is a substantial amount of cultivation in the area as a whole, for it is characterized by numerous upland plains and basins, some fair-sized, some very small. All are floored with alluvium and are capable of cultivation. The whole area may be conveniently divided into three for the purposes of description (1) the central highlands ; (2) the northern hills and plateaux ; (3) the southern slopes.

J.1. The Central Highlands

The central portion of the highland consists, roughly speaking, of a series of peaks lying somewhat irregularly around the largest of the upland plains—that of Lasíthi itself. The highest peak is Mount Dhíkti (7,047 ft.) and there are several that exceed 4,500 ft. These peaks are sharp and bare, composed mostly of hard blue or grey limestone, running out in numerous jagged spurs and ridges often wooded or clad with scrub. The slopes of the summits are sometimes covered with large angular blocks. The western face of the massif is abrupt, falling to the plain of Pedhiádha and the basin of the Kolokíthis river (Plate 89). To the south, the fall is also steep, but it is irregular, and a whole series of upland hollows intervene between the main mass and the coast. Towards the north and east, the descent is more gradual and is marked by a series of spurs, plateaux and foothills.

Most of the peaks girdle the Lasíthi plain with a bare serrated wall of grey rock, broken in only a few places by cols serving as passes. The plain itself is one of the most striking physical features of Crete. It stands at about 2,850 ft. above sea level and measures roughly 5½ by 3 miles. It is far from simple in structure, being composed of one large oval depression with several more elevated mountain pockets, all enclosed within the barren encircling heights. The surface of the main plain is uneven, and its eastern end in particular has several limestone conical hills rising 700 ft. above the floor level. The floor is covered with alluvial soils, mostly clayey, washed down from the hills. The surface of the western portion is divided by irrigation ditches, known as *linias*, into squares with sides 600 yds. long. These irrigation ditches vary from 3 to 6 ft. in depth and from 6 to 12 ft. in width. In summer, water has to be brought to the surface by numerous windmills. The plain is tenable throughout the year and there are a dozen villages around its margins (Plate 88). Wheat, barley, and fruits such as pears, plums and mulberries, are grown. The largest village is that of Tzermiádhes (1,163). Good pasturage also exists on the plain, or in the small pockets which lie around and above it. Snow lies deep in winter, but disappears in early spring, and the flocks and a good many of the inhabitants migrate upwards in the latter season.

J.2. The Northern Hills and Plateaux

The large north-western spur of the central highland flattens out and extends between the steep valley of the Aposelémis to the west and the Gulf of Mállia to the east until it finally reaches the sea in Cape Khersónisos. The upland includes such basins as Krási and Mokhós, overlooked by the heights of Kefála Mokhoú (2,087 ft.) and Piryiá (1,903 ft.). Along the northern slope of the upland, stretches the well cultivated plain of Mállia. All this country is geographically a continuation of the upland areas of the eastern part of the Iráklion plain, but with a much higher average elevation. In general, villages are not very frequent. Mokhós, with 1,730 inhabitants, is the largest village, and Mállia has only 1,082 inhabitants ; there are others strung along the floor of the Aposelémis.

To the north-east lies the triangular peninsula that terminates in the bold promontory of Cape Áyios Ioánnis. This area, too, is essentially a spur of the Lasíthi Mountains. It is, however, separated

Plate 87. The plain of Mesará

The mountains of Asteroúsia can be seen in the distance.

Plate 88. The Lasíthi plain

The view looks southward over the plain towards the Dhíkti range.

Plate 89. The Lasíthi massif, from the west

The view is eastward from the village of Roussokhória towards the western slopes of the highland.

[Facing page 241

from the main mass by a depression in which flow the rivers Xíro and Péra, the former southwards into the Gulf of Merabéllo, the latter northwards to the Gulf of Mállia. The watershed between the two streams lies near Neápolis (population 2,391), and is 878 ft. above sea level. Economically, the depression is an important area with fine gardens and olive groves, and it is traversed by an important main road that links the two bays. The peninsula itself is composed mainly of light grey limestone and lies for the most part at about 1,900 to 2,300 ft. above sea level ; the highest point, Stavróso, reaches 2,605 ft. The two seaward sides are steeply scarred and broken by ravines ; the steeper slopes are bordered by talus heaps that reach to the sea. The coastal scenery is wild, barren and picturesque. Near the mouth of the Péra is the famous cave of Mílatos, a place of refuge—and of massacre—in troublous times. Along the east coast is the curiously shaped peninsula of Spinalónga about 400 ft. high. Many of the hollows in the limestone surface of the peninsula as a whole are fertile (e.g. that of Fourní), and there are numerous villages. To the south, the lower spurs of Lasíthi, mostly wooded, enclose upland plains and stretch down as foothills to the Gulf of Merabéllo and the isthmus of Ierápetra. Here, for example, is the fertile valley of the Kalopótamos which forms a rich area of gardens and cultivation, and which contains the fertile village of Kritsá (2,476).

J.3. The Southern Slopes

The southern slopes of the Lasíthi mountains are much steeper and wilder than those of any other side, but between the massive bastion of Aféndis Khristós (7,024 ft.) and the sea, there are numerous small upland basins or plains separated by high barrier ridges through which the rivers have cut deep, broken, ravines. These basins are well-watered and sheltered, and their villages grow grain, vines, olives, mulberries and other fruits ; among the villages are Pévki (458), Áno Viánnos (1,203) and Anatolí (836). Along the coast, too, there are some small plains with cultivation. From the sea, the country looks wilder than it really is because the fertile and well-settled upland hollows are hidden from sight. Over much of the area the vegetation is abundant, and consists mainly of ilex, myrtle, wild olive, and wild pear. In the east, the steep slopes are cut by the valley of the Mírtos which drains a wild upland basin, and approaches the sea through a gradually widening valley with several villages and a good deal of cultivation ; here is the village of Máles

(1,049).   Among the valleys that reach the sea in the west, the ravine
at Moní Árvi is one of the most remarkable natural features of Crete.
It forms a narrow chasm, over 1,000 ft. deep, between almost perpendicular limestone cliffs.   Many legends connected with Zeus
centre about this wild and extraordinary locality ; one explains the
chasm as the result of a thunderbolt.   Farther west still, the plain of
Áno Viánnos is perhaps the most important of the upland hollows,
and has probably been occupied since early times.   It lies at about
1,650 ft., and is partially drained by the Keratokambítis.   The
stream dries up in summer, but the plain is never without water and
its fertile soil is well cultivated.   Beyond the Keratokambítis, the
south-western foothills of Lasíthi continue to the valley of the
Anapodháris beyond which they rise to form the mountains of
Asteroúsia.

K.   THE ISTHMUS OF IERÁPETRA (Figs. 44, 45)

The isthmus of Ierápetra is the most marked gap in the long series
of hills and mountains that form the backbone of Crete.   To the
west lie the outlines of the Lasíthi massif, and on the east are the
mountains of Sitía rising with startling abruptness and regularity.
Between these two bastions of old resistant limestone rocks, the
isthmus forms for the most part a trough of less resistant Tertiary
marls and unconsolidated limestones.   The two containing walls
are bordered by depressions that correspond to great faults running
south-south-west to north-north-east across the island.   The
western depression is formed by an extension of the lower Kalo-
pótomos plain, separated by a watershed of 1,580 ft. from a small
valley that runs to the south coast.   The eastern depression provides
a broader and easier passage from coast to coast, its watershed being
only 413 ft.   The whole isthmus is in the shape of a parallelogram,
about 7 to 8 miles from coast to coast and about 6 miles from east
to west.

Across this parallelogram, and rather nearer the north than the
south coast, runs an irregular belt of hills, an extension of the south-
eastern spurs of Lasíthi.   The main ridge is a rocky and broken
crest of hard grey limestone and conglomerate, and it rises to
2,290 ft.   From it, on either side, numerous ridges and spurs
diverge, forming together a boss of tangled hill country.   Towards
the north, these spurs are deeply dissected by short ravines, and
reach nearly to the coast.   To the south, there is a greater extent

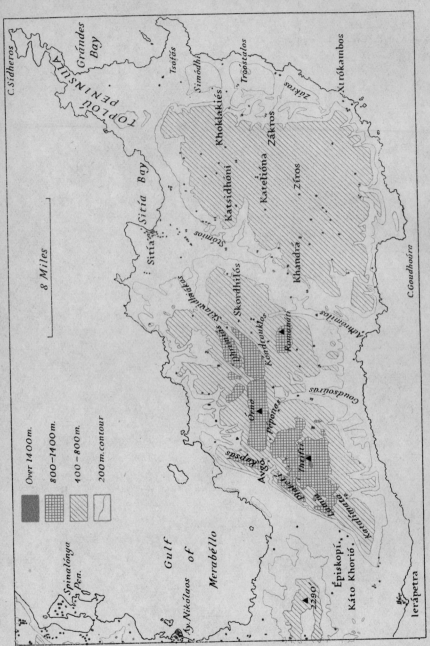

Fig. 45.   Settlement in the central and eastern parts of Lasíthi nomós (Crete)

Based on the 1 : 50,000 Crete, M.D.R. 408 (1943).

of broken hill country ; this is drained by a few intermittent streams which flow southward across the small plain that lies around the small port of Ierápetra (3,611). The plain is composed of brown pebbly sand and stretches for 3 miles or so along the coast where sand dunes and low reefs help to form a poor harbour.

The isthmus as a whole is rather stony and dry, but has fine olive groves and also grows cereals and other crops. The area is sparsely populated ; there is a line of villages in the western depression, but the most densely settled area extends in a belt from the plain of Ierápetra northwards along the eastern depression. Here in the east, for example, are the villages of Episkopí (539) and Káto Khorió (624). The few villages of the central hill valleys are surrounded by small fruit gardens. Much of the high ground in the centre is wooded, chiefly with pines, and over the remaining uncultivated areas there is a fair amount of low scrub.

L. The Sitía District (Fig. 45)

The great fault which forms the eastern limit of the isthmus of Ierápetra is flanked on the east by a long, steep-faced, line of hills rising well over 3,000 ft. The structure of the peninsula that lies to the east of this fault shows the final decline of the great Cretan mountain chain before it disappears below the broad gap separating it from Kásos and the other islands stretching to the coast of Asia Minor. The western part of the peninsula is highest, and here the mountains—after their subsidence in the isthmus of Ierápetra—recover something of their ruggedness and elevation, but farther east they become lower, and their general slope, though broken, is towards the east coast. Structurally the area falls into three divisions : (1) a rugged and irregular western mountain region ; (2) a long depression trending north-north-east to south-south-west, and bounded by faults ; and (3) a broad monotonous but uneven plateau sloping, with one large break to the coast. Each of the regions can be further subdivided, as will be seen, but the threefold division forms a convenient basis for description.

L.1. Western Sitía

This region consists mainly of a number of upstanding limestone blocks separated by valleys, but each block in turn is cut by sub-dividing valleys and headstreams so that the whole forms an area of very tangled relief. The greatest block is that of Thriftí Óros (4,839 ft.), which, with its radiating spurs, constitutes a great square-headed massif occupying most of the south-western corner of Sitía. The western border of the massif overlooking the isthmus of Ierápetra consists partly of the associated ridges of Plakotí (3,314 ft.) and Lamía (2,850 ft.) with their precipitous slopes, and partly of the blunter and more sloping boss of Katalímata (2,631 ft.). On the south, the Thriftï Oros massif is succeeded by low, rough and irregular hill country which is separated from the sea by a narrow coastal plain ($1\frac{1}{2}$ to 2 miles wide), uncultivated and barren. The intermittent streams that come down from foothills have cut furrows across the softer sediments of the plain.

East of the Thriftí Óros is a lower hill country through which flows the Goudsoúras, together with some other streams, to the southern coast. Here are a few villages with terracing and cultivation. Farther east still, rises the Romanáti block (3,074 ft.) a four-cornered blunt pyramid cut by gullies, and, like Thriftí Óros, sending spurs southwards to a narrow shelving coastal plain.

To the north, the Thriftí Óros-Romanáti uplands are separated by an east-west depression (the Avgó-Péponas-Kóndrouklos valleys) from a series of flat-topped mountain blocks—Kapsás (3,287 ft.), Órno (4,058 ft.), Dhrimiás (3,215 ft.). These masses are linked by narrow saddles and their spurs and ridges (of schistose rock) extend to the north coast where they fall for the most part steeply to the sea. In the valleys between these northern spurs, some villages are to be found, and here is a mixed cultivation of garden produce, vines, olives and cereals. Eastwards, the series is succeeded by the lower plateau of Skordhilós (about 2,300 ft.) with small villages and with cultivated valleys on its slopes.

L.2.   The Central Furrow

The depression that divides the uplands of eastern and western Sitía consists of two valley systems lying to the north and south of a low watershed. Broad, flat-topped and hilly, this watershed forms the only natural bridge between the eastern and western heights. It lies for the most part about 1,100 to 1,200 ft. above sea level, but rises to 1,476 ft. at one point, and slopes steeply to the large valleys that run north and south from it. The southern and shorter valley is that of the Adhrómilos which is predominantly an area of conglomerates and schists. Along the course of the river are several pockets of fertile soil brought down by side-streamlets, and about its lower part is a long narrow alluvial plain. Parallel to the eastern bank is a long narrow ridge (1,150 to 1,400 ft.)

which sinks as it proceeds southward. This shuts off another narrow valley parallel with the Adhrómilos and emptying into the sea to the south of it. The northern valley is that of the Stómios, and is a district mainly of white marls and limestone. To the east, the valley is flanked by the steep fall of the plateau of eastern Sitía, but the western slopes consist of long flat, sloping conglomerate terraces that fall from the edge of the plateau of Skordhilós. To the north of this plateau, across the important tributary of the Sklavidhiákos, stretches a flattish undulating lowland that slopes to the north-east from the highlands of western Sitía and falls to the sea in 100 ft. cliffs. This region belongs properly to the central furrow, and it is almost everywhere bare (save for some scrub), infertile and uninhabited.

In the furrow proper, villages are frequent ; rich orange, lemon and other fruit trees are to be found in the lower areas. Higher up, along the main and side valleys, there are terraces for the vine ; and, above these, olives and cereals are grown. The largest settlement is that of Sitía itself, a small port and a town of 2,170 inhabitants.

L.3. *Eastern Sitía*

The greater part of eastern Sitía is occupied by a limestone plateau which is cleft about four miles from the east coast by a long depression from north to south, practically isolating the eastern edge from the main mass. The general level of the plateau is about 2,000 ft., but individual heights rise to 2,687 ft. The limestone surface, particularly in the southern half, is varied by deep circular *doline*—flat, plate-like hollows with fertile soil and settlements. They are generally shut in by encircling limestone walls which shelter them from the wind, while the surrounding upland (i.e. the greater part of the plateau) is a barren and stony waste, clad only by low and scanty scrub, and exposed to the violent north winds. The largest hollow is the *polje* of Zíros right in the centre of the plateau. This is about 1 mile long and a quarter of a mile wide. It is floored by deep yellow clay soil, well cultivated and crossed by drainage ditches which empty into a swallow-hole situated at the south-west end. To the north, the surrounding limestone wall rises some 500 ft., but in the south it is only about 70 ft. above the *polje* floor. The village of Zíros itself has 742 inhabitants.

The southern portion of the plateau approaches at a level of

1,300–1,500 ft. to within a mile or so of the sea, to which it presents an abrupt, and in places a terraced, slope. Towards the north, the plateau likewise falls steeply to the lower land of the Toploú peninsula. In the north-west, however, below the steep edges of the limestone, is a belt of schists descending in a series of rounded convex steps to the shores of Sitía Bay ; here, settlements with a fair amount of cultivation are to be found. On the west, into the central furrow, the slope is steep, but here the edge of the plateau is broken by three large valleys : (1) the valley of Katsidhóni, (2) the upland depression of Katelióna drained by a gorge breaking into the Katsidhóni valley, and (3) the large upland basin of Khandrá. All three are fertile and cultivated ; the two latter are situated on ' bays ' of conglomerates with softer and more rounded forms than in the limestone areas around. Finally, on the eastern side, the edge of the plateau is cut by several deep east-flowing streams, and it falls in a descent of 900–1,600 ft. to the eastern cleft.

This depression runs along a belt of conglomerates which consist mainly of round, fist-size pieces of slate in a matrix of reddish-brown sandy earth, forming rich soil. The depression is not uniform in level, but consists of three valley-systems separated by ridges. The streams, after leaving the depression, turn east to the sea, cutting through the small eastern uplands. The valleys are those of Khoklakiés in the north, of Zákros in the centre and of Xirókambos in the south. They contain villages and are partly cultivated, but the district is capable of much closer cultivation.

These three streams divide the eastern uplands into four blocks, all fairly level and bounded by steep slopes. From north to south they are Tsofás (886 ft.), Simódhi (1,312 ft.), Traóstalos (1,640 ft.), and Zákros (650 ft.). Practically all of these uplands are bare, safe for stunted scrub. The coast is wild and desolate. The naked limestone steeps, terminating often in cliffs, are interrupted only by occasional gorges and ravines, and by small alluvial plains at their mouths.

Eastern Sitía includes yet another area—the triangular peninsula of Toploú to the north. It lies at a much lower level than the main plateau of eastern Sitía, from which it is separated by river valleys. From a height of 722 ft. in the south-west, it flattens out towards the north-east to levels of about 150 to 300 ft., except that it rises to form a minor ridge near the east coast (472 ft.). Its northern end is a fantastically shaped prolongation that terminates in Cape Sídheros, the most north-easterly point of Crete. The

Plate 90. Terrace cultivation near the village of Praesos in the basin of Khandrá

Plate 91. The Zákros gorge
The photograph was taken in summer when the stream-bed was dry.

Plate 92. Soúdha Bay

The view looks over the village of Soúdha and across the bay to the south coast of Akrotíri

Plate 93. Soúdha island, from the south-east

The south coast of Akrotíri can be seen in the background.

[Facing page 247

peninsula as a whole is covered mainly by low scrub and is little cultivated.

COASTS, ISLETS AND PORTS

The series of disturbances—dislocations, upheavals and subsidences —which have fashioned Crete in its present form were drastic in character. Owing to the abruptness of the mountains, the coasts of the island are for the most part steep, rugged and difficult, and, in several localities, wildly precipitous and grand. They are, too, peculiarly liable to ' fall winds ' or ' white squalls ' which, swooping from the heights, beat the sea into a fury (see p. 210). No Cretan port, not even Soúdha Bay, is exempt from these.

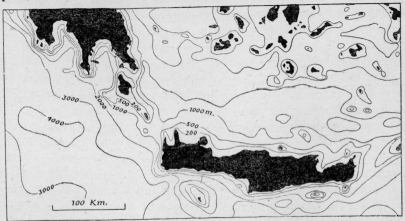

Fig. 46. Submarine depths around Crete
Based on *Enciclopedia Italiana*, vol. 17, p. 786 (Milano, 1933).

Not only are the mountains steep and high for the breadth of the island, but they fall away in great submarine declivities. Except on the north-east and north-west, where the island chains represent a former mountain belt connecting Crete with Asia Minor and Greece respectively, deep seas encircle the island. On the west, south and east, depths well over 1,000 fathoms are reached within 20 miles of the coast ; on the north, between Crete and the Kikládhes, the submarine declivities are less steep, but even here the sea-bed sinks to below 1,000 fathoms in the southernmost of the great Aegean basins. To the north-east and north-west, on the other hand, the depths average less than 450 fathoms (Fig. 46).

The north coast is the least precipitous, and is indented by bays of considerable extent, with stretches of low coast. Here are all the principal ports and harbours of the island ; there are few out-lying dangers and, generally speaking, depths of 100 fathoms lie about 3½ miles from the coast except near the projecting capes, where they seldom exceed a distance of 1½ miles offshore. A main road, suitable for traffic of all kinds, runs more or less parallel to this northern stretch of coast. The east and west coasts, despite several coves, are mostly steep and inhospitable, and have no important settlements along them. They are also without roads fit for wheeled traffic, other than cart tracks giving access inland. The south coast is also steep for the greater part and is likewise without good harbours, though there are anchorages in the several bays which afford shelter during northerly winds ; the depths, however, increase very rapidly offshore, and this limits the possibilities of good anchorage. There are but few good roads leading inland, none of first-class quality, and there is no main east–west arterial connexion.

For the convenience of more detailed description, the coast is here divided into ten stretches, and these are described in clockwise order under the main headings of north, east, south and west. The islets off the coast are described with their appropriate stretches. Finally, an additional section deals separately with the two main ports. The *Statistique du Mouvement de la Navigation*, 1938 (Athènes, 1939) gives details of the foreign and coastal trade of only two ports in Crete. Iráklion is the sixth and Khaniá the tenth port in Greece in respect of tonnage entered and cleared. Their details are as follows :

Entrances

Port	No. of vessels	Net tonnage	Cargo tons	Passengers
Iráklion	814	578,745	51,603	18,927
Khaniá	606	304,898	32,863	15,343
All Greece	41,931	19,810,603	4,135,106	1,012,263

Clearances

Port	No. of vessels	Net tonnage	Cargo tons	Passengers
Iráklion	814	578,745	47,148	18,394
Khaniá	606	304,898	17,462	15,688
All Greece	41,731	19,708,861	2,308,046	1,060,175

THE NORTH COAST

The North Coast of Khaniá Nomós (Fig. 47)

The 8 to 9-miles-long peninsula of Kórikos forms the north-western extremity of Crete, terminating in Cape Voúxa, and continued beyond in the islet of Ágria Graboúsa. The peninsula is about 2 miles wide at its neck ; it rises to 2,500 ft., and on both sides it presents precipitous faces to the sea ; it is almost completely uninhabited. Further east, there springs from the north coast the even more massive and striking promontory of Rodhopoú, 11 miles

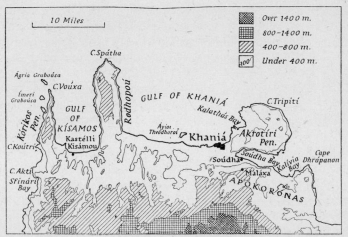

Fig. 47. The north coast of Khaniá nomós (Crete)
Based on the 1 : 50,000 Crete, M.D.R. 612 (1943).

long and 3 to 4 miles broad ; it rises to 2,454 ft. and terminates in the sharp point of Cape Spátha (1,200 ft.), the most northerly point of Crete. Its sides, especially the western, are girt by immense cliffs broken only by one or two small coves ; and, like Kórikos, it is almost completely uninhabited.

Framed by these two projections and by the mountains of Kísamos, lies the Gulf of Kísamos, some 10 by 6 miles. Its head consists of two bays (a smaller westerly and a broad straight-coasted easterly one) divided by a sharp, rocky, limestone spit. Both bays open on to a fertile and well-cultivated hinterland with a fair number of villages. In the larger eastern bay stands the ancient port of Kastélli Kisámou with an old mole and a harbour, but the latter is choked with sand which almost dries at low water. Overlooking the town is a ruined Venetian fortress.

Between Rodhopoú and Akrotíri, the next great peninsula to the east, lies the Gulf of Khaniá. The coast here is low-lying and consists of long flat curves, partly sandy and partly rocky, separated by higher blunt projections which are the ends of ridges from the uplands behind. The land around the gulf is well-cultivated and villages are frequent. Several streams with a fair flow empty into the bay, and about the middle, opposite a projection of which it is the apparent continuation, lies the islet of Áyioi Theódhoroi, barren, rocky and rising to 540 ft.; between it and the mainland are sunken rocks. Towards Khaniá the coast, though still low, becomes more indented with numerous small, rocky, fan-shaped peninsulas enclosing shallow, sandy coves. The town of Khaniá, with a population of 26,604 in 1928, stands on one of these small bays (see pp. 268–71).

To the east of Khaniá, the coast begins to trend north-eastward to form the circular peninsula of Akrotíri, some $6\frac{1}{2}$ miles in diameter and connected with the mainland by a narrow neck only $2\frac{1}{4}$ miles broad. The north-western flank is broken into by a deep oval bay (Kalathás Bay), at the head of which is a sandy beach ; the coast to the north of this bay is low. The remainder of the coast of Akrotíri is steep-to, bounded by precipitous cliffs and backed by rocky heights that reach 1,732 ft. in the east.

Between Akrotíri and the opposite coast of Apokorónas lies the bay of Soúdha, one of the safest and most commodious harbours in the Levant, covering some 6 by 2 miles. The entrance to the bay proper is constricted by the two islets of Soúdha off the north coast and by Cape Soúdha on the south coast. Along the north rises the steep and sterile slopes of Akrotíri. The head of the bay is low and marshy, and opens westward to the plain of Khaniá. The south coast, though as a whole more sloping, is dominated by the heights of Maláxa (2,014 ft.). The most important settlement on the south coast is Soúdha itself, with a population of 1,249 in 1928. There are a number of quays and piers, but the main wharf is a concrete pier, 738 ft. long, with depths of from 9 to 18 ft. at its inshore end, increasing (as a result of dredging) to 23 ft. at its outer end. A light railway (2 ft. 6 in. gauge) runs along the pier and continues for some distance inland (see p. 309). Here, at Soúdha, is the largest flour mill in Crete. On either side of the pier there are a number of wharves which can accommodate only lighters and other small boats (Plate 92). Less than a mile to the west of Soúdha is the subsidiary settlement of Azizié, with quays and a small pier, but the depths make them accessible only to small boats.

To the east, between Cape Soúdha and Cape Dhrápanon, is the large curving bight of Kalívia Bay. The western shores of the bight are low and are backed by fertile hills and valleys. Eastwards, it becomes irregular, steep-to and rocky, and so continues to Cape Dhrápanon.

The North Coast of Rethímni Nomós (Fig. 48)

From Cape Dhrápanon, the coast turns sharply southwards for about 9 miles and, together with the next 25 miles of coast eastward

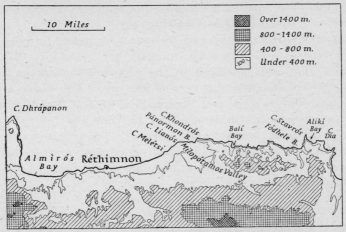

Fig. 48.   The north coast of Rethímni nomós (Crete)
Based on 1 : 250,000 Greece, G.S.G.S. No. 4410 (Crete) (1943).

(i.e. as far as Cape Lianós), forms a great bight ; Almirós Bay lies in the western part of this bight and Réthimnon Bay in the eastern half. The western side of the bight is rocky and precipitous and is backed by the uplands of Apokorónas which rise to a maximum of 1,736 ft. The southern coasts of both subsidiary bays are for the most part straight, flat and sandy, backed by the low irregular hills of the Réthimnon district. This sandy stretch is interrupted in the middle by a strip of 7 miles where rough limestone hills approach to form a rocky, and in places a high, coast. This part is indented by coves, and near its eastern end, on a small rocky peninsula, stands the port of Réthimnon with a population of 8,632 (1928), forming the third largest town in the island (Plate 94).

The town is surrounded by a Venetian wall largely in ruins, and immediately to the north is an old Venetian fort. A small harbour (400 by 250 ft.), formed between two moles, is situated off the eastern side of the town ; silting is continuous, but the entrance has been dredged to 12 ft., and there are depths of from 6 to 16 ft. within. Quays also extend southwards beyond the harbour, but the depths alongside are not over 1½ ft. The port is the outlet for the surrounding agricultural area ; local industries comprise two soap factories, an olive-oil refinery, a rope factory and small tanneries. The main exports are olive oil, soap, wine, silk and agricultural produce ; the main imports are potash, grain, timber and general merchandise. One of the few north-south roads in Crete leaves Réthimnon and proceeds southwards through Mélambes to Timbákion in the plain of Mesará (Fig. 59).

The sandy stretch to the east, beyond Réthimnon, terminates at Cape Melétsi, and from here onwards, for a distance of about 20 miles, the shore is backed by the limestone coastal range that shuts the Milopótamos valley from the sea. The coast here is high, bold and rugged, and indented by several secluded bays ; the chief of these are Pánormon Bay and Balí Bay, well sheltered but without good access to the interior. Towards the east, this rugged stretch terminates in several rocky capes, notably the conspicuous but low Cape Stavrós, the rugged and barren Cape Día, and Cape Panayía.

The North Coast of Iráklion Nomós (Fig. 49)

East of Capes Día and Panayía, the coast turns abruptly southwards for 4 miles, and here follows another of those notches which mark the coast of Crete, and give it its peculiar serrated appearance on a map. For over forty miles, the general line of the coast runs roughly due eastwards. At the western end of the stretch of coast lies the Gulf of Iráklion. Its western shore is formed by the rough and bold coastline that runs nearly due south from Cape Panayía, and is fringed in places by rocks. Its southern shore is low and sandy as far as Iráklion, a port with a population of 33,404 in 1928 (see pp. 265–8). Mount Yúktas (2,661 ft.), some 6 miles inland, is a prominent feature. East of Iráklion there are some low, rocky projections, and at 3 miles another small bend to the south, whence the coast runs almost due east to Cape Khersónisos. The whole of this stretch is low—rocky stretches alternating with sandy beaches— and is backed by slightly elevated sloping plains that lead to the

[*Facing page* 252

Plate 94. The port of Réthimnon

The view is from the old Venetian fort to the north of the town.

foothills of the Lasíthi (Dhíkti) mountains. Settlements here are not so frequent as to the west of Iráklion.

Some 6 to 7 miles offshore lies the island of Día. It is a limestone mass, with rather bare, low scrub, and it rises to 870 ft. near the centre. Its northern coast is precipitous ; its southern coast is also steep but is broken by four ragged indentations. The islet of Glaronísi lies about half a mile off the north-west coast, the passage between being almost closed by reefs. Nearly 2 miles off its eastern coast is the rock of Paximádhi, about 145 ft. high.

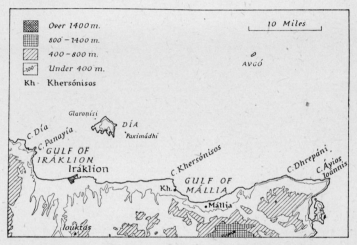

Fig. 49. The north coast of Iráklion nomós (Crete)
Based on 1 : 250,000 Greece, G.S.G.S. No. 4410 (Crete) (1943).
Kh. Khersónisos.

Beyond Cape Khersónisos the coast of Crete curves to form the Gulf of Mállia ; on the western shores of this is the ancient port of Khersónisos, with a population of only 700 in 1928. The ancient moles forming the harbour still exist, but the latter is now too shallow to be available. Mállia itself, with a population of 1,082 in 1928, lies at the head of the gulf about a mile inland. The shores of the gulf are indented with smaller bays lying between sharp points marking the ends of ridges. As Cape Áyios Ioánnis is approached, these ridges become steeper until they run out in high, steeply-scarped spines and fall boldly into the sea. Cape Áyios Ioánnis itself is 300 ft. high. About 18½ miles north-north-west off the cape is the island of Avgó (170 ft. high), steep-to and precipitous.

The North Coast of Lasíthi Nomós (Fig. 50)

Between Cape Áyios Ioánnis and Cape Faneroméni, 18 miles in a straight line south-eastwards, lies the large Gulf of Merabéllo, which reduces the island to its narrowest at the isthmus of Ierápetra. Its shores are sharply indented by numerous small coves, and, at its north-western and north-eastern sides, it is flanked by high cliffs, the termination of the ridges which are ranged around it.

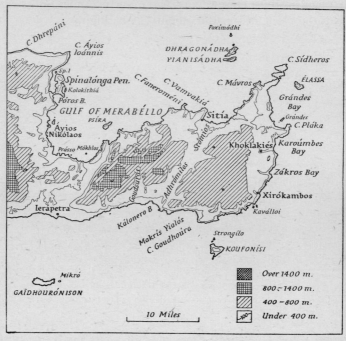

Fig. 50. The coasts of Lasíthi nomós (Crete)
Based on 1 : 250,000 Greece, G.S.G.S. No. 4410 (Crete) (1943).
Sp. I : Spinalónga island.

The stretch immediately south of Cape Áyios Ioánnis is striking because of its towering cliffs and the heights above. From the mainland, springs the curiously-shaped peninsula of Spinalónga—a sprawling, hilly mass that rises to 460 ft. It extends for 3½ miles parallel with the adjoining coast at a distance of about one mile, and is united to the mainland near its southern end by an isthmus barely 100 yards broad and only about 3 ft. high ; during strong northerly winds, the sea breaks over this. A boat canal, 15 ft. wide with a minimum depth of 3 ft., crosses the isthmus, and is spanned by a small drawbridge. Between the peninsula and the mainland is Spinalónga harbour, at the mouth of which there are a sandbank (over which there is a least depth of 12 ft.), and the little islet of Spinalónga, on which stands a ruined Venetian fort ; in 1935 there was a leper colony of about 250 on the islet. Before the outbreak of war in 1939, the harbour was used as a base by Imperial Airways, and had some petroleum facilities along its western side (Plate 96). Off the east coast of the peninsula lies the islet of Kolokithiá. To the south of the peninsula is the deep and beautiful bay of Póros, Next to Soúdha Bay, it is the finest natural anchorage in Crete, providing shelter from northerly and north-easterly gales.

Southwards along the west coast of the gulf is the port of Áyios Nikólaos, protected by the islet of that name (140 ft. high) and by the smaller Mikró Nísi (75 ft. high) to the north. The town itself had a population of 1,543 in 1928. Its small harbour (with depths of from 5 to 10 ft.) is protected by a mole. The industries of the town include a soap works and an olive oil refinery ; the town is also the commercial centre for the surrounding country, and exports olives, citrus fruits, carobs and large quantities of salt. The quayside is connected by a good road with the main north coast highway.

There are three other islands in the Gulf of Merabéllo. The largest, Psíra, is a rocky, crested islet of soft limestone, about 1½ miles long and 670 ft. high ; the smaller islets of Mókhlos (75 ft.) and Prásso lie close inshore. The head of the gulf consists largely of sandy beaches alternating with rocky projections ; there are but few settlements along it. Eastwards, towards Cape Faneroméni, the shore becomes very irregular, and the seaward slopes are mostly steep and often cliffed ; it, too, is a largely uninhabited coast.

Between Capes Faneroméni and Vamvakiá is an open bay (Faneroméni Bay) ; and beyond the latter is the still larger bay of Sitía, about 2 by 4 miles in extent. Its entrance is flanked by steep bluffs on either side, but its head is mostly flat and sandy. Inland, the valley of the Stómios occupies the central furrow that divides the plateaux of eastern and western Sitía. The little port of Sitía, with a population of 2,170 in 1928, lies on the western side of the bay, and is the eastern terminus of the main east–west coast road (see p. 310). Prominent landmarks are formed by the ruins of a Venetian fortress and the white tower of an old Turkish fort. The harbour works consist of a masonry pier 95 ft. long, with a masonry quay, 395 ft. long, to the south of the pier. There are depths of about 6 ft. off the end of the pier, which is used by schooners and other small vessels, and of 6 to 3 ft. along its southern side ; the northern side of the pier is silted up and is inaccessible even to boats. The quay to the south has a maximum depth of 3 ft. alongside. Cargo is carried by lighters to and from vessels anchored in the bay (Plate 97).

From Sitía Bay the uninhabited coast trends north-east, with numerous inlets and ragged cliffy bluffs to Cape Sídheros, the most north-easterly point of Crete ; there are sunken rocks close inshore. The curiously-shaped peninsula, which terminates in Cape Sídheros, has gently-sloping coasts, but is precipitous towards the east ; there are off-lying reefs and islets. Cape Sídheros itself is low, but close behind rises a sharp conical hill (686 ft.).

Facing the bay of Sitía, and 5 to 6 miles west of Cape Sídheros, are the Yianisádhes islands. The most southerly, Yianisádha, is an oblong block about 2 miles long (east to west) and nearly half a mile broad. It rises to 482 ft. and on the south it falls in steep cliffs to the sea ; on the other sides it slopes more gently, but has everywhere a hilly surface. To the north, across a half-mile-wide channel, lies Dhragonádha, the largest of these islands. It rises to 500 ft. and falls in steep cliffs to the north ; its southern shore, while gentler, is also fairly steep. Close north of it lies a rocky islet ; and, finally, some 1½ miles farther north still, is the small rocky spine of Paximádhi, the most northerly islet of the group. All these islands are composed of grey-black limestone, and have high, bold crests and outlines.

THE EAST COAST (Fig. 50)

The east coast of Crete can be divided into two parts separated by Cape Pláka. To the north lies the broad Grándes Bay, indented by several smaller bays and coves, with sandy beaches, separated by bluff rocky stretches and headlands ; offshore, there are outlying reefs both above water and awash. The whole hinterland is almost completely uninhabited.

The grey limestone island of Élassa, lying about 1½ miles offshore, is flat and high (over 330 ft.). Nearer inshore are the Grándes islands consisting of a narrow island about a mile long and 105 ft. high, together with an islet 30 ft. high off the south-west end, and another (8 ft.) off the north-west. On the mainland opposite the Grándes islands is a flat sandy beach, terminated on the south by the striking red hill of Palaiókastron. The promontory of Pláka is

Plate 96.   Spinalónga harbour

The view is northward towards Spinalónga island and Cape Áyios Ioánnis.   On the right is the peninsula of Spinalónga enclosing the harbour to the west.

Plate 97.   The port of Sitía

The view shows the quay from the south.

Plate 98.   The port of Ierápetra

The mountains of Sitía can be seen on the right.

Plate 99.   The coast near Trís Ekklisiés

The view was taken about half a mile west of Trís Ekklisiés.

[*Facing page* 257

fairly low and flat, and terminates in the cliffy headland of Cape Pláka, the most easterly point of Crete.

The cliffy southern shores of the Pláka promontory shelter a considerable bay to the south (Karoúmbes Bay), and from this point, south and south-westwards, the coast assumes a closed, desolate and forbidding appearance. It is formed by the steep, bare descents of the limestone plateaux of eastern Sitía, and, though there are several irregularities and rocky bays, the limestone wall is broken only in a few places by deep and narrow gorges. From north to south these breaks are : (1) the valley in which Khoklakiés stands, (2) that which leads from Zákros Bay, and (3) the valley which reaches the coast north of Xirókambos. Here are tiny coastal plains with settlements. Close inshore, and immediately south of Xirókambos, lie the Kaválloi islets.

THE SOUTH COAST

The South Coast of Lasíthi Nomós (Fig. 50)

Beyond Xirókambos the rocky and desolate coast curves rapidly south-westwards towards Cape Goúdhoura ; here, the inland heights of eastern Sitía fall steeply to the coast. Three or four miles offshore to the south lies the white cliff-girt Koufonísi, a limestone block covering about 2 sq. miles and rising to over 330 ft. in the interior ; to the north and south of it are some rocky islands and reefs, the largest of which is the islet of Strongílo to the north.

From Cape Goudhoúra westwards, the coast curves inwards to from a large bight, broken into two open bays—Makrís Yialós and Kaloneró Bay—and these in turn are articulated by numerous coves. The bays have high, rocky headlands, but towards the eastern end of each there are also considerable sandy beaches. Kaloneró Bay receives the river Adhrómilos which drains the southern part of the furrow that divides eastern and western Sitía. Westwards, the plateau of western Sitía overlooks the sea, leaving a barren and uncultivated coastal plain, 1½ to 2 miles wide. This is crossed by a number of deep and narrow watercourses, of which the Goudsurás is the largest. Offshore, there are rocks and reefs. The narrow coastal plain in turn merges into the lower land of the isthmus of Ierápetra. Here, the shore is low and backed in places by gravel and sand dunes. About the middle of this lower land lies the port of Ierápetra, with a population of 3,611 in 1928, the largest town on the south coast of Crete. It was the site of the

ancient city of Hierapytna, which attained some size and importance
in Roman times, and which had an artificial port formed by two
moles built of blocks of stone ; but the moles are now in ruins and
the harbour is for the most part filled up. There is, however, a
quay at the inner end of the northern mole with depths of from
7 to 8 ft. alongside. The only industries are an olive oil refinery
and a soap factory to the north of the town, and these are served by
a small pier that can accommodate small vessels up to 15 tons.
A wall with towers encloses the town on the landward side, and there
is a small Venetian fort southwards of the town. There are some
stretches of marsh in the neighbourhood, and, although much has
been drained, the district is still malarial in summer. A good road
unites it to the main north coast road, but lateral communication
along the south coast is very poor.

Some 8 miles offshore to the south lies Gaïdhourónison, about
3 miles long. Its eastern part has some hills, but most of it is
quite low and is composed of Tertiary formations. The islet of
Mikró lies off its eastern end.

The South Coast of Iráklion Nomós (Figs. 51, 52)

From the isthmus of Ierápetra westwards the coast has a slight
southerly trend, but runs roughly east–west with no large indentations. It is backed at varying distances by the southern
slopes of the Lasíthi mountains, which in places approach the sea
and which are furrowed into a confused hill country by streams
with deep gorges. As far as the valley of the Mírtos, the first of
these streams, the coast continues fairly low. Westward from here
appear white cliffs of gypsum and marls, surmounted by uneven
heights, though in places there are narrow coastal plains. At Árvi,
where a stream issues from a great perpendicular cleft, there is a
low, narrow coastal plain, and, close to the west, there is another
large plain flanking the fine open bay of Keratókambos. Immediately
west of this bay the river Anapodháris cuts through the mountains
in a gorge to reach the sea across a sandy beach. Beyond, the coast
curves to the south, enclosing the semicircular bay of Tsoútsouros—
a wild and picturesque part, where cliffs and a shingle shore are
backed by bold crags, and where the small Tsoútsouros stream
dashes to the sea from its narrow rocky gorge.

Westwards, the coast continues in the same general direction to
Cape Líthinon, the most southerly point of Crete. The shore is
here backed throughout by the Asteroúsia mountains which fall

with steep and sometimes precipitous rocky declivities into the sea ; the coast is ringed with reefs, and beaches are only occasional. There are several striking promontories, notably Capes Trikálas and Kefalás, the latter a high, rocky point projecting from the steep mountainous coast and terminating in a sheer precipice. Along this stretch there are some remarkable gorges in the little cove of Tris Ekklisiés, while Mount Kofínos (4,039 ft.), behind Cape

Fig. 51. The south coast of Iráklion nomós (Crete)
Based on 1 : 250,000 Greece, G.S.G.S. No. 4410 (Crete) (1943).

Martélos, forms a good landmark. To the west of Cape Kefalás is a long, flat, curving bay with sandy beaches and striking headlands and with confused hill country behind. The western extremity is sheltered by several rocky islets (among them Áyios Pávlos) and here is the well-known harbour of Kaloí Liménes or ' Fair Havens ', whence St Paul sailed to his shipwreck at Malta (Plate 100). The site of the old town of Lasea (with an ancient mole) lies at the north-east corner of the bay. St Paul's account of this shore is still relevant today : ' We sailed under the lee of Crete, over against Salmone ; and with difficulty coasting along it we came into a certain place called Fair Havens ; nigh whereunto was the city of Lasea ', and he adds that ' the haven was not commodious to winter in ' (*The Acts of the Apostles*, xxvii, 7–12). Cape Líthinon itself is a bold, conspicuous rock, and it marks the middle point of the south coast of Crete.

Beyond Cape Líthinon the coast turns sharply to the north to form

the bay of Mesará. The eastern shore of the bay, to the north of
the cape, is bordered by low white cliffs. Here is Matála, a port of
only 49 people in 1928, serving the larger Pitsídhia (653 inhabitants).
It is set in a little cove, with a small quay hewn out of the rocks,
and is accessible to vessels drawing less than 6 ft. To the north of
Port Matála the coast becomes lower as the Mesará depression opens
to the sea ; the coastal plain here is marshy in places.

In the middle of Mesará Bay lie the two Paximádhia islets.
The most westerly is a rocky, crested ridge rising to 1,160 ft. and
about 1½ miles long. Close beside it to the east lies a smaller and
nearly circular islet, also rocky and high.

The South Coast of Rethímni Nomós (Figs. 52, 53)

The north shore of the bay of Mesará is backed by the steep
outer slopes of the Mélambes and Asidhéroto mountains. It is an

Fig. 52. The south coast of Rethímni nomós (Crete)
Based on 1 : 250,000 Greece, G.S.G.S. No. 4410 (Crete) (1943).

exposed and difficult coast ; the high mountain hinterland is broken
by the valley of the river Platís, and here is the tiny village port of
Ayía Galíni with a population of 430 (1928). The harbour consists
of a small masonry pier about 50 ft. long, with a depth of 6 ft. at
the pier-head. On either side of the pier are small quays with
maximum depths of 6 ft.

At Cape Mélissa the coast curves to the north, and, from here to
the village of Khóra Sfakíon, it is mostly rocky, exposed, and backed

Plate 100. The bay of Kaloí Liménes

Plate 101. Frangokástello
Behind the ruined Venetian fort rises the eastern part of the Lévka Óri massif.

Plate 102. Khóra Sfakíon
The view shows the town nestling at the foot of the Lévka Óri.

[Facing page 261

by coastal ranges. These are most irregular ; in some places they recede, and small plains are found (as at Plakiás Bay with a small cluster of villages in its immediate hinterland) ; in other places the mountains closely overhang the coast. At several localities where streams from the inland valleys break through the fronting ranges, are the mouths of deep and picturesque gorges, e.g. where the Kissanós gorge opens on to the small bay of Límni. Towards Frangokástello, where there is a ruined Venetian fort, the ranges, while rising, retreat somewhat, leaving at their southern base a lower sloping strip, the seaward edges of which form white cliffs from 50 to 100 ft. high. On this stony, inclined plain, cultivation is possible, and here are several villages behind which craggy steeps rise. Inland from Khóra Sfakíon runs one of the few roads that cross the island from north to south ; it follows the depression that separates the central Lévka Óri from its eastern extension.

Káto, a small group of tiny islets, lies off Frangokástello ; and elsewhere along the coast between Cape Mélissa and Khóra Sfakíon there are above-water and sunken rocks.

The South Coast of Khaniá Nomós (Fig. 53)

From Khóra Sfakíon the general trend of the coast continues slightly north of west, and here follows the wildest and grandest part of the Cretan coast. The outer slopes and shoulders of the Lévka Óri fall to the sea in a confusion of gorges and towering cliffs. There are practically no beaches, but at the base of the cliffs, especially at the mouths of the gorges, there are sometimes narrow shingly strips and tiny plains. There is access to the interior only in one or two places. Four miles west of Khóra Sfakíon, and separated from it by cliffs falling sheer to the sea, is the promontory of Cape Moúros with a small bay on either side. In these bays are sandy beaches and on the eastern bay stands the village port of Loútra (with the islet of Loútra, 36 ft. high), but it is backed by almost impracticable steeps. ' It is the only bay on the southern side of Kríti ', says the *Mediterranean Pilot*, vol. IV, p. 28 (1941), ' where a vessel would be secure in winter ' (Plate 104).

The remainder of the coast as far as Cape Kriós has much the same character, but on a lower and more gentle scale. Westwards of Cape Pláka, the remarkable gorge of Roúmeli reaches the sea in the bay of Ayía Roúmeli ; the ravine opens on to a small, cultivated, gravelly delta, and the stream rushes over a steep pebbly beach into the sea. Farther west still, is Soúyia Bay, into which empties the river Dhrákou Póros ; this valley provides a routeway, through a narrow gorge, leading to the upland plain of Omalós. Besides these two, there are several other rocky bays into which narrow ravines open. A prominent feature in the west is the sandy spit terminating in a rocky bluff on which stands the small port of Palaiokhóra, also called Sélino Kastélli, with a population of 589 in 1928. The village is situated on a low and narrow peninsula, off the south-western extremity of which lies the small islet of Skistó

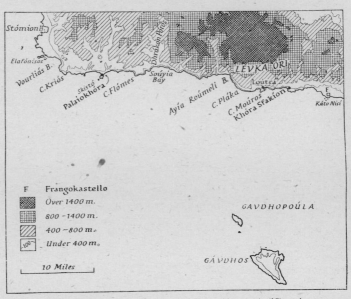

Fig. 53. The south coast of Khaniá nomós (Crete)
Based on 1 : 250,000 Greece, G.S.G.S. No. 4410 (Crete) (1943).

(40 ft. high). The village is on the bay to the east of the peninsula, and has a small pier, 80 ft. long and accessible only to small boats. A road of poor quality leads northward across the island to meet the north coast road near Máleme. Westward from Palaiokhóra, as far as Cape Kriós, the coastal uplands are of schist as opposed to the limestone of Lévka Óri, and consequently their features are softer and they present a more sloping surface to the sea.

Some 23 miles off the south-west coast of Crete lies the island of Gávdhos, triangular in shape and covering roughly some 12 sq. miles (Fig. 54). It rises to over 1,000 ft. Its western coast is a continuous line of high white limestone cliffs, but the eastern coasts are

Plate 103. The coast near Loútra

Behind rises the main massif of the Lévka Óri.

Plate 104.   Loútra harbour

Plate 105.   The port of Palaiokhóra (Sélino Kastélli)

lower though still rocky. The island has a barren appearance ;
there is little cultivation and only a few poor hamlets ; the population
in 1928 was 342. Copper and iron ore occur, and the former has
been worked in the past. Some 4½ miles to the north-west is the

Fig. 54. The islands of Gávdhos and Gavdhopoú la
Based on 1 : 50,000 Greek Islands, Gávdhos, M.D.R. 611 (1943).
A. Ámbelos : K. Kástri : K.S. Káko Spáthi : P. Panagoúla :
V. Vatsiana : X. Xenaki.

limestone islet of Gavdhopoúla, about 2 miles from north-west to
south-east, and half a mile wide. It rises to 440 ft., is steep-to,
and is uninhabited.

THE WEST COAST (Fig. 55)

For the most part, the west coast is cliffy and steep-to, backed by
the coastal heights of Sélinon and Kísamos, and fringed in places

by rocks and reefs offshore. There are several indentations. To
the north of Cape Kriós is the rocky and desolate bay of Vourliás,
bounded on the north-west by the narrow flat island of Elafónisos,
which is separated from the mainland by a very narrow channel ;
Low islet lies about half a mile off Elafónisos. To the north is the
small, deep bay of Stómion (' Outlet ') with a sandy beach lying
between sharp headlands and with a few settlements nearby ; this
corresponds with a break in the coast wall, and serves as an outlet
for the well-cultivated Enneakhoriá depression. Farther north still,

Fig. 55. The west coast of Crete
Based on 1 : 250,000 Greece, G.S.G.S. No. 4410 (Crete) (1943).
Sf. : Sfinári.

there follows a succession of capes and indentations until the bay
of Sfinári is reached ; the greater portion of the head of the bay
is rock-fringed, but at both ends there are stretches of sand. The
village of Sfinári lies behind the southern beach. Sfinári Bay, in
turn, is separated by Cape Aktí from Livádhi Bay in which there
are some tiny islets and rocks. North of Cape Aktí, the Kórikos
peninsula rises to 2,500 ft., and is wild and precipitous.

Off Kórikos lie the little peninsula of Tigáni and a number of
islands—all of Tertiary rock. Ímeri Graboúsa presents a steep face
to the north, where it falls to the sea in a precipice of 450 ft. ; the
south coast is gentler but is still fairly steep. Dangerous reefs
surround the island, and it has long been fortified. It is surmounted

by an old Venetian fortress which makes it very conspicuous from the west. Ágria Graboúsa, lying off Cape Voúxa to the north, is a bold and barren plateau with steep sides. Finally, some 6 miles to the west, lies the islet of Pondikonísi, a steep-sided, bare, conical rock of reddish colour, rising to 732 ft.

IRÁKLION (CANDIA)

35° 20′ N, 25° 09′ E. Population 33,404 in 1928

Iráklion is the largest town and the best equipped port of Crete. By tonnage of merchandise handled it is foremost among the ports of the Greek islands, and is surpassed only by Kérkira in the amount of shipping that enters and clears.

Approach and Access

The harbour lies on the south-eastern shores of the Gulf of Iráklion, a broad inlet in the northern coast of the island. The gulf affords no dangers to navigation, and anchorage in 15 to 25 fathoms can be found in the shelter of the western shores. Elsewhere the gulf is exposed, and in stormy weather large vessels frequently take shelter in the lee of Día island.

Detailed Description (Fig. 56 ; Plate 106)

The port has an inner harbour, accessible only to small vessels, and an outer harbour, larger but less well sheltered, to the east. The outer harbour has an entrance width of 670 ft. with a depth of 37 ft., decreasing to a general depth of about 22 ft. in the northern part of the harbour. The northern side is formed by a well-built breakwater-mole (7), which runs in a north-easterly direction for a distance of 3,110 ft. It is sufficiently broad (41 ft.) to take two-way motor traffic and vessels can lie alongside in over 27 ft. of water. The eastern side of the harbour is formed by a mole (6), some 1,900 ft. in length, but not sufficiently broad (24 ft.) for motor traffic. In the south-west of the harbour a 400 ft. quay (4), with depths alongside of 18–20 ft., is used by small merchant vessels, and a new south quay (5), still in course of construction, is used by coasting vessels moored stern-to.

The inner harbour was the original port of Iráklion and is formed by two short moles (1 and 3), both of which run in a north-easterly direction from the town water-front. The entrance width is 150 ft., with a depth of 9–10 ft., and the harbour can accommodate only about a dozen vessels of from 100 to 150 tons. The following table gives details of quays in both the Inner and Outer Harbours. The numbers 1–7 refer to Fig. 56.

Details of Quays in Iráklion Harbour

	Length (ft.)	Berthing space (ft.)	Depth alongside (ft.)	Height above M.W.L. O.S.	Remarks
Inner Harbour					
1. North Mole	900	900	6–12	6	Shore end (250 ft.) open timber piling Outer end (650 ft.) masonry
2. South Quays	1,100	700	6–7	3–5	Masonry ; 1 fixed 2½-ton crane
3. East Mole	980	680	9–12	6½	1 fixed 2½-ton crane
Outer Harbour					
4. South-west Quay	400	400	18–20	6½	Concrete blocks ; 1 electric travelling gantry crane
5. South Quay Breakwater	1,550 +	1,550 +	18	6½	Concrete blocks ; extensions in progress
6. East Breakwater-mole	1,900	1,150	16–27	6½	Concrete blocks ; 1 electric travelling gantry crane
7. North-west Breakwater-mole	3,110	2,400	27–39	8	Concrete blocks ; 1 electric travelling gantry crane

Port Facilities

Cargo can be discharged directly on to the breakwater-mole, but elsewhere lighters are used and there are normally about twenty in the harbour. For the most part, ships use their own derricks, but the port has probably five cranes (see table). There are at least four warehouses, cold storage at a distillery and ice factory in the town, and an area of some 9 acres near the south-west quay for open storage. Numerous slipways for small craft lie on the southern side of the outer harbour, and a machine shop that can undertake small repairs.

The Town

Iráklion commands the central corridor across the island between the mountain massifs of Psilorítis and Lasíthi. Before its destruction in 1941 it had a wide main street leading from the quay to the centre, but this belied the general style of the town, which was a maze of very narrow and crooked lanes, partly of Turkish aspect, though

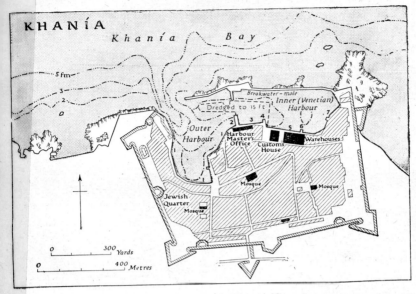

Fig. 57.   The port of Khaniá (Canea)

Based on British Admiralty Chart 1658 (1943).
Outer Harbour :   1. West, South and East Quays ;   2. South Mole.
Inner Harbour :   3. Main Quay ;   4. Western Jetty : 5. South Quay ; 6. East
Jetty ; 7. East Quays.

Plate 107.   Khaniá (Canea)

The view is from the lighthouse looking westward.   In the background are the
Lévka Óri.

[Facing page 267

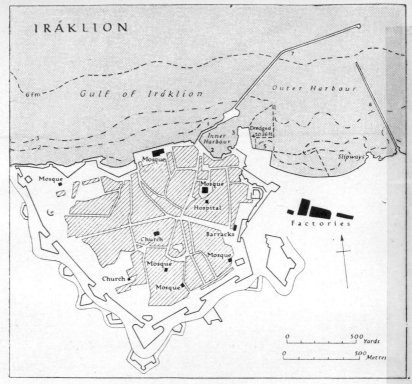

Fig. 56. The port of Iráklion (Candia)

Based on British Admiralty Chart 3691 (1943).

1. North Mole ; 2. South Quays ; 3. East Mole ; 4. South-west Quay ; 5. South Quay ; 6. East Breakwater-mole ; 7. North-west Breakwater-mole.

Plate 106. The Venetian fort and Inner Harbour at Iráklion (Candia)

On the left is the north mole and the fort at the entrance to the harbour ; on the right is part of the east mole. (See also vol. II, Plate 70.)

[Facing page 266

lacking the minarets of its fourteen mosques. The Venetian remains included several fine fountains and the damaged *loggia*. There were eight Greek churches, including a modern cathedral ; and there was a unique museum of Cretan (Minoan) antiquities, largely from Cnossus some three miles away (see vol. I, p. 428). Other buildings included the Prefecture, a small hospital, barracks, a Roman Catholic monastery and church, and an Armenian church. Iráklion is the seat of the eparchy of Témenos, of a nomarchy and a demarchy, and of the Archbishop of Crete.

History

The town was founded by the Saracens in the ninth century as Kandak (whence the name Candia) and has had a chequered history. Under Venetian domination it grew to some importance, and considerable traces of their occupation still remain in the fortifications that surround the town. It was finally captured by the Turks in 1669 after a three years' siege, and despite many insurrections they held it until 1912, when the island passed to Greece. During the German invasion of Crete in May 1941 the town was very badly damaged.

Trade and Industries

Iráklion has a large volume of trade by Greek standards ; it exports fruits, wine (the island was once famous for its malmsey), olives and olive oil, and imports wheat and flour, timber, coal and petroleum. Most of its trade is with Piraiévs.

Trade in 1937 (*thousands of m. tons*)

IMPORTS		EXPORTS	
Foodstuffs and agricultural products (chiefly wheat and flour)	10·4	Fruit, vegetables, nuts, etc.	22·2
		Olives and olive oil	1·5
Sugar	1·8	Alcoholic drinks	1·3
Timber and wood products	4·9	Miscellaneous	0·3
Minerals	1·5		
Metal goods	0·7		
Chemicals	0·8		
Miscellaneous	0·1		
Total	20·2	Total	25·3

Source : *Bulletin mensuel du commerce, spécial de la Grèce avec les pays étrangers*, Décembre, 1937, pp. 26–8 (Athènes, 1938).

The export trade is quite substantial, and for the year given exceeded the volume of imports. This position is most unusual for Greek ports, and unique in the case of the islands.

The industries are chiefly those relating to the processing of agricultural products, and the town contains oil and soap refineries, tanneries, distilleries, raisin-drying establishments and flour mills.

Communications

Road communications are adequate, though there are several bad sections. The road to Pérama, Réthimnon and Khaniá is in good condition, though it is unsuitable for heavy motor traffic. A road runs south-westward across the island to Timbákion and another eastwards to Neápolis and Áyios Nikólaos ; both of these can be used by motor traffic although their general condition is not good. Communication with other towns on the island is usually by coasting steamer, and a frequent service connects the port with the mainland of Greece. There are telephone and telegraphic communications with the important towns of Crete ; and Iráklion is connected by submarine cable with the mainland.

KHANIÁ (CANEA)

35° 31 N, 24° 02 E. Population 26,604 in 1928

Khaniá, the capital of Crete, has only a small harbour and the port handles little more than 50,000 tons of cargo each year. Nevertheless, it is fourth amongst the ports of the Greek islands.

Approach and Access

The broad bay of Khaniá, on the north coast of the island, is entered between Cape Spátha and Cape Tripití, some 24 miles apart. The coasts are bold and high, and Khaniá has been built at the south-eastern head of the bay on the only maritime plain of any considerable extent. Navigation presents few difficulties, except in the western approach to the harbour where there is a coastal bank on which lie above-water and sunken rocks. The regular passenger and mail boats anchor in the roadstead outside the harbour, where there is good holding ground in 20 fathoms. In bad storms, however, vessels normally go to Soúdha Bay, one of the safest and largest bays in the Mediterranean.

Detailed Description (Fig. 57 ; Plate 107)

The harbour is naturally poor and is formed partly by a ledge of rocks projecting westwards from the eastern promontory of a little bay. The ledge has been strengthened by a breakwater-mole on which a sea wall has been built. The entrance to the harbour lies between the end of the mole and the western promontory of the bay. A little less than 400 ft. in width, it has a central channel with a depth of 40 ft., but there is a marked shallowing immediately south of the entrance.

The harbour is divided into an inner and an outer portion by two short moles extending towards one another, and between which there is a passage of only 200 ft., with a depth of 15 ft. The outer, or western, harbour provides anchorage in about 20 ft. of water, shoaling rapidly towards the sides ; it is exposed to dangerous swell during northerly gales and there are no alongside berths. The inner, or Venetian, harbour has a quay along its southern side suitable for the berthing of small vessels. In 1939 the western part of the inner harbour was dredged to a depth of 15 ft., but the general depths elsewhere are from 8 ft. to shoal. Dimensions and functions of the various quays, all of which are constructed of solid-filled masonry walls, are given in the following table. The numbers 1–7 refer to Fig. 57.

Details of Quays in Khaniá Harbour

	Length (ft.)	Berthing space (ft.)	Depth alongside (ft.)	Remarks
Outer Harbour				
1. West, south and east sides	2,200	2,200	5–7	Masonry ; lighterage of general cargo ; 1 hand-crane
2. South Mole	160×26	320	6–13	General cargo by coastal vessels
Inner Harbour				
3. Main Quay	360	360	15	Masonry ; general cargo and passengers from coastal vessels
4. Jetty—west side	40	40	45	Masonry wall, solid fill.
head	23	23	45	General cargo by coastal
east side	160	160	15	vessels
5. Quay	520	520	4–5	Masonry ; lighterage of general cargo
6. Jetty	50×50	150	3–4	Masonry ; lighterage of general cargo
7. Quays	950	950	1–3	Masonry ; small craft only

Port Facilities

Port facilities are few. There are said to be three floating cranes with capacities of 8, 6, and 4 tons respectively, a hand-operated crane of 2 tons capacity and a 3-tons crane. Along the southern side of the Inner Harbour there are numerous warehouses. The normal harbour craft consist of ten lighters of from 20 to 25 tons capacity, two of from 5 to 10 tons, one steam tug and two motor-boats.

The Town

Khaniá was built by the Venetians in 1252 on the site of the ancient Cydonia (which gave its name to the quince), and was lost to the Turks only in 1645. It is compactly and solidly built, and is surrounded by massive and well-preserved Venetian fortifications, and on the southern side by a fosse, now dry and laid out with kitchen gardens. Most of its streets are narrow and crowded, but some have been widened lately ; the houses, often wooden, are low and whitewashed. The new quarter, outside the walls, is regularly planned and the suburbs have grown rapidly. Much damage was done to the town as a result of the German invasion.

Khaniá is the seat of government for Crete, and is a nomarchy and demarchy. Here too is a suffragan bishop : there are consular offices, military establishments, and the higher directorate of gendarmerie. Its Courts include those of Appeal, of First Instance, of a Justice of the Peace, and a Police court : there is also a Military court. Water is provided from springs in the suburb of Perivólia, at a place called Boutsounária, and from wells in the town. Electric lighting is supplied from the water-power of Lake Ayiá, and schemes have been prepared for the development of hydro-electric power.

Trade and Industries

Khaniá is the centre of one of the richest districts in Crete, and, although it is hampered by the lack of a good port, it has a considerable coasting trade. Among its imports there is no outstanding commodity, but the bulk of the exports are olives, olive oil and horticultural products.

Trade in 1937 (thousands of m. tons)

IMPORTS		EXPORTS	
Foodstuffs	12·5	Agricultural products	6·2
Sugar	1·6	Alcoholic drinks	0·2
Timber and wood products	1·9	Leather and skins	0·1
Minerals	0·4	Chemicals	0·2
Metals	0·6	Miscellaneous	0·1
Chemicals	0·6		
Miscellaneous	0·5		
Total	18·1	Total	6·8

Source : *Bulletin du commerce, loc. cit.*

The town has important olive oil and soap works, mills, tanneries, foundries, a government tobacco-cutting factory and a canning factory. There are, in addition, the native industries of cloth-dyeing, and wood, iron and leather working.

Communications

There is only one main exit from Khaniá, passing through the south wall of the town. This leads to the main motor road of the island, to Kastélli-Kisámou in the west and to Réthimnon and Iráklion in the east. A second road of poor quality strikes south-west to Palaiokhóra on the south coast (Fig. 59).

THE CRETAN PEOPLE

The Growth of Population

The population of Crete under the Venetians was estimated at about 250,000, and it is significant that in four centuries (1250–1650) there appears to have been little, if any, increase. After the Turkish occupation, the population declined rapidly at first and then recovered somewhat, and at the outbreak of the Greek War of Independence (1821) it was roughly 290,000, over one-half being Moslems. The succeeding disturbances and ensuing emigration nearly halved the number, and it was estimated by Pashley in 1836 at only about 130,000. Just before the next great revolution (1866) the number had increased to 210,000 according to Spratt in 1865 ; one-third of this total were Moslems. It has been estimated that over 50,000 people fled from the island during the years immediately following, but the greater degree of freedom and security granted under the Organic Statute of 1868 is reflected in the rise to a total population of 279,165 at the census of 1881. Of this total, 141,602 were males, and 137,563 were females ; 205,010 were orthodox Christians, 73,234 were Moslems, and 921 were of other faiths. The Moslem element predominated in the principal towns, of which the populations were—Iráklion, 21,368 ; Khaniá, 13,812 ; and Réthimnon, 9,274.

The general position between 1881–1911 is summarized in the following table :

Census	Christians	Moslems	Others	Total
1881	205,000	73,000	1,000	279,000
1900	270,000	33,000	500	303,500
1911	324,800	27,800	400	353,000

Some of these figures were probably exaggerated, as the total population at the census of 1913 was considerably below that of 1911. From 1913 onwards, the growth, as indicated by successive censuses, has been as follows :

$$1913—336,151$$
$$1920—346,584$$
$$1928—386,427$$
$$1938—441,687*$$
$$1940—438,000$$

* The figure for 31 December, 1938, was an estimate only.

The distribution of population by *nomoi* was as follows :

Nomós	Area in sq. miles	1928 Census		Estimates, 31 Dec. 1938	
		Total	Per sq. mile	Total	Per sq. mile
Iráklion	989	144,921	146	162,978	165
Lasíthi	737	61,813	84	75,914	103
Rethímni	582	67,674	116	76,141	131
Khaniá	927	112,019	121	126,654	137
Total	3,235	386,427	120	441,687	136

Source : *Annuaire statistique de la Grèce*, 1939, p. 30 (Athènes, 1940).

In 1928 there was a slightly larger number of females (52·5%) than males. The birth-rate was 26·50 per 1,000 inhabitants, as compared with 30·50 for the whole of Greece ; the corresponding figures for the death-rate were 11·31 and 17·0 respectively. Despite this growth in population, emigration has robbed Crete, like the rest of Greece, of many inhabitants. Nor was the exodus confined to the Moslem population. The youngest, most vigorous and enterprising men and women, discouraged by the hardness of life in the island and by the disorder of the years before 1913, sought their fortunes abroad. Students, politicians and business men found their way to Athens, but a good many of these returned to the island. There were other Cretans who went to foreign countries, and either remained abroad permanently or returned after years of absence. Remittances from abroad have provided a valuable source of income to the island. In 1912 the emigrants numbered 4,000. Latterly, however, the exodus has decreased, and the total number of emigrants in 1936 was only 148, composed of 92 who emigrated for the first time, and of 56 re-emigrants.

The Exchange of Populations

The Moslems, who numbered a third of the total population in 1866, progressively decreased with the decline in Turkish power. The emigrants went mainly to Asia Minor and to the islands nearby. The decrease was rapid under the autonomous regime (1898–1913), and particularly after 1909 (see p. 297). Finally, the exchange of populations between Greece and Turkey, after the Convention of Lausanne signed on 30 January 1923, brought about the final disappearance of the Moslem element. At the census of 1928 there were 33,900 refugees in Crete, forming 9% of the total population. Of these, some 32,671 had arrived after the Greek disaster at Smyrna in September 1922. As a result of the exchange, the number of Moslems who left the island (some 32,000) balanced that of the refugees.

Of these refugees, about 13,000 (some 3,500 families) were townsmen settled around Khaniá, Réthimnon, Iráklion, Ierápetra and Sitía. The remainder (approximately 19,000 individuals belonging to 4,760 families) were workers on the land. Some 62% of the total number of refugees were settled by the Refugee Commission; the work of the Commission was predominantly concerned with rural settlement, but some urban families were also settled, as the following table shows:

Rural refugees	19,316
Urban refugees	1,720
Total	21,036

The distribution of their settlements is shown in Fig. 58.

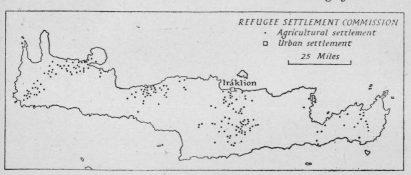

Fig. 58.   Refugee settlements in Crete

Based on a folding map in *Greek Refugee Settlement* (League of Nations, Geneva, 1926).

Town and Country

The people of Crete live for the most part in villages of about 200 to 500 inhabitants. In contrast with the rest of Greece, the Cretan peasant lives near his fields, and the greater number of villages are placed on the middle slopes of the mountains in the zone of olive groves. They are rarely more than 2,000 ft. above sea-level, but hamlets, occupied during the summer months for work in the vineyards, may extend up to 3,000 ft. Above this height there are only primitive huts for shepherds, and there is a good deal of seasonal migration. The main mountainous areas have less than 40 people per sq. mile, while on the restricted plains, where irrigation is practised, the density rises to 200 and over per sq. mile. The regional distribution of population is discussed on pp. 222–47. The populations of the three chief towns at the census of May 1928 were as follows : Iráklion, 33,404 ; Khaniá, the capital, 26,604 ; and Réthimnon, 8,632. Below this there was a great gap, for the next town in size was Ierápetra with only 3,611 people. There were altogether 51 communes in Crete (out of a total of 539), each with a population over 1,000. Of course, most of these communes comprised more than one settlement, and the number of separate settlements with over 1,000 inhabitants each was only 37 (Fig. 37).

According to the census of 1928, the working population of Crete numbered 127,109 out of a total population of 386,427. The predominant rural and agricultural character of the settlement is reflected in the occupational groups :

Category	Numbers			Percentages		
	Men	Women	Total	Men	Women	Total
Agriculture, Fishing, etc.	72,616	14,903	87,519	68·8	69·2	68·9
Industry, Mining, Quarrying, Transport	17,484	3,059	20,543	16·6	14·2	16·2
Commerce	9,028	384	9,412	8·6	1·8	7·4
Others	6,434	3,201	9,635	6·0	14·8	7·5
Total	105,562	21,547	127,109	100·0	100·0	100·0

Source : *Annuaire statistique de la Grèce,* 1932, p. 67 (Athènes, 1932).

Ethnic Composition

Crete, unlike the mainland, never suffered from large incursions of Slavs and Albanians ; but the presence of a number of Venetian surnames like Dandalis and Cornaro, or names such as Venetikos, or ones that contain Markos (such as Markoyannakis and Marko-dimitrakos), betray the mixture of Venetian blood in the island. The Saracen invaders were fully absorbed and only left their trace in a few Arabic names and in legends of treasures guarded by an Arab or a Saracen.

The Turks never settled in large numbers ; and the so-called Turks who were expelled after the Convention of Lausanne in 1923 were largely the descendants of Greeks who had turned Moslem. The village of Khalépa (in the south of the eparchy of Malevízion) was formerly a curious exception to the general rule, since it consisted largely of the descendants of Egyptian slaves who had been freed, and therefore contained a large negroid element. The small negroid community, however, was solidly Moslem and has disappeared since the exchange of populations.

Thus, in general, Crete is now inhabited by a population that is almost purely Greek in blood. The only considerable ethnic minority is that of the Armenians, who number over 6,000, mostly in Khaniá. There are a few hundred British citizens, chiefly Maltese and Cypriots, about two hundred Jews, and a sprinkling of Italians. The representatives of other nationalities are negligible.

Language

Greek is spoken throughout Crete, but there is a Cretan dialect which is perhaps stronger and more individual than any other save that of Cyprus. It has several features, which may have been produced, or at least have been affected, by the long Venetian occupation, but these peculiarities are by no means universal. Townspeople and educated villagers generally conform more or less to standard Greek pronunciation.

There are also some Cretan peculiarities of vocabulary. Sometimes the Cretan will use a Turkish word like *kalderimi* (cobbled road) or an Arabic word like *shamoudania* (candlestick), rarely or never heard on the mainland. Italian words are rare in standard Greek, but some, such as *kollatsioni* (breakfast), seem to be specifically Cretan. Not infrequently an ancient Greek word that has been abandoned or become unusual on the mainland is preserved in the Cretan dialect. Thus, the Cretan will use the old *tikhos* (wall), where a mainlander would say *douvari*. Sometimes a medieval word may be used, such as *takhini* (morning ; the regular word in *Erotokritos*). It may be remarked, however, that the Cretan will always understand the Greek speech of the mainland.

Literature

During the Venetian period, and mainly during the last 100 years of their rule, there flourished in Crete an interesting literature which was to have an important bearing on the development of modern Greek literature. The earliest poem of this medieval school was a paraphrase of Genesis and Exodus by Georgios Choumnos in the fifteen-syllabled ' political ' verse, but the school reached its acme during the fifteenth and sixteenth centuries. A series of Cretan dramas of this period is extant, of which the best known is *Erophile*, by Georgios Hortatzis, written about 1600 and clearly influenced by Italian writers such as Tasso. There are also Cretan comedies, such as the *Stathis* and *Fortunatus*, based on Italian models but introducing Cretan characters and local colour.

The most celebrated Cretan work, however, and the most quoted by modern Cretans, is the romantic love epic of *Erotokritos* by Vincenzo Cornaro, a native of Sitía. This poem describes the love of Erotokritos for Aretousa, the daughter of Heracles, King of Athens—an Athens of knights and tournaments. *Erophile* and *Erotokritos*, apart from their own literary value, are important because of the influence they exerted on Solomos when he was endeavouring to create a modern Greek literature that should not be out of touch with the people and the popular ballads. Somewhat less famous, but perhaps still more charming, is the pastoral comedy of Yiparis, showing the conversion to love of two shepherd girls, and marked by excellent characterization. Another of almost equal beauty is the *Sacrifice of Abraham*, in form a mystery play but in spirit a very sympathetic study of family life. This Cretan literature naturally contains a number of Italian words, but is in a fine vigorous language with many Cretan characteristics.

No account of Cretan literature is adequate without a reference to the *matinadhes* or *mandinadhes*, which are sung on most festive occasions. These consist of a series of rhyming couplets, which are answered by other rhyming couplets, usually didactic, amatory or facetious in tone. Two skilled performers will intone a long series of these couplets to a simple traditional tune, with the company repeating them. Many of the couplets are traditional, but a skilled singer will improvise them as he goes along. Any member of the company who is quick enough may insert a couplet of his own.

Literacy

Under Turkish dominion, education was extremely scanty in Crete as elsewhere in Greece, and no serious attempt seems to have been made officially to improve it until after the Pact of Khalépa in 1878, when more money was allowed for teaching purposes, and the Cretan Assembly voted in favour of primary and secondary schools similar to those within the kingdom of Greece.

At the present time, Cretan education stands at a fair level. The towns are quite well served, and nearly every commune has some kind of school. In 1920, the proportion of illiterates in Crete was 52·56% as against, for example, 40·75% in Central Greece and Évvoia. It must be remembered that the population contained in 1920 many adults whose schooling had stopped during the rebellions of 1866 and 1896. By the census of 1928 the position was as follows :

	Literate	Illiterate
Male	74·44%	25·56%
Female	40·7%	59·3%
Total	56·96%	43·04%

Art

The Cretans benefited in many respects from Venetian rule. Their towns acquired handsome buildings, and Venetian painting strongly influenced their own. A school of painting arose, termed the Cretan-Venetian school, which, together with that of Macedonia, produced a brilliant series of religious paintings, both ikons and frescoes. A curious but very important by-product of this school was the painter El Greco, whose Greek name was Theotokopoulos and who was alleged to have been born at the Cretan village of Fódhele, to the west of Iráklion. He was trained as a painter in Venice ; and, though his earlier works are strongly influenced by his studies under Titian, when he emigrated to Spain his figures began to show a Byzantine character which he must have learned as a boy in the Cretan-Venetian school of ikon painting.

Dress

The national dress of the Cretan man consists of a cylindrical cap or a kerchief for the head, a mantle of blue cloth embroidered

with black, gold and purple thread, a short purple silk sash, baggy
blue breeches and long boots of natural-coloured, or white, leather.
After the wars of 1912–13, 1914–18, and 1920–22, the younger
generation, partly for economic reasons and still more in imitation
of the Athenian, began to adopt European costume. Now, only
the older men wear the national costume except in the hill districts.
In 1940, there were left in Iráklion only four tailors capable of
making the Cretan costume.

In the Sfakiá district, where the younger men still to a large
extent wear the old costume, the head-dress is a fringed black
handkerchief. In Lasíthi also the black handkerchief is worn, but
without the fringe ; and the black handkerchief became regarded
as the typical headgear of the Cretan revolutionary in Turkish
times. In the uplands, the village priest is to be distinguished from
the rest of his congregation only by his clerical hat.

The dress of the women consisted of a kerchief for the head, a
short embroidered jacket, a simple blouse, a waistband, and a
flowing pleated skirt. This dress has almost died out except in
some of the mountain villages, such as Anóyia and Axós.

Dances

Cretan dances are vigorous and interesting, and are danced by
both sexes in common (contrary to the usual practice on the mainland). Of the mainland dances, only the *Kalamatianos* is generally
known, but, owing to the diffusion of refugees from Asia Minor,
most villages will produce somebody who can dance a *Sirtos* or
some other non-Cretan dance. The most widely known Cretan
dance is the *Pendozalis* or ' Five steps ', with two kicks followed by
a movement to the right. The dancers clasp each other by the
shoulders, and the time is gradually quickened till the dancers can
go no faster.

Other dances, as their names imply, are characteristic of special
districts. The *Khaniotikos* is like a mild *Pendozalis* (without the
initial kicks and the quickening time). Lasíthi is characterized by
a ' leaping ' dance called the *Pidhiktos*, the basis of which is a forward
and backward movement like that of the *Maleviziotikos* and the
Irakliotikos, but distinguished from these dances by the sudden
bounds into the air made by the leader.

HISTORICAL OUTLINE

EARLY HISTORY TO A.D. 1204

Before the birth of European civilization, Crete seems to have been an outpost of Egyptian and Asiatic culture. Its size and remoteness encouraged independence, its wealth was a source of power, its unique physical characteristics fostered a culture with clearly marked individual traits, and there arose in Crete a civilization which after 4,000 years seems astonishingly modern. It was presided over by dynasties to whom the collective name ' Minoan ' has been given, taken from the name of the semi-legendary Minos, a king whose reign lay on the border-line of history. These dynasts or series of dynasts seem to have held sway for something like 1,500 years (3000–1400 B.C.), during which time their civilization underwent considerable changes and finally fell into decadence. The remarkable discoveries at Cnossos (near Iráklion) have laid bare their ancient capital. Their power seems to have been based mainly upon the natural resources of the island, but to have maintained itself abroad by large fleets. They appear to have had colonies in Sicily and Asia Minor, and they played a large part in the development of the eastern Mediterranean. Most important was their connexion with Greece. The prominence of Crete in Greek legends—even though those legends may belong to a later time—and the superstitious reverence with which its mountains and plains were regarded by Greeks of the classical days are significant (see vol. I, pp. 129 *et seq.*).

With the coming of the Achaeans, and then the Dorians, there followed the dissolution of Cretan kingdoms into small and mutually hostile communities of the kind common on the Greek mainland. In Homer's time Crete was ' the island of the hundred towns ', and some of these can still be identified. From this time, Crete, weakened by division and discord, sinks out of the main course of history and does not appear again until Roman times. The Roman Republic was often called in to arbitrate in the endless quarrels between Cretan city-states, but the Romans for long shrewdly preferred to have Crete as an independent ally rather than as a subject state. Cretan archers and slingers were, during this period, valuable auxiliaries to the various mercenary armies of the mainland, and Cretan mariners turned their adventurous energies to piracy. As Rome extended and consolidated her eastern conquests, Crete, with its random lawlessness, became a thorn in the side of her empire. Assistance rendered to her arch-foe Mithridates, and the covert alliance with Cicilian and Pamphylian pirates, gave Rome an excuse to subdue Crete. After one signal failure this was accomplished by Quintus Metellus (henceforth called Creticus) in 67 B.C. Crete was thus the last of Greek-speaking lands to fall under Roman sway.

As a Roman province the island was included with Cyrene (eastern Tripoli) and became one of the granaries of the metropolis, being also famous for its wine and cheese. St. Paul and his disciple Titus began a work which ended in the complete conversion of Crete to Christianity in the early Roman Empire. At the partition of the Empire, Crete finally remained with the Eastern (Byzantine) half, but about A.D. 823 Arabs from Alexandria over-ran and destroyed most of its cities, but founded Rabdh el-Kandak (' Fortress of Suppression ') on the site of Candia (Iráklion). From this is to be traced the name ' Candia ' applied to the whole island by the Venetians, Italians, French and formerly by Englishmen, the ancient Greek title being ' Kríti ' (Κρήτη) and the Roman ' Creta.' The next century witnessed a long struggle between the Byzantine (Greek) emperors and the Arabs for the possession of the island, but in A.D. 961 it was definitely reconquered by the Greek Nicephoros Phocas. Under the Arab rule, Crete had become a great home for pirates and a slave-mart ; but, when they departed, the Saracens left little trace of their occupation on the island, and the Mohammedan religion, which had been forcibly imposed, was stamped out.

The Venetian Period, 1204–1670

After the conquest of Constantinople in 1204 by the Franks, Crete was sold by Boniface, marquis of Montferrat, to the Venetians. The value of the island as a means of controlling the trade-routes of the eastern Mediterranean was perhaps the leading motive for its acquisition by the Venetians, and they seem hardly to have anticipated the difficulties involved in its possession. The period of Venetian occupation falls into three parts : the first, about 160 years, was occupied in mastering the island ; the second, lasting for nearly another 200 years, saw the consolidation of Venetian power in the island, and the exploitation of its resources ; in the last, a period of 150 years, the decline of Venetian power before the Turkish onset resulted in the complete ejection of Venice, and in the transference of Crete to the Ottoman Empire.

The Venetian Conquest of Crete

The first opposition was from the Genoese—bitter commercial rivals of the Venetian State and rejected bidders for the island. They incited the Cretans to resist, and anticipated the Venetian occupation. In 1206, however, Iráklion (Candia) fell to the Venetians, and the Genoese retired to the western part of the island and held Khaniá. Fresh trouble arose when Marco Sanudo was called in to assist the Venetian cause. One of the freebooters licensed by the Venetian state, who had carved out for himself a realm in the southern Cyclades, he was now desirous of asserting his complete independence, and sided with the enemies of Venice. These and repeated other revolts of the islanders called forth energetic measures from the Venetian government. Some of the rebellions were serious and ended only by compromise. Khaniá was taken in 1290, but it was not until 1343 that the greater part of the island was subdued, though the Sphakiots held out in their mountains for 23 years longer. Not only did the natives rise against their Venetian masters, but the Venetian colonists themselves rebelled against the home government. The most important of these latter rebellions was that of 1361–64, which was fostered by the lack of representation and by the taxation to which the colonists were subjected.

Venetian Civilization in Crete

Whatever the original intention of the Venetians may have been, the opposition and difficulties they encountered imposed on them a policy of strictness. The rigorous suppression of the lawless and independent islanders, the supplanting of these as far as possible by Venetian colonists, and the organization of a strong government, became in their eyes indispensable for the secure tenure of the island. As early as 1212 a party of Italian colonists arrived in Crete, and they were followed by numerous other bands under state encouragement. The land was divided into State, Church and private property. The latter was given to Venetian nobles, 545 families in all, as fiefs, that is to say, on feudal conditions of rent in kind (one-seventh of the produce) and warlike service. A governor-general, with a large staff of military, judicial, financial, and civil officers and troops, controlled the island from the capital of Candia (Iráklion).

Conscious first of the danger and then of the profit of their enterprise, the Venetians devoted much energy to the development of

their possession and the consolidation of their power. Castles were
built on commanding sites all over the island. Even the remote
and wild south-western region had its castles at Sfakiá and
Frangokástello. Roads were built and bridges constructed ; fine
town and country houses arose ; agriculture was encouraged (the
wines of Crete again became noted) ; salt-works flourished ; and
Crete became one of the most profitable possessions of Venice.
Fine churches arose, and Pope Alexander V (1410) was the son of a
Cretan mason. But the whole of this system rested on a state of
slavery. The Cretan peasantry were for the most part broken-
spirited serfs whose labours went almost entirely to the enrichment
of their lords. The proud and free-spirited mountain chiefs were
duped and treated with ferocious brutality. To oppression by a
cruel and degenerate nobility was added religious persecution.
The Greek Orthodox religion was discouraged, and the Roman
Catholic was the official Church. Enforced agriculture yielded
diminishing results. At this time Crete produced insufficient wheat
for its own needs. Sugar-cane was introduced by the Venetians but
proved a failure. Many Cretan families, amongst them the best,
left the island.

Warnings and protests uttered by influential Venetians received
little attention in the decadence of the Venetian state until it became
apparent that the Turks were bent upon the capture of the island.
The loss of Crete would have dealt a death-blow to Venice, who
relied largely on its trade and revenues. Some attempts at reform
and amelioration were made. But the Venetians relied far more on
strengthening their hold, and carried out the series of remarkable
fortifications which survives, especially along the north coast, to
this day. The island of Spinalónga was fortified in 1526. In
consequence of an alarming but fruitless descent of the Ottoman
Khair Eddyn upon Áyioi Theódhoroi (1538–9), Candia (Iráklion)
was fortified and by 1566 was considered impregnable. Again, in
consequence of Turkish raids into Soúdha Bay, the islet of Soúdha
was fortified (1572–8), and so in 1584 was the island of Ímeri
Graboúsa. These fortifications, like those of Khaniá and Áyioi
Theódhoroi (apparently completed earlier), were designed to secure
Venetian military and naval supremacy. They were also meant to
serve, in case of necessity, as *points d'appui* for a second conquest
of the island. The finest brains and skill which the Venetians could
command were enlisted in their construction ; they are models of
design and construction, and remain prominent after three and a

half centuries. Particular attention was paid to dockyard and naval requirements, as maritime ascendancy was vital.

In spite of this and a slight improvement in the condition of the natives, Venetian rule in Crete was doomed. Like most oppressive systems it left little positive trace behind it except archaeological remains. The Venetian influence was confined mainly to the coastal towns and the neighbouring lowlands. Large settlements of Italian soldiers are said to have been made in eastern Crete (Sitía), which was more accessible, but the physical type was quickly merged in that of the islanders, and the mountaineers remained practically unaffected. The chief relics of the Venetian period are : the towns of Khaniá, Rethímnon, Iráklion, and Sitía, which are full of Venetian remains ; the numerous more or less ruined forts and country houses ; and the relics of some roads and bridges.

The Decline of Venetian Power

After the conquest of Constantinople in 1453 by the Turks, it was clear that the new Ottoman power aimed at reoccupying all the borders of the former Saracen empire. For the conquest of Greece and the Levant, maritime supremacy would have to be wrested from Venice, and to this end the conquest of Crete was necessary. The enterprises mentioned above were preliminary attempts in this direction, but they were abortive, and serious operations were not undertaken until 1645, when a force of some 50,000 Turks laid siege to the fortress of Áyioi Theódoroi on the island of that name. Repulsed from here, they landed in the south-west corner of the bay of Khaniá and, while blockading the bay of Soúdha (the anchorage of the Venetian fleet), laid siege to Khaniá, which they took. In the next year (1646) Réthimnon suffered the same fate, and, in spite of the vigorous naval defensive measures of the Venetians, by 1648 little remained to them of the island except the town of Iráklion and the island fortresses around the coast. The investment of Iráklion began in 1648 and lasted for over 20 years, being one of the most famous sieges in history. The hero of this scene was Thomas Morosini, Venetian admiral and general, but the Turkish general, Mehemet Kuprili, of Albanian descent, who ultimately took command of the Turkish forces and brought the siege to a conclusion, also proved himself a notable warrior. The beleaguered were several times succoured with money and military and naval reinforcements from Italy and France, for the imagination of Europe was stirred by this latter-day crusade ; but all efforts were useless, and in 1669 Morosini capitulated and was allowed to evacuate the town with honour. By the treaty of capitulation the whole of Crete was abandoned to the Turks, Venice retaining only the island fortresses of Ímeri Graboúsa, Spinalónga and Soúdha. Any intention of reconquest which may have been implied in the reservation of these posts was afterwards abandoned by Venice, and Ímeri Graboúsa was sold to the Turks in 1692, while the two others were lost 23 years later in the final struggles of the Venetians with the Turks.

TURKISH RULE, 1670–1821

Crete now was wholly Ottoman, and was styled by them Kirit or Kirid. The Cretans themselves had connived at Turkish occupation. To them in their misery a change even of tyrants seemed a relief, and, despairing but not forgetful of freedom, they welcomed the future. They were, in the nature of things, doomed to disappointment.

The conquest of Crete by the Turks was the high-water mark of their imperial achievement. The weakness of their empire became apparent when they succeeded to European possessions. There were special reasons why their failure should be more glaring and more complete in Crete than elsewhere. The conquest of the island had involved the loss of much blood and treasure, and there was a natural desire to recoup at its expense. Crete was an island and distant from the central government, and its governors had a comparatively free hand. With the growth of weakness and corruption at the capital, the governors were elected more and more capriciously, and their tenure of office became even more insecure. Crete was a prize for the favourites of the hour, and the lucky ones had to get rich quickly or not at all.

From the first there was no real peace. In the Cretans, the Turks found a people differing totally from themselves in race, language, and religion, and one in whom the fires of independence, however damped, were not utterly extinguished. The usual paraphernalia of Turkish rule were instituted. The island was divided into three *pashaliks* with centres at Iráklion, Khaniá and Réthimnon. The *pasha* of Candia (Iráklion) was also governor-general of the island. The *mufti* administered religious, the *cadi* civil law, and there were imperial treasurers. In theory, there was religious toleration. But the governors, weak and greedy, were at the mercy of their fierce janissaries, who occupied the chief villages, pillaged, bullied, and maltreated the inhabitants, and sometimes even deposed their rulers. The Christian religion was discouraged, and the law was subverted. Unnameable atrocities against Christians went unpunished. Churches were converted into mosques, and thousands of Cretans hastened to turn Moslem, some genuinely, some nominally only to secure safety. By dividing, the Turks subdued : the Cretan Moslems were accorded the upper hand and the protection of the law ; the Christians were deprived of both. Bitter hatred arose between the two Cretan sects, and the worst oppressors of their countrymen were Cretans. The Christians alone had to pay a heavy capitation tax, and were plundered by Turk and Cretan Moslem without redress.

Mehemet Kuprili in the seventeenth century did something to restore the chief fortified places ; later rulers allowed fortifications, roads, bridges, and all public works to fall into ruin. The Venetians had left the island well organized and, materially at least, civilized ; under the Turks, it became one of the worst governed and most deplorable wastes of the empire. The spirit of the people as a whole had been broken by the Venetian yoke, and they sank easily into deeper slavery and despair. The Sphakiots alone defied the foreigners. Russia, with Mediterranean aspirations, encouraged them to revolt, which they did under a native chieftain in 1770. But internal dissension and jealousy—the last infirmity of Hellenic patriots—were their ruin. Certain also of their number had been bribed by the Turks. The rising was suppressed with cruelty, and the Sphakiots, though they remained nominally independent, were forced to pay the capitation tax with the rest of their compatriots.

THE CRETAN PROBLEM, 1821–1913

Main Elements in the Problem

Such was the state of affairs during the first period—roughly 150 years—of Turkish rule. In 1821, the outbreak of the Greek War of Independence marked the beginning of a new era in Crete, and the dawn of a new hope. From the formal cession of the island to them in 1670 until the beginning of the nineteenth century, the Turks had had a free hand in Crete. Though the most detached of Turkish possessions, it had so far attracted little attention in Europe. Great Britain had always been interested in Turkey owing to her Levantine trade, and there had been an English consul in Crete since 1520. But, towards the beginning of the nineteenth century, other great European Powers were becoming aware of the vital importance of Crete to all Mediterranean schemes, and the decline of Turkish power was viewed with varying feelings. The year 1821 markes the debut of Crete into European politics. From that year its future became a part of the Balkan problem as a whole, and its history was merged more and more in that of Greece. In Crete was fought out in miniature, though not always in clarity, the battle of liberation and self-determination. The years 1821–96 marked the most painful period of this process. The following features are traceable in it : the growing decay of Turkish power disguised under a semblance of liberality and reform ; the growing self-consciousness of the Cretans, exhibiting itself in ever more violent actions and reactions ; and the growing consciousness among the European Powers of the nature and urgency of the problem, leading to continually more drastic interference. The history of these years is one of such confusion, violence, and complication that some preliminary analysis of the forces and motives operative in it is necessary if it is to be intelligible.

Moslem and Christian. At the outbreak of the War of Independence the Cretan population consisted of about 300,000 persons, of whom over half were Cretan Moslems, a small proportion were actual Turks (officials, militia, etc.), and quite a few were foreign residents (foreign consuls, merchants, Jews, etc.) ; the rest, perhaps 120,000, were Christians of the Orthodox Greek Church. In this population were all the elements of discord. The greater mass of the peasantry were ignorant, subservient and poor. The rich land-owners, merchants and townsmen had interests often conflicting with those of the common people. The dwellers in the towns were peculiarly liable to the excitements of faction and intrigue. The Sphakiots, and mountaineers generally, were independent lawless, fanatical, something of bullies to their own less warlike countrymen, not incorruptible, and led by chiefs often jealous of one another. The Turkish rulers were alternately ferocious and amiable, capable and weak, but almost always corrupt and time-serving. These were permanent, if personal, factors in the situation. Others changed or arose with the change of time and circumstance.

The antagonism of the two sects was always present. In times of unrest and excitement, it mounted to fanaticism leading to extreme horrors of violence and massacre. In times of peace, Christian and Moslem were capable of living together ; family mixed with family, church stood alongside mosque. In general, as long as the Moslems had the support of the Turkish government, they pursued an anti-national policy. Assuming to themselves all privileges and powers permitted to them, they aped the Turkish despots and stopped at no corruption or brutality. As Turkish power waned, they clamoured and bid ever more strenuously for support. The Christians underwent a reverse process. Harassed and bullied in their evil days, they gradually gained confidence, clamoured for equality, priority, and then for sole authority. From humility they ascended to arrogance and occasionally allowed themselves fanatical reprisals. The chief instigators in this movement were the priests, who, with growing impunity, taught the duties of religious intolerance and Panhellenism. Schools, too, became centres of propaganda.

The ' Black-coated gentry '. With the growth of education and intercourse with Athens—and through Athens with European ideas and culture—there arose in the cities of Crete a class of ' black-coated gentry ', mostly ex-students from the University of Athens, often teachers or necessitous lawyers who dabbled in politics and ' reform '. They were in close touch with Athenian politicians and with the agents of the Orthodox Church, and were a grievous burden to the country in difficult times. Yet they were instrumental in the intellectual and political awakening of the people, and, if their practice was generally bad, their theories were good. The schemes of reform framed under their influence show an enlightened understanding of the needs of the island, and, in time, most of these were carried out. The concessions and reforms which they claimed may be summed up as follows : political self-expression ; judicial and legal reform ; fiscal reform (revision of taxation so as to encourage trade ; release from capitation and military service exemption taxes) ; religious freedom ; educational reform ; liberty of speech and press ; the official use of the Greek language ; and finally a vigorous policy of public works and economic development.

The history of the nineteenth century shows a series of far-reaching concessions granted by the Sultan to the Cretan people. But as they were mostly extorted by fear and under pressure, so they were evaded or curtailed in practice and were never worth much more, as practical reforms, than the paper they were written on. The Turks complained that they granted all necessary reforms, remitted all unnecessary taxes, and treated all alike with justice and tolerance ; and in fact during the nineteenth century Crete was one of the most lightly taxed and loosely governed of Turkish provinces. They said that the chief causes of unrest were the poison of Panhellenic ideas disseminated by priests and teachers and the desire of revolution fostered by unscrupulous debtors, who hoped to evade their public or private obligations.

The Attitude of Greece. Meanwhile the attitude of Greece towards Cretan affairs was full of difficulty. A distinction, somewhat artificial, must be made between Greek government and the Greek people or individual Greek politicians. The Greek state, emerging from the War of Independence as a free European state, found itself in a continual state of latent hostility with Turkey. An era of Panhellenic propaganda was inaugurated in the whole Aegean world. What is now termed ' irredentism ' was preached throughout all Greek lands as the ' Great Idea '. In these wider movements, and until larger and nearer questions were settled, Crete and its affairs were a side issue. Crete was an island and therefore the prize of sea power. It was remote, and therefore less urgent. Its affairs were complicated, and many aspects of Cretan affairs made the acquisition of the island of dubious advantage.

Nevertheless it was an idea with which successive governments and politicians eagerly coquetted. Not only did the general state of Graeco-Turkish relations at any given time have a great influence on the official Greek attitude towards Crete, but Crete had a great reflex influence on those relations. More than once, declarations of ' Union ' made in Crete, and the demands of self-elected Cretan deputies to take a place in the Athenian Chamber, proved highly embarrassing to the Greek government ; and several times Crete came near to embroiling Greece and Turkey in war. Crete, too, was a great drain on the Greek exchequer. The budgets of 1881–98 show that one-third of Greek borrowings within that period were due to interference in Cretan affairs. As a general rule, however, the official attitude of Greece was non-committal. The Greek state did what it dared, and it dared more as time went on, but on the whole it preferred to canvass for the support of the Powers and to wait on time for a solution.

The hands of the Greek government were sometimes forced by public opinion. The Cretan cause was very popular in Athens. The reasons were largely sentimental, but they had a practical side also. There was an element of hero-worship in the veneration of the Athenian for the Cretan patriot. At a distance, the hardy mountaineers of Crete, struggling against impossible odds, and enduring the horrors of a barbarous and heathen tyranny, seemed to the mainland Greeks symbolic of unconquered national hope and national misfortune. To sympathy were added considerations of advantage. The Church, the learned professions, the military and civil services, politicians, merchants, and even outlaws, had much to hope from the acquisition of the island. Many refugees from Turkish oppression found ready homes and audiences in Athens. Some of these were genuine patriots, some were undesirables. But the effect was the same. The Cretan, who had a reputation for bravery and independence, was a favourite, and the current of Greek popular opinion set ever more strongly towards decisive intervention in Cretan affairs.

The Attitude of the Great Powers. But as the affairs of Crete developed and tended more and more to become involved in Athenian politics, the attitude of the Great Powers also changed and developed. Approaching the question, first with little knowledge but with a large amount of preconception and prejudice dictated usually by their imperial interests, these Powers for a long time played no very enlightening part in the drama. Into the kaleidoscopic changes of the policy of Great Britain, France, Russia and Italy with regard to the Turkish empire as a whole, and Crete and the eastern Mediterranean in particular, it is unnecessary to enter. Most of these powers were embarrassed by previous undertakings or already existing interests. To see the Cretan question except through these glasses was not to be expected of them. Great Britain, for instance, with her large commercial commitments in the Levant, had a particular interest in the fate of Turkey. Her policy was, on the whole, one of bolstering up Turkey as far as possible, or agreeing to her dismemberment only if it could be done with safety to all concerned. Russia also had an interest, now in maintaining, now in overthrowing, Turkish power. Some, realizing the peculiar geographical situation of the island and its strategic value, dreamed of it as the possible basis for Mediterranean power ; others hoped for its exploitation. Few thought at first of Crete itself and the welfare of its people. The results were disastrous. Unlucky ' solutions ' were followed by unluckier ' solutions ' of these ' solutions '. Hopes were encouraged now in one, now in another, Cretan party, and nearly always those hopes remained unrealized. Since European policy was almost entirely guided by conflicting interests and mutual antagonisms external to the island itself, that policy was seldom for the good of the islanders.

The Cretans seemed abandoned to their fate, yet ever the sport of great storms. When at last the Great Powers awoke to the full seriousness of the situation and their consciences, no less than their interests, became involved, there followed periods of alternate petulant irritation and hysterical sentimentality. Crete became the material and moral sore of Europe, which righteousness and policy alike bade heal. Once, however, the position was realized, the solution was found. The process of emancipation was difficult, partly owing to the state of Cretan affairs and partly owing to the disposition of the Powers. It was slow, but on the whole it was wise, cautious, and humane. The end of the nineteenth century saw the problem well under way to settlement. It is difficult to say which side emerges with the least dimmed reputation—Crete, or the Great Powers who redeemed her.

The importance of naval power in settling Mediterranean problems was never more strikingly illustrated than in this period of Cretan history. The part played by Greek and Turkish naval forces is significant enough, but the presence of naval flotillas of the allied Great Powers was in the end conclusive.

The Greek War of Independence

The outbreak, in 1821, of the War of Independence in Greece found a ready response in Crete. The Sphakiots, ordered by the Turks to surrender their arms as a measure of precaution, refused and rose in rebellion. Massacres of Christians as a reprisal led to a general rising and to the blockade of Khaniá by the insurgents. The dispatch of a leader by the mainland Greeks led to jealousy and dissension among the Sphakiot chieftains, and the insurrection languished. After the arrival in 1822 of an Egyptian general, with a fleet and 7,000 Albanian troops, the issue was not in doubt. Stern measures of repression led to the end of the revolt in 1824. It was in this revolt that some 300 Cretans, mainly old men, women and children, were smothered by smoke in the cave of Melidhóni above the Milopótamos valley. After Navarino in 1827, the Greek insurgent leaders of the mainland induced the Cretans to try again. They sent armed support to Ímeri Graboúsa, fostered the rebellion from that point, and declared a general blockade of Crete. The British fleet, however, intervened in 1828, dismantled Ímeri Graboúsa on the grounds of its being a piratical nest, and raised the blockade. In the same year hostilities died down, and an armistice was declared.

Egyptian Rule, 1830–40

By the Treaty of London (22 January 1830), Crete was excluded from the newly formed kingdom of Greece and was given to Mehemet Ali of Egypt. The islanders, however, were allowed a flag, free navigation, and the collection of their own taxes. This arrangement was unpopular with all parties in Crete. Nevertheless, Mustafa Pasha, an Albanian and the first Egyptian ruler, was at first just and lenient. Later, Mehemet Ali tried to impose his monopolies on the island, offended the Moslems, subverted justice, imposed new taxes, and obliterated former concessions. The use of Albanian gendarmerie throughout the island was a constant source of irritation. In 1833, non-cultivation of land was made punishable by reversion of the land to the state. As the population at that time was insufficient to cultivate all the land, this was felt to be particularly oppressive, and an assembly held in that year sought and obtained some redress. The execution of ringleaders, followed by measures which some regard as severe, others as impartial, kept Crete in tolerable peace and content for eight years. But the Moslems were restive for their loss of power, and the Christians for want of more. The latter, infected with current ideas of liberty and national government, agitated in Greece, where a central committee was formed to watch over their interests and to strive to prevent Crete again falling under Turkish sway.

Nevertheless, after the Turco-Egyptian war, the Great Powers (except France) restored Crete to Turkey in 1840. At this, a rising was started by the disappointed Sphakiots, but it was speedily suppressed by the Turkish government. In the famous ' National Assembly of 3 September 1843 ', which gave to Greece its constitutional government, Cretan representatives were admitted together with those of Thessaly, Macedonia and Epirus. This was the first formal recognition of the claim of Crete to form part of the Greek kingdom, but the decision of the Greek government of that day was against an attempt to incorporate the island.

The Organic Statute, 1868

For the next seventeen years Crete nursed her troubles in comparative silence. The rule of Vely Pasha, himself a Cretan, was on the whole humane, but compulsory road-making, religious dissensions, and above all Panhellenic propaganda, led in 1858 to a convention of some 8,000 Cretans at Perivólia near Khaniá. The time was well chosen, for Turkey was occupied with a war in

Montenegro. The incipient rebellion was, however, quashed by the recall of Vely Pasha, and reforms were promised.

Then followed a series of incidents typical of Cretan affairs. The new governor was avaricious and time-serving; and the promised reforms did not materialize. Dissensions amongst the Cretans continued; a petition to the Sultan in 1864 was neutralized by a counter-petition. Two successive bad agricultural years increased the discontent and unrest, and in 1866 a second assembly at Perivólia addressed complaints to the Sultan. The demand was at first for reform, and an imposing schedule of political, administrative, judicial, fiscal, and agricultural improvements was made out. Later, the Panhellenic agitators and politicians who were the ring-leaders became emboldened. Enlarging their demands, they applied to some of the Great Powers for sanction to unite Crete with Greece, or, failing that, for drastic reforms. The British government pointed, in reply, to the unsatisfactory condition of the Ionian Islands handed to Greece by Great Britain two years before, but they promised reforms. In reality, however, both the British and French governments supported the Turk, and the Porte played its usual game of make-believe and procrastination. Propaganda by priests and *agents provocateurs* in Crete, and by Cretans in Athens, and the preparations of the Turkish governor for war, precipitated revolt. In Greece, the Cretan demands aroused the keenest popular sympathy; and, though the government was obliged to preserve an official attitude of indifference, numerous volunteers left Athens unhindered for Crete.

A period of guerrilla warfare followed. The siege of the monastery of Arkádhi, full of women and children, and the subsequent massacre by the Turks, made a profound impression. British public opinion was listed on the side of the Christian rebels, and the British government with difficulty maintained its pro-Turk policy. The Greek government also was almost forced by popular clamour to intervene. While British and French individuals rendered practical aid to the Cretans, the British government reluctantly considered the proposal for Cretan autonomy, but finally opposed it as against the other Powers. There followed a series of obstinate refusals on the part of the insurgents to negotiate, and brutal massacres and devastations on the part of the Turks, who, however, also suffered serious reverses and losses. The vacillation and contradictory policies of the Powers, the false hopes and prejudices of the rebels, and the ferocity and fear of the Porte, at last brought exhaustion. The

Porte reverted to reconciliation, and the Organic Statute of 1868 promised a more efficient administration, considerable official recognition and power for Christians, a popular paid assembly, religious safeguards, and fiscal reforms. But the revolt continued half-heartedly ; the main insurgent leaders returned to Athens, though a fresh chieftain left Athens with reinforcements for Crete. The rebels counted on Athenian sympathy and perhaps on outside interference, but Turkey meanwhile threatened war upon Greece unless she abandoned her policy of mischief-making in Crete. A conference of the Powers, called by Bismarck in 1869, definitely rejected the idea of union. Greece reluctantly had to abandon her dreams of Cretan annexation and war with Turkey. The claim of Cretan deputies to sit in the parliament at Athens was rejected, and, all hope being gone, Crete became quiet for a time.

Continued Unrest, 1869–98

The smouldering fires flickered up once or twice, but it was not till 1876, when Turkey was preoccupied in war with Russia, that the ' patriotic ' party ventured to demand the reality of the reforms promised in 1868. The demand, repeated in 1877, was reinforced by a meeting of Cretans in Athens. Revolt was decided upon, volunteers went to Crete, and another ' General Assembly ' demanded autonomy. The hostilities which followed were not serious, as the Turks lacked men and the Cretans food, and finally the offer of Great Britain (through her Consul) to arbitrate was accepted. But by the Treaties of San Stefano and of Berlin (1878) Crete was left with Turkey on condition that the Organic Statute was to be applied in good faith.

The disappointment of the Cretans was intense, and, in view of the changed attitude of Great Britain at this time and the depression of the Panhellenists, the idea of a British protectorate was mooted and gained some support in the island. Crete had, however, to be satisfied with the Pact of Khalépa (1878), a modification of the Organic Statute of 1868. By this pact, which marked the highest point of Liberal Turkish reform in Crete, the privileges granted under the earlier statute were confirmed and extended ; the Christians had now for the first time a slight advantage, and new concessions—such as a free press, official use of the Greek language, improved education and taxation and public works—were granted. This constitution was given practical effect by the next Turkish ruler, and there was no further trouble for seven years.

The sentiment for union with Greece was not dead, but, in defer-
ence to Athenian wishes, the Cretans forbore to push their claims
in 1881, when Greece had to choose between Thessaly and Crete,
and it was Thessaly that became part of the Greek kingdom. In
1886, however, seizing a favourable moment, the irreconcilables
again tried to force union with Greece, but this came to nothing.
   Meanwhile, internal politics in Crete continued to produce trouble.
Faction and the petty tyrannies of rival political parties awoke
discord in 1889, and the disappointed party raised once more the
cry of ' Union '. Greece discouraged the movement, but strife,
once kindled, awoke the old enmities, and Christians and Moslems
began mutual outrages. The Sultan adopted a rigorous attitude ;
the Pact of Khalépa was virtually repealed ; neither the Powers nor
Greece intervened, and, though there was no serious revolt, unrest
and discontent prevailed. A Christian governor-general (vali) was
appointed in 1895 to quieten this unrest. The enraged Moslem
minority thereupon resorted to violence ; the Christians retaliated ;
things went from bad to worse until, in May 1896, a street fight in
Khaniá began the series of events which ended Turkish rule in
Crete. The death-bed repentance of the Porte produced a promised
revival of the Pact of Khalépa, but both Christians and Moslems
now thoroughly distrusted the Turks who, early in 1897 attacked
the Christians of Khaniá and burnt their town quarter. The
Christians thereupon occupied the Akrotíri peninsula and proclaimed union with Greece. Meanwhile, popular opinion in Greece
—where there were numerous influential Cretans resident, besides
large numbers of Cretan refugees—rose to boiling point. A naval
and military expedition was dispatched, with orders to expel the
Turks and to annex the island. The admirals of the five European
Powers who were present in force, acted as a steadying influence.
Then followed a serio-comic chain of events in which, acting as
arbiters, the admirals alternately tried to appease and to punish the
belligerents, now aroused to extreme fanaticism. Relying perhaps
on the favourable intervention of the British government and on the
undoubtedly favourable state of public opinion in England, Greece
now committed herself to a war with Turkey on the Cretan issue.
   There followed, however, a period of enforced quietude under
the guns of the allied warships. The settlement of the Cretan
question was now seriously occupying four of the Great Powers
(Germany and Austria had withdrawn), but for eighteen months no
conclusion was reached. The chief ports were occupied by European

troops, Iráklion by the British, Réthimnon by the Russians, Sitía and Spinalónga by the French, Ierápetra by the Italians, Khaniá by all four. The Moslems were confined to the towns, the Christians occupied the country and the villages. The continued delay and artificial restraint were trying, and there was much political agitation by the Christians throughout the island. In September 1898 a Turkish attack on the British in Iráklion was sternly suppressed by Admiral Noel, and soon afterwards the last Turkish troops left the island. This hastened the decision of the allies. In November they offered the post of High Commissioner of Crete to Prince George, second son of the king of Greece, and in December he arrived in Soúdha Bay in that capacity. The fleets withdrew, but the allied garrison remained, and, under the watchful eye of the Powers concerned, the experiment of autonomy was cautiously inaugurated.

Autonomy, 1898–1913

The next period of Cretan history has been called a transition or preparation period for Greek rule. In retrospect it certainly is seen to be so, and the appointment of Prince George may be taken as indicating, from the beginning, the same purpose. It is more likely, however, that the question was at first deliberately left open. Caution was needed in view of the difficult nature and inexperience of the Cretans ; a Graeco-Turkish war and perhaps a Balkan conflagration were not to be risked ; experience of the new regime was needed before any final judgment could be formed. Nevertheless, from this time, the current of affairs set towards union with Greece. The solution of the Cretan question was ultimately bound up with one man, M. Venizelos (see vol. I, pp. 210 et seq.).

Eleutherios Venizelos was the outstanding figure of this period of Cretan affairs—the disturber, the breaker, the reconciler, the champion of the Cretan cause. Born in 1864 at Mourniés, near Khaniá, he was a graduate of the University of Athens ; he came to Khaniá as a lawyer in 1886, and quickly made his mark. The next year he was elected a member of the Cretan Assembly, where his novel defence of the rights of minorities and his unwavering moral courage gained him a reputation for disinterested honesty and ability. In 1888, his leadership of the Cretan Liberal party evoked the opposition of the rival party, a difference which led to the troubles outlined above (see p. 294). During the stormy ten years which followed, Venizelos played a leading and unflinching part in the conduct of affairs. He was in this period a convinced ' Unionist '. At the head of the Christian irreconcilables on the Akrotíri peninsula (see p. 294), and again at an Assembly in 1897, he maintained, at considerable risk to himself, a resolute attitude on this point. Later, when the allies decided upon autonomy, and Prince George became High Commissioner, he gave way in the interests of peace. He threw himself into the working of the new regime, but it was his personal influence which finally decided in this period that Crete should go to Greece.

The new High Commissioner was at first personally popular with the Cretans, and displayed some tact if not always discretion. When he failed in the latter his chief adviser, M. Venizelos, encouraged him to better things. Prince George soon came to dislike his guardian. A new constitution was elaborated on the basis of former regimes, but with important Liberal modifications. M. Venizelos played a large part in the reorganization, and, whatever his final purposes, strove to educate his countrymen in self-government. The good work was helped by the work of Sir G. Chermside at Iráklion, and Crete began to prosper. Postal, police, and monetary changes were introduced, and in 1900 the British troops were withdrawn from Iráklion. The Moslems were the chief sufferers, and left the island in large numbers, and soon they numbered only one-ninth of the population and were confined mainly to the towns.

But the breach between Prince George and Venizelos grew wider. Both probably had the same end in view—union with Greece—but M. Venizelos saw better how to procure it in face of the internal and external difficulties. The self-willed and autocratic young prince would not be taught. Sides were taken, and a personal affair threatened to become a public disaster. Accusations of various kinds were brought against the statesman, false motives were attributed to him, and an attempt was made to wreck his career. Increasing arbitrariness, and neglect of an allied warning to act constitutionally, combined with the failure of a petition to the Great Powers for ' Union ', led in March 1905 to the opposition, under M. Venizelos, taking to the Lévka Óri (at Thérisson). The revolting party proclaimed union with Greece. After much negotiation and strong military measures by the allies, the insurgents gave way, but Prince George felt his position had become impossible and he resigned in 1906. This created a delicate situation. The firm action of the ' union ' party, led by Venizelos, in refusing in advance to accept a foreign High Commissioner caused the allies to leave the decision to the King of Greece. M. Alexander Zaimis, a leading Greek politician, was chosen, and another strong link was thus forged in the chain of union.

A spell of quiet followed. Order was restored ; the hellenization of the public services was allowed to proceed (e.g. Greek replaced Italian officers in command of the gendarmerie), and in July 1908 the allies, satisfied that the island might be left to solve its own fate, began to withdraw their troops. But the Young Turk revolution of 1908, and the Balkan events accompanying it, upset the harmony. The excited Cretans again proclaimed ' Union ', and took vigorous steps to give this decision practical effect. M. Zaimis had in the meantime tactfully left the island. Greece could now have taken over Crete with little danger, for Turkey's hands were full, and the Powers were disposed to allow union. The Greek government, however, maintained a cautious and correct attitude, and, in spite of strong popular pressure, nothing was done. The aggressive attitude of the new Turkish government, which tried to revert to the regime of ten years before, was quashed by the Powers, but feeling was intensified in Greece, and war was with difficulty averted. At this period, great tact and restraint were displayed by the allies, by the Greek government, and by Venizelos. The latter, who always had a fine appreciation of the larger issues involved in the Cretan question, showed his statesmanship not only in enlisting all sympathies—even the most powerful—in his cause, but even more by his patience in biding his time and in not alienating those sympathies by rash patriotism. In this year and the following (1908–10), he showed the highest powers of generalship, alternately pushing and withdrawing his party's demands. Upon the final withdrawal of the allied troops from Crete in 1909, the hot-headed action of the Cretan patriots in proclaiming ' Union ' again brought about delicate relations between Greece and Turkey. The Powers, meanwhile, restrained their premature enthusiasm.

The settlement of the Cretan question was assured with the entry of Venizelos into Athenian politics. Invited by the Military League to become its political adviser, the Cretan statesman in 1910 became the Prime Minister of Greece (see vol. I, p. 211). Already, before his election, he had averted fresh Graeco-Turkish complications by influencing three of his Cretan compatriots to forego their seats as deputies in Athens ; and again in 1912, at the height of his popularity and power, he dared to incur odium and misrepresentation in his native island by refusing, in the interests of Greece, to allow Cretan deputies to sit in the Chamber at Athens. On the outbreak of the First Balkan War, however, his opposition vanished. Greece declared war on Turkey on 18 October 1912. On 14 October, Venizelos had already admitted Cretan deputies to the Greek parliament. The union of Crete and Greece was accomplished. M. Stephen Dragoumis was appointed High Commissioner to continue the administration on the basis of the previously existing regime. Crete was formally given up by the Sultan in the Treaty of London (30 May 1913). On 1 December 1913, King Constantine unfurled the Greek flag in Crete, and the long-desired union was consummated. For some years Crete was administered on provisional lines, to avoid undue dislocation and to effect a transition from the old to the new regime. M. Loukas K. Rouphos was the last High Commissioner, and during 1914–15 Cretan administration was in the main assimilated to that of the Greek kingdom.

CRETE AFTER 1913

With the union, the history of Crete became merged in that of Greece as a whole (see vol. I, pp. 213–38). During the war of 1914–18, the island solidly supported Venizelos in his struggle with King Constantine ; and it was in Crete in 1916 that Venizelos initiated the rebellion that led to the setting up of his provisional government at Thessaloníki ; Cretans formed the backbone of the army of this provisional government in 1916.

From 1919 to 1935, the Cretan voters, with very few exceptions, followed their national leader, Venizelos. The loyalty of the island to Venizelos and the Liberal Party was further strengthened by his success at Versailles. The Asia Minor disaster was attributed to the king and the Popular Party ; and Cretans welcomed the establishment of the Republic in 1924. In due course, when the Liberal elements in the Services revolted against the existing regime (1935), the Cretans naturally joined the rebellion under Venizelos. It was, however, short-lived, and in the following year Venizelos died (18 March). During the dictatorship of Metaxas, from August 1936 onwards, the Liberal party did not raise its head, and a slight attempt at rebellion in the prefecture of Khaniá in 1938 produced no reaction in the rest of Crete. Nevertheless, the dictatorship was unpopular there, though Metaxas gained support by his firm stand against Italy in October 1940.

On 23 April 1941, in consequence of the German invasion of Greece, the king and the government moved from Athens to Crete ; and the German attack on the island by parachute troops began on 20 May. After the king and members of the government had escaped over the mountains to the south coast and thence taken ship to Egypt, the island was defended by Imperial and Greek troops, under General Freyberg, who fought with great gallantry against overwhelming odds ; and on 1 June came the decision to withdraw British forces from the island. The Cretan division had been trapped on the Albanian front, and so took no part in the battle of Crete, but the civilians rendered great service and suffered for their loyalty accordingly. Khaniá, Iráklion and other places were severely damaged as a result of the German invasion. It was not until the summer of 1945 that Crete was again free.

ECONOMIC GEOGRAPHY

AGRICULTURE

General Features

Agriculture is the main occupation of the people of Crete. In 1940, some 101,000 out of the total working population of 148,000 were engaged in agriculture (this figure includes a small number of fishermen), compared with 24,000 in industry, mining and communications. The area of cultivated land in 1937, the last year for which detailed figures are available, comprised 410 sq. miles, that is, only about 13% of the total area, an even lower proportion than that of Greece as a whole (18·5%). It must be remembered, however, that these figures do not include the land devoted to olive groves or to orchards, which provide a large part of the island's food. Just over one-half of the cultivated area was under cereals (53·70%), almost exactly one-quarter was devoted to vineyards (25·37%), and under one-fifth to vegetables (18%). The yield of crops per acre is on the whole very slightly higher in Crete than in mainland Greece, but the figure is nevertheless among the lowest in Europe.

As in the case of mainland Greece, the physical environment presents considerable difficulties to the farmer. Only 120 sq. miles of the total area of 3,220 sq. miles consists of fertile, cultivated plain. The lowlands are for the most part undulating, even hilly, and the valleys are narrow and steep-sided. As a result, much cultivation takes place on laboriously terraced hill-slopes, or in small sheltered pockets of level ground.　Many of these terraces are of ancient construction.　The scrub-covered limestone uplands provide spring pastures for herds of sheep and goats, but there are also extensive barren, stony wastes.　Aspect and shelter from the winds (particularly from the *Ostro*, a south wind which often does much damage) are both important factors.　The long summer drought makes irrigation essential, but while the innumerable springs usually form centres of garden-cultivation, irrigation is not on the whole adequately developed.

Most of the arable land is divided into small holdings worked by their proprietors.　In 1930, there were 90,000 holdings, of which 44% were under 1 hectare (about 2½ acres) in size, and a further 44% were between 1 and 5 hectares ; less than 100 farms exceeded 100 hectares.　Many of the little farms are made up of a number of scattered ' parcels '.　Near the village are vegetable gardens and orchards, clustered round a group of springs.　Next comes the zone of vineyards, on the terraced hillsides ; higher up come olive trees, either scattered or in small groves, while farthest away are patches of cereals occupying small pockets of fertile soil.　There is a good deal of migration amongst the agricultural population.　In some districts there are numerous hamlets up in the hills near fertile hollows or springs, where the lowland peasants have holdings. The peasants go up to these hamlets in early summer and return with their harvests in autumn.　In other places, permanent settlement is in the upper plain, and cultivation takes place near the coast. Many of the lowland villages keep herds of goats and sheep, which during the spring and summer months feed on distant upland pastures.　Cattle are kept primarily for draught purposes.　Farming standards are on the whole low, and implements are frequently primitive ; wooden ploughs are commonly used.　Over most of the island, therefore, agriculture is small-scale, the chief aim of the farmers being to feed their own families.　The Cretan peasant has a diet very similar to that of the mainland dwellers, consisting mainly of bread, olives and wine, supplemented by a variety of vegetables, milk, cheese and honey.　Meat is rarely eaten, except by wealthier people in the towns.　Crete is less dependent on imported food than are many other parts of Greece, although in 1938 some 16,000 tons of wheat, 3,000 tons of sugar and 1,800 tons of rice, together with small quantities of dried vegetables and coffee, were imported from abroad ; an unspecified quantity of food also came from mainland Greece.

The larger holdings are found in the principal plains and richer valleys, notably in the neighbourhood of Iráklion and Khaniá, in the Lasíthi plain, and in the Mesará plain. There is some cultivation for export ; the crops include grapes for wine and for drying (in 1938 some 24,000 tons of raisins and sultanas were exported abroad), oranges and mandarins, and olives (in 1938 some 10,000 tons of oil were exported abroad). Considerable quantities of these commodities, particularly of olive-oil, are also sent to mainland Greece. Other commercial crops, such as tobacco and cotton, which are important in mainland Greece, are of little significance in Crete ; only 1,400 acres were devoted to them in 1937. To assist these commercial growers, a number of co-operatives, both voluntary and compulsory, have been established. Wine-producers are for the most part organized into voluntary co-operatives, designed to market the wine, to improve its quality and reputation, and to erect co-operative factories. All growers of citrus fruits belong to compulsory co-operatives, and each producer is obliged to deliver his entire crop to the co-operative. Citrus fruit is exported through the Union of the Cretan Citrus Growers' Association, which has a monopoly of the trade. The co-operatives are also prepared to purchase surplus quantities from the small subsistence farmers.

Agricultural education and research is not very adequately developed in Crete. An agricultural school was established at Áyioi Dhéka in the early 'thirties. It trains about fifty students annually ; these are intended to give agricultural instruction throughout the island. Two semi-gymnasia, at Arkhánai (Iráklion) and Kolimbári (Khaniá) were converted into agricultural schools in 1930-1.

Cereals

The following table summarizes the average annual acreage and production of cereals during the years 1936-8 for each *nomós* and for Crete as a whole :

	Iráklion		Lasíthi		Rethímni		Khaniá		Crete	
	Area (acres)	Output (m. tons)	Area (acres)	Output (m. tons)	Area (acres)	Output (m. tons)	Area (acres)	Output (m. tons)	Area (acres)	Output (m. tons)
Wheat	12,619	5,520	7,341	2,310	5,115	1,831	7,723	2,996	32,798	12,657
Barley	23,410	12,280	13,256	4,819	7,034	2,708	8,188	3,274	51,888	23,081
Mixed corn	7,076	3,193	2,668	1,064	6,493	2,489	5,399	2,117	21,636	8,863
Maize	14	6	59	31	37	18	183	98	293	153
Oats	17,315	7,623	4,804	1,521	5,942	2,339	6,605	2,677	34,666	14,160
Rye	5	3	37	19	217	102	928	338	1,187	462

Source : *Statistique Annuelle Agricole et d'Elevage de la Grèce*, 1936-8 (Athènes, annual).

Both the area devoted to wheat cultivation and the total yield are little more than half those of barley. Oats, too, are more important than wheat. Crete, like the Aegean islands, is thus different from mainland Greece, where wheat occupies nearly four times as great an area as barley. The reason for the small wheat crop is the limited area of suitable soil. In general, cereals are grown where the soil is too poor and the ground too rough for vines and gardens ; the cornfields thus form small scattered patches, and cultivation and harvesting are carried on under conditions of great difficulty. The most important wheat areas are the plain of Mesará (which in Roman times was one of the imperial granaries), and in some of the upland plains. As wheat flour forms a substantial part of the diet, considerable quantities have to be imported.

Olives

The olive is the most important single item in the agricultural economy of Crete. In 1937, the island produced 32,000 tons of oil and 2,500 tons of table olives, or rather more than a third of the output of all Greece. In addition to supplying local needs, a substantial surplus is exported, amounting as a rule to about 20,000 tons of oil, both to the Greek mainland and abroad. The oil remaining in the crushed olive residues is normally extracted and used in soap-making.

The olive trees grow throughout the island at heights ranging from sea-level up to 2,500 ft., and in favoured localities may even be found up to 3,000 ft. The largest groves are in the neighbourhood of Khaniá and Iráklion. For the most part, little attention is given to the cultivation of the trees, and harvesting and extracting methods are primitive. In recent years, however, some growers, particularly in the Iráklion districts, have adopted more scientific methods, including the application of fertilizers.

Vines

In 1937 there were 67,000 acres of vineyards in Crete. Like olives, they are widely distributed and grow from sea-level to over 3,000 ft. on warm south-facing slopes. There are few villages, even in the upland hollows, without a belt of vineyards lying beyond the gardens and orchards. The best varieties of grape are to be found in the areas around Iráklion and Kastélli Kisámou.

The grapes are grown for wine-making, for table use, and for drying, as shown in the following table, which gives the average annual yield for the years 1936–8 for each *nomós* and for Crete as a whole :

	Iráklion		Lasíthi		Rethímni		Khaniá		Crete	
	Area (acres)	Yield	Area (acres)	Yield	Area (acres)	Yield	Area (acres)	Yield	Area (acres)	Yield
Grapes for wine	13,375	138,380 hl.	5,053	37,630 hl.	5,925	37,340 hl.	10,097	165,960 hl.	34,450	379,310 hl.
Grapes for table use	3,761	715 tons	390	55 tons	661	93 tons	635	139 tons	5,447	1,002 tons
Grapes for drying	18,777	1,444 tons	3,211	256 tons	1,200	75 tons	2,032	271 tons	25,220	2,046 tons

Source : *Statistique Annuelle Agricole et d'Elevage de la Grèce*, 1936–8 (Athènes, annual).

Cretan wines have been famous since medieval times ; Malvoisie, produced from grapes grown in the district of Malevízion, has long enjoyed a high reputation. The best wines, both white and red, still come from this district. Other good wines come from the Arkhánai, Kastéllion and Sitía districts, while rougher wines are produced in the Mesará and Lasíthi plains. The yield of wine varies between 350,000 and 450,000 hectolitres annually, rather more than 10% of the total Greek production. About half is shipped to the mainland, and a certain amount to foreign countries. A small amount of spirit is manufactured locally from the skins and seeds.

About three-quarters of the grapes grown for drying are for sultanas, the remainder consist of raisin grapes (*rozákia*). Crete is the only part of Greece which produces raisins. Nearly all sultanas and raisins produced are exported, and the high quality of the crops has ensured a steady market. Few currants, however, are produced. Table grapes (including black, white and red varieties) are of fine flavour, and are mainly exported.

Other Fruits

A number of other fruits are widely grown, especially citrus fruits, melons, figs, almonds and carobs. Citrus fruits are to be found especially in the plain of Khaniá, and in the sheltered valleys. The best groves are on level ground, while less productive trees are found on gentle hill-slopes near springs. Cretan oranges, which are noted for their size, flavour and thin skins, totalled some 32 millions in 1937, of which 27 millions came from the *nomós* of Khaniá. Mandarins, which require more shelter than oranges and are of very high quality, totalled some 33 millions in 1937 ; most of these also come from Khaniá. They are picked half-ripe in

December and exported. Lemons (6 millions) and citrons (nearly 4 millions) are less important. Nearly all this fruit is exported. Carobs (locust-bean trees) are widely grown, and appear to thrive in dry rocky areas near the coast. The trees are few, scattered and grow almost wild. In 1937, Crete produced about 26,000 tons of these beans, that is, about nine-tenths of the Greek total ; about half was exported, mostly to France. The beans are used mainly as fodder, but some are used for human consumption.

Mention may be made of almonds, both sweet and bitter varieties, which are scattered throughout the vineyards and cultivated fields, especially in Lasíthi. Walnuts, too, are fairly common in most parts ; while chestnuts are found in western Crete and figs in most upland gardens. Other fruits include apricots, peaches, medlars, pomegranates and quinces, while in upland districts, such as the Lasíthi plain, most northern fruits are grown.

Vegetables

Nearly every Cretan village has vegetable gardens nearby, for, while pulses and bread form a staple part of the food, the Cretans' diet depends largely on fresh vegetables for such small variety as it has. Some 32,000 acres were devoted to the production of dried vegetables, mainly beans, lentils and chickpeas. Of the 16,000 acres producing fresh vegetables, a third is planted with potatoes, although the climate and soil are rather dry ; melons, cucumbers, tomatoes, onions, artichokes and garlic are also grown.

Livestock

The following table summarizes the average number of livestock in each *nomós* and in Crete as a whole during the period 1936-8 :

	Iráklion	Lasíthi	Rethímni	Khaniá	Crete
Horses	2,081	329	823	2,044	5,277
Mules	4,035	3,026	1,904	3,189	12,154
Asses	18,690	8,087	8,720	6,994	42,491
Cows	11,435	7,382	6,640	8,217	33,674
Other cattle	9,814	3,288	3,595	4,249	20,946
Sheep	137,086	47,110	116,036	146,309	446,541
Goats	91,635	64,014	55,302	83,168	294,119
Pigs	15,055	10,901	10,666	12,138	48,760
Poultry	410,120	149,502	115,755	237,175	912,552

Source : *Statistique Annuelle Agricole et d'Elevage de la Grèce*, 1936-8 (Athènes, annual).

Sheep and goats form an important item in the economy of Crete. They are able to graze the high mountain pastures which would otherwise be wasted, and provide both meat and milk, as well as a small amount of wool and hair. Some 300 tons of butter is made annually from ewes' and goats' milk, and a considerable amount of cheese ; notable cheeses include *mizithra* and a type of gruyère known as *graviera*. Most villages combine pastoral pursuits with cultivation. The flocks are kept at low levels during the winter, and migrate in early spring to the plateaux and upland basins in the mountain masses.

Cattle are small in size and of poor stock. They are kept primarily for field work ; in fact, only about 6,000 out of the 53,000 cattle present in the years 1936–8 were not classified as beasts of burden. Owing to the absence of lowland pastures, these animals are fed chiefly on grain, carobs and straw, although a small amount of vetches, lupins and other fodder crops is grown. It is estimated that in the years prior to 1939 the annual output of cows' milk was about 12,700 tons, compared with 15,300 tons of ewes' milk and 11,200 tons of goats' milk. Butter and cheese are never made from cows' milk in Crete.

A number of Cretan horses and ponies are to be found in the lowlands and about the towns, but are owned only by the wealthier peasants. Mules and asses are kept in considerable numbers as pack-animals and are invaluable for transport purposes over the rough tracks of Crete ; there are, in fact, eight times as many asses as horses in Crete, and more than twice as many mules.

Pigs live in an almost untended state round the villages, and in some parts graze in the oak woods. The breeds are extremely poor, and the meat is said to be ill-flavoured.

Crete, in common with the rest of Greece, has little organized veterinary control and livestock inspection. In each of the four Cretan *nomoí* there are two State veterinary surgeons, appointed by the Veterinary Branch of the Greek Ministry of Agriculture. Each of these surgeons has an assistant, but clearly the numbers are quite inadequate.

Cretan honey has been famed since the earliest times, and forms the chief sweetening agent in the peasants' diet. The numerous aromatic plants of the maquis and phrygana provide a collecting ground for the bees, and the honey is dark and well-flavoured. In 1937, there were 3,200 modern hives with movable frames and 90,000 of the primitive ' skep ' variety ; it is estimated that the former produced 30 tons of honey in that year, the latter 264 tons.

FISHING

Fishing is not of any importance in Crete, although the island lies in a rich fishing area. This is partly because of the inhospitable nature of the coasts, and partly because of the sudden violent storms. Returns are given for the two main ports of Iráklion and Khaniá in 1936 as follows :

	Landings of sea fish (tons)	Fishing vessels		Number of fishermen
		Number	Total tonnage	
Iráklion	206	46	169	238
Khaniá	192	58	172	215

Source : *Statistique sur la pêche en Grèce pendant l'annèe* 1936 (Athènes, 1938).

Most of the Cretan fishermen, however, are not wholly employed in the industry, for many of the inhabitants of the small coastal villages engage in fishing to supplement their diet. Fishing is carried on inshore, particularly in partially sheltered waters such as Soúdha Bay. It is practised by hand-line from small boats, or by a lamp and spear at nights, or by nets operated by two or three boats. The commonest varieties landed include *palamídhes* (a variety of tunny), *glossía* (a small sole), *sardhélles* (sardine), *kefalía* (a type of grey mullet), and *barboúnia* (red mullet). During April, mackerel visit the waters near the island in large shoals, and are netted, especially in the Soúdha Bay region ; soles are netted on the bar between Cape Soúdha and Soúdha Island. The waters off Spinalónga are visited by shoals of sardine in spring.

MINES AND QUARRIES

Although in ancient and medieval times Crete was the source of a considerable variety of minerals, the extractive industries are restricted at the present time to a small amount of quarrying for local building material and for road metal.

There are small deposits of copper ores on the islands of Gávdhos and Elafónisos ; lignite occurs in the Áyios Vasílios valley, and iron ore near Kastélli-Kisámou and Ravdhoúkha ; while elsewhere there are small deposits of chrome, lead and zinc. Some of these have been worked to a slight extent in recent years. Their exploitation has been hindered by the small-scale nature of the deposits, by the poverty of most of the ores, by the inaccessibility of the sites and the inadequacy of transport facilities, and by the lack of capital.

Apart from supplying local needs for building and road construction, Cretan quarries provide lime for agricultural purposes, grindstones for grain-mills and for oil-presses, and whetstones for which the island has long been famous. Gypsum occurs fairly widely, and is extracted at Sitía for use in the wine industry ; some 9,400 tons were produced in 1938. Salt is obtained on the coast, especially at the head of Soúdha Bay.

INDUSTRIES

Less than one-sixth of the working population of Crete, or some 24,000 people, is engaged in industry, mining and communications. The small-scale nature of the various manufactures is shown by the fact that there were more than 5,000 separate enterprises. About one-third of these were concerned with the preparation of foodstuffs —flour-milling, olive-crushing, wine production and grape-drying— usually by the growers themselves as farm and village industries ; about one-quarter were concerned with the manufacture of goods from hides and skins.

Food Industries

Most of the enterprises are hand-operated, but some mills are built near streams and run by water-power ; the disadvantage of these is that most of the streams are greatly reduced in volume, or even disappear, during the summer months. Larger grain mills are at Iráklion, Khaniá, Soúdha and Ierápetra ; the largest of these, at Iráklion, is reported to have a crushing capacity of 75 tons a day. Most villages have small wooden hand-presses for olive oil ; larger oil mills are at Khaniá (ten in number), at Iráklion (seven), and at Kritsá. The olive residue after crushing is used for soap-making, mostly at Iráklion, but also at Khaniá and Réthminon. Some 2,500 tons of soap are exported abroad annually. The main raisin-drying and packing factories are at Iráklion and Khaniá. In addition to widespread production of wine, most of which is used for local consumption or sold to co-operative societies, there is a number of distilleries at Khaniá and Iráklion which make brandy, methylated spirits, and a spirit known as mastíkha.

Miscellaneous Industries

The light industries are operated on a small scale to supply local needs. Tanneries, using both local sheep and goat skins and imported hides, are found at Iráklion (nine) and at Khaniá (six), and there are some twenty-three smaller works ; few of these have machinery. There are tobacco factories at Iráklion and Khaniá, a carob bean factory at Khaniá and a macaroni factory at Iráklion. The manufacture of pottery, particularly of great olive and wine jars, has been carried on in Crete since ancient times, but today only rough pottery for local requirements is produced. There are brick-works and tile-kilns at Iráklion and a cement works near Réthimnon. There are small textile factories in Khaniá and Iráklion. In the towns, notably Iráklion and Khaniá, there are iron and steel foundries which make oil presses, waterwheels and tools (using imported pigs and billets), several printing works, furniture factories, refrigerating plant and other small-scale enterprises.

Handicrafts

Although the local peasant industries cannot now compete with cheap imported articles, some of these activities are still carried on in various parts of the island. Many houses have spinning wheels and looms, and the finer materials made include silk sheets, the shot-silk Cretan sashes, and fine silk shirts worn on ceremonial and festive occasions. Coarse textiles, notably striped rugs, are made from wool and goat-hair. A certain amount of lace-making is carried on at Khaniá, and during recent years peasant embroidery, which had declined considerably during the latter part of the nineteenth century, has become of increasing importance. Other domestic industries include the making of baskets, saddles and pack-frames. Wood-carving is commonly practised by shepherds, who use the wood of stunted mountain trees to make carved spoons, distaffs, ikons, etc. The village of Thrapsanós (Pedhiádha) specializes in the manufacture of pottery, especially of the big olive-oil jars or ' pithoi '. The potters of Thrapsanós, using a technique practically identical with that of the ancient Minoan potters, travel round Crete during the summer months.

Power

Few power stations operate in Crete, and the greater part of the country is without electricity. The chief power stations are at Khaniá and at Iráklion. At the former town the main station has three turbo-generators of 400 h.p. each, producing 3-phase A.C., of 500 volts, 50 cycles. In winter, two of the generators are worked by water and produce sufficient power for the district around ;

in summer it is only possible to work one generator by water, and for part of the time a 200-h.p. diesel motor takes over. There is a second power station, with two generators of 300 and 500 h.p., both worked by diesel motors. The main station at Iráklion is operated by two diesel motors, with an installed capacity of 1,350 kW, producing A.C. of 127–220 volts. There is also a small emergency power station, details of which are not known. The other Cretan power stations are at Réthimnon (diesel, 100 h.p., voltage 220, D.C.), Ierápetra (voltage 220, D.C.), and Sitía (voltage 2 × 110, D.C.).

COMMUNICATIONS

The inadequacy of the system of communications is one of the major handicaps to the effective economic development of Crete. The mountainous nature of the island, with so many engineering difficulties, is against the development of railways and modern roads ; capital, moreover, is lacking. The system of communications consists, therefore, of a few poor motor-roads and of a considerable length of tracks and bridle-paths.

There are no railways in Crete except for a few short isolated sections of narrow-gauge line near Iráklion, near Soúdha Bay and near Kastéllion in the centre of the island. The Iráklion line, of metre-gauge and with a total length of 7½ miles of track, was laid from Iráklion harbour to quarries some 5 miles distant. It was used to transport blocks of stone during the building of the eastern mole, which was completed in 1930, but does not seem to have been used since. The line at Soúdha Bay, of 2 ft. 6 in. gauge, runs from the main pier (along which it is double track) to quarries near Azizié, where there are several spurs. There is no information about the two short disconnected mineral lines near Kastéllion.

A number of projects have been mooted at various times to provide the island with a railway system. For example, a route for a single-track, narrow-gauge line was surveyed from Iráklion to Mesará in 1910, but the single tender proffered was rejected. Other schemes have likewise failed owing to the large amount of capital needed.

ROADS

The following table gives the length of the various categories of roads for each *nomós* in Crete in 1938, together with the average length of road per square mile of area (see vol. II, pp. 319–20) :

Mileage of Roads in Crete

Nomoi	National	Provincial	Municipal	Total	Miles of roads per sq. mile
Iráklion	180	38	22	240	0·25
Lasíthi	94	16	—	110	0·15
Rethímni	118	22	14	154	0·26
Khaniá	151	89	31	271	0·29
Total	543	165	67	775	0·24

Source : *Annuaire Statistique de la Grèce*, 1939, pp. 233–4 (Athènes, 1940).

The average length of road per square mile is considerably higher than that for Greece as a whole (0·17 miles), but even so it contrasts unfavourably with other Balkan countries and markedly with west European countries. The steep rocky hills, narrow, shut-in valleys and plains, and steep-sided gorges all make road construction difficult. Sudden rain storms, especially in winter, may sweep away considerable stretches of mountain roads ; tracks in the alluvial plains become thick mud, and swollen torrents often destroy bridges. Many roads and tracks are thus impassible in winter.

Surfaces and Widths

The best roads in Crete, prior to 1941, were markedly inferior even to minor English roads, but considerable stretches were widened and re-surfaced during the German occupation. Only the main national roads, notably that along the north coast, have metalled surfaces, usually of a poorly-laid water-bound macadam. This is extremely dusty in summer and muddy in winter. Prior to 1941, no road could take more than one line of heavy traffic, although ordinary cars could pass with care in most places. The narrowness of many roads is accentuated by the frequent sharp bends, especially on those which cross the mountains. No bridge can take vehicles of more than 7 tons with safety, and most of them much less. The bridges are for the most part of wood, with some of arched stone ; the latter are of considerable antiquity.

Geographical Description (Fig. 59)

The main roads may be divided into two groups. The great lateral (west-east) road runs along the north coast from Kastélli-Kisámou to Sitía ; it links up the most fertile parts of the island and the chief ports and towns. On the whole, it follows the coast closely, but where the hilly peninsulas project northwards

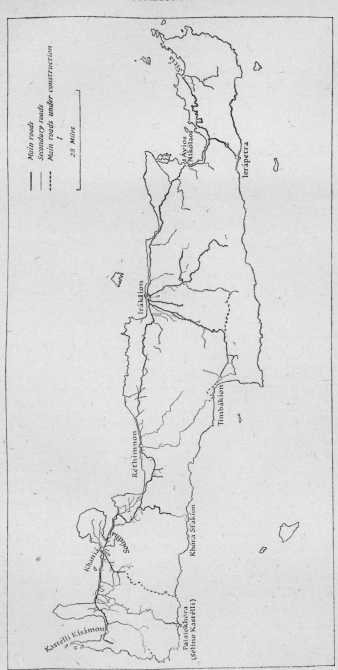

Fig. 59. The roads of Crete

Based on 1 : 25,000 Greece, G.S.G.S. No. 4410 (Crete) (1943).

(Rodhopoú, Akrotíri, Cape Dhrápanon and Cape Áyios Ioánnis) it cuts inland across the base of each peninsula. Between Réthimnon and Iráklion, where the limestone ranges lie close to the sea, it runs inland along the valley of the Milópotamos at a distance of some 5 miles from the sea. There is no south coast road, owing to the proximity of the steep mountain ranges to the sea.

The north to south transverse routes across the island radiate mainly from Khaniá, Réthimnon and Iráklion. Several of these roads, notably those from Iráklion to Pómbia, to Pírgos and to Káto and Áno Viánnos, and that from Khaniá to Alikianoú, do not reach the south coast. The only motor roads which do cross from the lateral road to the south coast are (1) from Máleme (west of Khaniá) to Palaiokhóra, (2) from Vríses (east of Khaniá) through the great Áskifos gorge to Khóra Sfakíon, (3) from Iráklion to Timbákion on the shores of Mesará Bay, and (4) from the shores of the Gulf of Merabéllo across the narrowest part of the island to Ierápetra. Most of these transverse routes have to cross difficult passes, and are frequently interrupted in winter. From them branch numerous short cul-de-sac roads, usually of extremely poor quality.

Tracks

There are some thousands of miles of tracks and paths. Some of these are paved with flat stones, and short stretches near villages are cobbled ; but the majority are either of bare rock or of beaten earth, the last dusty in summer, muddy in winter. There were some 5,000 horses, 12,000 mules and 42,000 asses in Crete during the years 1936–8, and a considerable number of the 47,000 cattle kept for draught purposes were used for hauling rough carts. The isolated hill villages depend entirely for transport on their mules and asses.

POSTS, TELEGRAPHS, AND TELEPHONES

Postal Services

Autonomous Crete was admitted in 1902 to the International Postal Union, and issued its own postage stamps until the war of 1914–18. Since then, its postal system has formed an integral part of that of Greece. In 1938, there were 110 post offices in Crete, giving an average of one for every 4,015 inhabitants, compared with one for every 5,063 in all Greece.

Telegraph Services

In 1938, there were 828 telegraph ' bureaux ' in Crete, although many of these were simply telephones where telegrams could be forwarded to be telegraphed at the main towns. The telegraph lines on the whole duplicate the main telephone network, and are often carried on the same poles. Equipment is serviceable although antiquated.

Telephone Services

The telephone network in Crete is fairly extensive, although except in Iráklion and Khaniá it is a rather antiquated hand-operated one. These two towns have automatic systems installed by Siemens and Halske. The E.E.T. (Hellenic Telephone Company), which operates in mainland Greece, is responsible only for the systems in these two towns, the rest of Crete being under the Ministry of Communications.

The main telephone line runs parallel to the north coast, from Kastélli-Kisámou in the west to Palaiókastron in the east, linking up the principal towns. From this line, extensions cross the island to a number of points on the south coast ; the main junctions are at Khaniá, Réthimnon, Iráklion and Sitía. Numerous single-line extensions branch off to the various villages. Most of the smaller settlements have only a single instrument, usually at the post office, and in districts where there is more than one, extensive use is made of the ' party-line ' system. During their occupation, the Germans extended the system, particularly in the Akrotíri peninsula, and elsewhere increased the number of lines between the main towns.

Prior to 1942, according to the *Bureau de l'Union Internationale des Télécommunications*, there were four fixed radio transmitters situated near Khaniá and a fifth at Iráklion. These were as follows :

Station	Call sign	Frequency kc/s.	Wave length (m.)
Iráklion	SYC	75	4,000
Khaniá	SXN	375	800
Khaniá	SXN	425	706
Khaniá	—	443	677
Khaniá	SXN	500	600

Source : *Nomenclature des Stations Fixes*, published by the *Bureau de l'Union Internationale des Télécommunications* (Berne, 1942).

These stations communicated with fixed land points, and with the exception of Iráklion which could be used for private messages to mainland Greece, were for official use only.

The only aeronautical station in Crete prior to 1942 (when a number were installed by the Germans) was the Iráklion Aeradio station (call sign SWH, frequency 333 kc./s.), opened for official use only in 1940. Prior to 1939, there was a medium-wave transmitter (600/1,000 m., 750 watts), and a direction-finding apparatus, installed on S.S. *Imperia*, lying in Spinalónga harbour. These were used by Imperial Airways Aircraft, which passed over Crete on their scheduled route to and from the East.

There were no broadcasting stations in Crete prior to 1942.

During the German occupation, several powerful radio transmitters, wireless telegraph stations and radio direction finders were operated in Crete and on adjacent small islands.

Submarine Cables

The following submarine cables link Crete with the rest of Greece or with other countries :

Between	Date opened	Length (nautical miles)
Iráklion-Alexandria	1871/3 (relaid 1933)	419
Iráklion-Siros island	1878	137
Khaniá-Zákinthos island	1873	255

Source : *Nomenclature des câbles formant le réseau sous-marin du globe*, published by the *Bureau de l'Union Internationale des Télécommunications* (Berne, 1939).

The first two of these cables were owned and operated by British Cables and Wireless, Ltd., the third was owned by the Greek government but operated by this company. It has been reported that the cable between Khaniá and Zákinthos was interrupted and has not since been repaired. A cable between Sitía and Rhodes was taken up in 1935. Local cables are reported to exist between Khaniá–Réthimnon–Iráklion–Sitía and between Khaniá–Iráklion. The condition of these cables is doubtful, and they are not listed in the *Nomenclature des câbles*.

BIBLIOGRAPHICAL NOTE

1. Four works belonging to the last century are well worth reading although they are now out of date :

R. Pashley, *Travels in Crete*, 2 vols. (Cambridge and London, 1837).

F. V. Raulin, ' Description physique de L'île de Crète ', *Actes de la Société Linnéenne de Bordeaux*, vol. 22, pp. 109–204, 307–426, 491–584 ; vol. 23, pp. 1–50, 70–157, 321–444 (Bordeaux, 1858).

T. A. B. Spratt, *Travels and Researches in Crete*, 2 vols. (London, 1865). This is a very interesting general account ; Capt. Spratt was responsible for the first Admiralty Chart of the island.

H. F. Tozer, *The Islands of the Aegean*, chapters 2 and 3 (Oxford, 1890).

2. A. Trevor Battye's *Camping in Crete* (London, 1913) has interesting descriptions, particularly of the natural history of the island.

3. The best general survey is volume II, part 3, of the N.I.D. *Handbook of Greece* (London, 1919).

4. An account of the coasts of Crete will be found in chapter 2 of the *Mediterranean Pilot*, vol. IV, 7th edition (London, 1941).

5. For a general account of the archaeology, see J. D. S. Pendlebury, *The Archaeology of Crete : an introduction* (London, 1939). A general historical summary is provided by J. H. Freese, *A Short Popular History of Crete* (London, 1897). See also W. J. Stillman, *The Cretan Insurrection of 1866–8* (New York, 1874).

6. Details of the population for 1928 will be found in *Population de la Grèce d'après le Recensement 15–16 Mai 1928*, Deuxième édition (Athènes, 1935).

7. The most useful topographical maps of Crete are : (a) the 1 : 50,000 Crete, M.D.R. 408, reproduced in 1942–3 by 512 Fd. Survey Coy., R.E., from Greek and German maps and partly revised from air photographs. The maps have a kilometre grid, latitude and longitude (from Greenwich and Athens) in margins, roads and tracks in red, water in blue. Contours are shown at 10 and 20 metres and then at intervals of 20 metres, except that the three most easterly sheets have contours at intervals of 50 metres to 200 metres and then at intervals of 100 metres ; (b) the 1 : 250,000 Greece G.S.G.S. Series 4410 (1943). The maps have a 10 kilometres grid, latitude and longitude (from Greenwich and Athens) in margins, contours at 100 and 200 metres and then at intervals of 200 metres, layer-shaded in purple, roads in red, water in blue.

Chapter IX

THE IONIAN ISLANDS

General Features : Kérkira (Corfu) : Levkás (Santa Maura) : Kefallinía (Cephalonia) : Itháki (Ithaca) : Zákinthos (Zante) : Bibliographical Note

GENERAL FEATURES

The Ionian Islands, in the conventional use of the term, include seven larger islands and numerous smaller ones lying off the western and southern coasts of Greece. The history of the name ' Ionian ' as applied to the group is obscure, but the islands are so called probably on account of ancient settlements of Ionian colonists there. The seven larger islands are sometimes described as the ' Heptanesus ', i.e., ' Seven Islands ', and they include, from north to south, Kérkira (Corfu), Paxoí, Levkás (Santa Maura), Kefallinía (Cephalonia), Itháki (Ithaca), Zákinthos (Zante) and Kíthira (Cerigo). The last named, together with its small neighbour Andikíthira, lies off the south coasts of the Pelopónnisos ; they are described on pp. 182–4. This chapter is concerned only with those islands strictly off the western coast. Administratively, the seven belong to five *nomoí* as follows (Fig. 2) :

Kérkira.—Kérkira together with Paxoí, Andípaxoi, Othonoí, Samothráki, Erikoúsa and smaller islets.

Kefallinía.—Kefallinía and Itháki together with Kálamos, Kastós and other islets.

Zákinthos.—Zákinthos together with some islets.

Préveza.—This mainland *nomós*, in Ípiros, includes Levkás together with Meganísi.

Attikí and Voiotía.—Strangely enough, this *nomós* includes Kíthira and Andikíthira.

According to present administrative usage, only the three *nomoí* of Kérkira, Kefallinía and Zákinthos are included in the term Ionian Islands.

GEOLOGY AND RELIEF

The islands lie on the continental shelf at no great distance from the mainland. Levkás is virtually a peninsula and the channel separating Kérkira from the mainland is, in the north, only two miles wide, while the eastern coast of Kefallinía, the most distant island, is only some 22 miles from the coast of Akarnanía. To the west of the islands, the sea bottom falls rapidly to 1,000 fathoms.

Structurally, the islands are isolated portions of a belt of folded

Fig. 60. The Ionian Islands
Based on the 1 : 1,000,000 G.S.G.S. Series 2758.

limestone (Cretaceous and Eocene), which follows in the main the direction of the folds of the mainland. From the southern end of Kérkira, the belt trends south-eastwards to the Gulf of Amvrakía, thence swinging west in an arc to Zákinthos where the south-easterly trend is resumed. The folding was probably contemporary with

the great Alpine movements of Tertiary times. It was succeeded
by much vertical earth movement and fracturing, often transverse
to the direction of the folds. The break in the folds near the Gulf
of Amvrakía, and their termination south of Zákinthos, may be due
to east-west faults parallel to those producing the Gulf of Corinth.
As a result of this movement and fracturing, the southern islands
resemble ' horsts ' rising abruptly from the sea. The limestones are,
generally speaking, succeeded to the east by progressively younger
formations at lower levels.

The structural and geological history is clearly reflected in the
present relief. The limestones, being more pervious and resistant
to water, form the high and rugged backbone of the islands, the
ridges generally trending south-eastwards and descending abruptly
in cliffs to the sea. The limestone reaches its maximum elevation,
5,315 ft., in Kefallinía ; the development is considerably less in
Kérkira, where the highest summit, Pandokrátor, is 2,972 ft., and
in Zákinthos it is 2,487 ft.

The more recent rocks, of Miocene and later ages, form the hilly
and lowland areas, and are of great importance in the life of the
islands because they are water-retaining and form more fertile soils.
They are well developed in the eastern half of Zákinthos, and in
central Kérkira. Owing to the summer drought, there are few
permanent water courses ; but springs and wells in these recent
formations provide sufficient water to maintain cultivation. On
the less exposed coasts, generally on the eastward and southern
sides, there are alluvial plains with rich soils.

CLIMATE

The climate of the Ionian Islands has the characteristic features of
the Mediterranean type—warm rainy winters and hot dry summers.
It resembles the climate of the neighbouring area of Central Greece,
except that it is modified slightly by proximity to the sea. As
between the individual islands, the general tendency is for both the
range of temperature and the annual rainfall to decrease towards
the south. It should be remembered that the following figures are
based upon observations at stations near sea-level, and that there
will be fairly considerable variations in other parts of the islands
according to altitude and exposure.

In Kérkira the average temperature in August is 79° F. and the
January average is as high as 51° F. The annual rainfall is about

Average monthly temperature (1900-29) in °F

	Jan.	Feb.	Mar.	Apr.	May	June	July	Aug.	Sept.	Oct.	Nov.	Dec.	Year
Kérkira	50·8	51·6	54·5	59·6	66·6	73·6	78·5	78·8	73·6	66·2	59·2	53·8	64·0
Argostólion	51·8	52·4	55·4	60·5	67·0	74·0	78·6	79·0	74·6	67·2	60·4	54·7	64·6
Zákinthos	52·6	52·8	55·6	59·8	68·0	75·1	80·3	80·6	75·2	67·8	60·8	55·6	65·4

Average monthly rainfall (1894-1929) in inches

	Jan.	Feb.	Mar.	Apr.	May	June	July	Aug.	Sept.	Oct.	Nov.	Dec.	Year
Kérkira	6·3	5·5	3·7	3·1	1·9	1·0	0·3	0·7	2·4	6·9	6·3	7·9	46·1
Argostólion	5·0	4·1	3·1	1·8	1·1	0·6	0·2	0·4	1·1	5·0	5·1	6·8	34·4
Zákinthos	7·1	5·2	3·4	2·1	1·2	0·3	0·1	0·4	1·4	5·1	8·1	9·2	43·9

Average number of rain-days (1894-1929)

	Jan.	Feb.	Mar.	Apr.	May	June	July	Aug.	Sept.	Oct.	Nov.	Dec.	Year
Kérkira	12·5	11·6	10·1	9·4	6·1	4·2	1·4	1·6	4·6	10·4	10·8	14·5	97·1
Argostólion	12·8	11·7	9·6	6·7	4·5	2·9	0·6	1·0	3·7	9·3	11·1	13·6	87·6
Zákinthos	13·8	12·5	10·5	8·0	6·0	3·6	0·8	1·4	4·4	9·9	13·1	16·5	100·4

Source : E. G. Mariolopoulous, *The Climate of Greece* (Athínai, 1938).

50 inches, three-quarters of which falls in the winter half-year. Kefallinía has a slightly higher average temperature than Kérkira, and, because of its greater distance from the mainland, a somewhat smaller range. There is also a marked difference in the annual rainfall, which is one-third less than that of Kérkira. The effects of this lower rainfall in Kefallinía are heightened by the greater areas of limestone, through which the rainwater percolates rapidly. Itháki, lying in the shadow of Kefallinía, has a lower rainfall and probably a more humid atmosphere. The more southerly Zákinthos has a smaller range of temperature than Kefallinía, but its rainfall is very much the same (see tables on p. 319).

HISTORICAL OUTLINE

The Medieval and Venetian Periods

At the subdivision of the Roman Empire, in the third and fourth centuries A.D., into western and eastern halves, the Ionian Islands passed into the possession of the Eastern, or Byzantine, Empire. Their exposed position at the entry to the Adriatic, however, soon involved them in attacks by raiders, and in political changes. In 1081, Kérkira and Kefallinía were captured by the Norman Robert Guiscard, who might have become the founder of a Norman dynasty in the islands but for his early death in 1085. During the twelfth century, there is mention of the islands amid the struggles of the Eastern emperors with the western powers, Sicily and Genoa, but it was not until the Latin empire was established at Constantinople in 1204 that the Venetians obtained possession of Kérkira (see vol. I, p. 169). The island soon passed, however, into other hands ; from 1214 to 1259 it was held by the Greek despots of Epirus, and between 1267–1386 it was held by the Neapolitan House of Anjou. During this period it suffered considerably from the inroads of various adventurers, and in 1386 it placed itself under the protection of Venice which held it until 1797.

To the south, the islands of Kefallinía, Itháki and Zákinthos formed the county of Kefallinía in the hands of Matteo Orsini, a member of an Italian family, who had made himself master here in 1194 (see vol. I, p. 178). After the fall of Constantinople in 1204, the country passed through a variety of confusing political vicissitudes, owning allegience to Venice, then to the principality of Achaia, and then to the Angevin power at Naples. In 1357, the county was granted out to the Tocco family who were leading personages at the

Angevin court, and who united Levkás to the other islands. Five members of the Tocco family succeeded each other, and it was under their sway in the fifteenth century that the court of Kefallinía was described by Froissart as a second fairyland. But family dissensions soon enabled the Turks to interfere, and the islands fell into Turkish hands in 1479. With the exception of Levkás, they were soon recovered by Venice, and held for over three hundred years (c. 1482–1797) ; Levkás did not become Venetian until 1684.

The Venetians exacted heavy contributions from the islands ; but they bestowed titles and appointments on the principal native families and won their adherence. The Roman Catholic Church was established, and there was a good deal of Italo-Greek inter-marriage. Greek was spoken only by the lower classes, who remained Orthodox.

The British Occupation

On the fall of the Venetian Republic in 1797, the Ionian Islands were annexed to France by the Treaty of Campo Formio ; but at the close of the following year the French were driven out by a joint Russian and Turkish force. In 1800, by treaty with the Porte, the Russian emperor created the ' Septinsular Republic ' ; but in 1807 the treaty of Tilsit declared the islands to be an integral part of the French empire, and they were incorporated in the ' Illyrian Provinces ' of Napoleon.

Kefallinía, Kíthira and Zákinthos were captured by the British in 1809–10, and Paxoí in 1814. Kérkira was strongly garrisoned by the French, and did not surrender to the British until after the fall of Napoleon. By the Treaty of Paris in 1815, Britain, Russia, Austria and Prussia agreed to place the ' Union of the Ionian Islands ' under the protection of Great Britain. The protecting sovereign was to be represented by a Lord High Commissioner, with authority to regulate the laws and general administration, and to supervise the drawing up of a constitutional charter. The seat of the Com-missioner was at the town of Kérkira, the capital of the Ionian Islands. He was represented in each of the other islands by a British resident, with local functions similar to his own.

The first Lord High Commissioner was Sir Thomas Maitland, nicknamed King Tom, with whose assistance a constitutional charter was drawn up and adopted by the Constituent Assembly in 1817. During the next 30 years, the islands enjoyed a period of peace and prosperity hitherto unknown to them. Life and property were made more secure and justice was administered fairly. The first good roads were constructed ; harbours and aqueducts were built ; trade and agriculture were encouraged, and educational institutions were established. The most important of these was the Ionian Academy with its fine library, founded at Kérkira in 1824, and amalgamated with the University of Athens after the return of the islands to Greece. Kérkira, it has been said, owes its olive trees to four centuries of Venetian rule, and its roads to the 50 years of the British protectorate. But in spite of the benefits of British rule, the firm but arbitrary administration of the High Commissioners aroused constant opposition among the natives.

In 1849 a liberal constitution was granted, including vote by ballot and a very extended suffrage. This opened up the way for nationalist agitations for the return of the islands to Greece. In 1858, Gladstone was sent to inquire into the situation on the spot, and failed to convince the islanders that what they wanted was reform rather than union. Finally, the Ionian Islands were ceded to Greece in 1864 upon the nomination of the Prince of Denmark, brother of the then Princess of Wales, to the Greek throne ; the political unity of the Heptanesus thereupon ceased to exist (see vol. I, p. 205).

The Twentieth Century

While the Heptanesians were celebrating the jubilee of their return to Greece in 1914, the status of the islands was in dispute between the kingdom of Greece and the principality of Albania. Then the war of 1914–18 broke out. The Serb army, assailed from the north, retreated across Albania, and in 1916, together with French forces, occupied neutral Kérkira which became the seat of the Serb government until the end of the war. After the war, the Greco-Albanian frontier was again in dispute ; and in 1923 the Italian delegate on the frontier commission appointed by the League of Nations, together with members of his staff, was murdered on Greek soil. In retaliation Mussolini, holding the Greek government responsible, sent a naval force to bombard and occupy the un-defended port of Kérkira. The ' Corfu incident ' was ultimately settled by the Council of Ambassadors ; Italy received full com-pensation for the murders, Greece received nothing, and the League suffered some discredit for its acquiescence in the settlement.

In the present war, after the Germans had saved Mussolini from disaster in his Greek campaign of 1940–41, and the Adriatic coastline

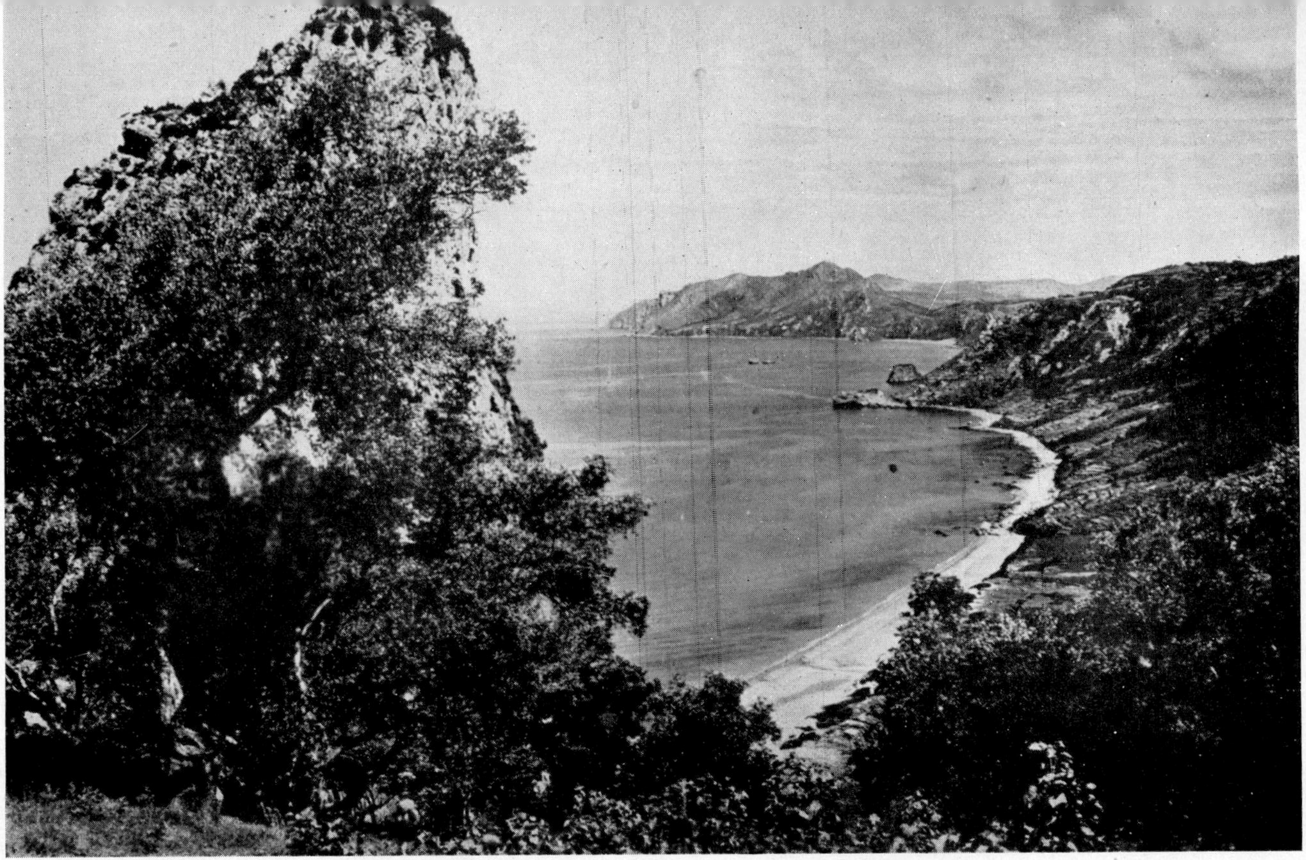

Plate 108. Áyios Yeóryios Bay, Kérkira (Corfu)

KÉRKIRA

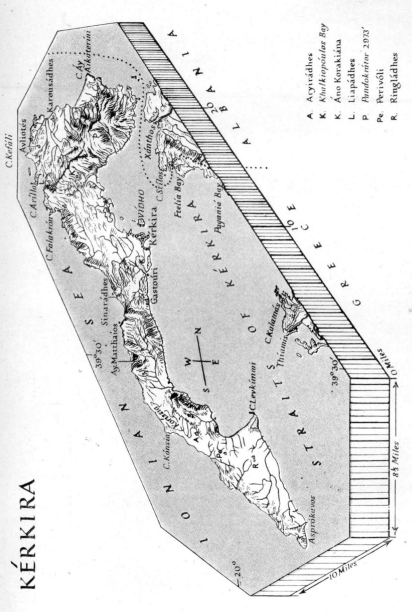

A. Aryirádhes
K. Khalkiopoúlos Bay
K. Áno Korakiána
L. Liapádhes
P. Pandokrátor 2973'
Pe. Perivóli
R. Ringládhes

Fig. 61. Relief diagram of Kérkira (Corfu)

Based on the 1 : 100,000 *Epiteliкós Khártis tis Elládhos*, Sheets Z2 (1936) and H2 (1940) and British Admiralty Chart 206 (1939).

was divided into segments over which Italy obtained either sovereignty or ' influence ', the Ionian islands ' reverted ' to Italy. In Kérkira, notices appeared claiming that the island had always been, and would always be, Italian. Italian currency and postage stamps were introduced and an Italian civil governor appointed. All but a few Greek officials were dismissed, including those of the courts of justice and the police, and their Italian supplanters issued orders in the name of the ' King-Emperor '. Communication with the Greek mainland was practically severed, and Greek traders from the mainland who arrived with permits from the Germans were turned back by the Italian authorities and their permits destroyed. The Italians began to fortify the islands ; but in September, 1943, after the Anglo-Italian armistice, they failed to defend them against German landings.

KÉRKIRA (CORFU)

The island of Kérkira lies off the coast of Ípiros. Its north-eastern corner is separated from the shore of southern Albania by a channel less than 2 miles wide. The island is about 37 miles long, and is 17 miles wide in the north but tapers southward. The nomós of Kérkira, which includes the nearby islets, has an area of about 246 sq. miles.

GEOLOGY AND RELIEF

In Kérkira, the limestones forming the foundations of the islands are not exposed so extensively, or elevated so considerably, as they are farther south. They occur principally in the north-eastern highlands and in the central Ayía Dhéka range (Fig. 62). These formations are very permeable, and resistant to erosion ; the relief is therefore bold and rugged, with stretches of high, waterless tableland, and deeply ravined slopes. In some areas, karst features appear, but they are not pronounced. The soils developed on the limestones are thin and light, with occasional heavier patches in small scattered basins. Around these calcareous rocks, especially in the north-west and centre of the island, there are extensive areas of more recent rocks—Tertiary sands, marls, clays, and loams. These are in general less permeable and more subject to erosion, forming lower hills and wider valleys. Though most streams dry up during the summer, there is usually sufficient water which can be obtained from wells for the irrigation of crops. The soils are

also richer and heavier. In the valleys there are also wide stretches
of alluvium which, when drained, become very fertile.

Fig. 62.   Relief and drainage of Kérkira, Paxoí and Andípaxoi

Based on the 1 : 100,000 *Epitelikós Khártis tis Elládhos*, Sheets Z2 (1936) and
H2 (1940).
The contours are at intervals of 100 metres (328 ft.).

The island can be divided into three regions : (1) the northern
highlands, (2) the central hilly region, and (3) the southern hills
and plains.

The Northern Highlands

Jurassic and Cretaceous limestones form a mountainous block, which is most extensively developed in the north-east but extends across the island to the west coast. On the south, this upland falls steeply to the centre of the island. In general, its summits decline in altitude towards the west. In the north-east, the Viglaes massif rises to 2,572 ft. ; to the west stands out a bold tableland dominated by the conspicuous summits of Lási (2,723 ft.), Stavroskiádhi (2,789 ft.), and Pandokrátor (2,972 ft.), the highest point on the island. The northern and north-western slopes are less abrupt, and are deeply cut by valleys. The western portion of this tableland is a level barren plateau about 2,300 ft. high and its surface is broken by small fertile depressions. Farther to the west, this limestone belt contracts and the summits are lower, e.g., those of Tsoúka (2,050 ft.) and Arákli (1,673 ft.). At its seaward termination, there are imposing cliffs on the north side of Liapádhes Bay. To the north-west of this belt lies a coastal zone of hilly lowlands and alluvial plains, drained by the Fónissa, and bordered by a low, swampy, coast.

The Central Hilly Region

This area is, in general, a segment of a basin facing towards the east and with the western rim falling steeply to the sea. This western ridge rises to 1,286 ft. in Áyios Yeóryios, and runs south-eastwards, across the island, its southern end being formed by the reappearance of the limestone in the Ayía Dhéka ridge. Immediately to the east of the western range lies the Rópa valley, some 5 miles long and from 1 to 2 miles wide, which was probably formed by solution and is covered by alluvial deposits. Owing to its gentle fall to the south, it was formerly swampy and extensively flooded during the rainy season, but it has now been reclaimed and is the most extensive cultivated plain in the island. It drains westward through a gorge to Érmones Bay.

In the east of this central region, the dip slopes are buried under Pliocene sands and clays, falling approximately into north-west to south-east hills. These are sometimes cut by transverse streams, but there are also small basins with interior drainage, often occupied by small lakes or swamps, now mostly drained. The most important river is the Potamós which flows northwards from the southern limestone range of Ayía Dhéka, in a valley which may be of tectonic origin, and then turns sharply eastwards across the plain to the sea north of the town of Kérkira.

The Southern Hills and Plains

The hilly land of the south is clearly marked off from the centre by the reappearance of the limestones which traverse the island and send off two branches along the western and eastern coasts. Both these descend steeply to the sea, the western being the higher and more broken. Between them lies the valley of the Mesongí, a basin filled with Pliocene clays and sands, and broken here and there by hillocks of conglomerate and areas of swamp where clays occur. The extreme south of the island is low with a range of conglomerate hills (Kavalóvouno) in the north-east, rising to about 1,000 ft. In the west is a low coastal plain of recent marine origin, in which lies the shallow salt water lake of Koríssia (3 miles long and up to half a mile wide) separated from the sea by only a narrow spit. The low hills continue to Cape Áspro (Blanco), the south-east extremity of the island ; on their north-eastern side, a triangle of low land runs out to Cape Levkímmi with a lagoon and salt pans nearby.

COASTS

The East Coast

The eastern coast of Kérkira extends for about 25 miles from Cape Áyios Stéfanos in the north-east to Cape Áspro (Blanco) in the south, and forms the western side of Kerkira Channel (Fig. 62). It falls into three main sections : (a) the north-easterly portion skirting the northern highlands ; (b) a lower central portion ; and (c) the coast to the south of Cape Sídhero.

(a) This portion trends in a general south-westerly direction from Cape Áyios Stéfanos to Ípso Bay. The coast is generally bold and steep-to, the land rising immediately behind to the Pandokrátor massif, and there are only a few small bays ; of these, the more important are those of Áyios Stéfanos and Karagiól.

(b) From Ípso Bay, the coast runs southwards and then eastwards to Cape Sídhero. This portion is generally low and marshy, and is broken by numerous small bays, in places bordered by mud banks. South of Cape Komméno, which is a small rounded promontory some 130 ft. high, lies Gouvíon harbour, entered by a narrow channel through mud banks, and now but little used. From Gouvíon to Kérkira, 3½ miles to the east-south-east, the coast continues to be low-lying. Offshore are the small islet of Gouvínon and the larger Vídho island (142 ft. high) together with some outlying rocks.

(c) In the neighbourhood of Kérkira, the coastline is higher, and the town stands on a rocky promontory which terminates in Cape Sídhero (see p. 328). To the south is the shallow Garítsa Bay, and beyond there is a narrow promontory which encloses Lake Khalkiopoúlos to the east, with the little islet of Pondikó (Ulysses) off its entrance ; the lake is now silting up. The coastline continues for 10 miles approximately in a southerly direction and then trends eastwards to Cape Voúkari (274 ft. high). Where it borders the Ayía Dhéka range, the land rises fairly steeply ; elsewhere, particularly west of Cape Voúkari, it is low. Some 3½ miles to the east is Cape Levkímmi, a long tongue of sand with shallows ; between the two points is Levkímmi Bay with low shores bordered by a narrow bank. South-west of Cape Levkímmi there are saltpans.

Some 6 miles to the south of Cape Levkímmi is Cape Áspro, the southernmost point of the island, with high white cliffs and with a sandy bank offshore extending for 2 miles to the east and south-east. Between these two capes the coastline is low, with banks and rocks offshore.

The West Coast

In contrast to the east, the land generally runs back steeply from the west coast, and except in the north there are few large bays. From Cape Áspro, the coast trends north-west for 13 miles to Alonáki Point ; the coast is low, and broken only by the low points of Megákhoro and Kónsia, with shallow water and rocks offshore. Nearly a mile to the south of Cape Kónsia are the flat and rocky Lagoúdhia islets. The coast then runs north-north-west for 4½ miles to Cape Faskiá, along the foot of the steeply sloping Garoúna mountains. Northwards, there is a small stretch of sandy beach, followed by an irregular rugged coast which continues to Cape Falakrón. North of Cape Áyios Yeóryios is the small bay of Érmones, into which flows the stream draining the Rópa valley. Liapádhes Bay runs in a mile to the north-eastward, and is dominated by the high land forming the south-western termination of the northern highlands. It affords shelter from northerly and easterly winds and vessels occasionally anchor here in depths of about 10 fm. Its northern shore, broken by two small coves (Spirídhon Bay and Alípa Bay) runs westwards to the bold precipitous Cape

Falakrón. To the north, opens the bay of Áyios Yeóryios with a sandy beach at its head, flanked on the north-west by the long tongue of land ending in Cape Arílla. The bay affords anchorage in 6–8 fm. but is seldom used. From Cape Arílla to Cape Dhrástis the hinterland is lower, and the coast, broken by a low tongue of land ending in Cape Kefáli, is marked generally by steep but lower cliffs, bordered by shallows, banks and rocks. Off this northerly stretch lies Graviá islet (218 ft. high), with outlying rocks, and the larger Dhiáplo islet (152 ft. high), cliffy and likewise with nearby rocks ; close off the south-western side of Dhiáplo lies the smaller islet of Dhiákopo, cliffed and rising to 100 ft.

The North Coast

East of the low, white projection of Cape Dhrástis, for 8 miles to Cape Ayía Aikateríni, the coast borders extensive plains, and is low and sandy, with shallows and rocks offshore. The higher land around Cape Astrakári divides it into two bays, Sidhári and Áyios Yeóryios, both of which provide anchorage. Cape Ayía Aikateríni, rising to 200 ft., is the northernmost point of the island. From here to Cape Spirídhon, the coast is shallow for half a mile offshore ; thence to Cape Áyios Stéfanos, it is generally higher, rising inland to the north-east highlands. The projecting points, Kassiópi and Várvaro, divide it into two bays, Áspro Bay and Volánas Bay ; being open to the north, these are infrequently used. One mile east of Cape Várvaro lies Tignoso, a rocky islet, and there are several other offshore rocks.

THE PORT OF KÉRKIRA (CORFU)

39° 36′ N., 19° 56′ E.   Population 34,193 in 1928

Kérkira has the greatest passenger traffic of all the island ports, and on the basis of net tonnage entering and clearing it occupies the fifth position in the list of Greek ports. The port is approached by a roadstead, protected from north-easterly winds by the islet of Vídho. It is open, however, to winds from a north-westerly or south-easterly quarter and at such times the working of cargo may be hampered and even suspended. Vessels unloading in the roadstead usually moor stern-to at the breakwaters and discharge into lighters. Anchorage is in stiff mud and clay in depths varying from 10 to 16 fm.

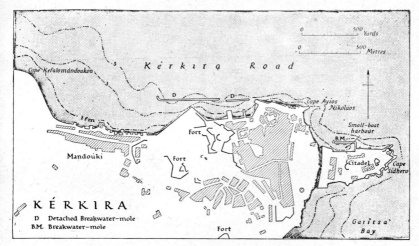

Fig. 63. The port of Kérkira (Corfu)
Based on British Admiralty Chart 1450 (1943).

Plate 109. The port of Kérkira (Corfu)
The view is from the north and shows the waterfront and the fort.

[*Facing page* 328

Plate 110. Paxoí and Andípaxoi from the south-east

In the foreground is Andípaxoi and in the background is Kérkira. Paxoí is in the middle distance, with the islands called Mongonísi and Kalkionísi off its southern end. On the south-east coast the small port of Gáïos and the off-lying islets of Áyios Ioánnis can be seen.

Detailed Description (Fig. 63 ; Plate 109)

The harbour lies between a detached breakwater-mole and the shore, and its depth is only sufficient for small vessels, ranging from 3 to 36 ft., with a depth of 6 ft. over the greater part of the area. The breakwater-mole runs from east to west and consists of two separate sections, 650 ft. and 1,500 ft. long. It is built of rough stone blocks, but small vessels can unload on to the structure. Work on a new breakwater, which it was proposed to construct east from Kefalo-mándoukon, has not yet been started. Alongside the quay forming the water-front north-west of the town, there are depths of from 9 to 10 ft. Two jetties project northwards from it for 250 ft. and can be used by small craft.

Port Facilities

Lifting appliances include a crane of 4 tons capacity on the customs house quay and two smaller cranes of 2 tons capacity. Normally there are numerous small tugs and lighters in the harbour and two 10-ton tank boats for supplying water. Small repairs to vessels can be carried out.

History

Kérkira stands on the promontory to the south of the harbour. The smaller promontory to the east, terminating in Cape Sídhero, is occupied by the ancient Venetian citadel, now a barracks and military hospital. The town is separated from the citadel by a wide esplanade, while to the south it extends along the shore of Garítsa Bay to form the suburb of Garítsa (otherwise Kastrádhes). The rocky peninsula of Palaiópolis was the site of the original town of Corcyra (or Cercyra), the ' tail ', founded by Corinth in the eighth century B.C. as a stepping-stone to Sicily and, in particular, Syracuse. The colony developed its trade and wealth rapidly, and broke with its mother-city ; the help given by Athens to Corcyra against Corinth was an immediate cause of the Peloponnesian War in 431 B.C. The town ultimately passed into Roman and Byzantine hands and became involved in the complicated politics of the medieval Greek world. Kérkira (or, in the Middle Ages and later, Corfu, the ' crests ', from the twin peaks of the citadel) was controlled by Angevins, Venetians, French, Turks, Russians, and, from 1815 to 1864 (when the Ionian islands were relinquished to the Greek Kingdom), by the British. In the war of 1914–18 the Serb army, assailed from the north, retreated across Albania, and in 1916 occupied Kérkira, which became the seat of the Serb government until the end of the war.

The fifty years of British occupation left good roads—though those of the town itself are narrow but well paved—buildings such as the Royal Palace, formerly the Governor's Residence, numerous statues and monuments, and the game of cricket. Until the end of the eighteenth century the ruling class of Kérkira was strongly Italian by descent, and bilingual in speech ; and even to-day Italian is still widely understood and there is a considerable Roman Catholic minority. In the Greek Church, Kérkira is venerated as the resting-place of the bones of the fourth century Cypriot St Spiridhon, brought thither in 1489, and carried solemnly through the town four times a year. There is a small Jewish colony in the town.

There are many churches, of which the tallest is that of Áyios Spirídhon ; the cathedral is dedicated to Panayía Spiliótissa, ' Our Lady of the Cave '. Other buildings include those formerly associated with the Ionian University, now disestablished. There is a large public hospital, a prison, and a thermic bathing-establishment. Classical remains are scanty and only a few of the old Venetian houses survive in this attractive town.

Kérkira is the seat of an eparchy, nomarchy and demarchy, of an archbishop and of a Roman Catholic bishop. It maintains Courts of Appeal and of the First Instance : it has the direction of gendarmerie, and had the first *Astinomía* in Greece, trained in a Police College under British direction. The Library of the former Ionian University is preserved, and there is a small museum in the Palace. Kérkira is also the seat of a School of Agriculture.

Trade and Industries

The trade of Kérkira is very similar to that of the other ports of Greece, the bulk of the imports coming from Greece itself. The exports are almost entirely made up of agricultural products, the chief of which are olives and olive oil.

The disproportion between exports and imports, which is the characteristic feature of the commerce of Greece, is well marked in the case of Kérkira, and the port derives its importance not so much from the bulk of its trade as from its commanding position at the entrance to the Adriatic. A large number of Italian vessels trading between Italy and the Near East call at Kérkira. In 1938 the total shipping entering and clearing amounted to 1.5 million tons, one-quarter of which was of Italian registration. The healthy climate

Trade in 1937 (*thousands of metric tons*)

IMPORTS		EXPORTS	
Foodstuffs and agricultural		Olives and olive oil	0·7
products	39·6	Fruit and vegetables	0·3
Sugar, etc.	0·8	Timber and wood products	0·1
Timber and wood products	1·4	Miscellaneous	0·3
Minerals	1·0		
Chemicals	0·3		
Paper and printed matter	0·6		
Textiles	2·6		
Miscellaneous	0·6		
Total	46·9	Total	1·4

Source : *Bulletin mensuel du commerce spécial de la Grèce avec les pays étrangers, Décembre* 1937 (*Athènes*, 1938)

and beautiful scenery of the island result in a considerable tourist industry—one of its principal sources of income—and large numbers of foreign travellers regularly visit the island. In 1938 the passenger traffic was 28,000 persons in both directions, only one-half of whom had come from, or were proceeding to, Greece itself. The only industries of note are the large numbers of small plants existing for the extraction of olive oil and the manufacture of soap.

Communications

The town has regular services to other parts of Greece and the Adriatic ports by Greek and Italian shipping lines. There is a cable service to the mainland and other Ionian islands.

POPULATION AND SETTLEMENT

In 1928 Kérkira had a population of 101,375, giving an average density therefore of 445 persons per sq. mile. It is thus the most densely populated of the Ionian Islands, and also one of the areas with the highest density in Greece. The distribution of population, however, varies considerably from district to district within the island, apart from the fact that the town of Kérkira and its immediate neighbourhood accounts for over one-third of the total (Fig. 64). Four main areas may be distinguished.

The north-eastern area

The higher surface of the limestone massif is waterless, and serves mainly for rough grazing, although there is scattered cultivation on the patches of heavier soil.   On the more broken slopes to the north-west there are a few small villages amid barren surroundings.

Fig. 64.   Settlements and communications of Kérkira, Paxoí and Andípaxoi
Based on the 1 : 100,000 *Epitelikós Khártis tis Elládhos*, Sheets Z2 (1936) and H2 (1940).
The dots show settlements but do not necessarily indicate individual houses.

In the clay valleys of the east, springs are more numerous, and there are notable concentrations of population, e.g., at Siniaís (2,237),* high up beneath Pandokrátor.   Farther to the west, near

* The figures in brackets after the names of towns and villages give the population according to the census of 1928.

the junction of the limestone and the more impermeable rocks, water is also plentiful, and there are several villages on valley slopes. The average density of population for this area is 228 per sq. mile.

The north-western area

In contrast to the north-east, the Pliocene formations are generally more retentive of water, and have heavier and more fertile soils, while there are also stretches of plains at lower levels. The area is therefore productive, and some districts are closely settled. In the south, there is a string of villages below the central ridge on the valley slopes or on the intervening ridges. It is noticeable that there are but few settlements on the alluvial river plains of the north. Villages like Karousádhes (1,364), Magouládhes (1,117) and Avliótes (1,018) stand on higher ground. The average density of population here is 337 per sq. mile.

The central area

This extends from the southern scarp of the northern limestone to the northern slopes of the Áyioi Dhéka range, and descends eastwards from the western coastal ridge. Here, the distribution of settlements, particularly in the northern portion, is largely around the margin of the lower land. In the north, settlements of any size are confined to the flanks of the higher northern and western borders. A group of large villages on the western slopes, well above the lower land (e.g., Liapádhes (1,065) and Yiannádhes (1,212), share in the cultivation of the drained Rópa valley. Farther south, soils are better and villages are more numerous on the ridges of the central hilly land, and on the ravined slopes of the Áyioi Dhéka, so that this is the most densely populated portion of the island. Excluding the town of Kérkira, the average density for the whole region is 350 per sq. mile.

The southern area

South of the Áyioi Dhéka, conditions at first resemble those to the north, but they gradually become harsher and less prosperous. This district has suffered from plague in the past, and the lowlands are unhealthy. Settlements are therefore largely confined to the highest elevations. In the north, they lie on the inner slopes of the coastal limestone ridges, with the Mesongí valley largely devoid of settlement except near Áyion Matthaíos (1,768). To the south, settlement is confined first to the spring line along the western

slopes of the eastern hills, and then practically to a string of villages
on the ridges overlooking the low plain of the south-east (e.g., around
Levkímmi (1,344). There is but little settlement on the western
coastal plain. The average density is about 290 per sq. mile.

AGRICULTURE

General Features

The cultivated land of Kérkira covers about one-quarter of the
total area of the island, but the productive area is greater because
this figure does not include olive groves and fruit orchards. On
the high limestone tableland of the north-east, the soils are generally
poor, and water is scarce. Consequently this is largely an uninhabited area of scanty scrub vegetation, sufficient perhaps to
maintain flocks of sheep and goats. Patches of better and moister
soils, carrying grain crops, occur sporadically in small basins, while
the vine is cultivated on the more favourably placed slopes. Elsewhere in the island, the lower hills, especially where they face
southward, are clothed with vineyards and with the ubiquitous
olive ; almonds and figs are also found. Finally, the lowlands
carry crops such as maize, wheat, barley, pulses and a little cotton,
as well as sub-tropical fruits such as oranges, lemons and mandarins ;
here, too, the vine is found. The general position is that the
islanders concentrate upon the production of wine and olive oil,
and to some extent oranges, for export, and rely upon imports to
supplement their grain supply and to provide sugar and other
commodities.

Main Crops

Of the cultivated area, one-third is in vineyards, slightly less
than one-third is in grain, and the remainder is accounted for by
vegetables (one-fifth) and fodder crops (one-sixth).

Vine. In 1938, the vineyards yielded more than one-half the
total value of the agricultural produce of the island. The grapes
are almost entirely used for wine ; a small quantity is grown for
the table, but none is dried. The grapes grown on the hill slopes
are better than those of the lowlands ; the red wine has a reputation,
and there is a considerable export to the mainland.

Grain. Of the grain crops, maize is the most important, accounting for nearly two-thirds of the total ; it is grown largely on the
central lowlands, and is a staple of the islanders' diet. Wheat

accounts for about one-fifth of the area under cereals, and in addition there are oats, barley, a little rye and meslin. The average production of maize and wheat is only about one-tenth of the island's requirements ; the balance comes from the mainland and abroad.

Vegetables play an important part in the local diet, and include potatoes, beans and peas. Lastly come the fodder crops (hay and clover) together with small quantities of miscellaneous crops like cotton.

Olive. In addition to these products of the cultivated area, there is the olive which is far and away the mainstay of the farmers of the island. Its predominance is a legacy from Venetian times, and conditions are very favourable to its growth. It is found throughout the island, wherever the slopes are not too steep or the soil is not too damp, particularly in the hilly centre and in the mountains up to about 1,500 ft. It has been estimated that there are some $3\frac{1}{2}$ million olive trees in the island. They grow in groves, and, unlike the practice elsewhere, are not pruned, so that they develop height and spreading branches. They receive little attention beyond the piling up of earth around the roots to preserve the moisture. The trees yield every other year, and there is usually a good harvest every 8 to 10 years. The fruit begins to ripen in November, and is collected as it falls to the ground, for the high branches are beyond reach. It has been said that, with more rational treatment, the area occupied by olives could be reduced by at least a half without affecting the total yield. During recent years the yield has varied greatly from year to year ; between 1935–8 it averaged about 8% of the total Greek production. The olives are crushed mainly in primitive presses, though there are also a number of power-driven presses on the island. The oil is of good quality ; much is consumed locally, and the rest exported mainly to other parts of Greece. A small quantity of table olives is also produced.

Fruits. Besides the olive, other fruit which can stand the long dry summer do well. The chief of these are oranges, lemons and mandarins. They are grown mostly on the lower land near the coast, and the oranges, particularly those grown around Benítses, are well flavoured. Other fruits include figs, grown on the drier stony slopes, and almonds.

Livestock

The livestock of the island include cattle, producing milk and a certain amount of soft cheese. Cows and oxen are also used as working animals more extensively than horses, though there are also horses, asses and some mules for transport purposes. In the supply of milk and cheese, sheep and goats, grazed on the uplands, play an important part. There is also a small number of pigs on the island.

ADJACENT ISLANDS

Paxoí

To the south of Kérkira, at a distance of about 8 miles, lies the island of Paxoí (Figs. 62, 64). It is a limestone mass about 6½ miles long by 2 miles wide, and rises to about 750 ft. above sea level. Its coasts are bold, particularly on the western side which rises in white cliffs. Adjoining the southern end, and separated by narrow channels, are the off-lying Mongonísi and Kalkionísi. Paxoí itself is well covered by olive groves among which small settlements are scattered. The total population of the island in 1928 was about 3,000, and the largest settlement was the little port of Gáïos (with 530 inhabitants) on the eastern coast. The harbour has a wharf with a depth of 10 ft. alongside, and the approach to it is sheltered by the two small islets of Áyios Ioánnis and Panayía. Farther north along the east coast are the tiny ports of Longós and Lákka. Despite a great shortage of water, the island is moderately fertile, and produces some of the best olives in Greece, as well as almonds and vines ; the few springs are near the shore so that the inhabitants have to rely on rainwater cisterns.

Andípaxoi

About a mile to the south-east of Paxoí is the small island of Andípaxoi. It is fairly level, but rises near its northern end to about 350 ft. There are cliffs along the west and south coasts, but on the east coast there is a little bay near the only village, and here small vessels with local knowledge can anchor. There are a few rocks lying close offshore, and about half a mile to the south are the Dhaskália rocks.

Samothráki, Othonoí and Erikoúsa

These three islands, together with several small islets and rocks, lie on a bank extending about 15 miles off the north-western end of Kérkira (Fig. 60) ; all are inhabited. Samothráki rises to 500 ft. and is surrounded by rocks. Othonoí (Fanós) island, the largest, rises to 1,289 ft. and is covered with pine trees ; its western side is precipitous and it slopes eastward. Erikoúsa (Merléra) rises to 440 ft. at its northern end ; its northern and western sides are cliffed and fringed with rocks, the cliffs of the north coast being white ; on the south side is a small sandy bay used by small craft.

LEVKÁS (SANTA MAURA)

The island of Levkás, sometimes called Santa Maura or Leucadia, lies off the coast of Akarnanía immediately south of the Gulf of Amvrakía. It measures some 20 miles from north to south, and is about 5 to 8 miles broad. Its area is about 113 sq. miles. It is separated from the mainland by mud banks forming a kind of sub-merged isthmus ; a canal was cut through these in the seventh century B.C. by the Corinthians, and was again, after a long period of disuse, opened by the Romans. During the British occupation, a new 16 ft. deep ship canal was proposed (1844) but was only partially excavated. In 1903, however, an improved canal was completed, thus rendering navigable the channel between the island and the mainland.

GEOLOGY AND RELIEF

The main feature of the relief is a lofty limestone upland extending the whole length of the island in the west (Fig. 65). It rises to heights of 2,000 and 3,000 ft. and culminates in Mount Stavrotós, 3,744 ft. For about 3 or 4 miles to the north of Stavrotós is the highest and widest part of the upland with an average elevation of about 2,800 ft. ; the general character of this massif resembles that of the Pandokrátor area in Kérkira ; its undulating surface is marked by many basin-shaped depressions with good soil.

From this main upland in the west, several spurs and foothills run eastward, separating a number of fertile plains. The largest plain is that to the south-west of the town of Levkás, at the north-eastern end of the island. It is largely a product of winter streams, and its regular water-supply comes from strong springs which flow in several places at the foot of the hills ; there are also wells here and there on the plain. This adequate water supply is an important factor in the fertility of the plain. To the south is the upland basin of Livádhi, about 1,000 ft. high. The basin measures some 1½ by 1 mile, and has fertile red soil. It has no surface drainage outwards through its steep rocky borders, but only some *katavóthra*, and much of it is flooded in winter. In summer it can be tilled. Farther

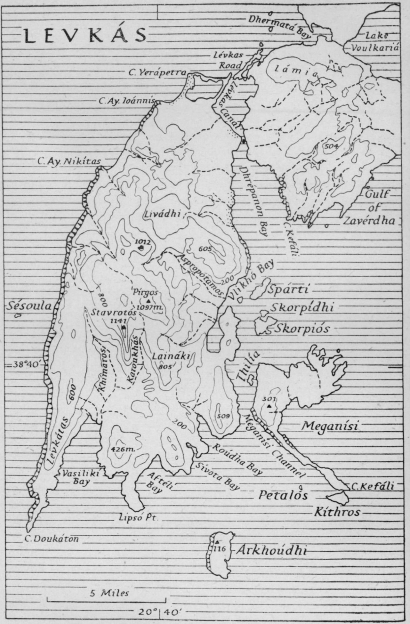

Fig. 65.   Relief and drainage of Levkás (Santa Maura)

Based on the 1 : 100,000 *Epitelikós Khártis tis Elládhos*, Sheets θ 3 (1910) and
θ 4 (1932) and British Admiralty Chart 1867 (1938).

The contours are at intervals of 200 metres (656 ft.).

south, is the fertile plain of the lower Aspropótamos, and this extends southwards along the northern coast of Vlikhó Bay. Finally, in the extreme south, is the plain of Vasilikí, through which the Khímaros and its tributary the Karoukhás flow. There are springs here and a good water supply.

The intervening spurs and foothills are a good deal lower than the western upland ; they rise to about 2,600 ft. in the Laináki hills of the south, and to 2,000 ft. in the Skáros ridge which reaches the coast opposite the island of Spárti. The western part of the Skáros ridge flattens out into an undulating surface cut by deep water-holes and fissures ; this plateau surface, which stands at about 1,500 ft., drops steeply to the Livádhi basin on the east. These two ridges, like the smaller subsidiary ones, include a number of little basins with good soil ; the marls and sandstones that outcrop beneath the limestone give rise to many springs.

COASTS AND PORTS

The lofty limestone ranges of Levkás give the coast its characteristic features of cliffed promontories and deep inlets. In the north-east, the island is separated from the mainland only by mud-banks, crossed by the Levkás canal. Towards the west, for 1½ miles to Cape Yerápetra, the most northerly point of the island, the coast is a shingle beach which in most parts has become as compact and solid as rock, and which encloses a large lagoon with a depth of about one foot.

The west coast of the island runs south-south-west for 22 miles in an almost unbroken line of cliffs, eventually terminating in the bold promontory of Cape Doukáton ; some 1½ miles off this coast lies Sésoula rock, 114 ft. high. Along the whole of this coast, the limestone ridges have been sharply faulted and subjected to powerful erosion from the Ionian Sea. On *the south coast*, numerous bays lie in the shelter of long, bare promontories ; the largest, Vasilikí Bay, provides shelter and good anchorage, while to the east are the deep but less important bays of Aftéli, Sívota and Roúdha. Along the *east coast*, occasional fertile plains break the line of bold, coastal mountains ; near one of these flat stretches, Vlikhó Bay forms a narrow indentation (Plate 117). Off this eastern side lies Meganísi, and north of it lie the islet of Skorpiós (186 ft.), Skorpídhi, and Spárti (110 ft.) together with small islets and rocks. In the north, the long inlet of Dhrépanon Bay separates the island of Levkás from the mainland. From this bay, the Levkás canal leads north-wards for almost 4 miles to Dhermatá Bay, and is navigable for vessels drawing 14 ft.

The Levkás canal is dredged to 15 ft. over a bottom width of 48 ft. and a surface width of 96 ft. Depths decrease with northerly winds and increase with southerly winds, but the variation is not more than 1 ft. Currents vary with the prevailing winds and are from ½ to 1½ knots. The channel is marked by buoys, but its deeper parts are more clearly defined by the light yellow colour of the water. The nature of the shores on either side of the canal are shown on Fig. 66. The northern entrance lies between a breakwater-mole and a citadel (Plate 111). The southern entrance lies between two ruined moles covered by from 4 to 10 ft. of water ; between these moles is a width of 165 ft. and a depth of 23 ft.

The town of Levkás, sometimes called Amaxiki, had a population of 5,083 in 1928 and is situated on the west side of the canal three-quarters of a mile within the northern entrance ; the harbour at the town is a triangular enlargement of an angle in the canal and covers an area of some 15 acres. Vessels drawing 13 ft. or less can anchor at the town quay which is about 500 ft. long and is equipped with bollards and a crane. Two other quays are situated at the northern entrance of the canal. One is along the inner side of the breakwater and is about 12,000 ft. long with depths of up to 15 ft. alongside ; the other, with similar depths, but only about 200 ft. long, is at the ruined fortress or ' citadel ' on the east side of the entrance. Larger vessels lie in the Levkás Road in the south of Dhermatá Bay, and discharge into lighters. The port exports grapes, wine, currants, olive oil, valona and wool.

A good road leads southwards from the town along the eastern side of the island and another runs south-south-west to Lazaráta and so south to Vasilikí Bay. The embankment along the west side of the canal carries the only road to the mainland, via the ferry or floating bridge opposite the citadel. On the mainland, the causeway continues north-eastward to the roads that lead to Vónitza, Préveza and beyond.

POPULATION AND SETTLEMENT

The population of the eparchy of Levkás (in the *nomós* of Préveza) was 28,331 in 1928. The eparchy includes Meganísi and some adjacent islets, and the population of the island of Levkás itself

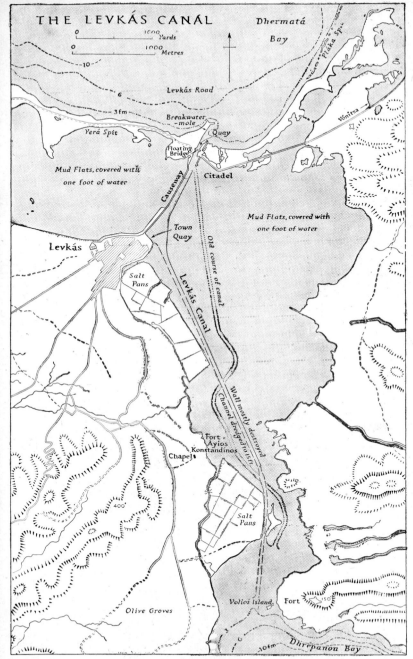

Fig. 66.   The Levkás canal
Based on British Admiralty Chart 1609 (1938).

Plate 111. The northern entrance to the Levkás canal

In the right foreground is the breakwater-mole connected to the town by a
causeway ; to the left of the entrance is the citadel (*cf*. Fig. 66).   Behind the town
the slopes rise to the main mountain mass of the north of the island.

Plate 112.   The town of Levkás (Amaxiki)

The view shows the town quay, with the root of the causeway on the extreme right.
Note the salt-pans to the left of the town.

[*Facing page* 341

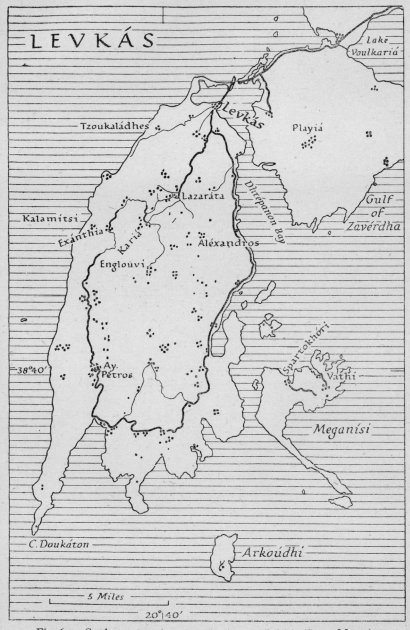

Fig. 67. Settlements and communications of Levkás (Santa Maura)

Based on the 1 : 100,000 *Epitelikós Khártis tis Elládhos*, Sheets θ 3 (1910) and θ 4 (1932).

The dots show settlements but do not necessarily indicate individual houses. For key to roads, see Fig. 64.

was 26,691. The inhabitants of the town of Levkás (Amaxiki) numbered 5,083 (Plate 112). The villages around the town are situated not on the plain itself but on the olive-clad heights behind— a relic of the days of piracy. The next largest settlement after Amaxiki, was that of Kariá (2,058) situated not in the plain of Livádhi, which its villagers cultivate, but high on the eastern side, some 500 ft. above. In the south, the third largest settlement, Áyios Pétros (1,192), stands likewise not on the plain of Vasilikí but higher up, some distance to the north-west. Vasilikí itself, however, with 508 inhabitants is a coastal settlement on the bay of that name.

What is true of these three largest settlements is, generally speaking, true of the island as a whole. The villages are set not on the plains, but amid the hills. It is difficult to generalize, but the average village includes about 500 to 600 people. A few villages, like Englouví (915) and Exánthia (1,226) are larger, while there are some smaller settlements that do not each 100. Fig. 67 indicates the general dispersion of settlements in the island.

AGRICULTURE

The chief agricultural areas of the island are the lowlands ; but the upland basins also have moderately fertile, well-watered soils and for this reason cultivation carried on at high altitudes is a feature of Levkás. Here and there along the seaward slopes of the western highland are areas of Tertiary marls and clays which are also exploited by neighbouring villages. The agriculture of the lowlands and the lower slopes of the eastern hill-country is concerned primarily with the growing of vines, olives and citrus fruits, but at the higher elevations the olive does not flourish, and grain and legumes assume greater importance. Vineyards, however, reach considerable altitudes, and, for example, around the village of Kalamítsi on the western side of the island, the slopes have been terraces for vines to heights of 3,000 ft., and the soil is often laboriously carried to the ledges by the villagers. Similarly, the Livádhi basin produces good crops of currants along its margins ; when the bottom lands of the basin have dried after the winter floods, the inhabitants of the village of Kariá descend to till the newly-dry, fertile stretches for grain and vegetables. The tableland north of Mount Stravrotós also has some viticulture, but it is not prosperous, and cultivation here is concerned mainly with cereals and legumes, especially lentils.

Plate 113. Vlikhó Bay, Levkás

The view is westward, over the village of Palaiokatoúna (B) and Neokhóri (C), to the slopes of Mount Eláti.

Plate 114.   The villages of Marandokhóri and Évyiros in southern Levkás

The view is southward towards Aftéli Bay.   Marandokhóri (B) is on the edge of the plain, while Évyiros (C) is high on the western slopes of the peninsula which forms the eastern side of Aftéli Bay.— In the foreground the women are washing clothes at the village spring (A).

The main products of the island are the olive and the vine, together with grain crops, and a variety of miscellaneous crops. The chief areas for the cultivation of *olives* are the plains and foothills of the north-east and south-east of the island ; the groves here extend up to heights of 1,500 ft. The crop is not important on the western side of the island. The pivot of the island's economy however is the growing of *vines*, both for wine and currants. The island produces a dark red wine which is not so fiery as that of Kefallinía. The currant, introduced about 1860, has become an important source of wealth. The chief *grain crops* are wheat and barley, but some oats and maize are also grown. These crops are fairly widely distributed, but, even so, the island does not produce enough grain for its own consumption, and a good deal has to be imported. At the lower elevations cattle are pastured amid the olive groves and on the fallow lands. The chief animals, however, are sheep and goats which graze those slopes that are too steep or too poor for tillage.

Adjacent Islands

Meganísi

Meganísi is irregular in form ; at its south-western end a long narrow strip of land, projecting nearly 4 miles south-eastwards, terminates in Cape Kefáli and forms a deep bight with the main portion of the island ; the shores of this bight are everywhere bold and the water is deep. The island is hilly, rising to 988 ft., and the valleys are cultivated. Water is scarce. On the northern and north-eastern sides of the island are several deep islets with accommodation for coastal vessels. The two chief anchorages are the bays of Spiliá and Vathí, with the villages of Spartokhóri and Vathí at their heads ; their populations in 1928 were 749 and 891 respectively. The middle stretch of the eastern coast is cliffed. Off the low-lying northern stretch is the islet of Thilía (30 ft. high). Off the southern extremity of Meganísi is the islet of Kíthros ; it rises to 186 ft. and has a steep coast. Three-quarters of a mile west-north-west lies the barren rock of Petalós (Plates 115 and 117).

Kalámos

The island is about 7 miles long ; a limestone ridge extends the whole length, rising to about 2,460 ft., and decreasing in height towards the south. The coast is bold and generally steep-to. The village of Kálamos, situated on the eastern side of the island, had a population of 965 in 1928 ; a rudely constructed mole forms a small harbour which provides accommodation for a few small vessels. The island is cultivated and produces excellent wine.

Fig. 68. Islands east of Levkás (Santa Maura) and Itháki (Ithaca) Based on the 1 : 100,000 *Epitelikós Khártis tis Elládhos*, Sheets θ 4 and I 4. The contours are at intervals of 200 metres (656 ft.).

Kastós

This island consists of a narrow limestone ridge about 5 miles long, rising to about 430 ft. Sarakíniko Bay on the west coast, and Kastós harbour on the east, are the indentations principally used. The village of Kastós had a population of 301 in 1928. Parts of the island are cultivated and the whole is studded with Valona oaks.

Plate 115. Vathí Bay on the north coast of Meganísi

Vathí Bay is the long indentation, with the village at its head, in the centre of the view.

Plate 116. The island of Kálamos

The view is from the south-west and shows almost the whole of the island; the village of Kálamos is along the point seen in the right centre of the photograph. Voúrkos Bay lies between the island and the mainland which rises to the uplands of Arkananía (see pp. 36-40). Part of the village of Mítikas appears on the coast at the extreme left of the view.

[Facing page 344

Plate 117. Vlikhó Bay, Meganísi and adjacent islands

The view is south-eastward from the summit of the Skáros ridge. In the middle distance is Meganísi, with Kíthros beyond it and Thiliá off its north-western end. In the right foreground is Vlikhó Bay. The long island in the right, are, the southern end of Spárti, Skorpídhi and Skorpiós. In front of Meganísi, from left to right. To the left of the entrance to Vlikhó Bay is the islet of Madhourí (cf. Fig. 65).

Offlying islets include Práso on the east, 26 ft. high and covered with low scrub, and Prováti, 140 ft. high, on the north. Two miles to the west is the islet of Formikoúla, 45 ft. high, flat-topped and surrounded by reefs.

Átokos

Átokos rises to about 1,095 ft., and is steep-to all round. Its three peaks, nearly all the same height, are conspicuous and form excellent landmarks. The island is mostly covered with brushwood, but a portion is cultivated, and a few sheep and goats find pasturage.

Arkoúdhi

Arkoúdhi rises to about 440 ft., and is rocky and generally steep-to, with cliffs on the western side. There are few settlements and it affords pasturage for a few sheep and goats.

The Ekhinádhes Islands

These limestone islands lie off the coast in the north-western approach to the Gulf of Pátrai. They consist of three groups, and range in size from islets capable of supporting settlements to rocks which are barely awash (Fig. 68).

The Northern Group (Dhragonéra Islands). This group consists of Dhragonéra itself, together with about a dozen other islets and several above-water rocks. They are generally steep-to with navigable channels between them. They are covered with large stones and scrub and with a few wild olive trees ; some patches are cultivated during portions of the year on all but the smallest islands. Dhragonéra itself rises to 413 ft. The other main islands are Pondikó (223 ft.), Prováti (226 ft.), Tsákalo (49 ft.), Kárlo (259 ft.), Kalóyiros (128 ft.), Sofía (147 ft.), Lambrinós (203 ft.), Fílippos (93 ft.), Pistrós (144 ft.), and Práso (42 ft.).

The Middle Group. The main island in this group is Petalás. It is hilly, rocky, and reaches a height of 832 ft. ; there are a few small patches of cultivated ground. Its western coast is steep and rocky, with considerable depths close offshore. The eastern side is also steep and, about the centre, precipitous ; here the cliffs are about 60 ft. high and there are several caves. The island is separated from the mainland by shallow sandy flats covered by dark weeds. To the west of Petalás lies a group of four islets, the largest of which is Módhi (Stamothi) which rises to about 230 ft.

The Southern Group (Kourzolárie Islands). This group consists of four islands : Oxía, Kounéli, Mákri and Prómonas. The largest island is Oxía which is rugged, precipitous and steep-to on all sides ; it rises to 1,380 ft. Kounéli is also steep and rocky, but it rises to only about 80 ft. Mákri and Prómonos, on the other hand, are higher and reach 417 and 472 ft. respectively.

KEFALLINÍA (CEPHALONIA)

Kefallinía, with an area of 277 sq. miles, is the largest of the Ionian Islands. The island is roughly quadrilateral, with a long peninsula projecting to the north, and another in the west connected to the main portion by a narrow isthmus. From its northern point to the south-east the island measures approximately 31 miles. Its greatest width is about 22 miles.

Geology and Relief

Structurally Kefallinía and Itháki are formed of limestone which has been folded into three parallel ranges trending approximately from north-west to south-east. The crest of the outer fold, which falls steeply to the west, is represented by the western peninsula : the middle fold, a broad and fractured anticline, forms the central mountain range of Kefallinía : the easterly fold appears in Itháki and south-east Kefallinía (Fig. 70).

Since Tertiary times, these formations have undergone much faulting and elevation, which has given to the coasts their characteristic rectilinear outline. The continued occurrence of earth tremors is evidence that stability has not yet been reached. These limestones, of Cretaceous-Eocene age, are porous and resistant to erosion and give to the islands their generally rocky and sterile character. Their relief consists of smooth rounded summits, steep slopes cut by ravines, and karst-like solution basins frequently filled in part by stiff red clays, the product of weathering. In the intervening troughs and on the flanks of the folds, younger formations have been deposited. These consist of marls and clays which, being less permeable, have undergone greater erosion, and form the lower hills and plains. These areas, owing to the presence of better supplies of water and more fertile soils, are, together with the alluvium of the valleys and coasts, the most intensively cultivated parts of the island.

The island can be subdivided into three main areas which form

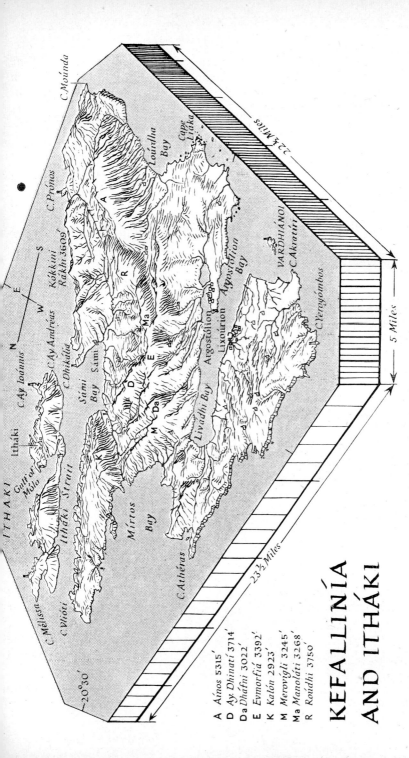

KEFALLINÍA
AND ITHÁKI

A   Aínos 5315'
D   Ay. Dhinatí 3714'
Da Dhafní 3022'
E   Evmorfiá 3392'
K   Kalón 2923'
M   Merovígli 3245'
Ma Manoláti 3268'
R   Roúdhi 3750'

Fig. 69.   Relief diagram of Kefallinía (Cephalonia) and Itháki (Ithaca)

Based on a map by J. Partsch in *Petermanns Mitteilungen*, Ergänzungsheft 98 (Gotha, 1890) and British Admiralty Chart 203 (1938).

[*Facing page* 346]

Plate 118.   The north-east coast of Kefallinía (Cephalonia)

The view is westward, from the slopes of Aëtós in Itháki across Itháki Strait, and shows the tableland of the northern peninsula. At the extreme left is the opening of the Pílaros valley.

Plate 119.   The peninsula and village of Ássos and the Venetian castle on the west coast of Kefallinía (Cephalonia)

convenient units for description : (1) the northern peninsula, (2) the
central mountains and plains, (3) the western peninsula.

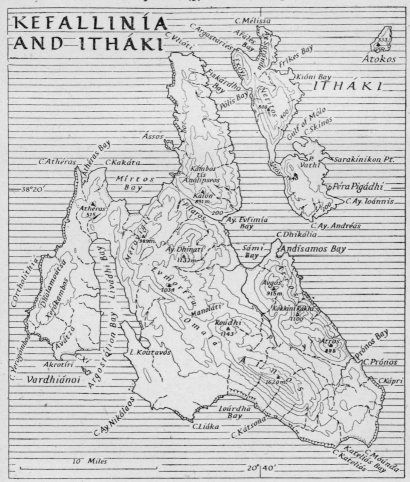

Fig. 70. Relief and drainage of Kefallinía (Cephalonia) and Itháki (Ithaca)
Based on the 1 : 100,000 Greece, Sheet I 3 (1943) by 524 Pal. Fd. Survey Coy, R.E.
The contours are at intervals of 200 metres (656 ft.).

The Northern Peninsula

    The northern peninsula is about 9 miles long, and nowhere more
than 4 miles wide. It is a continuation of the central range and,
like it, falls steeply to the west and less abruptly to the east. Its
northern end is a relatively low ridge, but to the south the crest

widens into a series of small tablelands, at progressively higher altitudes. It ends in the steep scarp of Kalón running approximately east to west. At the foot of the scarp is the Pílaros valley. Here are beds of clays and marls which make the valley a comparatively well watered and populous district.

The Central Mountains and Plains

The central division of the island consists of two limestone ranges separated by a depression filled with younger formation. The main range extends from Mírtos Bay in the north-west to Cape Kateliós in the south-east. To the east a parallel eastern ridge extends from Sámi Bay to the Póros valley.

The main range rises south of the Pílaros valley to form a jumbled mountainous mass of dry, poor limestone suitable for sheep grazing only. It culminates in the conspicuous triple summit of Ayía Dhinatí (3,714 ft.) which is separated by a high saddle from the Merovígli ridge. South of Ayía Dhinatí the main range continues through Evmorfía (3,392 ft.), Roúdhi (3,750 ft.), to Aínos (5,315 ft.) the highest point in the island. On the other hand, the upland is broken in places by depressions with gentle slopes. The largest of these, the high plain of Omalá, lying to the west of the main crest, is probable a solution basin in the limestone ; this plain descends along comparatively gentle slopes to hills and plains, rarely exceeding 500 ft., lying between Argostólion Bay and Loúrdha Bay. This well watered tract is one of the most fertile and populous parts of the island. Elsewhere the western slopes of the range descend sharply and are broken by only valleys and ravines.

The eastern ridge is about 10 miles long. It reaches a height of 3,610 ft. in Mount Kókkini Rákhi and then descends along a jagged crest to Mount Átros (2,903 ft.). Farther south it is broken by a gorge, 300–400 ft. deep, which is the outlet for the winter torrents. Beyond the gorge the limestone crest sinks below the Tertiary deposits which give rise to gentle hill country behind Cape Moúnda. On the east the ridge descends steeply to an almost harbourless coast but on the west the descent to the depression between it and the main range is less sharp.

The depression between the central range and the eastern ridge is drained in opposite directions by two rivers. The watershed between these two valleys is formed by the tableland of Piryí. The northern valley opens into the plain of Sámi. The southern valley is an enclosed basin of Tertiary marls and clays which, although well watered, is unhealthy and oppressive.

The Western Peninsula

The western peninsula of Páli was probably isolated by the foundering of Livádhi Bay and the erosion of the Tertiary formations. The core is a low limestone anticline, trending almost north to south and scarcely rising above 1,600 ft. (Athéras in the north, 1,690 ft.). The western, seaward edge is steep, running down direct to the precipitous coast. The gentler eastern slope is dissected into rounded summits, small plateaux or broad-topped ridges. To the south and south-east this limestone upland gives place to the lower and more developed relief of the Miocene sands, marls, and clays, fringed by a fertile coastal plain.

COASTS AND PORTS

The East Coast

Along the east coast of the northern peninsula, drowned valleys form small bays and coves which are however used by only local craft, except Fiskárdho Bay which has a small harbour with depths of $3\frac{3}{4}$–5 fm. and a small quay. About the middle of the coast is the large bight in which lie Áyios Evfimía Bay and Sámi Bay, each forming the estuary of a perennial stream. Áyios Evfimía Bay provides anchorage for small vessels in depths of 2–8 fm. but north-easterly and south-easterly winds cause a heavy swell and for this reason the harbour, which has a mole and a quay, is rarely used in winter. Sámi Bay, on the other hand, is sheltered from all but northerly winds and gives good anchorage in 12–15 fm. The village of Sámi (604) lies on the south-east side of the bay but its small mole is used by small craft only.

From Cape Dhikália to Cape Moúnda the coast has cliffs or steep slopes along most of its length. It offers anchorage only in Andísamos Bay (10–12 fm.) because Prónos Bay shoals to a shingle beach and its mole can be used by small vessels only and both bays are open to easterly winds which cause heavy seas.

The South Coast

The south coast from Cape Moúnda to Cape Liáka consists of cliffs except that Kateliós Bay and Loúrdha Bay have sandy shores, but both bays are fringed with banks and sunken rocks. Between

Cape Liáka and Cape Áyios Nikólaos the coast is low but it is encumbered with sunken rocks. North of Cape Áyios Nikólaos, Argostólion Bay extends north for about 11 miles and is known as Livádhi Bay in its inner part. On it are the two chief ports of the island, Lixoúrion and Argostólion.

The harbour at *Lixoúrion* is formed by two moles which enclose a rectangular area of about 27 acres with depths of between 6 and 13 ft.; the entrance is about 100 yds. wide and 12 ft. deep. The inner sides of the moles have quays but these can be used by small craft only ; large vessels anchor outside the harbour and discharge into lighters. Lixoúrion shares with Argostólion the greater part of the trade of Kefallinía and exports currants, wine and olive oil ; more than half the currant crop of the island is sent from this port. A ferry runs to Argostólion and a good road runs around the head of Livádhi Bay and links the port with the road system of the main part of the island (Fig. 71).

Argostólion has a natural harbour. The port lies on the east side of a short peninsula which extends northwards to enclose a narrow bay which is 1,300 yds. wide at its entrance and narrows southwards. Depths in the bay shoal from 13 fm. in its outer part to 7 ft. at its north to south and scarcely rising above 1,600 ft. (Athéras, in the head where a causeway separates it from Lake Koutavós (Plates 120 and 121). The eastern shore is steep-to but the western side is bordered by shallow water. The port consists of :

(a) a pier fronting a wine store ¾ mile north-west of the town. This pier is 130 ft. long and has a charted depth of 3 ft. at its head.

(b) a small harbour close north of the town. This harbour is enclosed by moles having three limbs, each 200 ft. long. The harbour area is about 1½ acres and the entrance is about 100 ft. wide with charted depths of 10 ft.

(c) the inner harbour fronting the town, where there are four piers and two landing places. Each of the piers is between 50 and 72 ft. long and has charted depths of about 3 ft. at its head ; this is also the charted depth alongside the face of the landing places. One of the piers has two ½-ton cranes but none of the terminals has rail connexion. The port has several lighters of 15 to 25 tons.

In 1943 the port had a daily steamship service to other Greek ports, a ferry to Lixoúrion, and good roads to the village around the

Plate 120. The town of Argostólion in Kefallinía (Cephalonia)
The view is from the western slopes of the central mountains and shows the harbour
and waterfront.

Plate 121. The causeway at Argostólion
The view is north-eastward over the causeway which separates Argostólion Bay
from Lake Koutavós. Beyond, the road which leads across the central range to
Sámi can be seen winding past three old mills ; to the left is the coast road leading
north.

[*Facing page* 350

Plate 122.   The Gulf of Mólo and the harbour of Itháki

The view is south-east from the slopes of the Neritos highland.   On the left are Cape Skínos and Skínos Bay.   In the centre is the harbour of Itháki (Port Vathí) and to the right of it is the main mass of the southern upland.   On the extreme right is the Aëtós ridge (*cf.* Plate 125).

borders of the central mountains. A road leads across the central range to Sámi on the east coast. The town has flour mills and an ice plant and it exports currants, wine and olive oil. North of the town are the so-called ' sea-mills ' of Argostólion. Here the sea pours into a swallow-hole in the limestone and the flow has been harnessed to provide power for two small mills.

Between Argostólion Bay and Akrotíri the coast is low in its eastern half and consists of two bays separated by Cape Xí, off which lies the island of Vardhiánoi. These bays are bordered by rocks and shoals.

The West Coast

Almost the whole of the west coast from Akrotíri to Cape Athéras consists of bold rock-fringed cliffs with small sandy bays. Athéras Bay also has steep rocky sides and is seldom used. The large bight named Mírtos Bay is also steep sided but has stretches of sand in places ; it offers no anchorage. On the eastern side of Ássos peninsula is a small harbour used in summer by local craft (Plate 119). From Ássos northwards to Cape Vlióti, the coast is largely bordered by cliffs, and with the exceptions of two islets and a few sunken rocks close inshore, it is steep-to.

POPULATION AND SETTLEMENT

The population of the island of Kefallinía in 1928 numbered 57,578, of whom almost exactly one-half lived in the eparchy of Kranaía which includes the chief town, Argostólion (8,293), and the closely settled hills and plains that lie between Argostólion Bay and Loúrdha Bay, as well as the high basin of Omalá. The hill and plain country has some two dozen considerable agricultural villages, such as Lakíthra (673), Svoronáta (1,066) and Metaxáta (706), grouped closely together on the marls which are well-watered by numerous springs (Fig. 71).

The limestone ridges of the central mountains are without settlements except for the round stone huts which are used occasionally by shepherds. Along the western slopes are Tertiary deposits, and a line of villages, lying at short intervals, extends from Kardhakáta in the north, through Dhilianáta and Farakl

áta, to Vlakháta and Lourdáta. Near the middle of this line of villages is the high basin of Omalá which has two large villages, Frangáta (657) and Valsamáta (1,007) as well as several smaller centres.

The centre and south of the western peninsula is also a well settled area of hills and broad valleys where clays and marls form fertile, well-watered soils, especially on the eastern side. Apart from the town of Lixoúrion (4,843) there are large villages such as Khavdháta (1,006), Kaminaráta (934) and Mantzavináta (758). The northern half of the northern peninsula is less closely settled but it

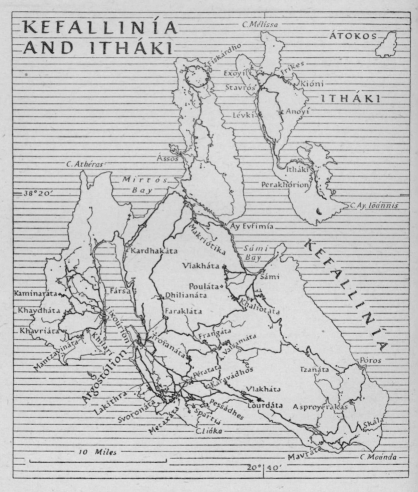

Fig. 71. Settlements and communications of Kefallinía (Cephalonia) and Itháki (Ithaca)

Based on the 1 : 100,000 Greece, Sheet I 3 (1943) by 524 Pal. Fd. Survey Coy, R.E. The dots show settlements but not necessarily individual houses. For key to roads, see Fig. 64.

has numerous small villages situated usually on hill-tops and ridges away from the coast. The southern part of this peninsula is a bare limestone upland and settlements are confined to the upper reaches of the valleys along its slopes. The Pílaros valley at its southern foot has two lines of villages along either flank. Along the northern slopes of the valley, clays occur at the foot of the limestone upland, but the southern side of the valley is drier.

The eastern side of the island is much less well populated than the western side. Even the central depression has only a relatively low density. A girdle of villages, which stand on the openings of valleys, lies around the hilly border of the plain of Sámi—Vlakháta (547), Pouláta (551), Khaliotáta (526) and Sámi (604)—and a line of hamlets lies on the Tertiary marls to the east of the river which flows north to Sámi Bay. The southern part of the central depression also has Tertiary deposits but, although they are well watered with good wells and some springs, they are not very fertile, and the area is sparsely populated. The tableland of Piryí, on the other hand, is much better settled with small villages which have usually less than 200 people.

AGRICULTURE

General Features

Kefallinia is much less productive than Kérkira, Levkás, and Zákinthos. The mountainous and infertile nature of much of the island is reflected in the fact that only about one-sixth of its total area is tilled. The limestone ranges are too dry, and the soil, even on the slopes, is often too meagre to permit tillage ; over much of their surface even the pasture is too scant and coarse to support cattle and donkeys, so that sheep and goats are the chief livestock. Yet, in many place swhich would be considered too poor for tillage in Kérkira, slopes have been terraced and soil collected laboriously to support vines, grain and olives. The chief agricultural districts are, the area of hill and plain between Argostólion Bay and Loúrdha Bay, the southern half of the western peninsula, the Pílaros valley, and the northern half of the northern peninsula.

Main Crops

Vine. The most important products of the island are wine and currants, which together account for about one-half of the total value of agricultural products excluding olives. The chief wine-growing districts are the hill and plain country of the west and southern part of the western peninsula, which produce a deep red wine. The western slopes of the central mountains behind Argostólion Bay, and the high plain of Omalá and its lower slopes, produce a rather sharp white wine. A sweet muscatel wine is also made, mainly in the southern part of the western peninsula. On these western slopes, terraced vineyards climb to heights of 2,500 ft. and sometimes even higher.

Grapes grown for drying into currants are also of great importance. Those grown in Kefallinía are smaller and sweeter than the products of Corinth and Zákinthos. The greater part of the crop comes from the southern part of the western peninsula where the clays and marls provide favourable conditions, especially around Lixoúrion. Another important currant-producing area is the northern half of the northern peninsula. Some are also grown in the plain of Sámi and on the adjacent slopes, but on the western slopes of the central mountains the crops are generally small.

Grain. Wheat and barley are grown in the valleys, on the lower slopes of the hill country, and where the soil is adequate in the upland basins. Some oats are also grown and indicate the hard conditions ; the island is too dry for maize to be a significant crop. As in the other islands the production of grain is inadequate for the needs of the population and much is imported.

Olive. Olives are much less important than in Kérkira and Zákinthos, but they are widely grown and well tended. They are most common in the southern part of the western peninsula and are also an important crop in the Pílaros valley and in the hill and plain country south of the Gulf of Argostólion, where the villages are surrounded by olive groves. Along the western slopes of the central mountains, olive trees are found up to heights of about 1,500 ft. but they rise to 1,600 ft. and more along the inner slopes of the high plain of Omalá and along the southern slopes of the Pílaros valley. On the eastern slopes of the central mountains the upper limit of cultivation would seem to be about 500 ft. lower.

Fruits. The chief fruit tree of Kefallinía is the fig, which is grown in all the hilly regions and sometimes extends to higher elevations than the olive. Oranges and lemons are grown in the gardens of the coastal districts, especially in the south-east where there is a good supply of spring water. The land is mostly too dry for temperate fruits. Apples are rarely grown and crops of cherries, plums and pears are small.

Plate 123. The island of Itháki (Ithaca) from the north

Plate 124. The Aëtós ridge and the Neritos highland, Itháki (Ithaca)
The view is northward, from the summit of the Aëtós ridge.

Plate 125. The Neritos highland, Itháki (Ithaca)

The view is south-eastward from the Exóyi ridge. In the foreground is the village of Stavrós and to the right of it is the cultivated land around Pólis Bay. Beyond is the main Neritos ridge with the roads to Lévki and Anoyí skirting it. In the distance (left) is Skínos Bay and Vathí Bay with the town of Itháki at its head. The Aëtós ridge is off the picture to the right (see Fig. 70 and Plate 122).

Livestock

The numbers of cattle on the island are small. They are mainly oxen and cows which are used as draught animals. Large numbers of goats are kept on the mountains and a good deal of cheese is made.

ITHÁKI (ITHACA)

GEOLOGY AND RELIEF

The island of Itháki is well-known as the legendary home of Odysseus. It faces the northern peninsula of Kefallinía across a narrow strait and has an area of 40 sq. miles. The island consists of a limestone range which reaches a maximum height of 2,650 ft. and falls steeply to the west but much more gently to the east. The Gulf of Mólo divides the island into two upland areas which are joined by an isthmus about 650 yds. wide and 300 ft. high (Fig. 70).

The northern upland area consists of the bare highland of Neritos which is a poor landscape of limestone rising to 2,650 ft. It falls steeply to the west coast but on the east it forms a broad undulating tableland in which erosion has produced basins and small troughs filled with *terra rossa*. To the north the upland falls steeply to a hilly foreland flanked by the two limestone ridges of Exóyi (1,722 ft.) and Áyioi Saránda (1,460 ft.) which form the two northern horns of the island. In this northern hill country the limestone is overlain by sandstone and clay, and, in contrast with the dry limestone ridges which surround it on all sides, has numerous springs.

To the south the upland descends to hills which occupy most of the central isthmus, but at the head of the Gulf of Mólo is the steep narrow ridge of Aëtós which rises to 1,247 ft. and is joined to the upland of the southern half of the island by a saddle over 400 ft. high (Plates 122–5.)

The southern upland is a broad, barren karst area which reaches a maximum height of 2,100 ft., and has depressions that are filled with lakes in winter. The summits rise only slightly above the general level, but southwards the upland drops rather sharply to a lower plateau area which has a general elevation of about 900 ft. and occupies the extreme south of the island. On the north-east the plateau descends along steep slopes to the valley behind the bay on which the town of Itháki stands. This is the only considerable area of lowland in the southern part of the island. Between it and the sea on the east is a range of low hills.

COASTS AND PORTS

The west coast of the island is steep-to and is backed by high land. The only considerable inlet is Pólis Bay where the entrance to the harbour is about 200 yds. wide ; there is a depth of 17 fm. in the middle of the harbour. The two northern horns of the island enclose Afáles Bay which has steep cliffs on its eastern side and a sandy beach at its head. The east coast is, in contrast to the west coast, much indented. From Cape Mélissa southwards it is high and steep-to as far as Fríkes Bay where there is anchorage in depths of 2 to 3 fm. Around the margins of the bay are several inlets which offer shelter to small craft. South of Fríkes Bay is Kióni Bay which is deep, but close to the shore the depths decrease to between 4 and 2 fm. The Gulf of Mólo is the chief feature of the east coast, for it contains, in addition to the port of Itháki, two bays which provide anchorages and have accessible beaches but no port facilities. The gulf itself is generally too deep for anchorage, but the channel is clear of danger. The harbour of Itháki is 2,300 yds. long and is 250 yds. wide at its entrance but it opens within to a maximum breadth of about 900 yds. The entrance is between 21 and 36 fm. deep, but within, depths decrease to between 6 and 19 fm. and to 1 fm. near the quays which lie at the head of the bay where the town of Itháki lies. Near the middle of the waterfront are a jetty with depths of between 3 and 6 ft. alongside. Ships generally discharge into lighters. South of the Gulf of Mólo the coast, although indented, provides no good anchorage except for small vessels.

POPULATION AND SETTLEMENT

The population of the island in 1928 was 7,183, of whom 3,265 lived in the town of Itháki. The majority of the remainder live in the hill country of the northern part of the island, between the Exóyi, Áyioi Saránda and Neritos ridges (Fig. 71). Here the sandstones and clays give fertile, well watered soils and the area has several considerable villages such as Stavrós (494) and Exoyí (354) and many smaller centres which give it a total population of about 1,700. The only other significant centres are, Kióni (734) on the bay of the same name, Anoyí (396) in poor surroundings near the centre of the northern upland, and Perakhórion (805) in the valley south of the town of Itháki. The only village on the steep western slopes of the island is Lévki (247) which stands on an isolated patch of Tertiary marl ; Áyios Ioánnis (59), farther south, is only a hamlet.

AGRICULTURE AND FISHING

The economy of the island is very similar to that of Kefallinía. It produces good olives, currants and wine, in addition to small crops of the usual grains, fruits and vegetables of the Ionian group. The most fertile part is the northern hill country where olives and vines do well. The limestone ridges and plateau areas are barren tracts with maquis plants such as the strawberry tree, lentisc and tree-heath, but where red earths have collected in valleys and depressions a little wheat is grown. For the greater part, the uplands offer only poor pasture for sheep and goats. The food production is not sufficient for the needs of the population. Fishing is an important supplement to agriculture and many are also employed in shipping ; some emigrate.

ZÁKINTHOS (ZANTE)

Zákinthos lies to the south-west of the entrance to the Gulf of Pátrai, its southern part being about 9 miles from the mainland. To the north it is separated by a channel of about 8 miles wide from the island of Kefallinía. Its extreme length is about $22\frac{1}{2}$ miles and its greatest width from east to west is about $13\frac{1}{2}$ miles. The southern and eastern coasts are considerably indented, so that its area is 155 sq. miles.

GEOLOGY AND RELIEF

The island is composed of two limestone ridges trending roughly from north-west to south-east, and an intervening depression filled with later (Pliocene) formations which in places overlie the slopes of the ridges (Fig. 72).

The Western Range

The western limestone range is the larger and more elevated, covering about half the area of the island. This anticlinal fold falls more steeply on the east to the central depression ; the western slopes are less abrupt, but they terminate in steep cliffs. In its central section the range rises to a general level of about 2,000 ft. Above this stand out low summits, culminating in Vrakhiónas 2,487 ft., the highest point in the island. The principal feature in the north is the tableland of Volímais, lying at about 1,450 ft., bordered by low summits, and descending in gentle slopes to the sea cliffs. The southern part of the range is dominated by the summit of Megálo Voúnó (1,980 ft.) which rises steeply from the plain on the east, and has deep valleys on the north and south, so that it is the most distinctive summit of the range. The southern end of the range is marked by particularly high and steep cliffs, sometimes exceeding 350 ft. Both these sections are cut by deep easterly-trending valleys. In contrast, the centre displays features which result more from chemical, than from stream, erosion. Thus its surface is a series of separate closed basins with undeveloped drainage, and gently rising, rather inconspicuous, summits. The whole area is an arid karst-like region of greyish limestone, with hollows filled with the products of erosion and with *terra rossa*, in which water tends to collect during the rains.

Fig. 72.   Relief and drainage of Zákinthos (Zante)

Based on the 1 : 100,000 Ionian Islands, Sheets K 3 and K 4 (1943) by 524 Pal. Fd. Survey Coy. R.E., and a map by J. Partsch in *Petermanns Mitteilungen*, vol. 37 (Gotha, 1891).
The shaded area shows very approximately the land above 100 metres (328 ft.).

The Central Plain

The central belt of the island is a foundered plain filled with later deposits. The beds are much disturbed and distorted, and the occurrence of earthquake shocks along the margins show that equilibrium has not yet been reached. The surface slopes towards the south and east, with low hills following approximately the general structural trend. The plain is well watered by streams from the flanks of the limestone ridges, and much of the lower ground is naturally swampy. However, drainage and reclamation have altered considerably its original character. The abundance of water and the heavier and more fertile soils make intensive cultivation possible, and it is here that most of the population lives.

The Eastern Ridge

The eastern ridge is lower and less continuous than the central range. The ridge has been broken into three sections. The northern section, which extends from Alikón Bay to the Tsiliví valley, falls sharply to the plain in the south-west and less abruptly to the north-east. Beyond the Tsiliví valley a small tableland rises to over 300 ft., falls precipitously to the coast behind the town of Zákinthos, and ends in cliffs at Cape Krionéri. The third portion forms the south-eastern peninsula of the island. It is dominated by the bold conical summit of Skopós (1,585 ft.) which rises in steep terraced slopes directly from the low cliffs south-east of Zákinthos Bay.

Coasts and Ports

The coasts of Zákinthos are, in general, steep and rocky. The south coast of the island forms the broad bight of the Gulf of Kerí which is flanked by rocky promontories but has a sandy beach and a low-lying hinterland at its head. The gulf is rarely used by ships, since the holding ground is bad, but Keri Bay, on the western side of the gulf, offers anchorage in depths of 7 fm. and the shore is a shingle beach. In the gulf are the two islands of Peloúzo and Marathón ; both islands are high. Peloúzo rises to 282 ft. and has a monastery ; Marathón is 488 ft. high and is terraced for crops and fruit. From Cape Marathiás to Cape Skinári, the northernmost point of the island, the coast is steep and fringed with cliffs almost everywhere. It offers no harbour. From Cape Skinári to Cape Katastári the coast continues rocky and occasionally forms cliffs but in the shelter of the latter cape is a cove where small coasting steamers sometimes anchor. Southwards the coast opens to Alikón Bay which gives access to the central lowland ; the shore has a sandy beach and salt pans. The stretch between Alikón Bay and Cape Krionéri is bordered by shoal water and the shore has alternating stretches of low cliffs and beaches. Zákinthos Bay is backed by steep slopes and affords anchorage in 7–10 fm. but is exposed to winds from north, through east, to south-east. In the angle of the bay is the chief port and town of the island (Plate 126).

The *port of Zákinthos* is protected on the north-east by a mole which is 600 yds. long and faced with masonry. About 200 yds. from its outer end the mole is enlarged by a quay area about 180 ft. long and 100 ft. wide but the whole of the inner side of the mole is quayed and has depths of between 11 and 18 ft. along its inner part and of 21 to 23 ft. along its outer part. The water fronting the town is shallow, or has rocks, except over a distance of 300 yds. close south of the foot of the mole, where there are depths of 6–9 ft. ; here are two $1\frac{1}{2}$-ton cranes for handling general cargo. At the southern end of the waterfront is a rock jetty which serves to prevent silting of the harbour by the stream which enters the harbour here. The port can repair boats, and the town and quays are lighted by electricity. The town is the terminal of several cables since it is the focus of telegraphic service in this part of the Mediterranean.

South of Zákinthos Bay the coast is backed by the sharp slopes of the eastern ridge and is fringed by sandy beaches with shoal water, and occasionally sunken rocks offshore, as far as Cape Yérakas.

POPULATION AND SETTLEMENT

The population of Zákinthos in 1928 was 40,469 ; the town of Zákinthos accounted for 12,063, or nearly one-third of the total. Most of the remaining two-thirds is concentrated on the central plain and on the slopes of the bordering highlands, which comprise approximately half the area of the island and have 54%, or, if the capital is included, 84% of the total population. The western limestone range and the south-eastern peninsula are sparsely populated and support about 6,500 persons only.

In the western highland the average density is less then 75 per sq. mile. The principal settlements are generally on the western slopes (Fig. 73). The most marked concentrations are around Volímais in the north and at the heads of the valleys which drain the south-western slopes, e.g., Áyios Léon (512), Agalás (458) and

Kerí (518). The basins of the central section are almost devoid of permanent habitations, though there are one or two small villages in the west. In the south-eastern peninsula, where the hills are lower and the limestones less in evidence, the density is somewhat higher.

Fig. 73. Settlements and communications of Zákinthos (Zante)

Based on the 1 : 100,000 Ionian Islands, Sheets K 3 and K 4 (1943) by 524 Pal. Fd. Survey Coy., R.E., and a map by J. Partsch in *Petermanns Mitteilungen*, vol. 37 (Gotha, 1891).

The dots show settlements but not necessarily individual houses. For key to roads, see Fig. 64.

The remainder of the island may be treated as a whole, since the other hills of the east are in the same category as the slopes of the western highland. The village lands are varied in character, including mountain grazing on the heights, olive groves, orchards, and fields on the lower slopes, and vineyards on the plain ; the villages are sited to enable these various areas to be worked most efficiently. A string of villages therefore extends along almost the entire eastern slopes of the highland, where springs are numerous and drainage is better. Some are among olive groves on the margin of the plain, others are scattered over the hillsides, and others lie in the mouths of the valleys. The upper limit of settlement is somewhere about 600 ft. A similar distribution is found on the western and south-western margin of the eastern hills, with the typical grouping of associated villages at ascending heights, e.g., Kato-, Meson-, and Ano Yerakári. Some villages are also sited on the higher ground of the plain itself, e.g., on the rise which separates the small northern portion from the main central plain. There are also a number of scattered dwellings on the plain, generally bordering the roads which traverse it ; on the whole, however, the concentration of settlement on the higher margins is marked.

AGRICULTURE

General Features

The cultivated land forms approximately one-quarter of the total area of the island. This is the highest proportion in all the administrative divisions of the Ionian Islands and is due to the greater expanse of late Tertiary and Pliocene formations in this island. The swamps of the central plain have been drained and brought under cultivation. The plain is mostly in vineyards which produce grapes for drying, but there are also grain fields, and pasture along the streams. The margins of the plain and the lower slopes of the highlands are given to olive groves ; higher up are arable fields and orchards. The greater part of the highlands are suited for grazing only, but in the higher valleys and the basins, where weathering has produced heavier soils, which retain moisture longer, there is some cultivation.

In comparison with the other Ionian Islands, the proportion of the cultivated land under cereals in Zákinthos is low (21%), but the most striking feature is the extent of the vineyards which occupy over half the cultivated area ; vines grown for currants alone account for 37% of the total.

Chief Crops

Vine. The characteristic feature of the agriculture is the great extent of the vineyards. Grapes are grown extensively for wine ; they occupy one-fifth of the cultivated area, which is approximately equal to the area under cereals. But much more land is given to grapes grown for drying into currants (37% of the total cultivated area) ; it is the smaller grapes that are made into currants. They are gathered in early August and dried, first in the shade and then in the sun ; the value of the harvest depends upon hot clear days during this period. Most of these vineyards are on the central plain. The output of wine and currants varies greatly from year to year. In 1934, a good year, 5,840 tons of wine were produced ; in 1936 less than a quarter of that quantity was produced. Similarly, the 1936 harvest of currants was 8,147 tons, but that of 1937 was 4,556 tons only. It is estimated that about four-fifths of this produce was exported, most of the currants going to Britain.

Grain. The principal, almost the sole, grain is wheat, which occupies about one-fifth of the cultivated area. In contrast to the other islands, hard varieties predominate and the yield is slightly higher, but the harvest is not adequate for the needs of the population and large quantities of grain have to be imported. Some oats and a little maize are also grown.

Fruits. Olives are another important item in the agriculture of Zákinthos, though not to the same extent as in Kérkira. The olive groves are mainly on the borders of the plain and the lower slopes of the highlands. As is usual, the harvest varies greatly from year to year ; the production of olive oil in 1937 was 6,370 tons, but in 1938 it was 2,584 tons only. Citrus fruits are also less important than in Kérkira but fresh figs and almonds are valuable crops.

Vegetables. A variety of vegetables is grown : tomatoes and potatoes occupy the largest areas, and onions, peas and beans are of some importance. Practically no industrial crops, with the exception of a little sesame, are cultivated. On the other hand, probably owing to the greater extent of heavier and moister soils, fodder crops are relatively much more important than in Kefallinía, and account for 15.7% of the cultivated area.

Livestock

The rearing of livestock is not important. There are 1,310 oxen and 754 cows on the island, but most of these are kept for labour. Only 88 horses are kept for labour and only 122 cows are kept for milk. Flocks of goats (17,509) and sheep (10,345) are grazed on the mountains, and provide milk from which all the cheese is made. The consumption of meat is low, even for the Ionian Islands. The number of pigs is less than one thousand.

BIBLIOGRAPHICAL NOTE

1. The basic works on the Ionian islands are four monographs by J. Partsch :
' Die Insel Korfu ', *Petermanns Mitteilungen, Ergänzungsheft* 88 (Gotha, 1887) ;
' Die Insel Leukas ', *Petermanns Mitteilungen, Ergänzungsheft* 95 (Gotha, 1889) ;
' Die Insel Zante ', *Petermanns Mitteilungen*, vol. 37, pp. 161–74 (Gotha, 1891) ;
and ' Kefallenia und Ithaka ', *Petermanns Mitteilungen, Ergänzungsheft* 98 (Gotha,
1890).

2. A more recent study, dealing primarily with the economic geography of the
islands, is E. Fels, ' Korfu, Kefallenia, Ithaka : ein wirtschafts- und kulturgeo-
graphischer Vergleich ', *Mitteilungen der Geographischen Gesellschaft in München*,
vol. 20, pp. 147–77 (München, 1927).

3. A detailed study of Kérkira is E. Fels ' Die Küsten von Korfu. Beitrag zur
Landschaftskunde der Insel ', *Mitteilungen der Geographischen Gesellschaft in
München*, vol. 16, pp. 21–114 (München, 1923). Descriptions of the coasts of the
islands are also given in the *Mediterranean Pilot*, vol. 3, chapters 2 and 3, 6th edition
(London, 1929).

4. The most useful topographical maps of the Ionian Islands are, (*a*) for Kérkira,
the 1 : 100,000 Corfu, G.S.G.S. Series 4165. The maps have a kilometre grid,
latitude and longitude (from Greenwich and Athens) in margins, contours in
brown at 20 metres interval, roads and tracks in red, water in blue ; (*b*) for the
other islands, the 1 : 100,000 Ionian Islands, which were drawn and reproduced
by 524 Pal. Fd. Survey Coy., R.E., in 1943. The maps have a kilometre grid,
latitude and longitude in margins, contours and form-lines in brown, water in blue.
The islands are also covered by the 1 : 250,000 G.S.G.S. Series 4088 (see
vol. I, p. 405).

Plate 126. The port of Zákinthos (Zante)

The view is westward, over the central plain, to the main limestone range. In the foreground is the harbour, enclosed by the mole and rock jetty, with the town at the foot of the precipitous slopes of the small tableland which backs it.

THÁSOS

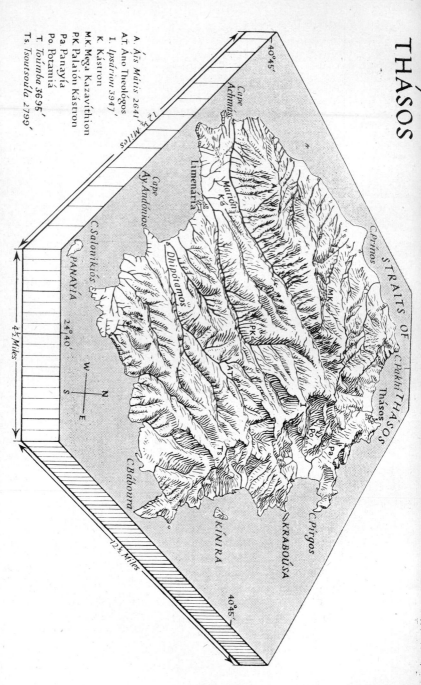

A. *Áis Mátis* 2641′
AT. Ano Theológos
I. *Ipsárion* 3947′
K. Kástron
MK Mega Kazavíthion
PK Palaión Kástron
Pa Panayía
Po. Potamiá
T. *Toúmba* 3695′
Ts. *Tsoutsoúla* 2799′

Fig. 74.   Relief diagram of Thásos

Based on the 1 : 100,000 G.S.G.S. Series 4087, Sheets C 4872 and C 5472 (1940) and British Admiralty Chart 1086 (1940).

[Facing page 365

Chapter X

THE THRACIAN ISLANDS

General Features : Thásos : Samothráki : Límnos : Áyios Evstrátios : Bibliographical Note

GENERAL FEATURES

The Thracian islands are a widely spaced group in the northern part of the Aegean Sea. There are four major islands—Thásos, Samothráki, Límnos and Áyios Evstrátios,—and the Turkish island of Imroz is geographically related to the group. Thásos and Samothráki lie close to the mainland of Thrace ; the former is only $3\frac{1}{2}$ miles south of Cape Ammódhis, while Samothráki is 24 miles from the Thracian coast. The islands are parts of separate *nomoí*. Thásos and Samothráki belong to the ' mainland ' *nomoí* of Kaválla and Évros respectively, while Límnos and Áyios Evstrátios are grouped with the Eastern Aegean island of Lésvos, which gives its name to the *nomós*.

GEOLOGY AND RELIEF

The deep northern basin of the Aegean Sea divides the group into a northern pair, Thásos and Samothráki, which are geographically related to the mainland of Thrace, and a southern pair, Límnos and Áyios Evstrátios, which are similarly related to the Turkish island of Imroz and the Gallipoli peninsula and which lie on a submarine ridge stretching south-west to the Sporádhes (Fig. 75). The northern basin stretches from the Gulf of Saros west-south-west towards Mount Áthos, but is embayed northwards towards the island of Thásos. The depth increases westwards and is over 600 fathoms south-west of Samothráki. This depression appears to be bounded by faults and is a region of fairly high earthquake frequency.

Thásos and Samothráki form an integral part of the Rodhópi massif and are built of Lower Palaeozoic and volcanic rocks. Límnos and Áyios Evstrátios are of a younger geological age and were probably folded during the Tertiary period. Both Thásos and Samothráki contain metalliferous ores, chiefly galena, calamine and blende. The southern islands, on the other hand, do not appear to possess any metalliferous deposits.

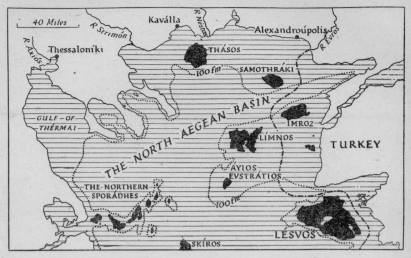

Fig. 75. The islands of the northern Aegean Sea
Based on the 1 : 1,000,000 G.S.G.S. Series 2758 (3rd edition, 1941).

CLIMATE

The climate is fairly uniform throughout the group. It is, in general, of Mediterranean type, modified by proximity to the coasts of Macedonia and Thrace. The temperature range is greater than in the islands farther south, and the summer drought is more prolonged. These ' continental ' features are most marked in Thásos and are least apparent in Límnos and Áyios Evstrátios. The highest summer temperatures reach 85–95° F in all the islands; the maximum usually occurs in August. The heat is very oppressive on the lower ground, especially on Límnos. North-facing coasts are generally cool and more pleasant, as they may receive winds from the high-lands of Bulgaria. The lowest temperatures are experienced in January, when they may drop to 22–25° F. At this time of the year the general southerly and south-westerly winds alternate with violent and very cold northerly or north-easterly winds from the mainland of Thrace. These gales, which may last several days, are sometimes accompanied by blizzards, but snow rarely lies long, except on the mountains. Short, sharp frosts are also experienced at this time.

The amount of rainfall varies with the relief; Thásos and Samothráki are very much wetter than the relatively low-lying Límnos. Most rain falls in the three months from December to

February. March and April are also fairly wet and dull, and a small rainfall, due mainly to thunderstorms, occurs through the summer. A marked feature of all the islands is the violence of the winds. Calms are rare, and winds are usually strong, especially in winter. In summer the winds are generally from an easterly or north-easterly quarter ; in winter they blow more often from the west or south-west as well as from the north-east. The north-east winds develop suddenly, attain a considerable violence and have short spells of treacherous calm, which may be followed by a reversal of wind direction. These gales are perhaps worst off Samothráki, where they are extremely dangerous to shipping and account partly for the isolation of this island. Furthermore, dangerous squalls descend from the hills to the shores of the island.

Consideration of the climate of these islands is hindered by the lack of statistics ; there is only one second class meteorological station (on the island of Límnos) in the group.

THÁSOS

The island of Thásos, the most northerly of the Thracian group, is a mountain mass, lying close to the shore of eastern Makedhonía. It has an area of about 154 sq. miles and is, at most, 14 miles from east to west and 16 miles from its most southerly headland, Cape Salonikiós, to its most northerly point, Cape Pákhi. Thásos is separated from the mainland by the shallow Straits of Thásos which, at their narrowest, are only 3½ miles wide. The small island of Thasopoúla lies near the middle of this channel.

GEOLOGY AND RELIEF

In its broad outlines, the geology of Thásos is relatively simple. The island consists of alternating beds of schist and marble, which have been arched up into an anticline trending roughly north-east to south-west. The two arms of the anticline were, however, very different. On the south, the beds are almost horizontal ; to the north they are sharply folded and bounded by a fault which runs across the island. A mineralized zone trends roughly north-south in the western part of the island, and has given rise in the past to an important mining industry. Kalirrákhi was the chief mining centre, and the most important minerals were calamine, galena and certain copper and iron ores.

The relief of the island is highest in its eastern half (Fig. 76). A lofty curving ridge lies concentric with the north and east coasts of the island. It reaches a general height of about 3,300 ft., and presents a steeply scarped face towards the north-east and east. In the west there is a more gentle descent, furrowed by the major streams of the island. Pyramidal peaks rise from the ridge. The

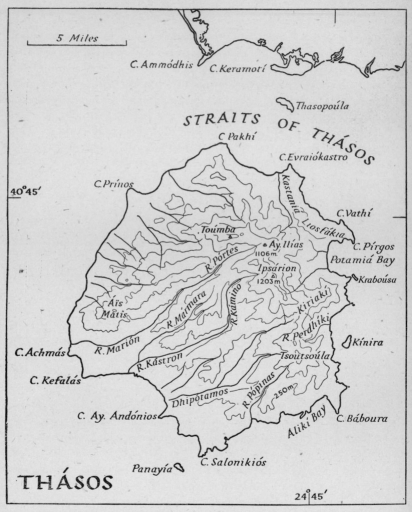

Fig. 76. Relief and drainage of Thásos

Based on the 1 : 100,000 *Epitelikós Khártis tis Elládhos*, Sheets △ XI (1934)] and △ XII (1933).

The contours are at intervals of 250 metres (820 ft.).

latter may be said to begin, at its north-western end, in the peak of Toúmba (3,695 ft.). The ridge extends eastwards for nearly two miles to Mount Áyios Ilías (3,628 ft.). From this point a spur stretches north-eastwards, and separates the drainage basins of Thásos (Limín) and Panayía. The main ridge, however, continues southwards, presenting a precipitous rampart towards the east, to Mount Ipsárion (3,947 ft.), the highest point in the island. Mount Tsoutsoúla (2,799 ft.) an inconspicuous summit 1¾ miles farther south, marks the south-eastern end of the main ridge. Another ridge, Kiriakí, extending north-eastwards from Tsoutsoúla separates the Potamiá from the Kínira plains. It includes Mount Kiriakí (2,434 ft.) and terminates in the tiny islet of Kraboúsa. South of Tsoutsoúla, the main curving ridge of the island becomes very much lower, before running out to the sea and terminating in the cliffs of Cape Báboura.

Within the curve of this mountain ridge is a broad plateau, which occupies the centre of the island and has a general level of about 2,000 ft. The outer portion of the plateau has been eroded into a number of ridges, which radiate to the south-west and west coasts. This erosion has been least in the south, where only short ravines score the steep plateau side. In the south-west and west the rivers are longer and their valleys are wider, leaving a fan-like series of irregular steep-sided spurs. These spurs maintain a height of 1,300–1,600 ft. until within some three miles of the coast, when they break away somewhat steeply and drop to the very narrow coastal plain. The highest point in this western plateau region is Áïs Mátis (2,641 ft.).

The main valleys lead south-west and west; those draining to other parts of the coast are merely ravines. The three longest and largest valleys have their heads high up on the plateau in the centre of the island, and flow to the south-west coast. These valleys are fairly broad and easy. Those farther north are narrower and more difficult, and are separated from one another by rough mountain ridges.

Two miles north-east from Áyios Ilías is the small, outlying hill mass of Liosfákia and Kastaniá, cut off from the main mass by the deep valley through which passes the high road from the town of Thásos to Panayía.

COASTS AND PORTS

There are few conspicuous headlands or indentations in the coasts of Thásos. Most of the bays are shallow bights, backed by narrow coastal plains. There are few actual cliffs, but the hills generally drop steeply to the sea.

The North-east Coast

Fronting the Thásos Straits, a shallow bay extends between Cape Pakhí (Cape Ommanney) and Cape Evraiókastro. Along its western side the bay is backed by steep hills, but to the east these give place to the flat plain of Thásos (Limín), a triangular area of a little over one square mile in area. In it is the port of Thásos (Limín), the most important in the island. The harbour is an artificial one, being formed by two moles extending from the shore. The moles have a combined length of over 1,000 ft. and enclose an area of about 6 acres. They are 10–15 ft. wide, but rise only about 4 ft. from the almost tideless sea. There is about 15 ft. of water inside the harbour. Coasting ships use this port and there was a frequent service to Kaválla on the mainland (Plate 127).

The town itself is on an important classical site. It has over 1,200 inhabitants and is growing rapidly. Greek refugees from Turkey were settled in a new quarter, and have greatly widened the activities of the town. It is a centre for the preparation of oil and tobacco, and has boat building yards capable of launching wooden ships of up to 300 tons. A motor road, 4 miles long, links Thásos with Panayía. South-east of Cape Evraiókastro a rugged coastline extends for some 5 miles and terminates in the anvil-shaped promontory which comprises Capes Vathí and Pírgos.

The East Coast

South of Cape Pírgos is Potamiá Bay, the deepest indentation in the coast of Thásos. It is backed by the largest plain in the island, an area of nearly 2 sq. miles. The villages of Potamiá and Panayía lie in the foothills to the west of the plain. At Skála Potomiás (Fig. 77) is a small coastal village and wharf, off which an anchorage may be obtained. The *skála* has a small jetty where the depth of water is 9 ft.

Two miles of rugged coastline, formed by the western spur from Mount Tsoutsoúla, follow (see p. 369), but the bay of Kínira is shallow and irregular, with only a few short stretches of flat land ; the village of Kínira lies on one of these. This stretch of the coast ends in Cape Báboura, the south-easterly point of the island.

The South Coast

Between Cape Báboura and Cape Salonikiós is one of the most rugged stretches of coastline in the island. The southern plateau drops steeply and the short valleys are deeply incised. Off Cape Salonikiós is the small, uninhabited island of Panayía, and east of the cape is the *skála* of Astoís. The coast is flatter between Cape Salonikiós and Cape Kefalás and considerable areas of plain occur around the mouths of the larger rivers. The village of Kástron, capital of the island, and its port of Limenária, lie on the largest of these alluvial tracts. An iron pier at Limenária served as the centre for the export of ore and is linked by a short mineral railway with the mines in the hills to the east ; ores were crushed and refined at Limenária and coasting ships maintained a frequent service to Kaválla. Potós, to the south-east, is a *skála*, and is connected with the inland village of Áno Theológos by an unmetalled road.

The North-west Coast

North of Cape Kefalás is a small area of plain, on which is situated the landing place of Skála Mariés whence an unmetalled road runs to Limenária. The north-western coast of the island is straight and smooth, except for the flat and sandy headland of Cape Prínos. To the north and south of this point are small stretches of plain between the ends of the ridges which come down to the sea from the interior plateau. Along this coast are *skálai* which serve the villages lying a mile or two inland. The chief of these is Skála Sotíros, which has a pier and a mineral railway linking it with the mining area of the interior. The *skálai* are linked by the unmetalled road from Kalirrákhi to Rakhónion.

HISTORICAL OUTLINE

The ancient Greeks developed the natural resources of the island, and in classical times Thásos became noted for its wine, oil, marble and minerals. In addition, the mines on the mainland opposite were exploited. A large town arose in the northern plain and ruins still indicate its size and splendour. From their forests the Thasians built a fleet, but the town was captured by Athens about 463 B.C. Later, Thásos fell under Macedonian, and then Roman, sway and was the provisioning base of Brutus and Cassius in their struggle against the triumvirs. Still of importance in Roman times—

particularly for its marble (cf. triumphal arch of Marcus Aurelius discovered in the island)—it later fell a prey to the disorders and piratical terrors of the Middle Ages.

After various vicissitudes, the Byzantine Emperor John V (Palaeologos) bestowed the island (along with Lésvos, Límnos, Imroz, Samothráki, and the town of Aínos) on Francesco Gattilusio, who had helped him to regain the throne in 1355. The Gattilusio family, originally Genoese, continued in possession until the fall of Constantinople (1453) and the subsequent conquest of Lésvos by the Turks in 1462. The island, on account of its predominantly Greek population, enjoyed the special privilege of being administered, under the archbishop of Maroneía, by nine minor Turkish officials aided by local elective councils.

The following centuries witnessed numerous piratical descents upon the island, and the fear of piracy became the chief preoccupation of the inhabitants. Agriculture was neglected, and the island fell into obscurity and poverty. The villages were withdrawn from the coasts and perched on secure heights inland. The population dwindled, and commerce vanished. Piratical depredations are recorded as late as 1854, and security is comparatively recent.

In the Greek War of Independence (1821) the Thasians enjoyed a momentary independence, but they hastened to place themselves again under the protection of the Sultan, thereby preserving for themselves their former privileges.

In 1824, Sultan Mahmoud II, wishing to conciliate his dangerous dependant, bestowed upon Mehemet Ali of Egypt certain of the revenues of Thásos as his private property. These revenues—the tithe on agricultural produce, the cattle tax, and certain mining and forestry rights—were devoted by Mehemet Ali to a charitable institution in Kaválla, his native town. Subsequently, the administration of the island passed into Egyptian hands and was governed by a *mudir*, assisted by a Greek Christian *proedros* elected by the islanders. There were, however, minor Turkish officials who collected such taxes as were not Egyptian—chiefly customs and military exemption (capitation) tax. The taxes payable to the Egyptian government were not heavy, and the chief value of the island to Mehemet Ali was the timber which its forests provided for his fleets. The Turkish taxes also were not excessive (the capitation tax amounted to a total of about £560 per annum), and the island on the whole was not much troubled by its governors. There was considerable local autonomy, and native officials had control of trade.

Agriculture

The olive and the vine are of great importance
they prepare and export olive oil and soap, and tl
a red wine which is free of the resin so common
Tobacco is a recent introduction, but is of a po
cultivation probably has little future. Honey is
mulberry is used for rearing silk worms. Cerea
their production is insufficient for the island. Sl
numerous and pigs are widely kept. Horses and
transport, but cattle are very few in number. Tl
forested, and timber has been an important sou
wealth. It was used for construction and boat bu
of resin and for burning for charcoal, which was
in considerable quantities to Constantinople.

Mining

Marble has been quarried at various times, and
of the chief products of Thásos. There are
workings along the south-east and south-west
ticularly on the peninsula of Alikí. More rec
Panayía have now been abandoned.

Herodotus relates that the island was once imp
which was mined in the eastern part of the is
times, the chief ores have been those of zinc, lead
which occur as impregnations in the marble and sch
the zinc ore, calamine, has been the most importar

In the nineteenth century the Turkish and Eg
attracted by tales of mineral wealth, examined the
ficial way. In 1904, the German firm of Speidel
concession near Vouves in the south-west of the
were started in 1905–6, and others were opened
near Sotíros. Mining had become a very success
outbreak of the war of 1914–18. In 1915, tl
transferred to a French-Belgian syndicate. The
carried on until recently, but its importance has
The reserves are too small for their exploitation to

The two chief mining areas are north-east of L
first opened up by the Germans), and near Sot
workings in these areas had been chiefly for coppe
spoil heaps have yielded valuable quantities of

Nevertheless, piracy and foreign rule combined to discourage
enterprise. At this time, Thásos formed part of the *vakuf* (Moslem
Church estate) of Kaválla ; on the Christian side it continued to be
subject to the Greek Orthodox archbishopric of Maroneía, on the
mainland opposite.

In 1902, the Young Turk government attempted in Thásos the
same policy of oppression and exploitation as it had adopted towards
the Dodecanese. Disorder was alleged to have broken out upon
a threatened increase of taxation, and on this excuse the island was
temporarily occupied by Turkish troops ; the Egyptian ascendancy
was restricted to rights over woods and mines, and the government
became Turkish. Discontent prevailed, and as a result of the
Balkan wars (1912–13) Thásos, along with other Aegean islands, was
assigned by the Great Powers to Greece in 1914 (see vol. I, p. 214).

Population and Settlement

The population of the island numbers about 11,500, and lives
mainly in villages. These consist of groups of houses, of two
storeys, scattered amongst their orchards and olive groves. They
are generally situated well inland, usually 2 to 4 miles from the sea
and at altitudes of 500 to 1,000 ft. They nearly all occupy hill sites
which are difficult of access, and often lie amid wooded ridges.
This is a survival from the time when piracy was rife ; only a
strong inland position afforded security from sea raiders. Thus
Panayía (1,092) and Potamiá (910) lie well back from the Bay of
Potamiá, and the majority of the villages are inland (Fig. 77).

The villagers are mainly agriculturalists. As there is little
cultivable ground in the upper valleys, they cultivate tracts of the
lower valleys and delta plains. With the coming of greater security,
the inhabitants of the inland villages have tended to migrate back
towards the coast and some of the *skálai*, formerly merely collections
of huts in temporary use, have become permanent settlements. In
the case of Limenária and Thásos (Limín) the *skálai* have outgrown
their inland bases of Kástron and Panayía. The inhabitants of the
villages tend to move towards the sea in winter and up to the
pastures of the plateau in summer. Groups of huts (*kalívia*), designed
to save the field labourers the long daily journey to and from the
village and its fields, have sprung up between the *skála* and the
village. There is thus in progress in Thásos a dispersion of its
former nucleated and typical Mediterranean settlement pattern,

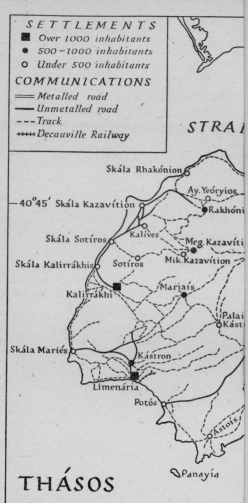

SETTLEMENTS
- ■ Over 1000 inhabitants
- ● 500–1000 inhabitants
- ○ Under 500 inhabitants

COMMUNICATIONS
- ═══ Metalled road
- ─── Unmetalled road
- --- Track
- ++++ Decauville Railway

STRA

Skála Rhakónion

Ay. Yeóryios

—40°45′ Skála Kazavítion

Rakhóni

Skála Sotíros

Kalíves

Meg. Kazavíti

Skála Kalirrákhis

Sotíros

Mik. Kazavítion

Kalirrákhi

Mariaís

Palai
Kásti

Skála Mariés

Kástron

Limenária

Potós

Astoís

THÁSOS

Panayía

Fig. 77. Settlements and commur
Based on the 1 : 100,000 *Epitelikós Khártis tis E.*
△ XII (1933) and *Population de la Grèce d'apr*
1928, deuxième édition (Athènes, 1935).

as well as a movement from inland, a
towards the sea. In this way the settl
times, when Thásos enjoyed a period o
restored. The village of Kástro, typic
settlements, is now almost deserted.

years. The veins contained calamine of varying degrees of purity, together with iron, copper and barium. The more southerly area was said to have been worked out 25 years ago, but there is reason to believe that other and similar deposits occur in a mineral belt stretching from north to south along the west part of the island.

Two light railways carried the ore from the mines to the coast. From the mines near Sotíros a line ran to Skála Sotíros. Coasting craft then conveyed it to Limenária which had crushing and refining plants capable of handling up to 20 tons of ore daily. Another short mineral line ran from the mines at Vouves to Limenária. The ore from other mining centres was conveyed by mule transport to the refinery.

There was no production from the mines of Thásos in 1938, and workings appear to have been abandoned. There are said to be important reserves of ore, but the metal content is reported to be low.

ADJACENT ISLANDS

Off the coast of Thásos are three small islands, which may conveniently be considered with it. Off Cape Saloníkiós is the small, low island of *Panayía*. It is difficult of access owing to its rocky coast and is uninhabited. The island of *Kínira* lies in the shallow bay of the same name. It is small, pear-shaped, and its longest axis is only ½ mile. *Thasopoúla* is slightly larger. It is a mile in length from north-west to south-east, and less than a mile in width. It is composed mainly of three hills, the highest of which reaches 360 ft. The islet is covered with scrubby vegation, and is probably deserted except for shepherds.

SAMOTHRÁKI

Samothráki, like Thásos, is mountainous and difficult of access. The island measures 14 miles along its longest axis and has an area of about 70 sq. miles. It lies 28 miles south-south-east of the port of Alexandroúpolis, and 16 miles north-west of the Turkish island of Imroz.

GEOLOGY AND RELIEF

Samothráki is the loftiest and, in some ways, the most impressive of all the islands of the Aegean Sea. It rises steeply from its relatively small base to the considerable height of 5,248 ft. in Mount Fengári. From whatever side it is viewed, Samothráki appears as an imposing pyramid. The island is a fault-bounded mass of almost rectangular plan to which have been added, at the eastern and western ends and along the northern margin, lowlying areas of Tertiary and recent sedimentaries and volcanics (Fig. 79). A very characteristic feature of the island is the regularity of its fault scarps (Fig. 78). That on the south-east is parallel with the margin of the North Aegean Basin and trends from east-north-east to west-south-west. A fault at right angles to this forms the eastern margin of the block. On the north-east, a fault trends west-north-west to east-south-east. The western side is formerly two separate faults, which meet in a broad angle. A short north-south fault lies behind the town of

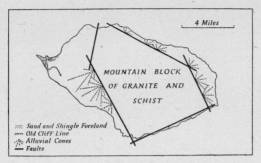

Fig. 78. The structure of Samothráki

Based on D. Jaranoff, ' L'île de Samothrace : Esquisse géographique ', *Bulletin de la Société Bulgare de Géographie*, vol. 6, pp. 61–84 (Sofia, 1939).

Samothráki (Khóra). This is met by a more southerly fault, parallel to that on the eastern side of the mass.

In the main, the mountain block consists of a fissile mica schist intercalated with bands of marble ; serpentine appears on the north. The schists appear to have been domed upwards allowing granite to intrude and form the core of the anticline. In places, erosion has removed the schistose cover, exposing the underlying granite. In Tertiary times, parts of the massif were covered by flows of trachytic lava, and the highest peaks of the island consist of caps of trachyte on schist. On the west, this lava flow has tended to obscure the boundary faults, and has formed the dissected hilly country west of the town of Samothráki (Khóra). The hills of Vríkhos and Turlí are formed of trachyte.

The throw of the faults which bound the mountains differs on the various sides. That on the south-east was greatest, so that the

southern, or downthrown, side is now deeply sunk beneath the
Aegean. On other sides the throw has been less. The rivers,
which have cut deeply into the margins of the mountain block, have
built up a series of alluvial cones, which are conspicuous features
along the south-west, north-north-east and east-north-east facing
scarps. Along the south-eastern side of the island, where the cliffs
are unusually steep, the rivers frequently fall direct into the sea and
the equivalent of alluvial cones here took the form of deposits on the

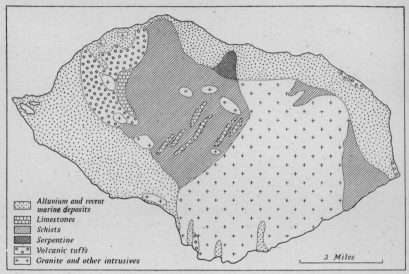

Fig. 79. The geology of Samothráki

Based on a folder map in L. de Launay, ' Etudes Géologiques sur la' Mer Egée',
Annales des Mines, vol. 13 (Paris, 1898).

sea floor. In the period that has elapsed since these deposits were
formed, the sea level has fallen relative to the land, and the rivers
have been forced to cut deep channels through the cones which they
had previously formed.

Beyond the trachytic area of the north-west of the island is an
area of Tertiary and Quarternary raised beaches, forming a series
closely comparable to that found around many other parts of the
Mediterranean Sea. The easily eroded material of the alluvial
cones, and that from other parts of the island, has been carried westwards by the current to form the low promontory of Cape Akrotíri.
Spits have grown outwards from the Tertiary cliff line, which is still
apparent, and have joined up to enclose two lagoons, cut off from the

sea by a single bar, through which the sea is able to percolate.   Cape
Akrotíri is still growing westwards.

A mountain ridge lies almost diagonally across the island from
north-west to south-east but it curves a little towards the south.
This ridge bears a marked resemblance to the mountain arc in the
island of Thásos (see p. 368) and contains the three highest points
of the island, Áyios Yeóryios, Ayía Sofia and Fengári, all over 4,500 ft.
From Fengári a ridge stretches southwards to the sea at Cape

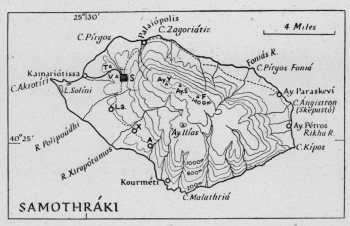

Fig. 80.   Relief, drainage, settlements and communications of Samothráki
Based on (1) a map of Samothráki by D. Jaranoff in the *Bulletin de la Société
Bulgare de Géographie*, vol. 6 Sofia, 1939) ; (2) *Population de la Grèce d'après le
Recensement du 15–16 Mai*, 1928, deuxième édition (Athènes, 1935) ; (3) British
Admiralty Chart 1087 (1940).
The contours are at intervals of 200 metres (656 ft.).
A. Alónia ; Ay. S. Ayía Sofía ; Ay. Y. Áyios Yeóryios ; F. Mount Fengári ; La.
Ládhiko ; S. Samothráki (Khóra) ; T. Turlí ; V. Vríkhos ; X. Xiropótamos.
For key to settlements and roads, see Fig. 77.

Malathriá, the most southerly point of the island.   This ridge,
together with the main ridge of the island, forms an immense
amphitheatre opening towards the south-west, the upper walls of
which are bare, craggy and precipitous.   To the north, the main
ridge drops steeply to the narrow coastal plain, but to the south
and east is a high plateau over 3,300 ft, which is sharply cut off on its
seaward edge by the still fresh fault scarps which bound the mountain mass.

Rivers are intermittent and are dry in summer, but the population
gets an adequate water supply from spring in the igneous rocks and
in certain water-bearing beds in the Quaternary deposits.   On the

northern fault line of the island is a thermal spring, which has deposited sulphur and formed terraces of travertine.

COASTS AND PORTS

Samothráki is one of the most inaccessible of the islands of the Aegean. The coasts are fault scarps, obscured on all sides, except the south-east, by spreads of alluvial material (see p. 378). The latter coast is straight and steep ; others are flat and shelving. Nowhere is there a safe anchorage, though the south-western side, which is sheltered from the prevailing winds, is the least dangerous. The only landing place on the island is Kamariótissa, 2 miles east of Cape Akrotíri. It was visited weekly by a steamer from Alexandroúpolis which waited for ten minutes off the village before continuing to Límnos, and every week the return ship from Límnos to Alexandroúpolis paid a similar call. The only export is olive oil ; the only imports are grain and dried octopuses to supplement the food resources of the island.

HISTORICAL OUTLINE

Noted in ancient times as the seat of a mystery cult and much visited by devotees, Samothráki in other respects seems to have stood apart from the main currents of history. This was largely owing to its economic unimportance and the danger of its coasts and seas. In general, its fortunes followed closely that of Thásos (see pp. 371–3). Near Palaiópolis, in the north-west of the island, there are striking ancient remains. Along with Thásos, the island passed in 1355 into the hands of the Gattilusio family, who erected several towns and fortifications, and with whom it remained until it was taken by the Turks about 1460. Up till this time the island supported a fair-sized population, but many of the wealthy inhabitants were taken to Constantinople, and the young men and women were sold as slaves. The population, however, rose again by immigration and may have amounted to 8,000 in the early part of the last century, and the island seems to have been on the whole little troubled by the Turks.

At the outbreak of the Greek War of Independence (1821) the Samothracians declared their independence, but after four months the Turks landed and almost exterminated them. About 400 refugees collected later on, but the population has never fully recovered. Owing to its poverty the island seems to have been left largely unmolested by pirates, but the capital, anciently on the north-west coast, is now situated high up and inland. After the Balkan Wars (1912–13) Samothráki was given with the consent of the Great Powers to Greece.

POPULATION AND SETTLEMENT

A hundred years ago the population of Samothráki numbered about 2,000. The population has since increased slowly and in 1928 it reached 3,866. During the past century the men of Samothráki emigrated regularly to the sponge fisheries of the Dodecanese. Many never returned to Samothráki, and sponge fishers were thus gradually lost to the island so that the industry is now extinct. On the other hand there has been much immigration from elsewhere in Greece.

Until 60 years ago the whole population was concentrated in a single village which, in the absence of any other, was called simply Khóra, or ' village '. This village lies below the western scarp of the highlands, but is cut off from the sea by the trachytic hills of Vríkhos and Turlí. The village is compact and built on a steep hillside. It was formerly the practice for the inhabitants to leave their village in March and live in temporary dwellings located wherever there was land suitable to cultivate. Gradually these residences acquired a semi-permanent character, and eventually became independent villages. In this way originated the settlements of Kamariótissa (which now has the only landing stage on the island), Palaiópolis (which occupies the site of a settlement of classical times), Xiropótamos, Kourméti, Ládhiko and Makriliés. This process still goes on and the village of Alónia was severed only recently from its parent village. Other such settlements are still deserted in winter, while at Ládhiko a few families linger on through the year.

Settlements are confined to the fringe of Tertiary and Quaternary deposits, and are compact groups of flat roofed houses. According to the 1928 census, 2,055 people lived in the town of Samothráki (Khóra) and the remainder were distributed in small villages, each with between about 100 and 500 inhabitants. The resources of the island are enough to support a much larger population, but, as long as external trade and intercourse are so restricted, only at a very low standard of living.

AGRICULTURE

The island offers little inducement to the cultivator. Soil is virtually lacking from the upper slopes, and is poor elsewhere. For this reason, cereal crops are little grown, and the chief cultivation is that of fruit trees. Fruit trees and olives are planted as the maquis is cleared, and the cultivation and pressing of olives is the chief occupation of the island. The walnut tree is also planted, and occasionally the oriental plane (*Platanus orientalis*), in the shade of which peach, almond, and sometimes cherry, trees grow. Oranges and lemons are confined to the southern side of the island, as the climate of the north is too severe for them. Cereals, for which the island is really unsuited, grow best in the flatter west of the island, but the yield is small, and the local production is never sufficient.

There are very few cattle in the island, though sheep and goats are of some importance. The island was once famous for its cheese, which was exported in quantity, but this trade has now ceased.

The forests have in the past provided a major industry in the island. The higher slopes of the mountains were formerly clothed with forests of evergreen oak (*Quercus coccifera*). The trees were cut and burned for charcoal, which was exported chiefly to Constantinople, but also to the mainland of Greece. The Constantinople market was closed when the island became Greek in 1913, and the charcoal-burning industry is now extinct. The forest laws now forbid the cutting of trees for charcoal. Maquis is cut as fuel but it grows again rapidly, unless the cleared land is planted with fruit trees.

The Samothracians are an example of islanders with little interest in, or dependence upon, the sea. The ancient sponge fishery is now extinct and only about 40 families, some 5% of the population of the island, engage in fishing.

LÍMNOS

The island of Límnos lies on the southern border of the North Aegean Basin, and faces Samothráki across a 23 miles wide channel. It is 12 miles south-west of Imroz and 38 miles west of Cape Helles. It is strategically the most important island in the Thracian group, and, with its excellent harbour of Moúdhros, can command the entrance to the Dardanelles. It is irregular in shape and deeply indented on the south by Moúdhros Bay. The island measures some 20 miles from east to west and 12–15 miles from north to south.

Plate 127.   The port of Thásos (Limín)

The view shows the north-eastern mole and the entrance to the harbour.   The
tip of the short south-western mole can just be seen at the extreme left of the view.

Plate 128.   The south coast of Samothráki

The great cliffs are due to faulting and not to wave action (see pp. 377-8).

LÍMNOS

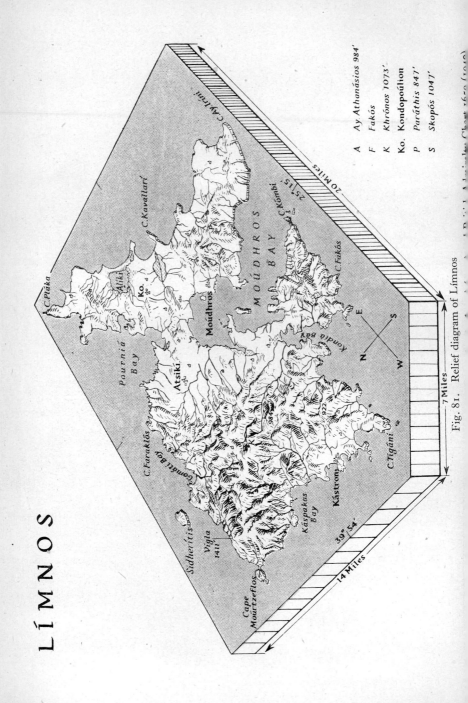

C. Plaka

C. Kavallari

Pourniá Bay

Alikí

Ko.

Atsikí

Moúdhros

C. Faraklós

Gomáti Bay

Sidherítis

Vígla 1411′

MOÚDHROS BAY

25′15′

C. Kómbi

C. Fakós

Kondiá bay

N

E

W

S

20 Miles

Káspakas Bay

Kástron

C. Tigáni

39° 54′

Cape Mourtzeflos

7 Miles

14 Miles

A   Ay Athanásios 984′

F   Fakós

K   Khrónos 1073′

Ko. Kondopoúlion

P   Paráthis 847′

S   Skopós 1047′

Fig. 81. Relief diagram of Límnos

Pourniá Bay on the north, and Moúdhros Bay on the south, approach
to within 2½ miles of one another, and almost sever the island. In
the south-west of the island is Kondiá Bay which stretches inland
and almost reaches Moúdhros Bay. On the north-east, a long
peninsula reaches out towards Imroz. Límnos has an area of
184 sq. miles, and is thus the largest island in the group. For
statistical purposes, both Límnos and Áyios Evstrátios are included
in the *nomós* of Lésvos.

GEOLOGY AND RELIEF

Límnos consists of a tabular area of sedimentary rocks, probably
Tertiary in age. They consist mainly of sandstones and con-
glomerates, into which Tertiary lavas have been intruded (Fig. 82).
It is to the latter that the roughness of the relief and coastline of
Límnos is largely due. The area west of Moúdhros and Pourniá
Bays is much the more hilly part of the island, though no part is

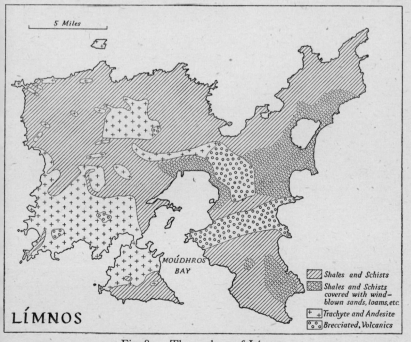

Fig. 82.   The geology of Límnos
Based on a map in H. de Launay, ' Etudes Géologiques sur la Mer Egée ', *Annales
des Mines*, vol. 13 (Paris, 1898).

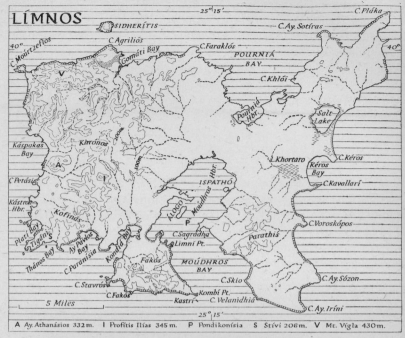

Fig. 83. Relief and drainage of Límnos

Based on the 1 : 50,000 Aegean Islands, M.D.R. 611 (2 sheets) (1944) and British Admiralty Chart 1659 (1940).

The contours are at intervals of 100 metres (328 ft.)

really mountainous. In the south-west a generally level surface is broken by a great number of volcanic peaks, with sharp and often fantastic outlines, and steep, often precipitous, slopes. The peninsula between Kondiá Bay and Moúdhros Bay, is dominated by the bold and rugged ridge of Fakós, the highest point of which is Mount Skopós (1,046 ft.). Many smaller volcanic hills lie along the west coast, and give it its rugged and indented character.

North of this region of scattered volcanic peaks is a highland with an average height of 800–1,000 feet. It consists of a series of irregular plateau surfaces which are interrupted by occasional peaks and dissected by deep and rugged ravines. Mount Vígla (1,410 ft.), lying close to the north coast, is the highest of the peaks, and also the highest point in the island. On the east, this wild region drops abruptly to the plain of the centre of the island.

The eastern region of Límnos is lower and flatter. The hills are rounded, with flattened summits, and, except in the south, rarely rise above 300 ft. East of the town of Moúdhros, a line of low volcanic hills stretches out to the sea at Cape Kavallarí. The plains in this part are low and often marshy, and in the north-east is the large salt marsh of Alíki which dries out in summer.

In the centre of the island is the plain of Moúdhros. It is flat, marshy near the coast and intersected by river courses.

There are no large streams in the island, and all the watercourses dry up in summer. Stream courses in the west are rocky torrent beds, often winding through deep and precipitous ravines. In the plains of the centre and east, the streams have cut vertical-sided, narrow courses through the soft sedimentaries, but towards the sea they often lose themselves in the sand. These plains have an arid appearance, but water is not really scarce. The water table lies near the surface, and each village has several shallow wells.

COASTS AND PORTS

The coast of Límnos is more irregular and indented than that of any other island in the group. It is fringed, particularly on the east, by shoals and reefs, which make navigation difficult. At the same time, the deep bays provide good anchorages, and make Límnos the most frequented and important of the Thracian islands.

Moúdhros Bay and Harbour

Moúdhros harbour is the most important in the islands and is one of the best anchorages in the Mediterranean (Plate 130). The bay and harbour are divisible into three parts :

(i) The entrance to Moúdhros Bay is between the lofty headlands formed by Mount Fakós on the west and Cape Ayía Iríni on the east. It is 3 miles wide from Kómbi Point to Cape Skio, and trends in a north-westerly direction for 4 miles. The bay is deep, and provides a safe anchorage at most times of the year.

(ii) The second division lies within the headlands of Cape Sagrádha and Limní Point. The bays shallows, and assumes a more northerly direction. Opening to the west is Ayía Paraskeví (Vourlídhia) Bay, to the west of the point of the same name ; this bay provides a safe anchorage. To the north, Moúdhros Bay is obstructed by Álogo island and Pondikonísia (Black Rocks). Passages on each side of these islands give access to the inner harbour of Moúdhros, the third division of this gulf. The East Pass, between Pondikonísia and Sagrádha Point, has a narrow deep channel, but the presence of shoals make it dangerous. The Middle Pass, between Pondikonísia and Álogo, is used more frequently. It is shallow and is obstructed by a bar which links the southern end of Álogo island with the mainland to the west.

(iii) The inner harbour, the third division, lies within the headlands of Cape Pávlos and Kaloyeráki Point, and is a rounded stretch of water 3 miles from east to west and 2½ from north to south, with the long narrow creek of Blenheim Cove opening to the west. On the south-west are the two small islands of Áyios Nikólaos and Tourkó ; the latter is linked to the mainland by a causeway. Ispathó island, a little to the north of Cape Pávlos, is also joined to the land by a causeway. There are over 10 fm. at the entrance to the inner harbour and although depths decrease northwards there are over 4 fm. in most of the harbour.

In 1915 Moúdhros harbour became the base for the Allied fleet operating in the Aegean and off Gallipoli. Hospitals and landing stages were built, and the faint signs of prosperity around the harbour date from this time.

The town of Moúdhros lies to the east and south-east of Cape Pávlos. The port facilities at Moúdhros are the best in the Thracian islands. There were formerly six piers on the eastern shore of the bay and seven on the west, but all except four of these have become ruined, or have been destroyed by the sea. The French pier, which has been partially rebuilt, is 400 ft. long and stone-faced. It is the chief landing place in the harbour. The Australian pier to the north is stone built and 245 ft. long, but has only 2–3 ft. of water alongside. The Town pier is also stone built, 100 ft. long and 15 ft. wide, with a depth of 3–4 ft. of water. No precise information is available about the dock facilities, but they appear to be very small. No shipping of importance uses the harbour. A motor road links the port with Kástron, the chief town of the island, and also with the extreme north-east of the island.

The West and North Coasts

To the west of Moúdhros Bay is the anchorage of Kondiá Bay. The west coast of Límnos is rocky and backed by high cliffs, but towards the south is the small circular bay of Platí which is used by local craft. The north coast, except for the inlet of Pourniá Bay, is equally rugged and inhospitable. Pourniá Bay somewhat resembles Moúdhros Bay in being divided by a headland and submarine bar into an outer bay and an inner harbour. It is exposed to northerly and north-easterly winds, which blow for considerable periods of the year.

The East Coast

The eastern coast of Límnos is, by contrast, flatter. Headlands are formed by hill ridges, but between them are sandy beaches. The largest of these is backed by the salt marsh of Alíki.

HISTORICAL OUTLINE

The chief importance of Límnos in antiquity lay, and still lies, in its possession of good harbours so situated as to command the main sea-routes of the northern Aegean. The chief of these routes is that to the Dardanelles, and the facts which underlie the legends concerning the connexion of the Argonauts and Límnos are no doubt essentially the same as those which today make Moúdhros Bay a point of strategic importance. The possession also of an almost impregnable fortress commanding the then most useful harbour (Kástron) was another circumstance of importance, and it was these two facts which underlay the evil reputation for violence and bloody deeds which clung to the island in ancient days. The island was of first-class importance to Athens for its Black Sea corn trade, and was held in succession by each of the powers—Persian, Macedonian, Roman—which struggled for supremacy in the Aegean. The island became Christian in the fourth century, and the bishop of Límnos who appeared at the Council of Nicaea (A.D. 325) was the predecessor of a whole line of Greek Orthodox dignitaries which has continued, apparently without interruption, down to the present day.

Along with the other islands of the northern Aegean, Límnos passed (about 1355) into the hands of the Gattilusio family (see p. 372), and in 1478 was taken by the Turks. It remained in the possession of the Turks until 1655, when it was conquered by the Venetians. The latter, however, held it for only a year, abandoning it after a three months' siege of the capital, conducted by the Turkish vizier Kiuprili. In 1770, the fortress was again subjected to a siege, this time by the Russian fleet under Count Orloff, who after two months, on the arrival of Turkish reinforcements, abandoned the attempt. Finally, in 1905, the port and fortress of Kástron were occupied, along with that of Mitilíni, by an international force as a means of persuading the Sultan to recognize financial control in Macedonia.

Turkish rule in Límnos seems to have been marked by nothing particularly untoward. A small garrison, besides the administrative officials, was stationed at Kástron, and the fortress, obsolete since the nineteenth century, was jealously guarded. The Turks revived the Roman use of Límnos as a place of banishment, and numerous broken viziers were resident at Kástron, in modern times.

In the First Balkan war (1912–13) Límnos, along with most of the other neighbouring islands, was seized by the Greeks, and their tenure was sanctioned by the Great Powers in their Note presented at Athens in 1914. During the war of 1914–18, it was used as a British naval base.

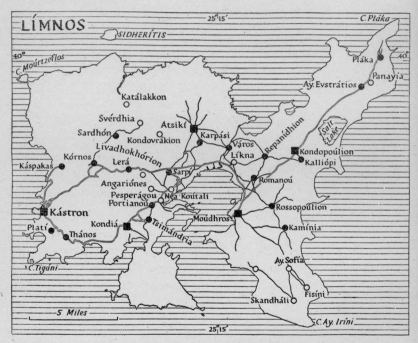

Fig. 84. Settlements and communications of Límnos

Based on the 1 : 50,000 Aegean Islands, Limnos, M.D.R. 611 (2 sheets) (1944) and *Population de la Grèce d'après le Recensement du 15–16 Mai, 1928*, deuxième édition (Athènes, 1935).

For key to symbols of settlements and roads, see Fig. 77.

POPULATION AND SETTLEMENT

Límnos is very much more densely peopled than the other islands in the Thracian group. In 1913 there were said to be nearly 23,000 inhabitants, of whom at least 2,000—probably nearer 3,000—were Moslems. The latter were removed to Turkey under the exchange of population of 1921–8, and Greek refugees were settled in their place. The population has been rising steadily, and in 1928 reached 23,611. This population lives in the chief town, Kástron, and in some 40 villages, many of which are very small.

Kástron (3,726) lies across the neck of a small but high peninsula, which is crowned by the ruins of a castle. The town, of small two-storied houses, lies on lower land to the east. The small bays north and south of the headland afford anchorages, but there are no harbour works. Much of the trade of Límnos is concentrated here. Motor roads run to Kondiá and Moúdhros, and to Káspakas (Fig. 84).

The villages of Límnos are, on the whole, poor and miserable. Some contain large houses, but most consist only of poor dwellings and uneven streets. Their rough appearance is due in part to the lack of good building stone in the island. Windmills are a feature of the villages and are squat, round and whitewashed. They either line the approach to the village or crown the ridges and heights behind. The most important town, after Kástron, is Moúdhros (1,795).

AGRICULTURE

Pastoral and agricultural pursuits are practically the only occupations. In proportion to its size, Límnos probably has more level and cultivable land than any other Aegean island, but the absence of forests and the consequent exposure to wind, together with the heat and lack of water for irrigation, affect agriculture adversely. The chief cultivated areas are the plain to the north of Moúdhros harbour, and eastwards towards Romanoú ; that at the head of Kondiá Bay ; the plains of Kástron and Thános in the south-west ; and the plain of Fisíni in the south-east. Elsewhere, there are small cultivated areas in the valleys of the interior, but much of the low ground is used only as pasture and is often marshy in winter.

The soil is light, thin and often sandy, and dries out quickly. The bulk of the cultivated land is under grain, chiefly barley but some wheat is grown, either alone or mixed with the barley. Vines are important in the valleys of the south of the island, but olive trees are almost completely lacking. Sesame is cultivated for its oil, which helps to make up for the lack of olive oil. Tobacco and a dwarf variety of cotton are crops of minor importance. Apricot almond, cherry and other fruits are occasionally grown in gardens, but the total fruit production is insignificant.

Pastoral pursuits are important and are dominant in the northern half of the island. There are large flocks of sheep, besides considerable numbers of goats. Bee-keeping, silkworm rearing and fishing are minor industries.

The exports of the island are almost wholly of agricultural produce, and consist of barley, wool, cheese, live-stock (particularly lambs),

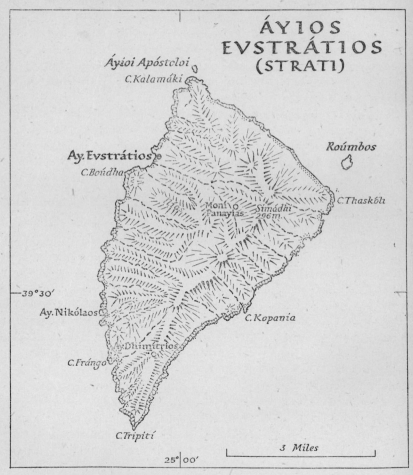

Fig. 85.   Áyios Evstrátios (Strati)

Based on the 1 : 50,000 Aegean Islands, M.D.R. 611 (1943) and British Admiralty Chart 1891 (1936).

For key and symbols of settlements and roads, see Fig. 77.

wine, spirits and tobacco. Olive oil, however, is imported, together with foodstuffs of tropical origin and manufactured goods.

ÁYIOS EVSTRÁTIOS (STRATI)

This island lies about 18 miles south-south-west of Límnos. It is a lonely rock in the open sea, almost at the centre of the northern Aegean. It lies within the 100 fathoms line which bounds Imroz and Límnos, and appears to be a part of the southern border of the North Aegean Basin. The island has an area of $17\frac{1}{2}$ sq. miles. The west coast, which is about 7 miles long, is slightly convex and has several small open bights and coves, with blunt promontories between them. The coasts are everywhere high, precipitous and forbidding. The island is occupied by a range of hills, which rise from the north corner in a series of irregular heights, reaching 973 ft. near the eastern angle of the island, Cape Thaskóli. The chain lies close to the east coast and sends out ridges towards the west. The island appears, like Límnos, to consist of a mass of younger sedimentary rocks, intruded by igneous masses which constitute the greater heights.

The population of the island is about 2,000, of whom 1,570 live in the only village of any size, Áyios Evstrátios, on a small sandy-shored bay on the north-west coast. This serves as the port of the island, and is visited infrequently by steamers and caïques from Límnos, Mitilíni and the mainland. In Turkish days, it was a subdivision of the *sanjak* of Límnos.

Fruit and vegetables are grown in the valleys. Pulse is a relatively important crop, but the Valona oak is the chief source of wealth in the island and considerable quantities of tanning bark are exported.

BIBLIOGRAPHICAL NOTE

1. Useful accounts of Thasos are H. de Coincy, ' L'île de Thasos ', *La Géographie*, vol. 38, pp. 405–26 (Paris, 1922), and A. Bon, ' L'île de Thasos : Etude de Géographie comparée ancienne et moderne ', *Annales de Géographie*, vol. 41, pp. 269–86 (Paris, 1932). Accounts of the geology of the island are given in L. de Launay, ' Description géologiques des Isles de Mételin et de Thasos ', *Nouvelles Archives des Mission Scientifiques et Litteraires, Paris*, vol. 1, pp. 127–75 *logique*, vol. 11, pp. 242–53 (Paris, 1888), and ' Etudes Géologiques sur la mer Egée ', *Annales des Mines*, vol. 13, pp. 157–316 (1898). A. Conze, *Reise auf den Inseln des Thrakischen Meeres* (Hanover, 1860) contains much material of general interest.

2. Samothráki is described by L. de Launay, *op. cit.*, and more fully by D.

Jaranoff, ' L'île de Samothrace : Esquisse géographique ', *Bulletin de la Société Bulgare de Geographie*, vol. 6, pp. 61–84 (Sofia, 1939). The article is in Bulgarian, with a summary in French. There is a scarcity of material on Límnos, though it is described by Conze. See also H. F. Tozer, *The Islands of the Aegean* (Oxford, 1890) and *Mediterranean Pilot*, vol. 4, 7th edition (London, 1941).

3. The most useful topographical maps which cover all the Thracian Islands are the 1 : 250,000 The Balkans G.S.G.S. Series 4088 (see vol. I, p. 405). Límnos and Áyios Evstrátios and covered also by the 1 : 50,000 Aegean Islands, M.D.R. 611 (see p. 487).

Plate 129.   The town of Kástron in Límnos
The view is westward and shows the town at the foot of the high peninsula crowned
by the ruined castle.

Plate 130.   Moúdhros bay and harbour
The view is westward, over the town, to the hills of the south-west of the island.

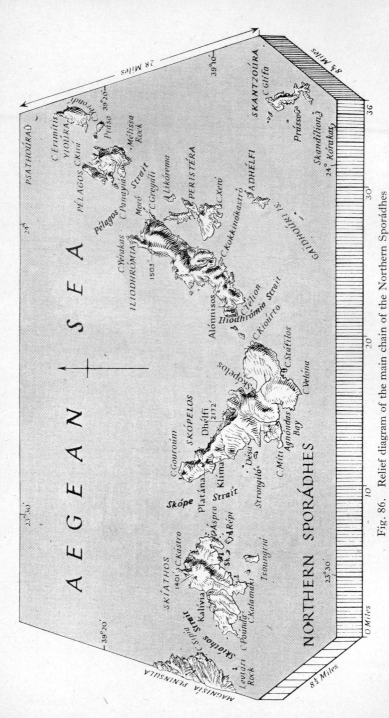

Fig. 86. Relief diagram of the main chain of the Northern Sporádhes

Based on the 1 : 100,000 Greece, M.D.R. 610/8584 (1943) and British Admiralty Chart 2072 (1937).

Chapter XI

THE NORTHERN SPORÁDHES

General Features : Skíathos : Skópelos : Iliodhrómia : Pélagos : Yioúra : Psathoúra : Pipéri : Skíros : Bibliographical Note

GENERAL FEATURES

The Northern Sporádhes consist of an arc of about six small islands, which continue the direction of the Magnisía peninsula of Thessalía, together with various outlying islets and the larger island of Skíros. The total area of the group is some 200 sq. miles. Most of the islands lie on a submarine ridge, which descends steeply on the north to the North Aegean Basin. The basal rock of the islands is schist, but this outcrops over only a relatively small area (Fig. 87). Above it, and forming the surface of most of the group, is massive, partly crystalline, limestone. There are also traces of volcanic rocks and serpentine. Many of the islands are high and rugged, with steep coasts, especially on the north and north-west. Although several of the islands reach considerable heights, the summits are usually rounded and are surrounded by hilly plateaux.

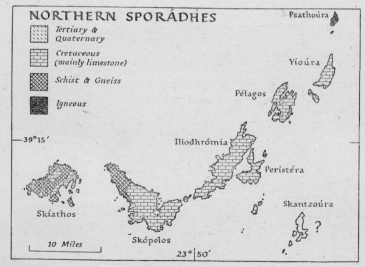

Fig. 87. The geology of the main chain of the Northern Sporádhes
Based on the 1 : 300,000 *Yenikós geologikos Khártis tis Elládhos*, Sheet, Evvoia (1924).

The climate of the Northern Sporádhes approximates to that of the mainland of central Greece, but is more equable. The winters are cooler than those of the Kikládhes and the rainfall is rather smaller, but the summer droughts is less pronounced. The islands are exposed to the cooling northerly and north-easterly winds in summer and to south-easterly winds in winter.

The Northern Sporádhes have retained a good vegetation cover, and their green appearance offers a pleasing contrast to the Kikládhes. The commonest trees are the Aleppo pine, with planes in the warm valleys and evergreen oaks. The forest cover has, however, been destroyed over large areas to provide wood for ship-building and charcoal burning, but a vigorous scrub growth has quickly replaced it, and the islands have not become barren and brown.

The total population of the group in 1928 was 13,521, of whom about 12,516 lived in the three larger islands of Skíathos, Skópelos and Skíros. Maritime interests are more conspicuous amongst the inhabitants of the Sporádhes than amongst those of the Kikládhes, and many go to sea. The building of trading vessels was formerly an important occupation, and fishing is pursued on a considerable scale. Agricultural products are, in general, similar to those of the Kikládhes, but agriculture is not so intensive. Tillage is relatively insignificant, and pastoral activities, especially cattle rearing, assume greater importance. The cultivated areas are mainly on the lower ground and are generally found on schist. The limestone heights are devoted to rearing cattle and especially goats. Only in Skópelos, Skíathos and Skíros is agriculture important.

Skíros alone has mineral resources of any importance. It has always been known for its marble, and chrome-iron has been worked from time to time. Manganiferous and copper ores are said to occur, and there are desposits of gypsum, china clay and lignite, none of which, however, is of more than local importance.

The importance of the Northern Sporádhes to Greece has always been out of proportion to their intrinsic economic value. In ancient times, when shippping was coastwise and the enemies of Greece lay in the north and east, these islands were of the highest strategic importance. The Magnisía peninsula and the north-east coasts of Thessalía and Évvoia generally are steep, exposed, harbourless and inhospitable. The Northern Sporádhes possessed harbours, water, wine and olives and, above all, timber. Skíathos especially, with its harbour, covers the entrance to the Trikéri channel and the north-eastern approaches to Greece. From their position and resources, therefore, these islands were capable of being either a northern maritime bulwark of Greece, or, conversely, in the hands of an enemy, a serious menace. To a naval power such as Athens, but even more to a continental invader like Alexander or Xerxes, their possession was the prerequisite of liberty or conquest. Skíathos served as the naval outpost of the Greeks against the hordes of Xerxes, and again in the Roman era it was the naval outpost of Mithridates against the Romans.

From the earliest times also these islands were the home of pirates. In their inaccessible and stormy seclusion and in their numerous harbours, the islanders found safe retreats, and piracy was not stamped out here till late in the nineteenth century.

In ancient times the resources (mineral and agricultural) of the islands seem to have been greater or relatively more important. For this reason also they were a continual bone of contention, and their possession was disputed by successive powers, Athenian, Macedonian, Roman. In the Middle Ages, Skíros was occupied by a member of the Ghisi family, and all the islands were held by the Venetians, Byzantine Greeks, and Turks in succession. They lay, however, aside from the main movements of history and were little troubled by their owners. Their chief energies were centred in piracy, and their robber wealth was itself often the prey of others. Their interests have always been largely maritime, and, though more naturally attached to Thessalía, they were incorporated in 1832 in the new kingdom of Greece. Their importance has diminished with the advent of steam ships, with the opening up of larger sources of supply (e.g., of chrome ores), and with the exhaustion of their timber. On the other hand, their agricultural products and cattle have come more to the fore, and their ships and sailors continue famous. As late as 1897, Skíathos served as a naval base for the whole of the Greek fleet in the war with Turkey ; and even today their position commanding the northern trade-routes, together with their harbours, give them considerable strategic importance.

SKÍATHOS

Geology and Relief

Skíathos covers an area of about 17 sq. miles and is separated from the Magnisía peninsula of Thessalía by a channel, about 2 miles wide. The dominating feature of the island is the large, dome-shaped mountain mass, which occupies its north-eastern half. It forms an undulating plateau of limestone, and its highest point,

Mount Stavrós (1,400 ft.), rises only slightly above its surroundings. The sides of the plateau slope gently at the higher levels, but lower down they fall more steeply and are furrowed on all sides by deep, well-watered ravines. To the north and north-west of the plateau a hilly terrace overlooks the sea, and to the east-south-east there is low hill-country. Towards the south, the round domed mass is continued by a broad ridge which narrows and sinks in height until it terminates in Cape Kalamáki. A deep depression, formed by two valleys running north and south to the coast, separates the uplands of Stavrós from lower hill-country to the west. Finally a

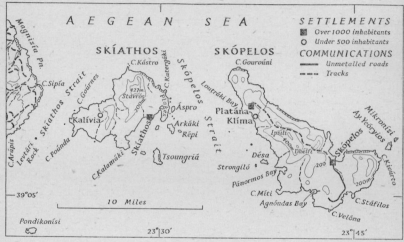

Fig. 88.   Relief, drainage, settlements and communications of
Skíathos and Skópelos

Based on the 1 : 100,000 Greece, M.D.R. 610/8584 and 9173 (1943) and British Admiralty Chart 2072 (1937).
The contours are at intervals of 200 metres (656 ft.).

ridge crosses the eastern extremity of the island, and between it and the Stavrós uplands is a small area of lowland lying north of Skíathos harbour.

The lowland of the western part of the island is mainly developed on gneiss. The rest of the island consists of marble and schist, on which has been laid down a great thickness of limestone. The features of Skíathos are soft and rounded, and inland communication is not difficult.

Coasts and Ports

The south coast of Skíathos, between Cape Poúnda and Cape Kalamáki, is indented by three small bays lying between the parallel

Plate 131.   The town of Skíathos, from the west

Plate 132.   The harbour of Skíathos

Plate 133. The island of Skópelos from the north-east

Plate 134. The town and harbour of Skópelos

Plate 135. The island of Skíros, from the east
In the foreground is the town of Skíros.

[*Facing page* 397

ridges of this part of the island. Farther east is a shallow and rather irregular bay, at the northern end of which a promontory encloses a deep, narrow inlet which serves as the harbour of Skíathos. A small islet protects the entrance to the harbour, and outside, in the bay, are the islets of Práso, Tsoungriá, Mikro Tsoungriá, Repi, Arkáki and Marangós, so that the harbour is safe from all winds. Off the eastern shore of the Plakes peninsula is the island of Áspro. The north-east coast, to Cape Kástro, the northerly extreme of the island, is steep and straight. The north-west coast is somewhat embayed but rough and exposed, and offers no anchorage.

Population and Settlement

On account of the dangers of piracy the medieval capital, Kástro, was located in an inaccessible position in the northern corner of the island. Here a small peninsula, girt with steep cliffs, juts into the sea. There are landing places for small boats on each side, but the narrow neck is cleft by a chasm. The ancient town is now, however, a wilderness of ruined houses and gardens. The modern capital, Skíathos, was established on the south coast in 1829. The town is well built and roomy and is backed by wooded hills. Except for the few shepherds who inhabit the offlying islands, and the dwellers in monasteries on the slopes on the eastern hills, the total population of 3,213 is largely confined to the capital.

Agriculture and Fishing

The chief area of cultivated land lies in the east and north-east, around the town of Skíathos. The low hills are covered with olive groves, and in the valleys there are vineyards and fruit gardens ; grain is also grown. The valleys of the western hill-country are only partly utilized. The uplands are well wooded and much is covered with a dense scrub of Kermes oak. The forests have been a source of wealth throughout its history and provided timber for shipbuilding. The men of Skíathos have long had a reputation for seamanship.

SKÓPELOS

Geology and Relief

Skópelos is the largest of the main chain of islands and has an area of 37 sq. miles. The western part of the island is composed of schists similar to those of Skíathos, but the centre and east are formed of limestone which overlies the schists (Fig. 87).

A high ridge runs from the north-western extremity of the island, Cape Gouroúni, to Skópelos Bay. It rises to a height of 1,155 ft. north of Platána and then gradually to its highest points, Mount Ipsilí (2,230 ft.) and Mount Dhélfi (2,172 ft.). These summits are featureless domes, but the ridge falls steeply to the sea on the north-east and has precipitous upper slopes towards the south-west. It is eroded on all sides by small streams. Beyond Skópelos Bay, a round hill mass continues the ridge until it falls in great cliffs to the strait between Skópelos and Iliodhrómia. The southern part of the island is composed of rolling hill country, and its greatest heights are not above 1,000 ft.

The chief plain of the island lies at the head of Skópelos Bay. It is a large, semi-circular depression, well watered and fed by numerous side streams. There are smaller plains at the heads of bays of the south-west and south-east coast. Streams and springs are numerous, and water is plentiful.

Coast and Ports

Except for Skópelos Bay, the north-eastern coast is straight, steep and harbourless from Cape Gouroúni in the north-west to Cape Kioúrto in the east. Skópelos Bay is a rectangular opening, 3½ miles wide and ½ mile deep, on which lies the chief town and port of the island. On the south-east coast, and protected by Cape Stáfilos, is the bay of the same name, which also affords a small anchorage ; an unmetalled road connects this bay with the town of Skópelos. On the south coast of the island, between Capes Velóna and Míti, is Agnóndas Bay, at the head of which is a cove where small vessels can anchor. North of Cape Míti is Pánormos Bay, which is narrow and sheltered, but it is too deep for an anchorage. Several islets and rocks—Paximádha, Plevró, Kasídha, Désa and Strongiló—lie off this rather rugged western coast.

Population and Settlement

Most of the population of Skópelos lives in the chief town and in two small villages in the north of the island. The town of Skópelos (4,075) stands on a hill on the western side of its harbour (Plate 134). It crowds up the steep hillside, but extends more openly towards the plain on the west. The houses are high and compactly built ; the streets are crooked and narrow. In the north are the two villages of Platána or Glóssa (1,414) and Klíma (497). They stand on high hillsides abounding in springs and overlooking the sea, and are the centres of a prosperous agricultural district. There are several monasteries and these, with a few small farming and herding settlements, contain the only other population.

Agriculture

The original forest cover has been destroyed, partly for ship-building. Its place has been largely taken either by dense scrub or by pasture. The hills of the south of the island, however, are still covered with forests of pine although the central ridge is mainly covered with scrub. The two more important agricultural tracts correspond with the areas of schist and are separated by the central limestone area. One covers the valleys and hillsides around the town of Skópelos ; the other is in the hilly, north-western part of the island. Fruit gardens often cover the valley floors, where not only typical ' Mediterranean ' fruits but also more temperate varieties, such as plums, pears and cherries, are grown. Vines cover the lower hillsides, and olive groves are found higher up. The north-western part of the island is particularly well-known for its fruit. Some tobacco is produced, but relatively little grain.

ILIODHRÓMIA

Geology and Relief

Iliodhrómia is a narrow island, 13 miles in length from north-east to south-west, and 24 sq. miles in area. The island is built of a mass of whitish limestone ; its relief consists of a single ridge which falls precipitously to the north-west coast. The eastern part of the ridge is high, reaching 1,590 and 1,508 ft. respectively in its two highest peaks. The mountains are scored by small ravines, but there are no valleys of any size and water is scarce. Farther south-west the island narrows, and the ridge becomes lower ; here are several isolated, rounded hills, one of which, Mount Kalavalos, lies at the extreme westerly point of the island and forms high cliffs.

Coasts and Ports

The north-west coast is rugged and high between Cape Yérakas and the islet of Manolás. South of the cape facing this islet are two small bays, which are exposed and provide only poor anchorages. Farther south the coast is still rough but somewhat lower, although the western side of Cape Télion is a line of cliffs. Much of the south-east coast is straight and rises steeply inland. The bays of

Patatíri, Miliá, and Tzórtzi, in the south-east serve as anchorages.
On the north-east coast behind Cape Yérakas is Firákon Bay, which
can shelter craft from westerly winds. But there are no good
harbours, and the bays offer only limited accommodation.

Fig. 89.   Relief, drainage, settlements and communications of Iliodhrómia,
Peristéra, Pélagos and Yioúra

Based on the 1 : 100,000 Greece, M.D.R. 610 (1943) and British Admiralty
Chart 2072 (1937).

The contours are at intervals of 200 metres (656 ft.).
For key to symbols of settlements and roads, see Fig. 88.

Population, Settlement and Agriculture

With the exception of a few herdsmen and charcoal burners, the
population of Iliodhrómia lives in the village of Alónnisos (1,005).
This lies on a steep limestone ridge in the south-west of the island.

It overlooks a small harbour, one of the several indentations on this part of the coast, but it is a poor, bleak village. The neighbouring islands are uninhabited, except when visited occasionally by herdsmen.

Most of the cultivation on Iliodhrómia is in the southern part where softer and more recent rocks occur. Pine forests still cover much of the north of the island, but over a larger area the trees have been destroyed and scrub has replaced them. Charcoal and timber have been exported from the tiny harbour of Áyios Dhimítrios, on the east coast, opposite Peristéra. Agriculture, especially the rearing of animals, is the chief occupation.

Adjacent Islands

Mikró and *Áyios Yeóryios* are two small islands in the strait between Iliodhrómia and Skópelos. *Mánolas* island lies off the north-west coast. Near the opposite coast is the much larger island of *Peristéra*, consisting of a waterless, featureless, limestone mass which reaches over 800 ft. It is covered with maquis, and is deserted except by a few herdsmen. Its northern peninsula approaches to within half a mile of Iliodhrómia, and with the latter island, helps to form the almost landlocked Vasilikó Bay. The water is deep, but, where it pentrates between the northern and south portions of Peristéra, is an inner cove where the water is shallower.

Likoréma, to the north-east of Peristéra, is a small schistose islet. *Adhélfi* and *Adhelfópoulo*, two small islands with a number of rocks, lie to the south. All consist of bare limestone and are uninhabited. South-east of these is the *Skantzoúra* group, composed of a large islet and a number of rocks. The main islet is 3 miles long and lies north-south ; its shores are rugged and devoid of harbours. It contains a small area of low, flat land, but the inmates of its monastery are the only inhabitants.

PÉLAGOS

The small island of Pélagos lies 4 miles north-east of Iliodhrómia and covers an area of $9\frac{1}{2}$ sq. miles. It is almost oblong in shape, but is penetrated on the north-east and south-west by deep and sheltered inlets. The greater part of the island consists of limestone, but in the south-east schist and gneiss appear. The relief of the island consists of two parallel ridges, along the north-west and south-east coasts respectively, separated by a central lowland extending from the bay of Planíti to Panayía Bay. The north-west ridge reaches the height of 1,247 ft. ; Mount Nissatika (1,312 ft.) the highest point in the island, lies at the centre of the eastern range (Fig. 89). Both coastal ranges fall steeply to the sea, and the east and west coasts are steep and cliff-bound. In the middle of the west coast, however, is a small funnel-shaped inlet, which opens on to the central plain of the island. Opposite this, on the east coast, is a small rounded harbour. A spur from the eastern hill range curves to the west, and encloses on the south the harbour of Panayía Bay. The entrance to this bay is protected by Pelérissa island, but the water is deep and not well suited for anchorage.

At the northern end of the central lowland is the bay of Planíti. This is entered from the north-north-east by a narrow channel about $\frac{1}{3}$ mile long, 4 fm. deep, and at one place only 90 yards wide ; it opens within to form two wider arms. Within these is abundant room, in water of 5 to 9 fm., but the entrance is rather difficult for sailing vessels.

The northern part of the central depression is cultivated, but the population is very small and forms an isolated and self-supporting community dependent on the monastery of Panayía.

YIOÚRA

Yioúra has an area of 6 sq. miles and is the last of the group of limestone islands. It is a small, sharply pointed island, wholly occupied by a single, jagged limestone ridge which runs from end to end of the island and reaches a height of some 1,650 ft. It falls away to the sea in rugged and inaccessible cliffs. Several ravines furrow the western flanks, and there is a tiny bay at the southern end, but otherwise there is hardly any landing place. The island is covered with phrygana scrub and is inhabited by wild goats. Its only visitors are herdsmen and charcoal burners.

To the south are three small, uninhabited limestone rocks of Práso, Koumbí and Pappoús.

PSATHOÚRA

Psathoúra, the most northerly of the islands, is flat and low and, unlike the rest of the group, consists of igneous rock (Fig. 87). It is frequented by fishermen, but does not appear to have a settled agricultural population.

PIPÉRI

Pipéri is an oval limestone mass, lying east of Yioúra. It is girt by steep cliffs and rises to a single, flat-topped ridge. The island is covered with pine forest. It has no harbours even for a boat, is difficult of access, and is uninhabited.

SKÍROS

Geology and Relief

The island of Skíros lies some 30 miles from the arc of the Northern Sporádhes, and is nearer northern Évvoia, with which, rather than with the Sporádhes, are its closest connections. It has an area of 78 sq. miles, and is thus by far the largest island in this group. It is long and narrow and is divided into two roughly equal portions by a low lying depression, about 2 miles broad, between Akhíli Bay on the north-east coast and the Gulf of Kalamítsa on the south-west. Most of the northern part of the island consists of limestone, overlying the schist, which is often revealed in the deeper valleys. The north-eastern hilly ridge consists of Tertiary sedimentaries (Fig. 13).

The north-western part of Skíros is a confused mass of hills, plateaux and valleys. The hills reach heights of over 1,000 ft. and have rounded caps with relatively easy passes between them. The plateau surfaces slope gently downwards towards the west coast, where they terminate in a short but abrupt ridge, while on the north-east they are bounded by a steep and narrow coastal range. There are numerous small glens in this northern part of the island, but only two lowland area of importance : (i) opening on to the coast near the town of Skíros, is the Áyios Dhimítrios valley which has a perennial stream, and, with the adjoining lowlands along the coast, is the largest area of lowland in the island ; and (ii) a semi-circular depression, known as Káto Kámbos, in the extreme north of the island ; it is connected with the Áyios Dhimítrios valley by a long, groove-like depression that runs north-east to south-west between the north-east coastal range and the plateau of the interior.

The central depression of the island is formed by two low and narrow valleys, each drained both to the north-east and south-west coasts. The more southerly of these valleys stretches between Áragma and Akhíli bays. It is straight, about 2 miles long, and from $\frac{1}{4}$ to $\frac{1}{2}$ mile wide. It is largely covered with wind-blown sand. The steep limestone-capped ridge of Kladhí (1,673 ft.) separates this valley from the second valley which is formed by two streams that descend from the northern hills and bend north-east and south-west respectively.   Together they form a single narrow and crooked glen with outlets in Akhíli Bay on the north-east and Linariá Bay on the south.

Fig. 90.   Relief, drainage, settlements and communications of Skíros
Based on a map by A. Philippson in *Petermanns Mitteilungen, Ergänzungsheft* 134 (Gotha, 1901) and on British Admiralty Chart 2048 (1939).
For key to symbols of settlements and roads, see Fig. 88.

The southern part of the island consists of a compact, oval, limestone mass, with flattened top and convex slopes.   On three sides the slopes are steep, but towards the south-west they spread out in low hilly spurs, one of which forms the large south-western promontory of the island. Erosion of the limestone of the plateau has formed a series of large, and often quite enclosed, hollows. The highest part, Mount Kókhilas, rises to 2,670 ft. Water courses have cut deep ravines in the lower slopes of the hills.

The water supply of Skíros is not good ; the northern half of the island is better supplied than the south and has a few good springs in the north-west, where the junction of the schists and limestones is laid bare on the steep slopes. The whole southern portion is arid, and the inhabitants rely on rain water caught in cisterns.

Coasts and Ports

The north-east coast of Skíros is formed of two stretches of straight exposed and rockbound coast, separated by a shorter stretch of curving, flat coast. The first lies between Cape Kártsino, the northern extremity of the island, and Cape Pouriá, where the coast bends away to the south. In the southern stretch of coast is the small, double bay of Akhíli, where there is a roadstead. South-east of Akhíli Bay the coast again becomes high and inaccessible.

The south-west coast, in marked contrast to the north-east coast, is irregular, deeply indented by bays, and fringed by islands. About 2½ miles west of Cape Lithári is Rénes Bay, a small cove ringed with hills. To the west the entrance to Trís Boúkes Bay is protected by Sarakinó and Platí islands ; this bay affords excellent shelter, but has no harbour works. A blunt ended promontory which ends in capes Mármara and Apoklístria, separates Tris Boúkes Bay from the Gulf of Kalamítsa. The latter is deep, semicircular in shape, and is protected by the island of Valáxa. A group of rocks lie between Valáxa and Cape Apoklístria. At the head of the gulf is Áragma Bay, with a white sandy beach and a good anchorage. Separated from it to the north-west by the ridge of Kladhí is the smaller bay of Linariá, where there is an anchorage and a small pier.

Between the Gulf of Kalamítsa and Cape Óros, the most westerly point of the island, are three small bays, Pévko, Áyios Fokás and Óros. The first has a small pier, where vessels tie up when loading marble.

From Cape Óros to Cape Kártsino are 7 miles of irregular coast, interrupted only by Kalógria Bay.

Population and Settlement

The population of Skíros is small in relation to the size of the island. Most of the 3,179 inhabitants live in the town of Skíros.

The town lies close to the sea on the northern slope of a steep, flat-topped hill which stands in the middle of the flat plain of the Áyios Dhimítrios river. The houses are flat-roofed and usually of two storeys ; the upper storey is usually constructed of wood. There is no harbour, but small boats can be drawn up on the sandy beach. Linariá, on the northern shore of the Gulf of Kalamítsa, is the chief port and has a population of 199. There are also a number of small settlements in the productive Káto Kámbos district in the north. Shepherds' huts and miners' settlements are found on the hills of the interior, but much of the hilly part of the island, particularly the southern half, is uninhabited.

Agriculture and Fishing

The hills of the northern half of the island have woods of Aleppo pine (*Pinus halepensis*) while the valleys have oleanders, evergreen oaks and maquis scrub. The southern half is less wooded, and is mainly covered with phrygana scrub. Skíros has a desolate and inhospitable appearance, and it is, relatively, one of the least productive of the Aegean islands. Where the limestone has been eroded and the schists are exposed, conditions are much better. For this reason the Áyios Dhimítrios valley is thus the most productive part of the island. The Áragma valley is largely covered with sand, but has some cornfields, and pasture. Káto Kámbos is devoted to cattle, sheep and other livestock. Fruit, vines and grain are grown in the narrow depression to the south-east. There is very little cultivation in the southern half of the island, and cattle rearing is of much greater importance. Fishing is of no importance and it is reported that the islanders have hardly any boats.

Mining

Skíros is relatively rich in minerals, though they have been little worked. The most important product economically has been marble. This has been worked behind Rénes Bay in the south, and Pévko Bay in the west, and from both there has been a small export. A medium-grade iron ore, comparatively rich in chrome, has also been worked in the north-west. There are deposits of lignite, gypsum, ochre and potting clay, which are said to be used by the islanders.

BIBLIOGRAPHICAL NOTE

1. The fullest accounts of the Northern Sporádhes are given in the N.I.D. *Handbook of Greece*, vol. 2, part 1, pp. 176–219 (London, 1919) and in the section on the Magnesian Islands in A. Philippson, ' Beiträge zur Kenntnis der griechischen Inselwelt ', *Petermanns Mitteilungen, Ergänzungsheft* 134, pp. 123–142 (Gotha, 1901). Some further details are given in the *Mediterranean Pilot*, vol. 4, chapter 6, 7th edition (London, 1941).

2. The most useful topographical maps of the Northern Sporádhes are the 1 : 100,000 Greece, M.D.R. 610/8584 and 9173 which were compiled and drawn by 524 Pal. Fd. Survey Coy., R.E., in 1943, from British Admiralty Charts, a map by A. Philippson in *Petermanns Mitteilungen, Ergänzungsheft* 134 (Gotha, 1901), the G.S.G.S. Balkans series (see vol. I, pp. 404–5), the 1 : 100,000 *Epitelikós Khártis tis Elládhos* (see vol. I, pp. 400–1) and air photographs. The maps have a kilometre grid, latitude and longitude (from Greenwich and Athens) in margins, contours in brown at 50 metres interval, roads and tracks in red, water in blue.

Chapter XII

THE KIKLÁDHES (CYCLADES)

General Features : The Eparchy of Ándros : The Eparchy of Tínos : The Eparchy of Síros : The Eparchy of Kéa : The Eparchy of Náxos : The Eparchy of Mílos : The Eparchy of Thíra : Bibliographical Note

GENERAL FEATURES

GEOLOGY AND RELIEF

The Kikládhes, or Central Islands, were, as their name suggests, regarded in classical times as a circle of islands around Delos. The group, however, is more irregular than this. It consists of the summits of two submerged ridges which continue the lines of Évvoia and the peninsula of Attikí (Fig. 93). The more northerly of these is an arc which includes Ándros, Tínos, and Míkonos (and continues through Ikaría and Sámos to Anatolia north of the Menderes river). The more southerly arc includes Kéa, Kíthnos, Sérifos, Sífnos, and Folégandros, and then bends abruptly through Síkinos, Íos and Amorgós towards the Turkish mainland. Páros and Náxos, the most massive islands in the group, are contained within the curve of this outer arc. Outside the arc are the volcanic islands of Mílos and Thíra, together with Anáfi and several islets and rocks.

The group as a whole stands on a submarine platform, which is rarely more than 150 fm. deep. A deeper channel separates the platform from Ikaría and the Dodecanese to the east, while to the north is a sharp drop to the greater depths of the Central Aegean Basin. To the south is a similar drop to the Southern Basin, beyond which lies Crete (Fig. 46).

There are about twenty major islands in the Kikládhes, together with a larger number of islets and rocks, most of them uninhabited. Taken together they have a total area of about 1,050 sq. miles. The group has over-all dimensions of 110 miles from north-west to south-east and some 60 miles from north-east to south-west.

The islands are, for the most part, rockbound and barren in appearance, and consist generally of plateaux of undulating surface. They are the eroded fragments of a former upland mass. Such lowlands and coastal plains as may once have existed have been very largely submerged, and only the highest levels remain above the sea. There are thus few alluvial plains, and the valleys are but the upper parts of the original forms. Bays are deep and rugged, but the waves have cut remarkably straight and precipitous coast lines, and in general there is a marked absence of sandy beaches. With one or two exceptions, therefore, the Kikládhes, with their rough, elevated, and even mountainous, interiors, their rocky valleys, their steep, and at times precipitous, coasts, have an inhospitable and inaccessible aspect, which is heightened by their prevailing barrenness and by an atmospheric clearness which reveals every detail. Nevertheless, the deep coves provide sheltered harbours, and at their heads are fertile, if small and sometimes marshy, plains. The water supply, though not abundant, is generally adequate. Streams, however, are seasonal and dry up in summer. Only in Ándros and Náxos are there rivers with a constant flow. The limestone areas are naturally drier than others, but springs are plentiful in regions composed of schist.

CLIMATE

The climate of the Kikládhes is naturally more equable than that of the mainland ; the conditions in individual islands within the group tend, in general, to become more equable with increasing distance from the mainland. Thus, the annual range of temperature at Ándros, close to the southern end of Évvoia, is 28° F. (15·6° C.) ; at Náxos, 80 miles to the south-east, it is only 23° F. (12·7° C.). The absolute maxima and minima of these two stations show a similar difference, the absolute ranges at Ándros, Síros and Náxos being 81°, 76° and 68° F. respectively. There is thus a general absence of strong contrasts in temperature, the only significant exceptions being in the valleys of some of the larger islands, such as Ándros, Náxos and Síros. There the valleys are usually cold in winter and hot and sultry in summer. Frosts are comparatively rare on the lower ground. They occur most frequently in Ándros ; at the Náxos station frost is virtually unknown.

The equability of the climate is to some extent due to the prevailing winds, which in winter blow most frequently from the south-west bringing warmth and rain, while in summer the islands are exposed to north-east gales for long periods at a time. The latter are exceedingly fierce, especially in the mornings and on the heights, where they prevent the growth of vegetation and even the movement of men and animals. They sometimes interrupt

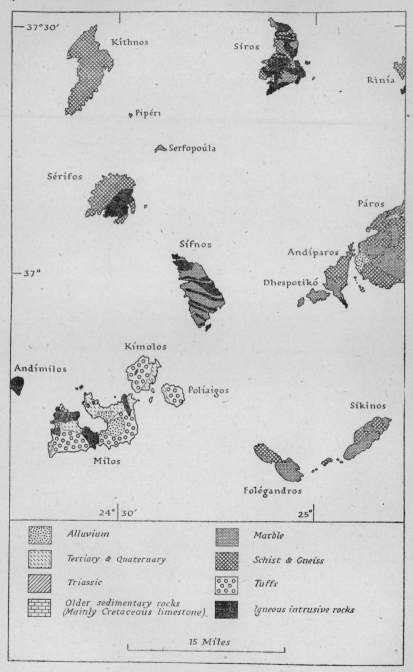

Fig. 91. The geology of the western Kikládhes (Cyclades)
Based on the 1 : 300,000 *Yenikós Geologikos Khártis tis Elládhos*, Sheet, Síros-Mílos.

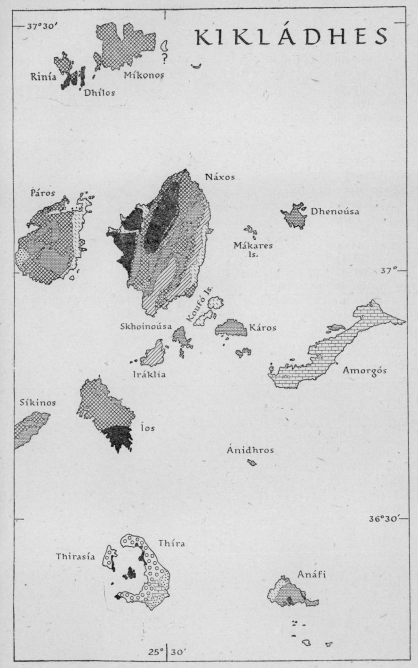

Fig. 92. The geology of the eastern Kikládhes (Cyclades)

Based on the 1 : 300,000 *Yenikós Geologikos Khártis tis Elládhos*, Sheet, Náxos-Amorgós.

communication between the islands for days together and, sweeping down over steep coasts, are a constant source of danger to coast-wise shipping.

Rainfall is concentrated in the winter months. The summers are never rainless, though the fall is slight in July and August. The total rainfall varies, and is much less in the southern, than in the northern, islands of the group. Ándros, the most northerly island, has 25 ins. and Thíra, the most southerly, has only 14 ins. The period of marked rainfall (over $\frac{1}{2}$ in. per month) lasts, in all islands, from October till May. Sleet and snow may fall in winter, but the latter never lies for more than a few days even upon the highest parts of Náxos and Ándros. The likelihood of snow diminishes in the southern islands of Mílos and Thíra. Relative humidity is generally low, ranging in Ándros from 78·7% in December to 58·3% in July. In Síros, it is even lower ; 72·9% in December and 52·4% in July. Thunderstorms are commonest in the winter months, particularly November, when they are accompanied by torrential rain, but they are nowhere as frequent as on the mainland of Greece.

HISTORICAL OUTLINE

The story of the Kikládhes is marked by unusual vicissitudes. This they owe not so much to their intrinsic value as to their insular character and their position—detached from, and yet associated with, the surrounding mainlands. Better known and of greater importance in the classical than in the modern world, they contained in Dhílos (Delos) one of the religious centres of Hellenism. Through a series of hands they fell to the Romans, under whose empire Dhílos again momentarily awoke, this time as a great slave-market and emporium for the Roman north-eastern trade, while other islands (e.g., Yioúra and Amorgós) were used as places of banishment. Lost to view in the Dark Ages—they apparently suffered no Slavonic invasion—the Kikládhes reappeared after the Latin victory over the Byzantine (Greek) Empire which was marked by the fall of Constantinople (A.D. 1204).

In accordance with the licence granted by the Venetian government to their nobility, the Kikládhes were seized by various Venetian and Genoese adventurers, who built up for themselves some twenty more or less independent island duchies and dynasties, the chief of which were those of the Ghisi in the north and the Sanudi in the central Kikládhes (see vol. I, pp. 177–8). These

Average monthly temperature (1900–29) in °F.

	Jan.	Feb.	Mar.	Apr.	May	June	July	Aug.	Sept.	Oct.	Nov.	Dec.	Year
Ándros	51·0	51·3	54·4	60·2	67·0	74·6	79·0	78·8	73·3	66·8	59·8	54·0	64·0
Síros	52·6	53·0	55·5	61·2	67·8	75·4	80·0	79·8	74·4	67·8	61·0	55·5	65·2
Náxos	54·4	54·8	57·1	61·7	67·0	73·0	76·8	77·2	73·4	68·2	62·4	57·4	65·2
Mílos	53·0	52·0	56·0	62·0	67·0	73·0	79·0	79·0	73·0	68·0	61·0	54·0	65·0
Thíra	51·0	51·3	53·8	58·5	64·6	71·5	76·0	76·2	71·5	66·0	59·7	54·4	62·7

Average monthly rainfall (1894–1929) in inches

	Jan.	Feb.	Mar.	Apr.	May	June	July	Aug.	Sept.	Oct.	Nov.	Dec.	Year
Ándros	5·0	4·1	2·7	1·1	0·7	0·4	0·05	0·06	0·5	1·6	3·5	5·3	25·0
Síros	4·0	2·6	1·9	1·0	0·7	0·2	0·03	0·1	0·3	0·6	2·9	3·6	19·1
Náxos	3·1	2·3	1·4	0·9	0·6	0·1	0·02	0·02	0·2	1·1	2·1	3·0	14·9
Mílos	2·9	2·3	1·3	0·5	0·5	0·3	0·0	0·03	0·3	1·1	3·1	3·5	15·7
Thíra	3·0	1·9	1·3	0·8	0·5	0·1	0·01	0·01	0·3	0·9	2·1	3·1	14·0

Average number of rain-days (1894–1929)

	Jan.	Feb.	Mar.	Apr.	May	June	July	Aug.	Sept.	Oct.	Nov.	Dec.	Year
Ándros	12·6	11·6	8·3	5·0	4·3	1·8	0·7	0·8	1·8	5·4	9·0	12·1	73·3
Síros	11·6	9·8	7·6	4·6	4·2	1·3	0·3	0·4	1·4	4·8	8·2	10·7	64·8
Náxos	12·1	10·9	7·9	5·2	4·7	1·8	0·4	0·4	1·8	5·1	8·4	12·6	72·2
Mílos	13·0	10·0	8·0	3·0	1·0	1·0	0·3	0·0	1·0	4·0	9·0	13·0	62·0
Thíra	10·7	8·6	6·5	3·9	2·8	0·9	0·1	0·1	1·2	3·8	7·1	9·9	55·6

Source : E. G. Mariolopoulos, *The Climate of Greece* (Athínai, 1938).

dynasties were semi-feudal in character, were based mainly upon the economic wealth of the islands, and were supported by considerable military and social force. Numerous fortresses and strong places, found on harbours or hills throughout the Aegean, were the work of these ' Frankish ' lords. Under them the islanders remained largely agriculturalists, sea-trade being a monopoly of their rulers, who, though well hated, preserved some degree of peace and external security while the mainland was devastated by ceaseless wars. So the Turks on their advent found here a submissive and industrious population, and the islands were spared the worse features of Turkish rule.

Most of these island dynasties succumbed to the Turks after the fall of Constantinople (1453), but some held out longer—Náxos till after 1550, Tínos till 1718. The Turks troubled the Kikládhes little : an official on a vessel anchored in Páros harbour collected a yearly tax, and if this levy was paid (and it was not burdensome) the islanders as a rule heard little more of their rulers. The seventeenth and eighteenth centuries, although they witnessed the final struggle between the Venetian and Turkish powers and the confusion, lawlessness, and wandering consequent upon them, were nevertheless the germinating time of liberty in these islands. The lands passed mostly into the hands of the peasants, and the sea was thrown open to trade and piracy. Piracy, which lasted with fluctuations down to the middle of the nineteenth century and yielded finally only to steamships, laid the foundations of Greek sea-power. The island seamen were conscripted for the Turkish navy, and became the sea-merchants of the Turkish empire.

To piracy and its effects must be attributed the numerous strong refugees and watch-towers scattered in fertile parts or near mines throughout the islands, while to this period belong the general abandonment of old coastal sites and the concentration into strong centres in inland, and often inaccessible, positions. So too in these years, as later in the struggle for freedom, many refugees from Turkish oppression in Crete and Asia Minor found a home in the Kikládhes and it was then that Tínos, with its settled government, received such a large access of population.

The eighteenth century saw the opening up of the Russian Black Sea trade for the Greeks, and the corresponding development of wine production in the islands, though it is true that this affected the Kikládhes less than some islands (notably those off the Asiatic coast) which had greater resources. In 1770, in consequence of the war between Russia and Turkey, eighteen of the Kikládhes were annexed by the former only to be ceded again to Turkey in 1774. In the War of Independence the Kikládhes as a whole played their part. The island seamen won naval battles for Greece, although some of the islands (Thíra, Ándros, Tínos and Síros), partly owing to the lightness of the Turkish yoke, at first refused to join the movement. In the treaty of 1832, the Kikládhes were incorporated in the newly formed kingdom of Greece. During the war and throughout the following century of Greek liberty the famous shrine of the Evangelistria in Tínos (founded in 1822), with its thousands of pilgrims from the whole of the Greek world, played an important part as a rallying point and centre for the dissemination of Hellenism ; and, whether consciously designed for this purpose or not by the patriotic Greek Orthodox clergy, it formed a remarkable parallel to the ancient shrine of Delos. A similar patriotic role was played by the once famous school of Sífnos, also conducted by the clergy, where numerous young Greeks found inspiration and revolutionary zeal. Having played its part in the achievement of freedom, it fell after 1830, like so many other patriotic institutions, into undeserved oblivion and decay. Theophilos Kaïres, a hero of the revolution, was a native of Ándros and a type of the new island patriot, in whom local and national patriotism were reconciled. It was during the War of Independence that refugees from Khíos, Psará, and other Asiatic islands founded the modern town of Síros, the island at that time being under French protection. The rise of Síros and its commercial prosperity symbolized the realization of Hellenism for the Kikládhes, as its decline upon the growth of Piraiévs symbolized their final absorption into the wider Greek nationhood.

POPULATION AND SETTLEMENT

As in other islands in the Aegean Sea, the population is beginning to assume a scattered pattern of settlement. During the medieval and modern periods of insecurity, a single large village, sometimes coastal but more often strongly placed a little inland, housed the entire population of each island. Recently, numerous villages have been colonized from these centres. In one or two islands, the outlying temporary huts are being converted into permanent dwellings, and new hamlets are appearing.

The villages are closely nucleated settlements ; some have been built in the form of strongholds. The streets are narrow, crooked and often vaulted over ; they are usually stone-paved, and where, as it often the case, the town occupies a hill-side, the streets become a series of steps. Good building stone is abundant, and the houses are usually large, square and well-built, but sanitation is primitive. The walls are white-washed or coloured in pale tints both within and without. In hill-side towns, the houses crowd box-like upon each other ; in Kéa, the roofs of the lower houses serve as footpaths for those at a higher level. Churches are conspicuous in most islands and are often large and fine.

The population of the Kikládhes as a whole numbered 129,702 according to the census of 1928 and it had increased to 146,987 according to the estimates of 1938.

AGRICULTURE AND FISHING

Statistics of the agricultural production of the separate islands are not available, but figures have been published for the *nomós* as a whole. The total area of cultivated land is 24,095,527 stremmes (5,951,595 acres), which form 12% of the total area. This figure may seem high, but the barren appearance of the islands is deceptive : there are few plains, but the numerous valleys are rich, warm, well-watered, and usually intensively cultivated ; their sides are often terraced to high levels ; advantage is taken of upland hollows, and even the barren and rocky areas afford some grazing for cattle.

The islands offer great contrasts in productivity ; the determining factors are geology and soils. The schist and volcanic areas are the most fertile ; the limestone and granite are often extremely barren. The agricultural output of the islands is of a high quality, particularly the vegetables, olives, wine and cheese. Irrigation, particularly of vegetable crops, is practised in many valleys.

Síros, Ándros and Náxos are noted for their vegetables, particularly potatoes, tomatoes and onions, and the production of these and also of pulses is very high for Greece (see table on p. 419). Tobacco is grown but is of slight importance. The grain chiefly grown is barley, either alone or mixed with wheat ; the latter is rarely grown alone. The production is not great, and some grain is normally imported. There is, however, an export of pulses.

Fruit growing is of greater importance. In Ándros, Náxos, Kéa and Sífnos, the well-watered lower valley slopes are clothed with fine groves, and the lemon, orange and mandarin, citron and almond crops of these islands are of considerable value. Practically all the islands produce wine of a fair quality and free of resin, but that of Thíra and Páros, and to a less extent that of Kéa, Ándros and Síkinos, is of considerable value and importance. The vines grow on lower sunny slopes and in upland depressions ; the decomposing tufa of Thíra is particularly suitable and olives occupy sheltered sunny slopes and depressions, though in many islands olive trees and fig trees are scattered about the hill-side terraces. Figs, however, are not widely grown.

Cotton and mulberry have been of some importance in the past, but the output is now very small, and the household industries which depended on them are declining. Oranges, lemons and vines have tended to replace industrial crops. The production of citrus fruits in 1937 amounted to :

8,773,000 lemons	1,962,000 mandarins
172,000 citrons	116,000 others
1,581,000 oranges	

The output of figs during the same year was

2,116 metric tons of dried figs
628 ,, ,, fresh ,,

Apples, pears, almonds, mulberries and nuts are of smaller importance. Tanning bark from Valona oak trees is also of some importance.

Agricultural holdings are small, rather smaller than the average for Greece as a whole ; 56% are less than 10 strémmata (or about 2½ acres) and 77% are less than 20 strémmata (or 5 acres). Only 6% of the holdings are larger than 12 acres.

All the islands support some live-stock, and the more barren the island the more important, as a rule, are its animals. The higher and barer areas are devoted to goats and sheep, and many islets and rocks are uninhabited save by shepherds with their herds and flocks. The methods employed differ in different parts. In the northern Kikládhes, cattle are kept in walled enclosures, single beasts often being tethered on the terraced plots on the hillside during the fallow period or after the harvest. In the southern Kikládhes, where there are larger semi-waste areas, the flocks and herds roam loose with herdsmen as on the mainland. Asses and mules are found in all islands, and are often the only means of transport. Horses are relatively few, and are not of high quality. Cattle and oxen are reared, and sheep are everywhere kept for their wool and meat.

Goats supply milk, and some islands have a reputation for their cheese. Young pigs are reared for their flesh, and poultry are widely kept. Pigeons are kept, partly because their droppings furnish a useful manure ; their dove-cotes are conspicuous features in many villages. Bee-keeping is also well-established.

In 1937 there were said to be 14,363 draught animals in the *nomós*. Oxen formed the greater part of this total, but there were 1,542 mules. Of the animals kept for either flesh or milk, goats were easily the most numerous, there being 106,995. There were 92,446 sheep, 14,065 donkeys, 12,232 pigs and 3,847 cows. There were nearly a quarter of a million poultry.

The total value of agricultural production of the islands, with the exception of meat for which statistics are not given, was 352,880,990 drachmae in 1937. Of this, almost two-thirds was accounted for by grain crops, pulses and vegetables.

Agriculture and allied pursuits are the chief source of wealth, followed by the manufacturing industries of Síros and the exploitation of minerals. But the peasant suffers from the remoteness of the islands from markets, his ignorance of prices prevailing on the mainland, and the uncertainty and instability of island conditions. He is thus often at the mercy of the middle-men and buyers who visit the islands.

Fishing is not of great importance, and is often left to men of other islands, although fish are plentiful enough. The sponge fishery has greatly declined in importance.

Síros is the only real industrial centre of the Kikládhes and has cotton spinning and weaving mills, ship-building and repair yards as well as minor manufactures. There is a pottery industry in Sífnos and Amorgós, and the potters from these centres sometimes work in other islands, returning home when their work is completed. The silk and lace industries of the islanders are now virtually defunct. Peasant crafts, however, linger on, and there is a small output of cotton and woollen goods in most islands.

Area under Chief Crops and Output in the Nomós of the Kikládhes,1938

	Area in Strémmata	Output in quintals	Value in Drachmae	Per cent. of cultivated area	Per cent. of total area of islands
Cereals					
Wheat	16,621	12,268	7,859,213	5·2	0·62
Barley	112,685	114,150	43,512,600	35·25	4·26
Mixed grain	53,750	36,756	18,994,500	16·82	2·03
Maize	505	574	291,300	0·16	0·02
Oats	1,295	865	343,000	0·40	0·05
Rye	950	1,142	522,200	0·30	0·04

	Area in strémmata	Output in quintals	Value in drachmae	Per cent. of cultivated area	Per cent. of total area of islands
Vegetables (Pulses)					
Haricot Beans	8,419	3,612	2,931,425	2·63	0·32
Broad Beans	2,420	1,737	1,315,860	0·76	0·09
Peas	5,114	2,546	2,093,150	1·60	0·15
Lentils	782	534	377,010	0·25	0·03
Other pulses	3,398	2,501	1,787,423	1·06	0·13
Vetch	117	181	83,250	0·04	0·004
Vegetables					
Potatoes	5,782	52,813	13,765,900	1·81	0·22
Cucumbers	5,074	43,388	7,522,700	1·59	0·19
Garlic	763	1,286	1,178,770	0·24	0·03
Onions	3,356	38,230	7,797,200	1·05	0·3
Tomatoes	7,686	65,269	11,954,950	2·40	0·29
Others	10,906	120,704	28,723,000	3·41	0·40
Industrial Crops					
Tobacco	3,880	1,714	4,520,150	1·21	0·15
Cotton	568	153	228,670	0·18	0·02
Sesame	660	188	390,740	0·21	0·03
Forage Crops					
Hay	44	102	17,000	0·01	—
Clover	87	293	75,175	0·03	—
Other forage crops	1,600	12,134	1,129,350	0·50	0·06
Viticulture					
Vine	61,019	84,021	25,710,820	19,09	2·3
Table grapes	11,308	23,648	6,502,500	3,54	0·43
Newly planted vineyards	850	—	—	0·26	0·03

Source : *Statistique Annuelle Agricole et d'Elevage de la Grèce*, 1938, p. 6 (Athènes, 1939).

Value of Agricultural Production in the Nomós of the Kikládhes, 1938

		drachmae	drachmae
Crops :	Cereals	71,522,813	
	Pulses	8,588,118	
	Vegetables	70,942,520	
	Industrial crops	5,139,560	
	Forage crops	1,221,525	
			157,414,536
Vineyards			32,267,320
Olives—table olives and oil			16,192,830
Fruit :	Citrus	7,336,910	
	Others	22,250,760	
			29,587,670
Animal products :	Milk	31,649,345	
	Cheese	36,290,295	
	Butter	1,132,110	
	Wool	3,071,090	
	Honey and beeswax	3,248,280	
	Eggs	14,796,514	
			90,187,634
			325,649,990

Source : *Statisque Annuelle Agricole et d'Elevage de la Grèce*, 1938, pp. 6 and 195 (Athènes, 1939).

MINING

The massif of which the Kikládhes form part has been extensively mineralized. Individual deposits, however, are small and cannot always be worked economically. Development has, in consequence, been spasmodic and the output fluctuating. Some deposits have been mined for centuries and are now nearly worked out. Lack of capital, transport factilities and enterprise have caused the abandonment of others, and the islands abound in deserted workings. The smaller enterprises, owned by individuals or small groups, are the most unstable ; those worked with foreign capital have been more successful. Emery working is a government monopoly, and only the pits on the island of Náxos are now allowed to operate. The salt works of Mílos and Náxos are also state-owned.

Iron ores occur in quantity in the more westerly islands of Kéa, Kíthnos, Sérifos and Sífnos, though only the deposits of Sérifos and Kíthnos are now exploited. Pyrites are found in Mílos, and manganiferous ores occur in most of the other more westerly islands. Silver, lead and zinc are also widely distributed through the archipelago, but the only workings in recent years have been on Sífnos and Andíparos. Emery is found on Náxos and Síkinos, as well as in islands outside the Kikládhes group, but is now produced from Náxos only. Other non-metallic minerals are worked—gypsum, sulphur, slat (a fuller's earth) from Kímolos ; pumice, from Thíra ; marble is worked on Páros, Tínos and Ándros ; material for mill-stones is quarried in Mílos. The gold of Sífnos and copper of Sérifos were once important, but are now worked out. Bauxite is of some small importance on Amorgós, but reserves are said to be small ; the deposits of Mílos have already been exhausted.

The emery and salt workings are owned and controlled by the Greek government. In other branches of the extractive industries, French capital is dominant. The iron mines of Sérifos, the most important single mining operation in the group, is owned by *La Société Française Seriphos-Spiliazeza,* and that of Kíthnos by *S.A. des Travaux Techniques.* The zinc has been worked by a French company, and the barytes by *S.A. d'Exploitation des Mines de Barytine Argentif.*

TRADE

The volume of trade carried on in the Kikládhes is small in relation to the population. Some islands are able to produce the bulk of their inhabitants' simple requirements, and their commercial contracts are very small. There is a good deal of purely local trade, carried on on a basis of barter, between the islands. Síros is a centre for this local trade ; it distributes flour, manufactures and colonial goods and absorbs a fair proportion of the surplus produce of the islands. Island products are taken by steam or by sailing vessels either to Síros or direct to Piraiévs. Síros is also a depot for the emery of Náxos, and also for certain other ores. The greater part of the inter-island trade is carried on in small Greek sailing vessels— caiques—or in the small steamers which ply between the islands. Minerals, however, are generally carried in vessels of heavier burden. All the inhabited islands are in frequent and regular contact by steamship with Síros and the mainland.

SUBDIVISIONS

The *nomós* of the Kikládhes is divided for purposes of administration into seven eparchies which form a convenient basis for description. A list of the eparchies is given below and their position is shown in Fig. 93.

(1) The eparchy of Ándros.

(2) The eparchy of Tínos.

(3) The eparchy of Síros, consisting of Síros and Míkonos and the smaller islands of Dhílos, Rinía and Yioúra.

(4) The eparchy of Kéa, consisting of Kéa, Kíthnos, Sérifos, and the less important Makronísi.

(5) The eparchy of Náxos, consisting of Náxos, and Páros and the lesser islands of Andíparos and Dhespotikó.

(6) The eparchy of Mílos, consisting of Mílos, Sífnos, Folégandros and Síkinos and the smaller islands of Andímilos, Kímolos and Políaigos.

(7) The eparchy of Thíra, consisting of Thíra, Íos and Amorgós, and the smaller islands of Iráklia, Skhoinoúsa, Koufó, Káros, Andíkaros, Dhríma, Dhenoúsa, Mákares, Kínaros and Anáfi.

The major islands of each group are described in detail and in the order given above. The lesser islands are described summarily. The many small and often uninhabited islets receive only incidental reference in connexion with the coasts of the major islands.

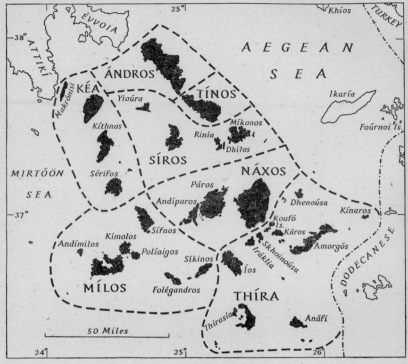

Fig. 93. Key-map to the Kikládhes (Cyclades)

Based on British Admiralty charts and *Population de la Grèce d'après le Recensement du 15–16 Mai*, 1928, deuxième édition (Athènes, 1935).

The names in large letters are those of the islands which give their names to the
eparchies. The pecked lines enclose the islands in each eparchy.

THE EPARCHY OF ÁNDROS

ÁNDROS

Geology and Relief

Ándros is the second largest island in the Kikládhes and is about
25 miles long but only about one-quarter of this in width ; it has an
area of 148 sq. miles. It is built throughout of fairly uniform rock—
a mica schist being predominant—veined with quartz. The latter
is often sufficiently developed to influence the relief, and the peaks
generally consist of quartz. A certain amount of marble occurs.
Though not of the best quality, it has commercial value. Iron and
manganese are associated with the quartz veins, and there has

recently been a small output of manganese ore from the north of the island.

The appearance of Ándros from a distance is that of a rugged and barren mountain mass. Its valleys are not at first visible, and this gives the island an inhospitable aspect. The island consists of a main ridge, which lies close to the straight and regular south-west coast of the island, and a series of transverse ridges which reach out to the north-east coast (Fig. 94). These lateral ridges thus form a series of barriers across the island, and divide it into a number of almost isolated sections, each with distinct physical and economic features. The ridges are broad and flat-topped, and terminate in large blunt promontories on the north-east coast. The intervening valleys run up to saddles in the main ridge of the island, which thus has an undulating profile. The most important of the transverse ridges is Pétalon, which joins the main ridge at its highest point, Mount Kouvárion (3,270 ft.), and almost bisects the island. Its broad, rounded, quartz-strewn back sinks gradually as it approaches the north-east coast. Almost exactly similar, though on a smaller scale, are the two more southerly lateral ridges, Yerakónas and Rákhi. To the north, the country is more irregular ; here the Áyioi Saránda ridge trends north-eastwards.

These four transverse ridges divide the island into five regions :

(1) The northern plateau lies north-west of the Áyioi Saránda ridge, and has a general altitude of about 1,000 ft. It reaches the sea in steep cliffs and forms rugged country dissected by deep, narrow and steep valleys running north to south. The only considerable area of low ground is the small plain of Gávrion on the west coast of the island (Plate 136). This northern plateau is the area of Albanian settlement in the island.

(2) Between the Áyioi Saránda and Pétalon ridges is a series of parallel valleys which, on the one hand, debouch on Vitáli Bay and, on the other, run up to the main watershed of the island which is here lower than elsewhere.

(3) The valley of Ándros lies between the high ridge of Pétalon and the lower, parallel ridge of Yerakónas. To the south-west the valley runs up to a low saddle across the main range of the island, and a metalled road crosses to Palaió-polis, the ancient capital of the island, on the south-east coast. The Ándros valley is itself divided into two unequal

portions by a low ridge, on the end of which the town of
Ándros lies. This latter ridge runs out into the bay of
Ándros, dividing it into two harbours of which the more

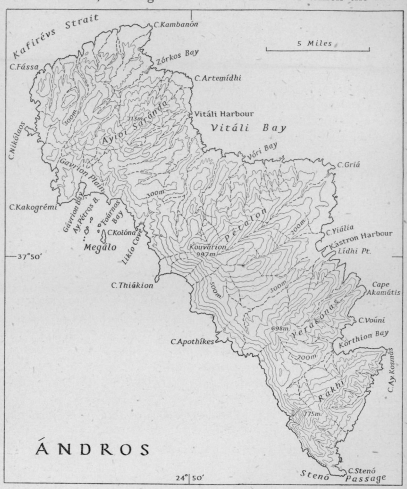

Fig. 94.   Relief and drainage of Ándros

Based on the 1 : 50,000 Aegean Islands, M.D.R. 611/9711 and 9712 (1944) and
British Admiralty Chart 1820 (1940).
The contours are at intervals of 100 metres (328 ft.).

northerly is that generally used by ships. The slopes of
the valley are gentle and well-watered and the valley
provides a considerable area of cultivable land.

(4) The Kórthion valley lies to the south-east of the Yerakónas

ridge, and although it is shorter than the Ándros valley, it is broader and forms a fair-sized plain. Like the Ándros valley, it is drained north-eastwards and is backed to the south-west by a saddle leading to the south-west coast which is here particularly rugged. The coast of Kórthion Bay is fringed with sand dunes, which threaten the land and impede traffic.

(5) The south-east of Ándros, beyond the Rákhi ridge, is a barren, uninhabited area.

Coasts and Ports

The coasts of Ándros are high and rugged. Along the straight, south-western coast, for 19 miles from Cape Stenó to Gávrion, the mountain ridge drops abruptly into the water. There is no coastal plain in this stretch, and only sometimes, where a torrent enters the sea, is there a small beach. The small plain of Gávrion lies between the main mountain mass of the island and the north-south ridge behind Cape Kakogrémi. From this point to Cape Kambanón, the coast is lower but not less rugged. It is broken by a series of small inlets and bays, separated from one another by rough, if inconspicuous, headlands. Landing is as difficult here as on the south-west coast, and in the whole length of the west coast from Stenó Point to Cape Kambanón, the only anchorage is the bay of Gávrion, and even this is interrupted by shoals and rocks, of which a small group, the Gavrionisa, lie in the middle of the bay. The port of Gávrion has a sufficient depth of water for small craft and there is a small pier (Plate 136). Roads connect it with Féllos to the north, and with the settlements along the west coast ; the latter road follows the Ándros valley to the chief town (Fig. 95).

The north-east facing coast of the island is made up of four bays of very unequal size. These are divided into two pairs by the headland of Cape Griá, in which the Pétalon ridge terminates. To the north-west of this point, the shallow Zórkos Bay offers few advantages. The broad, sweeping Vitáli Bay really consists of a series of minor headlands separating short creeks or shallow bays. To the south-east of Cape Griá are the two narrower, deeper, and economically more important, bays of Kástron (Ándros) and Korthíon. The harbour of Ándros (Kástron), although not good, is the chief port of the island and is in regular communication with the other islands and with the mainland. The harbour lies to the south of the spur on which the town stands and is about 800 yds.

long and 500 yds. wide with depths of between 4 and 14 fm. To the north of the spur is a larger, deeper (7–12 fm.) and more frequented bay which has a breakwater, 200 yds. long, in the north-west

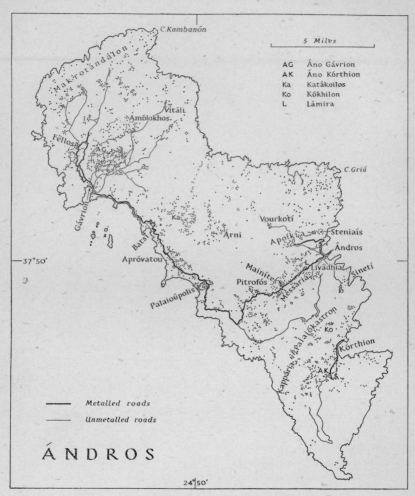

Fig. 95.   Settlements and communications of Ándros

Based on the 1 : 50,000 Aegean Islands, M.D.R. 611/9711 and 9712 (1944). The dots show settlements but not necessarily individual houses.

and a pier about 200 ft. long in the south-east ; depths alongside the breakwater vary between 3 and 26 ft. but alongside the pier they do not exceed 5 ft.

Population and Settlement

The total population of the island in 1928 was 17,593, of whom 2,069 lived in the chief town. The remainder were distributed over 89 villages. The degree of dispersion is thus seen to be very high (Fig. 95).

In the northern part of the island, the settlements are mainly pastoral and are scattered over the rocky hillsides. Here, the most important place is Gávrion (354), a comparatively isolated village on the eastern side of a good harbour in the north-west of the island. It is the centre of a fruitful plain, producing olives, onions and grain, but its trade is negligible and its harbour is little used. At the head of a valley in the Saránda ridge is the now ruined settlement of Ammólokhos, formerly the chief Albanian settlement in the island. Along the coast to the south-east are Batsí, Apróvatou and Palaiópolis, now small fishing villages, where formerly was quite a flourishing trade.

The most thickly populated part of Ándros is the valley in which the chief town lies. There are numerous small villages and scattered dwellings, having rich gardens and set around with cypresses. Ándros (Kástron) (2,069) itself lies partly on a rocky promontory which juts into Ándros Bay, and partly on the ridge inland from it. The seaward end is occupied by a fine Venetian fortress. Behind it lies the old town, a picturesque place with square red-tiled houses of all colours and decorated with much woodwork. The streets are narrow and marble-paved. Inland lies the new town with a market-place and with houses more widely dispersed.

The Kórthion valley is second only to that of Ándros as a centre of population. It contains numerous hamlets, with a total population of about a thousand. Kórthion (447) itself lies in a position similar to that of Ándros, but is farther from the sea. It consists of closely-built, white houses. It has some large storehouses and, higher up the valley, the large private houses of the more wealthy families of the island.

Agriculture and Fishing

The island is not fertile, but the schists in which the valleys are cut form rounded hillsides, often with very gentle slopes in their lower parts. Springs are very abundant. Cultivation can thus be carried to high levels, and every advantage which terracing and walling can offer is utilized.

The rocky hill country of the north is suitable, for the most part, for pasture only, and here cattle, sheep and goats are kept in considerable numbers. On the plain of Gávrion, which is treeless and in parts marshy, are the only meadows of the island ; in the lighter and drier parts, onions, grain and vines do well. In the hilly regions to the north and south of Gávrion are numerous olive groves. *Smigádi*, a mixture of wheat and barley, is also grown in the northern part of Ándros.

Other than a few hillside orchards and fields on the west coast, the only areas of cultivation in the southern half of the island are the valleys of Ándros and Kórthion, but the economic value of these is greater than that of the remainder of the island. The valley of Ándros is perhaps the most productive area of its size in the whole of the Kikládhes. In the irrigated valley bottoms are fine gardens of fig, orange, lemon, and many other fruit trees. Vines, which yield a good quality wine, are grown on the lighter soils. Cypresses and bamboo reeds are grown around the gardens to shelter them against the north-east winds. Above the tilled land are white villages, with fine churches. The higher slopes and terraces support pulse and grain, and here too olive and fig-trees thrive ; sometimes the latter are set amidst vines. Higher still, the stony hillsides are traversed by stone walls of rough and curious structure ; in the enclosures grain is grown, and after harvest, or in time of fallow, single animals are pastured. Bee-keeping is carried on, but the silk industry has now almost disappeared, and the mulberry trees have mostly been replaced with lemon.

THE EPARCHY OF TÍNOS

TÍNOS

Geology and Relief

Tínos, one of the best-known and, in some respects most interesting, of the Kikládhes, is neither a large nor a particularly fertile island. It has an area of 75 sq. miles. Its structure resembles that of Ándros, but is very much more complicated. The main Ándros ridge, interrupted only by the channel named Stenó, continues south-east along the length of Tínos, but is, on the whole, lower although it rises towards the south. The valleys, though small, lie behind the bays of the north-east coast and, like those of Ándros, run up to saddles in the main watershed. The lowest of these, the Ayía Marína Pass (666 ft.), forms, with the Kolimvíthra valley to the north and a smaller valley to the south-west, a depression that divides Tínos practically in half. The northern half is further divided by a less conspicuous depression which extends across the island from Pánormos Bay on the north coast.

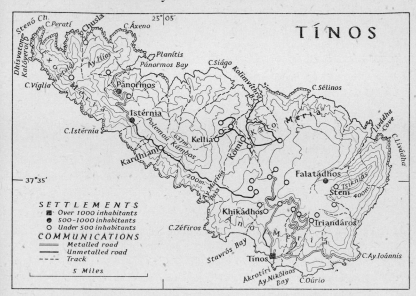

Fig. 96. Relief, drainage, settlements and communications of Tínos

Based on the 1 : 50,000 Aegean Islands, M.D.R. 611/9526 (1944) ; British Admiralty Chart 1815 (1939) and *Population de la Grèce d'après le Recensement du 15–16 Mai*, 1928, deuxième édition (Athènes, 1935).

The island is readily divisible into four regions, so distinct in their characteristics that three of them have acquired popular names :

(1) The central division of the island, known as Polemoú Kámbos, lies between the Pánormos and Kolimvíthra depressions. It is occupied by a dome-like mass of mica-schist, identical with that which composes the greater part of Ándros. This mass culminates in Polemoú Kámbos which reaches 2,090 ft. Many beds of marble occur in the schists, and the depression south-west of Pánormos Bay is very largely developed in these beds.

(2) The high plateau of granite and amphibolite in the south-east is known as Áno Meriá. It is dissected by rivers and is well populated. The amphibolites consist generally of a hornblende gneiss, but are in parts altered to serpentine.

Where this occurs, the more resistant rock forms high ridges. Thus, the Tsikniás ridge, the highest in the island, consists of a serpentine mass, which rises above the amphibolite plateau. Along the south-east coast, the mica schist again appears, but in the north-east, a mass of granite occupies rather higher ground and is surrounded, except on the seaward side, by the amphibolites. The boundary of the granite outcrop is emphasized by the Livádha river and by some of the tributaries of the Kolimvíthra river. Settlements avoid the granite but are not infrequent over the amphibolite outcrop.

(3) The north-western portion of the island, beyond the Pánormos depression, is known as Éxo Meriá. It is lower and more dissected and consists, in the main, of a similar outcrop of amphibolite, which in places has been altered to serpentine. The latter forms the Áyios Ilías ridge and the cliffs of the north coast each side of Chusla.

(4) The Kolimvíthra valley has been eroded along the junction of the schists of the centre of the island and the amphibolites of the south-east, and is the largest in the island. It is surrounded by rounded spurs, and forms a nearly circular depression, into the marshy bottom of which a radial system of streamlets converges ; the whole area is called Káto Meriá by the inhabitants.

Coasts and Ports

The south-west coastline of Tínos has many small indentations. Cape Zéfiros affords some shelter to Stavrós Bay which is a useful anchorage for small vessels and has a short mole. Tínos itself has the only harbour on this coast and the best on the island. It is formed by two breakwaters which enclose an area about 500 yds. by 350 yds. ; the harbour gives protection from all winds except those from the west. The entrance between the breakwaters is about 200 yds. wide and 6½ fm. deep ; within the entrance are depths of 18 ft., but the water shoals to the shore. Motor roads run east and north from the town (Fig. 96). To the south-east is Áyios Nikólaos Bay, which is also an anchorage. The south-east coast is in general rugged.

The north coast is rough and much indented, but contains three bays of some commercial importance. Pánormos Bay, in the north-west, is a secure anchorage. The small coastal settlement here has harbour works connected with the marble quarries in the hills behind, and a motor road runs to Istérnia. The bays of Kolimvíthra and Livádha are backed by small plains, but are otherwise unimportant.

Population and Settlement

Tínos is one of the more densely populated islands in the Kikládhes owing as much to the industry of the islanders as to any natural productivity. Venetian rule maintained itself longer here than on any other island (1390–1715), and Tínos enjoyed for centuries comparative quiet, stability and good government, and hence received a large access of population from less happy islands. These reasons account for the unusual persistence of Italian influences and the strong Roman Catholic element in the island.

In the towns and villages the houses are of white stone and show Latin influence. They are often of several stories, have balconies, outer flights of stairs, and flat roofs. Scattered settlements are rare, and even small villages are closely nucleated. The houses are built so close that the roofs often serve as footpaths. The streets below are narrow, dark, mostly paved with marble, and often vaulted over.

The chief town, Tínos (2,485), occupies a warm and sheltered position. It is on the site of the ancient capital but, during the less settled period of the Middle Ages, coastal settlements were deserted for inland sites, and Exópyrgo, in the centre of Áno Meriá, became the Venetian capital. The modern capital is built along the slopes between Áno Meriá and the shore and overlooks its harbour. It is white, clean and well-built with large orderly houses and a fine dominating church.

Most of the villages are small, but Pánormos (963), beautifully situated in a northern valley amid cypresses and orchards, and the centre of the marble industry, and Istérnia at the western end of the Polemoú Kámbos, may be mentioned. The population as a whole lives on the sheltered, south-western side of the island, in marked contrast to its distribution in Ándros. Settlements are strewn along the south-western face of Áno Meriá and the Polemoú Kámbos ridge, showing up from the distance as white patches amongst their grey-green olive groves.

Agriculture and Fishing

The steep, stony, and in parts arid, nature of the island does not make for fertility. Springs, though plentiful in the valleys, seldom develop into streams which can be used for irrigation. There are few valleys and the only considerable one, Kolimvíthra, is marshy. The highlands are exposed and support no forest ; much of the area is fit only for sheep and goats, for which the hardy plants and scrub afford scant pasturage. On sunny slopes, particularly the south-western face of Polemoú Kámbos, olives grow well, and vines are found on the warmer hill terraces. Wherever possible, terracing and walling have contained the scanty earth, and on such strips grain and pulse are grown. The most fertile parts are the uplands of Áno Meriá (except on the granite of the centre and north), the plain of Kolimvíthra and the Pánormos valley.

Fishing is only of very slight importance, partly, perhaps, owing to the lack of suitable harbours.

THE EPARCHY OF SÍROS

The eparchy of Síros comprises the islands of Síros, Míkonos, Dhílos, Riniá and Yioúra ; the islands are described in this order.

SÍROS

Síros, although neither fertile nor rich in minerals, is the best known, wealthiest, and most densely populated, of the Kikládhes. This is very largely due to its central position and its convenience as a port of call on important sea routes. The island extends from north to south for a little over 9 miles, and its maximum breadth is $5\frac{1}{2}$ miles ; its area is 33 sq. miles.

Geology and Relief

The northern part of the island is distinguished as Áno Meriá. It consists of a mass of schist of a greenish colour with considerable areas of marble. The former in general forms the higher ground. The relief consists of a mountain backbone which lies rather nearer the east than the west side and is arranged in a series of concentric, curving ranges (Fig. 98). The most easterly of these culminates in Mount Síringas (1,540 ft.) the highest point in the island ; the next culminates in Mount Pírgos (1,450 ft.). The mountains are close to the smoothly curving coast on the east, but towards the

Plate 136. Gávrion bay in Ándros

The view is northward over the small plain which surrounds the bay; in the background are the foothills of the Saránda ridge. The small port of Gávrion, with its pier, can be seen on the east side of the bay.

Plate 137. The town and harbour of Tínos

The view shows the inner part of the harbour within the breakwaters.

SÍROS

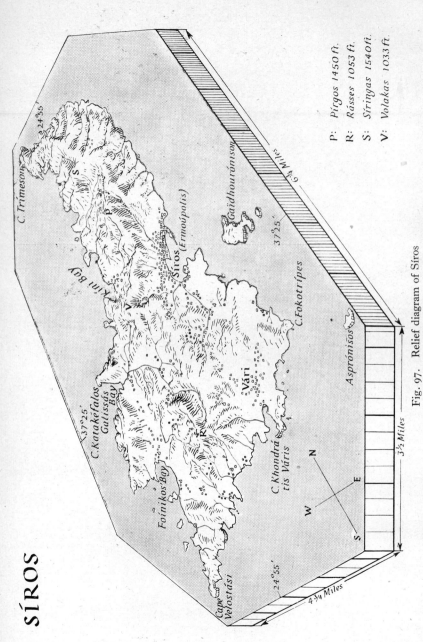

P: Pírgos 1450 ft.
R: Rásses 1053 ft.
S: Sirinyas 1540 ft.
V: Volakas 1033 ft.

Fig. 97. Relief diagram of Síros

Based on the 1 : 50,000 Aegean Islands, M.D.R. 611/7582 (1943) and British Admiralty Chart 1542 (1937).

west the slopes are gentler and terminate in numerous rugged promontories which enclose bays and coves. The drainage is mainly to the west. The only conspicuous river on the east is that which

Fig. 98. Relief and drainage of Síros

Based on the 1 : 50,000 Aegean Islands, M.D.R. 611/7582 (1943) and British Admiralty Chart 1542 (1937).

The contours are at intervals of 100 metres (328 ft.).

drains the Áno Síros valley and enters the sea at Síros. This northern part of the island is an area of barren hills, often striking in colour and form.

To the south is the lower, undulating country of Messariá, consisting mainly of the area of the amphibolite outcrops. The Vári plain in the south-eastern corner of the island is also in the same series. In the extreme south the schists again appear, and give a bolder relief, though by no means as high and rugged as in the northern region of the island.

Coasts

In the northern part of the island, the outer or eastern shore curves smoothly from the harbour of Síros (see below) to the most northerly point of the island, Cape Trímeson. The western shore, however, is broken by a series of headlands and small sandy bays, of which the most important are Mégas Lákkos, Aëtóu, Dhelfíno, Kíni and Galissás. To the south is the high, cliffed headland of Cape Atsinganókastro, with the islet-studded Foínikos Bay to the south. The south coast is straight and rugged, with a series of small bays, of which Vári Bay is the most important. From Cape Fokó-tripes northwards to Síros Harbour is a similar rock-bound coast.

The Port of Síros (Ermoúpolis)

37° 26′ N., 24° 56′ E.   Population 21,156 in 1928

For many centuries Síros was the principal port of Greece, the crossing place of sea routes from the western Mediterranean to the Levant and the Black Sea, from Thrace and Macedonia to Crete and Africa, and, like Dhílos in the age of classical Greece, the centre of the entrepôt trade of the many Aegean islands. But the rapid expansion of Piraiévs and other mainland ports from the last quarter of the nineteenth century gradually captured much of its trade, and today it has declined to the tenth place amongst all the Greek ports.

Detailed Description (Fig. 99). The harbour is formed by a bay, open to the east. A small peninsula which projects southwards from the northern side of the bay has been elongated by a breakwater some 1,300 ft. in length. The entrance is about 900 yds. wide and depths vary from 23 fm. to just over 13 ft. near the sea wall of the commercial basin. Good anchorage is available within the harbour and there is protection from most winds, except those blowing from the north and north-east. These, however, are seldom strong enough to prevent operations within the port. Large vessels can moor with their sterns attached to the breakwater.

The port falls naturally into four parts : a commercial harbour in the north, a small harbour in the west, a boat harbour in the south-west, and an outer harbour immediately inside the entrance (Fig. 99).

[*Facing page* 434

Plate 138. The town of Síros (Ermoúpolis)

The view shows the waterfront in the Commerical Harbour and the quarters on the hills behind (see p. 435).

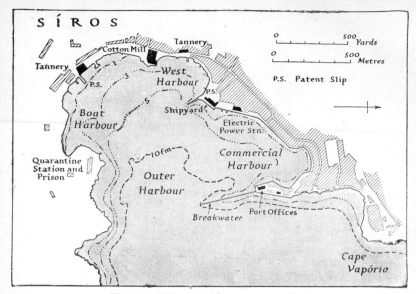

Fig. 99. The port of Síros (Ermoúpolis)
Based on official sources.

Plate 139. The Commercial Harbour at Síros (Ermoúpolis)
The view is southward and shows the breakwater and main quays. In the background are the prison and quarantine station (*cf*. Fig. 99).

The water-front of the commercial harbour is improved by a number of sea walls and quays that extend from the root of the breakwater around the northern part of the harbour. They provide some 3,700 ft. of berthing space in depths varying from 6 to 14 ft., although there are bollards for the end-on mooring of ocean-going vessels. The harbour is principally engaged in handling the general commodities that make up the trade of Síros. The small harbour in the west, used for the repair of coastwise and fishing vessels, has depths of only 3 to 10 ft., though just to the north-east, where two quays provide some 850 ft. of berthing space, depths increase to 16 ft. In the south-west the boat harbour has several small piers, amongst which are some for ship repairs, one for quarantine and another for prison landings.

Port Facilities. Two 1-ton hand-cranes and one sheer-legs of 50 tons capacity are thought to be the only lifting appliances available, and there are normally about thirty-three lighters with a total capacity of 2,500 tons. There are no docks in the port at present, though it is reported that a dry dock has been authorized. Two slipways, the larger of which can haul up vessels not greater than 4,000 tons, are maintained by two local ship-repairing companies. The more important is owned by *Cie des Forges et Chantiers de Syra.* Facilities for coaling and taking on fresh-water exist.

The Town. The town consists of three parts; the quayside quarter of Ermoúpolis, and, on two hills behind it, the old Catholic quarter (Áno Síra) on the southern hill, and the Greek quarter on the northern hill, Vrondádho. The Catholic population are the descendants of the Venetian and Genoese conquerors, who, after the Turkish occupation, lived under French protection. In 1821 they were reinforced by refugees from Khíos and Psára, who built Ermoúpolis and the Vrondádho quarter. A Roman Catholic cathedral dominates the southern hill, and the Greek church of Anástasis the northern. There are two hospitals, with a total of 100 beds, a large orphanage and a small museum. Síros, besides being the capital of the island, is a nomarchy (Kikládhes) and a demarchy; it has an Orthodox archbishop and a Roman Catholic bishop. As the judicial centre for the Kikládhes, it has Courts of Appeal, of the First Instance, of a Justice of the Peace, and of Police. It controls the gendarmerie of the Kikládhes. The town has a good water supply and electric lighting extends to the water-front.

Trade and Industries. The trade of Ermoúpolis is derived mainly from its position as the centre of the coasting trade between the Greek islands, and to a less extent from the tourist traffic, not only from abroad but also from the mainland of Greece itself. In 1938 the passenger traffic was about 23,000 visitors, and the total tonnage entered and cleared was just under one million tons. The great commercial activity of the port dates from the influx in 1821 of Greek traders who were driven from Khíos by the Turks, but the gradual economic development of the mainland and the territorial expansion of Greece gradually removed it from its pre-eminent commercial position.

Trade in 1937 (*thousands of metric tons*)

IMPORTS		EXPORTS	
Foodstuffs and agricultural		Minerals (stone, emery, etc.)	2·3
products	3·1		
Sugar	0·4		
Minerals	12·5		
Leather and hides	0·1		
Miscellaneous	0·3		
Total	16·4	Total	2·3

Source : *Bulletin mensuel du commerce spécial de la Grèce avec les pays étrangers, Décembre* 1937 (*Athènes,* 1938)

A certain amount of industrial activity, though on quite a small scale, is carried on in the town. The spinning and weaving of cotton is the most important occupation and a certain amount of raw cotton is imported from Cyprus, Egypt and America. The port has good ship repair plants and the town is also noted for *loukoúmi* (Turkish delight).

Communications. There are a number of roads suitable for motor traffic leading to the southern and western parts of the island (Fig. 100). Frequently steamer services connect with other islands and with Piraiévs, and many foreign lines call occasionally. Telegraph cable service, for the many islands of the Aegean, are centred on Síros.

Population and Settlement

Alone amongst the islands of the Kikládhes, Síros has distinct merchant and artisan classes, who live and are employed in and about the port of Síros. The merchants of Síros have a reputation for enterprise and capacity, and form a relatively wealthy class.

The northern part of the island is sparsely peopled. Settlements are most numerous in the valley north of the capital. In the hollows

and on the lowland to the west and south-west of Síros are many
small villages, including Kíni, Pagós and Galíssas. In the south
are Vári (875) on the edge of the plain which lies at the head of the
bay of the same name ; Khroúsa (139), on the edge of the plateau

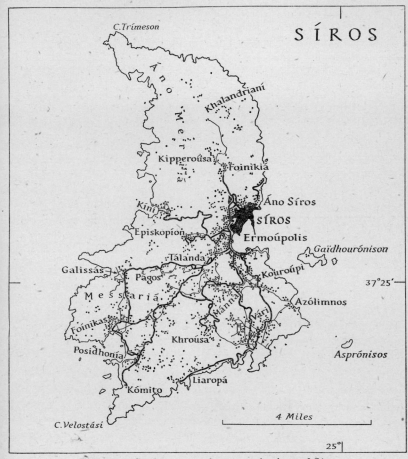

Fig. 100. Settlements and communications of Síros
Based on the 1 : 50,000 Aegean Islands, M.D.R. 611/7582 (1943).
For key see Fig. 95.

of the southern part of the island, amidst olive-clad hills overlooking
a fertile valley and the sea ; and the villages of Foínikos and
Posidhonía on Foínikos Bay, surrounded by gardens and fields.
Episkopíon (95) is a high village, beautifully situated overlooking
Síros.

Agriculture

The island has practically no natural vegetation except scanty heath on some of the hills, many of which, however, are quite bare. The Áno Meriá consists of mostly barren heights and supports a few sheep and goats. Cultivation is practically confined to the two southern sections, where the relief is gentler and the water supply is fairly abundant. The most fertile part is the hill country of the south, where the valleys are intensively cultivated.

Cultivation is more difficult in Messariá, where the stony hills have to be walled up and terraced. Olives and figs grow on the sunny hillsides, and grain on the narrow, rocky terraces. A mixture of wheat and barley, commonly used throughout the islands, is usually sown, with barley alone on the poorer land. Vines grow well on the lower land.

Adjacent Islands

About 1½ miles south-east of the entrance to Síros harbour lies the barren islet of Gaïdhourónison, on which is a lighthouse. Off the south-east corner of Síros is the small islet of Áspro. There are also several islets in Foínikos Bay on the south-western coast of the island.

MÍKONOS

Geology and Relief

The island of Míkonos, five miles south-east of Tínos, is a continuation, at a lower height, of the ridge of Évvoia. The general appearance of the island is that of a rocky tableland of no great height. The island is roughly triangular in shape, with its apex towards the east ; it is deeply indented on the north by the bay of Pánormos, and at the south-west corner, joined by a narrow isthmus, is a peculiar horn-shaped promontory, known as Anavoloúsa. The maximum length of the island from east to west is about 7½ miles and its breadth is about 6 miles ; its area is 29 sq. miles.

The geology of the island is little known, though it appears to be very similar to that of Áno Meriá in Tínos, comprising mainly gneiss and schist. Gneiss appears along the west coast, north and south of the town of Míkonos, and Tertiary and recent deposits occur in the central depression of the island. This depression, which resembles the depression across the island of Tínos, probably corresponds with some line of structural weakness.

The western half of the island is an undulating plateau, which reaches its greatest height in Mount Áyios Ilías (1,194 ft.) at its northern end (Fig. 101). To the east, a depression, occupied for half its length by the deep bay of Pánormos and for the rest by the valleys of two short rivers, divides this from the eastern part of the island. The latter is a similar undulating plateau, culminating near its eastern end in another mountain, also named Áyios Ilías (1,150 ft.).

The island is almost without rivers, and there is hardly a plain or valley of any size. Over most of its surface the granite forms low, rounded, and extremely rocky hills ; at lower levels the granite lies disintegrated in the form of boulders or sand.

Coasts

The coasts of Míkonos are everywhere rugged and indented, but they are without the high cliffs which characterize most of the other islands of the northern Kikládhes. The promontory of Anavoloúsa, in the south-west, is linked to the island by a low sandy neck of land on either side of which are Ornós Bay and Kórfos Bay. To the north, a broad bight occupies most of the west coast

Fig. 101. Relief and drainage of Míkonos, Rinía and Dhílos

Based on the 1 : 50,000 Aegean Islands, M.D.R. 611/9713 (1944) and British Admiralty Chart 1542 (1937).

The contours are at intervals of 100 metres (328 ft.).

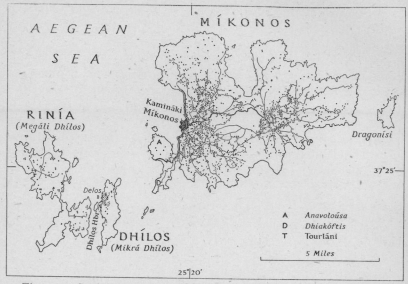

Fig. 102. Settlements and communications of Míkonos, Rinía and Dhílos
Based on the 1 : 50,000 Aegean Islands, M.D.R. 611/9713 (1944).
For key see Fig. 95.

of the island, and is divided by a blunt headland on which the town of Míkonos stands. This headland separates Toúrlos Bay in the north from Kórfos Bay in the south. The town of Míkonos has a small breakwater, and is further protected by the small islet of Áyios Yeóryios. The north coast is the highest in the island, but is broken by the deep bay of Pánormos which is completely exposed to the north, and appears to be little used. The south-eastern coast has several small bays and sandy beaches.

Off the eastern tip of the island are the Dhragonísi consisting of one islet and offlying rocks. Five miles to the south-east is the even smaller islet of Klitapodhiá. The Práso group of three islets lies off Cape Alogómandra and in the middle of the channel between Míkonos and Dhílos.

Population and Settlement

The total population of 4,188 is divided between the chief town, Míkonos (which has nearly one-half), and the settlements in the west and centre (Fig. 102). The former lies in the middle of the west coast, and is backed by low hills, which are carefully cultivated and set with numerous windmills. It is a prosperous and well-built town, in which Italian influence remains conspicuous.

Plate 140. The town and harbour of Míkonos from the south

Beyond the harbour is Toúrlos Bay and the granite plateau of the north-west of the island.

Plate 141. The waterfront at Míkonos

The view is south-westward. The root of the mole shown on the left of the harbour entrance in Plate 140 can be seen on the right and also the five windmill stumps behind it.

[*Facing page* 440

Plate 142. Áyios Nikólaos Bay, Kéa

This old view shows the bay from the south. In the foreground is Livádhi Bay, with Vourkári Bay beyond separated from it by a low point. In the background the long ridge of Cape Áyios Nikólaos flanks the entrance to the bay.

Plate 143. The waterfront at Korisía on Áyios Nikólaos Bay, Kéa

Agriculture and Fishing

The island is almost destitute of natural vegetation and has a dry and barren appearance ; the water supply is scanty. Nevertheless, the inhabitants make the most of the possibilities for agriculture. Terraces and garden-strips, built up among the granite boulders, mark out the hillsides in fantastic patterns, and in these strips fig-trees, beans and barley grow. Around the chief town, and in other more fertile valleys inland, there are a few irrigated gardens producing potatoes and a little tobacco and, on lighter and drier soils, beans and onions. Vines thrive on the warm slopes, and a good deal of wine is made, but there are few olives. The light, gritty soil of Míkonos is suited to barley, and a good deal is grown. Sheep are pastured over the uplands, and poultry and pigeons are numerous.

Owing to the poorness and small extent of the cultivable land, many of the islanders are forced to find employment on the sea, and the island has a relatively large number of sailing craft.

Mining

The minerals of the island have at various times been important. A barytes lode contains silver and lead and there are workable deposits of manganiferous iron ore. Mining was formerly important, and considerable quantities of iron and silver-lead ores have been extracted. But the good ores seem largely to have been worked out, and operations have long since been abandoned.

OTHER ISLANDS

The two small islands of Dhílos and Riniá, surrounded by several shoals and reefs, lie to the west of Míkonos, to which they belong geologically and physically. At its narrowest, the strait between Dhílos and Míkonos is about 1½ miles wide. Dhílos is separated from Riniá by an even narrower channel, generally about ½ mile across. North-west of Sïros is the small island of Yioúra (Fig. 103).

Dhílos

Dhílos is a rocky ridge of irregular outline, and measures 3 miles from north to south and ¾ mile across its widest part ; its area is about 2¼ sq. miles. It consists of granite, with a small outcrop of gneiss at its north-western end. The island is girdled by low but steep cliffs ; its surface is undulating and culminates near the centre in the hill of Kínthos, which, however, reaches only 350 ft. The granite and gneiss are everywhere exposed, but a little earth has collected here and there. Such patches have been enclosed by stone walls and are sown with grain by the people of Míkonos.

In antiquity Dhílos was one of the most famous islands in the Aegean. It was the traditional birthplace of Apollo and the centre of his cult, and perhaps for this reason became the meeting place and treasury of the Delian League, which Athens organized in the fifth century B.C. It became a great slave market under the Roman Empire, but its prosperity has vanished, and nothing now remains but a few ruins. The only inhabitants are an official or two and a few cultivators and herdsmen from Míkonos.

Rinía

Rinía is a larger island, deeply embayed on all sides (Fig. 101). Its maximum length, from north to south, is 4¾ miles and its breadth is 2 miles, but its area is only 6 sq. miles. Like Dhílos and Míkonos, it is a mass of granite and gneiss. The latter, which appears only in the north-western tip of Dhílos, occupies the whole northern half of Rinía. The junction of the gneiss with the granite of the southern half of the island is largely occupied by the deep gulfs of Misó Bay on the west and an unnamed bight on the east (Fig. 92).

Rinía is a low, undulating platform which attains a maximum height of 490 ft. in the north. The surface is treeless, intersected with stone walls, and cultivated here and there with crops and vines. Like Dhílos, the island is inhabited by only a few cultivators and shepherds.

Yioúra

Yioúra is a small triangular island consisting of a hilly mass with a maximum elevation of 980 ft. Its geological structure is similar to that of Ándros ; it consists of mica schist, with seams of marble and veins of quartz. The south and east coasts are straight and steep ; the north-west coast is less precipitous and rather more indented. Nowhere in the island is there a harbour. Off the south-eastern headland is the elongated rock of Gláros. Rocky, desolate, destitute of water and vegetation except brushwood and oleanders, the only inhabitants of Yioúra are a few shepherds and labourers, mostly in the service of the landowners of Síros.

Fig. 103. Relief and drainage of Yioúra

Based on the 1 : 50,000 Aegean Islands, M.D.R. 611/9536 (1943) and British Admiralty Chart 1817 (1944).

THE EPARCHY OF KÉA

The eparchy of Kéa comprises the islands of Kéa, Kíthnos, Sérifos and Makronísi ; the islands are described in this order.

KÉA

Geology and Relief

Kéa is 40 sq. miles in area and has a maximum length of 10½ miles and a maximum breadth of 5¾ miles. The island is compact in shape, and its coasts are fairly regular although they are broken by a few deep, narrow inlets, which form the harbours of the island. A feature of these inlets is that they are difficult to recognize from the sea, owing to their narrow, and often oblique, form and the high and steep slopes which flank the entrances. The interior of the island consists of a plateau with an average height of 1,450 ft. Ridges and peaks, such as Mount Áyios Ilías (1,840 ft.) rise above this level. The plateau is dissected by a more developed drainage system than is found on most islands. Deep valleys radiate from the central mountain mass and very small plains lie around the mouths of the larger rivers. There are no streams with a constant flow, but springs abound and water is plentiful, even at high levels, owing to the thick forest cover. The plateau drops steeply into the sea on all sides.

Like Ándros, the island consists of a mass of schists, which are generally greenish and rich in chlorite, and are intermixed with beds of poor marble.   There are also veins of quartz, which give rise in many parts to a layer of quartz debris over the surface.   The strike

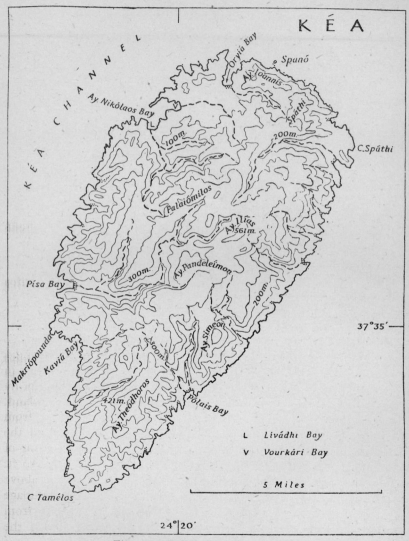

Fig. 104.   Relief and drainage of Kéa

Based on the 1 : 50,000 Aegean Islands, M.D.R. 611/9710 (1944) and British Admiralty Chart 1815 (1939).

The contours are at intervals of 100 metres (328 ft.).

of the schist beds from north-east to south-west has influenced the development of the rivers, which have their longest reaches in this direction. In such reaches the valleys are wide and open, but transverse reaches, in a south-east to north-west direction, are relatively narrow.

Coasts and Ports

The coasts of Kéa are steep, and they are broken by several small openings where the larger rivers reach the sea. Elsewhere small areas of plain occur at the mouths of other streams. On the straight south-east coast there is a small, exposed roadstead at Pólais, and 7 miles farther to the north-east is the deep Spáthi Bay. The coast between these two bays is rough, with only small, exposed coves. The north-east coast is steep and even more forbidding. Offshore is the islet of Spanó, and at the northerly point of the island is Oryiá Bay. This bay is narrow, and has a beach at its head, but it is exposed to north-easterly winds. On the western coast of the island, Kaviá Bay and Písa Bay afford anchorages, but between them is the rough and dangerous Makriópounda Point.

Áyios Nikólaos Bay in the north-west is the only well sheltered harbour in the island. The harbour consists of a double bay (Vourkári in the north-east and Livádhi in the south-west), and is entered between headlands which are 500 yds. apart. The customs house lies on the western shore of Livádhi Bay where there is the small village of Korisía. There is a good landing place with a mole. At the head of both bays are sandy beaches and shallow water. Several piers extend from the northern side of the harbour. The best anchorage is in the northern part of the harbour, where there is up to 15 fm. of water. There is ample room for large vessels, and this harbour has often been used as a naval base. It can accommodate a fleet, and its safety and convenience on the route through the Kafirévs Strait between Évvoia and Ándros have caused it to be selected as a coaling station (Plates 142 and 143).

Population and Settlement

As in other Aegean islands, the population, which was originally coastal in its distribution, was driven by fear of piracy into the interior, and the inland town of Kéa became the medieval centre of population and remains the capital. It is the only town in the island, and occupies a position of great natural strength commanding the valleys and passes of the north and centre of the island ; its population numbers about 3,000. A steep road follows the valley to Korisía and Vourkárion on the harbour of Áyios Nikólaos. The town of Kéa consists of solidly built houses on a steep hill slope, at a height of 1,000 to 1,200 ft., and it is backed by the windmill-

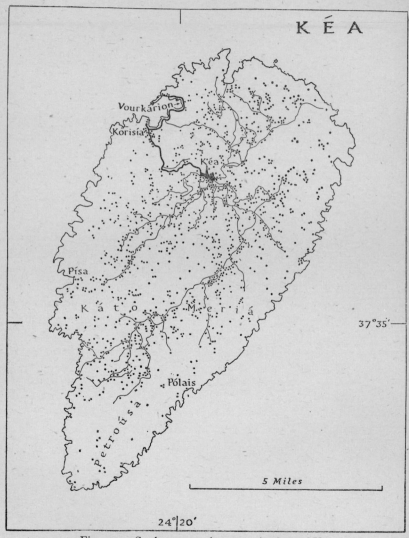

Fig. 105. Settlements and communications of Kéa
Based on the 1 : 50,000 Aegean Islands, M.D.R. 611/9710 (1944).
For key see Fig. 95.

crowned heights of Palaiómilos. The streets are narrow and dark, paved and often vaulted over.

The only villages are Korisía (295) and Vourkárion (241), both on Áyios Nikólaos Bay ; but a process of dispersion is going on. At first *stávloi*, rude cultivators' huts, were built as temporary shelters but later they gradually came to be occupied permanently. Much of the island is now dotted with these rough dwellings, which in some places have collected to form hamlets.

Agriculture

The flatness of the upland plateau, the damp atmosphere and the abundance of springs, make it possible to carry cultivation to higher levels than in most islands. The uplands and even the highest points of the island are covered with oak (*Quercus aegilops*), and the island has a fresh and green appearance. The forest cover tends to form and hold a soil, and, in parts, grain is grown around the roots of the trees. Wheat, barley and tanning bark (from Valona oaks) are the chief products of the higher parts. In the south, where small areas of limestone occur, pastoral occupations are important. Fig, almond and other fruit trees grow well on the valley slopes and below then are vineyards and groves of oranges and lemons. In the valley bottoms are irrigated gardens.

Mining

The island has been of some little importance as a source of minerals. Ores of iron, lead and silver occur in the south and have been extracted. In recent years antimony and lead have been more important, but these have now been abandoned.

KÍTHNOS (THERMIÁ)

Geology and Relief

Kíthnos, situated 7 miles south-east of Kéa, is 33 sq. miles in area. The general form of the island is that of a tableland with undulating surface and steep coast, lower than Kéa and with no pronounced peaks. It consists of two upland areas lying north-east and south-west, connected by a belt of lower land (Fig. 106). The north-western upland is 6 miles long and extends from Cape Kéfalos to Cape Kolóna. It is higher towards its southern end, and reaches 830 ft. in Mount Kakovólos. It lies close to the sea on the north-west and forms a straight and steep coastline. The southern upland is higher in its northern half but it sinks towards the south-

Fig. 106.   Relief and drainage of Kíthnos (Thermiá)
Based on the 1 : 50,000 Aegean Islands, M.D.R. 611/8213 (1943).
The contours are at intervals of 100 metres (328 ft.).

west. It has a gently undulating profile and lies along the middle of the peninsula it forms. Both flanks have numerous lateral ravines and streamlets, which issue on an extremely rugged coast. The belt which joins these uplands is 500 to 600 ft. high, but is featureless except for the large inlets on each side, two on the north-east and three on the south-west.

The island consists almost entirely of mica-schist with intercalated beds of marble ; in places, quartzite and hornblende schist occur. The island is rich in iron ore, and some asbestos also occurs. On the plain at the head of the western arm of Loutrón Bay are the hot springs which have given the island its alternative name of Thermiá. Considerable streams exist only in the centre of the island. They rise at the north-eastern end of the southern upland and flow westwards across the central belt of lowland. Here are the three longest rivers, which flow into the three small bays on the west coast.

Coast and Ports

The north-western and south-eastern coasts of the island are straight, steep and harbourless. The north-east coast is broken by two shallow bays, the more northerly of which is Loutrón Bay. The harbour is entered between two jutting headlands, but the bay expands within and offers a good anchorage except in north-easterly winds. The bay served to export the iron ore produced in the island, and there are facilities for loading vessels. Áyios Stéfanos Bay on the south-east coast is somewhat similar in form, but is rarely used. On the west coast three bays lie close together. Mérikha Bay, the most southerly, is a long, narrow, inlet, which provides good shelter. At its head is the village of Amos Meryion. To the north are Episkopí and Apókrousis bays.

Population and Settlement

Kíthnos is one of the poorest islands in the group. Dwellings are generally mean and thatched, and the people are poor. The population is almost wholly confined to the two towns, one north and one south of the river valleys of the centre of the island. Kíthnos, or Khóra (1190) lies about the middle of the central neck of land. It is built along a low exposed ridge at an elevation of about 500 ft. Roads run to (i) Loutrá, (ii) along the ridge to Dhriopís, and (iii) along the valley to Episkopí on the west coast (Fig. 107). Dhriopís (1,463) the chief town of the southern half of the island, is larger and a road follows the valley to Amos Meryion. Loutrá is a very

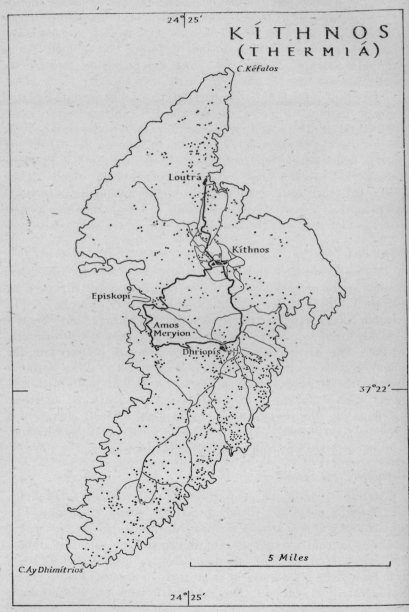

Fig. 107. Settlements and communications of Kíthnos (Thermiá)
Based on the 1 : 50,000 Aegean Islands, M.D.R. 611/8213 (1943).
For key see Fig. 95.

small coastal settlement. The agricultural population of the island lives mainly in these two towns, which are centrally placed for their respective halves of the island. Settlements, other than Kíthnos and Dhriopís, are very small.

Agriculture

There is little good soil, and the island is unproductive and nearly destitute of trees. The best parts are in the centre and around the two villages. There are fig trees and vineyards in the valleys of the west, and fruit also grows in some glens and hollows, but the chief crops are barley and pulse. Sheep, goats and pigs are relatively important, and cheese is also an important product.

SÉRIFOS

Geology and Relief

Sérifos is a barren, unproductive island lying 11 miles south-south-east of Kíthnos. It has an area of 29 sq. miles and consists of a dome-shaped mass of gneiss which rises in the centre to 1,585 ft. The area of high ground has been eroded by valleys discharging southwards to Koutalá Bay and eastwards to Livádhi Bay. The coast is steep and fringed by rugged inlets. Streams radiate from the central ridge, but areas of flat land are very small, the most important being a small marshy area at the head of Livádhi Bay. None of the streams is important and water is scarce.

Coasts and Ports

The western and northern coasts from Cape Kíklops in the south-west to Panayía Point in the north-east, are rugged and rock fringed. The numerous small bays are not backed by flat land of any extent, and there are no harbours. The south-eastern coast is even more irregular in its outline, but it contains the deep inlets of Livádhi Bay, Ambéli Bay and Koutalá Bay. Livádhi Bay lies near the chief iron mining area of the island, and is connected by light railway with the mines inland. There are three loading jetties for ore, and steamers can load at the rate of 1,200 tons a day. Ambéli Bay, to the west, has two loading jetties similar to those at Livádhi. Koutalá is the chief commercial port of the island. The bay is framed by high, rocky hills and is about $1\frac{1}{4}$ miles deep towards the north and about 600 yds. wide. Anchorage is good and can be used

in any weather.   There is a pier with limited loading facilities on
the western side of the bay.   The port is used for loading ore.

Population and Settlement

The chief town, Sérifos (1,621), is built on a conical hill over-

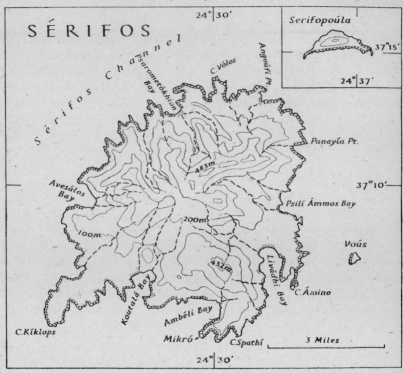

Fig. 108.   Relief and drainage of Sérifos and Serfopoúla

Based on the 1 : 50,000 Aegean Islands, M.D.R. 611/8212 (1943) and British
Admiralty Chart 1817 (1940).

The contours are at intervals of 100 metres (328 ft.)

looking the port of Livádhi (Fig. 109).   Its white houses cling to
the steep hillside, and its streets are steep and narrow.   Livádhi
itself has a population of 417.   There are several small villages in
the interior of the island.   On the hillside overlooking Livádhi are
mining settlements, and buildings connected with the mines.

Agriculture

The mountainous parts are bare and unfruitful, but the small
valleys support a little cultivation.   The island at one time produced

fruit and wine in small quantities, but agriculture has since become
entirely subsidiary to mining.

Mining

In the south-west of the island are haematite mines, which yield
an ore of some 50% metal content. In 1938, over 100,000 tons
were produced. Most of the workings are underground, though

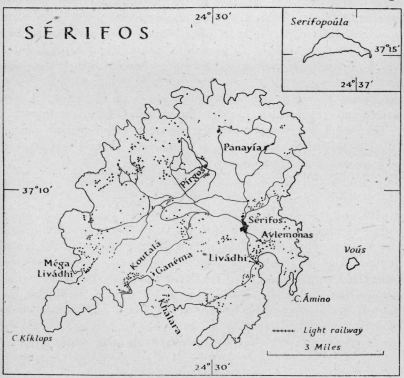

Fig. 109. Settlements and communications of Sérifos and Serfopoúla
Based on the 1 : 50,000 Aegean Islands, M.D.R. 611/8212 (1943).
For key see Fig. 95.

some are open-cast. About 400 men were employed. The ores
were sent by tramway to Koutalá and Livádhi for shipment. Reserves
have been estimated at 6,000,000 tons.

Adjacent Islands

About 4½ miles north-east of Sérifos is the islet of Serfopoúla
which rises to about 650 ft. and has steep cliffs along its southern

coast. It has pasture and a small area of cultivated land. Between Serfopoúla and Kíthnos is the islet of Pipéri which, like Serfopoúla, consists of marble. The islet of Voús rises sharply to 430 ft. about 1½ miles north-east of Cape Ámino on the east coast of Sérifos.

MAKRONÍSI

Makronísi lies between Kéa and the Attikí peninsula, from which it is separated by the Mandári Channel, which is only 1½ miles wide in its narrowest part (Fig. 16). The island is long and narrow and measures 8 miles from north to south. It consists of a single ridge which rises towards the north to a height of over 900 ft. The coast is steep and rough, but it is not interrupted by prominent headlands, except the northern and southern extremes of the island, Capes Tripití and Angálistros. On the eastern side is a shallow bight.

The island is without either landing place or permanent village. Its total population at the last census was only 38, and it appears to be little visited and little known.

THE EPARCHY OF NÁXOS

The two large islands of Náxos and Páros, with the small groups composed of Andíparos, Dhespotikó and Strongiló, lie at the centre of the Kikládhes group, and form a compact unit which has been recognized in the local name, Paronaxiá, given to the whole. The islands have the most varied relief and resources of any in the Kikládhes. Geologically, they are clearly related, consisting mainly of marble and gneiss (Fig. 92). They lie, furthermore, on a submarine shelf, cut off by deeper water from all other island groups.

NÁXOS

Geology and Relief

Náxos, the largest island in the Kikládhes, is 170 sq. miles in area. The dominant feature is the mountain spine, which extends along the whole length of the island from north to south and is unique in height, length and continuity in the Kikládhes. From the northern point of the island, Cape Stavrós, it rises within a short distance to a height of nearly 3,000 ft. From this point it runs south-south-westwards, only rarely falling below 2,000 ft., until it sinks to Cape Katoméri, the most southerly point of the island. Nearly 6 miles south from Cape Stavrós is the short transverse ridge of Mount

Koróna, which reaches 3,250 ft., and immediately to the south is a pass, and beyond it the narrow ridge of Fanára continues to the centre of the island. After a gap of about 2 miles, in which are the passes of Ay. Ioánnis and Ay. Marína separated by a small peak, is

Fig. 110.   Relief and drainage of Náxos

Based on the 1 : 50,000 Aegean Islands, M.D.R. 611/7938 and 7939 (1943) and British Admiralty Chart 1837 (1939).

The contours are at intervals of 100 metres (328 ft.).

Mount Zevs (3,305 ft.), the highest point in the island and in the whole of the Kikládhes. To the south, the ridge sinks gradually.

The ridge corresponds with a series of alternating beds of marble and gneiss, which stretch with remarkable regularity between the extremities of the island, and forms a significant divide. To the east a series of transverse spurs reach out to the coast in a direction a little north of east. They reach the coast in blunt headlands separated by deep ravines. The whole of this part of the island consists of marble, with only here and there an outcrop of gneiss.

West of the main ridge, however, the surface is composed mainly of gneiss, overlain towards the coast by Tertiary and later deposits and intruded, particularly towards the north, by granite. In the north there are lateral spurs and ravines, similar to those of the eastern division of the island. Towards the centre and south, these lateral ridges give place to broad plains, partly alluvial, and broken up by several ranges of low rolling hills parallel to the main spine. These hills, which are rounded, craggy and sometimes wooded, are quite distinct in appearance from the main spine, the hard sharp contours of which they throw into relief. These ridges enclose, about the centre of the island, the large, elevated basin of Trayía.

Coast and Ports

The coast of Náxos is very regular with few inlets of importance. The east coast from Cape Stavrós to Cape Katoméri is for the most part rugged and steep. There are no bays or harbours, and the only anchorage of importance is immediately to the south of the narrow promontory of Cape Moutsoúna. There is a jetty here, and vessels sometimes load emery, but conditions are difficult, and loading is impossible if there is a swell. The south-west coast is flatter, but is interrupted by the hill ridges which run out to the sea in low head-lands. Cape Prokópis, the westernmost point of Náxos, is formed by a small, square plateau, in the shelter of which is Náxos Bay. The western and southern shores of this bay are rocky and shallow ; near the town a quay has been built, but the water is deep enough for shallow-draught craft only. To the north-west of the town, the islet of Vákkhos has been joined to the mainland by a mole, and two other moles have been built to enclose two small harbours. There is a frequent and regular steamer service between the port of Náxos and the mainland, in addition to the boats which carry emery from the north-east coast. A motor road winds through the hills into the Trayía basin, and thence over the high pass across the main ridge of the island to Apíranthos (Fig. 111). Another motor road follows the north-west coast from Náxos to Mitriá in the Engarés commune. North-east of Náxos, the coastline again becomes high, rugged and harbourless, and closely resembles the east coast of the island.

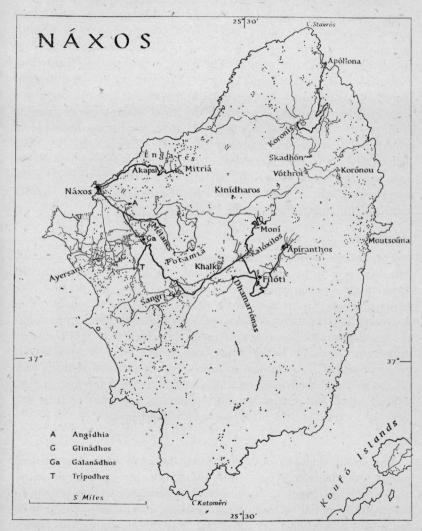

Fig. 111. Settlements and communications of Náxos

Based on the 1 : 50,000 Aegean Islands, M.D.R. 611/7938 and 7939 (1943).

For key see Fig. 95. The isolated portions of roads are joined by mule tracks which are not shown.

Population and Settlement

Náxos (2,160) the chief town of the island, lies at the north-east entrance to the only considerable bay in the island. The town is crowded, and the streets are narrow and dark (Plate 144).

Population is distributed over the whole island, but in the hilly country of the east there are frequently only isolated herdsmen's huts. Elsewhere the villages are generally large (Fig. 111). South and south-west of the capital is a group of villages situated mostly on the slopes around the plain. The most important are Trípodhes (888), Galanádhos (463), and Sangrí. The villages here are engaged chiefly in cultivation. In the centre and north-east of the island is a large number of villages in which the chief occupation is growing fruit trees. The Trayía basin is an olive producing region, and contains a considerable number of small villages. In the deep valleys of the north are a number of fairly large villages in which the economy centres on fruit cultivation. In the mining district of the north-east is the village of Vóthroi. Apíranthos (2,322), farther south, is the largest town in the island.

Agriculture

The forests which formerly covered Náxos have been cleared and now very little woodland remains. The highlands, especially those in the sparsely populated south-east, serve for grazing, and herds of goats, sheep and cattle roam freely over the hills. Pigs are reared in the patches of oakwood. Where agriculture is possible, the highlands produce crops of grain, of which barley is the most important. On the richer plain land in the west, vegetables are grown, particularly potatoes, tomatoes and onions and also tobacco. The slopes and well-watered valleys of the west have fine orange, lemon, citron and apricot groves. There is a surplus of fruit and olive oil for export, but the grain crop is inadequate.

Mining

The emery deposits of Náxos form the most important mineral product of the Kikládhes. The substance, an aluminium oxide, occurs in large, irregular masses, which are in some cases broken by the primitive device of heating and pouring cold water on to the rock. Some of the workings are open-cast, but the emery is also worked underground to depths of 600 ft. The output varies. In 1926 a total of 27,240 tons were produced. The output in 1938 was only 3,079 tons. At most, the industry has given employment to about

Plate 144.   The town of Náxos

The hill is crowned by a Venetian castle.

Facing page 458

Plate 145. Paroikía Bay, Páros

The view is northward and shows the town of Páros on the southern side of the bay.

Plate 146. The port of Páros

The view is north-eastward and shows the inner part of Paroikía Bay (*cf.* Plate 145). In the foreground are the two piers and the quays fronting the town. The west pier is about 75 ft. long and the east pier is about 325 ft. long, but depths alongside are small. In the background is Mount Taxiárkhis.

1,000 persons, but many of these were part-time employees. Emery production is a state monopoly, and production is now restricted to Náxos, though there are small deposits elsewhere in the Kikládhes. The emery was normally shipped to Síros, which has crushing mills and warehouses. Production appears to have continued under the Axis occupation.

PÁROS

Geology and Relief

Páros lies nearly 4 miles west of Náxos.   The island is 75 sq. miles

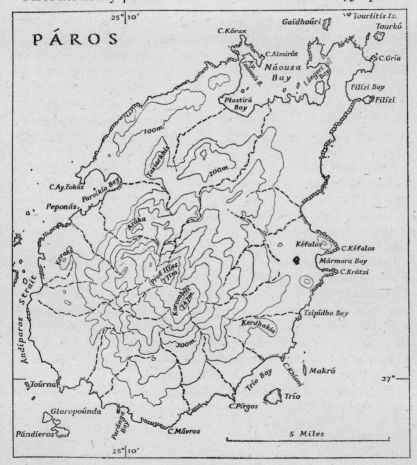

Fig. 112.   Relief and drainage of Páros

Based on the 1 : 50,000 Aegean Islands, M.D.R. 611/7941 (1943) and British Admiralty Chart 1837 (1939).
The contours are at intervals of 100 metres (328 ft.).

in area and is comparatively simple in relief and structure. Physically it consists of little more than a sharp and steep-sided ridge which rises to three evenly spaced peaks of very similar height (Fig. 112). Mount Profítis Ilías, the central peak, rises to 2,530 ft. ; the others are only a little lower. The central mountain mass does not approach the coast evenly all round. On the west, north-west and south-east it terminates somewhat abruptly in spurs, where the central ridge runs out to the sea. Between these spurs the coast is comparatively low. In the north-east it consists of comparatively recent sediments with low cliffs in places.

To the north-west of the main hill mass is a narrow ridge, stretching from north-east to south-west, developed mainly along an outcrop of marble. On its southern side a broad valley separates the ridge from the central hills. The extremities of the ridge form the north-western sides of the only two bays of importance in the island, Náousa Bay in the north-east and Paroikía Bay in the south-west. This depression forms an important route round the northern flanks of the mountains, and links the two most important plains of the island.

The ridges, peaks and tablelands are mostly of marble, which is hard and infertile. The granite regions, much smaller in area, are equally infertile, but the rich valleys and fertile lowlands are formed by erosion of the gneiss and schist, and the soft, dark, rounded hills of this material stand in sharp contrast to the bright and striking marble areas.

Páros is formed of alternating bands of marble and gneiss, with small intrusions of granite in the north and west ; in the east, Tertiary and later sediments overlie the older rocks. Much of the marble is inferior, but at lower levels the translucent white marble is of the highest quality. The alternating layers of marble and gneiss often give a curious streaked appearance to the hills. The white marble has formerly been worked. There are deposits of emery in the south, but they are not worked.

The drainage is of a simple radial pattern. Most of the rivers rise in the central ridge and flow by short straight courses to the sea.

Coasts and Ports

The coasts of Páros are nowhere as steep as those of Náxos. The island has two important harbours. On the north-west coast is Paroikía Bay, an inlet considerably over a mile in depth, and over half a mile wide at its entrance. The bay is not suitable for large

vessels, and, although there are two small piers, most of the loading
and unloading is done by lighters (Plates 145 and 146). Motor roads
connect the town of Páros with Náousa in the north, Lévkai in the
centre and Venetía in the south-west (Fig. 113).

Fig. 113.   Settlements and communications of Páros

Based on the 1 : 50,000 Aegean Islands, M.D.R 611/7941 (1943).
For key see Fig. 95.

Náousa Bay, 4 miles to the north-east, is one of the most commodious harbours in the Kikládhes.   From an entrance 1 mile wide,
the bay broadens eastwards and westwards behind low rocky capes
to a width of 2 miles and extends 1½ miles inland to a low shore.
Inshore waters are generally shallow and strewn with rocks, but in

the north-east and north-west are inlets sheltered from the north-west wind, to which the other parts are exposed. Trío Bay on the south-eastern coast is a good anchorage in summer, but is exposed to swell and strong winds in winter.

Population and Settlement

The population inhabits a number of large villages, but dispersion is also very evident (Fig. 113). Páros, the chief town (1,975) lies on the south-eastern side of Paroikía Bay and stretches up the gentle slope behind. It is the chief port of the island, and the centre of the western agricultural area. Náousa (959) occupies a similar position in the north-east, on the southern side of Náousa Bay. Several villages lie amongst the orange and lemon groves of the foothills to the south, of which the largest is Márpissa.

Agriculture

Páros is a barren island, and the highlands have at most a scanty covering of scrub. The cultivable land is not extensive, but is often rich, and this, combined with the mildness and dampness of the climate, explains the high quality of the limited output. The productive areas are the plains of the north-west, north and north-east. The low gneiss foothills of these parts have fine vineyards and olive groves. In the warm valleys of the east coast, where springs abound, are irrigated gardens containing orange, citron and other fruits, and considerable quantities of potatoes. The low, hilly coastal region of the north-east supports vines and grain. In the uplands of the interior sheep and goats are pastured.

ANDÍPAROS

Andíparos is separated from the island of Páros by the Andíparos Strait, which is a little over half a mile wide in its narrowest part. The centre of the island is occupied by a mountain mass which rises in Mount Áyios Ilías to over 980 ft. A long spine-like ridge reaches out to the south-east and forms the narrow promontory of Cape Petalídha. North of Áyios Ilías is a narrow small rounded depression, beyond which low hills continue to the northern extremity of the island. Andíparos consists predominantly of mica-schist and marble, with small areas of recent alluvium, particularly in the central depression. As is commonly the case, much of the hilly land is composed of marble.

The hills are scrub covered. Cultivable land is limited but productive and grain and vines are grown. A French concession has mining rights in the island, and formerly a considerable amount of zinc was produced. The mines now appear to have been closed. There are iron ores which do not seem to have been exploited.

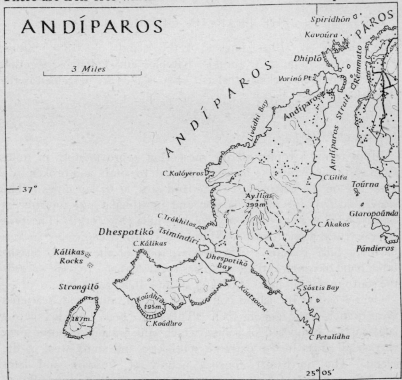

Fig. 114. Relief, drainage, settlements and communications of Andíparos
Based on the 1 : 50,000 Aegean Islands, M.D.R. 611/7942 (1943) and British Admiralty Chart 1837 (1939).
The contours are at intervals of 100 metres (328 ft.). For key to roads and settlements see Fig. 95.

Kástro, or Andíparos (612) is the only nucleated settlement. It lies in a depression near the northern tip of the island, and is so built that the backs of its houses form a circular wall, pierced by gates.

Adjacent Islands

The hilly, scrub-covered island of *Dhespotikó* lies close to the south-western side of Andíparos, and forms with the latter island a convenient anchorage in all except south winds. Dhespotikó consists almost wholly of marble.

Strongiló is even smaller, and is only an uninhabited rock. Off the northern point of Andíparos are the rocky islets of Dhipló and Kavoúra.

THE EPARCHY OF MÍLOS

The eparchy of Mílos consists of the islands of Mílos, Sífnos, Folégandros, Síkinos, Andímilos, Kímolos and Políaigos, together with certain other rocks and islets. The islands are described in the this order.

MÍLOS

Geology and Relief

Mílos forms a rough oblong measuring approximately 11 miles from east to west, and 5½ miles from north to south, and broken by a great bay on the north coast ; the land area is 62 sq. miles. The eastern half of the island is low and mostly flat but towards its eastern edge it rises to an area of low hills (Fig. 115). The promontory to the north-east of Mílos Bay is also occupied by an area of more hilly country. The western part of the island, on the other hand, is rough and hilly and has rocky coasts. It rises towards the south to the hill mass of Mount Profítis Ilías (2,464 ft.).

Over a half of the island consists of volcanic tuffs with scattered areas of more basic igneous rock. These have been extruded on to a land surface composed of schist, which still remains exposed over very small areas in the extreme south-east and south-west of the island. The north-east consists mainly of Tertiary and later deposits, and east of Mílos harbour is an area of ill-drained alluvial land (Fig. 91).

Coast and Ports

The eastern and southern coasts are fairly straight and regular, and the west coast is only slightly indented, but the north coast has three conspicuous headlands, Cape Váni in the north-west, Cape Spilás in the centre, and a blunt promontory which stretches towards Kímolos in the north-east. Between Capes Spilás and Váni, an opening leads into Mílos Bay.

The great inner *harbour of Mílos* is roughly oval in shape, the longer axis lying east to west. This harbour is one of the best in the Aegean. The entrance, between Cape Kalamária and Cape

Plate 147   Mílos Bay from the north

In the foreground are the Akrádhia islets and beyond is the entrance to the inner harbour between Cape Fourkovoúni and Cape Kalamária (see Fig. 115).   The peak on the right is Profítis Ilías.   The town of Mílos is on the extreme left of the view.

Plate 148.   Adhámas (Port Mílos)

Adhámas is the port of the town of Mílos (Kástro).   It has two piers : a wooden pier 100 ft. long at the west end of the town and a stone pier, 150 ft. long, at the east end ; the charted depths at their heads are 5 and 6 ft. respectively.

Plate 149. The village of Folégandros
The village is perched on a cliff which drops almost sheer for 1,000 ft.

Plate 150. The town of Kímolos

[Facing page 465

Fourkovoúni, is about a mile wide. The harbour is sheltered by high ground to the north, west and south-west, and except towards the east and south-east it has high and rocky shores and deep water. The harbour has at various times been used by naval vessels, but as a commercial port it has little value, although it is in regular communication by sea with Kímolos, with the larger islands to the

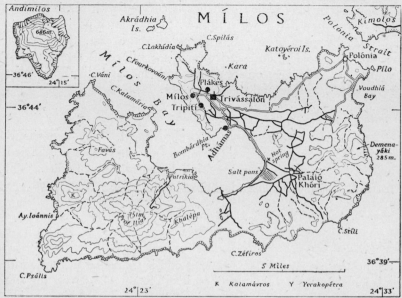

Fig. 115. Relief, drainage, settlements and communications of Mílos and Andímilos

Based on the 1 : 50,000 Aegean Islands, M.D.R. 611/7936 and 7937 (1943) ; British Admiralty Chart 2051 (1939) and *Population de la Grèce d'après le Recensement du 15–16 Mai, 1928*, deuxième édition (Athènes, 1935).
The contours are at intervals of 100 metres (328 ft.). For key to settlements and roads see Fig. 96.

north, and with Piraiévs. The chief settlement on its shores is Mílos (Kástro) which lies to the east of the entrance. There is a pier on the south-eastern side of the bay (Plates 147 and 148).

Other inlets round the coast of Mílos are rarely used except as refuge in bad weather. There is a small wharf in Voudhiá Bay in the north-east.

Population and Settlement

The hills of the western half of the island and the swampy land east of the harbour have confined the greater part of the population to the promontory north-east of Mílos Bay. Here Mílos itself

(788) and the village of Tripití (838) lie on the western side of the hill overlooking the harbour. A short distance to the east, and still on higher ground, are most of the other significant villages of the island, and the only motor roads in the island are in this area.

Agriculture

The western hilly region of Mílos is covered with scrub and the gullies are often filled with thicket. Little attempt is made to cultivate any part of western Mílos. In the east, the malarial swamps are avoided, and agriculture is confined to the low hilly country. Corn and cotton are grown, and vines and olive and orange groves occupy valleys and warmer slopes.

Mining

The mineral resources of Mílos are small. The deposits of bauxite are said to have been worked out. Barytes are quarried, and there are said to be some small kaolin and silica workings. The open-cast manganese workings appear to have been abandoned.

SÍFNOS

Geology and Relief

Sífnos has an area of 34½ sq. miles and is triangular in form, with its apex pointing to the north-west. The highlands lie towards the west, and consist of three parallel ridges, stretching mainly across the island. The two more northerly of these ridges trend almost east-west and reach heights of 1,535 and 1,627 ft. The most southerly trends north-west to south-east and is much larger and higher, reaching 2,280 ft., in Mount Profítis Ilías. South of this last ridge, its deeply furrowed sides drop to the south-west coast. Towards the south-east all the ridges coalesce and sink to form a plateau some 700 ft. high. In the south a small tableland with almost precipitous slopes lies between the bays of Vathí and Platíyialos.

The structure of the island is different from that of the others in this part of the Kikládhes, and resembles more closely that of Síros. It consists of great beds of marble, inset with schist. The strike of the beds is roughly east-west, and influences the drainage pattern at least in the north of the island. The high ground and ridges generally consist of marble ; the lower and more productive land in the east is mainly of schist (Fig. 91).

Haematite is found in the marble, together with ores of lead and zinc. There are many traces of mining in the north-east.

Fig. 116. Relief, drainage, settlements and communications of Sífnos

Based on the 1 : 50,000 Aegean Islands, M.D.R. 611/8211 (1943); British Admiralty Chart 1817 (1940) and *Population de la Grèce d'après le Recensement du 15–16 Mai*, 1928, deuxième édition (Athènes, 1935).

The contours are at intervals of 100 metres (328 ft.). For key to settlements and roads see Fig. 96.

Coast and Ports

The coasts of Sífnos are high and steep. On the western coast, only Kamáres Bay is of commercial importance ; it is exposed to the west, but has a small pier near the head of the bay. Áyios Yeóryios is a port of call for the island steamers and a metalled road links Áyios Yeóryios with Apollonía and Káto Petáli. Vathí Bay is a shallow lagoon-like inlet farther south. Between Kamáres Bay and Cape Fílippos are three further inlets but none of them has any commercial value. There is little break in the continuity of the cliffs on the east coast, but there is an anchorage in Kástron Bay. On the south-east coast are Fáros and Platíyialos Bays ; the former is sheltered but small.

Population and Settlement

Apollonía (619), the chief town, lies on the western edge of the plateau and at the foot of Mount Profítis Ilías. A mile to the north lies Artemón (597), the second largest settlement. Kástron and Áyios Yeóryios (Kamáres) are small coastal settlements.

Agriculture

The mountains are scrub-covered, and the most fertile part is the eastern plateau, which is carefully cultivated. Grain and garden crops are produced, and there are orchards, olive groves and vineyards.

Mining

Lead and zinc have been of some slight importance. Extraction of the latter appears now to have been abandoned and the lead is of very slight importance.

Adjacent Islands

Kitrianí, off the southern tip of Sífnos, provides only summer pasturage.

FOLÉGANDROS

Geology and Relief

Folégandros continues the direction of the Kéa-Sífnos line of islands. It has an area of 12½ sq. miles, and is 7 miles long. A constriction in the centre of the island divides it into two small oval tablelands. The south-eastern tableland occupies almost the whole of this half of the island. There is no coastal plain, and the table-

land rises to a height of 1,348 ft. in Mount Áyios Elevthérios.
Flanking the plateau on the north-east is the narrow ridge of
Palaiókastro (1,190 ft.). The south-eastern tableland is built of
marble which overlies schist. The western tableland consists wholly
of schist and reaches the height of 1,023 ft. in Mount Merovígli.
The water supply, especially in the eastern half of the island, is scanty.

Coast and Ports

The coast is high, particularly in the south-eastern half of the

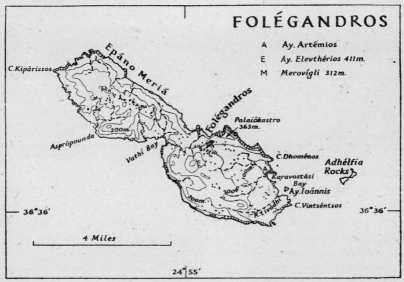

Fig. 117. Relief, drainage, settlements and communications of Folégandros
Based on the 1 : 50,000 Aegean Islands, M.D.R. 611/7933 (1943) and British
Admiralty Chart 2753 (1942).
The contours are at intervals of 100 metres (328 ft.). For key to settlements and
roads see Fig. 95.

island. At the eastern point of the island there is an anchorage in
Karavostási Bay. Landing is impracticable on all other parts of the
eastern half of the island. Vathí Bay is the southern constriction
in the centre of the island. The anchorage is exposed to the west.
The west coast of the island closely resembles the east coast in its
general ruggedness.

Population and Settlement

Folégandros, or Khóra (375) is the only centre and contains a very
large proportion of the population of the eastern part of the island.

Small, scattered settlements are, however, developing. Over the western part of the island are rude, single-roomed stone huts, which were used originally as temporary shelters, but are now permanently occupied. Folégandros itself lies at the head of a depression which leads up from Karavostási Bay, and is flanked by Mount Áyios Elevthérios and the Palaiókastro ridge. It is difficult of access, and formerly served as a place of refuge (Plate 149).

Agriculture

The two halves of the island are economically distinct. The eastern part, with its massive marble, is mainly covered with dry scrub, and serves to pasture sheep and goats. There is a little agriculture round the town of Folégandros and fruit is grown in the valleys. The western part, in contrast, is composed of schist. Springs are more abundant here and good harvests are obtained from the terraced hillsides.

Adjacent Islands

In the 6-mile stretch of water between Folégandros and Síkinos is a chain of small islets, composed of marble. The first, Áyios Ioánnis, lies off the mouth of the Livádhi river. The Adhélfia Rocks lie 2 miles to the north-east, and, between these and Síkinos, is the rather larger island of Khardhíotissa, which is occasionally used for pasturage. Close to the south-western tip of Síkinos are the rocks of Kalóyeroi and Káravos (Fig. 118).

Síkinos

Geology and Relief

Síkinos covers an area of 15 sq. miles. It is the most inaccessible of the Kikládhes, for, although its coasts are neither continuously steep nor so rockbound as those of Folégandros, the absence of important inlets, and the sudden squalls which are a feature of the island, make it very difficult of approach. A mountain ridge lies close to the north-west coast of the island. There is a steep drop to the rugged, harbourless coast on this side, but, on the south-east, torrents have eroded the gentler slope into several lateral spurs which extend from the main ridge to the coast. One of these ridges rises in Troulion to almost 2,000 ft., the highest point in the island. North of this ridge is the largest valley in the island, leading up to a relatively low col across the main ridge.

Like Folégandros, the island consists of a mass of marble and schist. The former covers something over a half of the island but rivers have in places cut through it into the underlying schist. The greater heights are usually of marble. As in Folégandros, the schistose areas are more productive and densely peopled.

Coasts and Ports

In spite of the transverse ridges which come down to the south-

Fig. 118. Relief, drainage, settlements and communications of Síkinos
Based on the 1 : 50,000 Aegean Islands, M.D.R. 611/9064 (1943) and British Admiralty Chart 2753 (1942).
The contours are at intervals of 100 metres (328 ft.). For key to settlements and roads see Fig. 95.

east coast, there are no deep bays and the island is almost entirely bordered by cliffs. Only Málta Cove in the north-east, and Skála Bay near the centre of the east coast, deserve the name of bay. The latter is the one generally used by visiting steamers.

Population and Settlement

The population is concentrated in Kástron, or Khóra (267), situated in the lowest saddle across the main ridge of the island. It commands a view over both coasts and grew as a place of safety from sea raiders. Outside the capital are a few huts which are

inhabited temporarily. The people of Síkinos are cut off from
outside contacts by their inhospitable coast, and are simple, poor
and frugal.

Agriculture

The soil is poor ; water and wood are scarce ; irrigation is not
practised, and the population is dependent on rain water. The
valley sides are terraced and cultivated as much as possible. Grain
and pulses are grown ; there are a few olive and fig trees.

ANDÍMILOS

This island, which is bare and uninhabited, consists of a single
trachyte mass, which rises steeply from the sea to a height of 2,250 ft.
(Fig. 115). It is occasionally used for grazing goats by peoples of
neighbouring islands.

KÍMOLOS

Kímolos lies north-east of Mílos, from which it is separated by a
little over half a mile of water. It has an area of 15 sq. miles and is a
rounded, compact island, with a small bay on the north-east coast.

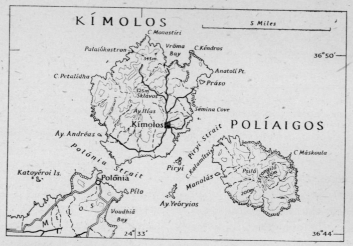

Fig. 119.   Relief, drainage, settlements and communications of
Kímolos and Políaigos

Based on the 1 : 50,000 Aegean Islands, M.D.R. 611/7937 (1943) ; British
Admiralty Chart 2051 (1939) and *Population de la Grèce d'après le Recensement du
15–16 Mai*, 1928, deuxième édition (Athènes, 1935).

The contours are at intervals of 100 metres (328 ft.).   For key to settlements and
roads see Fig. 96.

A hilly mass lies rather north of the centre, and reaches 1,132 and 1,066 ft. in the two peaks of Palaiókastron and Sklávos respectively. Except for a small strip on the east, where there are Tertiary and later rocks, the whole island consists of volcanic tuff, similar to that of Mílos. The almost complete lack of springs makes cultivation difficult, and the inhabitants have to rely on rain water which is collected in cisterns. There are several small bays and anchorages, but no good accommodation for large vessels. The harbour of the chief town, Kímolos, is a small creek on the south-east coast.

Almost the whole population lives in the town of Kímolos (1,959), which stands on a hill near the south-east coast (Plate 150). The hills are quite barren, and only the southern half of the island can show scanty fields of grain, bordered with loosely-built stone walls : a few olives, figs and vines grow in the valleys. There is, however, considerable maritime activity.

POLÍAIGOS

Políagos is a small, barren and uninhabited island consisting of a hilly mass rising to 1,214 ft. in the centre (Fig. 119). It is sometimes used for grazing stock by the people of Kímolos.

THE EPARCHY OF THÍRA

The eparchy of Thíra comprises the islands of Thíra, Íos, Amorgós, Iráklia, Skhoinoúsa, Koufó, Káros, Andíkaros, Dhríma, Dhenoúsa, Makares, Kínaros, and Anáfi ; the islands are described in this order.

THÍRA

Geology and Relief

Thíra, or Santorín, is the most interesting and spectacular island in the Kikládhes. The neighbouring islets of Thírasía, Aspró and Kaïméni cannot be considered apart from Thíra, for together they form the submerged crater of a volcano which is still far from extinct. Thíra itself is a crescent, convex towards the east, with long and clearly marked horns pointing west at both its northern and southern ends (Figs. 120 and 121). The slenderness and regularity of the crescent are obscured only by the oblong mass which thickens and broadens it towards the east and south-east, and contains the crystalline ridge of which the original island was composed. Neglecting for the moment this ridge as a now subsidiary feature, the island may be described as a hollow, truncated cone, which rises from an outer sandy beach of unusually regular form, at first gently and afterwards more steeply, to an inner concentric rim which, though broken by large gaps, undulates between elevations of 1,200 and 500 ft. (Plate 151).

This rim is narrow and on its inner, or concave, side it falls precipitously to the great basin occupying the former crater. The cliffs descend to the sea from heights averaging well over 700 ft. Sometimes the descent is sheer, sometimes it is in a series of gigantic steps, which represent successive volcanic deposits, leaving at their base one or two insignificant platforms and, except along the southern horn, hardly a single cleft or beach. From top to bottom the lateral interval is rarely more than 100 yds., and here and there earthquakes and weathering have formed rifts, later filled with white pumice, and immense outstanding bastions. The effect of these great encircling cliffs is heightened by the great and sudden depth of the waters at their base, by the hot springs which well up here and there below them, and by the still smoking peak of the central Kaïméni Isles. The varied forms and bizarre colouring of the cliffs, in which all shades and colours are represented in the strata, and the land slides and great boulders ever threatening to break loose from above, complete a scene hard to imagine or describe.

The outer surface of the cone, with its gradual slopes, is on the whole regular, but it is scored by numerous narrow and steep-sided ravines, cut by erosion through the pumice covering. At two places only is the uniformity of this outer front broken. Towards the south-east lies the rocky mass which represents the original, pre-volcanic core. Running as a ridge obliquely across the main crescent, slightly south of its extreme eastern curve, this mass, which has been partly overwhelmed by volcanic deposits, rises in Profítis Ilías to 1,887 ft. Continued towards the south-east by a saddle (Selláda), it terminates at the south-east in the height known as Mésa Vounó (or Áyios Stéfanos) (1,200 ft.), the high and steep sides of which form the only considerable rocky stretch on the whole outer coast.

Along the coast on either side of this ridge are the only two plains of Thíra. They are largely covered with fertile soil washed down from the neighbouring heights. In the more northerly plain near the coast stands an isolated rock, Monólithos. The southern plain has two small brooks which descend from the slopes of Mount Profítis Ilías. These are the only streams in the island. The narrow

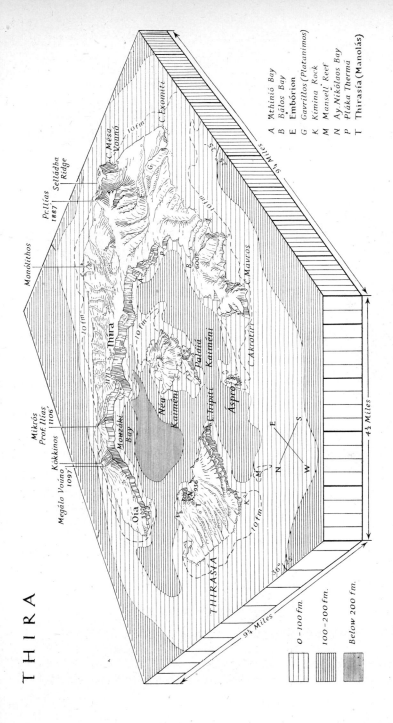

THIRA

A   Athinió Bay
B   Bálos Bay
E   Embórion
G   Gavríllos (Platanímos)
K   Kímina Rock
M   Mansell Reef
N   Ay. Nikólaos Bay
P   Pláka Thermá
T   Thirasía (Manolás)

Fig. 120.   Relief diagram of Thíra.

Based on the 1 : 50,000 Aegean Islands, M.D.R. 611/7940 (1943) and British Admiralty Chart 2043 (1937).

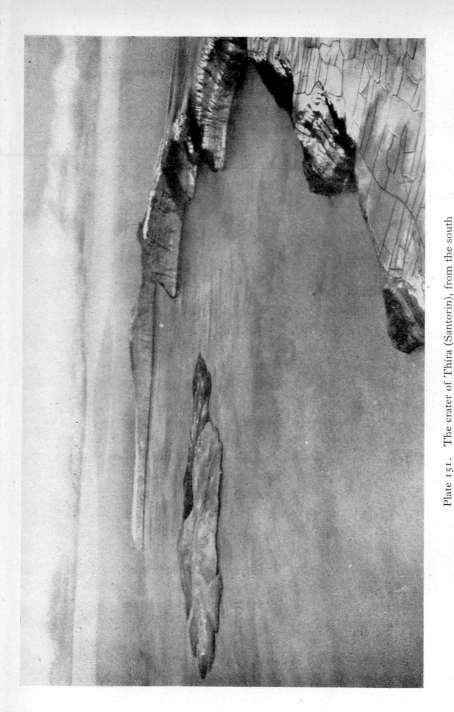

Plate 151.   The crater of Thíra (Santorin), from the south

The view shows the eastern rim of the crater, forming the main island, and within the crescent are the Kaiméni islands.   The town of Thíra can be seen perched on top of the cliff in the middle distance.

ravines referred to above are dry, except after rain. Then they are filled with roaring torrents, which endanger the paths and houses along them, and carry down much mud towards the coast ; but few of them reach the sea. The scarcity of water is one of the most striking features and serious problems of Thíra.

Thirasía shares in every way the characteristics of Thíra, and resembles it in everything except its smaller size. Thírasía is separated from the northern horn of Thíra by a channel a little over a mile wide, but of very considerable depth. Two and a half miles of water lie between Thirasía and Cape Akrotíri, the southern horn ; in the middle of this strait is the Áspro group of islets. These are small trachyte rocks, which are the only remnants of the original crater rim on this side.

The crater of Thíra is a remnant of a volcano which was active in Tertiary times. In the centre the caldera, the small islands of Palaiá Kaïméni, Mikrá Kaïméni, and Néa Kaïméni have been created by eruptions within historic times. Eruptions are known to have occurred in 46 B.C., A.D. 726, 1573, 1650 and 1707. In 1866 the volcanic plug known as Georgios was formed, but from that date until 1925 the volcano was quiescent. Then an eruption was preceded by a slight earthquake, but the first indications of volcanic activity was the heating of the water in the narrow strait between Mikrá Kaïméni and Néa Kaïméni, and fishermen were forced to leave the neighbourhood. On 11 July magma welled up and spread over the whole channel between the two islands. The first phase of this outbreak culminated in mid-September, and was marked chiefly by the explosive emission of gas and ashes. In the middle of October activity started again and was marked by an increased lava flow. This diminished in November and was not renewed until 7 January, 1926. Gaseous explosions and lava flows took place and activity did not finally cease until May. In the course of the eruption a flow of lava completely filled the strait between Mikrá Kaïméni and Néa Kaïméni and sent two delta-like flows into the sea on each side of the smaller island. Stones were discharged to a height of 1,600 ft., while flames shot up to a height of over 60 ft. The explosions took place rhythmically, ten or more following each other at intervals of about a second.

Coasts and Ports

The southern coast of Thíra, from Cape Akrotíri to Cape Exomíti, the most southerly point of the island, is formed by two shallow bays.

It has cliffs but is not rugged.   From Cape Exomíti to Kamári
Point the coast is flat and smooth, broken only by the precipitous
headland of Mésa Vounó.   The north-east facing coast, between

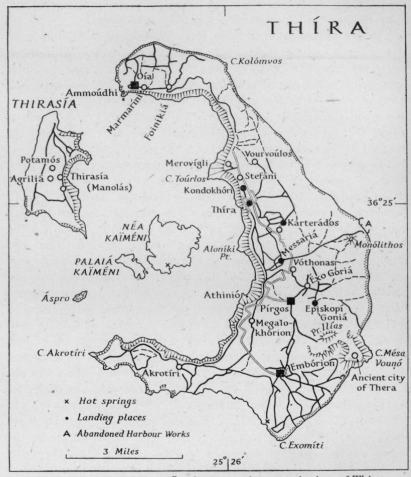

Fig. 121.   Relief, drainage, settlements and communications of Thíra

Based on the 1 : 50,000 Aegean Islands, M.D.R. 611/7940 (1943) and *Population
de la Grèce d'après le Recensement du* 15–16 *Mai,* 1928, deuxième édition (Athènes,
1935).

For key to settlements and communications see Fig. 96.

Kamári Point and Cape Kolómvos is straight and flat.   A little to the
north of Kamári Point harbour works were started but have been
abandoned ; two moles remain.   The northern coast of Thíra is
smooth and backed by low hills.   The outer, western coast of

Plate 152.   The town of Thíra (Santorin)

At the foot of the cliff is the *skála*, or landing place, whence a path zig-zags along the cliff face to the town on the summit.

[*Facing page 476*

Plate 153. Terraced lands on Thíra (Santorin)

The view shows the intricate terracing on the volcanic soils behind the crater rim. Note the absence of trees which is due to the arid nature of the soils.

Thirasía is in every respect like that of northern Thíra. Within the crater rim, the coast of both Thíra and Therasía is precipitous, dropping from heights of up to 1,000 ft. into depths of up to 100 fm. within 400 yds.

In spite of its appearance, Thíra offers little accommodation for ships, chiefly because of the abruptness of its cliffs on the inner side and the steeply shelving sea floor on the outer side. The landing place of Thíra, the chief town, is formed by a small natural platform at the foot of the cliffs. It is large enough to contain some houses, and is connected with the town above by a steep winding track. There is no anchorage owing to the depth, and vessels make fast to bollards cut in the cliff. Another landing place, Athinió, lies some 2 miles to the south, and there is a third, Marmaríni, just within the northern ' hook ' of the island (Fig. 121).

Population and Settlement

Settlements and dwellings in Thíra are usually on ground that is of no agricultural value. The villages are often pressed into narrow ravines, where they cling to the steep sides or are excavated out of them. Cement is much used in their construction, owing to the liability to earthquakes and the lack of timber. Cave dwellings also result from the absence of timber. These are often mere hollows in the soft tuffs and are faced with a wall having doors and windows.

Thíra is, after Síros, the most densely populated island in the Kikládhes. The town of Thíra (Pherá), however, has a population of only 680. It lies in a long line on the steep western rim of the crater, and partly down the face of the cliff (Plate 152).

There are large and flourishing villages on the fertile plain of the south-east and north-east of the island. The largest of these are Embórion (1,119), Pírgos (1,015), Episkopí Goniá and Karterádos.

Agriculture

Except on the rugged limestone mass of the south-east of the island, there is soil of varying fertility ; it is poorest on the more recent lava flows and best on the plains of the east. The most serious obstacle to agriculture is the scarcity of water. Trees are few and stunted, although cypresses, olives and figs are grown around the villages. Vegetable and grain crops are grown on the plains to the east, but the most important occupation is viticulture. Grapes are grown for the table and for wine, and vineyards cover most of the area of weathered pumice. This rock is a water-holding rock of some importance, and even in hot and dry seasons has sufficient moisture to keep the vines fresh. Considerable numbers of sheep and goats are kept on the island.

Íos

Geology and Relief

Íos is a compact island of some 40 sq. miles and lies 3 miles east-north-east of Síkinos. The coasts are everywhere less steep and more easily approached than those of Thíra, but the island is mountainous (Fig. 122). There are, however, considerable areas of low land. The hills constitute four distinct masses, each related more or less closely to the geology.

The southern part of the island, south approximately of Prásso and Kálamos Bay, is a plateau composed of granite. The land is of gentle relief, but is bare and strewn with boulders. To the north is the broad Pírgos mass consisting of schists. Its irregular surface reaches 2,410 ft. in Profítis Ilías. The sides of the mass fall away steeply, especially in the south and south-east, and are cut by deep ravines. To the north-east is Mount Áyios Ilías (1,575 ft.), which consists mainly of gneiss. From this summit a spur extends northwards, while on the south-west is a smaller spur that ends on a conical hill on which stands the chief town. The extreme north of the island is also made up of schist, with masses of marble along the north-east coast and in the interior (Fig. 92).

Numerous gorges and ravines furrow the sides of these hills, without, however, forming considerable valleys. The oval depression at the head of Íos harbour and enclosed by the northern and north-eastern hills is the most considerable area of plain. It possesses water even at midsummer and is the largest cultivable area. It is connected by passes with minor plains on the north and north-east.

Coasts and Ports

The coast of Íos is much indented. At the most southerly point of the island is Manganári Bay, which is used as an anchorage in northerly winds. The south-west coast is rugged, and near its western end has three considerable inlets. The middlemost of these is Íos harbour, one of the safest and roomiest in the Kikládhes. To the south-east is the larger, but less protected, bay of Milopótamos. The north-western coast offers no anchorage, and on the north-

Plate 154.   Íos Bay from the east

In the foreground is the *skala* or landing place.   On the extreme left is the entrance to the harbour, flanked by Cape Fanári.
In the background is the island of Síkinos.

Plate 155. Ayía Ánna Bay, Amorgós

The view is south-eastward and shows the villages of Aiyáli and Potamós on the shore and along the hill slopes respectively.   The track joining them winds along the ridge to the town of Amorgós.   Note the carefully terraced slopes.

east coast there are only the open and exposed bays of Theadhótis and Psátha. On the south-east coast, Tris Klisiés Bay is also used as a roadstead.

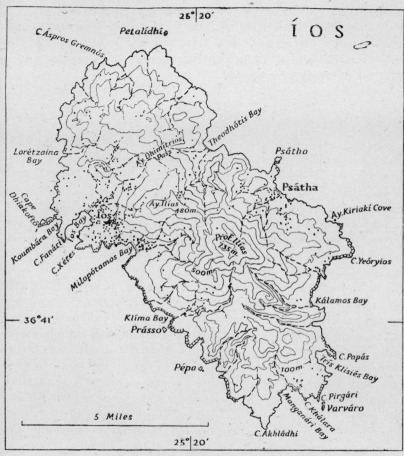

Fig. 122. Relief, drainage, settlements and communications of Íos
Based on the 1 : 50,000 Aegean Islands, M.D.R. 611/7932 (1943) and British Admiralty Chart 2753 (1943).
The contours are at intervals of 100 metres (328 ft.). For key to settlements and roads see Fig. 95.

Population and Settlement

As in most other islands, the population is concentrated in the town of Íos (1,472), built on the southern and eastern flanks of a conical hill in which one of the spurs of Áyios Ilías ends. Elsewhere are scattered dwellings on the lower slopes of the highland, especially around Psátha on the east coast.

Agriculture

Vegetation is scanty, and Íos is the least productive, for its size, of the islands of the Kikládhes ; the fertile areas are mostly small and isolated. Valleys are often terraced, but the only considerable area of arable land is around the harbour of Íos. Grain, pulses, olive oil and wine are produced.

AMORGÓS

Geology and Relief

Amorgós is a long, narrow island, measuring over 20 miles from south-east to north-west, and having an area of about 48 sq. miles. It is formed of a mountain ridge, which extends the whole length of the island, close to the south-eastern coast. At its extremities this ridge curves round to the north-west and transverse ridges form headlands. Between these are two broad bights, each interrupted by minor headlands and bays. Rivers are necessarily short in an island as narrow as Amorgós. There are three small areas of lowland, separated from one another by rugged highland, opening on to the north-west coast of the island. In the north is that behind Ayía Ánna Bay. South of Cape Áyios Iliás is the more fertile and important Katápola plain. Both these plains are well watered, but at the south-westerly point of the island the Kolofána plain is waterless. Owing to the shape and structure of the island, each of the two more northerly plains, and to a less extent the south-western one also, forms a distinct centre of cultivation and settlement, isolated from the others by the transverse heights and ridges, and the island is sometimes spoken of as though it were three distinct islands, Káto Meriá in the south-west, Amorgós in the centre and Yiáli in the north-east. Water supply is not abundant ; wells are scarce and windmills are used for pumping.

Coast and Ports

The north coast from Cape Vilakárdha, the most northerly point, to Cape Prásino, the most easterly, is high and bold. The south-eastern coast is similarly formed of high cliffs from which, during northerly gales, the wind descends in heavy squalls. There is no anchorage or shelter, and vessels normally avoid this coast. The north-west coast, from Cape Kalotéri to Cape Vilakárdha is irregular,

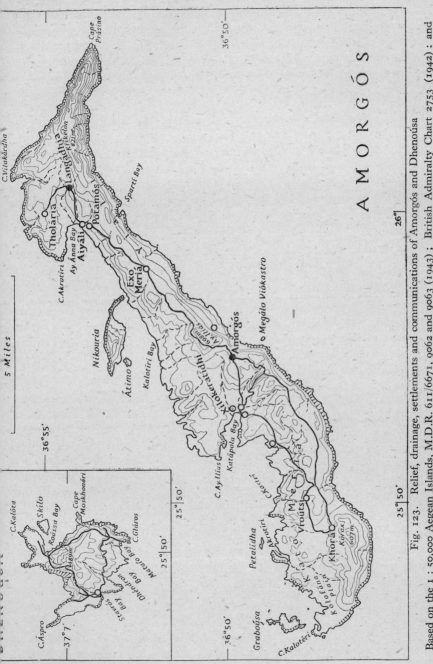

Fig. 123. Relief, drainage, settlements and communications of Amorgós and Dhenoúsa

Based on the 1 : 50,000 Aegean Islands, M.D.R. 611/6671, 9062 and 9063 (1943); British Admiralty Chart 2753 (1942); and *Population de la Grèce d'après le Recensement du 15–16 Mai, 1928*, deuxième édition (Athènes, 1935). The contours are at intervals of 100 metres (328 ft.). For key to settlements and roads see Fig. 96.

A M O R G Ó S

with small islands. Katápola Bay, immediately to the south of Cape Áyios Iliás, is the best anchorage on the coast, and can be entered easily. Kalotíri Bay, between the coast of Amorgós and the small, narrow, but very high, island of Nikouría, and Ayía Ánna Bay to the north of Nikouría, afford anchorages and have sandy beaches.

Population and Settlement

The population of the southern part of the island was formerly concentrated in Amorgós (Kástro or Khóra) now a village of 700 inhabitants. It lies at the head of a valley immediately to the south of Mount Áyios Ilías, and has access to the fertile valley and harbour below it to the west. It is a well-built and prosperous looking settlement but has been losing population to newly dispersed settlements in other parts of the island. In the Káto Meriá are several small agricultural villages. In the north, several villages are grouped around the plain of Aiyáli; the chief of these are Langádhia (545), Potamós (178), and Tholária (321).

Agriculture

Cultivable soil is confined to small areas. Lower slopes are usually well terraced, and grow olives; vines and fruit trees, grain and pulses are grown on high ground. Fruit, together with cotton and tobacco, are important on the small plain areas. The highlands support sheep, cattle and goats.

IRÁKLIA

Iráklia is the largest of the group of small islands which lies between Íos and Amorgós. It is a triangular island of about 7 sq. miles, composed of marble with an outcrop of gneiss in the south. Its relief is low and it has several inlets capable of serving as anchorages but the south coast is bordered by cliffs. It is scrub-covered, but has a small area of cultivated land and a population of 286.

SKHOINOÚSA

Skhoinoúsa is a small islet of low relief, composed entirely of marble. It has a population of 260. To the south are the small, uninhabited islets of Agrílos and Ofidhoúsa.

KOUFÓ ISLANDS

These two islands are low and almost contiguous; they have a combined area of about 5 sq. miles. They are composed of sedi-

mentary rocks of undetermined age and are comparatively fertile
and well cultivated. Áno Koufó, the more populous, had a total
population of 234 in 1928 ; Káto Koufó had only 27.

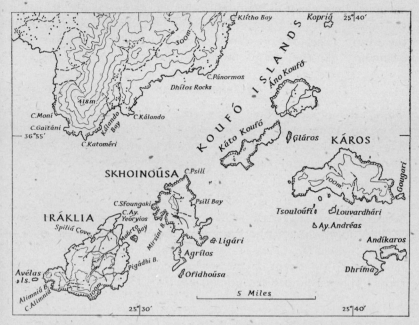

Fig. 124. Relief, drainage, settlements and communications of
Iráklia, Skhoinoúsa, Koufó and Káros

Based on the 1 : 50,000 Aegean Islands, M.D.R. 611/7939 (1943) and British
Admiralty Chart 1837 (1939).
The contours are at intervals of 100 metres (328 ft.). For key to settlements and
roads, see Fig. 95.

KÁROS

Káros is a high, barren island of limestone, 8 sq. miles in area. It is
without settled inhabitants and serves only to pasture goats. The
population amounted to 12 in 1928.

ANDÍKAROS AND DHRÍMA

Andikaros and Dhríma are small islands, composed of marble.
They have low relief, although the former is bounded by steep cliffs.
The population of Andíkaros was 7 ; Dhríma appears to have no
permanent population.

DHENOÚSA

Dhenoúsa is an island of irregular shape, with long promontories to the north-west, north and north-east (Fig. 123). The centre is occupied by a chain of rounded hills, consisting mainly of marble and schist. Zinc and copper ores have been worked in the hills of the west. Vegetation is scanty, and most of the island serves as pasturage. The population numbers 235.

MÁKARES ISLANDS

These are a group of three rocky islets, 5 miles west of Dhenoúsa. They are composed of sedimentary rocks, including limestone. The group appears to have no settled population, and probably provides only rough grazing for flocks and herds from Náxos.

KÍNAROS

Kínaros, the most easterly island in the Kikládhes group, lies some 7 miles north-east of Amorgós. It is about $2\frac{1}{2}$ miles long, rises to 1,050 ft., and has an area of $1\frac{1}{2}$ sq. miles. The coast is cliffed and mostly steep-to, except off the western end where are some sunken rocks. The island had ten inhabitants in 1928.

ANÁFI

Anáfi, and its adjacent islands are the most south-easterly in the Kikládhes. The main island lies 13 miles east of Thíra and 27 miles south of the western extremity of Amorgós. The extreme length of Anáfi is nearly 7 miles ; its breadth from north to south is about $4\frac{1}{2}$ miles, and its area is about 15 sq. miles.

Geology and Relief

The backbone of the island consists of a ridge which lies from east to west, with its crest rather nearer the northern than the southern coast (Fig. 125). The ridge culminates in Mount Profítis Ilías which reaches about 1,600 ft., the highest point of the island. To the north this peak is linked by a saddle with a steep mountain mass that occupies most of the northern angle of the island. Elsewhere the northern flanks of the ridge descend to the coast along fairly regular slopes which are cut by only short, straight, but deep valleys. The southern flanks of the ridge, on the other hand, are more dissected ; broad valleys alternate with intervening heights.

To the east, the ridge descends to the low isthmus which separates Kálamos Bay from Mégas Potamós Bay. To the east of this isthmus is a rugged promontory which rises to over 1,000 ft. in Mount Kálamos.

The geological structure of the island is complex. In the west the lower land between Mount Profítis Ilías and the sea is developed in sedimentary rocks, comprising sandstones, conglomerates, shales and some beds of limestone, which have been little folded. The centre

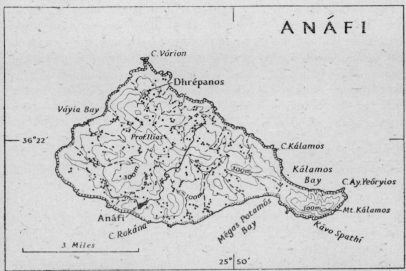

Fig. 125. Relief, drainage, settlements and communications of Anáfi
Based on the 1 : 50,000 Aegean Islands, M.D.R. 611/8210 and British Admiralty Chart 2836a (1944).
The contours are at intervals of 100 metres (328 ft.). For key to settlements and roads, see Fig. 95.

of the island consists of metamorphic schist, gneiss and marble ; granite has been intruded into the mass, and in the east is an outcrop of limestone. The promontory culminating in Mount Kálamos is a marble mass. Lead ore and haematite occur in the gneiss of the centre of the island, but the quantities are not sufficient to be of economic significance.

Coast and Ports

The coasts of Anáfi are regular and for the most part they are steep and fringed with above-water and sunken rocks. The northeast coast stretches for 6 miles from Cape Vórion in the north to

Cape Áyios Yeóryios. It is interrupted only by short, cliffed headlands. The intervening bays are shallow and backed by sandy beaches on which boats may be drawn up, but they have no protection and no harbour works. Kálamos Bay is rather deeper, but is not more sheltered than the others. It is backed by the low isthmus which links the island with its eastern headland. This eastern headland drops steeply to the sea ; on the south-east the land drops 1,300 ft. in less than 250 yds.

The south coast is even less broken by headlands, but is in general lower than the north-east coast. The blunt headland of Cape Rokána lies at about the centre of this coast. In its shelter is a small boat harbour, with a good landing place, which serves the village of Anáfi. The north-west coast resembles the south coast. It is backed by low hills and is without conspicuous headlands. In the centre of this stretch is Váyia Bay. Cape Vórion, at the northern extreme of the island, is a low, anvil-shaped promontory.

Population and Settlement

The population of the island in 1928 was 565. The people live mainly in the village of Anáfi, which lies on the slope of a conical hill, a little less than half-a-mile from the south coast (Fig. 125). The village stands at a height of about 500 ft. but is linked by a track with its *skála* on the coast to the east of Cape Rokána. There are scattered settlements in the lowlands of the west and in the sheltered valleys of the centre, but the only other settlement with any pretensions to being called a village is Dhrépanos. The only coastal settlement is the *skála* of Anáfi.

The islanders have little interest in the sea and do not engage in fishing or trade. The nature of the coastline restricts intercourse with other islands, and, although the inhabitants sometimes migrate to work on the mainland of Greece, Anáfi is one of the most primitive and self-contained of the islands.

Agriculture

The island is, however, not unproductive. The gentler slopes, valley bottoms and small plains around the coast are very productive. Slopes are terraced and sown with grain, and the western part of the island is almost wholly cultivated. The vine and olives are grown. Springs are numerous—a result of the varied structure—and gardens and orchards are well watered. The higher ground is covered with phrygana scrub ; goats are kept on the hills, but there are few cattle. The agriculture of the island suffices for its few inhabitants. There is very little trade with other islands or the mainland.

Adjacent Islands

Some 1½ miles south-east of Cape Rokána are the two small low and uninhabited islets of Ftená which rise to 50 and 60 ft. respectively. A further three miles to the south-east lies Anafópoulo (Pakhía), and 1¾ miles to the east of it is Makrá. Anafópoulo rises to 740 ft. and Makrá to 420 ft. ; both are uninhabited.

BIBLIOGRAPHICAL NOTE

1. The fullest account of the Kikládhes in English is given in the N.I.D. *Handbook of Greece*, vol. 2, part 1 (London, 1919). The basic work, however, is A. Philippson, ' Beiträge zur Kenntnis der griechischen Inselwelt ', *Petermanns Mitteilungen, Ergänzungsheft* 134 (Gotha, 1901). A general summary by the same author is ' Die griechischen Inseln des Ägäischen Meeres ', *Verhandlungen der Gesellschaft für Erdkunde zu Berlin*, vol. 24, pp. 264–80 (Berlin, 1897).

2. Some account, mainly gazetteer in type, is given in French in a series of articles by H. Hauttecoeur published in the *Bulletin de la Société Royale Belge de Géographie* (Brussels). The volume and page numbers of the accounts of the several islands treated are : Amorgós, vol. 23 (1899), pp. 90–108 and 145–71 ; Ándros, vol. 19 (1895), pp. 429–58 ; Kéa, vol. 20 (1896), pp. 181–225 ; Kímolos, vol. 25 (1901), pp. 350–66 ; Kíthnos, vol. 21 (1897), pp. 417–47 ; Sérifos, vol. 24 (1900), pp. 533–58 ; Tínos, vol. 27 (1903), pp. 197–230 and 288–311 ; Thíra, vol. 28 (1904), pp. 413–31 and vol. 29 (1905), pp. 47–62. See also the *Mediterranean Pilot*, vol. 4, 7th edition (London, 1941).

3. Popular accounts of the islands are V. C. S. O'Connor, *Isles of the Aegean* (London, n.d.) and H. F. Tozer, *The Islands of the Aegean* (Oxford, 1890).

4. The most useful topographical maps of the Kikládhes are (*a*) the 1 : 50,000 Aegean Islands, M.D.R. 611. This series is based on Greek and German maps and British Admiralty charts, and was revised from air photographs of 1942–3. The maps were drawn and reproduced by 512 Fd. Survey Coy., R.E. They have a kilometre grid, latitude and longitude (from Athens) in margins, contours and form-lines in brown at 20 metres interval, metalled roads in red, other roads and tracks in brown ; (*b*) the 1 : 250,000 Greece, G.S.G.S. Series 4410 (for details see p. 315) and the 1 : 250,000 Aegean, M.D.R. 609. The latter were compiled and reproduced by 512 Fd. Survey Coy., R.E., in 1943 and have a 10 kilometres grid, latitude and longitude (from Greenwich and Athens) in margins, contours at 200 metres interval, layer-shaded in purple, roads and tracks in black, water in blue.

Chapter XIII

THE EASTERN AEGEAN ISLANDS

GENERAL FEATURES

The Eastern Aegean islands lie close to the west coast of Asia Minor. There are four large islands, namely, Lésvos, often called Mitilíni (623 sq. miles), Khíos (331 sq. miles), Sámos (190 sq. miles), and Ikaría (99 sq. miles), together with three groups of small islands, namely, Psará and Andípsara, off the north-west point of Khíos, the Oinoúsa or Spalmatóri islands in the Strait of Khíos, and the Foúrnoi islands lying between Sámos and Ikaría (Fig. 126). In addition, there are many scattered islets and rocks, most of which lie close inshore but are too small to be inhabited.

Geology and Relief

Geologically the Eastern Aegean islands are varied in character. Sámos and Ikaría, together with the mainland region immediately to the east of them, are apparently a part of the old crystalline block of the south Aegean, the scattered western remnants of which form the Kikládhes, southern Evvoia and eastern Attiki. The recent volcanic tuffs of Sámos may be comparable in significance to the volcanics of Méthana, Thíra and Kos and may mark the approach to the northern edge of the block which is bounded to the south by the arc of volcanic peaks extending from Méthana to Kos (see vol. I, p. 5). The Central Basin of the Aegean separates Sámos and Ikaría from Khíos (see vol. I, p. 9). The mountains of Khíos trend north to south, parallel to the ranges of the neighbouring Erythraean peninsula of Asia Minor, and Lésvos is also closely related to the nearby landmass. The geological relations of these islands to the mainland of Greece are obscure, but, whatever the original elements in the region of the Aegean Sea, the islands of its eastern shore were created by earth movements in Quaternary times. The generally straight trends of their coasts are probably determined by fracture lines, but the detail of the cliffed headlands, rocky bays and deep inlets is the result of differential erosion and a recent relative rise of sea level. The continued instability of the region is indicated by the frequency of earthquakes (see vol. I, p. 8).

Fig. 126. Key-map of the Eastern Aegean Islands
Based on the 1 : 1,000,000 G.S.G.S. Series 2758, Sheet J 35.

CLIMATE

The climate of the islands is mild for the latitude and, except in the low-lying and swampy districts, which are malarial in the autumn, is healthy and pleasant ; the winters are mild and wet, the summers are warm and dry.

The islands differ one from another according to their latitude, configuration, and their position with respect to the mainland ; mainland influences are stronger in Lésvos and Sámos than in Khíos and Ikaría, where the winters are milder and wetter and the summers are not so dry (see table on p. 491). The situation of the islands off the west coast of Asia Minor gives them certain features which are transitional between Western Asiatic and Aegean conditions. In comparison with regions of the western Aegean, the shores of the eastern Aegean are colder and wetter in winter and humidity is greater, but conditions are milder and less stormy than in the islands of the northern Aegean. The depressions which pass eastwards through the Mediterranean in winter tend to move through the Aegean Sea on a north-easterly track, passing into the Black Sea along the line of the Sea of Marmara. Thus the west coast of Asia Minor and the Eastern Aegean islands have more prolonged rainfall than places in eastern Greece. In this area the damp air rising at the warm front of the depression meets the edge of the mountainous land and is forced to rise further, and this orographical rainfall accounts in part for the larger totals (vol. I, Fig. 58). The amount of rain varies greatly according to conditions prevailing locally in Asia Minor, but it seems to average between 25 in. and 27 in. annually. The variability appears to be greatest in Lésvos where 17·4 in. were recorded in 1912 and 41 in. in 1900. Sámos, on the other hand, has a higher total rainfall and more rain days than Khíos or Lésvos owing to considerably higher figures between November and March. These higher figures may be due partly to the fact that the meteorological stations at Mitilíni and Khíos are on the east coast and are sheltered from the rain-bearing winds, while that of Sámos is at Vathí, which is exposed to westerly and north-westerly winds. During the summer months Sámos has less rain than the other islands. In all the islands, rain falls chiefly during the period from November to February, but the month of heaviest rainfall and the total amount differ from island to island. Winter cold and summer heat are tempered by proximity to the sea and although temperatures may reach 80°–90° F. in June, July and August and may fall to 18°–20° F. in January, such extremes are rare ; the summer average is about 70° F. and the winter average is about 45° F. Snow falls not infrequently but soon melts. Wind conditions vary greatly in the different islands, but in general these islands are more sheltered than those of the northern Aegean ; Ikaría has the most exposed position. In spring, summer and autumn, northerly winds prevail and calm days are few ; in

Average monthly temperature (1900–29) in °F

	Jan.	Feb.	Mar.	Apr.	May	June	July	Aug.	Sept.	Oct.	Nov.	Dec.	Year
[Smyrna	45·6	47·6	51·2	59·5	69·2	76·4	80·9	82·0	75·0	65·8	58·1	51·8	63·6
Mitilíni	47·3	48·9	52·3	59·1	66·9	74·7	80·0	79·2	72·6	64·5	56·7	50·4	62·5
Khíos	—	—	—	—	—	—	—	—	—	—	—	—	—
Sámos	48·6	51·3	51·6	59·2	67·6	73·8	78·8	78·1	72·5	66·9	59·0	52·5	63·3
[Athens	48·3	49·2	52·8	58·9	66·8	74·7	80·5	80·2	74·0	66·2	57·8	51·8	63·3

Average monthly rainfall (1894–1929) in inches

	Jan.	Feb.	Mar.	Apr.	May	June	July	Aug.	Sept.	Oct.	Nov.	Dec.	Year
[Smyrna	2·8	2·6	3·2	1·1	0·9	0·4	—	0·4	0·5	0·8	3·3	3·7	19·8
Mitilíni	4·2	4·1	2·8	2·7	1·1	0·2	0·1	0·1	0·4	2·0	3·5	4·8	20·0
Khíos	5·0	3·9	2·5	0·8	0·6	0·3	0·1	0·1	1·0	3·1	4·8	6·4	28·7
Sámos	5·4	5·5	4·6	1·1	1·0	0·2	—	0·1	—	1·9	5·4	7·7	33·0
[Athens	2·1	1·6	1·2	0·8	0·8	0·6	0·2	0·3	0·6	1·6	2·6	2·7	15·1

Average number of rain-days (1894–1929)

	Jan.	Feb.	Mar.	Apr.	May	June	July	Aug.	Sept.	Oct.	Nov.	Dec.	Year
[Smyrna	10·8	10·6	9·6	7·1	5·1	1·5	0·3	0·6	2·5	3·0	10·3	11·1	72·5
Mitilíni	11·1	10·4	6·5	6·5	5·5	2·8	1·2	0·4	2·1	7·5	8·5	12·9	75·5
Khíos	13·5	10·2	10·3	6·0	4·5	1·6	0·5	1·1	3·2	7·0	12·4	15·0	85·3
Sámos	14·0	14·0	12·0	9·0	3·0	3·0	0·5	1·2	1·0	6·0	10·0	14·0	87·7
[Athens	10·8	9·3	8·9	7·2	7·0	4·9	1·6	1·8	3·3	6·6	10·0	10·9	81·9

Source : E. G. Mariolopoulos, *The Climate of Greece* (Athínai, 1938).

winter, winds are variable but seem to come frequently from the mainland from an easterly, south-easterly or southerly quarter. Local winds, determined by the form of the channels and islands, are often strong and may be dangerous to shipping. Land and sea breezes are very well developed.

HISTORICAL OUTLINE

Historically, as well as physically, the islands reflect their position ; they have been linked, now with the Greek mainland, now with the Asia Minor plateau, but they have always played an active role in the economics and politics of the Aegean. The islands were excellently placed on the trade routes between Crete, the Hellespont and the fertile valleys of Asia Minor and they soon became the site of wealthy and important settlements. At the beginning of the fifth century B.C. they fell under the domination of Persia, but, breaking free during the latter part of the century, each was more or less closely attached to the Athenian League. Athens valued their friendship highly, since they lay on the flank of her grain route to the Black Sea, and in general she allowed them considerable independence in exchange for loyal support. In the first century A.D. the islands were organized as part of the Roman Province of Asia and under Roman, and later Byzantine, rule they continued to flourish. During the period of the troubled later Middle Ages, Saracens, Franks, Venetians and Genoese were attracted by the fertility of the islands and attempted conquest and settlement. The Genoese were successful and two big trading companies were established ; these were the Gattilusio in Lésvos and the Giustiniani in Khíos and Sámos (see vol. I, pp. 181–2). All three islands fell to the Turkish Empire in the fifteenth century and they were only finally recognized as part of Greece at the Treaty of Lausanne in 1923, though independence of Turkey and allegiance to Greece was declared during the Balkan War of 1912–14.

LÉSVOS

Lésvos lies at the mouth of the Gulf of Edremit. The Muselim Channel, which is 5 to 6 miles wide, separates it from the mainland on the north ; Mitilíni Strait, on the east, is 8 to 11 miles wide but is shallower and more irregular in form. A stretch of open sea separates Lésvos from Khíos and the Karaburun peninsula of

Plate 156. The village of Stípsi in Lésvos (Mitilíni)

The village is near the centre of the view, which is northward. In the foreground are the olive groves and terraced lands of the villagers ; in the background are the western slopes of the Lebétimnos massif.

Plate 157. The plain of Eressós in Lésvos (Mitilíni)

This plain is the largest area of flat land in the west of the island and is closely settled and well cultivated, in contrast with the bare slopes of the hill-country of volcanic tuffs behind. The town of Eressós lies above the plain at the entrance to a high pass through the mountains.

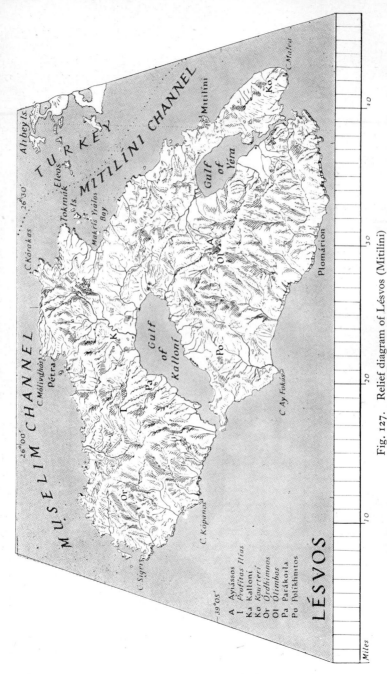

Fig. 127. Relief diagram of Lésvos (Mitilíni)

Based on the 1 : 50,000 Lésvos (6 sheets), M.D.R. 167/8222–27 (1943) and British Admiralty Chart 1665 (1940).

Asia Minor 20 miles to the south. Lésvos is the largest Greek
island after Crete and the seventh largest island of the Mediterranean.
Its greatest length, from Cape Sígri to Cape Maléa (west-north-west
to east-south-east), is about 44 miles and its greatest breadth, from
Cape Kórakas to Cape Áyios Fokás (north-north-east to south-south-
west), is about 23 miles. The island is, however, cut into by two
great gulfs opening from the south coast—the Gulf of Yéra and
the Gulf of Kalloní ; these reduce the land area to about 623 sq.
miles.

<h3 style="text-align:center">GEOLOGY AND RELIEF</h3>

Lésvos is a fragment of the neighbouring mainland. The Muselim
Channel and the Gulf of Edremit are roughly at right angles to the
Strait of Mitilíni and all three are probably determined by fracture
lines ; the rock types and structures of the island can be closely
matched on the mainland. Geologically, Lésvos can be roughly
divided along a line running north-north-east to south-south-west,
from Makrís Yialós on the Mitilíni Channel, along the east coast of
the Gulf of Kalloní, to Khokhlakáris Bay (Fig. 128). To the west

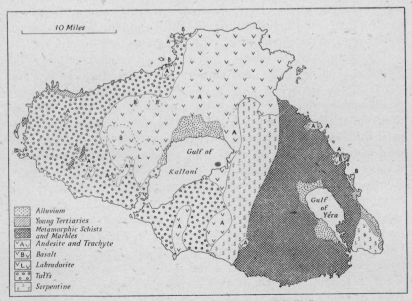

Fig. 128.   The geology of Lésvos (Mitilíni)

Based on maps by (1) A. Philippson in *Petermanns Mitteilungen, Ergänzungsheft* 172
(Gotha, 1912) and (2) L. de Launay in *Annales des Mines*, vol. 13 (Paris, 1898).

of this line the island, except for a patch of marine Tertiaries on the western promontory, is composed of volcanic rocks ; to the south-east of the line a variety of rocks appear.

North of the Gulf of Kalloní the island is built of andesite lavas, changing in the region due west of Kalloní to the more basic forms of labradorite and basalt. Tuffs, the consolidated ash of these lavas, form the westernmost part of the island and extend in a broad band eastward along both north and south coasts. The south-eastern region is of more complicated structure and is composed of older rocks consisting of an alternating series of crystalline limestone (marble), and slates and schists. The crystalline limestones are varied in character, some are pure white, some are streaked with yellow, others are red or grey or black. North and south of the town of Mitilíni, and around the Gulf of Yéra, they cover wide areas and are of great thickness. A wide belt of serpentine, running almost completely across the island, divides the volcanics from the crystalline sedimentaries, and serpentine again forms the southern part of the peninsula between the Gulf of Yéra and Mitilíni Strait. Small masses of andesite and basalt occur along the east coast and account for the largest of its rocky promontories and headlands. Here and there between these headlands are small patches of alluvium, but the only large alluvial stretches are to be found on the shores of the Gulf of Yéra and the Gulf of Kalloní.

The scenery of the island reflects its geological structure. The west has a barren look ; the outlines are sharp, trees are few, and much of the surface is bare rock. The east seems, by contrast, green and fertile, for although the limestone hills rise higher and their upper slopes are as devoid of soil as the volcanics of the west, their middle and lower slopes carry trees, and the schists form lower land with a thin soil cover supporting a vegetation which is relatively dense for Mediterranean lands.

There are no extensive lowlands ; along the north and north-west shore of the Gulf of Yéra there is a stretch of alluvium, and another small stretch forms a low-lying marshy area on the west coast just north of the entrance. Around Parákoila on the west coast of the Gulf of Kalloní recent alluvium gives good fertile land, but the most extensive alluvial plain of the island lies at the head of the Gulf of Kalloní. Much of this is marshy, and a large salt lake exists in winter though it dries in summer.

The island can be divided into three regions : (1) the plateaux of the south-east, which are dominated by the limestone massif of

Fig. 129. Relief and drainage of Lésvos (Mitilíni)

Based on the 1 : 50,000 Lésvos (6 sheets), M.D.R. 617/8222-27 (1943) and British Admiralty Chart 1665 (1940).

The contours are at intervals of 200 metres (656 ft.).

Ólimbos ; (2) the central volcanic highlands which stretch from west of the Gulf of Kalloní to the north coast and culminate in Lebétimnos ; and (3) the tangled hill country of the volcanic tuffs in the west.

The Ólimbos Massif

The Ólimbos massif is a broad east-west ridge with a serrated crest, rising to 3,175 ft. The eastern part of the ridge is built of a great thickness of marble, and the summit itself is a shining conical marble peak which falls away to the north in a sheer precipice 600 ft. high. Southwards, the Ólimbos highland extends to the coast in forbidding uplands which have a general level of more than 1,000 ft., rising in peaks to 2,000 ft. and deeply dissected by ravines. Much of it is built of schist and serpentine and the lower slopes carry a dense maquis vegetation of arbutus, myrtle and broom. The northern and eastern flanks of the main ridge are seamed by deep parallel canyons cut into the limestone ; these form very difficult but often very beautiful country between Ayíassos and the Gulf of Yéra. To the north of the Ólimbos massif, the ground descends to a wide plateau, 500–800 ft. high, lying between the Gulf of Kalloní and the east coast. The surface of the plateau has for the most part gentle slopes and was once well forested. In spite of the deforestation which this more accessible region has suffered, it still carries extensive patches of Black pine (*Pinus nigra*) forests, and planes, chestnuts and poplars grow in the valleys and around the gulfs.

The Central Highlands

The central highlands, lying west of the Gulf of Kalloní, form a broken belt running south-south-west to north-north-east. In the south the highland rises steeply from the west coast of the gulf and has a very irregular surface, with bare heights and sharp peaks. Northwards, it is continued through still more broken country to the Lebétimnos massif, a bare and striking ridge overlooking the north coast and rising to the towering peak of Mount Lebétimnos (3,175 ft.) (sometimes also called Mount Áyios Ilías or Ólimbos). Northward and north-eastward the ridge drops to flat plateaux which present to the coast steep edges, much dissected by ravines. Southwards, a huge amphitheatre has been eroded in the volcanic rocks which collects the drainage to the Gulf of Kalloní in a complex series of parallel headstreams.

The Western Hill Country

The hill country of the volcanic tuffs of the west has a very barren look, with stony irregular peaks rising to about 2,000 ft. The most impressive of these is the sharp conical peak of Mount Órdhimnos (1,680 ft.), crowned by the monastery of Ipsilón. The porous nature of the soil and the long drought of summer make vegetation in this region sparse. The heights are bare, the lower slopes and plateaux carry stunted prickly oak and juniper scrub, and here and there Black pines, but near the sea *Origanum*, *Agnus castus*, and other maquis species grow. The streams are marked by oleander and near the north-west coast brambles and briars fill the valleys.

Drainage

The river systems of Lésvos are in the main simple ; short swift streams have cut narrow valleys in the highland edge. The valleys often have almost precipitous sides in their upper courses, but some of them widen out farther down and in these the soil of the valley bottoms gives fertile land near the coast. In winter the streams are full, rushing torrents, but many of them, especially in the west, dry up in summer. Yet there is no serious water shortage in the island, for there are good perennial springs. Hot springs, like earthquakes, bear witness to the instability of the region. Thermí, on the east coast north of Mitilíni, has a perennial spring which flows at a temperature of 122° F. and contains sodium, magnesium and traces of other salts ; Políkhnitos, south of the Gulf of Kalloní, has a similar spring at a temperature of 185°.

There are two small basins of inland drainage on the plateau north of the massif of Ólimbos ; the eastern, and larger, is at 2,500 ft., the western, and smaller, is at 600 ft. The centre of each is a reed-grown marsh with open water in wet weather.

COASTS

The East Coast

The east coast from Cape Tokmák to Cape Maléa (Cape Zeïtín) forms the western shore of Mitilíni Strait. The strong northerly winds, which are so prevalent in the region, funnel down the straits and make conditions difficult for small boats, but the passage offers deep water. Cape Tokmák, the most north-easterly point of the island, is an impressive cliffed headland overlooking the northern entrance to Mitilíni Strait where it is narrowed by the Tokmákia

(Tomári) Islands on the west and the Alibey group of islands on the east. The Eleos islets lie in the centre of the passage between the two island groups. South of Cape Tokmák lies the wide sweep of Makrís Yialós, bordered by cliffs of volcanic rock. Along the southern shore of this bay the old crystalline rocks of south-eastern Lésvos reach the coast, and the cliffs from here to Militíni are cut in alternate stretches of crystalline limestone and schist with the boldest promontories built of recent volcanics, andesite or basalt. The water is deep offshore, and there are no real harbours, but small *skálai* afford anchorage provided the wind is not onshore. They also give the inland villages, with which they are linked by rough hill paths, a means of communication alternative to the uneven surfaced road which runs parallel to the coast, but at a distance of some miles inland. Mandamádhos, Valtzíkion, Mistegná, Thermí and Pámfilla all have *skálai* in sheltered coves. At Mitilíni there are two harbours with quays (see pp. 501–4). South of Mitilíni the coast trends south-east in a bold, almost unbroken sweep to Cape Maléa. The water is deep offshore and the land rises steeply, but not precipitously, from the sea to the wild hill country of the peninsula between the east coast and the Gulf of Yéra. Mount Kourterí, at the south-eastern end of the peninsula, rises to 1,730 ft.

The Gulf of Yéra

The Gulf of Yéra opens, through a narrow, steep-sided channel, from a bight on the south coast between Cape Maléa and Cape Válvi (Fig. 129). The channel is about 4 miles long, and, though it is in places only half a mile wide, the fairway is 4½ fm. deep. Strong northerly winds of long duration are said to decrease the depth by about two feet. At Pérama (= a ferry), a ferry carries the traffic of the road from Mitilíni to Plomárion across the channel. There are several small piers at Pérama. The gulf itself is an oval sheet of water measuring 4½ miles from south-south-east to north-north-west and 3 miles from north-east to south-west. It has regular shore lines fringed on all sides, except the south, by a narrow shingly beach. The average depth of the gulf is about 7 to 10 fm. and its mud bottom gives good anchorage ; the best and most sheltered anchorage is in the north-east of the bay.

The South Coast

The south coast from Cape Válvi to Cape Vromoúsa has in its

eastern part alternating stretches of cliffs and steep slopes. The coast trends slightly north-west in a series of shallow bights fringed by sandy and shingly beaches, and separated by rocky headlands. Some of these bights give shelter to shipping in northerly gales, but all are exposed to heavy seas if the wind is in the south. Mersiniá roadstead (Pétra Bay) has an entrance 2 miles wide but it is partially blocked by two small islets.

Plomárion lies immediately to the west of Cape Mérikhas, the southernmost point of Lésvos. It is a small port with a considerable coastal trade, but it has no good harbour. However, the anchorage lying between Cape Mérikhas and Cape Potamós, is sheltered to some extent from northerly winds. The town lies at the foot of a steep hill and the buildings extend up the slopes and along the valley to the north. It is the seat of one of the three bishoprics of Lésvos and of one of the four eparchies, and Plomárion and Mitilíni are the only two demes of the island. Plomárion is actively engaged in the manufacture and export of soap ; some flour milling and boat building are also carried on. It has a good water supply from wells, and from a reservoir fed by springs in the hills. It is linked by telephone and telegraph to other centres in the island and good roads lead to Mitilíni, via the ferry at Pérama or round the northern shore of the Gulf of Yéra. Another road leads inland to the villages on the south-western side of the Ólimbos massif and continues by a hill track to Políkhnitos.

Khokhlakáris Bay is at the western end of an unbroken sweep of coast fringed by shallow banks between Cape Potamós and Cape Áyios Fokás (Voúrkos). It affords anchorage during offshore winds but is exposed to the south ; a road leads inland to Vrissá and Políkhnitos. From Cape Áyios Fokás to Cape Kalloní the coast trends north-west ; it is high at first but the land is lower near the mouth of the Gulf of Kalloní.

The Gulf of Kalloní

The Gulf of Kalloní is entered by a channel running south-west to north-east between Cape Vromoúsa and Cape Mákara. The channel is 2½ miles long and half a mile broad at its northern and southern ends. The sides of the channel are rocky and steep, but the shores of the gulf are in general low and sandy. The southern part of the gulf is 2 to 3 miles broad, but northward it widens to about 4 miles across. There is sheltered anchorage in depths of between 4 and 10 fm., and the gulf is much frequented by local shipping. Xenorodo Bay, at the north-eastern end of the gulf, is most used and small vessels find good shelter from all winds from north-east, through east, to south-west, at Límni in the south-east corner of this bay. The gulf is surrounded by hills backed by mountain land, and is sometimes lashed by heavy squalls descending from the surrounding heights. The low-lying land round the shores is fertile and cultivated, and scattered settlements are grouped into small villages. On the south-east, Skála Polikhnítou is linked to the upland village of Políkhnitos and has salt works and olive refineries ; Parákoila, almost opposite on the north-west coast, is the centre of a fertile area. At the head of the gulf there is a group of small settlements and villages, the two most definite of which are Kerámion and Kalloní (often known as Akhirón). A road runs round the head of the gulf linking the coastal settlements with each other ; and from Kalloní a road goes to Pétra on the north coast and another eastwards to Mitilíni (Fig. 131). Kalloní has telephone and telegraph communication with the rest of the island.

The South-West Coast

The south-west coast from Cape Mákara to Cape Sígri is cliffed, rocky and backed by highland. Skála Eressoú, linked by a fair road to Eressós, has a good anchorage in 7–10 fm. of water off a fine beach, and gives shelter from north-east winds.

Port Sígrion is a useful harbour in the oblong bay, protected on the west by the islets of Sígri and Sedhoúsa, and sheltered at its northern and southern end by Cape Elaía and Cape Sígri. It can be entered from the south on either side of Sedhoúsa islet, but the entrance from the north between Sígri island and Cape Elaía is shallow and rocky. The harbour is an important naval point in the Aegean, but it is too remote and its hinterland is too infertile for it to have much commercial importance. Sígrion is only a village and is situated on a projecting point on the eastern side of the harbour. It is connected to the general telegraph system, and is linked by road to Eressós to the south-east and by a road along the northern flank of the central highlands to Míthimna on the north coast. There is regular communication by air to Athens.

The North-West Coast

The north-west coast from Cape Elaía to Mólivdhos is diversified by a series of rocky headlands and small coves ; spits extend seaward from some of the headlands, and there are rocks offshore. There is no harbour, but here and there temporary anchorages provide shelter from south-west winds. The village of Pétra lies at the head of a small bay, and a breakwater was built in 1933 to increase the safety of the anchorage. Cape Mólivdhos is a well marked headland with steep irregular cliffs.

Míthimna (population, with Mólivdhos, 2,303) is built on the southern side of Cape Mólivdhos. Its picturesque and narrow streets climb steeply to a castle on the summit. There is an anchorage in 10–20 fm. in the roadstead but the water deepens rapidly offshore. The headland gives shelter from easterly winds but throughout much of the summer, when northerly winds prevail, there is an unpleasant swell in the roadstead. The plain of Míthimna, though small, is fertile ; vines and fruit are grown and figs are produced in sufficient quantity to be exported. Míthimna is the capital of an eparchy and is connected by telegraph and telephone to the other population centres of the island. A metalled road follows the coast south to Pétra ; thence a road runs westward along the hills to Ándissa and Sígrion, another climbs to a pass in the central highlands and zigzags down to Kall#oní, and a third runs along the southern flanks of the Lebétimnos massif to Kápi and Mandamádhos and then southwards to Mitilíni. A road, which is no more than a mule track in parts, climbs the northern slopes of Lebétimnos and runs eastwards to Klió and Kápi (Fig. 131).

The North Coast

The north coast from Cape Mólivdhos to Cape Kórakas is straight and steep-to. From Cape Kórakas to Cape Féros, a great rocky promontory juts north-east, forming the northernmost part of the island. A deep bight sweeps south-eastward from Cape Féros to Cape Tokmák and the entrance to the Mitilíni Strait. The lava cliffs of the north coast offer few openings inland, and there is little communication in this area between the coast and the interior.

THE PORT OF MITILÍNI

39° 06′ N, 26° 32′ E. Population 27,870 in 1928

Mitilíni is the chief town of Lésvos and lies on a small peninsula on either side of which is a small harbour. Large vessels cannot enter and usually anchor in the roadstead, where, however, they are exposed to southerly winds.

Detailed Description (Fig. 130 ; Plate 159)

The northern harbour is the larger of the two, with an area of about 40 acres and a depth of 42 ft. across its 1,200 ft. entrance. It shallows rapidly towards the head of the bay and is therefore used by only small vessels. Some protection is given by two breakwaters composed of partially submerged boulders. On the west side of the

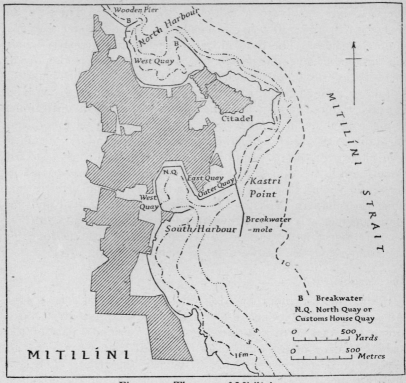

Fig. 130. The port of Mitilíni
Based on British Admiralty Chart 381 (1940).

harbour there is a quay, fringed with sunken rocks lying on a narrow bank ; the southern shore is a gravel beach and the eastern side is foul and dangerous.

The southern harbour is the more frequented and is used by vessels not exceeding 800 tons and with a draught of less than 16 ft. It is composed of an outer and inner harbour. The outer harbour is open to the south, but is protected on the eastern side by a breakwater-mole extending southwards for 1,500 ft. As yet it is unfinished

Plate 158. The entrance to the Gulf of Yéra in Lésvos (Mitilíni)

Plate 159. The North Harbour at Mitilíni
The view is north-westward from the citadel (in the foreground) and shows the
quayed western side of the harbour and the gravel beach which forms the shore on
the south side. The breakwaters are just off the view.

Plate 160. The town of Míthimna (Mólivdhos) in Lésvos (Mitilíni)

The view is from the south and shows the town extending along the southern side of Cape Mólivdhos and the castle crowning the hill. In the background the mountains of the Turkish Troad can be seen across the Muselim Channel.

Plate 161. The Ándissa valley in Lésvos (Mitilíni)

The view looks down on Ándissa Bay from the road to the town of Ándissa which lies at the head of the valley.

[Facing page 503

and only the first 700 ft. from the root provide berthing space. The depths at the entrance are about 40 ft., shoaling to 6 ft. The coast on the south side of the peninsula is quayed. The inner harbour is open to the south-east and has an area of 23 acres ; the entrance is 330 ft. wide and 22 ft. deep. The following table gives details of the quays in the port.

Details of Quays in Mitilíni Harbour

	Length (ft.)	Berthing space (ft.)	Depth alongside (ft.)	Remarks
North Harbour				
1. Wooden Pier	180	200	0–10	General cargo
2. West Quay	1,300	500	6	Masonry (?)
South Harbour				
3. Breakwater-mole	1,500	700	24	Masonry blocks on rubble ; not completed
4. Outer Quay	1,000	1,000	22	Masonry blocks on rubble base
5. East Quay	1,200	1,200	20	Masonry with concrete quay paving
6. North Quay	950	950	12–20	Masonry with stone quay paving ; one 3-ton crane
7. West Quay	1,150	1,150	22	Masonry blocks on rubble base

Port Facilities

Normally there are about 70 fishing boats which can be used as lighters, about 35 lighters with a total capacity of 1,500 tons, and ten pontoons with a combined capacity of 1,000 tons. Apart from several privately-owned warehouses in the town, there are said to be 7 acres of open storage space on the harbour quays. Lifting appliances are limited to one crane of 3-tons capacity. There are no repair shops ; supplies of coal and fuel oil are usually small and water is supplied by lighters.

The Town

Mitilíni is on the site of the ancient town ; this was originally built on an island, which was later joined to the shore by a causeway, on either side of which was a harbour. The peninsula so formed, with its medieval fortress (Kástro), is mostly uninhabited. The town extends from the neck of the isthmus to the foothills in a very attractive manner. Its churches include a cathedral, and there is a mosque. There are said to be two good hospitals. As a nomarchy the town controls not only its own island but also those of Límnos and

Áyios Evstrátios : it is also a demarchy, and the seat of a bishop. Its courts of justice include the *Plimmeliodhikíon* for the eparchy of Límnos, as well as local courts. Mitilíni gets its electric lighting from a Diesel-operated plant of 1,350 h.p., and its water from the local Mount Ólimbos and from wells. Sanitation in the town is reported to be poor.

Trade and Industries

There is a great disparity between the exports and imports of Mitilíni. Imports largely consist of essential foodstuffs like wheat and flour and such items as coal, timber and cement. Exports are very small in quantity and are largely taken up by consignments of olives and olive oil.

Trade in 1937 (*thousands of metric tons*)

IMPORTS		EXPORTS	
Foodstuffs and agricultural products	11·2	Fruits and vegetables	0·4
		Olives and olive oil	1·0
Vegetable oils	2·0	Metals	0·2
Timber and wood products	2·5		
Sugar, molasses, etc.	1·1		
Minerals	0·6		
Chemicals	0·2		
Miscellaneous	0·5		
Total	18·1	Total	1·6

Source : *Bulletin mensuel du commerce spécial de la Grèce avec les pays étrangeres, Decémbre* 1937 (Athènes, 1938).

The total tonnage of shipping entering and clearing was 0·6 million tons in 1938. In the same year the passenger arrivals were just over 21,000 and the departures were slightly more than this figure. The only industries are olive pressing and oil refining, soap manufacture and carpet making.

Communications

Roads on the island are for the most part bad, but some are suitable for motor traffic, e.g. the road from Mitilíni to Kalloní and Míthimna. Regular steamship services connect the port with Khíos, Piraiévs and Thessaloníki. There is a telegraph and island telephone service, and also a wireless station.

HISTORICAL OUTLINE

Lésvos to the south, and Límnos to the north, flank the main approach to the Hellespont. Lésvos, in addition, lay athwart the sea routes to some of the most important valleys of Asia Minor. The island formed a base sufficiently large and fertile for the successful exploitation of the opportunities the position afforded, and Lésvos early grew rich and powerful.

Classical History

According to tradition, Lésvos and the neighbouring coastlands of Asia Minor received a large immigrant population from Boeotia at the time of the Dorian invasions of peninsular Greece (1100–800 B.C.). Lésvos soon became one of the main centres of population of the ' Aeolian ' Greeks, as they were called in contrast to the ' Ionian ' Greeks who established themselves at the same time a little farther south. The town of Mitilíni, with a sheltered situation and, for that day, a good harbour, grew into an important settlement, and in its turn began to establish colonies in Thrace, in the Troad, and as far afield as Naucratis in Egypt. In the seventh century B.C. it was among the most developed regions of the Aegean, politically and socially as well as economically, and Greek literature was permanently enriched by two Lesbian poets—Alcaeus and Sappho. In the sixth century the island, involved in strife with its neighbours, fell an easy prey to Persia, who having conquered Lydia, turned anxious eyes on the Aegean lands. Persian domination was ended by the Ionian revolt of the fifth century, and Lésvos became a member of the Delian League headed by Athens.

In the Hellenistic period, Lésvos served as a base for the Persians against the Macedonians under Alexander the Great, but later it aided the Macedonians against Rome. Rome triumphed and the island was administered as a part of the Roman province of Asia, but in the following centuries the important links with the Byzantine Empire were by sea.

Medieval and Modern History

In the early Middle Ages, when chaos prevailed in much of mainland Europe, the island enjoyed with the rest of the Eastern Mediterranean area a period of prosperity based largely on sea-borne trade.

From the eleventh century the history of Mytilene, as the island was then called, was again a turbulent one ; its fertility and its position attracted all comers. In 1091 it fell into the hands of the Seljuks for a short period ; in the twelfth century it was repeatedly attacked, and sometimes occupied, by the Venetians ; in 1224 it was recovered by the Byzantines, who gave it in 1354 to a Genoese trading company, the Gattilusio. In 1462, Mytilene fell to the Turks, who, in spite of many attempts by the ' Franks ' to wrest it from them in the later fifteenth century, held it securely until the twentieth century. The Turks garrisoned the forts and a certain number of Turks settled in the island, but the Greeks were the more energetic element in the community and they gradually displaced the Turkish peasants from the more fertile areas. The priests, through church and school, encouraged the consciousness of kind among the Greeks and kept alive the Greek language and culture. Nevertheless, the men of Lésvos played no part during the Greek War of Independence (1821-9), pleading their close proximity to Turkey as the excuse for their inactivity. Thus during the nineteenth century the island remained part of Turkey, but the Greek element asserted itself more and more, and it became a centre from which Hellenization spread to the coastlands of Asia Minor. European powers also began to appreciate the importance of the position of the island. Sígri harbour occasionally sheltered units of foreign fleets, and English, French and Italian merchants began to frequent the port of Mitilíni. By the outbreak of the Balkan war in 1912, it had become one of the most important islands of the Mediterranean.

The Greeks secured the island in 1912, but at the outbreak of the war of 1914-18 the Turks had not recognized the change of ownership. It was unofficially recognized by the Great Powers as Greek, and in 1914 it was occupied by the Allies. It was restored to Greece under the Treaty of Sèvres (20 August 1920), and the restoration was confirmed by the Treaty of Lausanne (24 July 1923) after the disastrous Greek campaign in Asia Minor (see vol. I, p. 219).

At the beginning of the Balkan War the Greek population was said to number about 117,000 and the Turkish 13,000 ; the Turkish element has been almost entirely deported as a result of the exchange of populations which took place following the Convention of Lausanne (see vol. I, p. 379). More than 90,000 Greek refugees from Anatolia poured into Mitilíni during the years 1914-22 in two main waves, one following the entry of Turkey into the war, and one following the Greek defeat at Smyrna. Until arrangements could be made to send them on to mainland Greece, or to settle them on abandoned Turkish farms in the island, or to establish them in the small local industries, they suffered great hardships. Largely as a result of the substantial refugee element the political sentiment of the island from 1923–41 was strongly republican.

The importance of the position of Lésvos (the old name of the island was restored after Greek sovereignty was established) was seen in the fact that Lésvos, like Khíos and Límnos and the eastern frontier zone of Dhithikí Thráki was under German, not Italian, control during the occupation of 1941–4.

POPULATION AND SETTLEMENT

The Greek official census of 1913 gave the total population of Lésvos as 142,142 (Greeks 121,842, Moslems 20,000, Jews 300). After the entry of Turkey into the war of 1914–19, some 95,000 Greek refugees from Asia Minor came to the island, but many of them re-emigrated to the Greek mainland and the death rate among those who remained and among the islanders during the war was high, so that estimates of population in 1918 range from 160,000 to 200,000. Recent censuses suggest that this was an over-estimate. In 1920 the population of the island was 117,000 and by 1928 it had grown to 137,000 ; an estimate in 1943 was 154,000. The town of Mitilíni has grown rapidly ; in 1920 the population was 18,314, in 1928 it was 27,870. The figure for 1928 included some 30,000 refugees, of whom about one-half were in the deme of Mitilíni ; most of the remainder were scattered in the villages. The island is now almost entirely Greek ; in 1928, 120 Armenians and 15 Circasian families were recorded among the refugees, and in 1936 there were said to be three Jewish families.

The population is largely rural, and Mitilíni is the only town with more than 10,000 inhabitants, but the country people live in villages rather than in scattered farms. Apart from Plomárion (6,481) and Míthimna (1,405) the modern villages avoid the coast (Fig. 131). Prehistoric and classical sites are often coastal, but the population gradually moved away from the shores during the long centuries of political unrest in the Aegean Sea, when pirates raided and pillaged coastal towns. Most of the inland villages have small *skálai* in the nearest sheltered cove, sometimes with a few houses clustered round the landing. The modern Plomárion was once such a *skála* (then with the name Potamós), serving the upland village of Plómarion some miles inland. Since the Balkan Wars the population has tended to move from the highland village to the coast and the coastal settlement has developed into a flourishing township which has not only robbed its parent village of most of its inhabitants, but also of its name. As Potamós grew it became known as Néon Plomárion and now it is even officially referred to as Plomárion, and the upland village today is small and unimportant except that its beautiful surroundings attract holiday-makers. In most parts of the island, although there are some signs of growing *skálai*, no large scale return movement to the coast seems to be in progress. The inhabitants of the upland villages, however, move down, as they have always done, to cultivate the fertile patches of lowland near the shore.

The upland villages are surprisingly numerous and their size and prosperous appearance reflect the fertility of the land, in spite of its hilly character. The villages are most numerous in two regions —the south-east and the north-west ; the plateau country between the Gulf of Kallóni and Makrís Yialós is very sparsely populated and Ayía Paraskeví (4,549) is the only settlement of any size. There are three groups of villages in the south-east : (1) the settlements of the south-east coastal plain, (2) the settlements around the Gulf of Yéra, and (3) the hill villages of the massif of Ólimbos. The flourishing settlements of the rich olive growing district along the shore of Mitilíni Strait cling to the foothills at least two to three miles inland, and are linked to their *skálai* by rough and stony tracks. Mistegná (1,322), Thermí, Pámfilla (2,198), Mória (2,235) and Áyios Marína are typical in situation and character. On the upland edge of the alluvium around the head of the Gulf of Yéra are several scattered settlements and farms, together with the hamlets of Kheramnía and Íppios, which are often given collectively the name of Yéra. Pérama, on the small alluvial plain on the western shore of the entrance channel, has already been mentioned. Of the highland villages, Loútra (1,799) is in the south-eastern peninsula, and the Ólimbos massif is ringed by Ayiássos (5,679), Palaiókipos (2,073), Papádhos (1,319), Skópelos (3,384), Playiá (1,395), Vrissá (2,003), Políkhnitos (7,256) and Vasiliká (3,384). Most of the villages of Ólimbos are in the upper valleys and consist of a single village street, with its few shops and cafés ; side alleys lead off to the scattered farms of the wooded slopes. Políkhnitos, famous for its mineral springs, has oil presses and a small weaving industry ; it is in rather desolate country. Ayiássos, lying at the head of a narrow ravine, commands views of some of the most beautiful

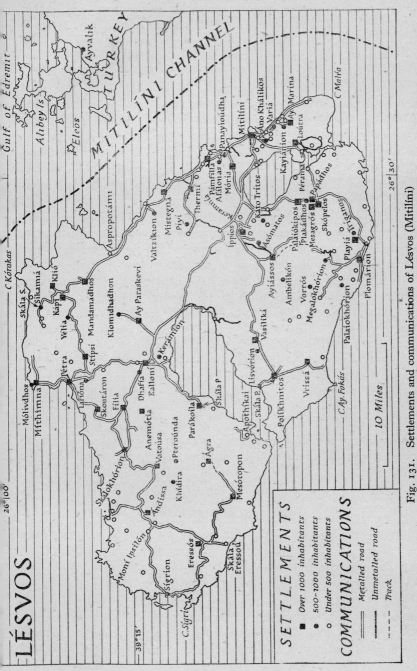

Fig. 131. Settlements and communications of Lésvos (Mitilíni)

Based on the 1 : 50,000 Lésvos (6 sheets), M.D.R. 617/8222-27 (1943) and *Population de la Grèce d'après le Recensement du 15-16 Mai, 1928*, deuxième édition (Athènes, 1935).

country in the island. It is a charming little village ; the houses are built largely in wood with overhanging tiled roofs, water is abundant, trees give shade, and there is an impression of coolness and freshness even on the hottest summer day.

The villages of the north and west of the island are on the whole barer and less attractive than those of the south-east ; trees are fewer but there are, nevertheless, some very flourishing settlements. Parákoila, on the western shore, and Kalloní (Akhirón) (3,365) at the head, of the Gulf of Kalloní, are group settlements which are similar in situation to those on the Gulf of Yéra and, like them, their names are collective. From Kalloní a road runs across the highland to Pétra (1,700), a small village in a fertile green plain near the north coast. The village takes its name from a grey, rocky spur of the hills which rises in its midst. It was perhaps originally a fortress, for it dominates the main gap through the central highlands, and is an important route centre. To the west the villages lie amidst stony hills, but they usually have access to fertile valleys. Typical villages of this type are Fília, Anemótia, Vatoúsa and Ágra, which command valleys high in the central mountains. Eressós (2,892) and Ándissa (Telónia) (2,930) lie respectively at the southern and northern end of the high pass which separates the central highlands from the massif of Mount Órdhimnos.

In the north-east of the island the two little villages of Klió and Kápi cling to the eastern slopes of Lebétimnos and a little to the south, in a broad, flat, stony valley, lies Mandamádhos (3,060). Mandamádhos is an example of a settlement which has moved inland ; the early village was on the coast, but the present one is out of sight of the sea at an altitude of 450 ft. It is linked by difficult stony tracks to several small *skálai* in bays to the north-east and south-east.

AGRICULTURE AND FISHING

Relatively few people are gainfully employed in forestry and fishing in Lésvos ; it was estimated that there were between 500 and 600 fishermen in 1936 and most of these were also small-scale cultivators. Many fewer are entirely engaged in forestry. Thus it is probable that over 20,000 families gain their living mainly by cultivating the land. The holdings belong, for the most part, to peasant proprietors and are small and scattered, making the introduction of modern methods of cultivation and marketing extremely difficult, especially

since transport is still slow and primitive. The co-operative
movement, in both compulsory and voluntary forms, is growing,
but in Lésvos it is not yet important. Few of the holdings provide
a full livelihood and the peasants are usually seamen, fishers, traders
or small-scale industrialists as well as agriculturists.

Only some 15% of the total area of the island can be cultivated.
Except in a few favoured places the soil is everywhere thin, though
rather better soil develops on the schists of the south-east. Good
deep, fertile soil is only to be found around the shores of the two
gulfs, in small patches along the south-eastern coastlands, around
Míthimna and Pétra on the north coast plain, and on the lower
slopes and in the bottoms of some of the wider valleys. Cultivation
is most intensive around the gulfs, along the south-east coast, around
Míthimna and Pétra and near Ayíassos.

Olives are by far the most important crop in Lésvos. In recent
years olives and olive oil have accounted for about 70% of the total
value of agricultural produce and Lésvos is one of the chief olive
districts of Greece. During the years 1931–5, Lésvos produced, on
an average, about 13,000 tons of oil annually. Of this, 9,000 tons
was exported and about half the export went direct to foreign ports.
The olives are mostly grown on the lowlands of the east, south-east
and south coasts, particularly in the coastal region north of Mitilíni
and in the hills and valleys around the gulfs of Yéra and Kallóni.
The trees are planted over great areas, closer together in the damper
valleys but more widely spaced on the slopes ; from afar the groves
have the appearance of grey-green forests, while from near at hand
they look like endless orchards. On the hillsides much of the
olive-growing land is terraced ; each tree is surrounded by a little
semi-circular containing wall which makes cross-country walking
extremely tiring. In the volcanic areas of the north and west,
olives are also grown, but here they are found mainly in isolated
groves in the more fertile valleys. The olive trees receive some
pruning, but otherwise they grow almost wild and little or no
fertilizer is used. Edible olives are harvested in October and
November ; those for the oil press are gathered from October to
the end of January. For the most part, the method of gathering
the olives is primitive ; the fruit is allowed to become ripe enough
to fall and is then picked up from the ground, or sometimes the
trees are beaten with sticks to bring the fruit down. In either case,
much of the fruit is bruised and the amount and quality of the oil
is decreased in consequence. Most of the olive growers still have

backyard presses ; there are primitive steam presses in most of the villages of the olive-growing districts, and bigger and more up-to-date factories are established in the capital and at Pérama and Plomárion. After the oil has been extracted, the waste material still contains a considerable percentage of oil, and this is used in the manufacture of rather poor quality soap for the local and eastern Mediterranean market. Of the 160 soap works in Greece with an average production of 25,000 tons per annum, seventeen are in Lésvos, but details of their location and production are not known. Caustic soda for soap making must be imported, and in recent years a considerable amount of olive waste has also been imported.

Other fruits of importance are, figs which are grown principally around Pétra and Míthimna ; pears which, along with other temperate fruits (apples, plums and cherries), grow in great orchards around Ayíassos ; and oranges, which grow in well-watered sheltered valleys, particularly around the Gulf of Kalloní. Vines grow in south-facing valleys around the Gulf of Kalloní, around Eressós, and also in the plain of Míthimna. The greater part of the production of the vineyards is used to make wine, though some table grapes are produced ; the vintage comes at the end of July for table grapes, but some varieties of grapes for wine may be harvested as late as the beginning of September. White and red wine of fair quality is produced, but it is insufficient for the needs of the islanders and very little is exported. Chestnuts yield an abundant harvest and they are exported from Mitilíni. The acorns of the Valona oak (*Quercus aegilops*) are gathered for the valuable tanning material which is made from their cups. Some 900 metric tons of acorns were registered in the market in 1938 and the export is considerable.

Industrial crops occupy about 15% of the cultivated area ; tobacco, cotton and sesame are the most important. Tobacco is not of a particularly good quality, but it is grown in considerable quantity along the shores of the southern gulfs ; about 300 metric tons are exported.

Cereals are grown in greater quantity in Lésvos than in the other eastern Aegean islands, but even Lésvos does not produce more than one-third of the wheat it needs. Wheat and barley are the most important cereals ; the strains grown are rather poor and the cereal crops are largely confined to the higher stonier ground which will not yield a more productive money crop. The patches of cultivation are often tiny, and the crop is so small that the grain is usually reaped by sickle and carted on ass or mule back to the threshing floor to be threshed with a hand flail. The greater part of the cereal production is in the valleys of the northern and western highlands.

Vegetables, particularly beans, cucumbers, melons and tomatoes are also of some importance. Beans are grown in all parts of the island, but melons and tomatoes are grown chiefly on the tiny alluvial plains of the coast, and on the bigger areas of lowland around the Gulf of Kalloní.

Livestock are not of very great importance. Although there are more cattle in Lésvos than in any other of the eastern Aegean islands, they are mostly used for draught ; the milk yield is very poor. Sheep and goats are more numerous ; large flocks of sheep are reared for their wool and milk, and surplus lambs are killed for meat. The meat consumption of the islanders is low but even so they do not produce enough for their own needs. *Yiaoúrti*, a junket made from sheep's milk, forms, however, a staple part of their diet and helps to make up for the small amount of meat and animal fat eaten. Small quantities of wool, and cheese made largely from sheeps' milk, are exported. The shepherds have permanent homes in the mountain villages but the flocks, which are as a rule small, are taken to graze from place to place. Horses, mules, asses and camels are used mainly as transport animals ; very few are yoked to the plough.

Fishing is mainly of domestic importance. There is plenty of fish in the surrounding waters, and most islanders fish to supply their own larders. Mullet, sardines, lobsters and octopuses are the most plentiful, and all are prized as food. Commercially, however, fishing is of minor importance, though Lésvos plays a bigger part in the fishing industry than its neighbours. In 1936, the port of Mitilíni contributed 900 tons to the total catch of 1,579 tons taken in the Aegean islands. The total catch for the whole of Greece in the same year was 9,600 tons. There is a small factory for packing sardines in brine at Mitilíni.

MINING

The island is poor in minerals. Alum occurs in the hills west of the Gulf of Kalloní and in the north around Lebétimnos ; it was of great importance in Mediterranean trade during the Middle Ages, since alum was the principal mordant used by the Italian dyers, but the mines are now little worked. Talc is found near Plomárion. The only mineral of any real economic importance is magnesite, which occurs in an area measuring some 2½ miles by 6 miles near Vasiliká. Three companies from Athens, and one from Vólos, mine in the region and the output in 1938 was 18,690 metric tons ; this represented about one-ninth of the total production of this mineral in Greece.

KHÍOS

Khíos measures 31 miles from north to south and varies from 8 to 18 miles from east to west. It lies off the coast of the Erythraean promontory of Asia Minor and within the 100-fathom line. It is separated from the mainland by Khíos Strait, which is 4½ miles wide in the south and broadens to 11 miles in the north. The channel is only 35–40 fathoms deep and is broken by rocks and islands, so that the character of the strait suggests that the island is merely a fragment broken off the mainland ; this suggestion is borne out by the rocks and structure of the shores. It would seem that recent faulting has shaped the island and created the channel.

GEOLOGY AND RELIEF

Structurally Khíos can be divided into three regions :

(1) The north-west, where old semi-crystalline rocks outcrop (Fig. 132) ; (2) the central region, which is built of a great thickness of folded limestone ; (3) the south-east, where there is a belt of sandstones and clays of upper Tertiary age.

The North-west

The rocks of the north-west are argillaceous schists and greywacke which may be of Palaeozoic age. Although much of the area is over 1,000 ft., the hills are smooth in outline and the valley sides slope gently ; here is a region of soft rolling hills. Since the rocks, and the soils which weather from them, are in the main impermeable, surface water is abundant. Numerous parallel streams run radially from the centre of the area to the coast, and most of them have some water even in the height of summer (Fig. 133).

The Central Region

The limestones of the central region are variable in character. Immediately above the schists are thick beds of red limestones often intercalated with beds of schists, or even conglomerates, and succeeding these red limestones comes a younger, grey, chalky limestone of great extent and thickness. This coarse, chalky limestone outcrops at the surface over the greater part of the island.

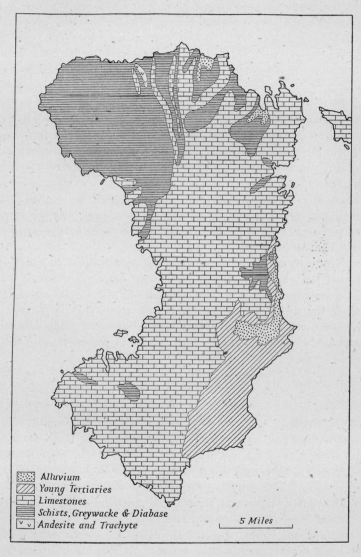

Fig. 132. The geology of Khíos

Based on a map by A. Philippson in *Petermanns Mitteilungen, Ergänzungsheft* 172 (Gotha, 1912).

This limestone region offers a marked contrast to the north-western area ; the hills rise sharp and bare to an irregular line of rugged summits. The ranges trend roughly north and south but are much broken ; in the south and centre they are roughly parallel but in the north they fork and diverge. They are highest in the north where the twin pyramidal peaks of Profítis Ilías, in the Pelinaíon mountains, are only some 3 miles from the coast and rise precipitously to 4,255 ft. Steep escarpments flank the central mountains on the west, and here the coastal plain is narrow. On the east, they descend in great craggy cliffs to wide plateaux. A rough plateau, more than 1,300 ft. high, reaches the coast between the Kámbos of Khíos and Kolokithiá Bay. The region to the north of Kolokithiá Bay, though not quite so high, is also bold and rugged country. Deep ravines with precipitous sides dissect the limestone mountains and plateaux ; they are the characteristic result of water erosion in limestone rock, particularly in a Mediterranean climate, but their development has probably been helped by faulting. The height of the chain decreases to the south. Low, flattened spurs spread out south-westward, but bare rock, ravines and escarpments are still characteristic of the region.

As a result of the great surface extent of limestone and the long-continued deforestation, Khíos is a bare land. Forests of Black pine (*Pinus nigra*) occur in big patches on the lower and middle slopes of the limestone mountains, particularly behind Khíos and on the north coast, but they are nowhere extensive. The limestone uplands carry little vegetation but phrygana covers the surface in favoured spots.

The South-East

The south-eastern area is very different from the central region. The sandstones and clays form a band, 3 to 5 miles wide, extending inland from the coast. The rocks are relatively unresistant to weathering and they have been eroded into a belt of irregular, low, rounded hills. The only large stretch of alluvium forms a plain, the Kámbos, which sweeps around the town of Khíos ; it extends southwards along the coasts and then south-westwards as the flood plain of a broad valley. Water is plentiful in this south-eastern region ; the bigger streams flow at least until the late autumn, there are perennial springs, and in the Kámbos a good water supply is obtained from deep wells.

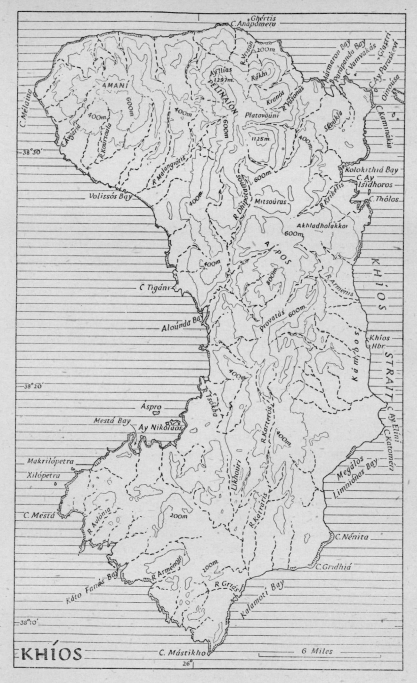

Fig. 133. Relief and drainage of Khíos

Based on the 1 : 50,000 Khíos (3 sheets), M.D.R. 614/7982-84 (1943) and British
Admiralty Chart 1645 (1943).

The contours are at intervals of 200 metres (656 ft.).

Coasts

The coasts of Khíos do not, in general, show much variation. They are characterized by rocky headlands alternating with small bays, high cliffs, and deep water offshore (Fig. 134).

The East Coast

The east coast has the greatest structural variety and therefore the greatest variation in its features. The north-east headland, with its three rocky capes—Cape Vamvakás, Cape Ayía Paraskeví, and Cape Kaminákia at the northern entrance to the Khíos Straits— is a bold cliffed feature cut in limestone rock. The western entrance to the Khíos Straits between Khíos and the Oinoúsai islands is only about a mile across but there is a clear channel with a depth of 15 to 20 fm. About a mile south of the entrance are two deep inlets ; the name of the northern one, Kolokithiá Bay (the gourd), is suggestive of its shape. At the head of this bay a small patch of argillaceous schist appears and it may be that the bays are due to differential erosion, the schists being less resistant than the limestone to wave attack. Southwards of these bays the coast is bold and steep. The rocky hill country closely approaches the sea and forces the road from Kardhámila to Khíos to hug the coast. Vrondádhes is a straggling fishing village with an open roadstead. A steep, difficult zigzag road runs inland across the mountains to Volissós (Fig. 136). From Vrondádhes to Cape Ayía Elíni, a precipitous limestone promontory south of Khíos, the sea has eaten into the softer shales, alluvium has been deposited and the coastland is low, green and fertile. It is fringed offshore by a shallow bank which broadens, south of Khíos harbour (see pp. 520–1), to a width of 1,000 yds., but beyond it the sea deepens rapidly.

The southern entrance to Khíos Straits between Cape Katoméri and the mainland of Asia Minor is about 5 miles wide ; it is obstructed by the two small islets of Panayía and Páspargos, but the passages between Panayía and Asia Minor and between Páspargos and Khíos are clear of dangers except for narrow coastal banks.

The South-east Coast

The south-east coast from Cape Katoméri to Cape Mástikho is made up of two big bays separated by a headland bounded on the north by the steep white cliffs of Cape Nénita and on the south by the less conspicuous cliffs of Cape Gridhiá. The northern bay,

KHÍOS

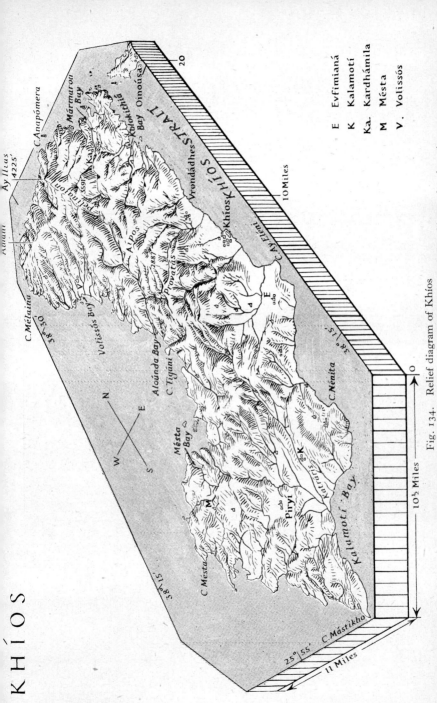

E   Evfimianá
K   Kalamotí
Ka. Kardhámila
M   Mésta
V. Volissós

Fig. 134. Relief diagram of Khíos

Based on the 1 : 50,000 Khíos, G.S.G.S. No. 4360 (2 sheets) (1942) and British Admiralty Chart 1645 (1943).

[Facing page 518

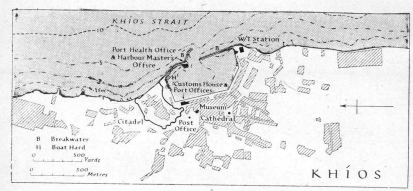

Fig. 135.   The port of Khíos

Based on official sources.

Plate 162.   The port of Khíos

The view shows the southern part of the harbour

Megálos Limniónas, is a great bight cut into the fertile Tertiary rocks. In its northern part it affords a convenient anchorage, during northerly winds, for vessels waiting for better weather to navigate the entrance to the Khíos Straits. The southern bay, Kalamotí Bay, has gentle, well-wooded, northern shores, but limestone outcrops midway along the bay and gives steep cliffs in the southern part. These cliffs culminate in the bold headland of Cape Mástikho, so called from the chief product of its hinterland, the gum mastic.

The South-west Coast

Along the south-west coast between Cape Mástikho and Cape Mestá, the limestone plateau ends in bold cliffs. Since this coast is transverse to the trend of the folded limestone it is indented, and has small coves alternating with rocky promontories. The water is deep offshore but there is a strong and uncertain current off Cape Mástikho and round the rocky islet of Venétiko. There is no anchorage for large vessels along this coast, but small vessels with local knowledge can find shelter at Káto Fanás, from which a rough track leads inland to Piryí and thence there are roads, fit for wheeled traffic, to Khíos.

The West Coast

The west coast juts seawards in its southern and northern stretches between which there is a great bight some 5 miles deep and about 11 miles from north to south. The character of the coast is similar to that of the south-west, especially in the south, since it also is cut in limestone. The water is deep close inshore, and rocky headlands alternate with tiny coves. The northern part of this coast is slightly smoother, and the 10-fm. line is some hundreds of yards offshore. There are only two anchorages worthy of mention : Mestá Bay, on the southern shore of the bight, gives slight shelter from northerly winds to small vessels, and the Volissós roadstead (south-eastward of an islet connected to the coast by a narrow reef) affords the only anchorage for larger vessels. A rough track, linking the south-eastern region to Volissós, skirts the shore of the bight and a road links the anchorage to the village. From Volissós, mule tracks lead to the north coast and a difficult mountain road zigzags up and down the limestone mountains of the interior to Vrondádhes on the east coast. During south-easterly gales, strong squally winds blow down from the highlands of the north-west peninsula and make the passage between Khíos and the island of Psará dangerous.

The North Coast

The north coast is steep and straight in the west and is cut by numerous small valleys. In the east, where limestone alternating with bands of schists reaches the coast, it is rockier and more indented. Cape Anapómera, the northernmost point of Khíos, is the seaward end of a rocky spur of the Pelinaíon mountains. Two inlets, Mármaron Bay and Parápanda Bay, separated by a promontory, give precarious shelter to small vessels, and Mármaron serves as a *skála* to the town of Kardhámila. Both bays are exposed to the north, and during southerly winds strong squalls blow down the valleys, making conditions dangerous to ships anchored in the bays. From Kardhámila a mule track leads along the northern foothills of the mountains, keeping some miles inland ; another crosses the mountains to Volissós ; and a metalled road runs southward to Vrondádhes and Khíos.

THE PORT OF KHÍOS

38° 22′ N, 26° 08′ E. Population 22,122 in 1928

The town of Khíos is the most important settlement on the island, and on the basis of shipping its port ranks next to Síros, although its imports are much smaller.

Detailed Description (Fig. 135 ; Plate 162)

The harbour is rectangular in shape and covers an area of 56 acres. It is entirely artificial and is sheltered by two breakwaters, each measuring about 2,000 ft. in length, and leaving an entrance channel 300 ft. wide. A depth of 25 ft. of water exists in the north-western section of the harbour ; elsewhere there is a depth of from 10 to 12 ft., except along the southern quay and the two breakwaters. The sides of the harbour are quayed and measure in total some 5,000 ft. Vessels usually moor stern-to on the quays and discharge into lighters. There are few port facilities apart from two large warehouses and two hand-cranes of 3 tons capacity.

The Town

The charming little town is dominated by the thirteenth-century castle (Kástro), near which is the old Turkish quarter. One of the town's possessions is the Korais Library. It has also a School of Agriculture, a hospital, a large leper-station, and an orphanage. Khíos is the seat of an eparchy and a nomarchy, of a bishop, and of a Court of the First Instance. It is a station for the Royal Hellenic Navy. The town is lighted by electricity ; the problem of getting enough drinking water at the height of summer is one that has engaged much attention.

Trade and Industries

The exports of Khíos include wines, fruit and vegetables, among which oranges and lemons are the most important individual items. The island is famous for its export of gum mastic, a resin from which a popular liqueur is distilled and which is used in the preparation of certain varnishes. Among the imports, timber and wood are outstanding, considerable quantities of wood being used in the manufacture of packing crates and boxes for the fruit export trade. In common with most of the ports of the Greek islands, a large proportion of its trade is handled through Piraiévs.

Trade in 1937 (thousands of metric tons)

IMPORTS		EXPORTS	
Live animals (number)	1,691	Fruit	6·8
Wheat, cereals and flour	1·0	Vegetable oils	0·2
Sugar	1·0	Timber	0·2
Leather and hides	1·2		
Timber and wood products	3·1		
Metal products	1·3		
Dyes and paints	1·1		
Miscellaneous	0·2		
Total	8·9	Total	7·2

Source : *Bulletin mensuel du commerce spécial de la Grèce avec les pays étrangeres,* Dècembre 1937, pp. 26–8 (Athènes, 1938).

In 1938 the total shipping entrances and clearances amounted to almost one million tons and the passenger traffic to about 25,000 persons in each direction. A few small industries catering for local requirements operate in the town, but none is of great importance.

Communications

Several roads suitable for motor traffic lead north and south from the town (Fig. 136), and there are frequent steamer services to the other islands and to the mainlands of Greece and Asia Minor. Italian vessels trading with the Dodecanese frequently call at Khíos.

Five cables provide telegraph communication with the mainland
and other islands.

HISTORICAL OUTLINE

Classical History

The history of Khíos is complicated and obscure in many of its
details. About the end of the Bronze Age (1100–800 B.C.) it was
colonized by Ionian Greeks, and it became one of the twelve leading
cities of the confederacy of Ionia. The north-eastern and south-
eastern regions of the island were green, fertile and productive ;
wines, figs and gum mastic were Chian specialities in classical times.
The valleys of Anatolia were equally productive and Khíos was well
situated to take part in the trade and commerce of the Aegean.
The islands of the coastal cities of the neighbouring mainland grew
rich, exchanging their products for the goods of the Black Sea coast,
Greece, the Levant, Egypt, and even the western Mediterranean.
The islands, and especially Sámos and Khíos, were the carriers of
this trade. It is significant that Khíos was closely linked, not with
Phocea opposite to her but with Miletus opposite to Sámos. Khíos
and Miletus were the bitter rivals of Sámos and Phocea. The early
prosperity of the island allowed its cultural progress ; iron welding
was known here in the seventh century. A school of epic poets
lived at Volissós and produced an accepted text of Homer ; they
were perhaps responsible for the tradition that the island was Homer's
birthplace. Chian sculpture in the sixth century had a wide reputation and influence.

The strategic position and wealth of Khíos attracted the Persians
and in 498 B.C. the island fell to them. It played, however, an
active part in the Ionian revolt ; and, throughout most of the fifth
century B.C., Khíos generally belonged to the naval empire of
Athens, though it remained locally autonomous and even from time
to time established complete independence. Alexander of Macedon
and Mithradates of Pontus each dominated the island for short
periods. The men of Khíos helped the Romans in their eastern
war, and were rewarded by the grant of an almost independent
status under Roman rule.

Medieval and Modern History

In the early days of the Byzantine empire Khíos remained rich
and flourishing, and its industry and commerce were little disturbed,

except by an occasional Saracen raid. When the power of Byzantium began to wane, the island lost the benefit of its protection and was temporarily occupied by the Seljuk Turks (1089–92), and by Venetians (1124–5, 1172, 1204–25). In 1304 the Zaccaria, a powerful Genoese family already established in Phocea, were granted commercial privileges by the Byzantines, and the Zaccaria later came to rule the island. In 1346, it was given into the hands of a Genoese trading company, or *maona*, which was reorganized in 1362 under the name of ' the Guistiniani '. This company exploited the alum mines of the mainland and the mastic trade of the island, but the islanders maintained independence in local affairs. In 1415 the Genoese became tributary to the Ottomans, but they were not finally driven out from the island until 1566.

During the long centuries of Turkish rule, Khíos was especially privileged. The Turks garrisoned the capital, but the Greeks remained in full control of their domestic politics ; they were represented at Constantinople by a Chiote ; they used the Greek language even in correspondence with the Turkish government ; and they remained members of the Greek Orthodox Church. Economically, the island developed unhindered apart from the south-eastern region, where the valuable mastic crop was a Turkish monopoly. On the outbreak of the Greek War of Independence Khíos did not at first revolt, but a band of Samiote patriots landed on the island in 1822. After defeating the Turkish garrison, they were joined by some ardent spirits in Khíos in proclaiming union with Greece. The Turks, baulked elsewhere in Greece, took full revenge in Khíos. They descended on the island in force ; the men were massacred and the women and children were sold as slaves. The figures given of those massacred and deported vary from 30,000 to 80,000 ; at any rate the island seems to have been largely depopulated, and a few survivors escaped to Síros and other islands. At the end of the war, the Eastern Aegean islands and Crete were returned to Turkey ; Khíos was pardoned, an amnesty was granted to survivors, property was restored, and all the old privileges were re-established. The island was recolonized from Greece and Asia Minor, and slowly began to recover. Then in 1881 a further great disaster befell the island ; much of it was devastated by an earthquake. Almost the whole of the town of Khíos was destroyed, and many of the villages of eastern Khíos suffered severely ; about 4,000 to 5,000 people are said to have been killed and some 40,000 more were rendered homeless.

Throughout the Balkan Wars, Khíos was occupied by the Greek fleet, but at the end of the war Turkey refused to give up her claim to the rich islands of Khíos and Lésvos. Relations were still strained and no settlement had been reached by the outbreak of the war of 1914–18. Khíos was recognized by the Allies as Greek, and was occupied by them during the war, but a settlement was only finally achieved in 1923 at the Treaty of Lausanne. Khíos has since been strongly Republican in sympathy ; and it was Khíos which General Plastiras, who conducted in a masterly fashion the retreat of the defeated Greek army in Asia Minor, used as the base for his revolt which brought about the abdication of King Constantine in 1922 (see vol. I, p. 220).

POPULATION AND SETTLEMENT

The population of Khíos was given as 68,704 in 1910, but before the massacre of 1822 it was estimated at 100,000 ; the vast majority of the inhabitants were Greek. In spite of recolonization full recovery was prevented by the great earthquake of 1881, and by emigration to the United States and to Egypt in the early years of the twentieth century. When the island became Greek, emigration was checked by the Greek military service laws. Since 1920 the population has increased.

Census	Population	Density per sq. mile.
1920	63,235	70·15
1928	75,680	83·94
1938*	82,914	91·96

* Estimate

These figures give the population for the *nomós* ; the population of the separate islands in 1928 was : Khíos 72,452 ; Oinoúsai Is. 2,440 ; Psará Is. 788.

The town of Khíos is also growing ; it had 14,006 inhabitants in 1920 and 22,122 inhabitants in 1928. There were no minorities in the island ; 3,000 Moslems were repatriated to Turkey after the Lausanne Convention and the 1928 census recorded some 13,000 refugees in Khíos, of whom about 9,000 lived in the deme of Khíos.

The greater part of the population lives in small nucleated villages which are surrounded by a few cultivated fields and separated one from another by big stretches of mountain land. As in Lésvos, the villages tend to avoid the coast. The only real coastal settlements are Khíos and Vrondádhes, both of which face the Khíos Straits

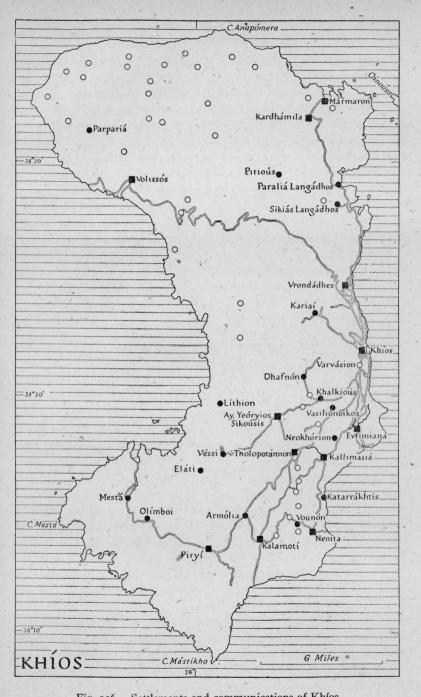

Fig. 136. Settlements and communications of Khíos

Based on the 1 : 50,000 Khíos (3 sheets), M.D.R. 614/7982–84 (1943) and *Population de la Grèce d'après le Recensement du 15–16 Mai, 1928*, deuxième édition (Athènes, 1935).

For key see Fig. 131.

and were therefore sheltered to some extent from Aegean pirates. Even Vrondádhes has its centre on a defensible spur of the plateau some miles inland, and it is only in recent years that houses have crept down to the coast and spread along the shore.

The little *skála* of Mármaron has recently shown a tendency to grow at the expense of the inland town of Kardhámila. Otherwise there seems no general movement to the coast, though most of the few and tiny villages of the north and west are linked by mule track to *skálai* in such sheltered places as the rocky and exposed coast offers.

The pattern of the settlement is clearly related to the geological structure. The density of population per sq. mile in Khíos is high in comparison with the average figure for the whole of Greece. Nearly all the population lives on the east coast plain and on the belt of Tertiary rocks in the south-east ; in these areas the density of population is very high but in the rest of the island it is extremely low. Apart from Khíos itself, there are only two settlements of more than 5,000 inhabitants—Vrondádhes (6,735) and Kardhámila (5,208), both in the east and both situated where small patches of argillaceous rock gives more fertile soil than the surrounding limestone. The south-eastern belt of Tertiary rocks has nearly all the remaining villages of any size ; Evfimianá (1,709), Kallimasiá (1,755), Nénita (1,580), Kalamotí (1,667) all occupy similar sites on hill spurs. They are untidy clusters of houses built solidly in stone and not more than two storeys high in an attempt to guard against earthquake damage. There are numerous smaller villages and this region, with Khíos and Vrondádhes, is the only really well populated part of the island. The inhabitants of Piryí (2,330) and the tiny villages of Olímboi, Mestá, Eláti and Véssi on the southern limestone plateau eke out a slender living herding sheep and goats. Áyios Yeóryios Sikoúsis (1,732) commands the one relatively easy pass in the southern part of the mountain range.

The limestone mountain belt in the centre and north of the island is almost entirely without permanent inhabitants ; a few shrines and shepherds' huts bear witness to the passage of occasional travellers. The north-western promontory, where slates and schists replace the limestone, is remote rather than infertile. It is cut off from the south-east by the mountain barrier and faces the emptiest part of the Aegean Sea. There are, however, some tiny villages on the hill slopes overlooking the west and north coasts but Volissós (1,450) is the only village of any size. It is situated about a mile inland from a fair anchorage and lies on the hill slopes above an extensive alluvial plain, the only one in the island apart from the Kámbos of the east coast.

AGRICULTURE AND FISHING

Agriculture is by far the most important occupation in Khíos ; according to an official estimate some 11,000 people (50% of the working population) are engaged in agriculture, fishing and forestry. The majority of the remainder are occupied in industries, mines and transport, and since mining is negligible in Khíos, and industries and exports are largely concerned with agricultural produce, the land certainly dominates economic life.

As in Lésvos, holdings are small, the majority being less than 2½ acres, and farm implements are primitive. Only in the coastal plain of Khíos and in the Kámbos is agriculture intensive. In these areas there is much garden and orchard cultivation around dwellings. All along the plain between Khíos and Vrondádhes there are scattered farms ; this area is an exception to the rule that in Khíos settlement is in nucleated villages. In the hills to the north and west of the capital, the lower slopes of the spurs and the valley sides are industriously terraced.

Fruits are the most important crops of the island. Citrus fruit, almonds, figs and carobs are produced in sufficient quantity to enter largely into export trade. The citrus fruits—mandarins, oranges and lemons—are grown mainly in orchards on the coastal plain and the Kámbos south of Khíos. The export of citrus fruits from Khíos is about 33% of the total export for Greece as a whole ; most of the remainder comes from Crete, the Kikládhes and the Ionian islands.

Almond trees grow scattered among the fields in the eastern plains and produce well, though sometimes violent winds during the flowering season seriously affect the crop. The export of almonds from Khíos in 1933 was about 1,000 metric tons or one-third of the total for Greece.

Olives are grown in orchards, and figs are grown in every village garden in and around the capital ; they are produced in sufficient quantities to enter into the home and export market. Khíos, unlike Lésvos, exports more table olives than oil.

Vines are grown on terraced hill slopes on the northern rim of the Kámbos, on the seaward slopes of the Evfimaniá peninsula and particularly in the little valleys of the north-west, north and north-east coasts. Chian wine was famous in antiquity and entered widely into Aegean trade ; the north-west of the island was then the wine-producing district. Modern wines are fiery and rather rough. They do not even suffice for local needs and very little wine is exported.

Carobs are grown in the hills around Kardhámila and on the hill slopes of the bays of the north-east coast.

Industrial crops play an essential part in the economy of Khíos ; aniseed, tobacco and, above all, gum mastic are the important ones. Tobacco was introduced in 1909. The climate and soil of the island suited the crop, and cultivation spread rapidly. Tobacco now occupies, however, less than 4% of the cultivated area and is of much less importance in Khíos than in Lésvos or in Sámos. Aniseed is grown locally and is used as a flavouring for cakes and, in particular, for the spirit *oúzo*, which is much drunk throughout the Greek islands.

Mastic is produced from *Pistacia lentiscus* (*var. Chia*), a special variety of the common shrub of the maquis *Pistacia lentiscus.* This variety does not grow wild, but is cultivated in small copses in the Tertiary hill district of the south-east ; twenty or more villages in this area are engaged in its cultivation and they have come to be known collectively as Mastikhokhória. The plant grows into a shrub 6–7 ft. high and yields nearly 5–8 lb. of a pearly green gum which exudes from slits made in the bark of the twigs. The harvest is from April to August. The gum is used in making *mastíkha*, a favourite liqueur ; it is eaten pure as a sweetmeat ; it is widely used as a general flavouring ; and it enters into the manufacture of various paints and varnishes. The gum mastic has been a valued product of the island throughout its history.

Cereal crops (wheat, barley and meslin) are grown in the south and south-east lowlands on land not wanted for commercial crops. They are thus confined mainly to the more barren hill slopes. Subsistence crops are grown in other parts of the island. Khíos is not self-supporting in cereal production ; the import of wheat, however, is small, but relatively to other islands Khíos imports large quantities of rice.

Vegetables and pulses are important crops. Beans are planted on about one-tenth of the cultivated area. Onions and tomatoes are also grown, and potatoes, a negligible crop in Lésvos, are important in Khíos.

Livestock. Khíos has, in proportion to its size, more goats, fewer sheep and many fewer oxen and horses than Lésvos. These facts reflect the mountain character of the country. The south-western plateau is the pastoral region of the island, but a special strain of sheep, giving large milk yields, is bred and pastured near the capital. These ewes will give $4\frac{1}{2}$ to $5\frac{1}{2}$ pints of milk daily, and they usually drop two, and sometimes three, lambs. Lambs often weigh about 56 lb. when two months old and the surplus stock is killed for meat. Hides and skins are tanned locally. The tanning industry has grown beyond the capacity of the island to produce raw materials, both hides and skins, and tanning materials—valona, pine bark and chemicals—are imported.

Fishing on a commercial scale is unimportant. The majority of the fishing boats belong to Kardhámila and Vrondádhes.

MINING

There are few important mineral deposits in Khíos. Small quantities of antimony, zinc and manganese occur in the north-west, but none of these deposits is worked. Lignite of good quality occurs near the town of Khíos but the mines produce only some 25 to 30 tons a day, though their potential production is considered to be great. The red limestone makes good paving flags.

ADJACENT ISLANDS

There are two island groups near Khíos, the Oinoúsai Islands off the north-east coast, and Psará and Andípsara off the north-west coast.

The Oinoúsai Islands

The Oinoúsai Islands lie in the northern entrance to the Khíos Straits. There are two islands, Oinoúsa ($5\frac{1}{2}$ sq. miles) and Pashá (*c.* 1 sq. mile) and five islets : Vátos, off the south coast of Pashá ; Arkhondó, Avlóni and Pondikó, in the channel between Pashá and Oinoúsa; and Práso, near the centre of the channel between the north-eastern cape of Khíos and Oinoúsa. The passage between the north-eastern cape of Khíos and the north-western cape of Oinoúsa, is about 2,000 yards wide and 15 to 22 fm. deep. The islands as a group lie north-west to south-east and extend for $7\frac{1}{3}$ miles towards Asia, leaving a passage $4\frac{1}{2}$ miles wide and 45 fm. deep between Pashá and the Kara Burun peninsula.

Oinoúsa itself is about 5½ miles long from north-west to south-east and consists of semi-crystalline argillaceous mica schists which have weathered into convex hills rising at the western end of the central ridge to over 500 ft.   The coasts are steep and indented.   Pashá is separated from the eastern end of Oinoúsa by a narrow strait. Pashá is nearly 2 miles long from north-north-west to south-south-east ; its coasts are steep ; and its hills rise to 330 ft.   Arkhondó,

Fig. 137.   Relief, drainage, settlements and communications of the Oinoúsai islands
Based on the 1 : 50,000 Khíos, Sheet 2, M.D.R. 614/7983 (1943) and British Admiralty Chart 1645 (1943).
For key see Fig. 131.

Avlóni and Pondikó, lying between Pashá and Oinoúsa, are placed so that they enclose two harbours which are roomy and secure in north-easterly gales.   The northerly harbour, Bogázi Bay, though more difficult of entry, is safer than Port Pashá to the south.

The importance of the islands lies in their position commanding the entrance to the Khíos Straits.   In classical times they were, as their name implies, famous for their wine ; today, they have but few settlements and their total population is only 2,440.   Most of the inhabitants are in the tiny village of Oinoúsa near the centre of the main island.

Psará

Psará lies about 11 miles west of the most westerly point of Khíos. It measures about 5 miles from north to south and 3 miles east to west ; its area is approximately 16 sq. miles. The island is bare and rugged. A range of hills runs parallel with the east coast and swings westward in a rectangular bend near the north coast. The

Fig. 138. Relief, drainage, settlements and communications of Psará
Based on the 1 : 50,000 Aegean Islands, M.D.R. 611/9537 (1943).

range continues into the north-western peninsula as broken hill country. The north and east coasts are, in general, steep, straight and approximately at right angles to each other. The south and west coasts are indented, with bold headlands separating deep bays which have sandy beaches at their heads. The little town of Psará is in the south-west of the island on a tongue of land which projects seaward and ends in a conical hill rising to 421 ft. and crowned by an ancient castle. The town lies north of the hill and the spit, and two moles built out from the coast enclose a protected harbour which has been dredged to 13 ft. The bay gives excellent shelter in summer from north-east winds, but is dangerous in a southerly gale.

During the War of Greek Independence the Psariotes played an active part on the sea. A large Turkish force descended on the island and killed most of the inhabitants ; the survivors fled to Síros and Évvoia. The island was recolonized from Khíos and it remained Turkish until the Balkan War of 1912. At the 1928 census the inhabitants numbered 788 ; most of them lived in or near the capital, and cultivated vines, figs and mulberries on the fertile patches in the small valleys.

Andípsara

Andípsara lies 1½ miles west of the south-west cape of Psará. It is a hilly island about 4¼ sq. miles in area. Its coast is steep and unbroken except for a small bay on the east coast. At the head of this bay a little cultivation is attempted by people coming over from Psará. South of the south-eastern cape of Andípsara is another small islet, and several rocks are scattered round the north and north-western coasts. Temporary shelter can be found from north winds off the southern shore of Andípsara but the island offers no good anchorage.

SÁMOS

Sámos lies slightly north-west of the mountainous peninsula of Samsun Dag (the ancient Mykale) in Asia Minor and is separated from it by the narrow Sámos Strait. Like Ikariá, it seems to be a part of the old broken crystalline block which forms the Kikládhes. The extreme length of the island from Cape Gátos to Cape Katávasis is about 28 miles, and the extreme breadth from Cape Kolóna to Cape Avláki is about 12 miles ; the area of the island is approximately 190 sq. miles.

Geology and Relief

The oldest rocks of the island are the crystalline schists which outcrop below crystalline limestone and are often interbedded with it in the south, and in a narrow strip along the north coast (Fig. 140).

Plate 163. The village of Sklavia in Khíos
The view is from the Khíos–Piryí road.

Plate 164. A street in Kalamotí, Khíos

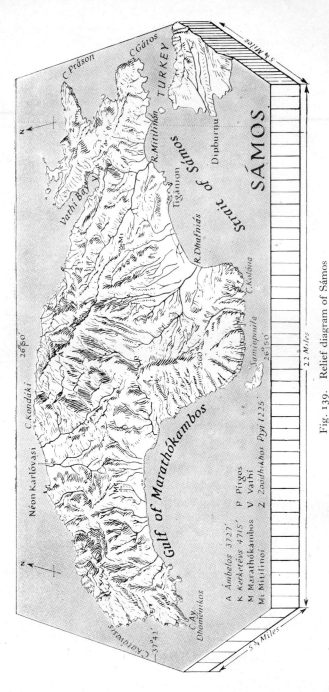

Fig. 139. Relief diagram of Sámos.

Based on the 1 : 50,000 Aegean Islands, M.D.R. 611/9486–87 (1943).

The greater part of the island is covered by thick massive limestone which are finely crystalline marbles varying in colour from blue-black through light grey to gleaming white. In places, a yellow-brown dolomite also occurs. Two belts of Tertiary rocks cross the island. In the west a great spread of coarse limestone conglomerates and clays stretches from the plain of Karlóvasi to the Gulf of Marathókambos, with here and there volcanic rocks and porphyries. In the east, from the coast at Vathí Bay, a narrow band of Tertiaries widens southward. Here the yellowish-white limestone deposits of pebbles and clays are banked up against the slopes of the central

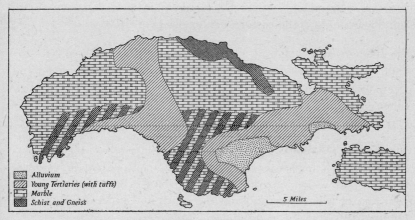

Alluvium
Young Tertiaries (with tuffs)
Marble
Schist and Gneiss

5 Miles

Fig. 140. The geology of Sámos

Based on a map by A. Philippson in *Petermanns Mitteilungen Ergänzungsheft* 172 (Gotha, 1912).

and eastern highlands and spread over the plain until they are overlain, in turn, by the great stretch of recent alluvium (stony in places), which forms the Kámbos, the plain of Sámos or Khóra as it is alternatively called. Smaller patches of alluvium are found around Vathí and at the mouths of the larger rivers.

The natural vegetation of Sámos is, for a Greek island, luxuriant. This is due partly to the extent of the relatively easily weathered Tertiary clays and volcanics, partly to the relatively heavy orographic rainfall of the north-westerly slopes, and partly to less complete deforestation. From the south the island appears as barren as its neighbours but from the north it seems green and fertile. Forests, largely of oak and pine (probably *Pinus nigra*), clothe the middle slopes of the Kerketévs and Ámbelos mountains, the higher slopes are bare and the lower slopes are cultivated. The valleys have planes, chestnuts and oleanders; the limestone scarps of the east, and regions where deforestation has taken place and cultivation has not followed, are covered by dense aromatic scrub.

The landforms of the island are clearly related to the rock structures; the crystalline limestones and schists form the highlands, and the Tertiaries form the lowlands. The island can be divided into five regions :

(1) The western highlands (the Kerketévs (Kerki) mountains); (2) the western lowlands, consisting of the Tertiary plain of Karlóvasi and Marathókambos; (3) the central highlands (the Ámbelos and Bourniás mountains); (4) the eastern lowlands between Vathí and Tigánion; (5) the eastern peninsulas (Fig. 141).

The Western Highlands

The western highlands, or Kerketévs mountains, rise rugged and precipitous from a narrow coastal plain to a height of over 4,000 ft. Three gleaming white peaks form the summit (4,715 ft.) and are made difficult of access by the steepness of the approaches.

The Western Lowlands

The western lowlands are crossed by a low east-west ridge of Tertiary hills which separates the plain of Karlóvasi on the north from that of Marathókambos on the south and links the Kerketévs mountains to the central highlands.

The Central Highlands

The central highlands are more extensive than the eastern highlands but are less rugged; their slopes are smooth and their sides are tree-covered. The highest summit, Óros Ámbelos (the Vine Mountain, 3,780 ft.) lies approximately in the centre of the island and commands a wide view; its gently sloping sides and rounded top make an easy climb. Southwards, the highlands form the salient promontory of Kolóna. The Bourniás mountains, rising steeply from the plain of Marathókambos to 2,560 ft., form a well marked chain ending abruptly at the coast and perhaps continued in the hilly island of Samiopoúla. A scattered group of conical hills, 1,000–1,500 ft. in height, fill the eastern part of the Kolóna promontory. Northwards from the Ámbelos massif, spurs and ridges extend to the north coast, making a region of low, detached, tree-covered hills rising in places, often associated with local outcrops of igneous rocks, to fantastically shaped splintered peaks.

Fig. 141. Relief and drainage of Sámos

Based on the 1 : 50,000 Aegean Islands, M.D.R. 611/9486–87 (1943).
The contours are at intervals of 100 metres (328 ft.).

The Eastern Lowlands

The eastern lowland is a region of irregular hills 750–900 ft. in height with wide troughs between them ; only in the south is there a true plain. The Kámbos of Khóra, an alluvial flat about 1 mile wide, stretches round the shore of Tigánion Bay west of Cape Foniás ; it is deeply cut by streams and is backed on the west and north by the steeply rising foothills of the central highlands. East of Cape Foniás the coastal strip is narrower, but still flat and lowlying, and here it is known as the Misokámbos.

The Eastern Peninsulas

The eastern peninsulas are formed by limestone scarps ; they are high and rugged with sharp crests, the northern one rising in Mount Zoödhókhos Piyí to 1,225 ft.

Drainage

The streams of Sámos have the general characteristics of mountain torrents. The great majority have short straight courses from source to sea, and deep narrow valleys cut by the swiftly running water during the winter. The only considerable stream of the Kerketévs mountains is the Seïtáni, flowing in a deep-cut consequent valley to the north coast with eastern and western subsequent tributaries draining the northern flank of the chain. Several longer streams rise in the Ámbelos highland. Two flow northward to the Karlóvasi plain ; while the Pírgos, the Dhafniás and the Mitilinón drain southward and help to build the alluvial flats of the south coast. These streams flow in deep-cut beds, even along their lower courses through the plains. In winter they are of considerable volume but by April the flow of water is much reduced, and, during the summer, evaporation and irrigation leave their beds completely dry. There are good perennial springs on the lower slopes of the hills in most parts of the island ; Vathí is supplied by springs in its neighbouring hills, and Tigánion from the springs of Evpalínos the supply of the classical town of Sámos.

COASTS AND PORTS

The approaches to the island are clear of dangers and the coasts are generally steep-to ; even in eastern Sámos, where the land is lower, the shore is rocky with high cliffs. There are three ports : Port Vathí and Karlóvasi on the north coast and Tigánion on the south coast. These ports are linked by regular steamship services with Piraiévs and with the ports of the neighbouring islands and Asia Minor.

The North-east Coast

The north-east coast from Cape Kótzikas to Gatítsa Point is the most indented in the island. High, rugged and bold promontories jut far out to sea, their line being determined by the structure of the interior (Fig. 140). Cape Kótzikas and Cape Dhaskalió are bold cliffed headlands separated by a deep bay which affords sheltered anchorage but is little used because of the remoteness and poverty of the hinterland. About Cape Dhaskalió lie five small islets, all steep-to, rocky and uninhabited. The high and rugged peninsula of Dumúz Burnú ends in Cape Práson, the north-easterly extremity of the island, and rocky shoals continue its line out to sea. A great bight with steep, indented and uninhabited shores lies between Cape Práson and the southern promontory terminating in the bold headlands of Cape Gátos and Gatítsa Point.

The South-east Coast

The south-east coast from Gatítsa Point to Cape Aspró forms the northern shore of Sámos Strait which is only a mile wide at its narrowest part. Apart from a rocky shoal with a depth of water of 5 fm. nearly in mid-channel, the passage has a depth of 17–40 fm. The coast of the island between Gatítsa Point and Cape Katsoúni is indented and at Molabraím there is an anchorage with good holding ground though the depth is considerable. Misókambos Bay between Cape Katsóuni and Cape Foniás, and Tigánion Bay between Cape Foniás and Cape Aspró, are wide curving bights with sandy stretches along their shores ; they are fringed by banks at a depth of less than 5 fm.

The harbour of *Tigánion* has an entrance about two cables wide between Cape Foniás and a breakwater built west of the port as a protection from southerly winds. Vessels can tie up by the stern to the bollards on this breakwater. In the north-western part of the anchorage an inner harbour is formed by a mole built on the eastward side. The village of Tigánion (2,501) lies round this inner port ; it has an ice plant, a power station, a flour mill and a tobacco factory (Plate 165). Steamers of several Greek lines plying between Piraiévs and the islands call regularly. There is telegraph and telephone communication with the rest of the island and fair roads run across the lowland, north-eastward direct to Vathí and north-westward via Khóra and Mitilinoí to Vathí (Fig. 142).

The South Coast

The south coast from Cape Aspró to Cape Áyios Dhoménikos can be divided into two sections : the broad promontory where the central highlands come down to the sea, and the wide sweep of the Bay of Marathókambos. The bold headland of Cape Kolóna at the eastern end of the promontory is the southernmost point of Sámos. Between Cape Kolóna and the rocky islet of Samiopoúla off the western shore of the promontory there is no good anchorage, though the submarine slopes are less steep than on the west and north coasts. The depths in the Gulf of Marathókambos are considerable and the outer edges of the narrow bank fringing its shores are steep-to. Nevertheless, vessels with local knowledge can find anchorage at several places though squalls sweep down from the mountains and even with moderate northerly winds they may be violent enough to be dangerous to shipping. The *skála* of Marathókambos lies between two breakwaters at about the centre of the bay and is linked to the inland village by a short mule track.

The West Coast

The west coast between Cape Áyios Dhoménikos and Cape Seïtáni is everywhere cliffed and rocky and backed by steep, in parts precipitous, slopes rising to the Kerketévs mountains. The prominent headland of Cape Katávasis is the westernmost point of the island. Along the whole of the west coast the offshore water is deep ; the 100 fm. line is only a few cables offshore.

The North Coast

The north coast from Cape Seïtáni to Cape Kótzikas has also steep submarine slopes. It is a closed, evenly curving, cliffed coast, but the two most frequented harbours of the island lie on it—Port Karlóvasi and Port Vathí.

Port Karlóvasi is an artificial harbour constructed at the western end of Karlóvasi Bay and in the lee of Cape Pangózi. It is formed by two breakwaters and is considered safe for vessels with local knowledge and of not more than 18 ft. draught. Greek steamers plying between the islands and Piraiévs usually call and the port has good road connections with the three villages which form the commune of Karlóvasi and lie slightly inland.

Plate 165.   The port of Tigánion, Sámos

In the foreground is part of the outer harbour and beyond, separated from it by a mole, is the inner harbour. Behind the village is the sweep of Tigánion Bay ending in the cliffs of Cape Áspro.

[Facing page 538

Plate 166. The coast near Vathí, Sámos

Plate 167. The port of Vathí, Sámos

The view is south-eastward and shows the quay, the lower town (Káto-Vathí) and the upper town (Áno-Vathí) on the hill behind.

[*Facing page* 539·

Port Vathí lies at the eastern end of the north coast. The Gulf of Vathí is a deep inlet sheltered by the promontory of Kótzikas. At the head of the gulf lies an oval stretch of water measuring one mile from west-south-west to east-north-east and half a mile broad. It is approached from the north-west by an entrance channel two miles long. Though squalls sometimes sweep down from the surrounding wooded hills, and a heavy swell may develop in the harbour with a north-westerly wind, the port and the entrance channel are sheltered and safe in nearly all weather for vessels of any size. Depths at the entrance are over 30 fm., but towards the harbour at the head of the bay they decrease rapidly. Merchant vessels usually anchor off the town in 3–10 fm. of water. There are few port facilities except for a quay along the water front where the depth is only 6 ft. and at which vessels lie stern-to. The town has two parts : Apano-Vathí and Límni or Káto-Vathí. The lower town, Káto-Vathí, is built along the eastern side of the harbour ; it is a modern town with well-built white houses and the streets, though narrow, are well paved and clean. The town has administrative importance as the capital of the island and the seat of the nomarch and it has some manufactures concerned mainly with processing the natural products of the island. There are 45 tanneries, 14 of which are equipped with machinery. The hides and skins produced locally were the foundation of the industry but these are now supplemented by a considerable import, the most valuable import of the island. There are 15 oil presses, 5 wine factories, 3 tobacco factories, soap and sulphur factories, a flour factory with a capacity to mill 26 tons of flour per day, an ice plant making 5 tons of ice per day, and a power station. Vathí ranks as one of the leading ports of Greece but is the least important of them ; the amount of cargo which it handles annually is less than 20,000 metric tons. Trade figures for a typical year are given on p. 540.

Greek and Italian shipping lines call regularly at Vathí and link the island with Marseilles, Piraiévs, and the ports of Crete and other Greek islands, Egypt and Asia Minor. From Vathí there are submarine cables to Khíos and the mainland of Asia Minor, telegraph lines to Karlóvasi and Tigánion, and telephone communication with all the bigger settlements of the island. Metalled roads lead westward along the north coast, north-west along the Kótzikas peninsula, south to Tigánion, and south-west to Mitilinoí, Khóra and thus to other centres. Motor omnibus companies run services along these roads.

Trade of Vathí, 1933

EXPORTS				IMPORTS			
Cargo	Total Export (metric tons)	Per cent. Total* Export of all Greece	Direct Foreign trade in foodstuffs	Cargo	Total Import (metric tons)	Per cent. Total Import of all Greece	Direct Foreign trade in foodstuffs
Wine	} 6,966	9·6	4,748	Hides and skins and mft. leather	1,068	17·0	—
Wine lees			52				
Tobacco	958	2·8	952	Wheat	5,267	1·2	2,938
Olive oil	} 763	2·7	67				
Olive residue			71	Rice	204	1·0	—
Raisins	—	—	14	Pulses	109	0·6	58
Almonds	2	0·2	2	Sugar	273	0·5	213
				Wood products and mfts.	768	0·5	—
				Sulphur	273	2·4	—
				Chemical and Pharm. products	126	0·2	—

* The population of Samos forms 0·9% of the population of the whole of Greece.
From official sources.

HISTORICAL OUTLINE

Classical History

In the Bronze Age Sámos seems to have been part of the cultural province of Asia Minor and it was not until the eleventh century B.C. that the island received its Greek inhabitants, the Ionians. The position of Sámos enabled it to achieve early prosperity ; it was linked to Attikí by the island chain of Ikaría, Míkonos, Tínos and Ándros, and it commanded the entrance to the two most important valley highways of Asia Minor—the Kaÿster, with Ephesus near its mouth, and the Meander with Miletus as its city.

By the seventh century B.C. the Samians had become wealthy middlemen facilitating exchange between the Aegean and the Near East. A struggle for dominance developed between Sámos and Miletus, and for a time the mainland city, by reason of the size and resources of its hinterland, won. With the rise of the powerful Persian empire, the situation altered, and the insular position of Sámos, giving greater security, became an asset. In the sixth century, under the tyrant Polycrates, Sámos reached the zenith of its power as one of the leading cities of Ionia. The ancient city of Sámos was not on the site of the modern capital, Vathí, but near Tigánion where the remains of temple, Kástro, theatre, aqueducts and cistern can still be seen. A flourishing school of sculptors grew up ; Samian pottery became prized all over the Aegean ; and the island claims to be the birthplace of the philosopher Pythagoras. Throughout the classical period, Samos was for the most part either a free or tributary ally of Athens, and, when it later fell to Rome, it enjoyed at first almost complete autonomy. Disloyalty to the Empire led to the loss of many privileges, but the island remained rich and famous for its wine and its pottery.

Medieval and Modern History

During the Byzantine period Sámos was linked administratively, not with Asia Minor but with the Kikládhes, and had importance as the head of this military district of the Aegean. The Venetians seem to have ignored the possibilities of the island but the Genoese trading company of the Guistiniani, which had acquired Khíos, ruled Sámos from 1346 to 1453. During the struggles preceding the Turkish conquest in 1453, Sámos was almost completely depopulated, and remained nearly uninhabited until the middle of the sixteenth century when it was recolonized largely by settlers from Albania.

The Samians played an active part in the War of Greek Independence, and were in consequence much disappointed when, by the terms of the peace treaty, the island was not included in the new Kingdom of Greece. Britain, France and Russia, however, guaranteed the island virtual autonomy under the Turks ; its ruler, the Prince of Sámos, though appointed by the Porte, was to be an Orthodox Greek Christian and was to be assisted by a locally elected Assembly which had complete control over internal affairs. Sámos flourished economically and the state of the Greeks of Sámos was certainly better than that of their compatriots on the mainland. But local politics, coupled with unwise administration by the Princes, and with lack of interest and perhaps even bad faith on the part of the Porte, created difficulties. The power of the Prince declined ; the Assembly of Sámos was often at loggerheads with the Porte ; and in 1911, after open hostilities had broken out, the Turks took control of the island. During the Turkish-Italian war, it was regarded as Turkish, and the Italians shelled the island. On the outbreak of the First Balkan War, union with Greece was proclaimed, and in 1913 this union was formally recognized. Sámos now forms one of the three *nomoí* of the *dhiamérisma* of the Aegean islands and has two eparchies, Sámos and Ikaría.

POPULATION AND SETTLEMENT

An estimate of the population of Sámos in 1912 was given as 50,900, of whom the great majority were Greek ; about 300 were Moslem and 350 were Jews. When the island became Greek (1913), emigration was checked, and, during the war of 1914–20, Sámos also received some refugee Greeks from Asia Minor. The population of the island in 1928 was about 60,000, of whom about 7,000 were refugees. In 1940 the population was reported to be about 54,000. Sámos is the most densely populated island of the Eastern Aegean.

Port Vathí is the only deme, and, although there are 49 communes, only 14 of them have a population of more than 1,000. The population of Vathí has grown in recent decades : in 1920 it was 6,143, and by 1928 it had become 8,636 ; the figures for 1940 are not available.

The comparative absence of true coastal settlements is, as in the other Aegean islands, testimony to the prevalence, until the nineteenth century, of piracy in this area. Apart from Port Vathí and Tigánion, both of which are of recent growth, even the trading settlements lie a little inland. Apáno-Vathí (5,677), the old settlement, is built on the steep slopes of a hill dominating the harbour and is about half a mile inland. Karlóvasi (6,875), the largest commune, includes three separate inland villages, and a port of recent and, as yet, small growth. Palaión Karlóvasi (508, including Port Karlóvasi) is the old village on the steep western slope of a tiny valley some way inland ; the port is closest to this settlement. Méso Karlóvasi (1,371) is also a little inland and about a mile west of the old village. Neón Karlóvasi (4,996) east of the Karlóvasi stream is now the largest of the three. The commune has an important tanning industry consisting of about 70 establishments, 7 wine factories, a tobacco factory and an electric power station. Most of this industrial activity is centred in Neón Karlóvasi. Marathókambos (2,988), in the south, also lies inland on the southern flanks of the Tertiary ridge and trades through its *skála* on Marathó-kambos Bay. The *skála* has few residents, yet Marathókambos ranks as the fourth port of the island. There are a few coastal fishing villages, Kokkárion (1,536) on the north coast is the largest (Fig. 142).

The inland settlements are for the most part route centres. Mitilinoí (5,519), the largest one, lies on the eastern edge of the central highlands and at the junction of route ways north-east to

543

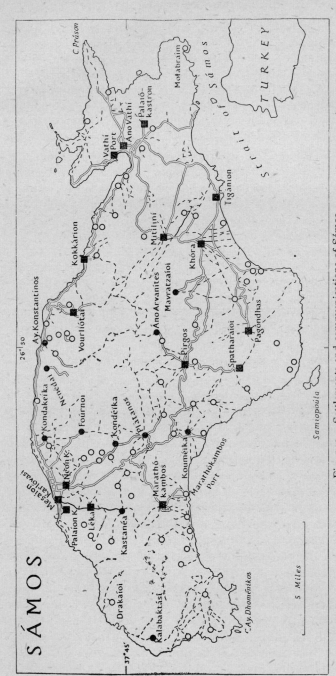

Fig. 142. Settlements and communications of Sámos

Based on the 1 : 50,000 Aegean Islands, M.D.R. 611/9486–87 (1943) and *Population de la Grèce d'après le Recensement du 15–16 Mai, 1928, deuxième édition* (Athènes, 1935).

For key see Fig. 131.

Vathí, north to Kokkárion and south to Khóra and the Kámbos. Khóra (2,079) the old capital, is a prosperous village on the Tertiary hills overlooking the plain. Palaiókastron (1,233) is the only big settlement in the eastern peninsula; and it really belongs to the eastern lowland, for its position is on the route from Vathí to Mísokambos and Molabraím. The southern part of the central highlands have three important hill villages : Pírgos (1,561) commanding the pass between the Ámbelos massif and the Bourniás mountains ; Pagóndhas (2,436) on the eastern slopes of the Bourniás range ; and Spatharaíoi (1,214) on its western slopes. The western mountains have a very sparse population huddled into a few tiny mountain hamlets, of which Dhrakaíoi and Kalabaktási (Priniás), on the north-west slopes, are the only two of any size.

Agriculture and Fishing

Sámos is better endowed agriculturally than most Aegean islands, for the soils developed on some of the Tertiary and volcanic rocks of the foothills and the lowlands are most productive. Sámos is probably for its size the wealthiest of the Aegean islands and its wealth depends primarily on its agriculture, for that is the basis of its considerable trade and of its small manufacturers.

Vines are grown on the lower slopes almost all over the island except in the extreme west which is too steep and barren for their cultivation. Now, as in antiquity, Sámos specializes in the production of wine, and the vine occupies a greater fraction of the cultivated area than any other crop. Vine-growing is especially concentrated on the well-watered fertile soils of the schists of the northern coastal strip, and here, on land suitable for terracing, the vineyards reach a considerable altitude. The foothills around the Kámbos of Khóra are also important vine-growing districts. The vines are carefully tended and are sprayed frequently to control pests. The greater part of the production of the vineyards is used for wine making. The grapes are rich and sweet, and the grapes for wine, largely muscatel grapes, are allowed to dry slightly in the sun before they are pressed ; this practice makes the Samian wine sweet and heavy. In bad seasons, raisins are added to the wine to give this quality. The wine is largely exported ; about 7,000 metric tons leave Vathí annually, and half of this goes direct to foreign markets, largely to Italy and France where it is used for making vermouth and for blending. Both muscatel and black grapes are also grown for drying, and a few grapes are grown for table use. The organization of the marketing of the produce of the vineyards is in the hands of a co-operative society, the Sámos Vine Growers' Association. All vine growers in the island, whether they are owners or only lease-holders of the vineyards, must be members of the Association, and all the produce of the vineyards must be delivered to it.

Tobacco is the second crop of the island and occupies about one-quarter of the cultivated area. Tobacco growing became important when, in the last decade of the nineteenth century, phylloxera reduced the yield of the vineyards to about one-third of what it had been. The rich soils of the lowlands are well suited to tobacco cultivation, though according to modern standards the quality of the tobacco is not high. A considerable proportion of the crop is made into cigarettes locally, but the production is greater than the local demand. Egyptian buyers are particularly active in Sámos.

Fruit trees, together with the vineyards, give the island a fertile appearance. Above the vineyards, and along the edges of the fields and vineyards, olive trees grow and there is an export of olive oil and its associated products. Carobs flourish, particularly on the ridge between the plains of Karlóvasi and Marathókambos ; apples and pears grow on the higher slopes ; and fig, mulberry, almond and citrus fruit trees are planted in more sheltered situations and around the houses. Citrus fruits are not produced in Sámos on the same scale as in Khíos, but the mandarins and oranges grown go far to supply the local market, though few are exported.

Cereals are comparatively unimportant ; only about one-quarter of the cultivated acreage is under cereals as compared with about two-thirds in Lésvos. Wheat and barley of poor quality are the commonest cereals, and are grown especially in the Kambós of Khóra. Rye is grown on the stony mountain soils of the western region ; a much greater acreage is under rye in Sámos than in Lésvos, while in Khiós the rye crop is negligible. Oats and a small amount of millet are also grown.

Vegetables and pulses are grown around the villages ; the most important crops are onions, tomatoes, potatoes, cucumbers and beans. Onions do well on the light soils of the western mountains and are grown for market around the remote village of Dhrakaíoi.

Livestock are not important in Sámos. Goats are the only animals kept in quantity ; from their milk some cheese is made and they

provide the greater part of the wool. The small number of plough-
ing animals is due to the small acreage of cereal cultivation ; vineyards, tobacco plantations, and fruit orchards are cultivated without
animal labour. Although the island is extensively forested, the
forests are too remote and the slopes too steep to support pigs in
large numbers.

Fishing is carried on by many families to supply food for their
own table but the fishing industry is not important in Sámos.

MINING

Although minerals occur in the island they are not yet worked nor
have the deposits been throughly explored. Iron ores (mainly
haematite) are widely distributed and where they occur in the
crystalline limestones they often contain zinc. The Kerketévs
mountains may be rich in minerals ; calamine and galena are found
near Dhrakaíoi in what appear, from surface indications, to be
large deposits ; emery and traces of copper also occur. A bed of
lignite exists near Karlóvasi but it is too small to be worth exploiting.
Clays in the same neighbourhood are suitable for making tiles and
earthenware, and are used to some extent.

IKARÍA

Ikaría is approximately 25 miles long from Cape Dhrápanon (or
Cape Fanári) in the north-east to Cape Pápas in the south-west.
Its breadth varies from 6 miles in the west to $3\frac{1}{2}$ miles in the east
and the area of the island is 99 sq. miles. It lies 12 miles west of
Sámos and 29 miles east of Míkonos, and would seem to form part
of the chain of islands spanning the Aegean from Évvoia through
Ándros, Tínos, Míkonos, Ikaría and Sámos to the Mykale peninsula
of Asia Minor.

GEOLOGY AND RELIEF

The geological structure of the island has not been investigated in
detail but the island seems to be made largely of crystalline schists
with, in places, a capping of thick blue limestone. A range of
mountains runs the whole length of the island, the crest lying parallel
and near to the south coast (Fig. 143). The range is sharp all along

IKARIA

Fig. 143   Relief and drainage of Ikaría

Based on the 1 : 50,000 Aegean Islands, M.D.R. 611/9715–16 (1944).
The contours are at intervals of 100 metres (328 ft.).

its length, and rises at intervals to well marked peaks. The highest peaks are in the north-east ; Fárdhi (3,420 ft.) is the highest point of the island and Ipsilís (Lofty) (3,365 ft.) is in the same massif. At the south-western end, Mélissa (the Bee) (3,390 ft.) dominates the range. The southern face of the mountains is steep, and for long stretches it falls to the coast in great rock precipices. The northern slope is gentler ; innumerable spurs and subsidiary ranges stretch northward from the main range, the highest of the ridges running parallel with the west coast. Although the mountain spine in the north-east is about midway between the north-west and south-east coasts, and the highest peak in the island is in this region, the land falls rapidly north-eastwards and the north-east promontory is a region of relatively low hills. The true lowlands of Ikaría are small ; one is near the north-eastern end of the island, the other occurs along the curving bay in the centre of the north coast. The northern hill country is, however, in many parts low with gentle slopes, and isolated upland plains and small enclosed basins are found even close up to the mountain crest.

Stony mountain soil has developed on the northern hills, but the steepness of slope, together with the resultant torrent action of the streams, makes the southern region rather bare of soil cover. There were formerly considerable forests on the middle lower slopes, especially in the north of the island, but these have been much reduced by charcoal burners. Oaks, beeches and pines, with planes in the valleys, are still found in the less accessible areas, with maquis in the damper lower regions where there has been deforestation, and phrygana, often very poor and sparse, in drier areas. The higher slopes are for the most part bare rock.

The river system is simple. The east-west mountain range is the main watershed ; the north-south spur along the west coast is a subsidiary one. The rivers flowing south and west are extremely short and rapid ; they have cut a parallel series of deep ravines in the mountain slopes. The northward flowing rivers are somewhat longer, especially in the west. All are torrential ; in winter they come down in spate but in summer they dry up completely or shrink into a series of pools. The rivers of the north-west, with a short plain stretch near their mouths, are particularly liable to flood ; their mouths get blocked by trees uprooted by the torrents in their mountain tracks. The island has abundant supplies of good fresh water ; there are numerous springs in the valleys and on the hill slopes.

Coasts and Ports

Ikaría has, in general, an almost unbroken coast line which is especially steep-to in the south and west ; there is not one harbour or even a good anchorage.

The South-east and South Coasts

The south-east and south coast from Cape Dhrápanon to Cape Pápas is steep and cliffed throughout its entire length.   It is indented by tiny rocky bays separated by bold headlands.   There is no shelter from southerly winds and, with prevailing northerly winds, the high mountains behind often cause considerable squalls offshore, Southward and westward of Cape Kalomeriá, however, is a wide, sandy bay which, at its northern end, gives the best shelter from northerly and westerly gales.   Áyios Kírikos (Angériko) Bay, six miles south-west of Cape Dhrápanon, affords temporary anchorage in quiet weather.   Áyios Kírikos (944) is the capital of the island and of the eparchy of Ikaría, and is the main port of the island. Steamers call from Piraiévs, Sámos, Síros and other Aegean islands and there is a considerable amount of coastal shipping.   The town lies at the foot of a ravine descending from the mountains above ; it has a power station, a flour mill and an olive press and is in telephone and telegraph communication with Evdhílos.   There are submarine telegraph or telephone cables to Sámos and the other islands.   A rough track follows the coast to Pírgos and mountain roads cross to Livádha and to Evdhílos on the north coast.

The North-west and North Coasts

From Cape Pápas to Cape Armenistís (Cape Strefóni) the coast trends north-eastward.   The water is deep offshore and the coast is high and rocky.   A few short torrents interrupt the straight line here and there, but there is no shelter and no anchorage.   From Cape Armenistís to Cape Evdhílos the coast trends due east and here the water deepens offshore more slowly.   Evdhílos is a small port and appears to be the main inlet and outlet for goods for the north of the island.   It exports charcoal and potatoes, and a Greek island steamship line calls weekly linking it with Sámos, Síros and Piraiévs.   The village of Evdhílos lies in the hills about half an hour's journey from the port, but in recent years the *skála* has been growing relatively much faster than the village.   In 1928, the population of Evdhílos, including both village and *skála* was 826,

A track runs eastwards across the mountains to Áyios Kírikos and another mountain track runs southward to Manganítis. Westward a coastal road links the *skála* to the villages of western Ikaría.

Eastward from Cape Evdhílos the coast trends north-east and the water again deepens rapidly offshore. The coast is exposed and high but small vessels with local knowledge can anchor under Cape Áyios Fokás (Gonáti). Cape Dhrápanon is a bold prominent headland but its hinterland is low.

HISTORICAL OUTLINE

The exposed character of the coasts of Ikaría and the absence of ports, combined with the infertility of the mountainous hinterland, has given the island a relatively uneventful history. It seems to have been part of the Athenian maritime empire, and exported wine to the capital. In the Middle Ages, it belonged nominally to the dominant power in the archipelago and there are medieval fortifications, probably Genoese, near Evdhílos. However, even pirates found few settlements worth plundering, and the island was left largely to its own devices ; its inhabitants, perhaps as a result of their isolation, gained a reputation for wild barbarism. From the sixteenth century onwards, the island paid tribute to the Turks and was organized as a part of the *sanjak* of Khíos though there was a large measure of local government.

After the Greek War of Independence, though Ikaría was popularly grouped with the Dodecanese, it was not occupied by the Italians, and was seized by the Greek Navy at the outbreak of the First Balkan War in 1912. In 1914, the Great Powers adjudged the island to be Greek, and it has since been administered from Greece, at first direct from Athens but now as part of the *nomós* of Sámos.

POPULATION AND SETTLEMENT

The total population of Ikaría according to the 1928 census was 10,783. According to the 1940 census, the results of which were not published until after the Italian occupation, it was 10,719. The island is an eparchy in the *nomós* of Sámos and has three principal communes : Áyios Kírikos, Dháfni and Evdhílos.

The commune of Áyios Kírikos (2,958) includes Áyios Kírikos itself (944) and eleven other small villages of the north-eastern region. All are hill settlements and the two largest, Pírgos in the north-east and Livádha overlooking the north coast, are connected

IKARÍA

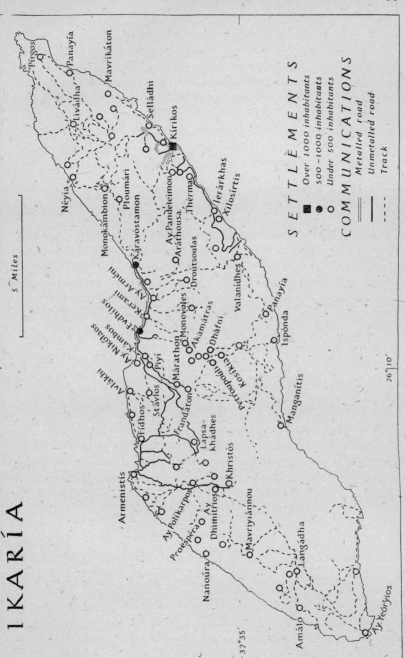

Fig. 144. Settlements and communications of Ikaría

Based on the 1 : 50,000 Aegean Islands, M.D.R. 611/9715–16 (1944) and *Population de la Grèce d'après le Recensement du 15–16 Mai, 1928,* deuxième édition (Athènes, 1935). For key see Fig. 131.

by tracks to Áyios Kírikos. Evdhílos (614) is the centre of the Méssarea, the richest part of the island, and is the only large settlement here, although in the hills around it are groups of huts ; these are too small to be *sinoikismoi* but are collectively known as Méssara. Dháfni (322), situated near the centre of the island, has several oil presses and in the wild highland of the western part of the island are some tiny villages, often high on the spurs of the mountains. All the settlements of Ikaría, even the villages of Áyios Kírikos and Evdhílos as distinct from their *skálai*, characteristically avoid the coast and seek safety inland.

AGRICULTURE

The plains and hilly lowlands of the north (especially the region of the extreme north-east around Cape Dhrápanon) and the coastal and inland plains of the Méssarea, are fertile and well watered and are under vines and potatoes. Wine is a traditional product of the islands, but now a variety of grape, which when dried makes a very well flavoured black raisin, is grown. Potatoes were introduced in the nineteenth century, and Ikariá, like Náxos, is one of the main areas of production in the Aegean. The ravines of the south coast are sheltered, warm and well watered, and, wherever there is space, have walled gardens growing olives, figs, oranges, lemons, nuts and temperate fruits such as pears and cherries. Cereals are not grown in any quantity, and much of the food for the islanders must be imported.

Livestock is not important but the islanders raise cattle, and flocks of sheep and goats are pastured, very little tended, in the mountains. Bee keeping is common and honey and wax are among the island products.

MINING

The mineral resources of the island may be considerable but are, as yet, unexplored and unexploited. Emery was once worked in small quantities, but, with the development of the Náxos mines, the output of Ikaría became insignificant and finally ceased. Iron ore deposits near Áyios Kírikos were also worked for a time, but the mining of more accessible supplies has made mining of ore in Ikaría uneconomic in present circumstances.

ADJACENT ISLANDS (FOÚRNOI ISLANDS)

The Foúrnoi islands lie south-west of Sámos and south-east of Ikaría and about half way between them (Fig. 126). This group of twelve islets and rocks, covering about 11 sq. miles, are bare and barren with steep rocky coasts; the sea is 40–60 fm. deep close inshore. The coasts are much indented with numerous small coves which give the islands their name (Foúrnas = oven). Foúrnoi, and Fímaina to the west of it, are the only two islands of any size (Fig.

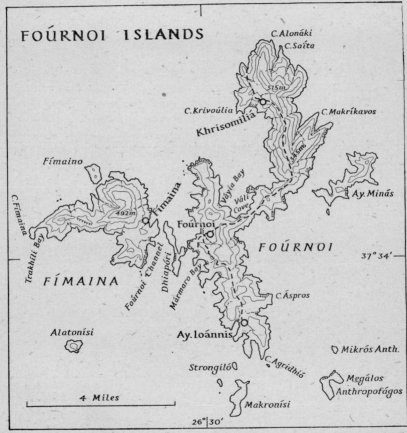

Fig. 145.   Relief, drainage, settlements and communications of the Foúrnoi islands

Based on the 1 : 50,000 Aegean Islands, M.D.R. 611/6667 (1943) ; British Admiralty Chart 1537 (1940) ; and *Population de la Grèce d'après le Recensement du 15–16 Mai*, 1928, deuxième édition (Athènes, 1935).

The contours are at intervals of 100 metres (328 ft.). For key to settlements and roads see Fig. 131.

145). *Foúrnoi* itself lies roughly north to south but has an extremely irregular outline ; a great bay, 60 fm. deep, opens north-westward and nearly cuts the island in two. This bay has a rocky bottom and is open to northerly gales, but in the south-east of this bay, Váli Cove forms an anchorage. The water in this cove, however, is more than 20 fm. deep except very close inshore. The island rises at its northern end to 1,690 ft. and much of the interior is rough and rugged hill country.

Fímaina lies a little west of Foúrnoi ; it is triangular in shape and sharp in profile, with hills rising to 1,615 ft. *Áyios Minás* lies close to the east coast of Foúrnoi and though of fair size is rocky and barren. The *Anthropofágos* (Cannibal) group, off the south-east of Foúrnoi, has three small islets. *Makronísi* lies off the southern point of Foúrnoi. *Dhiapóri* (Kisíra) islet lies between Fímaina and Foúrnoi, and *Alatonísi* is south of Fímaina.

The islets are poor ; they produce only a little grain, a little honey, and a few pigs and rabbits. Fish is abundant off the coasts but the waters offshore are difficult to navigate and this, together with their depth and the lack of safe anchorages along the coast, deters fishermen. The shepherds of Sámos sometimes bring flocks over to pasture in the spring and the seamen of Ikariá occasionally put in for shelter. In the past, marble quarries were worked by Samians on Foúrnoi, and marble was exported from a small *skála* known as Marmarokopió (marble quarry) on the west coast. The only permanent settlement is at Foúrnoi on the western hill slope of Foúrnoi island overlooking the southern shores of the great bay. The population of the whole island group in 1928 was 973 ; the majority of the inhabitants live in Foúrnoi village. The group was occupied by Greece at the same time as other Eastern Aegean islands and it forms part of the *nomós* of Sámos.

BIBLIOGRAPHICAL NOTE

1. The fullest account of the Eastern Aegean Islands is given in the N. I. D. *Handbook of Greece*, vol. 2, part 2 (London, 1919). Some account of the geology and relief is given in A. Philippson, ' Reisen und Forschungen in westlichen Kleinasien ; Heft 2, Ionien und das westliche Lydien ', *Petermanns Mitteilungen, Ergänzungsheft* 172 (Gotha, 1912). The coasts are described in the *Mediterranean Pilot*, vol. 4, 7th edition (London, 1941).

2. A popular account of the islands is H. F. Tozer, *The Islands of the Aegean* (Oxford, 1890).

3. The most useful topographical maps of the Eastern Aegean Islands are : (a) for Lésvos, the 1 : 50,000 Lesvos, M.D.R. 617/8222-7, which were drawn and reproduced by 19th Fd. Survey Coy., R.E., in 1943, from Greek maps

dated 1934 and revised from air photographs of 1943. The maps have a kilometre grid, latitude and longitude (from Athens) in margins, contours in brown at 20 metres interval, roads and tracks in red, water in blue ; (*b*) for Khíos, the 1 : 50,000 G.S.G.S. No. 4360 (2 sheets) which were copied from a Greek map of 1937, and the 1 : 50,000 Khios, M.D.R. 614/7982–4 which were compiled, drawn and reproduced by 514C Fd. Survey Coy., R.E., in 1943. The maps are in the same general style as those for Lésvos except that M.D.R. 614 has unmetalled roads, tracks, all names and other detail in brown, and G.S.G.S. No. 4360 shows contours at 40 metres interval ; (*c*) for Sámos and Ikaría, the 1 : 50,000 Aegean Islands, M.D.R. 611, details of which are given on p. 487.

CONVERSION TABLES

METRIC AND BRITISH UNITS

It is customary to think of the ' metre ' and the ' yard ' as representing unalterable units of length. This is not so. The metre was originally intended to be the 10,000,000th part of the earth's meridional quadrant. But the accurate determination of this length proved to be extremely difficult—partly for technical reasons, and partly because of different conceptions of the ' figure of the earth '. In view of these difficulties it became necessary to define the length of the metre in terms of suitable metal bars measured under specified conditions of temperature, pressure, humidity, etc. Similar standard bars were also used to define the length of other units such as the yard. As all these metallic standards are subject to change, conversion tables differ according to the date of comparison between different bars. The tables that follow are based on the comparison between the yard and the metre made in 1895. This made 1 metre equivalent to 39·370113 in.

Metric System : List of Prefixes

Deca means ten times.
Hecto means a hundred times.
Kilo means a thousand times.

Deci means a tenth part of.
Centi means a hundredth part of.
Milli means a thousandth part of.

In abbreviations the Decametre, etc., is Dm., and the decimetre, etc., dm.

Note on ' Nautical ', ' Geographical ' and ' Statute ' miles

A British ' nautical mile ' is the length of the minute of the meridian at any given latitude, and is therefore a variable unit. It is given in feet for Clarke's 1880 spheriod by the formula :

$$60771 \cdot 1 - 30 \cdot 7 \cos 2 \text{ Lat.}$$

This is the sea mile of the scale of latitude and distance of the Admiralty Charts. From the above formula it will be found to vary from 6,046·4 ft. at the equator to 6,107·8 ft. at the poles, being 6,077·1 ft. at latitude 45°.

The so-called ' international nautical mile ' of 1,852 m. or 6,076 ft. is the length of the minute of the meridian at latitude 45° on the international spheroid. This corresponds to the 6,077 ft. for Clarke's spheroid.

A ' geographical mile ' is a fixed unit, being defined by some as the length of a minute of the equator and by others as that of the minute of the meridian at latitude 45°. According to the former definition its value on Clarke's spheroid is 6,087 ft. and according to the latter 6,077 ft. The round figure 6,080 is usually adopted for the purposes of ordinary navigation.

The British ' statute mile ' measures 5,280 ft.

LIST OF CONVERSION TABLES

Table 1. Length

Nautical mile	Statute mile	Kilometre	Metre	Yard	Foot	Inch	Centimetre
1	1·152	1·853	1853	2027	6080*	72,960	185,300
0·8684	1	1·60934	1609·34	1760	5280	63,360	160,934
0·5396	0·621372	1	1000	1093·61	3280·84	39,370·1	100,000
0·0005396	0·0006214	0·001	1	1·09361	3·28084	39·3701	100
0·0004934	0·0005682	0·0009144	0·914399	1	3	36	91·4399
0·0001645	0·0001894	0·0003048	0·3048	0·33333	1	12	30·48
0·0000137	0·0000158	0·0000254	0·0254	0·02778	0·083333	1	2·54
0·0000054	0·0000062	0·00001	0·01	0·0109361	0·032808	0·393701	1

* This is the customary British practice, and not the 'international nautical mile' which Great Britain has not adopted.

Table 2. Area

Square mile	Square kilometre	Hectare	Acre	Square metre	Square yard
1	2·58998	258·998	640	2,589,980	3,097,600
0·386103	1	100	247·106	1,000,000	1,195,990
0·003861	0·01	1	2·47106	10,000	11,959·9
0·0015625	0·0040469	0·404685	1	4046·85	4840
0·00000039	0·000001	0·0001	0·000247	1	1·19599
0·00000032	0·00000084	0·0000836	0·000207	0·836126	1

Table 3. Yield per Unit Area

Tons per acre	Metric tons per hectare	Quintals per hectare
1	2·51071	25·1071
0·398294	1	10
0·398294	0·1	1

Table 4. *Volume and Capacity*

Kilolitre	Cubic metre	Cubic yard	Bushel	Cubic feet	Imp. gall.	Litre	Pint
1	1·000027	1·30799	27·4969	35·3157	219·976	1000	1759·80
0·999973	1	1·30795	27·4962	35·3148	219·970	999·973	1759·75
0·764532	0·764553	1	21·0223	27	168·178	764·532	1345·43
0·0363677	0·0363687	0·0475685	1	1·28435	8	36·3677	64
0·028316	0·028317	0·037037	0·778602	1	6·22882	28·3160	49·8306
0·0045460	0·0045608	0·0059461	0·125	0·160544	1	4·54596	8
0·001	0·001000	0·001308	0·027497	0·035316	0·219976	1	1·75980
0·0005682	0·0005683	0·0007433	0·015625	0·020068	0·125	0·56824	1

Table 5. *Weight*

Ton	Metric ton or millier	Quintal	Kilogram	Pound
1	1·01605	10·1605	1016·05	2240
0·984207	1	10	1000	2204·62
0·0984207	0·1	1	100	220·462
0·0009842	0·001	0·01	1	2·20462
0·0004464	0·0004536	0·004536	0·453592	1

Table 6. Temperature : Equivalents of Fahrenheit and Centigrade Scales

°F.	°C.	°F.	°C.	°F.	°C.	°F.	°C.	°F.	°C.	°F.	°C.
100	37·7	79·25	26·25	58	14·4	37·4	3	17	−8·3	−4	−20
99·5	37·5	79	26·1	57·2	14	37	2·7	16·25	−8·75	−5	−20·5
99	37·2	78·8	26	57	13·8	36·5	2·5	16	−8·8	−5·8	−21
98·6	37	78	25·5	56·75	13·75	36	2·2	15·8	−9	−6	−21·1
98	36·6	77	25	56	13·3	35·6	2	15	−9·4	−6·25	−21·25
97·25	36·25	76	24·4	55·4	13	35	1·6	14	−10	−7	−21·6
97	36·1	75·2	24	55	12·7	34·25	1·25	13	−10·5	−7·6	−22
96·8	36	75	23·8	54·5	12·5	34	1·1	12·2	−11	−8	−22·2
96	35·5	74·75	23·75	54	12·2	33·8	1	12	−11·1	−8·5	−22·5
95	35	74	23·3	53·6	12	33	0·5	11·75	−11·25	−9	−22·7
94	34·4	73·4	23	53	11·6	32	0	11	−11·6	−9·4	−23
93·2	34	73	22·7	52·25	11·25	31	−0·5	10·4	−12	−10	−23·3
93	33·8	72·5	22·5	52	11·1	30·2	−1	10	−12·2	−10·75	−23·75
92·75	33·75	72	22·2	51·8	11	30	−1·1	9·5	−12·5	−11	−23·8
92	33·3	71·6	22	51	10·5	29·75	−1·25	9	−12·7	−11·2	−24
91·4	33	71	21·6	50	10	29	−1·6	8·6	−13	−12	−24·4
91	32·7	70·25	21·25	49	9·4	28·4	−2	8	−13·3	−13	−25
90·5	32·5	70	21·1	48·2	9	28	−2·2	7·25	−13·75	−14	−25·5
90	32·2	69·8	21	48	8·8	27·5	−2·5	7	−13·8	−14·8	−26
89·6	32	69	20·5	47·75	8·75	27	−2·7	6·8	−14	−15	−26·1
89	31·6	68	20	47	8·3	26·6	−3	6	−14·4	−15·25	−26·25
88·25	31·25	67	19·4	46·4	8	26	−3·3	5	−15	−16	−26·6
88	31·1	66·2	19	46	7·7	25·25	−3·75	4	−15·5	−16·6	−27
87·8	31	66	18·8	45·5	7·5	25	−3·8	3·2	−16	−17	−27·2
87	30·5	65·75	18·75	45	7·2	24·8	−4	3	−16·1	−17·5	−27·5
86	30	65	18·3	44·6	7	24	−4·4	2·75	−16·25	−18	−27·7
85	29·4	64·4	18	44	6·6	23	−5	2	−16·6	−18·4	−28
84·2	29	64	17·7	43·25	6·25	22	−5·5	1·4	−17	−19	−28·3
84	28·8	63·5	17·5	43	6·1	21·2	−6	1	−17·2	−19·75	−28·75
83·75	28·75	63	17·2	42·8	6	21	−6·1	0·5	−17·5	−20	−28·8
83	28·3	62·6	17	42	5·5	20·75	−6·25	0	−17·7	−20·2	−29
82·4	28	62	16·6	41	5	20	−6·6	−0·4	−18	−21	−29·4
82	27·7	61·25	16·25	40	4·4	19·4	−7	−1	−18·3	−22	−30
81·5	27·5	61	16·1	39·2	3·8	19	−7·2	−1·75	−18·75	−23	−30·5
81	27·2	60·8	16	39	3·75	18·5	−7·5	−2	−18·8	−23·8	−31
80·6	27	60	15·5	38·75	3·3	18	−7·7	−2·2	−19	−24	−31·1
80	26·6	59	15	38	3·3	17·6	−8	−3	−19·4	−24·25	−31·25

Table 7.   Pressure :   Equivalents of Millibars, Millimetres of Mercury, and Inches of Mercury at 32° F. in Latitude 45°

Mercury in.	Milli-bars	Mercury mm.	Mercury in.	Milli-bars	Mercury mm.	Mercury in.	Milli-bars	Mercury mm.	Mercury in.	Milli-bars	Mercury mm.	Mercury in.	Milli-bars	Mercury mm.
27·02	915	686·3	27·82	942	706·6	28·62	969	726·8	29·41	996	747·1	30·21	1,023	767·3
27·05	916	687·1	27·85	943	707·3	28·65	970	727·6	29·44	997	747·8	30·24	1,024	768·1
27·08	917	687·8	27·88	944	708·1	28·67	971	728·3	29·47	998	748·6	30·27	1,025	768·8
27·11	918	688·6	27·91	945	708·8	28·70	972	729·1	29·50	999	749·3	30·30	1,026	769·6
27·14	919	689·3	27·94	946	709·6	28·73	973	729·8	29·53	1,000	750·1	30·33	1,027	770·3
27·17	920	690·1	27·97	947	710·3	28·76	974	730·6	29·56	1,001	750·8	30·36	1,028	771·1
27·20	921	690·8	28·00	948	711·1	28·79	975	731·3	29·59	1,002	751·6	30·39	1,029	771·8
27·23	922	691·6	28·03	949	711·8	28·82	976	732·1	29·62	1,003	752·3	30·42	1,030	772·6
27·26	923	692·3	28·05	950	712·6	28·85	977	732·8	29·65	1,004	753·1	30·45	1,031	773·3
27·29	924	693·1	28·08	951	713·3	28·88	978	733·6	29·68	1,005	753·8	30·48	1,032	774·1
27·32	925	693·8	28·11	952	714·1	28·91	979	734·3	29·71	1,006	754·6	30·51	1,033	774·8
27·35	926	694·6	28·14	953	714·8	28·94	980	735·1	29·74	1,007	755·3	30·53	1,034	775·6
27·38	927	695·3	28·17	954	715·6	28·97	981	735·8	29·77	1,008	756·1	30·56	1,035	776·3
27·41	928	696·1	28·20	955	716·3	29·00	982	736·6	29·80	1,009	756·8	30·59	1,036	777·1
27·44	929	696·8	28·23	956	717·1	29·03	983	737·3	29·83	1,010	757·6	30·62	1,037	777·8
27·46	930	697·6	28·26	957	717·8	29·06	984	738·1	29·86	1,011	758·3	30·65	1,038	778·6
27·49	931	698·3	28·29	958	718·6	29·09	985	738·8	29·89	1,012	759·1	30·68	1,039	779·3
27·52	932	699·1	28·32	959	719·3	29·12	986	739·6	29·92	1,013	759·8	30·71	1,040	780·1
27·55	933	699·8	28·35	960	720·1	29·15	987	740·3	29·94	1,014	760·6	30·74	1,041	780·8
27·58	934	700·6	28·38	961	720·8	29·18	988	741·1	29·97	1,015	761·3	30·77	1,042	781·6
27·61	935	701·3	28·41	962	721·6	29·21	989	741·8	30·00	1,016	762·1	30·80	1,043	782·3
27·64	936	702·1	28·44	963	722·3	29·24	990	742·6	30·03	1,017	762·8	30·83	1,044	783·1
27·67	937	702·8	28·47	964	723·1	29·26	991	743·3	30·06	1,018	763·6	30·86	1,045	783·8
27·70	938	703·6	28·50	965	723·8	29·29	992	744·1	30·09	1,019	764·3	30·89	1,046	784·6
27·73	939	704·3	28·53	966	724·6	29·32	993	744·8	30·12	1,020	765·1	30·92	1,047	785·3
27·76	940	705·1	28·56	967	725·3	29·35	994	745·6	30·15	1,021	765·8	30·95	1,048	786·1
27·79	941	705·8	28·59	968	726·1	29·38	995	746·3	30·18	1,022	766·6	30·98	1,049	786·8

INDEX

PRINTED UNDER THE AUTHORITY OF H.M. STATIONERY OFFICE
AT THE CHAPEL RIVER PRESS, ANDOVER, HANTS